A SOCIAL AND RELIGIOUS HISTORY OF THE JEWS

By SALO WITTMAYER BARON

Second Edition, Revised and Enlarged

High Middle Ages, 500–1200: Volumes III–VIII

VOLUME V

RELIGIOUS CONTROLS AND DISSENSIONS

COLUMBIA UNIVERSITY PRESS 1957

New York

LIBRARY OF CONGRESS CATALOG CARD NUMBER: 52-404

PUBLISHED IN GREAT BRITAIN, CANADA, INDIA, AND PAKISTAN
BY THE OXFORD UNIVERSITY PRESS
LONDON, TORONTO, BOMBAY, AND KARACHI

MANUFACTURED IN THE UNITED STATES OF AMERICA

CONTENTS

A SOCIAL AND RELIGIOUS HISTORY OF THE JEWS: HIGH MIDDLE AGES

RELIGIOUS CONTROLS AND DISSENSIONS

XXIII

COMMUNAL CONTROLS

As in all other periods of Jewish history, the external framework of the worlds of Islam and Christendom within which Jewish life developed tells only half the story. Eminently significant, indeed far more decisive than would appear from the perusal of either contemporary Hebrew records or most modern Jewish historical works, the varying environments essentially set the conditions and delimited the area within which the Jewish community could continue its historic progression. In constant interplay, in an unceasing process of tension and harmonization, the Jewish people's will to persist and its age-old traditions and institutions met, and adjusted themselves to, the newer needs and drives of the expanding or contracting Christian or Muslim societies. That in the process its own world outlook and mode of living necessarily underwent great changes is self-evident. Yet, after the first major adjustments to the rule of Islam, these transformations were so slow and gradual that they readily escaped attention. To the masses of Jews, Jewish life in the ninth and tenth centuries appeared to differ but little from that of the second or third century, with which many had familiarized themselves through intensive study of the Talmud. The leaders' staunch insistence upon the unbroken continuity of Jewish law, the general perseverance of folkways and rituals, greatly contributed to that illusion of sameness. Psychologically even more than in reality, the new life seemed to differ from the old only in minor details or some quantitative aspects, but not in the basic quality of its outlook and its dominant values.

Convictions of this kind were further strengthened by Islam's peculiar evolution. The more the new religion fell heir to the ancient Graeco-Roman and Persian civilizations, the more it absorbed and synthesized the cultures and institutions of the conquered populations, the more it confirmed the impression of similarity, if not complete identity, of the ancient with the newer modes of living. At the same time, its failure to integrate more fully the religious minorities into the fabric of the new states, and its studied effort to segregate them culturally and socially from the Muslim majority, forced these "infidels" continuously to fall back on the resources of their respective historic traditions.

Rare indeed, among both Jews and Christians, was the sentiment of "belonging" to a particular Muslim state which seemed to bend all its efforts on humiliating them and, on principle, denied them all opportunity of serving it in the army or public office. True, unlike their Christian compatriots, who often looked longingly to some Christian power across the frontier or welcomed approaching Crusaders, the Jews had no reason for being actively disloyal. But their primary loyalty belonged to their own religious community. To all intents and purposes most Baghdad or Isfahan Jews felt greater physical kinship, spiritual and cultural affinity, and even community of interest, with their coreligionists in Cairo or Cordova, Constantinople or Rome, than they did with their Muslim neighbors in adjacent localities. Nurtured by the ubiquity of social and religious prejudices, discriminatory taxes, and consciously derogatory regulations, this solidarity of the Jewish people strengthened the hands of its leaders and infused new vigor into its traditional communal structure.

Conversely, Jewish communal and intellectual leaders emphasized the spiritual foundations of their people's unity, the need for separation from the ways of Gentile nations, each individual's duty to share in the community's burden, and his right to reap part of its rewards. Even men like Abraham Maimuni who felt quite "at home" in the Muslim environment and drew a sharp line of demarcation between Islam and the "idolatrous" creeds condemned by Bible and Talmud, agreed on the basic needs of Jewish segregation and autonomy. "Do not separate from the community," Saadiah Gaon had exclaimed in an exhortatory letter, "for one who isolates himself will strive to fulfill all his desires and brook no contradiction. . . . All the nations rely upon chariots and horses, but your defenses consist only of the Lord's Torah and its sages." Nor was this to be but a temporary task. "Our nation of the children of Israel," the gaon added in his philosophic treatise, "is a nation only by virtue of its laws. Since, then, the

Creator has stated that the Jewish nation was destined to exist as long as heaven and earth would exist, its laws would, of necessity, have to endure as long as would heaven and earth." To foster separation he and other leaders tried to prevent Jews from having recourse to the state's administrative authorities or judges in their quarrels with fellow Jews. An early, fairly typical Aramaic formula of a Jewish court edict read: "He who goes to the nations, denounces [a fellow Jew] and tells untruths about him, shall be excommunicated before the Lord of Hosts, the God of Israel." An even more remarkable decision was made by Sheshna Gaon within half a century of the Muslim conquest (before 689). "If an official or tax collector," the gaon decreed, "orders a community to issue bans for his own purposes and needs . . . and it is impossible to resist the compulsion, such enforced bans are null and void, and may be disregarded." This declaration of passive resistance remained the communities' major safeguard against extortionist state officials.[1]

WORLD-WIDE LEADERSHIP

External and internal pressures thus converged, strengthening both the independence of Jewish inner life and the unity of world Jewry. Continuing on a higher plane the Sassanian traditions, Babylonian Jewry now enhanced its preeminence, because far larger masses of Jews were united under one empire. Its direct influence now extended from India to Spain. The Caliphate's laws, too, setting up "unbelievers" as the main source of imperial revenue, further strengthened these bonds. More consistently than their Sassanian predecessors, the caliphs entrusted to the Jewish community the task of collecting the Jewish poll tax, thus making it one of the important governmental agencies.

To increase that agency's efficiency and to facilitate its dealings with other organs of government, centralization in a few focal points became a vital necessity. Again building on Persian foundations, the caliphs declared the exilarchs the spiritual and, in many ways, the temporal rulers of all Jews in the empire. To make that choice more palatable to Jews, they imposed upon themselves the severe limitation of appointing only members of the exilarchic family to that high office and of respecting, within this narrow range, the preferences of the Jewish community as expressed by scholars gathered at its leading academies. Although there still remained some leeway in choosing one of two contending brothers, which lent substance to occasional outcries by opponents that a particular appointee had "purchased" his office by bribing officials, succession usually followed the rule of primogeniture.

Even after an uncontested election, the caliph and his advisers expected substantial contributions from the exilarch-elect. Lavish gifts accompanied the latter's first appearance at court which in time developed into a major ceremony, with large Jewish crowds accompanying their new chief to the royal residence. No full text of a caliph's decree of appointment of an exilarch has been preserved, but it probably resembled roughly the decrees issued in favor of Nestorian *catholicoi,* the recognized leaders of the most influential Christian denomination. Such a charter issued by Al-Muktafi II in 1138, was addressed to the *catholicos* and read in part:

> Thou art empowered to act as their [the Nestorian Christians'] head and the head also of all those Greeks, Jacobites, and Melkites, whether represented here [in the delegation] or not, who might oppose them in any country. . . . Following the precedent sanctioned by the imams his predecessors, in their dealings with the *Catholicoi,* thy predecessors, the Commander of the Faithful does also hereby bestow upon thee and upon thy followers the statutory prerogatives: thy life and property and those of thy people will be protected; great care will be taken in the promotion of your welfare; your ways of interring your dead will be respected and your churches and monasteries will be protected. . . . That we shall be satisfied with you by your payment of the capitation tax, levied upon the males of your community who have passed the age of minority and who are rational and solvent. . . . The Commander of the Faithful was also gracious to be willing to mediate between the different Christian communities in their lawsuits in order to exact justice from the strong in favor of the weak. . . . Be thou worthy of all these favors granted to thee, which fulfill the desires of thy soul, and set up prayers and invocations for the Commander of the Faithful as a token of thy gratitude and a sign of thy allegiance.

Very likely the reference to sectarian divisions was either totally absent or appeared in highly diluted form in the Jewish charters even after the rise of the powerful Karaite schism. Otherwise these provisions lent themselves to almost literal repetition in the caliph's confirmation of a newly designated exilarch.[2]

In this way, the princely family which, with some justice, claimed an unbroken line of succession from King David, was now perpetuated in office for several more centuries. It became the longest-lived dynasty in history. According to Ibn Lahi'a, an exilarch himself pointed out this obvious contrast between the Muslims who had slain their Messenger's grandson, Ḥusain (in the battle of Karbala in 680), and the Jews who held the occupants of the exilarchic office inviolable, despite the lapse of seventy generations since David. The ninth-century Zaidite, Al-Qasim ibn Ibrahim likewise pointed to the exilarchic family as a classical example of *waṣiyya,* or the hereditary transmission modified by testamentary disposition. Certainly no prince of captivity was ever murdered by Jews. Even executions by outside powers, such as had occurred under the Sassanians, are rarely recorded under Muslim rule. Bearing in mind the Qur'anic praises of the ancient "prophet" David, the very Muslim officials addressed the exilarch as "our lord, son of David." Compared with the numerous caliphs (beginning with 'Umar I himself) and viziers who died at the hands of assassins, the personal security of exilarchs, even if occasionally deposed and banished, stands out in high relief. The sporadic depositions, too, as a rule resulted from internal Jewish conflicts, rather than from arbitrary acts of government, such as bedeviled the orderly succession in the leadership of Christian sects, deprived of the continuity of a hallowed hereditary dynasty.[3]

Like the Nestorian *catholicos,* but probably higher in rank, the exilarch was assigned a seat in the chief imperial council, serving as a sort of minister for Jewish affairs. Both religious chiefs speedily removed their residence from Ctesiphon to the new capital of Baghdad. This privilege was denied, for instance, to the Monophysite patriarch in 912. Such proximity to the caliphal court not only made the exilarch available for consultation at the call of ruler or vizier, but also enabled the Jewish leader to secure audiences with these high dignitaries whenever the interest of the Jewish community required it. Understandably, each audience with the caliph himself was invested with an elaborate ceremonial; one of these is graphically described by Nathan the

Babylonian. It also had to be secured by preliminary negotiations with the vizier, abetted by bribes, and accompanied by costly gifts to the monarch himself. It is small wonder then, that, to quote Michael Syrus, "our [Christian] leadership is different from that of Zoroastrians and Jews. The latter call their chiefs 'kings' enjoying hereditary dignity. They pay their taxes to those chiefs; such never was the case with us." Many a legend was current, even among the Arabs, concerning the Jewish princes' power and wealth, and reflections of their glory fell upon the Jews all over the world. Isidore of Seville probably had exilarchs, rather than the South Arabian converts, in mind, when he accused the Spanish Jews of the effrontery of speaking of "I do not know what king of the tribe of Judah who holds sway in some extreme regions of the East." An Egyptian leader, Ḥisdai, claimed to "rule over the people of the Lord by virtue of the authority invested in me by our master, the prince of captivity, under the scepter of whose kingdom we and all of Israel dwell." There was sufficient substance in the realities of exilarchic power, even in its decline, for Exilarch Daniel ben Ḥisdai to enjoin his coreligionists, in 1161, to excel "in the observance of the laws and judgments of our God and in the love of your king," that is, himself. Even in the far West, Nissim bar Moses of Marseilles still saw in the prince of captivity in the thirteenth century the personification of "Judah's rod" and exhorted his coreligionists to see to it that "he may still possess greatness and government, and no one should rebel against his words." [4]

Grandiloquent assertions of this type glossed over, but could not entirely conceal, certain basic weaknesses in the structure of the exilarchate. To begin with, from its reestablishment under Muslim rule, some branches of the exilarchic family were under a cloud of suspicion. After the conquest of Persia, 'Umar I had given Exilarch Bustanai one of the captive daughters of the Sassanian king, Khosroe, or more likely Yazdegerd III, assassinated in 651 (Ibn Daud). Since there existed no clear documentary evidence of her manumission, her children, according to Jewish law, had an uncertain status. Friends of her descendants, who had interveningly become the reigning exilarchs, argued that it was unlikely for a leader like Bustanai to marry a captive woman without first granting her freedom. But opponents sneered at the legitimacy of their descent, just as the anti-Maccabean faction of the Second Commonwealth had cast a slur on the genealogical purity of John Hyrcanus and his descendants, because John's mother, allegedly taken captive, had been disqualified to continue as a priest's wife. Even Sherira did not hesitate to emphasize the superiority of his own Davidic descent without that blemish. Nor are the circumstances which led to the transfer of authority to the descendants of the Persian princess altogether clear. This change occurred some time after the decease of the vigorous exilarch Solomon bar Ḥisdai, best known for his efforts to raise the standing of the academy of Sura by appointing new leaders in 733 and 759. Perhaps Solomon had displayed excessive loyalty to the 'Umayyad dynasty, and the new 'Abbasid ruler, Al-Manṣur, after 767 appointed Zakkai bar Akhunai of the Persian line, Zakkai establishing his residence in the new capital of Baghdad.[5]

More portentous was the conflict between 'Anan, founder of the Karaite schism, and his brother, Ḥananiah (about 767) which, as we shall see, resulted in the permanent separation of the Karaite sect from the main body of Rabbanites. In 825, another controversy between David ben Yehudah and his brother Daniel, allegedly a Karaite sympathizer, led to Caliph Al-Ma'mun's momentous decision. According to later but generally well-informed chroniclers, the caliph, evidently combining in this case his religious liberalism with his anti-Jewish leanings, decreed that "if ten men of whatever creed, be they Jews, Christians, or Magi, should get together and constitute an authority over themselves, no one should prevent them from so doing." This decree caused consternation particularly in Christian circles, since it opened the gates to endless sectarian subdivisions. The issue was resolved when Dionysius, for more than a decade the recognized head of the Jacobite Church, visited Al-Ma'mun in Baghdad in 829 and secured a compromise which greatly curtailed the freedom of forming new congregations without the approval of the established authorities within each major denomination. While neither Barhebraeus nor Denys of Tell-Mahré, who graphically describe the progress of these negotiations, mention anything about their effects on the Jewish community, its leadership, too, must have felt strengthened by this modification of the original decree. To close the ranks against the threatened atomization of the eastern communities in that period of great sectarian divergences, the exilarchs sought the undivided support of the two great Babylonian academies. We do not know what concessions they were forced to make, but there probably is some truth in the obviously exaggerated assertion of Samuel ben 'Ali, the twelfth-century geonic opponent of the exilarchate, that "in the days of David ben Yehudah the Exilarch, they [the exilarchs] were removed from royal service and joined once more the sages and the academies, but they were not admitted until they accepted in writing the conditions of the academy which had installed them." This statement is literally inexact, but it correctly mirrors the prevailing trend toward the increasing superiority of the scholarly leaders.[6]

Exilarchic authority soon was further circumscribed by the rise of the Jewish banking families in Baghdad to economic and political power. Because they had the ear of statesmen, especially during Ibn al-Furat's recurrent vizierates, they often played the role of unofficial Jewish spokesmen. Nor did they always exercise the necessary restraints in the internal conflicts, which began to multiply in the tenth century. In one such controversy between the exilarch Mar 'Uqba and the Pumbedita academy over the revenue from the province of Khorasan, the leading bankers, Joseph ben Phineas and his son-in-law, Neṭira, took the side of the academy. As a result, the exilarch, who had been in office for more than twenty years (since 890), was now deposed and banished to Kirmanshah in Persia (about 912). According to the story reported by Nathan the Babylonian with the usual anecdotal elaborations, 'Uqba succeeded in ingratiating himself to the caliph, then on a visit in Kirmanshah, by greeting him daily with a new Arabic poem. As a result he was recalled to Baghdad and reinstated in office. Probably more important was some change in the general administration, and the temporary loss of influence by Neṭira and his faction. But another shift brought back Neṭira's unofficial leadership, and 'Uqba was now banished entirely from the confines of the Caliphate. He was told that "in the case he entered it [Baghdad], Islam should be more appropriate for him," that is, he would be treated as a convert to Islam. For some four year, until Neṭira's death in 916, the exilarchic office remained unoccupied, thus underscoring both its weakness and the power of the plutocracy. Soon after Neṭira's death, however, at a time when Ibn al-Furat was out of office, a new exilarch was installed, over the protests of the academy of Pumbedita. Under the vigorous leadership of David ben Zakkai, 'Uqba's cousin, the exilarchate reasserted for a time its full authority. After some three years David secured also the recognition of the Pumbedita scholars, who in his subsequent struggles proved to be his staunchest supporters.[7]

As we shall presently see, David succeeded in weathering the storm of his sharp conflict with Saadiah Gaon, although Saadiah had found an active supporter in David's brother Ḥasan-Josiah, whom he declared counter-exilarch. Before long the government intervened, and Josiah was banished to Khorasan; only his descendants ultimately secured the exilarchic office. Such dissensions within the exilarchic family, abetted by the absence of a strictly regulated form of succession, played into the hands of its geonic and other opponents.

Neither David nor his immediate successors, however, could lend effective guidance to the Jewish communities during the anarchy which engulfed the Caliphate toward the end of David's regime. After the restoration of more orderly conditions, the exilarchate reasserted itself, on a somewhat reduced scale, in the eleventh century. Hezekiah, one of David's descendants, who had become exilarch before 1021, actually succeeded in combining with this function the office of head of the academy for some twenty years (1038–58). Exilarchic prestige still shone brightly more than a century later, when Benjamin of Tudela enthusiastically described its power and glory under Daniel ben Ḥisdai, whom he observed from close range. An ancient law allegedly going back to Mohammed, the world traveler declared, had ordered

> that every Mohammedan or Jew, or one belonging to any nation in his [the caliph's] dominion, should rise up before him (the Exilarch) and salute him. . . . And every fifth day when he goes to pay a visit to the great Caliph, horsemen, Gentiles as well as Jews, escort him and heralds proclaim in advance, "Make way before our Lord, the son of David, as is due unto him." . . . Then he appears before the Caliph and kisses his hand, and the Caliph rises and places him on a throne

which Mohammed had ordered to be made for him, and all the Mohammedan princes who attend the court of the Caliph, rise up before him. And the Head of the Captivity is seated on his throne opposite to the Caliph, in compliance with the command of Mohammed to give effect to what is written in the Law—"The scepter shall not depart from Judah. . . ."

Exilarchic authority still extended, according to Benjamin, over Mesopotamia, Persia, Khorasan, Yemen, and regions in the Caucasus and Siberia. These assertions, though clearly exaggerated, are by no means controverted by the attacks leveled at Daniel's successor, Samuel (of Josiah ben Zakkai's line), by the ambitious Gaon Samuel ben 'Ali. The gaon not only dismissed the reigning prince as a man "who had never read nor studied nor attended a scholar, but had merely achieved power through money and through the help of government," but also assailed the exilarchic office as such. Israelites in the dispersion, he declared, "have neither a king nor war, nor anything that would necessitate a king. They need, therefore, only one who would lead them, enlighten them, teach them the commandments of their religion, hand out justice, and decide for them the law." Curiously such an outstanding student of the law as Maimonides held the exilarch in higher esteem than the gaon. In deference to the highest office in Jewry, he once read an exilarchic letter before the entire communal leadership of Fusṭaṭ, assembled at his home on the Feast of Tabernacles. Both reader and congregation remained standing during the entire recitation.[8]

Exilarchic revenues varied with the changing power constellations and the effectiveness of general caliphal controls. In their heyday in the ninth and early tenth centuries, the princes of captivity enjoyed a wide range of taxing authority. Not only their ardent admirer, Nathan the Babylonian, but also such an outsider as Al-Qasim ibn Ibrahim described in some detail these fiscal operations. According to Al-Qasim, the exilarch received 1⅓ dirhems for every animal ritualistically slaughtered, and 4 dirhems for every marriage license, decree of divorce, or permit to build a house. He was in charge of raising all illegitimate Jewish children and foundlings, from among whom was mainly recruited his large retinue of courtiers. His tribunal enjoyed high judicial authority which, however, he soon had to share with the heads of the academies. True, Al-Jaḥiẓ (died 869) claimed that "neither the *catholicos* nor the *ras al-galut* [exilarch] has any right in Muslim lands to condemn defendants to prison or flagellation. They can merely impose fines or prohibit intercourse with them." But this was a clear exaggeration, owing to the author's rationalist and anti-foreign biases, of the temporary weakening of exilarchic authority under Al-Ma'mun. Similarly, if Ibn Ḥazm, writing in Spain after 1013, sweepingly declared that "the prince of captivity wields no power whatsoever over Jews or any other persons; he merely bears a title which carries with it neither authority nor prerogatives of any kind," he reflected the wishes of western Arabs to see Spanish Jewry completely independent of a chief residing in Baghdad. This certainly was not true of most eastern communities even in the eleventh century. Well-informed Al-Biruni, Ibn Ḥazm's distinguished contemporary, went to the other extreme in calling the exilarch "the master of every Jew in the world; the ruler whom they obey in all countries." [9]

ACADEMIC INDEPENDENCE

Behind the frequent clashes between geonim and princes of captivity loomed deeper issues than mere personal ambitions. Not at all comparable to the contemporary Western conflicts between state and church, they were not struggles between temporal and spiritual leaders (both offices combined spiritual with temporal authority) but rather a reflection of the age-old drive of the scholarly class for supreme control over the Jewish community. Suffering many setbacks in the course of history, this drive, carried on by the ancient Pharisees and talmudic sages, was now renewed against the semimonarchical power of exilarchs and continued under changed conditions against the emergent Western plutocracies.

In the vanguard of these scholarly groups marched the members of the two venerable academies of Sura and Pumbedita, whose heads now assumed the proud title of *geonim* (contracted from "heads of the academy, the pride [*geon*] of Jacob"). As in the talmudic age, these distinguished teachers exercised broad communal controls. In time, they were assigned definite administrative districts in Babylonia and vicinity, the regular income from which supplied a sizeable portion of the academies' budgets. We hear, for instance, that Sura's revenue from its district amounted at one time to 1,500 gold dinars ($6,000) annually, of which the rich city of Baṣra contributed 300 dinars. Both schools received in addition substantial voluntary donations from the outside. It appears that, following an ancient injunction of the Usha academy, many a pious Jew sent a double tithe (*ḥomesh*) to these great schools of learning. Direct state subsidies are recorded only in Egypt and Palestine under Faṭimid rule, but the caliphs of Damascus and Baghdad seem to have extended some formal recognition to the gaonate of Sura in 658, and to that of Pumbedita about 830. Although the exilarchs for a long time enjoyed the right of appointing and deposing geonim, their choice was greatly restricted by the wishes of the academies themselves, which, as a rule, preferred members of several distinguished scholarly families. True, unlike the exilarchic office and, to some extent, also the leadership of the Palestinian academies, the gaonate was not strictly hereditary. With the exception of Hai, who even in Sherira's lifetime began sharing the burdens of administration, no son immediately succeeded his father. Naḥshon bar Zadok had to wait some fifty years, Naṭronai bar Hilai fifty-three years, and Dosa bar Saadiah seventy-one years before they attained leadership. Nevertheless, there was decided preference for scions of six or seven well-established families. Only the combination of a great national emergency and Saadiah's superlative abilities made possible the appointment of this outsider, hailing from Fayyum in Egypt to the gaonate of Sura.[10]

The early history of the two geonic academies and their relations with the exilarchs are still full of obscurities. It appears that "the fortunes of Sura and of the exilarchate intimately and inseparably intertwined." Located at a considerable distance from both Damascus and Baghdad (as previously from Ctesiphon), its academy interfered but little with the exilarchic administration. Even in the judicial sphere the exilarchs' "judges of the court" could adjudicate litigations with undisputed authority. In fact, frequent depositions of Sura geonim by exilarchs in the seventh century are cited by our main chronicler, Sherira, as the chief reason for his inability to reconstruct the former's succession to the end of the first millennium of the Seleucid era (689 C.E.). Nor was there overt opposition when Exilarch Solomon bar Ḥisdai appointed scholars from Pumbedita, R. Samuel (730–48) and the famous R. Yehudai bar Naḥman (760–63), to the gaonate of Sura.[11]

In contrast thereto, Pumbedita was only twelve parasangs (some forty miles) from Baghdad, and could well become a thorn in the flesh of the central administration. The princes of captivity tried, therefore, to dominate it through pliable appointees. In one case, the exilarch's relative (possibly son-in-law) Naṭronai I ruled the academy with such an iron hand that many members departed and joined the academy of Sura (719). Later a great scholar, Aḥai of Shabḥa, author of *She'eltot,* was passed over, undoubtedly because of his "excessive" independence, and the exilarch's secretary appointed instead (about 748). More serious was an attempt, in 771, by R. Malka Gaon to replace the reigning exilarch, Zakkai bar Aḥunai, by another member of the exilarchic family, Naṭronai bar Ḥabibai, a distinguished scholar in his own right. This controversy, possibly connected with the long-smoldering conflict over the legitimacy of the exilarchic line descended from Bustanai and the Persian princess, ended in the exilarch's decisive victory. R. Malka was deposed and soon thereafter died, while Naṭronai left Babylonia and settled in Spain. His arrival in the West was to become a milestone in the intellectual evolution of Spanish and Provençal Jewry.

Half a century later, however, the controversy between David ben Yehudah and his brother Daniel, followed by Al-Ma'mun's decree of 825, turned the scales in favor of Pumbedita. At first, to be sure, the academy itself was presided over by two rivaling geonim, Abraham bar Sherira and Joseph bar Ḥiyya. But when peace was restored by Joseph's temporary return to the vice-presidency, the academy could invoke the new royal decree and assert its total independence. The exilarch now had to concede the judicial and fiscal authority of the two academies, and to co-operate in securing governmental recognition also for Pumbedita. This is probably the meaning of the aforementioned statements by Sherira and Samuel ben 'Ali concerning the lowering of the dignity of the exilarchate. Both these geonim wrote with the aid of records preserved in their own academy of Pumbedita-Baghdad. This official recognition was accompanied by the allotment to Pumbedita of one third of the gifts sent to either academy. In time, even this inequality was removed. More significantly, as part of the settlement, the academies were assigned separate districts, in which their heads appointed the local judges and collected Jewish taxes without interference from the exilarchic bureaucracy. Ultimately, even judicial decisions of the exilarchic court required confirmation by a gaon.[12]

Notwithstanding these perennial bickerings, the world-wide prestige and influence of the two academies grew with the general expansion of Jewish settlements and the strengthening of the bonds of the Caliphate during the eighth and ninth centuries. Their correspondence soon reached out to the most distant regions of the Muslim world and beyond it. Ibn Daud was shown a pamphlet addressed more than two centuries earlier by Saadiah Gaon to "the congregations of Cordova, Elvira, Lucena, Bajjana [?], Kalsana [?], Seville, and Merida, the great city, and all the Jewish communities in its vicinity." The power and authority of the geonim, too, exceeded that of their predecessors under Persian rule. They substituted for the capital jurisdiction, which (except in Spain) they did not possess, other sufficiently severe sanctions to deter any but the most powerful or daring individuals from infractions of the established order.[13]

Among the severe penalties they could inflict upon the guilty were excommunication, flogging in public (even without regard to the criminal's ability to sustain such a punishment as was required for the talmudic *malqot* or *makkot*), and disqualification from testifying before courts, the rabbinic counterpart to the modern suspension of electoral rights. In fact, while incarceration of offenders never played a great role in the Diaspora communities, flogging was in frequent use. By changing from the biblical flagellation with thirty-nine stripes, to which they no longer felt entitled, to the rabbinic *makkat mardut* (flogging for rebellion), the rabbis actually aggravated that penalty. We possess a graphic description of a public flagellation in a responsum written by Sherira or Hai in 997. After tying the convict's arms and feet, the bailiff, acting under the supervision of the court, administered thirteen strokes each to the culprit's right side, left side and back. At the outset and during each intermission the court made the unfortunate recite scriptural verses, particularly relevant to his crime or bearing on flagellation as a means of forgiveness. Either before or after, he also was forced to confess his guilt and to pray, "Let my flogging be an atonement for my sin." The court, too, joined in this prayer for forgiveness. This elaborate religious ceremonial may have reduced the opposition of the Jewish public to this cruel performance, accustomed though it was to its daily repetition among its neighbors.[14]

Flogging was far overshadowed in both importance and frequency by the communal anathema which was at times more permanently injurious and could even serve as a sufficient substitute for the extreme penalty. Following ordinances issued by Naṭronai bar Hilai and Sherira, Maimonides succinctly stated that one found guilty of a capital crime should "receive a heavy flogging and then be excommunicated in a public ceremony before Torah scrolls, which excommunication must never be revoked." The horrors of such a permanent anathema can easily be visualized from one of Palṭoi Gaon's responsa. Explaining that anyone defying the court's will for more than thirty days after the imposition of a milder ban (the so-called *niddui*) should be placed under the severe *ḥerem,* the gaon briefly described the latter:

> This is to be done with respect to the excommunicated person: Announce publicly that his bread is the bread of Cutheans, his wine the wine of libation [of an idolater], his fruits are untithed and his books are the books of sorcerers. Also cut his show-fringes and impede his livelihood. Do not pray with him, do not circumcise his sons, and do not teach his children in the synagogue; do not bury his dead; do not associate with him in either obligatory or voluntary association. Pour a cup of water after him, and treat him with contempt and as a stranger.

All this was doubly underscored by the solemnity of a synagogue proclamation with the blowing of horns which impressed even the Muslim, Jaḥiz. A tenth-century Palestinian poet was quite right in comparing the lot of such an outcast with that of a leper banished outside the walls.[15]

In some areas, formerly under Byzantine domination including Palestine, the communal authorities occasionally inflicted corporal punishments other than flogging. Transgressions against sexual morality, in particular, were often punished by shaving off the hair of the culpable women. In the case of priests marrying divorcées, Ṣemaḥ Gaon informs us, Palestinian, but not Babylonian, judges at times resorted to the drastic penalty of cutting off the culprit's thumb, in order to prevent him from moving away to another locality and participating there in synagogue services administering priestly blessings.[16]

Local variations of this type were minimized by the great power of the central authorities in Babylonia. Inasmuch as the central leadership was often coresponsible for the taxes owed the state, it and its local appointees were invested with the power of collecting the combined state and communal revenue from Jewish taxpayers. Petaḥiaḥ of Ratisbon found, for instance, that the Jewish chief in Mosul was gathering annually a gold dinar from every Jewish resident of the city and dividing that income equally between the state treasury and the communal chest. If half a dinar was less than what the treasury alone expected to receive in poll taxes from "unbelievers" (we recall Abu Yusuf's three classes subject to taxes ranging from one to four dinars), the Jewish authorities must have either broadened the tax base by including individuals freed from the governmental levy, or else made up the difference from other, indirect forms of taxation. The community, and not the state, also inherited the property of any member who died without heirs, or whose natural heirs had been converted to another faith. The decree of 923, which specifically excluded converts from any share in the estates of Jewish relatives, merely formalized an ancient practice, going back to a reputed saying of the Messenger himself, "The infidel does not inherit from the Muslim, nor the Muslim from the infidel." This injunction was doubly remarkable, as it ran counter to the express provision of the Qur'an in favor of blood relations.[17]

Both the legally enforceable revenue and the large voluntary donations were used by the academies for the maintenance not only of the gaon and his high court, but also of an extensive educational system, which included provisions for the support of students. While we do not possess any precise statistical data, it appears that in prosperous times the academies attracted large numbers of pupils, probably reaching the size of Sura's alleged enrollment of 800–1200 in the third century. Around Hai Gaon were assembled students from all over the Muslim world, Byzantium, and southern Italy. Since many gifts merely accompanied inquiries to one or the other gaon, Nathan the Babylonian was doubtless right in asserting that "the exilarch had no share in the offerings and contributions sent by the communities of Israel to the academies." Sometimes donations were sent without designation of the recipient. In this case, Sura, the "exilarchic academy," long received two thirds, until the gradual rise of Pumbedita in the ninth and tenth centuries established full equality. The vigorous gaon Kohen Zedek seems to have secured such equal treatment during Sura's temporary weakness about 926. In joint formal gatherings, however, Sura retained her precedence. Its gaon was always seated to the right, that of Pumbedita to the left of the reigning exilarch. Apart from such extraordinary occasions as the installation of a new exilarch, the colorful pageantry of which was graphically described by Nathan the Babylonian, such joint sessions were convoked annually on Sabbath *Lekh lekha* (the third Sabbath after the Feast of Tabernacles). Since in Islamic times these joint sessions took place at the exilarchic see, the geographic proximity of the Pumbedita academy must have given it an early advantage in the number of attendants and the geonim's personal following. After 890, Pumbedita's transfer to Baghdad, combined with the general weakening of exilarchic controls, lent it a preeminent position which was only temporarily checked by Saadiah's brilliant leadership of Sura (928–42). After Saadiah's death Sura had to suspend all activities for about forty-five years. Reestablished after 987, it had to make strenuous efforts merely to maintain equal status with its sister academy.[18]

Both academies studiously imitated the ancient seats of Jewish learning and, indirectly, the Sanhedrin itself. They consisted of seventy-one members and staged their public sessions in the Sanhedrin's hallowed semicircle. Each academy's vice-chairman was called by the venerable name *ab bet din* (father of the court). The leaders underscored this historic continuity in their official correspondence. Writing to Barcelona, then the leading community in Christian Spain, Amram ben Sheshna, gaon of Sura, sent it greetings "from us and from R. Ṣemaḥ, the judge of the gate, the heads of the *kallahs,* and from all the ordained scholars who are in the place of the Great Sanhedrin, and from the candidates who are in the place of the Little Sanhedrin." At the same time the academies also renewed the Babylonian semiannual assemblies during the months of Adar and Ellul. These sessions usually attracted large masses of eager students who wished to review their rabbinic studies during the preceding five months, and to listen to the authoritative exposition of new legal decisions by the geonim and their associates.[19]

Appointees of either exilarch or gaon usually served as local judges of the Persian-Babylonian communities, receiving fees for each judicial transaction. This right, originally granted by the government to the exilarch alone, was apparently after 825 delegated to the geonim in their respective districts. A certificate of appointment, now extant, authorized the judge "to dispense justice and to supervise all matters of Law, those pertaining to the prohibited and permitted things and those to the fear of heaven." The broad concluding sentence, "And he [the judge] is herewith empowered to deal as he sees fit with anyone refusing to submit to his judgment," may readily be understood in the light of the vast discretionary powers generally given also to the Muslim *qadhis,* according to the principle of *ta'zir.* By this latitude Muslims and Jews wished to enable the judge to reform a sinner after actions considered unethical, although not illegal. The local *dayyan* (judge) thus became the forerunner of the medieval "rabbi." Both academies retained their judicial supremacy, however. Each of their tribunals, often designated the *bet-din ha-gadol* (supreme court), served as a court of appeals, sometimes controlling even such distant communities as Kairuwan.[20]

GROWING DISCORD

That authority began to decline in the tenth century. Intermittent strife among the leaders contributed greatly to the weakening of their power. Apart from unavoidable clashes among incompatible personalities, there was, in particular, an almost permanent, latent antagonism between the exilarchate and gaonate.

Among the prolonged public quarrels, that between Exilarch David ben Zakkai and Saadiah Gaon was the most far-reaching. Although forewarned about Saadiah's boundless ambitions, David defied precedent and appointed this outstanding newcomer to the supreme scholastic office in Sura. He merely imposed upon the gaon an unusual oath which, if we may believe a later polemical assertion, included the pledge that Saadiah "would not transgress my words, nor conspire against me, nor recognize anyone else as prince of captivity, nor side with any of my opponents." The clash between the two strong personalities, each claiming supreme control, soon became unavoidable, however. Catching something of the spirit of the Muslim doctrine of the hereditary transmission of the prophetic soul, which later was to play a great role in the world-outlook of Halevi, Saadiah soon developed the theory that

> God does not leave His people in any generation without a scholar whom He inspires and enlightens so that he in turn may instruct and teach the people, and make it prosper through him. And the occasion thereto has been what I have personally experienced by what God, in His grace, has done for me and for the people.

The clear implication here that he was called upon to lead world Jewry was soon reinforced by a spurious genealogy. Saadiah suddenly claimed that his ancestry went back to Ḥanina ben Dosa, which must have evoked in every talmudist's mind an association with Rab's story of the divine voice announcing daily from Mount Horeb, "The entire world is being sustained on account of My son, Ḥanina." Ḥanina's forebears in turn were traced all the way back to the biblical Shela, son of Judah. This family background was obviously intended to point up Saadiah's superior descent from Judah, while the exilarch's Davidic lineage was tainted at its source by Judah's illicit relations with Tamar. Such exorbitant claims were doubtless justified in the gaon's mind by his life's dream of reunifying world Jewry under a single leadership, that of each generation's outstanding scholar. This dream was shattered, however, not only by the resistance of the exilarchic party, supported by the Pumbedita academy, but even more by the Caliphate's accelerated dissolution in Saadiah's last years. When the gaon died broken-hearted ("of melancholia") in 942, both his academy and the exilarchic office were in a state of eclipse.[21]

On other occasions, too, the Pumbedita leaders bitterly fought those of Sura. Apart from personal rivalries, disagreements often arose from the two schools adopting different halakhic principles. Although Babylonian supremacy had been firmly established, the halakhic differences, carried over from the talmudic age, between the Palestinocentric Suranic academy and the more independent school of Pumbedita still accounted for many peculiarities in law and custom. Formulas in prayer (for instance, *Ahabah rabbah* or *Ahabat 'olam*), the attitude toward the Palestinian Talmud, whose authority as a work implementing the Babylonian Talmud seems to have been early accepted in Sura but denied in Pumbedita until the days of Hai Gaon, and various halakhic minutiae revealed the distinctiveness of the two main schools of thought. It was not without reason that Naḥshon Gaon scolded the scholars of Kairuwan because they had ventured to address a question simultaneously to him and to the academy of Pumbedita. On account of the distance of twenty-eight parasangs (of about three and a half miles each), he declared, "we do not know what they write and they do not know what we write, and in so far as it is only a matter of opinion, we may see it one way, and they another way, and the name of God may be disgraced there." Even more dangerous disagreements arose when a Babylonian gaon and a prominent scholar of another country were consulted simultaneously. In his reply to an inquiry on the delicate problem of resurrection, addressed from Yemen to both Samuel ben 'Ali and Maimonides, the Baghdad gaon sharply attacked certain implications in Maimonides' earlier writings. Forced to more clearly define his eschatological doctrine, which he did in a special Treatise on Resurrection, the sage of Fusṭaṭ here, as well as in a letter to his beloved disciple, Joseph ben Yehudah, curtly dismissed his opponent's uncritical and philosophically untenable interpretation of talmudic passages. Obviously, such differences of opinion played into the hands of Karaites who contended that the Rabbanite *halakhah* could not possibly be based on authentic tradition, if its defenders' interpretations diverged so widely from one another.[22]

Conflicting decisions appeared the more dangerous as the geonim were used to issue sentences with undisputed authority. Self-assertive Saadiah, in particular, used to conclude his responsa with phrases, like "What we have ordered and decided must not be departed from." His opponent Aaron ibn Sarjado actually prescribed on one occasion that the elders of the recipient community assemble to read his reply. If in doubt about any point, he told them, they should ask him, but otherwise his decision must stand. "They must not deviate from it either to the right or to the left." Even mild Sherira Gaon exclaimed with total abandon, "He who opposes anything of what they [the geonim] say, is like one opposing God and His Torah." [23]

On the other hand, the practice of consulting more than one academy may actually have enabled distant communities to evade the responsibility of choosing among rivals. In periods of Babylonian-Palestinian tension, especially, inquirers may have considered it a part of wisdom to take counsel with leaders of both countries rather than show partiality. Perhaps Khagan Joseph was somewhat disingenuous in the naiveté of his assertion that, although the Khazars lived at a distance from Zion, they were looking "to the sages of Israel, the academy in Jerusalem and the academy in Babylonia" for the solution of their problems, including their messianic expectations (Kokovtsov, *Perepiska,* p. 25).

All these difficulties were of minor consequence, however, compared with the general deterioration of Babylonian life in the middle of the tenth century. The financial conditions of the academies, even previously far from satisfactory, now necessitated recourse to means which led to the further lowering of their prestige. The political or economic disturbances had so greatly reduced their regular revenue that the geonim had to appeal more and more frequently to friends in many lands for financial assistance. A number of such letters of solicitation have come to light. Only Saadiah succeeded in asking for funds in such a restrained and veiled language that its import, although unmistakable to his disciples, eluded modern scholars. Few other writers, even when they were of the rank of Sherira, were able to preserve the dignity of their exalted office. Of course Sherira, as well as his predecessor Nehemiah, son of Kohen Zedek, wrote under exceptional circumstances, when the Pumbedita academy had been reduced to a shadow of its former self. Nehemiah's prolonged struggle with the magnate, Aaron ibn Sarjado—here the all-powerful Baghdad plutocracy invaded even the hallowed precincts of the academy—together with the general anarchy in the metropolis, accounted for this unexampled decline. We may realize the poignancy of Sherira's situation when in 987, the very year he composed his famous Epistle, he complained that he had been left with but a single pupil during the month of Ellul. To underscore their mourning for the bygone glories of the semiannual *kallah,* master and pupil studied by themselves the talmudic tractate previously assigned for that convocation.[24]

Like the exilarchate, both academies regained their prestige in the early eleventh century. They were fortunate in having at that propitious time vigorous leaders in Sherira's son, Hai Gaon of Pumbedita, and in the latter's father-in-law, Samuel ben Ḥofni of Sura (died in 1013). This upsurge was checked after Exilarch Hezekiah's death in 1058. Subsequently the fate of each institution depended largely on the personality of its leader. Before long, to underscore their independence from the exilarchic office, the geonim secured direct confirmation of their election by governmental authorities. One such formal investiture of the gaon Daniel ben Samuel ibn abi ar-Rabia' by the Muslim chief justice in 1247, even led to riots by the hostile Muslim populace, and their sharp repression by the government. The diploma, issued on this occasion and probably typical of many earlier governmental investitures of exilarchs and heads of academies, read in part:

> I have appointed thee leader of the folk of thy community, over the folk of thy faith, which hath been abolished by the Mohammedan law, that thou mayest lead them within the boundaries of their religion. Thou shalt order them regarding those things commanded by their religion and those things forbidden by their religion. Thou shalt decide between them in their conflicts and legal disputes according to their religion, and the praise of God be over Islam.[25]

PALESTINE'S SELF-ASSERTION

Far more important than these internal bickerings was the new international situation. The Caliphate's progressive disintegration and the growing political antagonisms among the Islamic states affected also their Jewish subjects. The decline of Iraq's cultural hegemony stimulated the intellectual self-assertion of the Palestino-Egyptian and Western centers of learning. With the increasing elimination of Jews from international commerce, the necessity of maintaining close uniformity in civil law also diminished, while the increasing importance of local trade demanded its adaptation to local needs and usages. Sectarian movements within the Jewish mass settlements added to the centrifugal forces. All these particularist tendencies finally brought about the organizational dissolution of world Jewry into loose territorial units.

Understandably, the old rivalry between Palestine and Babylonia became the starting point for these separatist movements. After the rise of Islam, Babylonian hegemony was long fortified by the unity of the new empire centered in the Euphrates Valley. Since naming of high officials in prayers had become a symbol of allegiance under both Byzantium and the Caliphate, the Babylonian leaders insisted that in all countries prayers must be recited "first for the scholars of Babylonia." Informed about Eldad the Danite's report concerning the homage paid to the Babylonian academies among the remote tribes of Israel, Ṣemaḥ bar Ḥayyim Gaon of Sura explained this custom historically. During the First Exile, he declared, "the chief sages and prophets were deported to Babylonia, where they founded centers of learning and an academy on the Euphrates from the days of Jehoiachin, king of Judah, to the present day. Here rests the chain of wisdom and prophecy, and from here the Torah radiates to the whole people." In the early decades of the 'Abbasid Caliphate, Yehudai Gaon (who was soon extolled as the model teacher, not only because of his great learning and piety, but also because he had never taught anything he had not learned from his teachers) and his disciple, Pirqoi ben Baboi, tried to force North African Jewry to follow the Babylonian rather than the Palestinian Talmud. The fact that under Roman and Byzantine oppression the Palestinians had to modify certain Jewish laws and observances, now provided a pretext for the contention that every Palestinian deviation from Babylonian regulations had been forced upon Jewry by Roman intolerance. Louis Ginzberg has shown how unjustified was in most instances this denunciation of age-old Palestinian customs, and how it was abused as a political stratagem to promote Babylonian hegemony. But it carried great conviction with a people long inured to the idea of its perennial martyrdom in exile, and the innumerable legal and liturgical changes resulting therefrom. Was not Saadiah Gaon, in reply to Karaite attacks, prepared to attribute the very composition of the Mishnah to the growing dispersion and the ensuing fear of ancient rabbis that the Oral Law might be forgotten? [26]

Hostile enactments of Byzantine emperors against the traditional Jewish liturgy lent a semblance of truth to these assertions. Not only did Justinian's outlawry of the *deuterosis* seriously affect homiletical exercises and the teaching of Oral Law, but at one time the Empire seems to have forbidden also the recitation of such basic Jewish prayers as the *Shema'* and the *'Amidah.* Its ruling circles apparently suspected these unitarian prayers as aimed at the Trinitarian dogma. Babylonian leaders now censured, therefore, even such an old divergence, already debated for nearly a millennium, as the Palestinian insistence upon the recitation of *Shema'* while standing upright. Since the Babylonians had consistently allowed the worshipers to remain seated, Amram Gaon scolded all "those who believe that they are performing an act of supererogation by standing at the invocation of the Kingdom of Heaven. In fact, however, this is but a mistake and an aberration on their part, and it is nothing but ignorance and foolishness." Amram himself and other geonim, as we shall see, tried to stem the growing ritualistic diversity by issuing official prayer books and trying to persuade all Jewish communities to follow them closely in their services. But the Palestinians refused to budge even in such an overt challenge to liturgical uniformity as was inherent in their triennial cycle of weekly scriptural lessons. Undismayed, they continued to celebrate their very festival of the Rejoicing in the Torah not at the end of each Feast of Tabernacles, but on the completion of their cycle after three or three and a half years.[27]

Such Palestinocentrism was not limited to the inhabitants of the Holy Land. The glories of the past and the undying hopes for future redemption had tied the destinies of the whole people with the Land of Promise by links which external developments could weaken, but never completely sever. Sometimes this Palestinian orientation reached curious extremes. A much-debated preacher reemphasized the external signs of mourning which had long served as constant reminders of the loss of the ancient sanctuary, and then added on his own:

> Even if men of eastern lands and those banished [to the islands of the sea] require moisture during the *Tammuz* season, they must not pray for rain except when Palestine needs it, too. For if one were to permit them to pray whenever they need precipitation, even during the summer, they might believe that they are living in a country of their own. But they ought to look upon themselves as living in a hostelry [temporary shelter], while their heart turns to the land of Israel. Prayers for rain must come, therefore, in their stated time.

The preachers' only concession was to allow congregants to insert a request for water in their individual recitations of the *Shome'a tefillah* (He who listens to prayer).[28]

Curiously, the geonim themselves could not escape the impact of the Jewish people's unrelenting attachment to the Holy Land. When the new economic evolution under the Caliphate and growing Jewish participation in international trade and banking had made some ancient talmudic business usages obsolete, the heads of the academies themselves fell back on the Jewish claim to the land of Israel as a means of facilitating the far-flung transactions. According to talmudic law, one could issue to an agent a letter of authorization to collect funds from a debtor or depositary only if it was accompanied by the transfer of a parcel of land to the agent. Now few Jews owned land. Some early Babylonian teachers enacted, therefore, an ordinance (*taqqanah*), enabling Jewish businessmen to use for that purpose the ideal claim of each Jew to the possession of four ells of Palestinian soil. As a gaon explained it, "the land may have been occupied [by Gentiles] for many generations, but we have the old legal maxim that [ownership of] land is never lost by illegal seizure, and hence Israel still holds title to it [the Palestinian land]." While there were minor differences in the application of that legal fiction between the Palestinophile academicians of Sura and their more Babylonian-minded colleagues in Pumbedita, they all agreed on the underlying inalienable claim of the Jewish people to its ancestral land. This principle was accepted also by Alfasi and grudgingly recognized by

Maimonides. Nor was it in any way denied by the author of an apparently Western responsum, quoted by Rashi, who explained the fictitious transfer of the four ells of land as relating to an ideal claim of every individual, dead or alive, to four ells of space around him.[29]

In practice, however, the division between Palestine and Babylonia went so far as to necessitate the erection of separate synagogues of the Palestinian and Babylonian rituals throughout the Orient. Such synagogues are recorded in Fusṭaṭ, Damascus, Ramleh, and probably also in Tiberias and Baniyas. Even the supreme influence of Maimonides, whose codification of the liturgical observances otherwise enjoyed uncontested authority from Morocco to Syria, did not suffice to bring about a full rapprochement. His attempt to introduce Amram Gaon's prayer book into the synagogues of Palestinian rite was frustrated by the congregants' stubborn adherence to their traditional worship. The only concession his son, Abraham, was able to obtain in 1211, was the acceptance by the "Palestinian" synagogue in Fusṭaṭ of the annual reading of the Pentateuch from an ordinary copy. But the congregation continued to recite in addition the weekly portion according to the triennial cycle from a scroll of the Law. This at a time when the triennial cycle had been abandoned by decimated Palestinian Jewry itself after 1099. Similarly tenacious was the adherence of some "Palestinian" synagogues to the daily recitation of the Ten Commandments. Theoretically given up in ancient times because of its abuse by "heretics," this rite was revived at an unknown date, if indeed it was ever completely suppressed in practice. Now "Palestinian" congregations in Egypt defied both the talmudic record and the Babylonian insistence on conformity, causing no little difficulty to later rabbinic authorities. The issue was still under debate in modern times.[30]

Curiously, one significant ritualistic change was adopted in Palestine under the impact of Western rather than Babylonian scholars. From ancient times the Jewries of the dispersion had celebrated two days of each holiday, because of the possibility that news of the proclamation of a new moon in the Holy Land might not reach them on time. Palestine, however, relied on its immediate access to this information and observed only one holiday even on the first day of Tishre, the New Year. Hai Gaon ineffectually tried to persuade his Palestinian contemporaries living at some distance from their main academy to accept the two-day New Year celebration. Through Ḥananel of Kairuwan, however, his opinion became known to Isaac Alfasi in Spain and embodied by the latter in his code. "All follow therein the Babylonian custom," the Spanish jurist sweepingly declared, "even in every Palestinian locality, except at the seat of the Council [main academy]." So impressed were some Provençal scholars by that decision of three celebrated jurists that, upon their arrival in Palestine, they influenced the local communities to observe two New Year days. Obviously Palestinian Jewry after 1099 was in no position to resist a request for greater ritualistic strictness voiced by pious pilgrims from the lands of their conquerors.[31]

Of more than passing interest are also the differences between the two countries in the equally tenacious domain of family relations. According to an ancient Palestinian custom, weddings of virgins were usually set for Wednesdays, while widows or divorcées were married on Thursdays. The latter day was preferable, because it enabled busy farmers and artisans to set aside three days (together with Friday and Saturday) for a brief honeymoon. In the case of a virgin, however, Wednesday was more advantageous to a bridegroom claiming his bride's lack of virginity, for on the morrow of the wedding he could submit his case to a court of justice, which in Palestine sat only on Mondays and Thursdays. In Babylonia, on the other hand, courts were more readily available on other days and, hence, there was no need to distinguish between a virgin and widow. We may also understand why Palestinian Jews, even after Yannai's reform, abstained from using for betrothals money secured from a Sabbatical year's produce, whereas the Babylonians, who had never observed the year of fallowness, had no such compunctions. The Karaite, Qirqisani, was evidently mistaken in reversing that order.[32]

On the other hand, environmental influences explain, for instance, why Palestine adopted the Roman custom of betrothal through a ring, which remained unknown in Babylonia. Conversely, Babylonian Jewry, apparently resisting Parsee standards of ritualistic purity, refused to practice ablutions after each sexual impurity, a practice considered obligatory in the Graeco-Roman environment, where bathing had long lost much of its ritualistic quality. Curiously, under the Caliphate the Babylonian geonim themselves propagated the adoption of such ablutions even on the Day of Atonement. Already Yehudai Gaon reassured his inquirers that this observance ought not to be considered an imitation of Gentile ways which, indeed, it no longer was from the ritualistic standpoint. Kohen Zedek actually justified it as the "sanctification of the name of the Lord before the nations." Ultimately, in the days of Maimonides, the distinction shifted to new boundaries; "All the Jews living among Arabs," declared this much-traveled jurist-philosopher, "practice ablution, and all the Jews living among the uncircumcised [Christians] do not practice ablution." [33]

Babylonian supremacy, firmly established in the eighth and ninth centuries, suffered a sharp decline in the following generations. The growth of the Palestinian Jewish population, which gradually made up for the severe losses inflicted by Byzantine rulers, as well as the increasing appreciation of Palestinian poetry and linguistics, slightly restored the balance in favor of the Holy Land, until the establishment of the Latin Kingdom of Jerusalem. Although the famous struggle between the Palestinian leader, Aaron Ben Meir, and the Babylonian chiefs, represented by Saadiah, over the right of fixing the calendar ended in 922 with the apparent victory for Babylonia, Palestine remained an increasingly independent focus of Jewish life. The very delegation of the defense of the Babylonian standpoint to a new arrival from Egypt who, while still in Palestine, had already evinced certain misgivings about the calendar regulations in that country, must have revealed to keen observers the intrinsic insecurity of the Babylonian chiefs. Saadiah was not guilty of a gross overstatement when he claimed that the outcome of that controversy might affect the very foundations of world Jewish unity. "It is more important," he pleaded with Egyptian friends, "than trade and daily bread and every urgent business." And yet only his initiative and fighting spirit stirred the complacent Baghdad leaders to decisive action.[34]

Not surprisingly, therefore, the lines were not too sharply drawn. We may believe the Karaite Sahl ben Maṣliah that "some Palestinian residents followed the Babylonian leaders, while some Jews of Babylonia followed the Palestinians." Previously, Babylonian leadership itself had recognized Palestine's supremacy in all calendar regulations. As late as 835, an exilarch had declared that in this matter "we always rely on them [the Palestinians] so that Israel shall not break asunder into independent cliques." But now, partly owing to the difference of some fifty-six minutes in the visibility of the moon on the respective horizons of the two countries, Ben Meir decided to proclaim Marḥeshvan and Kislev of 4682 (921) deficient (of twenty-nine days each), while the Babylonians, following the accepted computation, declared both months to be of thirty days duration. The result was that the New Year of 4683 was celebrated in Palestine on a Tuesday, and in Babylonia on Thursday, causing great confusion particularly in cities which had congregations of both rites. This muddle evoked adverse comments even from such an outsider as the Christian chronicler Elijah bar Shinaya of Nisibis. In his letter to the Egyptian disciples, Saadiah implored them, "Take pity on the people of Israel . . . that they may not eat leavened bread on Passover [which ended two days earlier according to Ben Meir], nor eat, drink and work on the Day of Atonement." Ben Meir's faction, however, seems to have held out despite all these fulminations and bans. Saadiah's victory, if any, was decidedly short-lived. Palestine's effective control over the calendar in 1083, almost on the eve of its destruction by the Crusaders, is clearly reflected in the Scroll of Abiathar. Even Saadiah's attempt to eliminate from the prayer book the long-accepted phrase, *Ve-Or ḥadash 'al Ṣiyyon ta'ir* (O Cause a New Light to Shine Upon Zion), was prompted by philosophic rather than anti-Palestinian motives. He was clearly disavowed by Sherira, head of the more Babylonia centered school of Pumbedita, who asserted that both academies had always continued to recite that prayer.[35]

Certainly, with the progressive dissolution of the Caliphate and the expansion of the Diaspora, the Holy Land's glamorous memories and messianic future carried greater appeal to the more distant Jewries than did Babylonia's historic achievements, buttressed though they were by the authority of the Babylonian Talmud and gaonate. To Palestine and not Babylonia went those streams of pious pilgrims, like the French Jew robbed of his wealth by a feudal lord, or the Jew of Russia who had come from Salonica speaking only his Slavonic dialect, whose letters of introduction have been found in the Cairo Genizah (Mann, *Jews in Egypt,* II, 165 f.). All through the years, moreover, Babylonia herself furnished a steady contingent of ascetic "Mourners for Zion" and other emigrés to the Holy Land, led by such outstanding leaders of both the Rabbanite and Karaite communities as Aḥai of Shabḥa and the descendants of 'Anan.

PRIMACY OF SCHOLARS

After the extinction of the patriarchate (about 425), Jewish leadership in Palestine was recruited exclusively from academic circles. Only the Karaites made use of the arrival of 'Anan's descendants to reestablish the patriarchal office, although almost all their truly influential Jerusalem leaders were scholars, rather than dignitaries of Davidic origin. Among the Rabbanite majority, heads of the Tiberian academy, later transferred to Jerusalem (nominally it still was called the academy of Tiberias in the eleventh century) and subsequently to Tyre, held undisputed sway.

Even the arrival of Exilarch Mar Zuṭra III in the Holy Land after 491 did not change this primacy of scholars, for he himself merely assumed the position of head of the academy. Apart from the fear of antagonizing the Byzantine officialdom, which had become deeply suspicious of the secular, hereditary patriarchate, he may have faced the opposition of the local leaders who still remembered the old rivalry between the two ruling families in Palestine and Babylonia. On the other hand, none of the later Babylonian settlers until the middle of the eleventh century played a leading role in Palestinian affairs. Not even Aḥai of Shabḥa, who, disgruntled by the exilarch's failure to appoint him gaon in a Babylonian academy, had emigrated to Palestine after 748, seems to have been elected to the presidency of the Tiberian academy. Curiously, despite their signal achievements in biblical learning, Hebrew philology, and poetry, the Palestinian academicians have remained but shadowy figures until the sudden appearance of their vigorous chief, Ben Meir. But we owe most of our information about him to his controversy with Saadiah and the partial preservation of the correspondence exchanged on this occasion. Otherwise even his life and career are shrouded in darkness.[36]

While staving off, with greater or lesser success, the Babylonian encroachments, these heads of academies left few personal marks on the history of the communities under their jurisdiction so long as Palestine remained a province of the Baghdad Caliphate. Only after the establishment of the Faṭimid regime in Egypt and Palestine in 969 did the Palestinian academies begin to exercise supreme authority in teaching and administering Jewish law. Just as the Faṭimid rulers for the first time set up a rival "caliphate" (even the Spanish 'Umayyads were, until that time, satisfied with the title "the Caliphs' sons"), so did the Jewish spiritual leaders under their suzerainty arrogate to themselves the high-sounding title of *geonim*. This self-assertion had the full blessing of governmental authorities, including such Jewish officials as Palṭiel and Manasseh. Under the latter's influence the government extended a direct subsidy to the academy. Discontinued after Al-Ḥakim's intolerant outburst in 1012, this subsidy was nostalgically referred to in a letter of solicitation by the head of the academy, Josiah. Subsequently, too, the Jewish grandees of Fusṭaṭ and Alexandria continued to extend a helping hand, financially, as well as through intercessions with the caliph's advisers against abuses by local governors. At time they even had to take sides in the recurrent internal conflicts among members of the Palestinian academies themselves. In the eleventh century, finally, teachers of note arose in the Holy Land, who could aspire to real leadership beyond the confines of their own country. Under the four successive geonim, Solomon ben Yehudah (1027–51), Daniel ben Azariah (1051–62), Elijah ben Solomon (1062–83), and the latter's son Abiathar (1084–1109), the academy regained for a time some of its ancient splendor.[37]

Yet even in this period of relative glory, the academy membership suffered from an intellectual anemia, especially in the area of Jewish legal studies, which mattered most. During the tenth and eleventh centuries the greatest contributions to biblical, linguistic, and philosophic studies, too, were made by the distinguished array of Karaite scholars who were often sharply critical of their Rabbanite colleagues. Solomon ben Yehudah, the most prolific letter-writer among the Palestinian Rabbanites, certainly could not stand comparison with such illustrious contemporaries as Hai Gaon in Babylonia, Ḥushiel, his son Ḥananel, and Nissim bar Jacob in Kairuwan, or Samuel ibn Nagrela in Spain. In fact, Solomon himself acknowledged Hai's supremacy by sending his son, Yaḥya, to Baghdad to study under the great gaon.

Similarly, the Palestinian student Nathan ben Abraham quickly gained a reputation for extraordinary learning among his fellow citizens in Palestine, merely because he had spent a few years in Kairuwan as Ḥushiel's disciple. Upon his return to the Holy Land, Nathan immediately obtained a high-ranking office at the academy, forcing an older member voluntarily to renounce a long-established seniority. Before long he even reached out for the gaonate itself. Residing in the country's administrative capital, Ramleh, Nathan quickly secured both a considerable public following and governmental support. Aging Solomon ben Yehudah hurried to Ramleh, but after a dramatic scene in the local synagogue, described in one of his letters, he was forced to leave the Sabbath services. Nathan's partisans, allegedly bribed by him "with money, clothing, food and drink," became so vociferous that, in order to avoid great public disorder and the ensuing intervention by the local police, the gaon withdrew to another synagogue. But it was precisely governmental intervention, obtained by Solomon's friends in Cairo, which after some three years (1039–42) quelled the uprising. Nathan had to be satisfied with the vice-presidency—in his case more nominal than real.[38]

More remarkably, Solomon himself seems not to have been a native Palestinian, but a fairly recent arrival from Fez, that great center of both Rabbanite and Karaite learning which had been supplying distinguished intellectual leaders to many older communities from Babylonia to Spain. Nor was Solomon's immediate successor a "local boy who made good." Daniel ben Azariah, a descendant of the Exilarch David ben Zakkai, had for unknown reasons left his Babylonian home and settled in Jerusalem. Despite the opposition of the local vested interests, which still found expression in the Scroll of Abiathar written about forty years later,

Daniel was elected gaon. But reminiscent of his Davidic descent, and perhaps also emulating his kinsman Hezekiah who was at that time occupying the offices of both exilarch and gaon in Babylonia, Daniel assumed the high-sounding title of gaon and *nasi* (patriarch). He was apparently successful in securing also the backing of the Fusṭaṭ Jewish dignitaries, and soon ruled the Palestinian communities with an iron hand. "Ever since we arrived in this holy place," Daniel himself asserted, "we have been guiding, with God's help, all of Israel in Palestine and Syria, and adjudicating their affairs, as well as those of distant arrivals. Prayers are recited for us in all cities and villages." [39]

Understandably, this coup d'état evoked widespread opposition in the country and elsewhere. To remove the stigma of usurpation, Daniel himself argued in a letter addressed by him to a "Western" (probably Moroccan) correspondent that the Bible had reiteratedly mentioned the duty of obedience only in connection with the Davidic house, of which he was a member. He also stressed the *de facto* acceptance of his authority by all Palestinian communities, and the peace and order reigning there which had also accrued to the benefit of the Western pilgrims. Evidently to appease the opposition, Daniel, whose protracted poor health boded ill for his longevity, recognized Elijah ha-Kohen as Father of the Court (vice-president), and therewith as his heir apparent, in preference to any of his three sons, then still in their early childhood. He also tried to assure himself of the unflinching support of all newly appointed local judges by making them take an extraordinary oath of loyalty. We possess the text of one such remarkable pledge signed by Joseph ben Shemariah of Barqa in 1057. Apart from promising not to speak evilly of any person, but especially not of the members of the holy academy, Joseph declared:

From now and for ever I shall love the loyal adherents of our lord, Daniel, the great Patriarch and Head of the Academy the "pride of Jacob," and the loyal adherents of our master, Elijah ha-Kohen, Father of the Court of all Israel. I shall hate their haters, and shall not cooperate with anyone opposing them in any action of enmity and hatred. I shall also stay away from those excommunicated by him [Daniel]. All these conditions I have taken upon myself voluntarily and not under duress . . . by invoking the revered and awesome name of the Lord of Hosts, without any mental reservations now or in the future. Should I fail to live up to any of these conditions in full or in part, I shall consider myself excommunicated by the Supreme Court.

Many Near Eastern Jews, moreover, must have felt flattered by the extraordinary spectacle of two scions of the house of David simultaneously combining in their hands the two highest offices of Babylonian and Palestinian Jewry.[40]

After Daniel's death, however, neither his young sons nor his nephew Josiah, who had come together with him from Babylonia, seem to have played any prominent role in the affairs of the academy or the country at large. Perhaps the public or the influential groups in the imperial capital were disturbed by Daniel's high-handed methods. In any case, Daniel's sons were too young to be considered for any immediate appointment. The leadership now reverted to the local academic family of priestly ancestry. Elijah, the new gaon, was son and grandson of high academy officials before the regime of Solomon ben Yehudah.

Nevertheless, this reversion to the old order was far from smooth. Daniel's son David moved to Fusṭaṭ at the age of twenty in 1078, and there he established a rival exilarchate (1082–94). David's brother, Samuel, first accepted, and later gave up, his post as "Third" in the Palestinian academy, and moved to Damascus to head an academy of his own. Neither did Daniel's relations in Babylonia receive gracefully this transfer of authority to the priestly family. A century later Exilarch Daniel ben Ḥisdai still claimed that "it is matter of common knowledge that the chain of ordination had been broken for many years since the demise of our lord, Patriarch Daniel . . . and the priests called after him have behaved irresponsibly." The exilarch refused to honor these priestly leaders with the title gaon, since Hai Gaon had refused to apply it even in referring to Solomon ben Yehudah. Most threatening was another echo of that controversy, in Daniel ben Ḥisdai's remark that "from the days of our ancient forefathers the academy of the Holy Land had no share in Egypt [its support]." If accepted, this view might have dried up the most important source of financial assistance for the Palestinian academy.[41]

Daniel may have alluded here to an old source of friction which came to the fore again after Elijah's ascendancy in 1062. The ever turbulent "Babylonian" congregation in Jerusalem seems not to have accepted that change gracefully. Already in the eighth century it had forced the Palestinians to accept certain modifications in their liturgy. Now, headed by one Joseph, it demanded independent control over the distribution of charitable funds sent from Egypt for the poor of the Holy Land. It thus adumbrated the nineteenth-century struggles over the distribution of *ḥaluqqah* funds raised in the various countries of the dispersion. This effort reflected not only the simple self-interest of the Babylonians, but also their studied attempt to undermine the authority of "the head who is in Jerusalem." The geonic party reacted by appealing directly to the Faṭimid caliph in Cairo. In a letter, recently published, its spokesman argued that the Babylonians had been allowed to form an independent congregation only for purely ritualistic purposes, since their prayers and observances substantially differed from the local usages. But in all other communal matters they were subject to the authority of the head of the academy. "When two authorities are permissible," the writer added with reckless abandon, "there would be permissible three and even more [that is, the North African, Spanish, and Sicilian congregations might demand equal recognition], and this would lead to endless anarchy, to the robbing of lands and goods, to the rape of women, and the end of rights." [42]

Discounting these emotional outbursts, the Palestinian spokesman rightly sensed the dangers of internal disintegration which accompanied the rapid decline of the country. After the conquest of Jerusalem by the Seljuks in 1071, the academy had to be transferred to Tyre, which only in the broader sense could be counted as part of the Holy Land. When Elijah Gaon wished formally to sanctify the new moon in 1183, he had to proceed to Haifa on Palestinian soil. Soon thereafter he died, and his remains were carried with great solemnity "on the shoulders of men and not on horseback, a distance of three days" to Dalata in Galilee, where they were buried near the tomb of the second-century sage, R. Jose the Galilean.[43]

With Elijah's son, Abiathar, to whose Scroll we are indebted for this report, in fact for much of our knowledge of the period, the Palestinian gaonate to all intents and purposes went out of existence, unsung and unmourned. Not only was Palestinian Jewry now greatly reduced by the Crusaders' intolerance, but in the interim there had also arisen new centers of world Jewry, which no longer looked for guidance to the leaders of either Palestine or Babylonia.

PROGRESSIVE DECENTRALIZATION

David's attempt to establish an exilarchate in Egypt was a clear demonstration of the weakened controls of the two main centers. Understandably, the Muslim chiefs were duly impressed by his descent from the royal house of David. They were prepared to let him establish himself as a rival exilarch and thus help to eliminate whatever little influence the Baghdad princes of captivity still exerted over the Jews of the Faṭimid Empire. Personally, David was a ruthless, intriguing politician of the type then fairly common among the Near Eastern viziers. As such he merited Abiathar's sarcastic stress on his Davidic descent making him "related to Ahaz, Manasseh, Ammon, Jehoiachin and their ilk." On the one hand, he probably was greatly aided by his influential Karaite father-in-law, Moses ben Aaron ha-Kohen. On the other hand, this very marriage, at the beginning of his occupancy of the high office, with a sectarian lady who had reserved to herself the right to observe Jewish law in Karaite fashion, must have greatly antagonized even the "legitimist" Rabbanite circles. Combined with his high-handedness, fiscal exactions, and other personal defects, his flouting of public opinion led to his ultimate downfall. His regime lasted, therefore, only some twelve years (1082–94). In this short span of time he not only proved extremely ungrateful to his former benefactors and embroiled the community in serious controversies, but by his antics he also seriously undermined the authority of all Jewish leaders.[44]

Possibly at that time originated the legend of the appointment of a hereditary Jewish leader from the house of David by an early Faṭimid caliph, a legend which was to be repeated, with many romantic embellishments, by the seventeenth-century chronicler Joseph Sambari. Exaltation of Davidic origins naturally enough increased during more turbulent, messianically fraught periods.

At such times even an outright impostor, like one Shem Tob who had produced forged documents to prove his exilarchic-Davidic ancestry, was allowed to travel through Palestine, Egypt, and Syria, appoint judges and generally administer communal affairs. He did it so efficiently and so greatly earned the gratitude of the public that, when after two years his fraud was discovered, he was allowed quietly to depart for Byzantium. He never reached his destination, however, but died on the way. More legitimate members of the exilarchic house, too, began roaming through the Near Eastern countries, in search of employment or, rather, of charitable support. But their communal influence was very slight. As honored pensioners they were often on the payroll of the real communal leaders, the so-called *negidim* (princes), who held sway over Egyptian Jewry for more than half a millennium. In this important office some dim memories of the ancient "ethnarchs" of Egyptian Jewry now came back to life. That original Hellenistic title had, in fact, been used by the ancient Greek translators of the Bible to render the Hebrew designation of *nagid*.[45]

Such regional chiefs were now to be found almost everywhere in the Jewish world. Apparently the first to establish a rivaling provincial authority was an exilarch himself. We recall that, on his deposition from office as a result of the protracted controversy with an opposing geonic faction and his banishment from the Caliphate (about 912), Exilarch 'Uqba proceeded to Kairuwan, the young metropolis of the new Faṭimid empire. Here, according to Abraham ben Nathan ha-Yarḥi (of Lunel, early thirteenth century), he was assigned "a seat of honor near the ark in the synagogue and, after the recitation of the weekly sections reserved for priests and levites, the scroll of the Law was brought to his seat" for him to read the third section *(Sefer ha-Manhig,* fol. 32 No. 58). This signal honor, theretofore restricted to kings and officiating exilarchs, underscored the community's recognition of the hallowed leadership of the new arrival. 'Uqba apparently continued to style himself exilarch for the rest of his days, although he did not transmit that dignity to any of his heirs.

In later years there sporadically appeared leaders without claims to Davidic or, for that matter, any other distinguished ancestry, who served as semiofficial representatives of the Kairuwan Jewish communities before the government. Probably they owed their dignity not to any formal appointment or election, but merely to their wealth and political connections. Perhaps beginning with Abraham ben Nathan ibn 'Aṭa (early eleventh century), some of them called themselves *negidim,* probably after the title had been resuscitated in Egypt. This title was also acknowledged by the Babylonians. When Exilarch Hezekiah addressed the local leader, Jacob ben Amram, he spoke of himself as the "head of all the dispersed communities of Israel," but called Jacob "our mighty and noble *nagid,* lord and teacher, head of the phalangies of Israel." In the flowering Hebrew epistolary style these titles did not have quite the connotation they carry in the English language. They nevertheless expressed a measure of recognition of Jacob's provincial leadership. The new academies established in Kairuwan likewise enjoyed considerable independence. They heeded Samuel ben Ḥofni Gaon's call, addressed to the Kairuwan leader Joseph ben Berakhiah, and asking that geonic messages be publicly recited. They also constantly raised funds for the support of the Babylonian and, to a lesser extent, of the Palestinian academies. Yet even the staunch pro-Babylonian Nissim bar Jacob did not hesitate to introduce into his academy the observance of a *shabbata de-rigla* (the first Sabbath of the festive months of Adar and Ellul), which had long been the exclusive prerogative of Babylonian schools. Nissim even had occasion to answer a legal question from a Palestinian (Tyrian) student, R. Zadok, which, but a few decades earlier, would have seemed like carrying coal to Newcastle.[46]

Stimulated by 'Uqba's example in Kairuwan, the Faṭimid caliphs, upon expanding their realm to Egypt and Palestine, welcomed such independent Jewish leaders also in their newly acquired provinces. Since their armies were accompanied by a southern Italian named Palṭiel, an astrologer and purveyor of supplies, they allowed this influential adviser to become the main representative of Egyptian Jewry. We need not accept the sweeping assertion by his descendant, Aḥimaaz of Oria, that Palṭiel had become the spokesman over "the communities of the people of God living in Egypt, Palestine, Palermo [Sicily], Ifriqiya [north central Africa] and all the kingdom of Ishmael [the Faṭimids]." Nor do we have to postulate his identity with either the leading general,

Jauhar, or the influential statesman, Ibn Killis, as has been suggested by modern scholars. But he undoubtedly played a considerable role at least in internal Jewish affairs and in shaping the more permanent friendly relations between the Faṭimids and their ever more numerous and affluent Jewish subjects.[47]

It is very doubtful whether Palṭiel himself revived the ancient title of *nagid,* or established a permanent office of any kind. Despite the exaggerations inherent in most family traditions—even in our more critical age, these must as a rule be taken with a considerable grain of salt—Aḥimaaz himself nowhere clearly states that Palṭiel had held the post of *nagid.* Nor does his description of the synagogue service, attended by Palṭiel, indicate more than the congregation's general acclaim of a distinguished benefactor. There is no hint, for example, that the entire congregation remained standing, while the scroll of law was brought to Palṭiel—a special privilege accorded to reigning exilarchs. Nonetheless, Palṭiel may indeed have indirectly laid the foundations for the Egyptian institution of *nagid,* as it gradually emerged in the eleventh century.[48]

In any case, notwithstanding the general Near Eastern penchant for perpetuating offices within the same family if not necessarily by direct primogeniture, Palṭiel apparently was not followed by his descendants, except perhaps by his son Samuel mentioned briefly by our chronicler. But we have only an uncertain reference to a *nagid* Samuel (probably Samuel ben Ḥananiah) in whose presence the Cairo court took action concerning an Egyptian Jew's estate in Aden. The identity of these early leaders is the more questionable, as most of Palṭiel's descendants seem to have lived in Italy. Only a century after the Faṭimid conquest there appears something like a dynasty of *negidim,* founded by the influential court physician, Yehudah ben Saadiah, who was followed by his brother Meborakh, and the latter's son Moses. Between them these three officials held the reins of government for some three quarters of a century (about 1065–1140). Even their status, however, depended entirely on the whims of caliphs and viziers, and on no less whimsical shifts in public opinion. A newcomer, like David ben Daniel, succeeded through a political intrigue not only in temporarily dislodging Meborakh, but also in having him imprisoned for many years. By another shift, Meborakh came back to power in 1094, and remained *nagid* to the end of his life. But after the death of his son, Moses, the office, or at least its authority, was transferred to another court physician, Samuel ben Ḥananiah, perhaps best known for his friendship with Yehudah Halevi (about 1140–59). Even if formally appointed by the caliphal administration, these leaders did not yet enjoy exclusive jurisdiction. The head of the newly established academy of Fusṭaṭ, Maṣliaḥ (1127–38), styling himself *gaon,* often issued independent decisions. In 1139, one Solomon is recorded as having appointed judges. Twenty-two years later Netaneel Gaon received his assignment from the Babylonian Exilarch Daniel ben Ḥisdai. We even possess a remarkable decree of appointment of an Egyptian *nagid* himself by an exilarch, although the identity of both officials is far from certain.[49]

After 1160, there existed no generally recognized *nagid* in the country. For a number of years one Zuṭṭa (Sar Shalom) held that office against mounting opposition, but his authority was speedily overshadowed by that of the newly immigrated Maimonides. When the great sage threw his unmatched prestige in the community and his court contacts into the scale, Zuṭṭa was deposed (about 1075). The office remained unoccupied for a long time, since Maimonides himself, though by far the community's most influential member, apparently refused any official appointment. Some of his legal decisions were countersigned by a purely honorary *nasi,* Yehudah ben Josiah. Finally Maimonides' son, Abraham, was formally invested with the office of *nagid.* His authority, and that of his descendants, grew with the progressive weakening of both the Palestino-Syrian and the Babylonian centers. Real communal power was now wielded by the five or more generations of *negidim* from the house of Maimonides who dominated Egyptian Jewry from 1205 until after 1409, and by their successors until the conquest of Egypt by the Ottoman Turks in 1517. According to David ibn abi Zimra, the *nagid* had been supported by the Egyptian communities in a princely state, "so that he may devote his entire time to administering justice among them and representing them before the king and the authorities. Like the exilarch he is entitled, by virtue of a royal grant, to flog and to imprison them." This statement correctly mirrored the conditions during the last three centuries of the

Middle Ages. In the earlier period, however, the *negidim* faced a formidable array of competitors in and outside the country, and exercised only as much control as they could secure through their personal talents, wealth, or court connections.[50]

Internal dissensions in Babylonia's exilarchic family led to the formation of another Jewish provincial administration in Mosul. Zakkai ben Azariah, like his brother Daniel barred from succession to the exilarchic office by the long reign of Hezekiah from David ben Zakkai's line, likewise left Baghdad and founded a new branch dynasty which was to rule over Mosul Jewry for some three centuries. Petaḥiah of Ratisbon, visiting the city a century and half later, found there two cousins, David and Samuel, in full control of the Jewish community. They not only collected taxes from their constituents, but also maintained one of the very few Jewish prisons on record, to which they were allowed to commit both Jewish and Muslin culprits. Remarkably, despite his family's absence of a century and a half, one of these cousins, Samuel, was called back to Baghdad, to take over the exilarchate after the death of Daniel ben Ḥisdai in 1174. Here he became embroiled in his aforementioned conflict with Samuel ben 'Ali, whose letters denouncing the exilarch apparently carried little appeal in the latter's home community of Mosul. In itself, Samuel ben 'Ali may not have been unjustified in leveling at his opponent the accusation of insufficient learning. When Al-Ḥarizi visited Mosul in 1216, he had words of high praise only for Exilarch David (probably the same man whom Petaḥiah had observed some forty years earlier), but he sharply ridiculed the low intellectual level of the rest of the community. In 1288, another David (ben Daniel), styling himself "the great prince, head of the dispersed communities of Israel," joined in excommunicating the European arrival, Solomon Petit, for his anti-Maimonidean agitation. In this epistle David proudly enumerated his ancestors back to Josiah, David ben Zakkai's brother, and beyond.[51]

More sporadically we also hear of new regional chiefs in Aleppo, Damascus, and Yemen. On his visit to Yemen Benjamin found two brothers, Ḥanan and Shalmon, who, as *nesi'im* in possession of a genealogical record proving their Davidic ancestry, divided the country between them. They paid more or less equal allegiance to the Jewish leaders of Baghdad, Cairo, and Palestine, although the political and spiritual ties between their country and the Faṭimid regime indirectly fostered their special attachment to Egyptian scholars. Even the French of the twelfth century, we recollect, spoke admiringly of the "Jewish king" of Narbonne. The old provincial leaders of the Roman age were thus resuscitated in various lands. Some of them claimed Davidic descent, some assumed the office simply by virtue of their learning, wealth, or governmental connections.[52]

Spain was one of the few major Jewish centers under Islam where no leader exercised formal authority over the communities of the entire country. No such official spokesman is recorded during the Roman and Visigothic periods, when practically the whole Iberian Peninsula was united under the same public administration, and no permanent office of this type emerged during the relatively brief era of the Caliphate of Cordova. Even Ḥisdai ibn Shapruṭ exerted his beneficent influence without holding formal appointment as a Jewish chief from either the Jews or the government, although his title *nasi* must have conveyed to contemporaries the idea of at least semiofficial leadership. A more definitive attempt to superimpose a central authority occurred later in the tenth century. According to Ibn Daud, a prominent Cordovan silk manufacturer, Jacob ibn Jau, impressed the regent, Al-Manṣur, with some beautifully woven garments. In recognition for various services rendered to the government, the regent

> issued a document raising him [Ibn Jau] above all Jewish communities from Segelmessa [Morocco] to the river Duero on the border of the realm. He empowered him to adjudicate all their litigations, appoint their officials at his discretion and to collect all their taxes and fines resting on them. He gave him eighteen eunuchs beautifully clothed, and allowed him to ride in the royal coach. Thereupon all the [Jewish] inhabitants of Cordova, old and young, assembled and drew up a writ of princely dignity stating, "Thou shalt rule over us, as shall thy son and also thy grandson."

But after a year Al-Manṣur not only deposed Ibn Jau, but put him in prison, allegedly because he had failed to exact enough money from the Jewish taxpayers. Although soon liberated by Caliph Hisham, he never regained his full power in either political or Jewish affairs. When he died (about 990) he was nevertheless mourned by at least some communal leaders, including R. Ḥanokh ben Moses, whom he had opposed in the latter's famous controversy with Joseph ibn Abitur. Possibly this betting on the unsuccessful candidate had undermined the acceptance of his leadership by the Jewish community.[53]

Thus ended the short-lived attempt to establish in the western Caliphate a regular counterpart to the eastern exilarchate. It was cut short by the Caliphate's speedy disintegration. Whatever local or regional Jewish leaders emerged in the eleventh and twelfth centuries found their authority circumscribed by the boundaries of the Muslim "petty princes," or by the Christian principalities. The most important among them, Samuel ibn Nagrela, to be sure, assumed the high-sounding title of *nagid* in 1027, perhaps with the approval of Babylonian or Palestinian leaders with whom he frequently exchanged friendly letters and on whom he occasionally bestowed of his bounty. But his formal authority extended only over the small principality of Granada.[54]

Not that there existed any fundamental opposition to comprehensive Jewish self-determination on either the Muslim or the Christian side of the frontier. In fact, from time immemorial Spanish Jewry had exercised even capital jurisdiction, a right invariably denied to its coreligionists in other lands. Joseph ibn Abitur, a tenth-century Spanish exile in Palestine, boasted of the fact that the grandfather of his grandfather (in the ninth century) had applied the four biblical-talmudic forms of execution to criminals, and for that reason had received the family name of Satanas (from *shoṭ anash,* the scourge of men). The native Spaniard Maimonides also informed his eastern readers that the law prescribing the execution of heretics was "being applied in all western countries with respect to many individuals." On the other hand, Ibn Daud lauded the "prince" (*nasi*) Joseph ibn Ferrizuel for having reduced the Karaites in the country and restricted their residence to a single small castle, while he could have condemned them to death. Such exercise of capital jurisdiction, however sporadic, was doubly remarkable, as talmudic law had long rationalized the Jews' political impotence and expressly taught that capital punishment could be inflicted only while the Temple was in existence. The Spanish deviation can best be explained historically by the Muslim conquest of Spain, which had left the large Christian population in possession of its traditional right to execute heretics. It would have been doubly incongruous for the conquerors to discriminate against Jewish *dhimmis,* their allies during the country's occupation. On its part, Spanish Jewry may have caught some of the Visigothic spirit of intolerance toward heretics. It must also have inherited from that era of endless persecutions and enforced secret profession of Judaism a particular hatred of informers, whose denunciations endangered the survival of entire communities. It had every reason, therefore, to cherish the prerogative of threatening both heretics and informers (often the same individuals) with the extreme penalty.[55]

FORCES OF INTEGRATION AND DISINTEGRATION

In their usual romanticizing vein, contemporaries explained the phenomenon of Jewish decentralization as the effect of an historic accident affecting four captives. According to Ibn Daud, four distinguished scholars, Ḥushiel, Shemariah, Moses, and one whose name had been forgotten, embarked in Bari (probably for the East) and were soon thereafter captured by an Arab pirate, Ibn Riyaḥin. On the corsair ship Moses' beautiful wife committed suicide to preserve her virtue. Subsequently the three men were sold to three different countries: Shemariah to Egypt, Ḥushiel to Ifriqiyya, and Moses to Spain. By founding great academies in their countries of adoption, these three men were responsible for the emancipation of Western learning from the control of the Palestino-Babylonian center. In itself this story is not necessarily unhistorical. Certainly the mention of Bari, rather than an eastern seaport as the point of departure; the reference to Ibn Riyaḥin, an Arab admiral recorded in Muslim sources as commanding an eastern Mediterranean squadron in 972; and Ibn Daud's admission that the fourth scholar's name had since been forgotten—all bear the earmarks of authenticity. Such new arrivals from the East, moreover, whether voluntary like Dunash ben Labraṭ, or involuntary, indeed helped fructify the cultural milieu among both Jews and Muslims of the western lands. In the same context, Ibn Daud himself recorded also the subsequent settlement in Spain of two sons of the exilarch-gaon Hezekiah. Ibn Daud might also have mentioned, as did Yehudah bar Barzillai a century earlier, that long before Moses, the exiled prince of captivity, Naṭronai bar Ḥabibai (Ḥakhinai or Zabinai) had laid the foundation for independent Spanish learning by recording the Babylonian Talmud for the benefit of his new fellow-countrymen. But of course, behind all these more or less accidental personal experiences operated strong sociopolitical and cultural factors, which slowly but inexorably brought about that gradual westward shift in the center of gravity of the Jewish people.[56]

Most contemporaries recognized the political basis of the separation between the different groups of Jewry. In Spain and North Africa, especially, the separatist tendencies of the local communities were greatly encouraged by the Muslim rulers, who wished to sever the connections between their own Jews and the Babylonian leaders. Long known from Abraham ibn Daud's chronicle, which explained the Spanish caliph's refusal to nullify Moses' redemption by the community of Cordova, because he "greatly rejoiced on hearing that the Jews of his realm would no longer depend on the Babylonians," this political motivation has been confirmed by such a Muslim writer as Abu Qasim ibn Ṣa'id. When Ḥisdai ibn Shapruṭ gained the caliph's highest regard, writes Ibn Ṣa'id, "by his superior mettle, perfection, and culture, he succeeded, through the kind intervention of the Caliph, in procuring the works of the Jews of the East." This separatism took deep root in the masses, as may be deduced from several characteristic incidents. Among Abraham Maimuni's letters we find an interesting complaint by Joseph ben Gershom, a French Jew then serving as third judge in Alexandria. Joseph had been deeply insulted by Hodayah Nasi, one of the xenophobe local leaders, who had not only excommunicated him personally and called him "the cursed, son of the cursed," but had attacked "all French Jews as heretics and apostates, because they ascribed matter and form to the Creator." One easily perceives here the repercussions of the anti-Maimonidean controversy and the sharp antagonism provoked among the oriental partisans of Maimonides by the southern French opposition to his extreme insistence on the immaterial essence of God.[57]

Joseph ben Gershom was perturbed by the *nasi*'s excommunication, but Abraham Maimuni, himself a *nagid,* allayed his fears by pointing out that many of these grandiloquent designations were entirely nominal. In Abraham's opinion, the talmudic regulations concerning the severity of bans imposed by a *nasi* no more applied to Hodayah's excommunication than did the Arabic title *ra'is* (head) assumed by numerous self-appointed leaders without any official authorization. "It is known among all men of reason and understanding," he added echoing his father, "that most of these titles which people use for one or another purpose are vain and senseless words applied by wise persons sparingly and with discomfort. Only pretenders in quest of power indulge them to excess, because with them rests all their greatness and dignity." [58]

Because until 1038 the personal authority of the leading Babylonian geonim had maintained the semblance of centralization at least in the intellectual sphere, the end of the geonic period has usually been dated by the death of Hai bar Sherira in that year. This great gaon was indeed so deeply revered from Persia to Spain that, regardless of the fully established independence of Jews in the various countries, his word still carried great weight in all legal, theological, and even communal affairs. Shortly before his death at the age of ninety-nine he addressed a letter to the community of Fusṭaṭ in Egypt, staunchly supporting a local leader against a powerful opposition. Such encroachments upon both local autonomy and the rivaling authority of the near-by Palestinian gaonate annoyed the leaders of the Holy Land. Solomon ben Yehudah bitingly repudiated that intervention as motivated only by prospects of financial gain for the leaders of Pumbedita "who wish to extend their boundaries and spread their net over the entire inhabited world." Yet Solomon himself, the most forceful of the Palestinian geonim, could not prevent his own academy from submitting legal inquiries to Hai's superior judgment. Such inquiries were usually accompanied by appropriate gifts. Solomon also sent, as we recall, his son Yaḥya to Hai for advanced study. R. Nissim, leading Kairuwan scholar who dispatched inquiries and donations to Baghdad, once had to appeal to an intermediary to secure an early reply from the overburdened gaon. On the latter's death the great Spanish poets, Samuel ibn Nagrela, formally an independent *nagid,* and Solomon ibn Gabirol, composed moving elegies, Samuel extolling, particularly, Hai's great influence through his spiritual "sons in every Muslim and Christian country." After 1038, however, this spiritual dependence likewise ceased. Each country or region now developed its own intellectual leadership on the basis of personal merit and popular acceptance, rather than formal office. Great teachers like Isaac Alfasi of Fez and Lucena and Maimonides of Fusṭaṭ speedily acquired an international reputation which far outshone that of the contemporary Baghdad scholars. Even in his lifetime Maimonides' name was formally mentioned in the prayers of distant Yemenite Jewry.[59]

Jewish communal history was made, however, not only by these great leaders, but also by a host of lesser officials in both the central and local administrations. Even in the more centralized eastern communities the exilarchs, patriarchs and heads of academies were assisted by numerous officers of lower rank, like "fathers of the court," "judges of the court" and others. On the local level, lay elders shared with professional judges, synagogue precentors, teachers, and scribes the management of the Jewish communities. At times the heads of academies associated their underlings in decisions they rendered to inquirers from various lands. When they faced difficulties and needed the moral support of larger groups they were particularly prone to mention their vast following. In his conflict with Saadiah, Ben Meir tried to assuage the ruffled feelings of the Babylonian leaders, and sent out a circular letter "to the numerous communities of our Israelitic brethren living in the provinces of Shinear [Babylonia]." In this conciliatory epistle he extended "a great salutation from Us and from Isaac, [father of] the court, from the large and small Sanhedrins sitting before Us, from the scholars, memorizers and all the rows of disciples, from the 'nobles and grandees,' from the judges, scribes and precentors, from the elders and the rest of the community of Israel living at God's sanctuary [Jerusalem]." Even more numerous were the categories of leaders and officials enumerated in the circular letter, apparently sent out by the Jerusalem academy to the communities of the entire country and the "Palestinian" congregations established in Egypt during the emergency period after 1071. Here no less than twenty-nine synonyms were used, many of them without any technical connotation, to indicate all the more important citizens of the Palestinian communities in both cities and villages. To make the measure full, the enumeration concluded with a salutation to "the rest of God's people, the great and the small." [60]

In Babylonia, to be sure, the appointment of the local judges was entirely in the hands of exilarchs and heads of academies. But even there, when a successor was to be selected, the academy membership and some communal elders had the opportunity of expressing their preference among rivaling candidates, although their choice was restricted by the operation of both the hereditary principle and the gradual advancement in rank, especially at the Palestinian academies. At times, these considerations were swept aside in favor of such desirable candidates as Saadiah or Daniel ben Azariah. In such contingencies the powerful, though entirely unofficial, influence of bankers, governmental advisers, and courtiers often decided the issue.

Regrettably, we know very little about the methods of election or appointment of local officials. Even in Babylonia the judges appointed by exilarchs depended on the good will of the communities. The local chiefs were supposed, according to Nathan the Babylonian, to write the prince of captivity either commending his choice and praising his appointee's behavior, or else to point out the judge's evil conduct and to ask for his recall, which was promptly granted. Very likely many of these officers were recruited from the learned and wealthy groups in the communities themselves, and from the outset owed their posts to the wishes of fellow members. In most communities visited by Benjamin there were three such elders. The warlike Jewish population of Palmyra was headed, not by military commanders, but by three civilian elders, among them "R. Isaac the Greek." In large cities there was a greater division of labor. In Aleppo, for instance, Al-Ḥarizi found a whole array of distinguished citizens, most of whom probably held some communal office. In Baghdad alone Benjamin recorded the presence of ten full-time officials, called by the traditional talmudic designation, *baṭlanim* (men of leisure). After enumerating their respective positions at various local schools,

Benjamin explained their title by saying: "They do not engage in any other work than communal administration; and all the days of the week they judge the Jews their countrymen, except on the second day of the week, when they all appear before Rabbi Samuel [ben 'Ali], the head of the Yeshiva Gaon (Jacob), who in conjunction with the other *baṭlanim* judges all those that appear before him." Many eastern communities also had such specialized officials as the "head" (*paqid* or *waqil*) of merchants, who, probably self-appointed, nevertheless depended on the good will and the use of his services by both local and foreign Jewish merchants. Adumbrating in many ways the later functions of foreign consuls, these officials exerted great influence also in general communal affairs. They often transmitted their dignity to their descendants for many generations. A regular dynasty of such "heads" held sway over the Jewish merchants of Aden during three centuries.[61]

Under western Islam and, still more, in Christian countries the leadership rested more fully in the hands of collective bodies. There were no central offices resembling the exilarchate or patriarchate. Heads of academies exercised control through the willing acquiescence of their constituencies much more than by virtue of any constitutional provisions. Even the more authoritarian Kairuwan *negidim* frequently sought the cooperation of other leaders. Perhaps typical of their other governmental acts is a letter, beginning with the salutation, "From Us, Prince of the Dispersion, Light of Israel, the elders, and the rest of our community." Even more diffused was the authority of the elders of the increasingly populous and influential communities of Morocco and Spain, where the "princely" position of Samuel and Joseph in Granada was quite exceptional. As a rule every major community governed its own affairs through men, lay and professional, of its own choice.[62]

Yet its fundamental community of interests and ideology prevented the atomization of the Jewish people into innumerable local units independently pursuing their historic careers. Ironically, the financial needs of the Babylonian academies, to which Solomon ben Yehudah had so unkindly alluded, proved to be a major cementing link between the various Jewries. Much of Hai's and Samuel ben Ḥofni's correspondence was prompted by the desire to enlist the financial support of distant communities. To place such financial subsidies on a more permanent basis, the geonim stimulated their correspondents to submit to them legal inquiries. On the basis of their uninterrupted traditions from ancient times, the geonim were indeed able to help the local leaders not only to overcome the general difficulties of rabbinic law, but also to resolve the often baffling conflicts between book learning and contemporary needs. By thus arousing the self-interest of communal elders and scholars, and by furnishing them authoritative and uniform guidance in their perplexities, the geonim helped maintain also the uniformity of Jewish law and outlook on the world. Whether writing on their own initiative or, more frequently, replying to inquiries, they spoke with a voice of authority which brooked no contradiction. Even addressing a distant community, against which they could not invoke the assistance of the secular arm, they freely used phrases like "if such questions should arise among you, teach and inform the people what we have decided for you and communicated to you about the custom of the two academies." In adopting new ordinances (*taqqanot*), they had the whole Jewish world in mind. Although Maimonides still expressed doubts about the binding force of such deviations from talmudic law, they were almost invariably accepted by world Jewry. On the other hand, catering to the spreading mania for titles and decorations, the Babylonian teachers, followed by their Palestinian and other confreres, lavishly awarded designations like "friend" or "elect" of the academy on individual patrons in foreign lands. At times they also appointed permanent representatives in charge of fund raising. If these local representatives happened to be men of great acumen and erudition, like Jacob ben Nissim of Kairuwan, the ensuing correspondence served to enrich learning as such.[63]

Ultimately, the geonim resorted to the old technique of the ancient patriarchate, and began sending out authorized messengers to collect contributions. One such lengthy letter of authorization, written in 1191, was found among the papers of Samuel ben 'Ali. It was issued in favor of Zechariah ben Berakhel, the Baghdad gaon's son-in-law and future gaon, who was embarking on a journey to his native Aleppo. Among other matters, Samuel wrote that, because of Zechariah's learning and piety,

> we have ordained him father of the court of the academy, and given him permission to judge and to teach, to release the first-born animals [by ascertaining their blemishes with reference to Ex. 13:2; Sanhedrin 5a], to expound the Torah in public, to set stated hours for study, to appoint interpreters, to have his sermons solemnly heralded in advance and followed by the recitation of the "sanctification of the name" of the Lord [prerogatives usually reserved for exilarchs and heads of academies], to be the first to leave and to enter, to appoint scribes, *ḥazzanim* [synagogue readers and preachers], leaders in services and heads of communities, and to protest any infractions in heavenly matters. Anyone daring to contradict him shall be excommunicated by him and separated from the rest of the people, for his word is our word, his hand is our hand, and his honor is our honor.

The arrival of such an honored guest was not only an occasion for a public celebration, but also for the revival of interest in the affairs of the academy which dispatched him and the fate of the communities which he had visited on the road. Like the delegates for Palestine relief in modern times, these messengers helped to bridge over the gap in mutual communications between distant communities, and to maintain living contacts among them in the spiritual domain, even where the economic and political connections had largely been severed by the imperialist clashes of the age.[64]

This constant exchange of ideas among the Jewries of various lands was promoted also by a great many private scholars. Extensive journeys for purely intellectual purposes had long become customary in the entire world of Islam. Despite occasional rivalries, even minor manifestations of xenophobia, foreign Jewish scholars were assured brotherly reception in most communities. According to the chronicler, Aḥimaaz, a ninth-century Palestinian visitor in Italy had no difficulty in securing an audience for his sermon, just as the chronicler's own ancestor, also named Aḥimaaz, had the opportunity to conduct services in Jerusalem. There he secured forgiveness for his countryman, Silano, who had been excommunicated on account of a prank he had played on the Palestinian preacher. A released captive, like Moses ben Ḥanokh, needed but quietly to reveal his acumen in Jewish lore to be raised speedily to the leading position in the rabbinate of Cordova. There probably was not too much exaggeration in Joseph ibn Abitur's assertion that he had refrained from proceeding sooner to Egypt, lest his arrival inconvenience some of his good friends there, "for our brethren the Israelites, may God guard them, in every locality they inhabit, whenever they see a man revealing familiarity with the Torah, run after him, neglect their businesses, and strain themselves [to extend their hospitality to him] in order to secure the reward from our God in heaven." And Ibn Abitur had then been living under the cloud of an excommunication imposed upon him during his struggle for supremacy with Ḥanokh ben Moses in Cordova! [65]

In short, confronted as it was by tremendous forces of disintegration operating in the turbulent world of the eleventh and twelfth centuries, the Jewish people was able to maintain its essential unity because of its unbreakable spiritual links. The geonic reinterpretation of talmudic law now became the common heritage of Jewish scholarship from Yemen to England. The Jewish community and its religious, social, and legal institutions emerged with renewed vigor from that era of great tensions, because once again they revealed great adaptability to changing needs and were pliable enough to allow for infinite local variations in detail, while maintaining unbroken continuity and unity in fundamentals.

BYZANTINE CONTINUITY

In the Balkans and other imperial possessions, more democratic forms of self-government had been inherited from the vast experimentation of the Graeco-Roman world. Administration by a council of elders, rather than by a single chief, had become the rule in most provinces of the ancient Roman Empire, except, for a time, in Egypt and possibly Rome. The greater geographic distribution of the Jewish communities, their somewhat equivocal status as organs of public law, and the ensuing preponderantly voluntary allegiance of members would have made controls by regional chiefs largely ineffective even if the small size of most western Jewish settlements had not converted them into tiny family-like units. In the larger cities the confluence of Jews from many eastern areas created incipient ritualistic disparities and other distinctions according to countries of origin, which led to the formation of more or less independent congregations. That is why even the great council of elders (*gerousia*) in ancient Rome probably exercised little authority beyond the confines of the imperial capital. Certainly, the Jewish elders of the new metropolis of Constantinople enjoyed but strictly local authority.

In his famous *Novella* of 553, therefore, Justinian threatened a number of communal leaders, rather than any single chief, with severe sanctions in case they tried to teach the "second law" or to prevent the plaintiff faction from reciting Scripture in Greek. Characteristically, the emperor professed ignorance of the respective positions held by these leaders functioning under his very eyes. Some apparently bore the simple designation of "elders" (*presbyteroi*), while others were called *archipherekitai* (the equivalent of the Hebrew *rashe ha-pereq,* heads of "chapters," that is sections of the academy), and still others *didaskaloi* (teachers). There evidently was no sharp distinction between purely religious and secular activities, despite occasional ancient precedents for such a division. Some elders were elected to office because of their wealth, social connections, or administrative abilities, while others owed their distinction to greater or lesser expertness in Jewish law. Probably in matters of great ritualistic concern, like the prohibitions enacted by Justinian, the experts' voices carried greater weight. But the actual imposition of bans on a recalcitrant minority doubtless presupposed a measure of cooperation with the less learned but influential elders, indeed with the communal membership at large.[66]

On his journey through the Balkans more than six centuries later, Benjamin of Tudela found as a rule collegiate bodies of two to five members in charge of all communal affairs. Councils of five existed only in the three largest communities of Constantinople, Salonica, and Thebes. Coming first to the latter city, the traveler observed that "they have scholars learned in the Mishnah and the Talmud, and other prominent men [literally: great men of the generation] . . . and there are none like them in the land of the Greeks, except in the city of Constantinople." In all three cities this leadership was headed by a rabbi, or even "chief" (great) rabbi, but only in Salonica did Benjamin report that the rabbi was "appointed by the king as head of the Jews." Probably the king had merely confirmed his election. On the council of Thebes sat also the rabbi's brother, on that of Salonica the rabbi's son and son-in-law. The distinct functions of the Balkan rabbinate are nowhere indicated, but here, too, its professionalization seems still to have been in its incipient stages. Only in the case of Salonica, perhaps because of the royal "appointment," Benjamin emphasized that both the rabbi and his son were "scholars." Neither the rabbis nor the councils however, exercised any controls beyond the confines of their own communities. Unlike Egypt, moreover, where the *negidim* served as representatives of Karaites and Samaritans as well, the influential Karaite community of Constantinople recognized no authority of the Rabbanite chiefs, who could merely retaliate with the double-edged weapon of excommunication.[67]

An interesting responsum, issued in the eleventh century by the sages of Bari, then under Byzantine domination, was subsequently often quoted by German rabbinic authorities. It was signed by no less than seven rabbis. These signatures, as well as the public presentation of that reply to the messenger of the inquiry, were further attested by six witnesses. But one must not rashly generalize from this document for the usual size and general procedures in the southern Italian and other Byzantine Jewish courts. Bari may merely have adopted a usage, then rapidly spreading through the Near East, of having more than the required minimum of two witnesses sign on such solemn writs as marriage contracts.[68]

Because ever since 398 the government had withheld recognition from the Jewish tribunals, except as voluntary courts of arbitration, the communal leaders could enforce their authority only through anathemas and other spiritual means. That is why Justinian threatened sharp governmental reprisals for the use of these ecclesiastical sanctions in violation of his order. At times, to be sure, communal authorities transgressed these bounds. According to Aḥimaaz of Oria, the scholar and wonder-worker Aaron of Baghdad (son of an alleged exilarch Samuel), immediately upon settlement in the city, proceeded to enforce discipline in the Jewish community:

A certain Theophilus committed a sin through criminal intercourse with a married woman. Aaron, before the assembled community, condemned him to death by strangulation. A man laid violent hands on a woman and killed her; the master decided this case with severity, and sentenced him to death by the sword. He then considered the homosexuality of a man who had intercourse with a male in the way of idolaters; his case was detected and became known; hence he was condemned to death by stoning. Again a man violated the Law of God through illicit relations with his mother-in-law; by order of the master the community assembled and put the criminal to death by fire.

If at all true, these obviously were extralegal proceedings; they resembled lynchings, rather than formal executions. Although the chronicler's intention obviously was to stress the application in Oria (as in Spain) of the four forms of capital punishment provided for in the Talmud—even there they had already become of merely theoretical import—he himself emphasized that the criminals' death was brought about by the "assembled congregation." Theophilus was admittedly saved by the city's governor who "drove off the multitude" because he hoped to persuade the culprit to accept baptism. All four crimes represented, moreover, violations of sex laws. By some stretch of imagination Aaron may have felt entitled to apply here the talmudic provision for the lynching of Jews caught *in flagranti* while cohabiting with "Aramean" (Gentile) women.[69]

In any case we must not generalize from conditions in Oria for those in the rest of the Byzantine Empire. We know that later on, under both Islamic and Norman domination, southern Italian Jews were in possession of an independent civil judiciary. Such was not the case in Byzantium's Balkan provinces or in Asia Minor. In Benjamin's days Emperor Manuel Comnenus removed even the exceptional right of Constantinople Jewry to be judged only before the higher court of the *strategos* of the Stenon, the section in which the Jewish quarter was located. Thenceforth they were to appear "before every court in accordance with the law." On one occasion, Maimonides explained the difficulty of judges hailing from Christian countries by their lack of practical experience in civil litigations, since Christian rulers had suppressed their civil jurisdiction. Jewish civil law had, therefore, become there as abstruse and theoretical as were the laws governing sacrifices among rabbis living under Islam. True, Maimonides referred here particularly to the "people of France." But "Franks" often embraced all Europeans, and the asserted absence of civil jurisdiction certainly was more in keeping with the situation in Byzantium than in western Europe.[70]

WESTERN DEMOCRACIES

Different patterns of communal cooperation developed in the Western countries under the combined impact of age-old traditions and the newly evolving peculiarities of Jewish status. From the Roman Empire the small and widely scattered Western communities inherited a greater measure of local autonomy than was enjoyed by their coreligionists in the East. Their greater distance from the Palestinian center, the difficulties of maintaining regular communications, and the ensuing paucity of Western pilgrims to the Holy Land or Palestinian visitors in the West—all forced most early pioneers in the western provinces to rely mainly on their own resources. Even such a tireless traveler as Paul had been discouraged from visiting Spain by the difficulties of the journey. Since the provinces north of the Alps and the Loire were quite inaccessible to all except the most daring civilian settlers from the East, few of the Palestinian patriarchs' regular *apostoloi* must have considered it worth their while to venture westward beyond Rome, and possibly some cities on the coast of Spain. Discounting the evident exaggeration in Samuel ibn Nagrela's proud assertion that "Spain had been a seat of Jewish learning from ancient times, ever since the days of the [First] Exile from Jerusalem," we may nevertheless assume that the *nagid*'s own and other western communities had shown considerable independence in their intellectual evolution during the preceding centuries. Self-reliance in communal affairs, which so greatly depended on the changing local situations, was even more imperative.[71]

Because of the communal freedoms, almost anarchy, which must have prevailed in all of Rome's western provinces, there was much communal experimentation. The very domain of tenaciously conservative synagogue rituals was permeated with local usages handed down from time immemorial, which appeared incomprehensible to many later Eastern arrivals, as well as to students of the Talmud. The absence of *mezuzot* (door-post inscriptions reproducing Deut. 6:4–9, 11:13–21) from Jewish homes—Jacob Tam claimed with obvious exaggeration that "until ten years ago there were no *mezuzot* in our entire country"—might still be explained by the fear of attracting attention in a generally insecure environment. But praying without head covering and phylacteries, the recitation of the *qaddish* (mourner's prayer) in the parents' lifetime, and many other deviations from talmudic practices, evidently stemmed from an independent local evolution, rather than from willful neglect. Only the city of Rome, which harbored a continuous Jewish settlement from ancient times, still maintained fairly close relations with the Holy Land. In emulation of the Palestinian organizational forms leaders of the Roman community adopted even the new titles of *nasi, gaon,* and *resh kallah,* the latter two borrowed by Palestine herself from Babylonia only a short time before. A Moses Nasi was found already by Jacob bar Yequtiel on his diplomatic journey to the papal capital in 1007–10.[72]

Such emulation of the Eastern quest for titles seems to have been short-lived, however. Only the title *gaon,* which was quickly losing its peculiar association with the presidency of an Eastern academy, became now fairly popular in Rome and elsewhere. The great lexicographer, Nathan bar Yeḥiel, who is recorded to have defied the ancient prohibition, and built a new synagogue in the very citadel of Catholicism, his father, and the latter's predecessor, Jacob, were all distinguished by this honorific title in an inquiry addressed to Nathan by Rashi, as reported by Isaac bar Moses of Vienna. But the papal administration paid them no heed. At least the Jewish elders welcoming Alexander III in 1165 were described merely as *stratores, scrinarii, judices cum advocatis* (elders, scribes, judges and supervisors). Whether these titles represented a division of functions between lay elders, professional or nonprofessional scholars and judges, and some permanently employed lesser communal servants, is nowhere indicated. Probably even a community of the size of Rome's, at that time embracing more than 1,000 Jews, had neither a large permanent communal board nor a sizeable staff. When Benjamin visited the city shortly thereafter he mentioned only six leaders by name; among them Daniel, "the rabbi," Nathan's grandson Yeḥiel, the pope's influential adviser, and Menaḥem, "head of the academy." More or less similar conditions are reflected in Benjamin's itinerary through the more populous settlements south of Rome. In northern Italy, with its slight and scattered Jewish population, even the larger communities of Lucca and Pisa had communal boards of but three individuals.[73]

Elsewhere, too, committees of three were preferred to the traditional councils of "seven best men," as they appear in the Talmud and, following it, in many medieval writings. Here it is merely a stereotype with little relation to reality. Even in the Byzantine centers of Rabbanite and Karaite life and later in the more populous Central European communities, the number seven was rarely attained. Such a literal student of the Talmud as Mordecai bar Hillel ha-Kohen may have tried to force through the rule that each community possess seven elders and three charity supervisors. The former were needed, in his opinion, at least for such major decisions as turning a synagogue into a profane building. But following Eliezer bar Joel ha-Levi's interpretation that even a single elected official could represent the entire community, he had to be satisfied with the concurrence in major communal undertakings of seven distinguished citizens, whether or not they held any office.[74]

Despite the break in historic continuity occasioned by the persecutions of the seventh century, the northern Italian Jewish communities, like the Christian municipalities of that area, carried with them many vestiges of ancient Rome. In a position to help develop some of the newer Jewish communal patterns north of the Alps, they found particularly receptive ears in southern France and the Rhinelands where the ancient communities of Marseilles, Arles, or Narbonne, of Cologne and Treves, had likewise salvaged some ingredients of their community life before it was submerged by the barbarian migrations. There is indeed a grain of historic truth in the old legend of the transplantation, by Charlemagne, of members of the Kalonymid family from Lucca to

Narbonne and Mayence. "Charlemagne" is evidently a symbol more than a person. This transfer may have begun under Pepin in Narbonne, and continued over several generations of contacts between the southern French and Rhenish communities. Italy, and through it Palestine, thus remained a permanent fountainhead of much of the new cultural and communal forms springing up in the nascent centers of Jewish life and learning in northern France, Germany, and England.

Visigothic Spain, on the other hand, which at first had likewise retained many Roman traditions, was soon engulfed by the Arab-Berber wave. By being incorporated into the world of Islam, most Spanish Jews came under the guidance of the Babylonian sages and permanently followed Babylonian, rather than Palestinian, teachings and observances. Ultimately, there emerged not only in law and ritual but also in the forms of communal organization a certain cleavage between these European communities, creating the broad distinctions between Sephardic and Ashkenazic Jewry. Once established, these divergences persisted after Spain's reconquest by the Christians, although the underground survival of Roman vestiges was now reinforced by the growing prestige of the northern Tosafists' talmudic learning. Many concepts and observances, interveningly developed in the Ashkenazic communities, were now unwittingly introduced also into Sephardic community life via the reinterpretation of talmudic law. In between lived populous, affluent, and culturally advanced Provençal Jewry, which often served as a bridge between the two branches of European Judaism. Culturally oriented toward its southern coreligionists, its communal life nevertheless retained many more vestiges of the ancient Roman-Palestinian tradition. It also was more deeply influenced by the communal observances and doctrines developed under the northern feudal order.[75]

Out of the welter of these manifold new adjustments evolved certain basic lines of evolution which were to differentiate the later European communities from all their predecessors. Because of the paucity of contemporary documentation, these early, perhaps chaotic, but fundamentally creative, trends are shrouded in almost total darkness. When these communities emerge into the light of history in the tenth century they appear as fully grown entities with such prominent leaders as Gershom bar Yehudah (died 1028) and Joseph bar Samuel Tob 'Elem (Bonfils). They certainly were much further advanced than their counterparts among the Christian burghers in the then nascent northern cities. Comparing the well-known decrees issued by Henry IV in favor of the Jews of Worms and Spires with similar enactments for the benefit of Christian merchants, B. Altmann has rightly concluded that "except for the similarly worded grants for commerce, the rights of the autonomous Jewries considerably exceeded the privileges of the citizens." From the entire tenor of these privileges, moreover, it is quite manifest that many provisions had been formulated by the Jewish petitioners in accordance with their long-observed customs and laws. Such drafting of laws by interested parties and their approval by the authorities after negotiations, usually accompanied by a regular give and take however variable in form, were a fairly permanent feature of medieval legislation. Apart from this qualitative difference, there was also the significant priority of the Jewish privileges by several centuries, since in their essence they were but modifications of rights already granted the Jewish settlers by Louis the Pious. The fact, moreover, that the Jews represented not only a different social class, but also a distinct religious denomination, enabled the rulers to assimilate certain Jewish rights, especially full judicial autonomy, to the immunities long secured by the Christian clergy in its early struggle for independence from the state. Jews were thus in a position to perform significant pioneering services not only in trade and agriculture, but also in the domain of community life.[76]

Perhaps the outstanding contribution to the development of the medieval city constitutions was made by the democratic processes gradually evolving in the Western Jewish settlements. Not having had regional chiefs even in ancient times, and scattered through many small, often sparsely populated towns and villages, the Jews of Western Rome's successor states had to rely upon their own local resources to meet the tremendous challenges of the backward, but rapidly developing environment. True, Charlemagne or Louis made an effort to organize all Frankish Jewry at least for purposes of state services and supervision. In his fulminations against the favors bestowed by the emperors upon the Jews, Agobard mentioned a *magister Judaeorum,* whose task evidently consisted in both controlling the Jews' fiscal contributions and protecting them against attacks. But this short-lived experiment left no permanent mark on either the Jewish communities or their relations with the Western states.

No similar official is, in fact, recorded until the later Middle Ages when, largely for fiscal purposes, the governments sought to establish centralized controls, but when, for that very reason, Jews vigorously resisted. The first Western community to be organized on a country-wide scale under governmental pressure was that of Angevin England, where royal control over Jews was more effective than in any Continental country. Out of the crucial decade following the bloodshed of the Third Crusade emerged also the new office of "presbyter," or "episcopus," of all English Jewry. Jacob, the first presbyter known to us by name, was appointed by Richard I, and then reappointed for life *per totam Angliam* by John I (1199). After a considerable time lag France followed with a chief rabbi in the fourteenth century, while Germany made similar but vain efforts to establish a chief rabbinate in the fifteenth and sixteenth centuries. Christian Spain, too, notwithstanding the example set by the earlier communities under Islam, seems not to have entrusted the management of Jewish affairs to regional chiefs until 1257, when James I appointed his secretary (*alfaquim*), Solomon, chief judge of Aragonese Jewry. Even there, however, the doctrine enunciated by Solomon ibn Adret, Solomon Alfaquim's contemporary, was doubtless shared by the majority. The Barcelona rabbi, himself formally under Solomon's jurisdiction, taught that "within its borders each community possesses the authority equal to that of the geonim." Certainly, before 1200, each Western community was sovereign in its own right, except where a larger city was surrounded by small isolated Jewish settlements. In this case the city's synagogue, cemetery, and other communal institutions serving the needs of the entire district, also buttressed the control of the city's elders over these dependencies in a way reminiscent of the authority exercised by the ancient Palestinian municipalities over their "daughters." [77]

Not that intercommunal cooperation was altogether lacking.

The communities' small size and dispersal, the necessity of their frequent consultation and negotiation with imperial or royal authorities, as well as their need to legislate on legal and ritualistic matters of common concern, demanded a frequent exchange of ideas and common action. At first such outstanding rabbinic authorities as Gershom or Rashi sufficed to give them a sense of common direction. Some ordinances attributed to Gershom doubtless merely reflected older observances, some others were the fruits of a later evolution. Even those which were enacted in his name were undoubtedly preceded by much intercommunal consultation. But neither Gershom nor Rashi seems to have presided over a regular synod convoked to issue ordinances. True, in one recension of the *Responsa* of Meir bar Baruch of Rothenburg, our main source for Gershom's ordinances, the ban is designated as "the ban of the ordinances of the communities." In another inquiry to Gershom there is mention of "communities assembled there," probably in a city along the Rhine (a Cologne fair?), which tried to aid a Jewish merchant in salvaging objects lost in a shipwreck. But even if both these passages were authentic records of Gershom's period, and not later reformulations, they would prove no more than some chance meetings of representatives from various communities. Similarly, the opening sentence in Rashi's ordinance (likewise preserved by Meir bar Baruch), "We the inhabitants of Troyes with the communities in its vicinity," hardly refers to a formal synod. If authentic, it merely indicates a public assembly of the Jewish inhabitants of Troyes, attended by a few leaders from among the numerous lesser communities of Champagne. Such a gathering may indeed have taken place in Rashi's time. Yet even without formal assent by their colleagues, the great authority enjoyed by both Gershom and Rashi insured general acquiescence.[78]

In time, however, the individual communities grew larger and more self-assertive; many of them were led by scholars of equal distinction. Hence all new joint ventures tended to become collective efforts. Witnessing the frequent assemblies of priests and laymen in Catholic synods, Jews may have been prompted to follow that example. The Champagne city of Troyes, especially, had long been a favored meeting place for Catholic provincial councils embracing the Champagne and neighboring districts. The first important French Jewish synods likewise convened in Troyes after 1150. Not all important French communities were represented, but even those absent were expected to subscribe to the synodal resolutions, as stated in their preamble:

Therefore have we taken counsel together, the elders of Troyes and her sages, and those of her vicinity, the sages of Dijon and its vicinity, the leaders of Auxerre, and of Sens and its suburbs, the elders of Orléans (?), and its vicinity, our brothers, the inhabitants of Châlon-sur Saône, the sages of the Rhine country, and our masters of Paris, and their neighbors, the scholars of Melun and Etampes, and the inhabitants of Normandy, and the shore of the sea, and Anjou and Poitou, the greatest of our generation, the inhabitants of the land of Lorraine; of those mentioned here, some have already agreed and from some we have not yet heard, but since the matter was pressing, we were confident [of securing their agreement], knowing that they are great men who listen to their inferiors, and that the decision is a correct one. If it were not written down, it ought to be placed on record.

Despite these soft words there was a metallic sound behind this pronunciamento. By wielding the powerful communal weapon of excommunication, the authors of such resolutions were able to enforce compliance not only by recalcitrant local minorities, but in extreme cases also by unwilling leaders of other communities. This certainly was the case in matters of religious and ritualistic concern, as stressed already by Joseph Tob 'Elem in his communication to the sages of Troyes, with reference to the rabbinic maxim concerning the mutual responsibility of all Jews for the behavior of each.[79]

We must not be misled into believing, however, that these regional gatherings, or even local communal councils, ran roughshod over minority opinions. In fact, protection of minorities became one of the major concerns of the communal leaders of that period—causing them unwittingly to make a major contribution to democratic processes, which was soon emulated in some city constitutions. Since governmental taxes loomed large in all Jewish relations with the outside world, safeguards against the undue imposition of burdens on individual taxpayers became extremely important. The pertinent talmudic legislation could be, and frequently was, subjected to divergent interpretations. Yet some rabbis insisted that voting in tax matters required unanimity, and that no one could be coerced to contribute more than his due share by a simple majority vote. Since the concept of a community acting as an "artificial person" apart from the totality of its members had only begun to crystallize in the minds of leading rabbis, the consent of individual taxpayers was considered indispensable. But once the general principle and methods of collection were unanimously adopted, no one was allowed to retract.[80]

Such procedures naturally presupposed great mutual confidence. They were possible only in those small direct democracies where the communal membership, rarely exceeding a few score persons, usually collaborated in family-like corporate groups. Only thus could one envisage the successful operation of a fiscal practice, occasionally recorded in the northern communities, that, after the vote on the tax rate, left actual payments entirely to the discretion of individual taxpayers estimating their own property or income. Of course, this emphasis on conscience was strongly abetted by religious sanctions, even threats of excommunication, against those abusing that privilege.

Another democratic feature of the medieval Western community could not readily be imitated by the Western cities; it depended too greatly on the intimate relationships prevailing in a small, well-knit group exercising police functions chiefly through moral and religious suasion. Even in ancient Palestine a Jew feeling aggrieved by his own leaders, or unable to secure justice because of the power of his opponent in litigation, could appeal to the public conscience by "interrupting the prayer." Cases of this kind occurred also under Western Islam. Only in Babylonia, whose communal administration was strongly centralized, did the rabbis try to prohibit all interference with orderly worship. A geonic responsum stated bluntly that "in Iraq one does not recognize that right, for there the public does not exercise supervision over law and order and only the court is entrusted with that function. The public must obey what the court ordains. . . . Everywhere else, too, where a judge is in charge of law and order, the plaintiff must turn to him, and not to the public." Even in Palestine, Morocco, or Spain, however, such appeals to public conscience were quite exceptional. They were never devoid of a slightly revolutionary character, resembling the interruption of prayers by a dissatisfied populace in some of the leading mosques. Even in Baghdad, we recollect, such a popular upheaval of mosque worshipers once forced the hand of a pro-Jewish administration. This is the less surprising since both synagogue and mosque served not merely as houses of worship but also as communal centers for the transaction of "secular" business. In the West alone, such interruptions became so frequent as to threaten the orderly synagogue services. Hence already in the days of Gershom it was found necessary to forbid disturbance of prayers on Sabbaths or festivals, or even of the morning and afternoon prayers on weekdays in the middle of services, unless the complainant had "thrice interfered with the evening service or the *completion* of the morning service" without success. Later rabbis allowed appeals to the public only at the end of services, but after three failures to secure redress, permitted the plaintiff to interrupt the prayers at any time. An exception had to be granted in matters of public concern, when any citizen could interrupt even holiday services.[81]

On the other hand, electoral democracy did not loom as a major issue. Elections to communal boards had frequently been practised in ancient Palestinian and other populous communities. But in the West groups averaging a few score adult males rarely required representation on boards via complicated electoral procedures, such as were to develop during the later Middle Ages. Most members relied on their learned and wealthy leaders to take care of all communal affairs and but occasionally render account to a general assembly readily available at almost any time after synagogue services. In this respect the Jewish community of tenth- or eleventh-century Germany and northern France resembled somewhat the ancient Israelitic municipality with its council of elders recruited from the heads of local clans. Now, moreover, the scholars were engaged in a drive for communal supremacy, far more comprehensive and successful than that of their ancient Palestinian or Babylonian predecessors. The presence in most communities of several learned and pious individuals, whose opinions enlisted unhesitating majority support, often rendered elections entirely superfluous. If such communal leadership revealed many "aristocratic" features, this was an aristocracy of learning based upon a fully democratic equality of educational opportunity.[82]

Because of these close local ties, on the other hand, there developed a certain amount of xenophobia aimed at new arrivals. There was no opposition in principle to immigration of foreign Jews. But the growing regimentation of medieval economy favored the interests of the local population against unfair competition of newcomers—and almost any kind of competition was considered unfair. Expanding, therefore, certain talmudic provisions intended for the protection of tradesmen in semifeudal Babylonia, Gershom and Rashi laid the foundations for a fairly ramified legislation concerning the *ḥerem ha-yishub* (ban of settlement). With this weapon it was possible to limit admission of new settlers to those who were likely to provide a living for needy coreligionists or increase the communal resources without serious damage to vested interests. Going beyond the talmudic regulations, new settlers were also made to contribute to local taxes and charities within two weeks after their arrival. At the same time the growth of medieval cities and of interurban trade made these restrictions quite burdensome. Faced by these confusing crosscurrents, the Paris rabbis addressed an inquiry to the older community of Rome as to how this ban was to be interpreted (about 1130). Not having shared with the northern Jewries the full impact of feudal regimentation, the Roman sages expressed amazement "at your request that we take sides in a matter which, not being customary in our country, is unfamiliar to us." Some northern rabbis, too, objected to these severe restrictions on the freedom of movement. Jacob Tam, for example, taught that "our ancestors had not introduced the ban of settlement except against overbearing individuals, informers, and those unwilling to submit to communal ordinances or to pay taxes along with others, but no ban is to apply to other persons." Isaac of Dampierre was even prepared to accept Joseph ibn Megas' ruling, understandable in the far more liberal economy of Muslim Spain, that no one should be denied settlement rights if his wares were cheaper or of better quality than those of the local merchants.[83]

Local variations in time and place thus influenced the application of that legal principle decisively, if unobtrusively and even imperceptibly to many protagonists themselves. For example, Gershom and Rashi used almost exactly the same language in interpreting the talmudic law. Yet there was a basic difference in the realities of their respective communities. The ancient rule that residence permits could not be refused to poll tax payers of the same government had applied to all Jewish subjects of the vast Sassanian Empire. Perhaps unwittingly, Gershom's interpretation sharpened these restraints and applied them to taxpayers of but a single feudal principality. For instance, in Gershom's own archbishopric of Mayence, permits were to be essentially limited to Jews already resident in Mayence. Wherever the state boundaries and those of the Jewish community roughly coincided, the community would thus enjoy full freedom in keeping away all outsiders. In the time of Rashi and his successors, on the other hand, Troyes embraced only a fraction of Jewish taxpayers of the counts of Champagne. Rashi's use of the same terminology allowed considerable freedom of movement at least within numerous larger and smaller communities of that prosperous county. With the progressive increase in the Jewish population and international trade relations and the simultaneous pulverization of feudal controls over many western areas, the restrictive laws could become a serious obstacle to Jewish migrations and international trade in western Europe. Hence came also the growing diversity of rabbinic opinion and the ultimate abandonment of any general regulation. By turning it into a *ḥerem,* a ban, the rabbis made it part and parcel of those communal restraints which each community was entitled to impose on its members by means of a self-proclaimed ban.

QUEST FOR SELF-DETERMINATION

Whatever forms Jewish communal administration assumed, whether it stressed individual freedoms or communal welfare, centralized controls or local self-government, aristocratic-rabbinic or democratic-popular supremacy, the main concern of both rabbinic and lay leaders was to stave off external interference. While under Islam the general principle of Jewish autonomy was fairly well respected and, except for some extralegal interventions by high-handed government officials, there was little meddling with the Jewish judiciary, Western attitudes were far more fluid. Wherever in a position to do so, Jews sought to secure privileges guaranteeing their self-government. Such protective regulations were enacted by the Carolingians, Emperor Henvy IV, and many other monarchs. But other sovereigns either refused formally to grant their Jewish subjects full autonomy or, more frequently, failed to live up to their own pledges. Since feudal lords, bishops, and city elders often competed with the royal power in exercising control over the Jewish communities, they also tried to arrogate to themselves, or their appointees, the right to adjudicate litigations among Jews. Northern communal leadership had to expend, therefore, much energy and money to ward off encroachments. Members, in particular, seeking positions of power or the settlement of their disputes with fellow-Jews through the aid of highly placed dignitaries of state or church, were threatened with severe reprisals, even with the awesome anathema. The main resolutions adopted by the Champagne synod, presided over by Jacob Tam, read:

1. We have voted, decreed, ordained and placed under ban any man or woman who cites a fellow-Jew before Gentile courts or exerts compulsion on him through Gentiles, be they prince or commoner, ruler or inferior official, except by mutual agreement made in the presence of proper witnesses.

2. If the matter accidentally reaches the ears of the king or other Gentiles, who exert pressure on a Jew, we have decreed, under ban, that the man thus aided by Gentiles shall save his fellow from their hands. . . . He shall make satisfaction to him in such a manner as the seven elders of the city will ordain.

3. We have also decreed, under ban, that no one must intimidate the "seven elders" through the power of Gentiles. Because the masters of wicked tongue and informers do their work in darkness, we have decreed to excommunicate them also for indirect action, unless they satisfy him [the injured party] according to the directions of the seven elders of the city.[84]

Paradoxically, the final resolution of that synod reads: "We, the undersigned, request all those that are in touch with the government to coerce, through the power of Gentiles, anyone who transgresses our commandments." This was, indeed, the general exception confirming the rule: the leaders alone were allowed for the common good to employ governmental coercion against members abusing governmental support for their private benefit. Perfectly realistic, this practice often placed the burden of decision on the governmental authorities which, when guided by enlightened self-interest, tried to strengthen the communal bonds among their Jewish subjects and imposed upon themselves strong self-restraints. Much too frequently, however, immediate interests and appetites, personal favoritism, and other all-too-human weaknesses interfered with the smooth operation of these general principles. This constant tug-of-war constitutes, in fact, much of the "political" history of the medieval Western Jewries. In this uphill struggle successes followed defeats and vice versa, but the perseverance of Jewish leaders and the active or passive resistance of the masses always salvaged a broad range of communal autonomy.[85]

Opposition to non-Jewish interference in internal Jewish affairs was reinforced by an ancient Jewish tradition which considered all government a concession to the fundamental imperfections of human nature. Without going the whole length of the scholastic theory of the state being merely the fruit of sin, though at the same time a remedy to sin, talmudic rabbis, followed by medieval jurists and philosophers, regarded the exercise of power by one man over another as but a deplorable necessity. Just as economic productivity enforced a division of labor and, hence, required a single manager to coordinate the diverse activities, so did public life, in the prevailing rabbinic opinion, demand the management of the state or city by a single leader. As usual looking back to the Bible in its talmudic reinterpretation, Maimonides declared that the election of a king had been the first of three commandments imposed upon Israel after its settlement in Canaan. Similarly, he merely summarized old biblical-talmudic law when he taught that the appointment of judges and officers (Deut. 16:18) in every district and city was a positive commandment at least for the land of Israel. Even foreign monarchs were generally recognized as instituted by the divine will. Commenting on an ancient proverb, "For the transgressions of a land many are the princes thereof" (28:2), Saadiah contended that "it stands to reason that a perfect government is only one that is in the hands of one man . . . , whereas a government by many is a visitation inflicted by God." We perceive here an echo not only of Plato's *Republic* but also of the political and economic realities in the contemporary world. Nor is it surprising to find the fairly autocratic gaon extol the monarchical regime which, in modified form, prevailed also in the contemporary Jewish community in the Near East, while the ascetic Baḥya and Abraham Maimuni stressed chiefly the personal insecurity of even kings, who lived in perpetual fear of assassination. Such fear, to be sure, was much more in order in Saadiah's Baghdad than in Baḥya's Saragossa, or still later in Abraham Maimuni's Cairo.[86]

As was the case with economic theory, the medieval rabbis failed to produce a comprehensive political doctrine concerning either state and government or the management of the Jewish community itself. They merely recognized the inherent differences between the various constitutional systems under which they lived, and agreed that, as long as Jews dwelled in exile, they had to obey all established authority. Even philosophers, therefore, were satisfied with a few generalities relating to man being a social creature dependent on cooperation with others and, therefore, subject to the will of a government above them all. On the other hand, their observation of contemporary political life convinced them that power had a demoralizing influence. A homilist, quoted in the relatively young *Midrash ha-Gadol* exclaimed, "Woe unto power, for it removes from its possessors the fear of heaven!" Maimonides, who had little use for many contemporary leaders, expressed a similar sentiment by saying, "No sooner do most of these Jews achieve positions of authority, than they lose the fear of heaven." He himself set an example in refusing to accept the post of *nagid,* although he freely restated the biblical prohibition of cursing a king and extended it also to heads of academies. Any such offense against a supreme "royal" or "spiritual-legislative" authority was punishable by flagellation. Almost all medieval thinkers, moreover, agreed with him that one ought not to seek power and dominion over one's fellow-men. Not only otherworldly writers like Baḥya and Abraham Maimuni, but also Saadiah, personally as ambitious and militant a leader as any produced by medieval Jewry, advised his readers to shun office.

He admitted that ambition and the quest for power was an innate characteristic of man. He ascribed it in particular to the impulsive faculty, one of the three basic faculties of man. Yet he demanded that here, too, man's cognitive faculty should control this subordinate propensity, and that he should not "manifest any eagerness for dominion or vengeance." The gaon merely conceded that, when called upon, a good citizen would fulfill his duty and assume whatever governmental responsibility may be demanded of him.[87]

We need not take all such assertions at their face value. Ethical sayings and theorems were often handed down from generation to generation. Attitudes of supererogation, at some time or other formulated by unworldly, power-shunning individuals renowned for their piety, were transmitted to posterity as shining examples of humility and exemplary behavior. Even men of different temperaments, or confronted with different social challenges, nevertheless felt impelled to pay lip-service to the teachings of those illustrious predecessors. Nor was it considered good form to admit that one's quest for office was prompted by personal ambition. For the most part, one had to mouth professions of unworthiness and to offer services for the public good at great personal sacrifice, even if one did not quite mean it. Assertions, therefore, such as made by Solomon ben Yehudah, "May the Lord fulfill my wish and bring forth a qualified and deserving man to take my seat," just as Hillel had succeeded the self-effacing sons of Batirah in ancient times (Mann, *Jews in Egypt,* II, 126), must be taken with a large grain of salt. Facing a serious attempt to replace him, the aged gaon fought bitterly, as we recall, for the preservation of all his prerogatives.

In the Eastern communities much of that struggle for power was obviated by the operation of the hereditary principle. Discussing the ancient Israelitic monarchy, Maimonides declared that "once anointed, the king acquires the crown for himself and his descendants for ever after. . . . And not only the monarchy but all offices and appointments in Israel are transmitted to one's son and grandson forever, provided that the son can fill the father's place in regard to wisdom and piety." In order to preserve the dignity of office, the old law excluded from the highest offices of king and high priest proselytes, women, and even certain craftsmen held in low esteem, such as butchers, barbers, bath-masters, and tanners. Moreover, according to the oriental etiquette, a high official was supposed to "lose face" before the public if he appeared in undignified attire, or performed some menial function.[88]

Exclusion of women and proselytes from public office, however petty, was evidently upheld in the Middle Ages, although active businesswomen often played a considerable role behind the scenes. The provision that even descendants of proselytes be barred until they had Jewish mothers had little practical significance. The few converts to Judaism who defied the sharp prohibitions of both Muslim and Christian law were quickly absorbed, the ancient racialist emphasis speedily melting away in the crucible of tremendous outside pressures. Our sources occasionally mention proselytes, but hardly ever speak of their children. There existed in no medieval community any identifiable group of descendants of proselytes, segregated in any way from the rest of the population. Nor was there any effort at endogamy.

Only socially was some stigma attached to non-Jewish origin. In the personal vilification of Saadiah Gaon which characterized the scurrilous pamphlet literature during his controversy with David ben Zakkai, his descent, too, was under debate. While Saadiah stressed his aristocratic ancestry, the opposition claimed that he was of proselyte origin and that his father had performed idolatrous services. But these vehement denunciations undoubtedly defeated their own purpose, and found little credence even among the exilarch's adherents. Of no more practical significance was the exclusion of members active in certain professions from eligibility to the highest offices. Repeated as a matter of legal theory also in medieval sources, it rarely influenced elections to communal boards. Much more significant was the contemporary deprecation of all manual labor, which Jews shared with Muslims and Christians especially in Eastern lands. It was considered a sign of the Suranic academy's utter degradation that, before Saadiah, one Yom Tob Kohen, a weaver, was appointed its presiding officer. Sherira's observation to this effect is the more poignant as he himself mentioned that Yom Tob was a son of R. Jacob bar R. Naṭronai who had presided over Sura for thirteen years. Yet Yom

Tob's appointment, "although he was a weaver," seemed understandable only "because there were not many scholars there." These prejudices were carried over into the Western communities, notwithstanding the gradual rise there of an influential artisan class in the cities. Even more decisive was the Jewish preference for learning and contempt for illiteracy which automatically favored scholars, regardless of their origin or economic standing. But in the ultimate sense it was the will of the community which determined the choice of its leaders.[89]

Without directly adumbrating the modern doctrine of the sovereignty of the people, even ancient rabbinic theory recognized that, no matter how sanctified it was by the divine choice, the king's regime ultimately depended on its acceptance by the Jewish community at large. A Jewish king, in fact, was not supposed to ascend the throne except by election of the Great Sanhedrin of seventy-one representing the whole people. These regulations pertaining to the monarchical regime were translated, with the necessary modifications, into the realm of communal legislation. An ancient teacher, R. Isaac, had already declared that "one must not appoint an elder over a community except after consultation with that community" (Berakhot 55a). Even in the autocratic Eastern regions the local judges appointed by exilarchs had to prove acceptable to their constituents; otherwise they had to be recalled after a brief tenure of office. From Palestine westward the communal majority had its way, through elections or otherwise, of choosing, or even deposing, its communal leaders. On the whole, it respected the hereditary principle by giving preference to worthy sons or brothers of former office holders. But in many cases newcomers from the ranks were given a chance to ascend the highest academic offices and, through them, to become the real powers in the community.

Medieval rabbis did not philosophize on that score. They were perfectly convinced that the most learned members had an inherent claim to being heard, and usually followed, in major communal decisions, as well as favored with respect to their share in communal burdens. Asked about the scholars' obligations to poll taxes and other governmental imposts, Naḥshon Gaon replied bluntly, "Even if the king and his viziers impose upon Israel a multitude of taxes and harshly oppress the public, one is forbidden to take anything from the rabbis." Summarizing the long-accepted law, Maimonides stated more broadly,

> Scholars do not personally go out together with the rest of the community and take part in the digging or building of a city and the like, lest their dignity suffer before the illiterate people. Nor does one collect from them contributions toward the construction of walls, the erection of gates, the wages of guards and the like, nor toward a gift for the king. They are not obliged to pay any tax, be it a general tax resting collectively upon the city's inhabitants or one imposed upon each individual. . . . Similarly if a scholar has merchandise for sale, he is allowed to sell it first, and none of the other market vendors is permitted to dispose of merchandise before him. Also if he has a litigation and appears in court among many other parties, he is given precedence and is seated [before the judge].

Maimonides, it should be noted, was one of the few rabbis of his time who tried to stem the professionalization of learning by insisting that Jews should pursue the study of the Law for its own sake and not for worldly gain. Joseph ibn Megas actually freed a rich landowner from all taxes, including thousands of dinars of land taxes in arrears, because he was a scholar. Even more consistently than in Eastern countries, the Western rabbis fought for complete tax immunities of scholars. Under Islam neither the rabbis nor the Christian churchmen, except monks living on charity like other beggars, were exempt from the poll tax. Only where the communities were responsible for the total amount of the state tax could they free their scholarly members by increasing the share of the others. In the West, on the other hand, they often succeeded in securing regular governmental exemptions for scholars. Apart from invoking precedents set by talmudic sages with the concurrence of Roman authorities, they were aided and abetted in this endeavor by the general tax immunity granted there to the Catholic clergy.[90]

In time, the widespread tax immunities proved unbearable to many communities squeezed dry by royal tax collectors. The very success of the rabbinic propaganda and the ensuing spread of rabbinic learning made too many members eligible, thereby disproportionately increasing the tax pressure on the unlearned members. Following Ibn Megas himself, who did not wish to see his own liberality unduly extended, Asher ben Yeḥiel and other rabbis decided that only full-time scholars, who spent few hours on earning a living, but not those principally engaged in secular pursuits, were entitled to such privileged treatment. Even more radically, Ḥananel of Kairuwan, followed by the Spaniards Naḥmanides and Nissim Gerondi, restricted that immunity to general taxes, but insisted that imposts resting on persons or property, especially poll and land taxes, had to be paid by scholars too.[91]

The most crucial problems arose, however, not from the internal administration of the community, but from its relations to outside powers. The ambivalence of the rabbinic theory in this respect has already been noted. On the one hand, it considered external interference as the major menace to Jewish autonomy and the very survival of the Jewish people. On the other hand, it demanded unquestioning obedience to established authority, especially to kings who, in the prevailing opinion of all three denominations, could not have come to power without the will of God. In Jewish law, particularly, the ancient compromise formula of *dina de-malkhuta dina* (the law of the kingdom is law) was more frequently invoked than clarified. Everybody understood that the law of the kingdom could not impinge upon the Jewish religious institutions or beliefs. A king, demanding conversion to another faith, or the wanton breaking of the Sabbath, or that of any other basic commandment, was to be resisted; in some cases he was to be fought to the last drop of blood. Even in civil affairs, where acceptance of "the law of the kingdom" apparently reigned supreme, some rabbis made serious reservations. No one questioned the king's authority to impose taxes on all subjects. Israel's king, for instance, was expressly given the authority to "impose a tax on the people for his needs or for the financing of wars, as well as to fix custom duties which one is forbidden to evade" (Maimonides). This prerogative doubly applied to the royal power with respect to Jews living in the dispersion who, the rabbis agreed, however erroneously from the standpoint of historic fact, had been admitted to the foreign countries under the condition that they would carry the full burden of taxation. Custom played a tremendous role, however. Just as Thomas Aquinas advised the countess of Brabant not to impose upon her Jewish subjects any but the customary taxes, so did Thomas's rabbinic contemporary, Meir bar Baruch of Rothenburg, declare any new and unaccustomed tax an illegitimate exercise of the royal prerogative. In such cases, he taught, the king acted not as a king but as a highway robber, and hence his law was not to be considered valid Jewish law. We also recall the Tosafists' protest against Philip Augustus' undue interference with French Jewry's long-customary freedom of movement.[92]

Who was to decide? Clearly, under the then existing power relationships no king treated such rabbinic qualifications as serious obstacles in the enforcement of his decrees. On its part, the Jewish public was likely to follow its rabbinic leaders' interpretation of the law and to offer at least tacit resistance to royal enactments considered illegal by the rabbinate. To all intents and purposes we have here a clash of rivaling sovereignties. On the royal side, the king's law, especially as relating to his Jewish "serfs," possessed undisputed authority. On the Jewish side, the *jus divinum* of Torah and Talmud was superior to any enactments by human beings, however powerful. Few Jews would have dissented from Maimonides' exclamation that their "Law alone is called divine; other laws such as the political legislations among the Greeks, or the follies of the Sabeans, are the works of human leaders, but not of prophets." In his *Epistle to Yemen* the sage of Fusṭaṭ waxed eloquent in extolling the "deeper meaning of its [the divine law's] positive and negative precepts," and its infinite superiority over the laws of other nations. "The tenets of the other religions," he declared, "which resemble those of Scripture have no deeper meaning, but are superficial imitations." Only the sagacity of the rabbis, combined with the general restraints imposed by custom upon rulers, prevented most of these theoretical conflicts from degenerating into regular miniature struggles between state and church, in which naturally the Jewish community would have succumbed. Here, too, the unflinching perseverance of the Jewish people and its leadership helped to overcome many a temporary crisis and to maintain the Jewish communal evolution on a fairly even keel.[93]

CITY WITHIN A CITY

Communal self-determination was facilitated by the penchant for segregated living characteristic of most medieval peoples in both East and West. Members of the same religious, ethnic, and professional groups preferred to live together for the sake of both convenience and the greater feeling of at-homeness. Notwithstanding the great freedom of movement and facilities for travel in the Muslim world, there were "Andalusian" and "Kairuwanese" districts in Fez, although their inhabitants' Sunni religion and Arabic speech differed but slightly from those of the native majority. Jewish living apart from the rest of the population was so much taken for granted that contemporaries but incidentally mentioned Jewish quarters, making it often difficult for modern scholars to ascertain their precise location.

Nor did the Jews in any way resent such topographical separation. Even in the East, where they mingled more freely with their Muslim and Christian neighbors and where they pursued diverse economic careers, they usually preferred to live among their own folk. Rabbinic law, trying to stave off the influence of Gentile ways of living, had long been a major force of segregation. It not only discouraged Jews from residing among non-Jews, especially on the Sabbath, but also objected to the sale or renting to Gentiles of dwellings in the Jewish street. The Jews themselves often hailed the assignment of special *juderias* in Spain as a distinct favor, particularly if the latter were located in fortified places and the ingress to them even of public officials was circumscribed by law. Similarly, Bishop Rüdiger of Spires considered the establishment of a separate Jewish quarter surrounded by a wall in 1084 as a means of attracting Jewish settlers and of enhancing the city's honor and trade. This was by no means watertight separation. Innumerable business, social and intellectual contacts between the Jews and their neighbors often breached these walls. Nor were all Jews necessarily living in their own quarters, or all non-Jews barred from residence there. Legislation enforcing such segregated living was yet to come. When it did come in the later Middle Ages and early modern times, it was a sign of the weakening of social barriers which the law then tried to reinforce—often in vain. Before 1200, however, the majority of Jews in almost every town voluntarily congregated in their own street or streets, where they could more fully enjoy the educational and religious facilities and the amenities of life amidst a like-minded and socially homogeneous group. Here they did not have to be constantly on their guard as to what impression their actions would create on hostile observers, but could unconcernedly go about their private or public business.[94]

Within that Jewish quarter Jewish law reigned supreme. Here the communal administration and the judiciary, as a rule enjoying the full confidence of their constituents, governed along lines hallowed by ancient custom and reinforced by legal sanctions which, everyone believed, were of divine origin. Behind that wall of law and custom, even more than behind any physical walls, life's drama was played out by most Jewish actors with little conscious attention to the clashes in the outside world. Enclosed in such spiritual or physical islands amidst vast, often tempestuous seas of three diverse but almost invariably strange if not hostile civilizations, the Jews felt greater kinship and revealed greater understanding for the problems and behavior of distant coreligionists than for the affairs of their immediate Gentile neighbors.

Nor was this attitude in any way resented by these neighbors. Only in modern times was the battle cry sounded that Jews lived in a "state within the state." When this form of separation began to be resented, it too was an overt sign of the breakdown of the accustomed separation of all citizenry into self-governing corporate groups, all of them forming miniature "states" of their own. In the Middle Ages unfriendly critics of Judaism may have assailed or ridiculed certain Jewish laws, particularly those derived from irrational ancient taboos. Less frequently, they also objected to excessive Jewish "legalism" as such, although the antinomian Pauline heritage had lost much of its plausibility even in the Christian world which was increasingly overloaded with liturgical ceremonies and canonistic casuistry. Antinomianism was altogether meaningless under the strongly legalistic Muslim civilization. The vast majority of non-Jews simply took it for granted that Jews would adhere to their own laws, even those which they themselves did not comprehend. On the Jewish part, it was precisely that portion of the Law which, as a talmudic sage observed, "the nations criticised and Satan disputed" to which each Jew was obliged to adhere unhesitatingly and without harboring any "evil thoughts." [95]

Equipped with the powerful instrumentalities of that law, and itself wholly under its control, Jewish leadership could steer a consistent course amidst the baffling currents in the evolving great civilizations. The people as a whole lived its own sheltered life, whose worthwhileness it never doubted. Firmly adhering to this way of life, it serenely confronted the "nations and Satan" in their unceasing attacks on Judaism.

XXIV

SOCIORELIGIOUS CONTROVERSIES

STARTING from different assumptions, Jew, Christian, and Muslim almost never penetrated the core of each other's faith. Although in Eastern lands they lived the same kind of life, spoke the same idiom, even studied the same works of science and philosophy, they nevertheless missed some of the crucial points in each other's religious outlook. Islam's combination of a world religion with political imperialism proved as incompatible with the Jewish syntheses of religious universalism and ethnicism as had been the cosmopolitan otherworldliness of early Christianity and the Roman imperial ecclesiasticism of the later Church.

Not that attempts at clarification were altogether lacking. The intellectually alert and, on the whole, rather liberal atmosphere of the Caliphate, only occasionally overcharged with currents of intolerance and religious persecution, was conducive to a free interpenetration of ideas. There certainly was no water-tight separation of the various religious groups. Even the most orthodox Muslim had to evince curiosity about the "people of the book," to whom his authoritative sources of tradition, the Qur'an and the *ḥadiths,* were professedly both deeply indebted and acrimoniously hostile. The Muslim sectarian and free-thinker, on the other hand, searching for flaws in the official doctrine, were happy to find ready-made weapons in the large Jewish and Christian armory of reasonings as to why these faiths consistently rejected Mohammed's message. The "infidels," on their part, had to keep on justifying to themselves, as well as to the outside world, why they refused to yield to the views of the majority, backed as these were by all the paraphernalia of power and success. In the process they unavoidably acquired some familiarity, however superficial, with the dominant religion. Nor could they avoid being affected by the fervent quest for new truths in religious, as well as scientific and philosophic, spheres which characterized the "Renaissance of Islam."

POLEMICS AND APOLOGIAS

Out of this blend of awakened mutual curiosity and missionary pressures, further stimulated by the general Near Eastern predilection for debating almost any issue, arose endless religious disputations. These were conducted on all levels, from popular altercations on the streets and in the bazaars to large public debates staged with all the fanfare of royal command performances. Harun ar-Rashid and Al-Ma'mun, especially, seem to have delighted in such public exchanges at court. All enjoyed listening to these exhibitions of mental prowess and quick wit, although doubtless they knew in advance that each disputation would end as it had started, with no party conceding defeat. A tenth-century Spanish Muslim, Abu 'Umar Aḥmad ibn Sa'id, reminisced about his experiences in Baghdad:

> I twice attended their [the philosophers'] assemblies. . . . At the first session there were present not only Muslims of all sects, but also agnostics, Parsees, materialists, atheists, Jews and Christians, in short, infidels of all kinds. Each of these sects had its spokesman, who had to defend its views. As soon as one of these spokesmen entered, the audience stood up reverently, and no one sat down until the spokesman took his seat. . . . We are assembled to discuss matters, one of the unbelievers declared, "you all know the conditions. . . . Each one of us shall use exclusively arguments derived from human reason." These words were universally acclaimed.

After two such sessions our Spanish visitor foreswore attendence at these "godless" assemblies. According to another Arabic report, a Jew appeared at a meeting of Muslim theologians, and entered into a debate with a Muslim divine concerning the Qur'an. He was allegedly silenced by Kabi (died in 929) only because of the latter's great reputation and the presence at those assemblies of all the renowned Muslim theologians of Baghdad. Widely publicized, too, but on the whole equally ineffective, were the numerous controversial tracts, designed principally to satisfy the cravings of an argumentative citizenry. "There hardly exists any other literature," notes such a connoisseur as I. Goldziher, "which deals with so many petty problems in a polemical vein, as do the Arabic letters." [1]

These were no mere games to most participants and onlookers, however. Many disputants were deadly serious, not because they were desperately trying to persuade their opponents, but rather because they strove to convince themselves and their adherents. Apologetic, rather than missionary, motivations are particularly manifest in the theoretical works devoted to comparative religion. With the widening of the geographic and historical horizons, the challenges of other faiths to Islam had to be met on a more rational level. Not surprisingly the first students of comparative religion came from the circle of translators of Greek classics, like Naubakhti, or from such students of world history as Mas'udi. Before long theologians and philosophers too had to take cognizance of the existing great varieties of religious experience. Abu Bakr al-Baqillani, an eminent exponent of the Asharite doctrine, was among the first to devote a large section of his theological work to all-embracing polemics against the major non-Muslim religions and even their sectarian subdivisions. In *Kitab aṭ-Ṭamhid* (Guide to Confuting the Various Heretics and Unbelievers), written about 980, he calmly but decisively attacked the doctrines of Zoroastrians, Brahmins, Christians, Jews, and even astrologers. Among the Jews he singled out not only the dominant Rabbanite group whom he called *Sham'atiyya* (adherents of the Oral Law), but also the Karaites, Samaritans, and the small but still fairly influential sect of 'Isawites. Christians and Jews responded in equally restrained fashion. Although John of Damascus (died about 752) initiated a series of Christian polemics against Islam, two more centuries passed before the distinguished Rabbanite and Karaite teachers of the tenth century, Saadiah and Qirqisani, took up the cudgels in behalf of Judaism.[2]

Not that all debates were conducted on a high, scientific plane. Street brawls, even minor pogroms, flared up at times against a weaker party which had held its own in a debate. Acts of violence occurred not only among members of major denominations, but also among lesser sects within the same faith, and even factions espousing different interpretations of Scriptural passages. Unlike the Christian minority, which never completely relinquished its missionary ideals, the Jews must have felt that they had little to gain from such intellectual encounters. While there undoubtedly always were individual Jews spoiling for a fight, and others who looked for an opportunity to strengthen the faith of their coreligionists, most of their leaders, particularly the usually staid and soft-spoken exilarchs, must have responded to such calls with utter reluctance and restraint. And yet it often devolved on the princes of captivity, as well as on the chiefs of the Christian hierarchy, regardless of their personal predilections and intellectual equipment, to serve as spokesmen for their respective religions. Two such command performances by exilarchs before Harun ar-Rashid and Al-Ma'mun are briefly described in contemporary Arabic letters.[3]

After a while these discussions became extremely repetitious, almost stereotyped, thus greatly lightening the burden of defenders of their faiths. A well-read controversialist could, without too much difficulty, anticipate the main arguments of his opponent, who could display his dialectical brilliance only in giving some unusual new twist to an old cliché or in finding a particularly happy or elegant phrase to express the same old idea. Jews were better off in so far as they recognized the sacred and divinely inspired character of neither the New Testament nor the Qur'an. Even a polemical writer like Simon Duran, who left behind a major Jewish anti-Muslim treatise, seems not to have studied the Qur'an, but was evidently satisfied with excerpts therefrom included in the writings of Averroës. Saadiah read it more carefully, but hardly ever referred to it directly. On the other hand, because of their general recognition of the Old Testament, both Christians and Muslims had to argue against its Jewish interpretations. The battle usually raged over certain key passages in the Hebrew Bible, Arabic translations of which may have existed in part even before Mohammed. To be sure, the penchant for second-hand knowledge and reliance on older authorities was too great even for savants of the rank and breadth of knowledge of Ibn Ḥazm. While his treatment of Pentateuchal passages betrays careful critical study, that of other biblical books is quite superficial. Only such later converts from Judaism as Samau'al ibn Yaḥya al-Maghribi, 'Abd al-Ḥaqq al-Islami, or, long before them, the more famous 'Ali aṭ-Ṭabari, a Christian turned Muslim at the age of seventy (about 838–48), had grown up with a truly first-hand knowledge of their Scriptures.[4]

ARGUMENTS FROM SCRIPTURE

From Mohammed himself the Muslim apologists inherited both their reverence for the Hebrew Scriptures and the view that the latter had been abrogated by the work of the Prophet. Following on a far lesser scale the Christian example, the few Muslim students of the Bible strained their ingenuity to detect in the Old Testament forebodings of the coming of their founder. Since the strictly messianic passages fit Mohammed less well, these controversialists often had to resort to such dangerous expedients as the *gemaṭria* to prove that certain biblical words or phrases, the numerical value of which totaled 92, really had Mohammed in mind. They explained, for example, that God's promise to Abraham, "And I will make of thee a great nation [*le-goi gadol*]" could only refer to Mohammed, because only under him did the patriarch's descendants become a truly great nation and because these two Hebrew words consist of letters aggregating 92 in value. Other words, (for instance, *gan* of the Garden of Eden) were found to have the numerical equivalent (53) of Aḥmad. If, on the other hand, in God's creation of the two "great [*ha-gedolim*] lights" the letter value amounted to 98, this biblical adjective allegedly symbolized both the Messenger's rise and his instituting the sixth day (Friday) as the weekly holiday (92 + 6). Not surprisingly, it was Jewish converts like Samau'al and 'Abd al-Ḥaqq who made extensive use of these numerical acrobatics from Hebrew letters.[5]

In this way, and also through the biblical locality of Paran, were detected hints of Mecca and the Ka'aba stone. From other passages one could deduce the future greatness of Ishmael and almost anything else one wished to find.

The Jews persist ['Abd al-Ḥaqq exclaimed] in denying Muḥammad's prophetic mission out of envy and obduracy; for indeed their books refer to him clearly. . . . With God's help, I shall refute them, and annihilate their doctrine with arguments which they themselves accept and cannot dismiss; for I am going to cast their own stones upon them, and flog them with their own assertions, taking my arguments from their twenty-four books [the Bible] which are alleged to be revelations.

Others, like Ṭabari, emphasized that Moses' prediction that God would raise a prophet "of thy brethren, like unto me; unto him ye shall hearken" necessarily related to Mohammed, rather than the Israelitic prophets or Jesus, for the latter were "from themselves, and not from their brethren." Samau'al ibn Yaḥya added that the passage would have been meaningless, if it referred to Samuel the Seer, as the Jews contended, for the Jewish people would have readily listened to a prophet confirming their tradition. But they had to be ordered to "hearken" to a prophet from a brotherly tribe who would come to abrogate their law. Of course, neither Jews nor Christians acknowledged these claims. The only prediction in the Bible the rabbis were ready to concede to Mohammed was the prophecy of Daniel relating to the "little horn" which was to uproot the three previous horns, that is the Babylonian, Persian, and Roman empires. Maimonides saw a particular pertinence in Daniel's accompanying prediction that the new prophet "shall think to change the seasons and the law" (7:25). But the sage of Fusṭaṭ hastened to add that "Daniel was divinely informed that He [God] would destroy this person notwithstanding his greatness and his long endurance together with the remaining adherents of his predecessors." [6]

Pointing out that things permitted to Noah and the patriarchs were forbidden by the Torah, the Muslim apologists argued that just as earlier revelations had been superseded by that on Sinai, so did the latter yield its place to the message of Mohammed. Moreover, they contended, close examination of the Hebrew Scriptures revealed many internal contradictions and dogmatic shortcomings, all attesting to their imperfect preservation. These deficiencies contrasted sharply with the alleged absence of all contradictions in the Qur'an, to which Mohammed himself had boastfully referred as a sign of its indubitably divine origin. Muslim apologists went to great lengths in glorifying the unmatched beauties of their Scripture and, like Al-Baqillani, emphasized its superhuman, miraculous qualities.[7]

Anticipating much of modern biblical criticism, Ibn Ḥazm stressed certain inaccuracies and inconsistencies in the Old Testament, particularly as relating to numbers, and exclaimed, "I have never seen anybody more ignorant of arithmetic than the person who compiled the Torah for the Jews." Since one could not ascribe such failings to God, the fault must rest with the Jewish tradition which, in many respects, was utterly unreliable. Unlike the Muslim *ḥadith,* Ibn Ḥazm contended, which could be traced back by a chain of reliable witnesses to the Messenger himself, Jewish tradition really went back only to Hillel. It was under the Maccabeans, some four hundred years after the destruction of the ancient kingdom, that the Torah spread among the Jews, becoming to all intents and purposes a new religion created by the rabbis. Jews thus had had many opportunities for falsifying their Scriptures to suit their biases, as for example in substituting Isaac for Ishmael in the story of Abraham's great hour of trial. In this way Ibn Ḥazm and others, utilizing the materials accumulated in age-old controversies between Jews and Christians, or with their own sectarian and free-thinking scholars, supplied a pseudo-scientific foundation for the Qur'anic accusation of Jewish "forgeries" of the Bible.[8]

As against Ibn Ḥazm who may be considered the first consistent, critical expounder of the theory of "falsification" (*taḥrif*) of Scripture, a more moderate school (according to tradition going back to the Jewishly informed cousin of the Prophet, Ibn 'Abbas, "the Arab rabbi") merely contended that the "people of the book" had placed erroneous interpretations on various passages in order to suppress their original allusions to Mohammed and Islam. In this respect the Christians were supposed to have been even greater culprits, since they actually eliminated all such references from their copies of the New Testament.[9]

Like many another controversialist before and after him, 'Ali aṭ-Ṭabari was oversanguine when he believed that he "did not leave the members of the protected cults any argument, any difficult question, any contentious point, that I have not mentioned and then refuted and solved." Here and there a *dhimmi* was persuaded by such altercations to join Islam, although the great majority of converts were doubtless drawn into the younger faith by more cogent pressures. Nor did most Muslim writers pursue primarily missionary aims. While there is no doubt that in oral encounters they tried hard to outwit their opponents and, if possible, make them acknowledge defeat, they addressed their controversial tracts principally to Muslim audiences which, especially in periods of religious tensions, were often wavering in their faith. Similarly, the defense of Judaism served as a means of stemming internal dissensions. Jewish scholars must have considered most Muslim reasonings spurious and ill-informed. They certainly looked askance at deductions made from questionable Arabic translations of biblical texts. Even such crucial passages as Gen. 16:10–12 were quoted by different Arab controversialists in at least eight different Arabic versions, all of which could rather easily be repudiated by their Hebrew opponents. The very fact that, unlike the western Christian missionaries from the school of Raymond Lull, none of the Arab writers made an effort to study Hebrew and, in their rare quotations of Hebrew words, had to lean heavily on Jewish friends (including converts), shows how little they were animated by genuine conversionist aspirations.[10]

Muslim claims that Mohammed's coming was predicted in the Bible caused the least difficulty to Jewish apologists. They merely had to stress the ordinary meaning of the respective scriptural passages and to point out that through *gemaṭria* one could prove anything. The Samaritan scholiast, Abu Sa'id ibn Abu'l Ḥusain (known to us also from a legal decision rendered on July 15, 1261), voiced a view widespread among Jewish apologists, when he objected, for instance, to the identification of Mount Paran with Hejaz on both geographic and exegetical grounds.

> How can any intelligent person [he asked] believe that the Holy Scripture foretells the appearance of one who will annul its precepts, allow what it forbids, and forbid what it allows? This is a flagrant calumny, and God knows best. I am not acquainted with any one who believes this, except one who has renounced the true faith and attached himself to him whom they have accepted.

Some enlightened Muslims themselves were aware of the specious nature of the accepted arguments. Ibn Qayyim ibn al-Jauziya (died 1351) conceded that it was highly unlikely that "Jews and Christians living in all parts of the world should have uniformly expurgated from their Scriptures the name" of Mohammed. Such reasoning, in his opinion, merely played into the hands of unbelievers. All that the Qur'an (7:156) wished to indicate was that the characteristic features of the Messenger and the time of his arrival had been clearly adumbrated in the Torah and the Gospels. It would seem inconceivable, he added, that the ancient prophets should have failed to foretell an event "the like of which the world had never seen, nor would see again until the hour of resurrection." Others admitted that each specific contention in support of the Muslim tradition might be rejected, but argued for the cogency of its total outlook, especially its view that Mohammed had attained the highest degree of prophecy. To which Sa'd ibn Manṣur ibn Kammuna calmly replied, "This is an argument based upon intuitive insight. It is difficult to convince of its truth an opponent who fails to detect that intuitive insight in his soul." [11]

More complicated answers had to be devised against the interrelated contentions of the Jewish falsification of the Bible and its abrogation by the Qur'an. Jewish apologists had to explain not only the contradictions and inconsistencies in Scripture which the newly awakened critical and philologically refined curiosity had easily detected, but also certain of its underlying philosophic, ethical, and legal concepts which no longer corresponded to the standards of the medieval intelligentsia. Clearly, stories like those of Lot and his daughters and Jacob's misrepresentations to Esau and Isaac, required explanation. Samau'al ibn Yaḥya argued, on natural as well as moral grounds, that a dignified elder like Lot, then one hundred years old, could not get so drunk two nights in succession as not to recognize his daughters and yet retain his sexual potency. He came, therefore, to the interesting critical conclusion that this passage must have been inserted into the Pentateuch by a priestly writer who wished to discredit the ancestry of both the Moabite people and the Davidic dynasty, descended from the Moabite Ruth. Jewish apologists had to find answers appealing to the new rational predilections of their readers. Even more difficult yet, as we shall see, was the task of squaring anthropomorphic passages in the Bible and its miracles with the refined speculative doctrines of medieval philosophy. On the other hand, orthodox Muslim polemists of the Asharite school, like Baqillani, stressed precisely the miracles performed by Mohammed as incontrovertible proof of his divine mission. Many of these miracles, he contended, had been performed in the presence of numerous observers. The few Jewish and Christian contemporaries, who had stubbornly repudiated them, could not be counted against the overwhelming majority of affirmative witnesses. Moreover, Jews and Christians had rightly disregarded denials by unbelievers, including Brahmins and Zoroastrians, of miracles performed by Moses. They cannot object, therefore, to the application of the same standard to miracles reported in the Qur'an. Some of these controversies went so deeply to the core of the Jewish outlook, indeed that of all revealed religion, that they fructified the whole range of Jewish thinking, and we shall have to refer to them in many connections.[12]

On the primary level, all Jewish writers argued for the eternity of their Torah and of Israel because of its observance of the Torah. The author of Midrash rabbah on Deuteronomy 30:12 had argued, we recollect, that the phrase that the Torah "is not in heaven" means that "you shall not say that another Moses will arise and bring us another Torah from heaven; for no part of it had been left behind in heaven." Recalling a prophecy by Jeremiah, Saadiah eloquently asserted that the Jewish people was, like its law, to endure as long as heaven and earth. He also analyzed the seven main arguments in support of the alleged abrogation of the Torah, and repudiated them one by one. At the same time he quoted a logical argument from his Jewish predecessors why one could assume neither the abrogation of laws enacted by God for eternity, nor that of laws clearly instituted by Him either for a special period of time or to fit certain specific conditions. The latter expired automatically without any new revelation and, hence, could not be "abrogated." To the eternal laws, on the other hand, belonged the Sabbath, which both Christians and Muslims had arbitrarily removed to another day and deprived of some of its fundamental functions. Jews always were particularly proud of their weekly day of rest. Occasionally they were called "people of the Sabbath" by their Muslim neighbors, most of whom considered Saturday an unlucky day because of its ancient folkloristic connections with Saturn. Even Ghazzali shared that prejudice, while the populace repeated a Persian proverb, "The Jews are welcome to Saturday." Jews, on their part, proudly emphasized in a Sabbath prayer that "of its rest the uncircumcised [some versions read: the Ishmaelites] shall not partake." Did not the Torah itself clearly enjoin Israel "to observe the Sabbath throughout their generations, for a perpetual covenant?" To be sure, some Muslims argued that even the last two words, *berit 'olam,* if not altogether a Jewish forgery, could mean only a long-term covenant, just as the provision concerning the Hebrew slave continuing to serve his master "forever" (*le-'olam*) really meant only "for a long time." But Jews easily shrugged off such forced explanations. More fundamentally, answering Muslim contentions that a large number of witnesses had attested each of the Messenger's miracles, Saadiah and, even more emphatically, Yehudah Halevi pointed out that, unlike any other revelation, that of Sinai was given in the presence of a whole people of 600,000 adult males in addition to women and children. A revelation, thus unanimously attested by a vast multitude, could not possibly be subject to error or alteration; whereas, for instance, Mohammed himself admittedly often changed his mind.[13]

With equal vigor the rabbis repudiated any suggestion that their ancestors had ever tampered with the text of the Bible. They even denied that there had been any involuntary alterations or corruptions owing to the passage of time. In his apologetic fervor, Maimonides outdid his colleagues in repudiating all such allegations, contending that

> First, Scripture was translated into Syriac, Greek, Persian and Latin hundreds of years before the appearance of Mohammed. Secondly, there is a uniform tradition as to the text of the Bible both in the East and the West, with the result that no differences in the text exist at all, not even in the vocalization, for they are all correct. Nor do any differences effecting the meaning exist. The motive for their accusation lies, therefore, in the absence of any allusion to Mohammed in the Torah.[14]

Jewish apologists admitted, of course, that the Sabbath had not been observed before the days of Moses and that neither the prohibition of marrying two sisters, which Jacob did, nor that of consuming the meat of forbidden animals had as yet been enacted. Sharp-witted Arabs argued that, by permitting marriage between an uncle and a niece and at the same time insisting on levirate marriage, the Bible had opened the way to incest. Upon the childless demise of that uncle the brother-levir would be bound to marry his own daughter. They also pointed out that, by prohibiting many animals for Jewish consumption, Mosaic law had run counter to the Creator's original intention that "every moving thing that liveth shall be for food for you" (Gen. 9:3). Jewish dietary laws were considered irksome also for practical reasons. Although less frequently than in Christian lands, we hear of Muslim complaints of Jews' selling to Gentile customers carcasses of ritualistically slaughtered animals found upon subsequent examination to be unfit for Jewish consumption. The poet, Abu Isḥaq al-Ilbiri, was not alone in objecting to the custom that "Jews slaughter at our markets, but you eat what they consider unfit for themselves." [15]

In answer, Saadiah and others drew a line of demarcation between restrictive legislation concerning matters previously allowed and the permission of things previously forbidden. The latter alone, representing the bulk of Christian and Muslim deviations from Old Testament law, was outright nullification, whereas the outlawry of formerly permissible acts, from which any individual could have abstained at will, was in no way an abrogation of the law or alteration of the divine will. This argument appeared sufficiently persuasive for Samau'al ibn Yaḥya to devote to it a lengthy reply at the very beginning of his anti-Jewish tract. Curiously, there was less controversy over the difference between God's revelation to Moses, and that given to Abraham, although Islam had long claimed to have restored the Abrahamic revelation to its pristine purity. Only obliquely did the author of the mystic "Letters of Rabbi 'Aqiba" explain why the Torah had not been given to any of the three patriarchs, each of whom had fully merited to be its recipient. Certainly, Abraham had been the first to relinquish the idols and had withstood ten severe trials, Isaac had submitted himself to sacrificial offering, and Jacob had at least kept himself and his household away from sin. Yet the Lord "did not reveal it [the Torah] to Abraham, because the offspring of Ishmael [Islam] are doomed to hell, nor to Isaac because the offspring of Esau [Christendom] are doomed to hell." In the case of Jacob, the homilist admitted, "the Lord hath chosen Jacob unto Himself, and Israel for his own treasure." But the patriarch had to be punished for arrogantly claiming that his "way is hidden from the Lord." [16]

Jewish apologists did not limit themselves to a defense of their position, but often went over to the offensive. In Muslim lands they could speak their minds freely with respect to Christians, but they had to be careful in assailing the dominant religion, since blasphemies against Mohammed were punishable by death. Even writing in Arabic, therefore, they used as a rule the Hebrew script. In their Hebrew writings they could use such circumlocutions as Ishmaelite, Qedarite, Hagari. More frequently they alluded to Mohammed as the "madman" (*meshugga'*) with obvious reference to Hosea's description, "The prophet is a fool, the man of the spirit is mad!" which may already have given currency to the Messenger's epithet, "obsessed," among his contemporaries. They also stressed Mohammed's moral laxity and sexual indulgences. For the Qur'an, whose "miraculous" nature belonged to the stock-in-trade of Muslim theologians, they often used the similar-sounding term, *qalon* (shame). A tenth-century Jewish writer opined that most of it had been written by Mohammed's Jewish companions, whose very conversion was designed "to save the people of the Lord, so that he [Mohammed] should not hurt them through his machinations." Vestiges of some avowedly misleading statements could still be detected in the Qur'an. The writer boasted that, if he chose to restore the book to its original form and trace each of its verses back to its sources, the Muslims themselves would recognize their error.[17]

In Arabic writings the Jewish counterattack was more indirect. Saadiah's repudiation, for example, of those who "deny that the prophet dies like all other human beings" was, despite Elijah, an oblique, though unmistakable, repudiation of Mohammed's alleged ascension. In the heat of his assault on the Muslim and Karaite celebration of the New Moon by observation (he accused the Karaites of consciously emulating Islam in order to curry favor with its rulers), Saadiah even asserted that, from its inception, Israel had possessed a permanent calendar ordained for it by God. This historically untenable view was repudiated even by such Rabbanite leaders as Maimonides.[18]

POLITICAL AND ECONOMIC ISSUES

Next to these scriptural and theological controversies there also arose heated debates on socioeconomic and political problems. Jews and Christians were often accused of unlawfully serving in public office, building new and enlarging old houses of worship, neglecting to wear their badges, and otherwise contravening the laws of the Muslim states. Ibn Ḥazm, in particular, who, as A. S. Tritton remarked, was "free with abuse for all who disagreed with him," doubly resented the rise of the Jewish statesman, Samuel ibn Nagrela, to power in Granada. The two men had had a religious altercation in their youth. But when Ibn Ḥazm learned that the hated Jewish statesman dared to write a controversial tract against Islam, he completely lost his temper. Claiming to have been unable to procure a copy of Samuel's pamphlet, he heaped abuse on excerpts therefrom in the manuscript of an unnamed Muslim's reply.

> A man who was filled with hatred towards the Apostle [reads a characteristic attack in Ibn Ḥazm's *Refutation*]—a man who is, in secret, a materialist, a free-thinker, a Jew—of that most contemptible of religions, the most vile of faiths . . . loosened his tongue . . . and became conceited in his vile soul, as a result of his wealth. His riches, his gold and his silver, robbed him of his wretched senses; so he compiled a book in which he set out to demonstrate the alleged contradictions in the Word of God, the Qur'an. . . . By God, his argumentation proves how poor is his knowledge, how narrow his mind, about which I already knew something. For I used to know him when he was naked, except for charlatanry, deprived of everything, except anxiety, void except of lies.

Ibn Ḥazm attacked also the Muslim rulers who, because of greed and insatiable ambition, enabled Jews to seize power. His sentiments were echoed by the Granadan poet, Abu-Isḥaq al-Ilbiri, whose incendiary attacks on Samuel's son, Joseph ("Do not consider killing them a treachery; treachery would be your condoning their misrule") greatly contributed to the anti-Jewish massacre of 1066.[19]

Such complaints were often heard also in Egypt and elsewhere. In a sweeping condemnation of the existing state of affairs Al-Asnawi, in his "Earnest Appeal against the Employment of Dhimmis," accused the latter, particularly the Copts, of regarding the land of Egypt as theirs only, deceiving the state, and appropriating Muslim estates including those of the *waqf*. Christians, rather than Jews, were also accused of inveterate enmity toward Muslims, and even of acts of arson against mosques and Muslim quarters. A *cause célèbre* based on such an accusation in Damascus in 1340 produced several anti-Christian pamphlets. Because of the interdependence of the fate of all "unbelievers," however, this agitation reflected on the Jewish status as well. Jews as such, on the other hand, were the targets of attacks (as voiced, for instance, by Ibn Qayyim al-Jauziya) aimed at their allegedly better concealed hatred of Muslims, their efforts to hurt the latter whenever possible, and their exploitation of the Muslim population through usury and other forbidden trades. In his "Book of Selections in the Uncovering of Secrets" Zain ad-Din al-Jaubari of Damascus (about 1250) assembled an imposing array of illustrations of dishonest practices by Jewish tradesmen and physicians. Evidently, as in Christian Europe during the same period and perhaps under its influence, Jewish success in business and medical practice aroused widespread professional jealousies. Ibn al-Hajj al-Abdari (before 1350) devoted a pamphlet to hair-raising stories about intrigues between Jewish physicians and disgruntled wives of patients, who conspired to kill their husbands slowly, and other equally picturesque accusations. This writer also warned his readers against patronizing Jewish apothecaries who would willfully sell them adulterated drugs. Nor were denunciations of Jewish magic arts absent from these controversies, nurtured by the growth of the Jews' own interest in occult practices.[20]

It should be noted that most of these polemical tracts date from the later Middle Ages, when progressive feudalization and economic contraction of Near Eastern society were conducive to both greater Jewish concentration on mercantile and medical occupations and the sharpening of economic rivalries. Hence, without any immediate Western influence, which increased after the Crusades and the commercial expansion of the Italian republics, some such similarities with Western conditions would have been perfectly natural. Because of their late date, therefore, these accusations are mentioned here with some hesitation. Yet, in view of the extreme paucity of extant early polemical writings and the often great repetitiousness characteristic of that entire branch of literature, we may assume that many of these sociopolitical arguments had also been voiced by anti-*dhimmi* writers before 1200. Had not Ibn 'Abdun in early twelfth-century Seville called for a general Muslim boycott of Jewish and Christian physicians, and even for a refusal to sell scientific books of any kind to unbelievers? Those Muslim obscurantists who objected to medical science as such were doubly aroused over the success of "unbelieving" doctors. That these accusations were not purely academic may be seen in the case of the famous statesman-historian Rashid ad-Din (ad-Daula). After serving five successive rulers devotedly, this converted Jew was accused before the Khan of having administered a wrong potion to the Khan's father some twenty months before and thereby accelerated the latter's demise. After a trial, in which ironically the testimony of a Jewish physician played a decisive role, Rashid was executed in 1318 together with his sixteen-year-old son, Ibrahim.[21]

These accusations had consequences which transcended the fate of individuals. With the universal penchant for generalization against minority groups, they undermined the status of all Jews under the rule of Islam. Zealous neophytes actually demanded complete cancellation of the long-accepted principle of toleration. Al-Ḥaqq al-Islami argued that, since the Jews had been guilty of falsification of Scripture and associating other powers with God, they had forfeited the privileges granted them as a monotheistic "people of the book." Less extremely, Sa'id ibn Ḥasan of Alexandria, upon his conversion in 1298, tried to prove from the Bible that the fortunes of the Jewish people had always fallen with the rise of their idolatrous temples, and risen on the latter's destruction. Hence, he declared, Muslim rulers, too, would fare better if they destroyed the infidels' houses of worship, and particularly the icon-worshiping Christian churches. Writing in Damascus in 1320, he predicted that the end of the seventh solar century after the *hejira* (1322) would prove to be a crucial period in the destinies of Islam, and suggested that the government convoke a congress of ten rabbis, ten priests, and a number of Muslim experts. At such an assembly in the king's presence he promised to demonstrate the existing forgeries in the Torah, Gospels, Psalms, and Prophets, and to prove that all of them had foretold the advent of Mohammed and postulated the destruction of all images and churches. Although the Muslim leaders approved of the project and the government allegedly issued six successive permits, for some reason the expected debate never took place.[22]

In this area of socioeconomic Jew-baiting, Jewish apologists were at a decided disadvantage. There undoubtedly were unscrupulous and dishonest Jewish merchants, physicians, and druggists, just as there were dishonest Muslims and Christians. The only cogent answer could have been supplied by detailed statistical comparisons with due attention to ratios in population, urbanization, educational level, and other social factors. But no such basic data were available. Although interest in sociological facts, doubtless stimulated by these religious controversies, was gradually awakening, and fourteenth-century Islam produced in Ibn Khaldun a distinguished social thinker, the compilation of simple statistical facts still was in its infancy.

Jewish controversialists could and did reciprocate in kind by condemning such entire classes of Muslims as their corrupt judges and officials. But whatever weight such statements carried with Jews, they probably made little impression upon the Muslim majority. Moreover, few if any of the Jewish controversial tracts ever reached a large Muslim audience. Even noncontroversial works like Saadiah's translation of the Bible, though known to Mas'udi, was not fully utilized even by such an Arab "specialist" as Ibn Ḥazm. Jewish authors so generally expected their books to be read by Jews only—the usual fate of Jewish anti-defamation literature—that as a rule they used the Hebrew script. This is the less surprising as even the Muslim author Aḥmad ibn Idris al-Qarafi (died 1285), interested in counteracting a popular Christian apologia, wrote, "We are mentioning all these matters of unbelief in order that the Muslim may learn to appreciate the more the blessings of his faith." Since there was little, if any, effective censorship of manuscripts (Sa'id ibn Ḥasan's proposal to censor Jewish books evidently evoked no response), even sharp Jewish attacks on the dominant faith could thus circulate rather freely, although their authors were subject to later reprisals on the slightest denunciation. Jewish apologists must often have felt discouraged by the general inefficacy of their efforts, but they blamed it, together with all other shortcomings of the Jewish position, on their people's exilic existence.[23]

In fact, the problem of exile appeared to be at the root of all peculiarly Jewish problems. The contrast between the great memories of the past or the still greater messianic expectations in the future, and the actual misery of national existence, was sharpened rather than mitigated by the rise of numerous Jewish individuals to positions of power and affluence. Muslim thinkers gloried in the unparalleled expansion of Islam, and saw in the very achievements of Islamic thought and science a proof of the superiority of their religion. But the Jewish position as a "people poor and lowly," was in peculiar need of a rationale. To add insult to injury, it was the Arab, supposedly the descendant of Ishmael and Hagar, the "son of a female slave," that wielded the greatest power over the legitimate offspring of Abraham. "Beneath the feet of slaves we bend" (Ibn Gabirol's *Selected Religious Poems,* trans. by I. Zangwill, p. 32) is the unceasing mournful refrain of Jewish poets and sages in Muslim lands.

Muslim polemists, particularly converts from Judaism, made full use of this political inferiority as proof of the Jews' religious inferiority as well. God's blessings to the ancient patriarchs were frequently cited as manifestations of the divine will realized only through the expansion of the sons of Ishmael. Mohammed's victory as such was often invoked as a miracle attesting his divine mission. "Who has ever claimed such a victory," asked 'Ali aṭ-Ṭabari, "in the name of God, since the creation of the world by God? . . . a victory which was realized in such a decisive and unquestionable way, in all the countries and regions of the earth, on sea and land, from the extreme Sus [Morocco] to the deserts of Turkestan and Tibet, by means of devotees and deeply pious leaders, and by proclamation in the name of the God of Abraham, Ishmael, Isaac, Jacob, and the rest of the prophets?" The very divine promise to the patriarchs, "All this land that I have spoken of will I give unto your seed, and they shall inherit it forever" (Exod. 32:13) could not in Ibn Ḥazm's opinion refer to Jews, who had lost the country, but to the Muslims who occupied it. Harping on this theme, Samau'al ibn Yaḥya interpreted God's blessing to Abraham, "And I will make My covenant between Me and thee, and will multiply thee exceedingly" (Gen. 17:2), as necessarily relating to the great expansion of Islam. He reinforced this argument with the similarity of sound between the blessing's last two words, *bi-me'od me'od,* and the name of Mohammed, as well as their equal numerical value of 92.[24]

Samau'al went further and contended that much of contemporary Judaism and particularly rabbinic law owed its existence to Jewish life in exile. He taught that, fearing the Jewish minority could not resist absorption by the nations if it were allowed freely to mix with them, the rabbis had departed from biblical law by prohibiting intermarriage with Gentiles and forbidding the consumption of meat slaughtered by non-Jews. In Samau'al's interpretation, the Torah had merely forbidden union with idolaters and consumption of pagan sacrifices. But the rabbis extended that prohibition to monotheists and their food, so as to keep their people in a state of permanent segregation. "This is the root," Samau'al exclaimed, "of that community's stubborn adherence to its laws, because it lives in strong opposition to the other communities." Of course, this is the voice of a self-hating former Jew who had long resented the shackles of Jewish law and his inability freely to mix with Muslims before his formal conversion. Certainly, the more orthodox Muslim thinkers and legislators, far from resenting Jewish segregation, encouraged it by their emphasis on distinguishing colors, opposition to intermarriage, and unflinching adherence to Muslim rituals.[25]

With the tide of individualism surging over the semicapitalistic society of the Arabian Renaissance, the difficulties of the individual, as we shall see, his rights and duties within the compass of his creed, individual conscience, and free will, reward and punishment and the all-embracing problem of sin demanded integrating answers from Jewish thinkers. That the cumulative effect of individual sins was responsible for the national misfortune, was argued just as frequently as that, conversely, life in Exile was conducive to human sinfulness and degradation. On the other hand, for Saadiah the Exile was not only an incentive to desist from sinning, so that Israel's repentance might accelerate redemption, but it served as a positive instrument of the divine government. The misery of the Jews, he declared, is to show that they believe in God not because He had made them great, but even when they are lowly, whereas the nations, though elevated by Him, "still did not believe, [and hence] the verdict against them was sustained." Saadiah's idea was combined by the anonymous tenth-century apologist, who may indeed have been his disciple, with the old aggadic doctrine of the Exile as an instrument of the divinely ordained Jewish mission. God preserved the holy people, he declared, "in order to make it study and teach all the nations law and judgment, and to try it through signs and miracles so as to find out what is in their hearts, whether they would obey his commands or not." [26]

Even more deeply preoccupied with the problem of the Exile was Yehudah Halevi. Living at the crossroads between Islam and Christendom, himself a native of either Tudela or Toledo reconquered by the Christians in his own lifetime, the poet-philosopher drew his great lesson from this world-historic clash between the two civilizations. He not only stressed, as had no Jewish philosopher before him, the impermanence of human power, but pointed out, as we recall, that even Muslims and Christians revered their saints and martyrs more highly than their kings and conquerors. For him the very powerlessness of the Jewish people was a sign of its selection. Differently, but even more cogently than Blaise Pascal, who thus contrasted Mohammed and Jesus, he could have stated, "Mohammed chose the way of human success, Judaism that of human defeat." [27]

At the same time Jewish leaders tirelessly told coreligionists that their sufferings had deep compensations. Maimonides, especially, himself the victim of a major religious persecution and confronted by a confused and despairing generation, reassured his readers that "our nation speaks with pride of the virulent oppression it has suffered, and the sore tribulations it has endured. . . . For the bearing of these hardships is a source of glory and a great achievement in the sight of God." Lest, however, some weak-kneed members despair of the ultimate outcome of that unending Jewish struggle for survival, he also reminded his correspondents in Yemen that "we are in possession of the divine assurance that Israel is indestructible and imperishable, and will always continue to be a preeminent community. As it is impossible for God to cease to exist, so is Israel's destruction and disappearance from the world unthinkable, as we read, 'For I the Lord change not; and ye, O sons of Jacob, are not consumed' " (*Epistle to Yemen*, pp. 26 f., 34 f., v ff., with reference to Mal. 3:6).

Such reasoning was not likely to impress power-hungry individuals even within the Jewish community. It fell flat on the ears of Muslims, brought up on the strong blending of religious and political aspirations, and believing that their empire's wordly and military successes were an integral part of the manifest destiny of their faith. Starting from such different premises, the champions of both religions talked at rather than with one another, and, as is usual, their disputations persuaded only those who had already been persuaded. Converts from genuine conviction were very rare. Even Sa'id ibn Ḥasan admitted that the initial impetus to conversion had come to him from an illness and a dream promising recovery if he were to recite the first sura of the Qur'an. On the whole, Ibn Kammuna, the distinguished thirteenth-century philosopher, who discussed the merits of the three faiths more dispassionately than any of his contemporaries, was right in asserting,

> We have not found anyone until today who would adopt Islam without being impelled to it by fear, the striving for a respected social position, the threat of a high tax or imprisonment, the love for a Muslim woman, or some other motives like those. We have never heard of a man who, familiar with his own faith as well as with Islam, of reputable social standing, well-to-do and God-fearing, would convert himself to Islam, if not for the above or similar reasons.

Even unbelieving Jews remained Jews, because of their general agnosticism or their belief in the "equivalence of proofs," which left the superiority of either faith hanging in the balance. Ibn Ḥazm attacked on this score both a Jewish skeptic and a Jewish deist. The latter, in particular, had frequently disputed Ibn Ḥazm's views: "Whenever we invited him to embrace Islam, and sought to dispel his doubts and refute his arguments, he would say: 'Conversion from one religion to another is buffoonery.' " [28]

RELIGIOUS LIBERALS AND ZOROASTRIANS

Ibn Kammuna's plea for mutual toleration and recognition of existing differences was not altogether unique. Muslim mystics, too, were often prone to overlook denominational differences and stress the common beliefs of all faiths. Some, like Ibn Hud of Damascus, attracted Jews and Christians, as well as Muslims, to their sermons. Ibn Hud asked any new disciple: "Upon which road [shall I guide you]? the Mosaic, the Christian or the Mohammedan?" Perhaps because of this liberality he proved more effective in converting Jews than some of his fanatical confrères. He aroused thereby the animosities of the Jewish community of Damascus which, by playing on his weakness for wine, exposed him to public contumely. There were others, however, who were entirely uninterested in converting Jews to Islam. At the height of the Renaissance of Islam, agnosticism in various forms was rampant. Among the spokesmen of nihilism in both religion and society was the ninth-century thinker, Ar-Rawandi, allegedly the son of a Jew. While much of his thought and activity is hidden behind the cloud of constant aspersions by enemies, it appears that his philosophy was for a time quite the rage in Baghdad and its vicinity. We shall see that he also exerted some influence on Jewish writers of the period. Of a different type was the later skeptic Abu'l 'Ala al-Ma'arri (973–1058), who in many of his poems expressed his disdain for all established religions. In one poem he sang,

> Ḥanifites [Muslims] have erred, Christians walked wrong paths,
> Jews were confused, Magians lived the life of illusion.

In another vehement outpouring he wrote,

> Religions are falsehoods, and tales one tells,
> A Book of Revelation [Qur'an] is invoked as authority
> A Torah or a Gospel;
> Every race believes in certain lies,
> Has any race ever monopolized the truth?

Not unjustifiedly modern scholars have traced back to the intellectual ferment which had generated an Ar-Rawandi, Al-Ma'arri or certain negativistic Qarmatian sectarians the tract *De tribus impostoribus,* which referred to Moses, Jesus, and Mohammed as mankind's three greatest deceivers. According to an eleventh-century version, the Qarmatian chief Abu Tahir (died in 932) had allegedly stated, "In this world, three men have corrupted the people: a shepherd [Moses], a medicine man [Jesus], and a camelier [Mohammed]. The camelier was the worst juggler, the worst conjurer of the three." [29]

Abu Tahir's purported statement reflects, indeed, the prevailing concentration of the sectarian agnostic and atheistic circles on attacking Islam rather than Judaism. With a freedom unknown in the West, the Dahriyya and other religious radicals threw down the gauntlet before the dominant Islamic circles, abetted though these were by the intimate alliance between the state and the mosque. In their attacks they included polemics against the Old Testament and the Gospels more for the sake of consistency and because official Islam itself had acknowledged the latter's basically revealed character, than because of any intrinsic interest in spreading their teachings among the religious minorities. In fact, unlike the sectarians, the *zindiqs* seem to have refrained from overt propaganda. True to their basic argument that "human reason is full of uncertainties" (Saadiah), most of them doubtless preferred to expatiate on their philosophic doubts in circles of close friends and disciples, rather than espouse them militantly among the masses, whose intellectual equipment they often held in utter disdain. This very lack of militancy, and the relatively small number of intellectuals living in the rarefied atmosphere of detached philosophic speculation, largely accounted for the relative mildness of the official reaction to their preachment.

Understandably, the Jewish community felt little endangered by assaults stemming from those quarters. It could dismiss them as an internal affair of the Muslim world. Only in so far as there appeared skeptics in their own camp, did the Jewish leaders have to take cognizance of their arguments. At the height of sectarianism and free thought in the ninth and tenth centuries, one heard of some such Jewish spokesmen for skepticism in its various shades, though none of their works have been preserved. They were sufficiently numerous and influential for Saadiah to devote to them many paragraphs in his major philosophic work. Among the causes of internal Jewish deviations from orthodoxy he had found "a word that a person hears from the mouth of the godless that touches his heart and unnerves it, so that he remains for the rest of his life in this state of nervous prostration." But these Jewish radicals seem to have been even less militant than their Muslim counterparts. They must have realized that, as a struggling minority, the Jewish people could far less afford any weakening of its faith, and that by undermining the latter they might cause the people itself to die in its roots. Certainly, the time was not yet ripe for the evolution of a secular Jewish nationalism. Individually, too, a Jewish agnostic could fare much better by converting himself outwardly to Islam, and continuing to cherish his agnostic beliefs, without the stigma and the disabilities attached to his continued membership in the Jewish community. Since all that was legally required for conversion to Islam was the recitation of the brief Muslim credo, his conscientious scruples could easily be overcome. There is no way of telling how many Jewish converts to Islam left their ancestral creed merely because they had lost all belief in God and revealed truths, and joined the dominant religion for practical reasons. In any case, the few skeptical Jewish voices were silenced by occasional calm philosophic arguments, rather than by direct communal action.[30]

No more serious appear to have been the attacks on Jewish monotheism by the representatives of dualism, both Zoroastrian and Manichaean. To be sure, our Jewish information is limited to sources almost exclusively written west of Iran, the main battleground of dualism's struggle for survival. In that country, the impact of the raging religious controversies was indeed conducive to the formation of Jewish, as well as Muslim, sects and influenced individual writers of more orthodox persuasion, such as Ḥivi ha-Balkhi. Yet, having weathered the Zoroastrian influences in Achaemenid and Sassanian Persia while the dualist doctrines enjoyed the enhanced prestige of political success, Jews were less likely to succumb now, when the Zoroastrian mobedhs fought their losing battle for survival against the onrushing forces of Islam.

On the other hand, this very progress of Islam enraged the Zoroastrian spokesmen against all monotheistic religions. A ninth-century Pehlevi author, Mardan Farukh, devoted no less than two chapters of his controversial tract, "The Decisive Solution of Doubts," to a critique of some basic concepts in the Old Testament. These chapters corresponded in size to the space allotted by him to the critique of the Qur'an, whereas he deemed Christianity and Manichaeism worthy of only one chapter each. Undoubtedly the old and influential Jewish community of Isfahan and other major cities appeared to this apologist for a decaying civilization a greater threat than even the expansive missionary faiths of the two other minorities.[31]

Whether he used an existing Persian translation of the book of Genesis, or had to rely on a Syriac version, Mardan Farukh saw the Bible essentially through the eyes of Muslim controversialists, and borrowed more than one argument from the *zindiqs*. Of course, he utilized also some of the old materials accumulated in his ancestors' religious controversies with Jews and Christians in the Sassanian Empire, materials which had doubtless furnished in turn many a weapon to the early Muslim apologists. As a dualist, he was particularly concerned with the biblical cosmogony, including the creation of light which, together with its contrasting element of darkness, touched the very core of the dualist credo. The biblical descriptions of Adam and Eve, their sin, and their expulsion from the Garden of Eden, on the other hand, lent themselves to questioning on rationalist grounds. For example, God's query to Adam, "Where art thou?" and His apparent ignorance of what had happened until He was told by Adam, cast a shadow on His postulated omniscience. Nor was there any justification for Adam's misdeed reaching in its consequences "unlawfully over people of every kind at various periods." In short, Mardan Farukh concludes this line of attack, "I consider it, in every way, a senseless, ignorant and foolish statement." He also attacked many passages in Scripture relating to the story of the patriarchs. Viewing them not only in the light of the biblical text, but also of the embellishments by the Aggadah (known to him probably through its Muslim critiques), he could readily accuse the author of Genesis of outright anthropomorphism. In the much-debated story of the three angels' visit to Abraham at Mamre he saw an outright attribution to the Lord Himself of the consumption of food. Citing these and other examples, Mardan waxed rhetorical,

Now if he *be* a sacred being, of whom these are signs and tokens, that *implies that* truth is far from him, forgiveness strange to him, and knowledge is not bestowed upon him, but rather the fiend who is leader of the hell, prince of the den of the gloomy race, whom the perverted and devilish *people* glorify by the name of *Adonay,* and offer *him* homage.

One hears in these accusations a distinct echo of the ancient gnostic-Jewish controversies, which seven centuries before had led Marcion to relegate the God of the Old Testament to the position of a *demiourgos.* Such accusations were also voiced by Manichaeans whose influence, unlike that of Zoroastrians, had spread to the Christian lands and remained there a permanent heresy-generating force throughout the Middle Ages.[32]

Of all the Jewish apologists, only Saadiah took these accusations earnestly enough to devote to them several polemical references in his *Beliefs and Opinions.* Apart from his bellicose temperament, his observations of their impact on some Iranian Jews induced him to take a stand. He denied that light and darkness really were opposing principles and insisted that darkness merely connotes "the absence of light." But his main argument, reiterated in various forms, was that, once we depart from the principle of one godhead and subject it to numerical counting, there is no valid reason why we should limit it to two, rather than five or any other number of deities. Nor could the dualists, in his opinion, adduce any historical attestation of their teachings through a valid tradition supported by genuine prophecy and miracles: "They have never seen such mutually exclusive and distinct elements, nor how they could become united and comingled with each other." The gaon also took time off from his busy career to answer in detail some related strictures on the Bible voiced within the Jewish community itself by Ḥivi ha-Balkhi.[33]

By the tenth century the power of Zoroastrianism had already been broken, however. While individual Persians appeared even in Byzantium and Morocco, their religion ceased to engage the attention of the majority, except for those who happened to be interested in the history of religion. To the Jews in the Caliphate's western provinces or in Christian countries, the Zoroastrian faith never appeared as a serious rival or antagonist. Even Manichaeism could be dismissed as but an internal concern of the Muslim and

Christian faiths. Crushed between the millstones of Islam and Christendom, some Jews may actually have viewed the Manichaean agitation, both overt and concealed, as a welcome diversion for the wrath of their powerful antagonists. But such sitting on the fence often proved to be no less risky and uncomfortable.

JUDEO–CHRISTIAN POLEMICS

Controversies between Jews and Christians far overshadowed those with Muslims and adherents of other faiths in both frequency and intensity. Even in the Muslim world Jewish tenacity and increasing vigor under the Caliphate, compared with the steady decline of the other religious minorities, greatly infuriated the Christian leaders. Al-Jaḥiẓ had already observed that Christians were generally rather tolerant toward Magians, Sabians, and Manichaeans, "but when they come to speak of the Jews they brand them as obstinate rebels, not merely as people walking in error and confusion." At the same time he had also noted that the Jews were less liked (or more heartily disliked) by the Muslims than were the Christians. He explained that fact in part as the result of the historical clashes between the Jews of Medina and Mohammed, for "the enmity of neighbors is as violent and abiding as the hostility that arises among relatives." Above all, the fact that Judaism and Christianity shared the Old Testament as their revealed Scripture made their respective interpretations an urgent concern to both.[34]

Anti-Jewish polemics had, moreover, formed a much more integral part of the New Testament than of the Qur'an. Christian homilists preaching in their churches and quoting biblical passages were automatically led to think of Jews and their stubborn resistance to conversion. During the Holy Week, in particular, the Passion of Christ and his resurrection offered provocative themes for anti-Jewish assaults in theory and practice. We recall the need of a special protective legislation and the frequent prohibitions for Jews to appear in public streets, lest they further inflame the aroused passions. Nothing of the kind existed in the Muslim world. Garbled accounts of these anti-Jewish persecutions, reaching the Near East, were used there by polemists like Qarafi to demonstrate the general bloodthirstiness of the Christians and their religion. Three days were said to have been set aside every year in such cities as Barcelona, Marseilles, and Florence for indiscriminate assaults on Jewish passers-by and the plundering of Jewish houses. Initiated by the formula, "Jews have robbed your religion," this sanguinary period allegedly concluded with another solemn ritual in the churches (cited in Fritsch's *Islam,* p. 149). In contrast, even the clashes between Mohammed and the Jewish tribes of Medina were not commemorated at major Muslim holidays and led to few liturgical formulations. They had relatively little bearing on the later controversies between Muslims and Jews, whether in theological tracts or in street corner debates.

Christian apologias had behind them such a long and ramified history, reaching back to the days before Constantine but climaxed in the heated debates of the fourth and fifth centuries, that controversialists on either side had little to add to the ancient arguments. But repetition was generally considered a virtue. Unlike the modern mind, bent on originality of approach and ever novel interpretations, the medieval man, especially in Byzantium and the West, was very suspicious of innovations, which he often considered as smacking of heresy. The greatest medieval thinkers, Avicenna, Maimonides, or Thomas Aquinas, whom we in retrospect consider original minds and distinct innovators, would have rejected with horror any suggestion that they departed from the highway of their religious traditions. They merely wished to reformulate and, in some minor matters, adapt these traditions to contemporary exigencies. The last truly universal Council of the Church, the Trullan synod of 692, actually adopted a formal canon enjoining the clergy "not to interpret it [the Bible] in any way other than that explained in the writings of the Church luminaries and doctors." Outright apologists felt it doubly incumbent upon them to defend every minutia of their accepted beliefs and rituals. To them, arguments borrowed from predecessors were welcome weapons. No less a figure than John of Damascus, considered by the Greek Orthodox Church one of its greatest apologists, insisted that he had contributed nothing new. Hence we shall not be surprised that after Aphraates and St. Ephrem in the Eastern churches, after Eusebius and Chrysostom in the Byzantine world, and after Jerome and Augustine among the Latins, all Judeo-Christian debates were mere variations on old themes.[35]

Equally conservative in their general approaches, Jewish controversialists were nonetheless at a considerable disadvantage, for they had to rely largely on their own ingenuity. They were unable to fall back on the Talmud itself, which, in contrast to the ramified anti-Jewish argumentation in the patristic letters, contained but few overtly anti-Christian polemics. Nor did they have at their disposal many written apologias. If at times they benefited from previous debates, local disputes of recent vintage were normally better remembered than more penetrating reasonings advanced in remote districts and periods. These difficulties have bedeviled modern investigators as well. Since but few discussions were committed to writing, and of those recorded few are now extant and still fewer published, it is almost impossible to trace the literary indebtedness of each author. On the other hand, even where we find very similar reasonings, even formulations, they do not necessarily prove direct borrowings. The all-pervading identity of both challenges and methods could easily lead to similar, and yet wholly independent, elaborations of the same fundamental ideas.

There was a basic difference, however, between the Judeo-Christian discussions carried on under a Muslim, and those under a Christian regime. In the Great Caliphate, especially when appearing before Al-Ma'mun's entourage and other mixed audiences, the Christian spokesmen had to assume a sweetly reasonable tone, appeal to general philosophic considerations, and but moderately use Scriptural proofs based on their own allegorical interpretations. On the whole, they had to follow here the models laid down in the alleged debate at the Sassanian court of the fourth century, and to repeat some of the moderate views expressed by Eastern Fathers, like Aphraates. Written Eastern apologias, too, few of which are preserved, lack much of the bitterness and vehemence which characterize many controversial tracts, homilies, and poems written by apologists in the Byzantine or the Western world. Eastern Jewish polemics, too, written overtly and for public consumption, were generally restrained. Saadiah merely reiterated the general Muslim and Jewish objections to Christian trinitarianism, while his contemporary, the Karaite Qirqisani, briefly disposed of the rise of Christianity in his chapter describing the origins of the great Jewish sects. Only later did he add several pages devoted to an "account of Jesus, and exposition of the teaching of Christians," together with a "refutation" thereof. In the more heated atmosphere of the Crusades and Almohade intolerance, Halevi and Maimonides aimed sharper barbs at the Christian faith, but neither they nor any other Jewish writer under Islam felt impelled to produce a special treatise against Christian dogmas or rituals. Most of the openly apologetical Jewish literature, beginning with the *Sefer ha-Berit* (Book of the Covenant), by Joseph Qimḥi (or Qamḥi, *ca.* 1110–75), was written under the more intemperate clime of Western controversy.[36]

Christian authors recorded with particular relish debates with Jews in border areas, where the reputed defeats of the Jewish representatives helped to promote the Christian mission or at least to underscore the Christian missionary successes. An interesting disputation allegedly took place, for example, between the bishop of Zafar Gregentius and a Jew Herban in the religiously embattled arena of pre-Islamic southern Arabia. Regrettably, this debate is available to us only in the distorted report by Gregentius, probably further sharpened by later copyists as well as by its Slavonic translator. Yet, even when viewed through these colored glasses, the Jewish representative appears to have argued his case with considerable freedom and judiciousness. The Christian author admitted that Herban had conceded defeat only as a result of the miraculous appearance of Jesus himself. There is no way of telling what other pressures were applied in that debate, which took place in the presence of the local ruler apparently some time between 510 and 520. The bitterness occasioned by this disputation and its aftereffects may well have been coresponsible for the anti-Christian measures shortly thereafter adopted by the Jewish king, Dhu-Nuwas.[37]

In Christian countries the heat of the debate rose and declined together with the general intensification or diminution of tensions. In periods of great crisis, as under Heraclius in the Byzantine Empire, in the Visigothic kingdom of the seventh century, and during the age of the Crusades, anti-Jewish polemics increased in number and vehemence. In most other periods, too, anti-Jewish sermons were preached, vituperative poems written, and controversial tracts circulated, but much of that literature was mechanically repetitive and had a certain aura of unreality about it. True, not only those temperamentally inclined to missionizing, but ordinary Christian clerics and laymen as well, often considered it a good deed to persuade a Jew of the superiority of Christianity. But the most important objective at all times remained the strengthening of the faith of the Church's own adherents.

On the Jewish side the idea of mission had long been abandoned, and all apologetical writings were almost exclusively aimed at reinforcing the faith of the Jews themselves. That is why they were usually composed in Hebrew, or in an Arabic written in the Hebrew alphabet. In the Christian environment Jews refrained altogether from circulating formal replies until the twelfth century. At that time the sharp tensions of the Crusades, combined with the greater articulateness and philosophic training of the Jews, especially in the Provençal border areas between Islam and Christendom, induced Joseph Qimḥi and his son David to indulge in open polemics. Curiously, among the defenders of Judaism there appeared also a family of Hungarian proselytes, Abraham, Isaac, and Joseph, possibly a father and two sons. At the same time, as a permanent minority on the defense, Jews evinced strong apologetic concerns even outside their polemical literature. We shall, indeed, detect an apologetic undertone in most Jewish writings of the period, even though these were devoted to the glorification of Jewish doctrines and observances much more than to the disparagement of the outside world.[38]

The Church's missionary pressures were to become increasingly heavy in the later Middle Ages. Before 1200, the enforced attendance of Jews at conversionist sermons in their own synagogues still was in its early stages. But subtler methods were always used. A typical autobiographical narrative by Hermann, a twelfth-century Premonstratensian monk, describes how he had grown up in Cologne as Judas son of David ha-Levi, had married early, and entered business. On a trip to Mayence at the age of twenty (in 1128), he was persuaded to extend a loan to the bishop of

Münster. Since in his youthful inexperience he had failed to secure a pawn, his father, on the urging of friends, sent him immediately to Münster to collect his debt. As was customary at that time, the bishop entertained his guest and the latter's old Jewish companion for twenty weeks in his castle until he paid up. During that period, the young Jew was subjected to various forms of persuasion, from a public disputation with Abbot Rupert of Dentz to friendly talks with the unlearned but deeply pious house steward, Richmann. The latter made the greater impression. No sooner did Judas return home than he decided to leave his young wife, kidnap his seven-year-old brother, and return to Münster. Upon his formal conversion (some time before 1136), he joined the Premonstratensian order. By 1150 he was serving as abbot of the monastery of Scheda, where he died in 1198 at the age of ninety. We even have a medieval adumbration of the famous Mortara affair of 1858. After listening to religious debates with the duke's chaplain at the home of her wealthy parents, a Jewish girl named Rachel fled, or was abducted, to a nunnery in Louvain. Parental protests were heeded by the bishop of Louvain, but he was overruled by Archbishop Engelbert of Cologne and an ecclesiastical assembly (about 1220). At the instance of the Abbot of Clairvaux, the latter's decision was sustained by the pope. The new convert, called Sister Catherine, was said to have performed miracles, and her "martyrdom" was long celebrated by the Cistercian order on every May 4. We also recollect the story of the boy convert who allegedly scolded William II of England for his liberality in allowing the forced converts of 1096 to return to the Jewish fold. Such conversions must often have taken place even in the more staunchly orthodox communities of northern France and Germany, and many more in the Mediterranean countries.[39]

On the other hand, there were conversions to Judaism not only in such countries as Hungary, where Christianity had not yet struck deep roots, but also in older Christian lands—despite the mortal peril to both the proselyte and his collaborators in that "crime." It is never easy to ascertain whether the converts acted out of conviction or because of some romantic attachment, as allegedly was the case with two Cistercian monks before 1200, and with an Oxford deacon who suffered death by burning in 1212.

Others seem to have done it from political-utopian motivations nurtured on biblical stories. Such nebulous yearnings apparently animated Count Raymond of Sens when, according to the obviously garbled account of Ralph Glaber, he observed Jewish laws and customs and called himself a Jewish king. He thus not only provoked an attack on Sens by King Robert the Pious, but at least indirectly contributed to the anti-Jewish reaction on the part of that king which was to place all of French Jewry in great jeopardy.[40]

Notwithstanding the ready availability of information, however willfully distorted, from converts, few Christian apologists revealed direct knowledge of living Judaism. Certainly none of Aphraates' successors in the East approximated his familiarity with Jewish law and contemporary Jewish life. Nor could Jerome's Latin-writing successors at all compare with that foremost Christian Hebraist who, despite his anti-Jewish fulminations, maintained many close contacts with rabbinic teachers. For the most part, Byzantine and Western writers on Judaism simply quoted alleged Jewish views from previous anti-Jewish polemics. The image of the Jew, of his beliefs, rituals, and social life, had become so standardized that not even Isidor of Seville or Julian of Toledo, who lived in the midst of large and vigorous Jewish communities, made any efforts to get acquainted with the realities of Jewish life.[41]

Even in dialogues pretending to be debates between Christians and Jews the latter are, as a rule, shadowy figures without flesh and blood. Not that actual debates were rare. Sometimes they were ordered by rulers, as that between Priscus and Gregory of Tours, recorded by the latter. Despite the threats overhanging Jewish spokesmen, private exchanges also took place, at least in calmer periods, although few of them were mentioned even in passing as was the disputation attended by Alcuin in Pavia. Many published dialogues also give the impression of being based, at least to some extent, upon real altercations between their authors and Jews. The famous *Disputatio Judaei cum Christiano* by Gilbert Crispin, abbot of Westminster, seems to reflect in part arguments presented by a living Jew (possibly Simon the Pious of Treves), some time before 1092, and as such it belongs among the earliest Anglo-

Jewish records. True, the same abbot also produced a more imaginary controversial tract against a heathen philosopher (*Gentilis*). Yet his Jewish apologist speaks with a more authentic voice, which reminds us somewhat of Tryphon of Justin Martyr's ancient dialogue. Apparently the Jewish interlocutor's questions stirred the abbot deeply and not only stimulated him to compose the companion piece against the philosopher, but also gave impetus to Crispin's friend St. Anselm of Canterbury to complete in 1098 his major treatise on incarnation, *Cur Deus Homo*. Not until the disputations reported by Meir bar Simon about 1245 and by Naḥmanides in Barcelona in 1263, however, do we possess any authentic Jewish record. In all previous cases we are limited to reports by Christian controversialists such as Gregory of Tours, with the Jews invariably on the losing side.[42]

A distinct branch of anti-Jewish literature, among Christians and Muslims alike, consisted of writings by Jewish converts themselves. On the one hand, their information about the Jewish religion was more direct and authentic. Most of them, to be sure, were recruited from the uneducated classes, which were more familiar with Jewish superstitions than with the refined teachings of the rabbis. But for that very reason the converts represented a cross section of the Jewish masses with whom the Christian world was in more direct contact than it was with the frequently cloistered rabbinic leaders. Even if kings and dignitaries of state and church had Jewish business or political confidants, these were not necessarily learned men, except perhaps in the Franco-Jewish communities of the eleventh and twelfth centuries. On the other hand, the apostates from their former faith often hated it with an unbridled hatred. In their accusations they went to extremes rarely found among native Christians.

Petrus Alphonsi (born in 1062) was indubitably the most learned and influential among them. A former rabbi and physician, known as Moses Sefardi, Peter contributed significantly to the transplantation of Eastern mathematics to the Western countries, especially Spain and England where he spent many years of his life. He also used much folkloristic material current among his Jewish and Muslim compatriots, compiling a collection of tales to which he gave the characteristic title, *Disciplina clericalis*. Probably to justify his own act of conversion at the age of forty-four, prompted by Alphonso I of Aragon who served as his godfather, he composed a *Dialogus Petri cognomento Alphonsi, ex Judaeo Christiani, et Moysi Judaei,* whose arguments were frequently repeated by later controversalists, including Peter of Cluny.[43]

Occasionally converts, especially if they had adopted Christianity under duress, genuinely tried to penetrate the mysteries of their new religion and to contrast them with their inherited concepts. Such insecure converts searching for the truth appear especially in the remarkable autobiographical presentation by Jacob son of Tanumas, himself a convert during the critical age of Heraclius. Here we listen to an alleged debate among recent forced converts in North Africa after the suppression of Judaism by the emperor in 634. Despite Jacob's self-avowed unreliability, we perceive in that discussion echoes of troubled consciences by people who tried to make peace with the inevitable. Understandably, Jacob claimed that, as a result of his persuasive arguments, these neophytes underwent a full and genuine conversion, although he admitted that his efforts had substantially been aided by the intervention of the provincial governor, Sergius.

Notwithstanding the constant repetition of major themes, popular imagination could invent a great many new details, especially in the ever-growing literature on the lives of saints. Here popular fancy often ran riot in describing the saints' sufferings at the hands of Jewish enemies and their ultimate success in converting these very foes. While, as we shall see, Muslim story-tellers often preferred purely secular subjects, those under Christendom, even if themselves not recruited from the clerical profession, preferred religious themes. Compared with these hagiographic romances, the secular narratives had but a slow and belated growth in Western lands. Before long these stories of saints also penetrated the folk plays. Among these ancestors of the modern drama, generally dominated by passion plays, there was also considerable room for martyrologies in which Jews appeared as the natural villains.[44]

In essence, it made little difference what literary or dramatic forms were chosen. Whether they appealed to the Christian intelligentsia, itself largely clerical in the West, were addressed to powerful monarchs or noblemen, or spoke to the masses of the urban or rural populations, the major apologias harped on essentially the same themes. As of old, the main controversy raged about the coming of the Messiah, the nature of Christ, the doctrine of Trinity, and the abrogation of Jewish law. At the same time, much fault was found also with contemporary Jewish ways of living and reputed national characteristics.

CHRISTOLOGY AND TRINITARIAN DOGMA

In the controversy with both Islam and Judaism, the Christian teachings concerning the divinity of Christ played a supreme role. In the case of Jews, the debate also raged over Jesus' messiahship and the question whether the Messiah had already come or was to come for the first time at some future date. Neither of these lines of reasoning was at all new. In all fundamentals and many details the debaters could fall back on the accumulated arguments voiced by Church Fathers and rabbis for many generations. Only here and there was a new point added, or an old one elaborated, in the light of new concepts in philosophy and law.

The Christian side lay great emphasis on proving to the Jews that their Messiah, long predicted by the ancient prophets, had come in the person of Jesus. Unlike the Muslim apologists who had to construe far-fetched *gemaṭrias* and other risky hermeneutical methods to find in the Old Testament allusions to the coming of Mohammed, the Christian controversialists could readily invoke well-known and authentic passages predicting the arrival of a redeemer. The only question was whether that redeemer was the founder of Christianity. Proofs to this effect had already been assembled in ancient collections of "testimonies," and medieval writers merely had to refer back to this much-exploited field. The most telling argument, at least since the days of Constantine, was the fact of Christian expansion. The biblical predictions that in the messianic age all nations would join the religion of Israel seemed to be nearly accomplished by the vast conquests of the Christian faith which was professed, if not in the entire world, at least in the main areas of the old *oikumene*. This argument, to be sure, lost much of its force after the expansion of Islam. It made no sense at all in Muslim countries, where the Christians themselves were but a tolerated minority. But in Byzantium and the West it still was rather frequently repeated.[45]

Jewish spokesmen had no difficulty in countering these claims. They pointed out that the reign of universal peace, foretold by the ancient prophets for the messianic age, had never become a reality. There certainly were more wars in the Middle Ages than under the *pax Romana*. At times they could even claim that "the scepter" had not departed from Judah itself and that some Jews, like the kings of southern Arabia and Khazaria or the exilarchs, continued to hold political sway over the Jewish people.

In Muslim countries Jews did not hesitate to admit that their ancestors had been coresponsible for Jesus' crucifixion. Some writers may have been irked by certain Muslim theologians who, in their anti-Christian zeal, denied that Jesus had ever been executed. Qirqisani somewhat bitingly commented, "that the Rabbanites plotted against him until they killed him and crucified him." Even Maimonides limited himself to a derogatory statement, more remarkable for its acerbity of language than for its clarity. Contending that some sectarians were most effective in raising claims to prophecy and founding a new faith, he observed:

> The first . . . was Jesus the Nazarene, . . . a Jew because his mother was a Jewess, although his father was a Gentile. For in accordance with the principles of our law, a child born of a Jewess and a Gentile, or of a Jewess and a slave, is legitimate (Yebamot 45a). Jesus is only figuratively termed an illegitimate child. He impelled people to believe that he was a prophet sent by God to clarify perplexities in the Torah, and that he was the Messiah that was predicted by each and every seer. He interpreted the Torah and its precepts in such a fashion as to lead to their total annulment, to the abolition of all its commandments and to the violation of its prohibitions. The sages, of blessed memory, having become aware of his plans before his reputation spread among our people, meted out fitting punishment to him. . . .
>
> Quite some time after, a religion appeared, the origin of which is traced to him by the descendants of Esau, albeit it was not the intention of this person to establish a new faith. For he was innocuous to Israel, as neither individual nor groups were unsettled in their beliefs because of him, since his inconsistencies were so transparent to every one. Finally, he was overpowered and put a stop to by us when he fell into our hands, and his fate is well known.[46]

Evidently, the sage of Fusṭaṭ wished to convey here the idea that the Christian religion was really the creation of the Roman Empire, which embraced Jesus' preachment without his will or foreknowledge. Qirqisani, too, unhesitatingly stated that "as for the religion of the Christians which they profess today, it was Paul who introduced and established it. He was the one who invested Jesus with divinity, and he claimed to be a prophet ordained by his lord Jesus." The Muslim, Qarafi, spoke even more disparagingly of Paul, "the evil spirit of the Christians." This sharp dichotomy between the founder and later Christianity, often voiced by medieval Jewish writers, was not the result of modern historical criticism which recognizes that the very name *Christiani* originated only after the death of Jesus, but rather of the chronological confusion in the ancient rabbinic sources which had placed Jesus among the disciples of Joshua ben Peraḥiah in the second pre-Christian century. If the ancient sages, much closer to the scene, could thus be mistaken about Jesus' time, one need not be astonished by the medieval writers' chronological misconceptions.[47]

Generally, they were none too exacting nor well informed about the chronology of the Second Commonwealth. While Chrysostom undoubtedly exaggerated the apologetic import of biblical chronology, there is no question that the talmudic and medieval rabbis were quite hazy about the sequence of generations before the Maccabean age. This came to the fore also in the constant Judeo-Christian debates on the meaning of the messianic prophecies of Daniel. The crucial prediction of that prophet, generally believed to have preached in the days of Nebukadrezzar, that from the building of Jerusalem seven weeks would pass before the anointed prince would come (Dan. 9:24–25) was usually computed to refer to a period of seven times seventy years, or a total of 490 years. According to a broad Christian calculation, the predicted prince was Jesus, born some 490 years after the Exile. The rabbis rejected that chronology, especially by referring to the old rabbinic telescoping of the entire Achaemenide domination over the Jews to thirty-four years. Relying on that rabbinic miscalculation, even Saadiah allowed himself to blame the Christians for their willful "mistake" of claiming "that the government of the Persians over Palestine existed for a period of something like 300 years before that of the Greeks" and that there were altogether seventeen Persian kings. "However," the gaon asserted with perfect conviction, "I have refuted this contention on their part from the text of the Book of Daniel itself, [pointing out] that it was impossible that between the time of the government of Babylon and that of the Greeks more than four Persian kings should have ruled over Palestine." But whatever were the merits of these chronological controversies, few, if any, Jews were persuaded by the Christian identification of the prophetic messiah with Jesus.[48]

On much safer ground was Saadiah's philosophic argument against the divinity of Jesus. Unlike Jesus' messiahship, which appeared almost as an internal controversy between Judaism and Christianity, the Trinitarian dogma was under direct attack by Muslims, dualists, and skeptics. To answer these numerous criticisms the Syrian Christians, and after them other Eastern philosophers of religion, increasingly elaborated the doctrine of divine attributes. Contending that the very nature of God requires the three basic attributes of existence, power, and knowledge, Christian thinkers saw therein a philosophic justification for the doctrine of Trinity, combined with the overriding unity of God over and above His three attributes. In addressing Jews and Christians the medieval apologists adduced scriptural proofs from the Old Testament. Invoking, for example, the very Jewish credo of "Hear, O Israel," the Christian teachers pointed out that "the Lord our God, the Lord is one" (Deut. 6:4) really shows the three-in-oneness. They also argued that such plural forms as "Let us make man in our image" (Gen. 1:26), indicate that God had co-makers in the process of creation which could only refer to His son. Petrus Alphonsi, quoting a kabbalistic treatise, stressed that Jesus' final word on the cross, *Eloi* (my God), instead of the plural *Elohai,* could be understood only as the second person in the Trinity addressing the first. Moreover, the very Tetragrammaton, God's ineffable name, really consists, in Petrus' opinion, of three divine names, *Yah, Hu,* and *Vah,* combined into one. Further tying up the messianic with the christological argument, some apologists fell back upon the old aggadic concept of the Messiah's preexistence. They contended that the Messiah could not be an ordinary human being, since he was compared with the morning star, and that star had been created two days before Adam. Much stress was also laid upon the biblical phrases relating to the creation by means of the divine "word," which Philo had already identified with the *logos* as the intermediary in the process of creation, whereas the ancient Christian teachers had elevated it to a position coequal with God himself.[49]

Against such reasonings Saadiah was in his own element. Combining expert knowledge of Hebrew philology with the dialectical techniques of contempoary *kalam,* the gaon could disprove one such argument after another on philological or philosophic grounds. He insisted that the words "spirit" and "word" (in II Sam. 23:2) were nothing but "things specially created by God," and claimed that the Christian interpretation of these terms was obviously owing to "unfamiliarity with the Hebrew language." Plural forms, moreover, were often found in the Bible in connection with such distinguished persons as Balak, Manoah, or Daniel, without relating to actions by more than one person. Similarly, he discounted the story of God's appearance to Abraham at Mamre (Gen. 18:1–2) which, following Muslim controversialists, Mardan Farukh had cited as a blatant instance of Jewish anthropomorphism, and which had lent itself to Christian identification of the Lord with the three persons appearing before the Hebrew patriarch. Saadiah explained this chapter as simply referring to the Lord's light shining upon Abraham and warning him of the arrival of the three angels, and continuing to shine after their departure. The gaon further inquired as to why one should limit the divine attributes to existence, power, and knowledge, and not include also God's ability to hear and see. We shall later note that, despite Saadiah's partial rejection, the doctrine of divine attributes was to fructify much of medieval Jewish and Muslim thinking about God. Similarly, in their repudiation of the Christian teachings about the Messiah, Jewish thinkers were forced to rethink and reformulate their own traditional concepts and to develop an even more ramified messianic doctrine than had existed in ancient times.[50]

ATTACKS ON JEWISH LAW

No less challenging was the Christian repudiation of Jewish law. True, the old Pauline and Gnostic antinomianism no longer carried much weight with churches bent upon cultivating an extensive ceremonial law of their own. It mattered even less in a Muslim environment whose dominant religion emphasized law as much as Judaism. The Christian attack was now concentrated, therefore, not on law as such, but rather on specific laws to which Jews attached great significance.

According to some Christian apologists, contemporary Jews emphasized above all other laws those relating to circumcision, the Sabbath, and Passover. There is no justification for that distinction from the standpoint of rabbinic law, for all six hundred and thirteen biblical laws are equally binding. Perhaps in tacit opposition to some such discrimination between important and unimportant laws which certain Jewish individuals may have drawn for themselves, Maimonides contended that making such a distinction constituted King Manasseh's greatest sin. But it was an historic reality, to some extent admitted by the rabbis themselves, that the Jewish people were often ready to sacrifice their lives to avoid idolatry, and in order to comply with the commandments of circumcision and the Sabbath. That is why, a rabbi exclaimed, the latter two commandments have remained a permanent possession of the Jewish people, whereas many other commandments (that relating to phylacteries, for example), for which Jews had not sacrificed their lives, have often fallen by the wayside. In any case, Christians who may have learned of such debates within the Jewish community claimed that all commandments had since been replaced by the belief in Christ.[51]

Understandably, circumcision was not under attack in the Muslim world, where the majority of the population was circumcised. There the Christian leaders themselves were on the defensive not only against Muslims and Jews, but also against the Christian Copts and Abyssinians. In his appearance before Al-Ma'mun, Theodore abu Qurra merely argued that Christianity had reverted to the older practice from Adam to Abraham and replaced the "sign" of circumcision by baptism. As late as the fourteenth century the Armenian polemist, Gregory of Tathew, could offer no cogent argument against Muslim debaters who pointed out that Jesus himself, along with Abraham and the other prophets, were all circumcised. In Christian countries, however, that "mutilation," already denounced by Paul, was often decried as Cain's sign and an appropriate penalty for the "stiff-necked" people, whose stubbornness had not diminished in the course of ages. The Sabbath idea, as such, could not be attacked because both Christians and Muslims had likewise adopted it, but the rigid forms of its Jewish observance were sharply denounced. Rather than a welcome day of rest, such enforced abstention from work was deemed to be another penalty inflicted by God on a recalcitrant people. At times the controversy over the Sabbath degenerated into crude folkloristic tales. According to a widely repeated story, a Jew who had fallen into a sewer on Saturday refused to be drawn out lest the Sabbath rest be violated. In reprisal, the local authorities prevented his rescue on Sunday as well. Christian writers heaped equal scorn on the Jewish ritualistic restrictions on food and many other laws. At times they still reiterated the old denunciations of the Jewish sacrificial system which had allegedly been still another divinely imposed penalty, although Jews had ceased sacrificing animals ever since the fall of Jerusalem, and even before that time had limited that ritual exclusively to the sanctuaries of Jerusalem and Leontopolis.[52]

We must bear in mind that, unlike circumcision, which few Western Christians wished to emulate, the Sabbath and Passover rites still carried great appeal to many sectarian and some orthodox Christians everywhere. In fact, Saint Caesarius of Arles held up the Jewish Sabbath observance as an example for the Christians to follow. Most other churchmen, however, often had occasion to fulminate against such "aberrations" as attendance at synagogue services on Sabbaths and the consumption of unleavened bread by superstitious parishioners. Agobard scolded those members of his diocese who preferred to listen to Jewish, rather than Christian sermons. He also claimed that, because of their excessive familiarity and constant living together, some Christians celebrated the Sabbath with the Jews, while they violated the Sunday with illicit work. Christian writers tried to prove, therefore, that the

Jews themselves had often broken the Sabbath commandment, especially in wartime. John of Damascus pointed out that both Elijah and Daniel had fasted on the Sabbath and that all Jews performed circumcision on that day. The Spanish controversialist, on the other hand, cited to the same effect Joshua's attack on Jericho and the Maccabean revolt.[53]

On the whole, however, these were but pinpricks. In essence, state legislations in both the Christian and Muslim worlds respected the Jewish ceremonial practices. So long as Jews were tolerated at all, they were allowed to adhere to their religion and cultivate their mores according to their ancestral tradition. The denunciations may have impressed, therefore, the relatively few Jews who had already become insecure in their orthodoxy, but they passed largely unnoticed by the majority. Their purpose obviously was not so much to convert Jews as to reassure the Christians themselves that biblical law could safely be disregarded, since many Mosaic provisions must be understood in a purely allegorical sense, while others, actually imposed upon the Jewish people, had been abrogated by the new dispensation. To the former argument the Jews replied quite simply that allegorical interpretations can offer subsidiary insights, but leave the binding nature of the commandments' ordinary meaning totally unimpaired. Jews also sharply repudiated any abrogation of their law by either Jesus or Mohammed. In fact, they no longer repeated the doctrine of some early teachers that with the advent of the Messiah the reign of law would also pass, faint echoes of which were still found in the talmudic literature. On the contrary, Maimonides made it a special point to emphasize the unrestricted validity of all Jewish laws also in the messianic era.[54]

Admittedly, the problem of Jewish observance did not really loom large in the Judeo-Christian controversy. Jewish apologists (for instance, the two Qimḥis) took little notice of that accusation. Among Eastern Christians there was more resentment of the continued adherence to Jewish practices by converts than by professing Jews. They sometimes actually pointed an accusing finger at the laxity of many Jews. A proverb cited in the Latin translation of Al-Kindi's renowned apology paradoxically claimed that "A Jew is not [quite] a Jew, until after he turns Saracen;

hardly any of them cultivates his law, except when he accepts another." [55]

Jews and Muslims often reciprocated by assailing the Christian worship of icons and the cross. Sa'id ibn Ḥasan cited the wrathful exclamation of the Deuteronomist, "Cursed be the man that maketh a graven or molten image" (27:15), translating the crucial term, *pesel* (image) by *ṣalib* (cross). He also explained that among Achan's booty which had caused Joshua's defeat was a golden cross (7:21). An early thirteenth-century Muslim polemist repeated at some length a legend aimed at the True Cross, which had played such a fateful role in the days of Heraclius. It was allegedly a Jew, Itmar, who had buried three ordinary crosses in the dirt and subsequently dug up one for Empress Helena, claiming with the aid of a fabricated miracle that it was the very cross on which Jesus had died (Fritsch, *Islam,* p. 140).

Here, too, these arguments and counterarguments nurtured new thoughts. While the antinomian attack of Graeco-Roman heathens and early Christians had already been met by the Jews with a renewed insistence upon the law as the "fence for the Torah," the new challenges relating to specific rather than to general norms stimulated much rethinking of the traditional rationales. In some ways they helped to fructify the speculations on the meaning of the *halakhah* in general and of the reasons for specific commandments in particular, and thus they aided in the development of a new philosophy of Jewish law.

SOCIOPOLITICAL JEW-BAITING

In attacking contemporary Jewry Christian spokesmen, unlike their Muslim counterparts, had to come to grips with the Old Testament doctrine of the Chosen People. The biblical references were too numerous and unequivocal to be interpreted away by simple exegetical methods. Medieval churchmen were able, however, to fall back on the ancient Christian concept that, with the advent of Christ, the Jewish people was rejected by God and Christendom became the new chosen people. This conviction was so deep-rooted that, even without direct polemical intent, writers could refer to Christians as the new Israelites. Moderate Sidonius

Apollinaris described the Jewish convert Promotus as "a Jew by race, who preferred to be regarded as an Israelite through faith, rather than through blood." Similarly, when Paulus Alvarus embarked upon the reconversion of Bodo-Eleazar, he concluded his first letter in very friendly terms. "I pray that you may always be happy, most revered and most beloved brother by nature, not by faith." Less equivocally, he later replied to Bodo in a lengthy tirade,

> Which of us better deserves to be distinguished by the name of Israelite? You, who as you say have been converted from idolatry to the worship of the supreme God, and are a Jew not by race, but by faith, or I, who am a Hebrew both by faith and race? But I am not called a Jew because a *new name* has been given me which the mouth of the Lord hath named (Isa. 62:2). Abraham is my father not because my forbears descended from that stem. For those who expected the Messiah to come, and received him when he came, are more truly Israel than those who expected his coming yet rejected him when he came, and have not ceased to hope for him; because you are still awaiting him whom you have most certainly already rejected. The Gentiles, however, who are daily being converted to the faith of Israel, take their place in the people of God, while you obviously still adhere to the error of the Jews.

Isidore of Seville ingeniously interpreted the ancient separation of Israel and Judah as an adumbration of the breach between Christianity and Judaism, and he saw in the prophecies concerning the former's ultimate reunification a prediction that, at the end of days, all Jews would be converted to the Christian faith and thus rejoin "Israel." In time, there developed a certain nuance between the three terms Hebrew, Israelite, and Jew. Bernard Blumenkranz, an assiduous student of the Latin polemical literature, has observed that in these writings "the term 'Hebrew' is a neutral designation, 'Israelite' a noble term, whereas 'Jew' often carries with it a pejorative connotation." Had not Melito of Sardis as early as the second century used some fanciful etymologies to prove that *Israel* were the Christians who "saw God" (a variant of Philo's interpretation), *Judaei* stood for adherents of the synagogue of Satan, and *Ishmael,* the obedient, designated those who obeyed their own lust? By a curious inversion he identified Edom with the Jews, "red" with the blood of Christ.[56]

Jews paid no heed to these reinterpretations of ancient texts. With his claim of the eternity of the Jewish people and its law, both vouchsafed by the divine promise, Saadiah repudiated not only the Muslim-Christian contentions concerning the abrogation of that law, but also the Christian methods of interpretation. If, as has been suggested, the ancient rabbinic doctrine of election had already been stimulated by Paul's denial of the Jews' chosenness, the medieval Jewish thinkers and exegetes could calmly reiterate the old rabbinic rationales and support them by citing scriptural passages in their ordinary meaning. They cared very little about the Christian accusation of their literal, "materialist" understanding of the Bible. While having their share of allegorists, they reiterated the ancient adage that, no matter how ingenious hermeneutical elaborations may be, "Scripture never departs from its ordinary meaning." In detail, moreover, expert students of the Hebrew Bible could point out many mistakes in quotations therefrom current in Christian letters. In an anonymous polemical tract a Jewish writer emphasized that the very Gospels contained such misquotations. On one occasion he caustically referred to Jesus as a "poor man" who did not know his *Shema'*, and yet was acclaimed as a messiah by his disciples.[57]

These ancient controversies received new meaning as a result of the changed status of Jewry. In ancient times there was little to distinguish a Jew from a Christian in the socioeconomic sphere. Hence the economic element played a very minor role in the numerous ancient altercations. Now, however, even in the Near East the Jews' progressive urbanization and entry into world trade and banking caused an outcry against alleged Jewish financial domination. Such harangues became doubly meaningful in the Christian West from the Carolingian age on. In the Frankish Empire, we recall, there were relatively few Jews, but most of them served as mercantile and cultural mediators between East and West, an occupation which was both financially lucrative and politically influential. For this reason Agobard and his successors raised the battle cry against "Jewish insolence" and drive for power, abetted for selfish reasons by Christian rulers and noblemen. This battle cry has never subsided since. Later on it received further nourishment from the growing Jewish concentration on moneylending. No matter how much the Church itself fostered Jewish "usury" in order the more effectively to suppress Christian moneylending, the Jews' public indulgence in an occupation which, even where it was morally reprehensible still appeared financially and socially rewarding, lent itself to extensive exploitation by their enemies. While we find no reference to Jewish usury among Church Fathers, not even Chrysostom, who spared no possible invective against his Jewish fellow-citizens of Antioch, Agobard and Peter of Cluny initated that long series of tirades against Jewish economic exploitation which have ever since marred all Judeo-Christian relations. Moreover, Peter's greater contemporary, St. Bernard of Clairvaux, equated usury with "Judaizing." [58]

Here Jewish apologists were at a considerable disadvantage. They could argue formally, as did the anonymous Western author, that charging interest to Gentiles had expressly been permitted by God's revelation to Moses. Rejecting the claim of a Christian contemporary that, according to the Psalmist, all usury had been forbidden, our author declared that King David could not possibly have contradicted the revealed word of the Torah. Before him Joseph Qimḥi had quoted a Christian spokesman as contrasting contemporary Jewish usurers with the numerous Christian anachoretes who preferred solitary living in forests and deserts to the enjoyment of worldly goods. In reply, the Jewish apologist pointed out the rigid abstention of Jewish moneylenders from usurious transactions with fellow-Jews, which alone had been outlawed in the Bible. They avoided even the "dust of usury" in these business dealings, whereas Christians applied various methods of evasion. "Moreover, it is known that many Christians lend money on usury to both Jews and Christians." Christian ascetes, on the other hand, are but one of a thousand or ten thousand, while the rest of the people "are all immersed in worldly pursuits." Another Jewish apologist, Meir bar Simon, we recollect, was to argue quite sensibly that taking interest was an economic necessity and that, were it not for Jews, even the king of France would have been unable to raise necessary funds. Not surprisingly, however, such replies fell flat upon the ears of Christian moralists and debtors of all classes.[59]

Curiously, such assaults upon Jewish domination were combined in the Christian world with unrelenting emphasis upon Jewish serfdom. Unlike the Muslim controversialists, for whom the combination of Jewish subjection and governmental protection was mainly an historical fact, the Christian spokesmen had inherited from such revered teachers as Augustine the doctrine of perpetual Jewish serfdom as a God-inflicted penalty for the stiff-necked repudiation of Christ. Originating from a biblical simile, that phrase was constantly reiterated in ecclesiastical circles, and from there spread to the secular rulers as well. Isaac's blessing of Esau, "And thou shalt serve thy brother" (Gen. 27:40) originally reflected but the actuality of Israel's dominion over Esau-Edom in the days of David, Solomon, or Jehoshaphat. Now it was reinterpreted to mean that the new Israel in the spirit, as the younger brother, would dominate the older brother, Israel in the flesh. Since both the Hebrew term *ta'abod* and the Latin *servies* have the double connotation of serving and being in bondage, they could be understood to mirror Jewish political powerlessness and dependence on the good will of Christian masters. The Toledan Council of 694, which spoke of the Jews being *perpetuae servituti subacti,* still voiced merely the old homiletical exaggeration. Before very long this doctrine was to assume the character of a genuine political and legal concept of universal import. "There is no more dishonorable nor serious serfdom," exclaimed St. Bernard of Clairvaux, "than that of the Jews; they carry it with them wherever they go, and everywhere they find their masters" (*De consideratione,* 1.3 in *PL,* CLXXXII, 732).

Here Jewish controversialists did not disagree. True, all Jews were convinced not only of the ultimate redemption of their people, but also that God would avenge all wrongs committed against them. An old legend attributed to Jethro a warning to the Pharaoh of Egypt which sounded a refrain often voiced in Hebrew letters. "But, sire," the wise Midianite elder was supposed to have warned the king, "he who ever put forth his hand against Israel has invariably been punished." But the rabbis were the last to minimize the sufferings of the *galut.* While under Christendom they were spared the irony of being enslaved to the son of a slave, Ishmael, the reality of living in Exile with all its insecurity and alienage loomed even greater in Western Jewish minds as a result of the recurrent massacres and expulsions. If there was any controversy on this score at all, it referred only to the cause of the Exile. To Christians the Jewish dispersion appeared as a clear-cut divine infliction for the Jewish rejection of Christ. Jews, on the other hand, merely prayed in general terms, "Because of our sins we have been exiled from our country," definitely repudiating the idea that these sins had anything to do with the appearance of Jesus. Joseph Qimḥi argued that the Davidic monarchy had ceased with the first fall of Jerusalem, and that the rulers of the Second Commonwealth were either priests or foreigners like Herod. Hence Jacob's blessing of the scepter not departing from Judah referred only to the Davidic monarchy before the first fall of Jerusalem, and could not possibly relate to Jesus. The ancient Jews were fully entitled, therefore, to repudiate Jesus' messiahship. The Torah itself, moreover, in his opinion, gave the reason for the subsequent Jewish dispersion: "Because we have relinquished the Law of our God, his commandments and ordinances, not because of a sin relating to Jesus or any other matter." Otherwise some specific warning would have been included in the original divine admonitions, for no one can legally be punished unless he had been forewarned. Nevertheless the Lord had promised the Jewish people its ultimate redemption, and interveningly had preserved it through eleven (twelve) centuries of life in exile. In fact, the prophet Elijah had already hinted that the Torah, which had been compared to fire (Deut. 33:2), would not be extinguished by many waters, but endure forever. By emphasizing that the fire of the Lord would lick up the water on Mount Carmel (I Kings 18:38), Elijah indicated that "the fire of our holy faith would consume the water, that is Christian baptism in the waters of their sin. And God answered him through fire, and thus preserved for us our holy faith." [60]

Not surprisingly, our apologist no longer referred to the existence of a Jewish monarchy in his day. After Khazaria's downfall and the eclipse of the exilarchate this argument no longer carried much weight. Previously, however, Christian apologists had to resort to daring subterfuges to controvert it. While Isidore of Seville had declared the Jewish claim of a remote Jewish kingdom a figment of imagination, his successors, Julian of Toledo and

Paul Alvarus, conceded the fact itself; but they argued that this was not a genuine monarchy because it had no temple, sacrifices, or priests (Julian), or because the king was not of Jewish descent (Alvarus). Elaborating the latter reasoning, Christian of Stavelot contended that the Khazars were of Hun rather than Jewish ancestry, embraced also many Christians, while their neighbors, the Bulgars, had altogether embraced Christianity.[61]

Understandably, no one now accused the Jews of "atheism." Early Christian apologists occasionally referred to such arguments formerly advanced by Graeco-Roman pagans, but they could not denounce Jews for not recognizing the gods of the Empire. However, they, and particularly the gnostics among them, sometimes claimed that Jews were worshiping the wrong kind of god. A variant of that theme, Jewish "misanthropy," also was repeated now in a novel key. Since the Church itself strongly promoted segregation, Jewish separation as such was resented less than certain of its forms, such as insistence on ritual food. The Jewish prohibition of pork products, especially, was declared an unreasoning form of the Jewish feeling of superiority, underscored, for those who knew about it, by the old aggadic symbolism equating Rome with a pig. Toward the end of our period the re-emerging "blood accusation" served as another illustration of alleged Jewish hostility toward non-Jews. It mattered little that in ancient times the Christians themselves had been the primary targets for these denunciations. Curiously, for a long time, the Jews did not take the accusation too seriously. Except where it led to direct executions or massacres of Jews, as in Blois, it was ignored in Hebrew letters. To most Jewish contemporaries it appeared as but a phase of the general popular hostility which they had come to expect from their Christian neighbors. Nor did it as yet play any important role in the general Judeo-Christian debate, although in the overheated atmosphere of the Crusades the Jews likewise often reciprocated with curses and invectives rather than calm argument.[62]

Deep suspicions were nurtured by the Church's frequent allusions to "perfidious" Jews. Originally, this term was used merely in the meaning of "unbelieving" Jews. But in time it increasingly conveyed to listeners the notion of Jewish underhandedness and proneness to cheating. Combined with the denunciation of Jewish usury and economic exploitation, it doubtless helped evoke the image of the ever-hostile Jew, waiting to pounce upon unwary Christians. It is small wonder, then, that medieval art often presented the Jew under the symbol of a scorpion, with the implied warning that the faithful had better keep at a safe distance from its deadly sting.[63]

In time the alleged Jewish alliance with demonic powers also began to play a major role in fostering suspicions among the Christian masses. The more segregated Jewish life became and the more the Jewish mores differed from the Christian, the easier it was to equate such mysterious conduct with an alliance with Satan. Jewish economic successes and, even more, the efficacy of Jewish doctors, perhaps underscored by the lower rate of mortality in the Jewish quarter, could well be adduced as further "proof" of the Jew's compact with demons. Such allegations sounded doubly plausible, as the Jewish religion was often denounced as the child of Lucifer; the "Synagogue of Satan" had become a standardized phrase among Christian teachers, and the Jews were supposed to be impatiently awaiting the arrival of anti-Christ. It is true that in the period under review this accusation was not vigorously pressed; perhaps the audiences on both sides felt too much awe and reverence for the demonic powers. Yet there were enough incendiary possibilities in this line of reasoning for David Qimḥi strenuously to deny any connection between Jews and fallen angels, and to explain that the Isaianic prophecy relating to *Helal ben Shaḥar* (day-star, son of the morning; 14:12) was aimed at Nebukadrezzar, not Lucifer. Clearly such denials, if at all known to the Christian public, made no impression. Jew-baiting thus became permeated with magical ingredients which deeply colored the emotional reactions of medieval Christians, and which have ever since seriously handicapped understanding among the two faiths.[64]

Other accusations could be taken more lightly. If, as a heritage of classical Jew-baiting, medieval Christians occasionally repeated phrases relating to Jewish laziness, audacity, proneness to leprosy, and the like, these denunciations were so completely devoid of solid factual basis that they must have carried little conviction.

Certainly no medieval Christian could blame Jews, as had the ancient Graeco-Roman writers, for their "laziness" in observing a weekly day of rest, although Jewish abstention from work went much further than the requirements of either Church or Mosque. Leprosy, which had once served as a fanciful explanation of the Jewish exodus from Egypt, must have become quite meaningless when Jews were but infrequently represented in the European leper colonies. Still, more or less mechanically repeated by such churchmen as St. Ambrose and St. Theodoret of Cyrrhus, this accusation implying both that the Jews had lied about their Exodus from Egypt and that they had always been the special object of wrath divine, is rarely echoed in later literature. This despite the fact that after the Crusades, as J. J. Walsh observed, leprosy was to become "almost as much of a folk disease as tuberculosis came to be towards the end of the nineteenth century." Not that the medieval man had medical statistics at his disposal, or that he refrained from exaggerating individual cases. Yet in the long run the fact that fewer Jews appear to have suffered from that scourge and that the numerous lepers of all classes became the subjects of pity rather than condemnation, must have blunted the edge of this accusation.[65]

Somewhat more significant was the repetition of the Graeco-Roman accusation of Jewish lasciviousness. Sex morality among Jews was undoubtedly more strict and more rigidly enforced than among the medieval Christian masses if for no other reason than the necessarily greater emphasis upon family life in a minority struggling to survive against tremendous odds. At least north of the Alps and Pyrenees, sex relations between Jews and Christians were categorically outlawed. Nonetheless such transgressions must have occurred much more frequently than is recorded in the sources. Any single affair between a Jew and a Christian woman could easily lead to the condemnation of the whole Jewish community as a salacious group. At times Jewish seductions were advanced as a reason why Jews should not be allowed to employ Christian domestics, and soon also as a justification for the introduction of a special badge so as to obviate any mistaken identity. On the other hand, Jewish and non-Jewish authors occasionally mention love affairs between Jewish women and Christian paramours. Caesarius of Heisterbach tells with considerable relish how an English cleric, after seducing a Jewish girl, persuaded her to accept baptism, whereupon both joined the Cistercian order. According to him, many Christian young men evinced special preference for beautiful Jewish girls. More, in the circles which mattered most, namely among the clergy, the very emphasis of rabbinic law upon the duty of procreation must have appeared as catering to the baser instincts of human nature. The more ardently Western churchmen preached celibacy for their own priests and the more seriously monks and nuns took their vows of chastity, the more likely were they to look askance at the rabbis who publicly extolled the virtues of early marriages and even demanded that a wife after ten years of barren marriage be divorced by her husband, so that each might try again to fulfill the duty of providing progeny for the Jewish people. True, these demands were never enforced. Yet, the idea that procreation was not only a matter of individual bliss, but also a high moral obligation, ran counter to the very fundamentals of the Christian preachment.[66]

In reply, Jewish apologists emphasized the stricter standards of sexual morality prevailing in the Jewish community. "Jewish families are pure," exclaimed Joseph Qimḥi, "and their women are modest in their entire behavior. Even children are severely scolded by their parents for using profane language. In contrast thereto, Christian society allows the public display of vice at street corners, without police interference. Even the majority of celibatarian bishops and priests are known to be steeped in debauchery." In the Muslim world, on the other hand, it was Arab licentiousness which served as the main target for Jewish attacks. The author of the *Zohar* doubtless merely repeated an old legend when he explained in a dramatic dialogue why the descendants of both Esau and Ishmael had rejected the offer, extended to them along with all other nations, to be recipients of the Torah. When Samael, Edom's (Rome's) angelic prince, transmitted God's offer to the warlike Esawites, they refused because they did not wish to submit to the prohibition of murder. Similarly, the licentious Ishmaelites rejected the offer of their angelic representative, Rahab, because they resented the prohibition of adultery.[67]

THE "REBEL"

All in all these accusations were not the primary cause of the growing tensions in Christian-Jewish, and to a lesser extent in Muslim-Jewish, relations, but rather rationalizations of animosities nurtured by other social and psychological wellsprings. Once voiced, however, and placed in wide circulation, they were repeated from generation to generation and became in turn further sources of infection. In time their mountainous accumulation became a burdensome heritage not easily to be removed, even after the original social causes had disappeared.

Jews had, of course, little to gain and much to lose from these protracted controversies. True, an anonymous Jewish polemist tells us that, after they had been shown the discrepancies in the Christian interpretation of the Old Testament, "I have seen Christian Frenchmen, pious and wise in their behavior, who for this reason converted themselves to Judaism." But such instances must have been very rare, and not at all to be compared with the numerical losses sustained by the Jewish community through conversion to either Christianity or Islam. On principle, too, Judaism had long ceased to be a missionary religion. It realized that the few conquests it might make would be very dearly compensated by increased animosity, perhaps even by violent retribution. Their spokesmen, therefore, including Saadiah, Halevi, and Maimonides in the Muslim world, and the Qimḥis under Christendom, debated the merits of the respective faiths entirely for internal edification. Most Christian and Muslim apologists, too, argued their case much more for the benefit of their own adherents than in order to convert unbelievers. A pseudo-Augustinian controversial tract, one of those numerous fabrications which were long in greater vogue than the Bishop of Hippo's authentic works, stated succinctly, "Let then the Christian pay heed, since the Jew does not want to listen!" In the case of Jews it was agreed that they were needed as witnesses for the Christian faith and that their remnant must be allowed to persist to the second coming of Christ. Only in border areas, or such as had recently been conquered from Islam, did Christian Crusaders feel it incumbent upon themselves to use spiritual and worldly means to bring

Muslims and Jews under their ecclesiastical tutelage and thus eliminate a potential "fifth column" after the renewal of hostilities. But in countries of deeply rooted Christianity, as in most Byzantine and Western lands, the debate was often purely academic, and most of these writings bear the earmarks of exercises in historical and systematic theology, rather than of any deep concern for direct conversion. Some polemists, like Bartholomew, bishop of Exeter (1180–84), warned his readers not to "engage in a debate over religion with them [the Jews] in the presence of unbelieving or inexperienced listeners." [68]

Nevertheless, there was much realistic substance in these diatribes. In most Muslim lands the resentment over the Jewish refusal to conform with the views of the majority was attenuated by the presence of numerous Muslim sectarians as well as Christians, Zoroastrians, and Sabians. There the Jews were not even the principal religious minority. In the intolerant Christian world, however, they were, for the most part, the sole recognized representatives of religious dissent. Naturally enough, their very ubiquity helped to nurture rebellious attitudes arising from the social or ideological unrest among the majority, too. However we evaluate the Jewish influences on Shi'ites or Ismailis under Islam, Nestorians or inconoclasts in Byzantium, and Albigensians or Passagii in the West, the very fact that they persisted in their different beliefs and interpretations of the Bible, as well as in their diverse rituals and modes of living, served as a stimulant to religious-minded individuals to rethink their own positions. That is why the accusation "Jew," hurled at one another by the Christian and Muslim sectarians, had a grain of historical truth, even if heresiarchs of both faiths had not borrowed some ideas from the Jewish interpretation of Old Testament teachings and institutions.

Paradoxically, Christian and, to a lesser extent, Muslim apologists now began arguing that the Jews themselves knew the truth but refused to admit it. Old Testament hermeneutics, however daring, were utilized to prove that the Jewish "materialistic" interpretation of Scripture was a deliberate falsehood. In time, Christian spokesmen, especially if recruited from among Jewish converts, liked to delve into the mysteries of rabbinic literature in order to prove the authenticity of the Christian message from these hostile sources themselves. It was only "stiff-neckedness," they taught, already stressed in the Bible, which prevented most Jews from acknowledging that truth. But what else could one expect from born rebels?

Jews now saw themselves robbed of their own history to an even greater extent than in their ancient debates. Their own Scriptural traditions were marshaled in such a way as to prove their stubborn falsification of either text or meaning. Their patriarch, Abraham, was appropriated as either an early preacher of pure Christianity, or the ancestor of the Arab tribes, the descendants of his really beloved son, Ishmael. Isaac's renowned sacrifice was replaced by that of Ishmael, or else made to serve as but a pale adumbration of the crucifixion of Jesus. The very Israelitic prophets now appeared merely as witnesses for those Jewish crimes and shortcomings which they denounced, but not for God's pity over His chosen people, or for His promise of its ultimate redemption. Conversely, while presenting Christianity as the new Israel, its spokesmen were prone to cite only the prophetic words of comfort, and not those of chastisement, for the ancient people.[69]

Nonetheless, unperturbedly and, despite prolonged sufferings, quite serenely, the Jewish people proceeded along its accustomed ways. Unabashed by the alarming cacophony of accusations of its religious and sociopolitical behavior, it confidently looked forward to the early realization of its messianic dream.

XXV

MESSIANISM AND SECTARIAN TRENDS

The focal position held by the messianic idea in the Judeo-Christian controversy was merely a reflection of the fundamental importance of that idea in Jewish theology and life. On dogmatic grounds, Christians were convinced that once Jews acknowledged the messiahship of Jesus, practically all of them would readily be converted to Christianity, particularly since, with the removal of the messianic hope, their position in exile would have become untenable. That is why Christian controversialists blamed the Jews for not recognizing Jesus as their Messiah unless they saw with their own eyes Moses and Elijah paying homage to him as their Creator. In many conversion stories, in fact, dreams involving Moses' homage to Jesus played a decisive role.[1]

Even more irksome to the Christian leaders was the "insolence" of the Jewish messianic expectation, which viewed the ultimate outcome of the people's perennial struggle for survival as consisting in its certain victory over all its foes. Its conviction that at the end of days all nations would recognize its supremacy seemed the more insufferable a challenge as it appeared so far-fetched and impossible of realization under the existing conditions of power. Yet it was this very certainty about the ultimate fulfillment of the ancient messianic prophecies, in defiance of all political realities, which served as a buoy for the Jewish minority in the darkest periods of its history. As the Jews' political and social standing sank lower and their prospects for the future became more desperate, so did the messianic hope permeate more deeply all Jewish consciousness and illumine more brightly the dark night of exile.

Jewish messianism took many forms. At the end of the talmudic era it already had behind it a long and ramified history. Fully developed by the ancient prophets, especially of the exilic and postexilic periods, it received ever new formulations and elaborations during the religiously exalted, while socially restless and politically unsatisfactory, late Maccabean and Herodian ages. Messianic speculation played an enormous role especially in the apocryphal and pseudepigraphic literature, the dominant conceptions of which, as we recall, were to a large extent responsible for the development of the Christ idea in the daughter religion. Though somewhat discredited within the Jewish fold through the rise of Christianity and toned down by the talmudic sages, the messianic expectation nevertheless remained one of the major pillars of the whole structure of Judaism. One cannot judge the importance of this ideology by the relatively small space allotted to it in the two Talmudim. In the Aggadah it always played a preeminent role and, whether outspoken or implied, it pervaded the entire fabric of Jewish thought and behavior.

With such a rich heritage from ancient times, medieval messianic thinkers could only elaborate, adjust, and modify its basic ideas. Because of the preservation, however, of a much larger body of writings and the much greater diversification of Jewish disciplines from the tenth to the twelfth centuries, these old thoughts received a new articulation which put them into bolder relief and, on occasion, made them more fully comprehensible. At the same time the new spirit of intellectual exploration generated some novel approaches in this field. Basically we must, therefore, consider the messianic idea during our period under the headings of the traditional apocalyptic-aggadic ideas, the new rational interpretations in the light of dominant trends in religious philosophy, the activist messianic movements aiming at the liberation of Jews from foreign domination, and, finally, the sectarian offshoots of these movements which used the messianic aspiration as a vehicle for religious and social reform.

APOCALYPTIC–AGGADIC MESSIANISM

During the world crisis which resulted in the startling rise of Islam and its rapid expansion from the Atlantic to India, there was a new outcropping of Jewish apocalyptic literature. As in the turbulent days of the Second Commonwealth, these apocalyptic visionaries preferred to attach their speculations to some revered biblical hero or else to attribute them now to some newly recognized authority of the talmudic age. Among the biblical prophets, the mysterious personalities of Elijah and Daniel attracted the greatest following. The talmudic story about R. Simon ben Yoḥai's escape from Roman retribution, his hiding in a cave for twelve years, and his flaming denunciation of worldly pursuits after his mystic experiences there elevated him as a natural spokesman of general Jewish mystic beliefs and particularly as the revealer of the mysterious personality and actions of the Messiah. R. Ishmael ben Elisha, too, held a high rank among the ancient mystics whom God allegedly used as mouthpieces to foretell the future of his chosen people. A number of apocalyptic writings attributed to these ancient personalities made their appearance from the seventh century on, and they achieved wide circulation. They were often accepted at their face value, not only by the gullible masses, but also by many recognized spokesmen of official Judaism. W. Küppers's characterization of the ancient apocalyptic authors applies equally to these medieval dreamers. "According to our notions they may appear in large measure to be but fanciful visionaries, compilers of older views, men of heretical propensities, or speculative philosophers, as well as purveyors of secrets, preachers and mystics. But at the same time they primarily are religious thinkers and, in a specific Jewish sense, theologians deeply attached to their religious tradition." Their extreme flights of fancy, combined with frequent realistic appraisals of changing historical situations, all hidden behind a consciously obscure verbiage of *vaticinia ex eventu* interspersed with predictions for the ultimate future, makes the chronological setting of these outpourings quite uncertain. But their frequent hints as to contemporary events and personalities, in so far as these are ascertainable from other sources, not only help to identify their approximate dates, but also to elucidate some obscure and otherwise unrecorded phases of the history of their people.[2]

One of the classics of that literature, the *Sefer Zerubbabel* (Book of Zerubbabel), reproduced an alleged vision of the rebuilder of the Second Temple who foresaw that this sanctuary, too, would be destroyed, but looked forward to the construction of a third and final Temple. The selection of Zerubbabel as the spokesman seems to have been connected with the political struggles of the day. According to an Arabic story extant in two versions, the exilarchic office, then being revived by 'Umar I, was occupied by youthful Bustanai. Because of the latter's immaturity, an unnamed old man had served as a sort of regent, but was removed by 'Umar who decided to enhance the power of the exilarchate, doubtless in return for Jewish aid in the conquest of both Persia and the Byzantine provinces. In the great messianic fervor created in the Jewish community by these world-shaking events, nothing would have appeared more natural than to select Zerubbabel, one of the revered founders of the exilarchic dynasty, as the chief spokesman of the forthcoming redemption. Many a contemporary was doubtless reminded of Zechariah's prediction, "The hands of Zerubbabel have laid the foundation of this house; his hands shall also finish it" (4:9)—a verse quoted in fact by the author of our Arabic narrative. Not that the exilarchic party expected Bustanai himself to be the Messiah. According to long-accepted expectations, the redeemer had already been born in ancient times and kept alive in obscurity in the very citadel of Antichrist, the city of Rome, and later Constantinople. This belief is reflected also in our Apocalypse. Yet the exilarchic family could bask in the reflected glory of both the Messiah and Zerubbabel, members of their own, the Davidic dynasty. Our author, moreover, added a mysterious woman, Ḥefzibah, likewise of Davidic descent, whose valor was to decide the pre-redemption campaign. This Deborah-like personality may have mirrored some living individual, perhaps Bustanai's mother during the years of his minority, who, though easily recognizable to contemporaries, is no longer identifiable today.[3]

Naturally enough, most of these writers were deeply preoccupied with the messianic problem to which, like their ancient predecessors, they often lent a cosmic significance. In some of their presentations the Messiah appears as not just an ordinary human being entrusted by God with the mission of redeeming His people from bondage, but rather as a superhuman personality of deep influence on the divine guidance of the universe. In reaction, however, to the christological emphases of their Christian neighbors, even these visionaries largely shifted the supernatural manifestations of the messianic evolution to the angelic, or demonic, hosts who were to predict and aid, or interfere with the realization of the messianic program. For the most part it is Archangel Michael, Israel's special guardian angel, or Meṭaṭron, who broadcasts the news of the forthcoming salvation. Angelic hosts are said also to have maintained the Jerusalem on high which, built at the same time as the earthly Jerusalem and its Temple, survived the lower one's destruction and was to become instrumental in the latter's restoration. In another remarkable vision, R. Ishmael is reported to have heard from Meṭaṭron that the angels called *Seraphim,* each endowed with six wings and sixteen faces, were constantly helping to mitigate the hardships of exile in order to maintain the Jewish people intact to the messianic era.

Why are they called *Seraphim?* [Meṭaṭron explained.] Because they burn [*sorefim*] Satan's ledgers. For every day Satan sits with Samael, the guardian of Rome, and Dubbiel [or Dummiel], the guardian of Persia, and writes down Israel's sins on ledgers, and hands them to the *Seraphim,* so that they be brought before the Holy One blessed be He, and Israel be eliminated from the world. But the *Seraphim* know the mysterious designs of the Holy One blessed be He who does not wish the downfall of Israel, the people of God. That is why they take [these ledgers] from Satan's hand daily and burn them in scorching fire in front of the exalted Throne, lest they enter into the consideration of the Holy One blessed be He when He sits on the seat of judgment and judges the whole universe.

Nevertheless some of the Messiah's superhuman qualities, so strongly emphasized in the pre-Christian apocalyptic literature and carried over into the Aggadah of the talmudic age, survived the restraints of the Judeo-Christian debate also in the medieval period.[4]

Jewish visionaries were particularly agitated by the problem of the signs of the approaching Messiah. In their great impatience to see the ultimate redemption in their own lifetime, they looked for extraordinary manifestations in either nature or international relations for forebodings of the approaching end of days. Although these "signs of the Messiah," too, had behind them accumulated lucubrations of many centuries, much room was left to the imagination of each individual and generation to add to those traditions and to adjust them to the outlook of their age. With the spread of astrological interpretations of human history, in particular, much weight was given to stellar constellations as indications of what the future had in store.

Numerous apocalypses concerned with the so-called *Otot ha-Mashiaḥ* (Signs of the Messiah) appear under different names, but they are essentially interrelated. They usually list ten successive portents. In one of the longest of these tracts, the following picture is drawn: As a first sign, there will appear three kings who will deny their own faith and pretend to be serving Israel's God, but in fact, they will merely mislead the people. Impious Jews will then despair of redemption and abandon their religion. "The world will be profoundly changed, and there will be no king nor prince in Israel . . . no heads of academies, no faithful shepherds, no pious and wonderworking people; the gates of Heaven will be closed, as will be the gates of earning a living." During nine months, moreover, these three kings will enact serious restrictions and impose tenfold taxes, those unable to pay being decapitated. They will also decree that all their subjects must deny the Lord, the Temple, and the Torah. Simultaneously, a people extremely ugly will arise at the end of the world, each with two skulls and seven eyes throwing glances of fire, and any onlooker will die of fright without a battle. As a second sign, God will produce extraordinary heat combined with pestilences. People will hide in caves, but myriads upon myriads will die, only the pious being saved. This will be followed by a third sign of a bloody dew falling on the world. Mistaking it for water, the Gentiles and Jews despairing of redemption will drink it and die. As a fourth sign, a dew of healing will descend to heal the people who had not been exterminated because of their wickedness. As a fifth sign, God will turn the sun into utter darkness for thirty days. During that period many Gentiles will take fright and secretly convert themselves to Judaism.

A sixth stage will come when Edom (Rome) will rule over the entire world for nine months, destroy many cities and impose severe taxes and other punishments upon Israel. At the end of these nine months will appear the Messiah ben Joseph under the name of Nehemiah son of Ḥushiel, accompanied by troops of the tribes of Ephraim, Manasseh, Benjamin, and parts of Gad. This messiah will start war on the king of Edom, kill him, destroy the city of Rome, remove some of the implements of the Temple hidden in the house of Emperor Julian, bring them to Jerusalem, make peace with the king of Egypt, but destroy the inhabitants around Jerusalem up to Damascus and Ascalon. In the seventh stage, Armilus or Antichrist will appear. Born from a union between evil men (or Satan) and a feminine marble statute in Rome, this demon, "twelve ells long and two ells wide, with slanted red eyes, golden hair, green footsteps, and two skulls," will declare himself the god-king of the Edomites and invoke the Bible he had given them as testimony for his messiahship. All children of Esau will believe in him. He will also send messengers to Nehemiah and demand that the Jews, too, should recognize him as a god. Nehemiah will refuse and, at the head of 30,000 troops, will wage war against him, but will fall in the ensuing battle. His corpse will be hidden by angels so that Armilus will not know the extent of his victory. This will be followed by a period of suffering for Israel, "the like of which had not been from the beginning of time." During that interval all the rest of doubting and weak-kneed Jews will abandon their faith, but Archangel Michael will save a remnant and keep it in the Judean desert for forty-five days. In the eighth stage, Michael will blow the horn three times. At the first sound, the Messiah son of David and Elijah will appear, bring back the pious Jews from the desert, and enter Jerusalem. Upon learning of their arrival, Armilus will collect the Gentile armies to fight the messiah, but he will be defeated and Israel will wreak vengeance on the former destroyers of the Temple. As the ninth sign, Michael will again blow the horn, the graves will open up in Jerusalem and God will revive the dead. The Messiah son of David will send messengers to Israel's remnant dispersed over many lands, and the Gentile kings will carry these survivors on their shoulders to the house of the Lord. In the tenth and final stage, Michael will blow the horn a prolonged blow and God will collect the lost Ten Tribes from their distant abodes. They will be accompanied by divine clouds and nurtured from divine springs on their way to the Holy Land.[5]

Here we find summarized the main ideas of the great natural

and human cataclysms which were to accompany the ushering in of the age of redemption. We have two messiahs: the fighting and dying messiah of the house of Joseph and Ephraim, and the final pacific messiah of the house of David and Judah. Other visionaries of the period restated clearly the old belief that the destruction of all enemies by the Davidic redeemer will be accomplished by supernatural means alone in line with the ancient prediction, "And with the breath of his lips shall he slay the wicked" (Isa. 11:4). Of course, the Messiah's "breath" could also be taken more concretely as a supernatural blow of such staggering power as to fell all enemies. This seems, indeed, to have been the understanding of most of the medieval visionaries. But all of them agreed that the Messiah son of David would not engage in any extensive warfare. As the chief antagonist appears Armilus, evidently a corruption of Romulus, representing the archfoe, Edom or the Roman Empire. Rome remained indeed the ultimate enemy even after the rise of Islam. In most of these tracts Ishmael is neither mentioned nor implied, obviously because these formulations had been fully crystallized before the appearance of Mohammed. Our descriptions of the various "signs of the Messiah" seem particularly related to events of the sixth century which, as we recollect, had evoked among Jews, Zoroastrians, and Christians alike the feeling of the approaching end of days. However, no century was devoid of elementary catastrophes, which in the imagination of a populace nurtured on these eschatological predictions readily assumed the character of cosmic cataclysms concomitant with the inception of the messianic era. Since, moreover, the entire inhabitable world, at least in so far as it entered the vision of the common man, was divided between Rome-Byzantium and Parthia-Persia, or Islam, every major war appeared to be a world war, which could be equated with the wars of Gog and Magog. Almost any age furnished, therefore, a sufficiently realistic background for the ancient messianic motifs to be readily readjusted to the tastes and predilections of each new generation of apocalyptic dreamers.[6]

While these outpourings of an overheated fantasy are generally extremely repetitious and often differ only in details, a unique tract of this genre originating from twelfth-century Spain made a strong impression also outside Jewish circles. In fact, it is extant only in its Latin version. Taking a clue from an astrological calculation of Abraham bar Ḥiyya (Savasorda), the author of that vision (attributed to the famous Toledan translator, Avendeath), predicted that, beginning on Sunday midnight of Ellul 29, 4946 (September 15–16, 1186) and lasting for three days, peculiar constellations of stars would cause extraordinary storms to rage from the extreme West to the extreme East. These storms would be followed by the successive appearances of five harbingers of the end of days: a prophet, walking justly and spreading enlightenment and morality among men; a short-lived warrior; an equally short-lived false prophet appearing with an allegedly revealed book among the Gentile nations; a comet bringing in its wake destruction, drought, and bloodshed, "the righteous and true men of faith will so severely be oppressed and suffer from persecutions that the synagogues will be disturbed"; and finally, a total eclipse of the sun. Regrettably, the fragment breaks off here, leaving unsatisfied our curiosity about the ultimate advent of the Redeemer.[7]

In contrast to this great concentration on the beginnings of the messianic era and the role of the two messiahs in its realization, there was relatively little speculation on either the nature of the Messiah's personality or of life during the messianic era. Here and there an apocalyptic or homiletical writer would strike the old note of the preexistent Messiah to whom even Moses paid homage. Such imaginary dialogue is included, for instance, in the vision of the "Jerusalem on high" of the medieval midrash *Bereshit rabbati,* which emanated from the school of Moses ha-Darshan in eleventh-century France. But this traditional view of the ancient visionaries now preoccupied principally the minds of the mystic *yorede merkabah* (descenders of the divine Chariot), who, in their constant visits to the upper spheres, claimed to have encountered there also the future redeemer of Israel. In their colorful descriptions of the Garden of Eden, particularly, they rarely fail to mention the presence there of the Messiah or, as in the case of the *Midrash Konen,* of the two messiahs and Elijah. But in these cosmic visions the entire problem of earthly redemption played, as we shall see, a relatively secondary role. Otherwise the Messiah's transcendental nature, already intertwined with strong human features in the ancient apocalyptic literature, was now less and less frequently stressed—obviously because of the Christian challenge. Even in the famous talmudic enumeration of the seven preexistent things, the Messiah not only ranks last after the Torah, repentance, the Garden of Eden, Gehenna, the Throne of Glory, and the Temple, but it is his "name," rather than person, which is said to have existed before the world's creation. In other words, only the messianic idea had emerged in God's primordial vision, but the particular person to whom its realization was to be entrusted was created, like other human beings, at a particular historical moment. Even our apocalyptic visionaries, who often invested the "anointed one" with miraculous features and made him live for centuries on end, only postulated his birth at the time of David (with the underlying idea of the king himself coming back to life to redeem his people) or immediately after the destruction of the First or Second Temple. This divine antidote to the destruction was reported by talmudic sages and medieval homilists with many variants, including the characteristic refrain that the Messiah was born in Bethlehem. They only differed as to the place of his hiding during that long preparatory period. Some believed that he was kept concealed in heaven, while others attributed to him a downtrodden earthly existence. Even Amulo was familiar with the Jewish belief that a messiah of the house of David had been born on the very day of the destruction of the Temple and that he had, ever since, been living in chains and with wounds all over his body in some Roman hovel. Most specific on this score is a vision attributed to Elijah, according to which the Prophet had learned that the Messiah would spend "400 years in the Mediterranean Sea, 80 years among the children of Korah, 80 more at the gate of Rome. Thereafter he would wander from one big city to another until the end of days." [8]

Most of the other, more earth-bound speculations on Israel's final redemption generally neglected, even if they did not deny, the Messiah's heavenly rank and superhuman characteristics. More remarkably, they also refrained from depicting the glories of the messianic age in any detail. This restraint was undoubtedly owing, in part, to the question, as yet unresolved in their minds, concerning the difference between that age and the eschatological world-to-come. This confusion which even in the talmudic period had led to the indiscriminate use of the term, *le-'atid la-bo* (the ultimate future) for both the Hereafter (*'olam ha-ba*) and the days of the Messiah (*yemot ha-mashiaḥ*), could more readily be cleared up by the disciplined philosophic speculation of the medieval scholastics than through the emotionally overcharged yarns of visionaries and preachers. In fact, the very term, *'olam ha-ba,* had sometimes been used in the Talmud interchangeably with the "days of the Messiah"; for instance, with respect to the novel agricultural divisions expected at the end of days. Notwithstanding Mar Samuel's pointed declaration that "the only difference between this world and the days of the Messiah consists in foreign domination," the confusion continued unabated into the late Middle Ages. In a letter to his beloved disciple, Maimonides himself had occasion to complain about the Yemenites who "confuse the world to come with the days of the Messiah." [9]

Even the colorful descriptions of the material and sexual delights of the life in the Hearafter included in the Qur'an and elaborated in later Muslim legends, did not greatly affect the Jewish image of the end of days. Typical of many other apocalyptic visions is the book of "Mysteries" of R. Simon ben Yoḥai, which, adhering very closely to the talmudic Aggadah, limits itself to the glorification of the new Jerusalem rebuilt and purified of all idols, indeed consisting of the Jerusalem on high brought down to earth. It would include the Temple built in heaven, among the decorations of which would be seventy-two pearls "shining from one end of the world to the other." All the nations would be guided by the light emanating from it. "Israel will live in security for two thousand years and consume the flesh of the Behemoth, the Leviathan and the *Ziv* [mythological bird]. After the Behemoth are slaughtered, the *Ziv* tears the Leviathan to pieces with its claws, and Moses slaughters the *Ziv.*" [10]

All this bliss would last only two thousand years, however. Like most of his contemporaries and successors of the Islamic age, our apocalyptic writer accepted the old aggadic scheme wherein the world would exist for only six thousand years, of which the last two thousand would constitute the days of the Messiah. Of course, in his time the pre-messianic eon had already lasted more than four thousand years (which had ended in 240 C.E.; Rashi, noticing this discrepancy, commented: "Because of our numerous sins many of these two thousand years have already passed, and the Messiah has not come"). The author of the "Mysteries" continued:

At the end of two thousand years the Holy One blessed be He will sit on the throne of justice in the Valley of Jehoshaphat. Instantaneously heaven and earth will disintegrate, the moon will be confounded and the sun ashamed, the mountains will dissolve, and the hills be removed, lest they remind Israel of its sins. The gates of Gehenna will open at the brook of Joshua, as will the gates of the Garden of Eden in the East on the third day, as it is written, "After two days will He revive us," which relates to the days of the Messiah lasting two thousand years. "On the third day He will raise us up, that we may live in His presence," this will be the day of judgment, and woe unto him who will die on that day.

God would commit to Gehenna the idolatrous nations and the sinners of Israel. But the latter would be released after twelve months. Then they would all live in the Garden of Eden and enjoy its fruits, for it is written "Thy people also shall be all righteous." [11]

None of this was essentially new. Not only were biblical passages here, as elsewhere, extensively quoted, and even more extensively alluded to, but even the aggadic interpretation of these passages had largely been anticipated by the homilists of the talmudic age. In fact, like most Jewish mystics trying to commune directly with the Deity and to divine His will, these visionaries adhered closely to the millennial traditions of their people. Even in their extravagant and uncontrolled dreams they sought merely to bring up to date the long accepted biblical-talmudic doctrines. Their originality usually exhausted itself in applying these ancient teachings to situations and personalities of their own time.

Remarkably, few of these apocalyptic writers attempted to set a precise date for the forthcoming redemption. Most of them were impatient enough to expect it to take place in the immediate future. The various "signs" they defined and the personalities they alluded to, under more or less transparent disguises, doubtless enabled most of their contemporaries to perceive that nexus. But the very form of the apocalyptic vision, especially if represented by an ancient spokesman like Elijah, Daniel, Ishmael ben Elisha, or Simon ben Yoḥai, militated against furnishing specific data of any kind. Thus style and fashion were far stronger deterrents than the discouragement of "pushing the end" on the part of the talmudic sages. That is why most of these visionary outpourings are so difficult to date, and why so many diverse hypotheses could be advanced by modern scholars on this score.[12]

In any case, from the standpoint of the general messianic expectation animating the Jewish people, these are all but variants of the same theme—a theme which had become clearly defined in the preceding periods. While great world tensions and specific sufferings of the Jewish people added new zest and immediacy to messianic speculations, they did not alter their fundamental character or content. In more quiescent periods there was less urgency in the messianic appeal, and some individuals may even have begun to doubt its necessity for the preservation of the Jewish faith. Like all other aspects of the Jewish tradition, the messianic hope, too, required now a new rationale in the light of the new "scientific" reinterpretations of all theologumena. But no authoritative spokesman of Judaism suggested that it could be altogether abandoned.

POETIC AND EXEGETICAL DERIVATIONS

Compared with the flights of fancy of these apocalyptic dreamers, the poetic license of even the most daring liturgical poets appeared rather tame and restrained. Following the example set by the authors of ancient prayers, most liturgical writers were satisfied with general complaints about their people's misery and oppression, and with doleful petitions for speedy deliverance. The same Saadiah Gaon who, in his commentaries on the Bible and even in his philosophic work, expatiated at some length on the details of the messianic expectation, was utterly restrained in his liturgical compositions included in his prayer book. "May it be Thy will, O Lord, our God," reads the beginning of one of his poems, "to note the plight of Thy people Israel dispersed over all lands, and the ruins of Jerusalem which has been lain waste, and the Temple which has been forsaken and abandoned like the desert. Mayest Thou be jealous for Thy holy name which has been desecrated among the nations, assemble the remnant of Thy flock from all the places to which they had become dispersed, and return

Israel to its abode and to the Palace restored to its due rank." Such a prayer could have been composed by any rabbi of the second century who, too, took little cognizance of contemporary elaborations of the messianic theme in the apocalyptic and hermeneutic letters. This remarkable self-restraint in avoiding all controversial and theologically questionable subjects in prayers destined for recitation by synagogue audiences generally characterized, as we shall see, the liturgical creativity of ancient and medieval poets, with the exception of the authors of *piyyuṭim*.[13]

For reasons to be explained in a later context, the *payyeṭanim* (liturgical poets) of the sixth to the tenth centuries endeavored to communicate to the synagogue audiences the main teachings of the Aggadah in poetic form. Themselves genuine homilists, they also felt free to expatiate on some of these older teachings by adding new ingredients of their own. Certain challenging verses of the Pentateuchal lessons recited during Sabbaths and holidays, as well as the accompanying prophetic selections (the *Hafaṭarahs*) stimulated the imagination of both homilists and poets, who were often distinguished from one another only through their differing literary media.

It is not surprising, therefore, to find especially in the liturgical poetry of the most prolific seventh-century *payyeṭan,* Eleazar Qalir, certain novel ingredients of messianic speculation unencountered in any prose writings available to us. Many poems, to be sure, do not go beyond the generally accepted doctrine. A series of *Geshem* compositions, attributed to Qalir, merely stresses the over-all messianic theme. Certainly one could appropriately pray for the resuscitation of the Jewish people while imploring God to provide rain for the dry soil. The lengthy poem *Adon mi-shamekha* (O Lord, from Thy Skies) describes in considerable detail the areas of the world from which the ingathering of Jewish exiles (including the Ten Tribes) was to take place. It uses as a rule the standardized biblical designations of these regions. Nor does the request included in another poem, that God "may hasten the return through Tishbi [Elijah] and the Angel Michael," in any way transcend the traditional view. But in one poem, beginning *Ba-Yamim ha-hem* (In Those Days), a phrase serving also as its constant refrain, Qalir contrived to depict the expected messianic happenings in a monthly sequence, into which he inserted most of the apocalyptic predictions known to us from the visions attributed to Elijah and Zerubbabel. But he differed from them in many details and altogether omitted such extravaganzas as the figure of Ḥefzibah. Nor did he mention Armilus. Apart from the relative novelty of this legendary personality in Jewish circles of that time, he may have felt compunctions about magnifying the role of a contemporary emperor like Heraclius into cosmic proportions. In fact, his poem reveals no overt traces of the great Perso-Byzantine war of the period and may have been written before its inception. If so, the authors of the Zerubbabel and Elijah apocalypses may have been greatly indebted to Qalir's fertile poetic imagination. Of course, all of them were nurtured from the undying springs of popular folklore transmitted by word of mouth and ever embellished by legions of unnamed dreamers. Certainly, by being included in the liturgy of the Ninth of Ab as an optimistic antidote to the succession of mournful litanies over the loss of the sanctuary, Qalir's poem, much more than the more obscure apocalyptic writings, helped popularize the details of that messianic folklore at the height of its febrile creativity during the transition from Byzantine to Islamic rule.[14]

Later poets were far less articulate. The tenth-century Italian author, Amittai ben Shefaṭiah, doubtless referring to the rise of the Italian republics, merely voiced the eloquent complaint, "Why do all my neighbors tend / To rise from their afflictions / Whereas I for years on end / Bewail the two destructions?" Even Solomon ibn Gabirol, profound mystic though he was, repeatedly reverted to the messianic theme only in general terms. In his philosophic *magnum opus,* in fact, he made no mention of the messianic hope, evidently because in the rarefied atmosphere of his neo-Platonic speculations there was little room for specific Jewish dogmas or, for that matter, for those of any faith. Otherwise he was less reticent. In an unguarded moment, perhaps with no intention of publicizing it, he even suggested that the Messiah would come at the conjunction of Saturn and Jupiter, thereby drawing the scorn of Abraham ibn Ezra, a far more distinguished astrologer. In his poetry, too, Ibn Gabirol frequently alluded to the messianic teachings of both the Aggadah and the apocalypses, without elaborating them. From the aforementioned talmudic aggadot he borrowed the Messiah's reputed name, Yinnon, and the eschatological role of Elijah-Phineas. One of his liturgical creations, recited in connection with the *Habdalah* (the prayer of separation between the outgoing Sabbath and the beginning week days), was entirely devoted to a petition that God might hasten the coming of the end. Each line ends with the symbolic name, Phineas. Ibn Gabirol was also familiar with such typically apocalyptic notions as that the Messiah was born in Bethlehem and that his father's name was 'Ammiel (my people of God). But he not only failed to elaborate these mystical hints, he also emphasized constantly that God's eschatological designs are a sealed book which only God himself would open in due course. In one of his remarkable *Ge'ulah* (redemption) poems, appropriately designed to be recited on Passover, the festival of liberation, or the immediately following Sabbaths, Israel asks: "How long till the turn of my fate shall draw near, / How long ere the sealed and the closed be made clear?" In another poem the author complained that, unlike previous redemptions, the one now forthcoming had not been precisely foretold. Abraham had been taken into God's confidence about how long his descendants would languish in the Egyptian bondage, Jeremiah had been informed about the duration of the Babylonian Exile, but "the third end from every eye is concealed. Every seeker flounders, every seer is disillusioned." It was this very disillusionment of all previous seekers which served as a mighty deterrent.[15]

Yet not for a moment did Ibn Gabirol doubt that the redemption would come at the stated time and that possibly it was nearer at hand than many people thought. Living in a messianically excited period, he seems to have shared the belief of many contemporaries that the Messiah would come at the end of the first millennium following the destruction of the Second Temple, that is in 1068. Viewing the millennial "night" of Exile, he saw something symbolic in the rise of Islam, that fourth apocalyptic beast of the book of Daniel, soon after "midnight," or in the sixth century after the fall of Jerusalem. With keen disappointment he noted, therefore, in a poem written toward the end of his short but rich life, that already 461 years of the Muslim calendar had passed (1069 C.E.), and yet the end was not in sight. His sense of urgency may have been enhanced by the tradition current among his Spanish-Muslin compatriots that if the Jewish Messiah failed to arrive within the following four decades (to 500 A.H.), the minimum of toleration theretofore extended to the Jewish *dhimmis* would be withdrawn.[16]

Be this as it may, the poet confidently, though impatiently, awaited the advent of the Redeemer. In another moving *ge'ulah,* he presented the Lord as exchanging thoughts with the people of Israel. After God's reassurance to the "daughter of Zion, tried in Sorrow's furnace" that He would keep His promise to the fathers, and Israel's urging the Lord, "whose name is linked with pardon," to come back, the dialogue continues:

GOD

Where'er thy sojourn, whosoe'er thy opponent,
I shall come myself thy cause to plead,
Against him who holds the bill of thy divorcement.
Like wall or tower of fire I guard thy seed,
Then wherefore weep or heart affrighted heed?

ISRAEL

Why do I weep? Because Thou keepest silence,
Though violence rages and, all uncontrolled,
The mob destroys, and we as slaves to strangers,
Master and man together, have been sold,
And no Redeemer do our eyes behold.

GOD

Who art thou thus to shrink from man in terror
And be dismayed because of mankind's scorn?
My angel I will send, as wrote the prophet,
And gather Israel winnowed and new-born:
This miracle shall be tomorrow morn.

ISRAEL

To gather my chieftains Thou hast set the time,
The day comes not, and of signs is none,
Nor see I Temple built nor any herald
Of Peace arrive to the martyred one—
Ah, wherefore lingers Jesse's promised son?

GOD

Behold, I keep the oath I swore to gather
My captives—kings shall bring their gifts to thee:
Created for a witness to the nations,
My martyred saints shall testify to Me—
Yea, Jesse's son Mine eyes already see.

[Variant of Zangwill's trans., pp. 28 f.]

Compared with this religious fervor, even the famous Zionide poems of Yehudah Halevi sound more terrestrial. In fact, Halevi, whose entire philosophy was permeated with the messianic ideal, viewed it more in its nationalistic and territorial than its cosmic implications. We must bear in mind, however, that in his entire outlook on life, history itself, that instrument of the divine government of the universe, possessed cosmic significance. We shall see presently how focal was the role played by the ideas of Jewish exile and political impotence, to be ended in the glorious restoration to Palestine, the land of all lands, in his reconstruction of world history. Of course, even in his most "secular" approaches, the poet could not divorce the destinies of Zion and the Jewish people from their religious world mission. Not in vain have many of his poems, too, become part and parcel of the synagogue ritual. One of his famous *habdalah* poems reproduces the anxious query of his generation, disappointed by the passage of the thousand years since the destruction of the Temple: "Where is the God of Elijah?" With masterly brevity the poet describes here the great miracles performed by Elijah and his disciple, Elisha, and then asks insistently, "The watchers for the signs foretold / When will they see the wondrous deeds? / How soon the miracles will they behold? / The work of the Lord,—for it is awesome." Admitting that Israel's sins were responsible for its prolonged sufferings, he nevertheless asked impatiently, "Shall mine iniquity for ever / Stand between me and Thee?" Similar references to Elijah and the Messiah abound in many *habdalahs* and other poems. In all this, however, Halevi took little cognizance of the aggadic and apocalyptic ingredients of the messianic hope; rather he adhered closely to the accepted fundamentals of the biblical and talmudic outlook. The same is even more true of the two Ibn Ezras, in whose poetry the messianic expectation, though always looming in the background, never occupies the preeminent place given to it, in their diverse ways, by Ibn Gabirol and Halevi.[17]

More frequently Abraham ibn Ezra was forced to allude to the messianic problem in his commentaries on relevant scriptural passages. While he and the other commentators could hide behind the cloak of objective exegesis and merely explain the meanings conveyed by the biblical authors, their personal biases nevertheless shone through. Understandably, it was the book of Daniel with its challenging predictions about the redemption of Israel which forced most exegetes to take a stand. Uniformly assuming both that Daniel had been divinely inspired and that he had prophesied in the days of Nebukadrezzar, they all sought a solution to the chronological puzzles of Chapters 7–9 and 12. Ibn Ezra felt impelled to preface his commentary with a warning:

> This book by a "man greatly beloved" contains weighty matters and prophecies, since fulfilled, or still awaiting fulfillment. Everything is said briefly and in riddles. It also contains profound allusions to the nature of the angels on high. But the commentators did not comprehend its deeper meaning, each trying his best but all ending in failure. They erred in their interpretation of the end; they were also confused about the vision of the beasts. . . . I propose to explain it in accordance with the rules of language.

By linguistic rules he meant the purely rational explanation of Daniel's obscure forecasts which he largely related to events of the Second Commonwealth and, especially, the Maccabean revolt. He refused to give them a messianic significance, and, despite his penchant for astrology, he rejected the astrological interpretations of Ibn Gabirol and Abraham bar Ḥiyya. "All who compute words or letters," he exclaimed, "after the manner of the *gemaṭria* pursue 'vanity and a striving after wind.' For Daniel did not know the end, how much less did those who came after" (on Dan. 11:30). On the other hand, more traditionally minded commentators usually saw in Daniel's visions precise predictions of the messianic end of days.

Other biblical books likewise lent themselves to messianic interpretation, even the apparently neutral Song of Songs being turned into a vehicle for eschatological prophecies by a commentator going under the name of Saadiah (wrongly identified with the gaon). The latter actually incorporated in his interpretation many ingredients of the apocalyptic expectation, including the story of Armilus, the names of the two messiahs, Neḥemiah ben Ḥushiel and Menaḥem ben 'Ammiel, and the sojourn of the righteous in the desert—incidentally, ideas which, as we shall see presently, were not altogether foreign to the gaon himself.[18]

Avoidance of the messianic issue was less possible in those prophetic and psalmodic passages where a messiah is quite clearly indicated. These verses had long been a battleground of Jewish and Christian apologetics. True, the biblical term, *mashiaḥ,* could often be interpreted simply as "the anointed" and made to refer to any king of Israel. Even Rashi, though generally traditionalist in his approaches and greatly indebted to the Aggadah, found this explanation applicable in most instances. But many other messianic prophecies could not so easily be dismissed. Unlike the Muslim allegations, largely derived from far-fetched *gemaṭrias,* about biblical allusions to Muḥammad or Aḥmad, Christian citations of "testimonies" for the coming of Christ were based, at least in part, upon genuine biblical expressions of the messianic hope. After all, much of the evangelists' reconstruction of the life and passion of Jesus had been determined by what they had read in the Old Testament. Jewish exegetes often controverted these testimonies by relating the biblical predictions to specific historic personalities. For example, "Immanuel" (of Isa. 7:14) was declared to be none other but the prophet's own son, while the "shoot out of the stock of Jesse" (Isa. 11:1) was said to refer to King Hezekiah. Because of its christological reinterpretation even Rashi refused to follow his rabbinic predecessors in viewing the Second Psalm as relating to the Messiah, but explained "Thou art my son" (v. 7) as referring to David who was as precious to God as a son to a father.

On the other hand, where no Christian testimony was involved, Rashi could give free rein to his aggadic propensities. He explained, for instance, Isaiah's reference to "Thus saith the Lord to His Anointed, to Cyrus" (45:1) by following a talmudic sage's denial that Cyrus was called the Messiah. According to this interpretation, it was God who addressed the Messiah about Cyrus.

Rashi himself supported that interpretation by reference to the masoretic punctuation of that verse. Curiously, this problem formed the subject of a legal-homiletical inquiry addressed to the sage of Troyes. In his reply Rashi wished mainly to forestall the question as to the existence of the Messiah in Isaiah's day. Evidently he did not believe in the Messiah's preexistence and, at the most, shared the view of those homilists who taught that the Messiah had been born at the time of the destruction of the First or Second Temple. Rashi simply pointed out that Cyrus, too, had not yet been born, and that in His omniscience God could inform the prophet of His speech, which was to be addressed to one unborn person about another. Similarly Rashi interpreted Isaiah's reference to Ephraim and Judah (11:13) as predicting that the two messiahs of the house of Joseph and David would not envy one another. Nor did he hesitate to utilize Daniel's chronological riddles for a calculation of the end. While merely equating the "ten horns" (7:7) with the ten Roman emperors preceding Vespasian, he accepted Saadiah's interpretation of "a time and times and half a time" (7:25) as relating to the ultimate redemption. But, more prudently than other forecasters, he figured out that the Messiah's arrival was due in 1352, some two and a half centuries after his own writing.[19]

Ibn Ezra went further than Rashi in looking for historical explanations. They both agreed, as we recall, in viewing Deutero-Isaiah's "Servant of the Lord" as a personification of the Israelitic people. But many overtly messianic passages had to be recognized as such even by the rationalist exegete (for instance, Isa. 55:4, 59:20). In one of his few direct anti-Christian polemics, Ibn Ezra rejected the Christian interpretation of Isaiah 40. While Moses ibn Chiquitilla explained these prophecies as relating to the Second Commonwealth, Ibn Ezra preferred to see "everything referring to our Exile, although there are in this book also references to the Babylonian Exile for remembrance." On other occasions, too, he stressed the differences of opinion on this score among earlier exegetes, both Rabbanite and Karaite. He mentioned, for example, that "the day of their calamity," three times occurring in the same verse (13) of Obadiah, had been related to the period of Hezekiah by the rationalist Rabbanite exegete,

Moses ibn Chiquitilla; to the Second Commonwealth by the eleventh-century Karaite thinker, Yeshu'a ben Yehudah; but projected into the messianic future by the equally "enlightened" tenth-century Karaite commentator, Jephet ben 'Ali. Following the Targum, Jephet also interpreted Hosea's prophecy (2:2) about the "one head" who will lead Judah and Israel, as referring to Elijah leading all Jews out of exile—an identification advocated also by David Qimḥi. Writing in the rather isolated Karaite community of Jerusalem, Jephet gave so free a rein to his messianic aspirations that a later disciple could compile a whole collection of excerpts from his messianic interpretations in a tract bearing the characteristic title, "Explanation of the Future." All of these differences of opinion merely illustrate the confusion among the rationalist thinkers of the period who, confronted with clearly messianic and eschatological statements in the Bible, could not quite reconcile them with their own "scientific" world outlook. To clear up that confusion at least in part became a major task of the leading Jewish philosophers of that age.[20]

MESSIANIC RATIONALES

Messianic ideology played a vital role indeed in all Jewish philosophy, the medieval thinkers devoting much ingenuity to systematizing and rationalizing the variegated traditions which had come down from the days of the Second Commonwealth and the Talmud. Jewish society likewise presented many a perplexing cross current. Some of the more rationalistic Jews, especially among the early Karaites, were inclined to interpret the messianic annunciations of the ancient prophets as fulfilled during the Second Commonwealth. These men also "call themselves Jews," caustically remarked Saadiah (*Beliefs and Opinions,* VIII.7, p. 247). To combat this view, Saadiah marshaled an imposing array of fifteen arguments, five each from Scripture, history, and personal observation—all predicated on the demonstration that many biblical descriptions of the messianic age had not yet come true. Some of these arguments, we recollect, were used by the gaon also against the Christian contention that these prophetic annunciations had been realized by the appearance of Jesus. Other Jews of a more worldly and political orientation saw in the messianic future only the realization of their people's political aspirations toward national independence and glory. Some of them avowedly preferred the messianic hope to the belief in the Hereafter. The official leaders could not find harsh enough words to condemn these notions.

Saadiah, especially, placed in the midst of these controversies, was quite outspoken. Summarizing very selectively the teachings transmitted by the Aggadah, he declared that the end of days would come either as a result of the people's universal repentance, or at the time originally set by the divine will. This means, that, by their conduct, the Jews might hasten the advent of the redeemer. But even if they should prove recalcitrant to the last, they still could not prevent his arrival at the appointed time. The real Messiah son of David may be preceded by one of the house of Joseph, if the end should come as a result of early Jewish repentance, but the son of David would, in any case, prove victorious over the enemies of Israel. He would, in particular, slay Armilus in Jerusalem, and usher in the golden era. To obviate ethical objections, the gaon made clear that Israel could not really be redeemed without prior repentance. The only difference was that, in the case of voluntary repentance, the Jewish people would hasten the end. Otherwise God would cause such widespread and unprecedented sufferings before the stated end that Israel would be forced to repent. Even after the advent of the preliminary redeemer, some such sufferings of short duration would materialize in connection with the great world war of Gog and Magog, and the appearance of Armilus who was to slay the son of Joseph. The latter's body would miraculously remain intact, however, until the resurrection ushered in by the advent of the final Messiah. During the incipient messianic era the righteous would suffer along with the others, just as Moses, Aaron, and Miriam had to undergo all the hardships of Egyptian bondage, and as the innocent of all ages are afflicted along with the guilty by famines, wars, and pestilences. In view of this belief in the terminal date having originally been set by God, it is not surprising to find that the gaon, under the stress of the raging conflicts of his day, embarked upon the venturesome enterprise of computing that date from biblical passages. Although generally writing on this subject with a studied obscurity that was open to a variety of interpretations by later medieval authors, he seems to have reached the year 968 C.E., a date which, if he were to live to a ripe old age, he could still have witnessed.[21]

Such quests for the terminal date were by no means limited to the turbulent and disintegrating Eastern Caliphate. Even in flourishing Cordova, the level-headed statesman and scientist, Ḥisdai ibn Shapruṭ, learned with joy of the existence of the Jewish kingdom of Khazaria. He saw therein the opportunity not only to answer the constant twitting of foes concerning Jewish political powerlessness, but also to find out whether in that remote country some memory might not have been preserved pertaining "to the computation of the miraculous end." In his reply the Khagan expostulated that, living far away from Zion, the Khazars had to rely upon the academies of Jerusalem and Babylonia for their guidance. He had only heard that, "because of our many sins the computations have gone astray . . . and we have nothing but the prophecy of Daniel to go by" (Kokovtsov, *Perepiska,* pp. 18, 25).

Saadiah's summary served as a guide for Hai Gaon when he was confronted by an awkward legal inquiry asking for a full explanation of the following: "How will redemption take place from beginning to end, as well as resurrection and the 'new heavens' [Isa. 65:17]?" In general, this last of the great geonim took a rather detached view of the legendary elements in the Aggadah, whose doctrines he felt free to accept or reject in accordance with the commands of reason. Yet dealing with this delicate subject, he was prepared, on the authority of his distinguished predecessor, to accept even such medieval innovations as the figure of Armilus. Apart from repeating with great lucidity Saadiah's famed exposition, eliminating specific arguments, but frequently referring to the biblical sources, Hai added a few ideas of his own. He was evidently influenced by the intervening events. On the basis of the talmudic legends written under Roman-Byzantine domination, Saadiah had already emphasized the great role of the hereditary enemy, Edom, in this final drama of history. But Hai viewed these ultimate developments as a succession of first a defeat of Ishmael by Ashshur, and subsequently that of Ashshur by Edom. "That is why," he taught, "when we see that Edom rules over the Land of Israel, we believe that our redemption has begun." One cannot help feeling that the gaon referred here to contemporary events, such as the incipient rise of the Turkish tribes and their spread in the eastern parts of the Caliphate, as well as John Tsimiskes' temporarily successful invasion of Palestine in 972–74. Combined with the general decline of Baghdad, these events may indeed have conveyed to sensitive and messianically overcharged minds the idea of the approaching end of days. Of interest also is Hai's view that, as soon as the Messiah ben Joseph will have established his regime in Jerusalem, the rulers of many countries would expel their Jews. They will argue: "Until now you have lived with us in loyalty, because you had neither king nor governor [of your own]. But now that you have a king, you shall not live in our country." With this modern-sounding accusation of the Jews' purported "divided loyalties" the gaon explained the presence of many Jews in the desert at the time of the advent of the final Redeemer.[22]

Perhaps taught by Saadiah's mistake, Hai and the subsequent Jewish thinkers on the whole refrained from "forcing the end." Apart from Rashi's hesitant effort, only Ibn Gabirol, who seems not to have been familiar with Saadiah's philosophic work, and Abraham bar Ḥiyya, who remained true to his astrological conception of history, still played with the idea that the end could somehow be figured out. Both leaned heavily on astrological factors. Bar Ḥiyya actually devoted to this subject the bulk of his "Scroll." Perhaps to indicate that he was interested in the quest as such and believed in its feasibility, but was far from convinced of the validity of his own solutions, he suggested such widely disparate terminal dates as 1136, 1230, 1358, 1403, 1448. Knowing well enough that such computations would evoke considerable opposition, Abraham began his treatise with a brief discussion of why, unlike details of ritual law, such matters were left to the discretion of each individual. "One ought, indeed, to investigate everything," he argued, "which stems from the Torah, does good to Israel in this exile, fortifies their heart in faith, or enhances their confidence and hope. One should set his heart on finding out its [the Torah's] hidden aspects and divulging its secrets." This argument failed to disarm the opponents. Abraham's underlying astrological conceptions were soon attacked and had to be defended, in fact they were considerably toned down in the letter he addressed to the influential Barcelona rabbi, Yehudah bar Barzillai. He also refrained from any detailed messianic predictions in his ethical treatise, *Hegyon ha-nefesh* (Contemplation of the Soul), where he merely gave a glowing description of the messianic age. The other thinkers, too, including Halevi and Ibn Ezra, looked askance at such attempts and left detailed messianic speculations of any kind to popular preachers, especially mystics. Maimonides stated it as a general advice: "In any case, neither the sequence of these [messianic] developments, nor their details are principles of the faith. Hence a man ought not to busy himself with *aggadot* and study at length the homilies concerning these and similar [irrelevant] subjects. Certainly, he must not consider them of prime importance, since they bring one no nearer to the fear or the love of the Lord. Similarly one must not compute the end." [23]

At the same time all Jewish philosophers, particularly those living in Muslim countries, assigned to the belief in a personal redeemer a focal position in their theology. In this respect they differed from most Sunni, though not Shi'ite, Muslim theologians, many of whom completely evaded the doctrine of the *Mahdi*. Even Ibn Khaldun still spoke rather disparagingly about the popular misconceptions and the authenticity of the pertinent traditions. "Only a small number of them is above criticism," he declared. In contrast, the historically minded Jew, Halevi, saw in the messianic belief the ultimate goal of all history. He used an old rabbinic metaphor, based on R. Eleazar ben Pedat's homily on a verse in Hosea (2:25), that "the Holy One blessed be He exiled Israel among the nations only in order to multiply proselytes," and likened Israel to a seed planted in the world's soil. At first invisible, it gradually transforms the soil itself and grows into a fruit-bearing tree. "In the same manner the law of Moses transforms each one who honestly follows it, though it may externally repel him. The nations merely serve to introduce and pave the way for the expected Messiah, who is the fruition, and they will all become his fruit." Even the less historically oriented Maimonides included the messianic hope in the thirteen basic tenets of the Jewish credo. Only in Christian countries, for reasons to be discussed below, did a certain reaction set in two centuries later.[24]

Curiously, despite his sharp opposition to messianic computations—his *Epistle to Yemen* was in part designed to counteract such premature hastening of the end—Maimonides found mitigating circumstances for Saadiah's attempt to calculate the time of the Messiah's expected arrival. In the days of the gaon, he contended, heretical trends so threatened to submerge Judaism that it was the gaon's great achievement to have stemmed this tide through all sorts of emergency measures. "He [the gaon] believed in all earnestness that, by means of the messianic calculations, he would inspire the masses with hopes for the truth." More surprisingly, the sage of Fusṭaṭ himself could not refrain from mentioning an old family tradition, "going back to our early ancestors who were exiled from Jerusalem," according to which "prophecy would be restored to Israel in the year 4970," or 1210 C.E. As in Saadiah's case, Maimonides may have expected to witness that day.[25]

On the other hand, popular conceptions concerning the days of the Messiah could not be fully countenanced by the rationalistic thinkers. Especially the folkloristic glorification of the messianic future by the Aggadah needed serious qualification. Saadiah and Maimonides selected from among the talmudic utterances those which minimized the eschatological character of the advent of the redeemer. They drew a sharp line between the this-worldly messianic era, in which national freedom, eternal peace and prosperity will be obtained and all nations will worship the true God of Israel, and the otherworldly incorporeal existence in the Hereafter. Maimonides, especially, waxed rhetorical on this score and concluded his Code with a lengthy peroration:

Let no one think that in the days of the Messiah anything in the order of the universe would be abolished, or there would be any change in the works of creation, but rather the world will continue along its accustomed ways. . . . Sages and prophets have looked forward to the days of the Messiah, not in order that they rule the world or hold the nations in subjection, nor that they be honored by the nations, or that they eat and drink and be merry, but solely in order that they be free to engage in study and the pursuit of wisdom and suffer from no oppression and interference, so that they may earn life in the world to come. . . . At that time there will be neither famine nor war, neither jealousy nor rivalry, for there will be abundance of all good things, all delicacies will be plentiful like dust, and the whole world will be exclusively dedicated to the knowledge of God. That is why Israel will be great scholars comprehending hidden matters and will attain the knowledge of their Creator within the capacity of man.

In fact, he was such a great believer in the power of reason that, almost in the vein of an eighteenth-century enlightened thinker, he considered the spread of knowledge the best antidote to war, "for the knowledge of truth removes hatred and quarrels, and prevents mutual injuries." For Maimonides, the messianic age thus was but a more propitious preparation for the world to come. There, and there alone, the souls of the righteous, divested of all worldly needs and desires, would live the eternal life of pure contemplation and knowledge. Maimonides, his son Abraham, and others took a positive stand against the excited popular fancy, nourished by talmudic folklore, and further inflamed by Qur'anic descriptions of Paradise. In his polemics against those who longed to partake of the meat of the Leviathan and of the wine of the grapes preserved from the six days of creation, Abraham Maimuni finally declared that all these talmudic legends were merely intended to attract the populace, "just as we attract the hearts of the little ones to learn the Torah in school during the week by distributing among them cakes and nuts on the Sabbath." This from one more deeply imbued with Sufi mysticism than even Baḥya! [26]

Not all philosophers agreed, however, about the absence of extraordinary changes in human nature after the advent of the redeemer. Saadiah, for example, more literally accepting the prophetic predictions, not only depicted the splendor of Jewish power at that time, when kings would be the servants of each and every Israelite, but he positively expected that every Jew, and even his servant, would feel a call to prophecy. The gift of prophecy would, in fact, serve as a test for a Jewish traveler in foreign lands. The gaon also expected the extinction of sin. Not by compulsion, but under the stimulus of the visible signs of divine grace, the Jews would voluntarily choose worship rather than rebellion. Maimonides' greater reticence sprang from his general philosophic outlook which, indeed, postulated immortality of the soul and personal salvation in the Hereafter, rather than bodily resurrection and national-messianic redemption. Anticipating the eloquent conclusion of his Code, he had combated in his first major work, the Commentary on the Mishnah, five divergent opinions which he briefly analyzed, and taught that "we do not ardently long for the days of the Messiah on account of their plentiful crops and their riches, nor in order that we may ride on horses [forbidden to the 'protected subjects' since the days of the Covenant of 'Umar], nor that we may drink wine to the accompaniment of musical instruments," but rather because at that time "the pious will foregather, and there will be the reign of goodness and wisdom." In another context, he also insisted that "the Messiah will neither add to nor subtract from the Law." In general, he considered it more prudent, as he advised an inquirer, Joseph ibn Jabir of Baghdad, not to indulge in speculations on the Hereafter. In line with this advice the sage of Fusṭaṭ allotted no space in his *Guide* to a discussion of the interrelated problems of messianism and resurrection, although among his "perplexed" readers there undoubtedly were many who required guidance in this matter. Yet when he wrote his special "Treatise on Resurrection" he advised his readers not to dispute the ordinary citizens about the delights of the world to come, provided they admitted God's incorporeality. Even more remarkably, he insisted upon both the messianic redemption and the resurrection of the dead as indispensable articles of faith. "Even if he [the Messiah] be delayed," declares daily the pious worshiper reciting the Maimonidean credo, "I shall each day wait for him to come." [27]

MESSIANIC AND SECTARIAN MOVEMENTS

Speculations of this type did not remain limited to scholarly circles which, in periods of great crisis, for the most part merely responded to popular pressures. We have seen how popular folklore, nurtured by yearnings of the masses and preachments by a host of anonymous homilists, forced the hands of even the rationalist thinkers and colored their messianic theories. On the other hand, once a scholar of distinction suggested, however timidly, a possible date for the advent of the Messiah, his computation sometimes evoked an immediate mass reaction going far beyond his wildest dreams.

One such widespread computation, reinforced by the sociopolitical upheavals of the age, led to a major tragedy of Cretan Jewry in the second half of the fifth century. Neither the precise date nor the detailed circumstances of that messianic movement are known. The Palestinian rabbinate had long been silenced, while that of Babylonia had likewise lost much of its articulateness. Even in earlier periods, moreover, they rarely reported events outside these two great centers of Jewry. Our information is limited, therefore, to a hostile description by the Byzantine chronicler Socrates. It appears that the combined impact of the Roman Empire's progressive dissolution, the waves of barbarian migrations which the excited fantasy of persecuted Jews readily magnified into wars of Gog and Magog, and the decline of both the Palestinian and Babylonian Jewish communities, had generated a mass hysteria conducive to the appearance of a messianic pretender. The belief in the approaching redemption was deepened by such computations as that the Exile could not last longer than the Egyptian bondage or a maximum of four hundred years. Hence the liberation could confidently be expected not later than in 468 C.E. That approximate date received further support from a talmudic legend which, harking back to the ancient chronologies of the book of Jubilees, had attributed to the prophet Elijah (appearing to one R. Judah, brother of R. Salla the Pious) the annunciation that the world would endure eighty-five jubilees, and that the son of David would arrive during the concluding fifty-year cycle. With their general penchant for *gemaṭrias,* some homilists found confirmation of that forecast in the Lord's assertion to Job, "Hitherto [*'ad po,* the last two letters have the numerical equivalent of 85] shalt thou come, but no further" (38:11), in which they saw a clear hint that the Exile would not outlast the eighty-fifth jubilee. The redemption was thus due sometime during the years 4200–

4250 A.M. (440–490 C.E.). In the non-Jewish world too, rumors had spread that Rome was destined to last altogether 1,200 years and that, hence, the end of the world would come in 447 C.E.[28]

It is small wonder, then, that a visionary appearing at that time in Crete found an immediate response among Jews. According to Socrates, this messianic pretender assumed the name of Moses, claiming that the Redeemer would be none other than Moses redivivus, and in the course of a year traversed the island from one end to the other. So effective was his preachment that the Jews neglected their daily affairs, allowed their possessions to be dissipated, and concentrated on preparations for their miraculous journey to the Holy Land. On the appointed day, they all assembled at the seashore and, at a given sign, many plunged into the Mediterranean, expecting to witness a repetition of the miracle of the Red Sea. But the waters did not separate for them, and many drowned, though many others were saved by local fishermen and sailors. "Moses" himself vanished from the scene, creating a legend that he was a demon bent on the destruction of Jews.[29]

Messianic currents spread with particular intensity to the Arabian Peninsula, where Jewish tribes, living in relative isolation, had assimilated many ingredients from the local Arabian folklore as well as all sorts of heterodox admixtures germinating in their own and in the neighboring Christian communities. H. Z. Hirschberg has marshaled an impressive array of sources and arguments to prove how deeply influenced Mohammed and the subsequent *ḥadith* were not only by general Jewish religious concepts, but specifically by the visions of the final redemption to be initiated by Elijah and fulfilled by a prophet-messiah. Some Jews actually recognized these pretensions of the new Messenger, while others insisted on the Messiah's indispensable Davidic descent. In accordance with older Jewish traditions, one of these Jewish followers of Mohammed, 'Abdallah ibn Saba, began preaching that the Messenger would reappear before very long to usher in the end of days, and that in the meantime, his son-in-law 'Ali, ought to occupy his place. 'Abdallah's preachment thus paved the way for the Shi'ite schism. long before it materialized as a result of the political breakup. Without altogether discounting the Christian factors in this evolution, we may readily admit that this overcharged messianic atmosphere among the Arabian Jews helped to create that intellectual and religious ferment out of which emerged the new faith.[30]

At the same time these trends, for which we possess largely later, insufficient, and partially dubious attestation, already adumbrated that mixture of messianic yearnings with heterodox beliefs and practices which was to characterize the Jewish sectarian movements under early Islam. In fact, it is difficult to speak of Islam as an entity in that period. Under the Caliphate there existed so many subsidiary religious currents that only Islam's great elasticity enabled it to maintain a semblance of unity until the more pacific period of consolidation. The sectarian habits of the western Asiatic and North African peoples; their inveterate differences in outlook and attitudes; the dissenting trends within Christianity and Zoroastrianism before the rise of the new religion; the rapid growth in population; the ever sharpening political conflicts—all contributed to the spread of great divergences in belief and action. Like Judaism, Islam paid less attention to the purely dogmatic than to the actional sides of religion, and hence the distinctions in theological fundamentals appeared less important than those in actual life. This fact, in connection with the far-reaching principle of *idjma'* (universal consent), by which the customs and beliefs of local majorities were declared to be authoritative interpretations of the law, helped keep the Muslim world together. Some sects, however, developed into serious schisms, with disastrous effects in the religious, as well as in the political field.

Such sectarian movements, reciprocally, affected Judaism, where the people's rapid growth and geographic expansion prepared the ground for increasing nonconformity. It had been much easier to maintain the unity of a persecuted minority in Palestine and Babylonia, under Rome or Persia, than that of relatively prosperous masses in a Jewish world extending over thousands of miles. The experiences of the Second Commonwealth were repeated now, although neither scope nor intensity of the sectarian clashes could rival those of the ancient period before the thorough and comprehensive reformulation of orthodox Judaism by the talmudic sages.

SAMARITANISM

Symbolically, the most ancient of these heterodox movements, Samaritanism, shared with talmudic Judaism the new uplift occasioned by the Renaissance of Islam. With this revival came back, however, some of its inner divisions as well. Their renascence under Baba Rabbah had sustained these sectarians even during the extremely turbulent century and a half before the rise of Islam. Baba was able to reestablish some sort of sanctuary on their holy Mount Gerizim which, never formally recognized by the government, was finally destroyed, in connection with one of the recurrent Samaritan uprisings, by Emperor Zeno in 484 (490). Instead a church in honor of the Virgin, as well as other Christian ecclesiastical buildings, permanently reminded the Samaritans of their political inferiority. To underscore it, the emperor built a tomb for himself, or for one of his sons, in front of the Church, forcing the Samaritan worshipers turning toward their holy mountain to pay unwilling homage to his memory. The Samaritans kept their peace only for a brief period. Both their own chroniclers and the more nearly contemporary Byzantine writers record their frequent uprisings (in 529, 556, etc.), combined with actual attempts at achieving independence under their own kings (Justus in the days of Zeno, Julian in those of Anastasius, 491–518). At times they cooperated even with the much-hated Jews in combating the hostile regime. With equal frequency, however, these two minority groups, as well as the no less severely persecuted Christian sectarians, went their diverse ways, greatly facilitating the tasks of their common oppressors. All this commotion can only be understood against the background of the prolonged Perso-Byzantine wars. On one occasion, as we recall, the Samaritans allegedly offered an approaching Persian army an auxiliary force of 50,000 men to be recruited from among them and the Jews (probably about 540). In reprisal the Byzantine rulers allowed their armies to decimate the Samaritan population, brought about innumerable forced as well as voluntary conversions, and issued many antagonistic laws which practically canceled the time-honored toleration of the Samaritan faith. If at one time even powerful Justinian found it necessary to backtrack and, in a special decree addressed to the Samaritans, speak of his willingness to forgive especially their rural population (whose fiscal contributions he could not readily forego), the unrelenting governmental pressures defeated all these attempts at reconciliation.[31]

With truly amazing vitality the Samaritans survived all these harassments and persecutions which would have broken the back of any other less resilient group. Reduced to a shadow of their former strength during the last century of Byzantine rule, to all intents and purposes outlawed by Justinian's decrees of 529 and 531 which declared them to be a Christian rather than a Jewish sect, the Samaritans quickly came to terms with the Arab conquerors. Their stories about Samaritan contacts with Mohammed and the latter's epistle guaranteeing them full toleration may be dismissed, however, as imitations of similar narratives, authentic and spurious, circulating among Jews and Christians. In fact, during the Arab conquest of Palestine they suffered severely.

Caesarea, which even in the fourth century had been one of their major strongholds, allegedly still numbered 30,000 Samaritans, along with 200,000 Jews, at the beginning of its seven-year siege. Evidently exaggerated, these figures nevertheless convey an idea of the populousness of both communities. But before the city fell, we are informed by the chief Samaritan chronicler Abu'l Fatḥ, most Samaritans had fled from it and other seaboard towns "to the east and never returned hither." Those who remained, as well as those who established themselves in the resurrected Samaritan diaspora in Egypt, Syria, and Babylonia, were treated by the new rulers as a Jewish sect entitled to the protection of the law. This remained the fairly consistent attitude of Muslim administrators and jurists. For a few decades the Samaritans were allegedly freed even from land taxes. On the other hand, there were occasional outbursts of Muslim and, after the Crusades, of Christian intolerance, which caused much bloodshed and forced conversion among the Samaritans as well. They were often victimized also by internal disorders and rebellions, especially during the anarchical tenth century. Their main center, however, in and around Shechem-Neapolis (now renamed Nablus) remained fairly intact. It was allowed to expand into neighboring Ramleh, founded in 716 and made the new seat of the district governor. To judge from Al-

Ya'qubi's equivocal statement, the city's main "protected" population about 891 consisted of Samaritans, while under the early Faṭimids a Samaritan and his son held high government posts there. In Shechem proper, Benjamin of Tudela found no Jews. There was indeed no Jewish community there in the preceding centuries, although some Jews seem sporadically to have settled in that district during the later Middle Ages.[32]

Most of the time Judeo-Samaritan relations were very strained. They had constantly deteriorated since the Jews had accused the Samaritans of yielding to Diocletian's decree enforcing idolatrous worship. Jewish leaders must therefore have welcomed Justinian's decision that these sectarians should no longer be considered members of the Jewish faith. In their unflinching determination to perpetuate their creed, on the other hand, the Samaritans sharply separated themselves from members of all other religions. Mere contact with a Jew, Christian, or Muslim sufficed to cause ritual impurity. According to Qirqisani, "if any person who is not one of them comes near to them they wash themselves." On the passing of any such "infidel," they allegedly dropped straw on his footsteps and burned it. They made themselves so inconspicuous that relatively few Muslim writers referred to them directly. More, although the Crusaders converted Nablus into a major stronghold, they paid little attention to this colorful community. Jews, too, studiously ignored them. Even such an ardent controversialist as Saadiah passed them over in silence. An old ban ascribed to Ezra, Samaritanism's sworn enemy, was now upheld. Although the talmudic sages had admitted that the Samaritans strictly observed the numerous laws they shared with the Jews—they had even at an unknown date adopted the Jewish computation of 613 commandments—the medieval rabbis not only prohibited the consumption of Samaritan food, but also denied these sectarians any share in the future resurrection of the dead. Because of their marriage laws, Jews refused Samaritan proselytes admission to the Jewish fold. Maimonides tersely summarized the Jewish view of Samaritans: "They have been found to be much inferior to heathens." [33]

Ancient controversies were now reinterpreted and new arguments added in the light of the issues raised by the Judeo-Muslim disputations. The age-old controversy over the respective superiority of the temples of Jerusalem and Gerizim lost little of its virulence, although both temples had lain in ashes for more than five centuries before the rise of Islam. Not only the main Samaritan group, but also their sub-sect, the Dositheans, continued to worship at Gerizim or its vicinity. Qirqisani, who mentions the latter group as still in existence in 937, also refers to another sectarian, Malik ar-Ramli (of Ramleh) who stood at the location of the ancient Temple of Jerusalem and swore "that cocks used to be sacrificed upon its altars." Jews reciprocated by denouncing Gerizim as one of the biblical *bamot,* which the ancient prophets had so persistently denounced. The accusation of an anonymous tenth-century controversialist that Samaritans practiced these rites "until the present day," gained in force as Samaritan leadership seems to have made allowances for sacrificing the Paschal lamb at home, even at some distance from the holy mountain. Perhaps it was this Jewish attack which decided the issue, still debated among such leading Samaritan apologists as Abu'l Ḥasan aṣ-Ṣuri, Munajja ibn Ṣadaqa, and Yusuf ibn Salama in the eleventh and twelfth centuries, in favor of exclusive sacrificial worship at Gerizim. From 1163 on, Paschal lambs were sacrificed on that mountain alone (from which Caliph Al-Manṣur had removed the remaining Christian structures built by the Byzantines). The veneration of this sacred site was perhaps further enhanced later by the Turkish prohibition of access to it, intermittently observed until 1832.[34]

Down to the sixteenth century the Samaritans also practiced the ceremonies of purification through ashes of a red heifer. One was found and donated to the community by a coreligionist of Damascus as late as 1348. Despite the carping of Jewish critics who considered the "Cuthean" priests successors of the illegitimate northern priests installed by Jeroboam, they also continued to revere their high-priestly family. In justification of its lineal descent from Aaron, they constantly composed new or brought up to date older chronicles. However artless and dry, these chronicles testify to the Samaritans' awareness of the essentiality of the historical argument for their religious independence. Until 1623–24 the line of their high-priests claimed unbroken succession from Aaron; later a junior branch assumed office under the Deuteronomic title *ha-kohen ha-levi.* At the same time, the majority of the people worshiped in synagogues similar to those of Jews.[35]

Even these debates depended to a large extent on mutual recriminations concerning alleged alterations of Scripture. "Jewish *ta'wil* [commentaries relating to content]," declared Munajja, "is against the Law and for nullifying its regulation. But the *ta'wil* of our predecessors is for the Law and for strengthening it and making it stricter." Despite the rabbis' admission that Samaritans strictly observed laws accepted by them, the differences in their interpretation of the biblical precepts sufficed to obviate almost all commerce between the two groups. Reciprocally, the Samaritans, by extending, for example, the biblical prohibition of castrating animals to all crops possibly produced by the use of such animals, excluded from sacrificial use practically all Jewish, Christian, or Muslim produce. The ritualistic and legal breach between the two groups, already far developed in ancient times, constantly widened itself through the repeated elaboration of legal minutiae on both sides. Ultimately, the Samaritans themselves, through the authoritative voice of Abu'l-Ḥasan, conceded the validity of "the things heard and the things handed down by tradition," and particularly, "the customs observed by a whole community in unison." But this principle, related to the Muslim *idjma',* could now serve only as a further rationale for Samaritan isolationism. More generally rejecting all prophets after Joshua, the Samaritans also had to expand the Muslim distinction between "messenger" and prophet. Only Moses was considered qualified to bear the former designation. That is why they spun many old and new legends around the birth of Moses, writing one book after another under this title.[36]

Moses restored to life, or one of his descendants, was to be the final Redeemer. The book *Asatir,* entirely devoted to divulging the so-called "Secrets of Moses," ends with a triumphant messianic oracle. After describing the twenty-three princes who will successively arise to rule the land of Israel, for the most part bringing havoc and destruction, the author asserts that "a prince will arise who will write the Law in truth, the rod of miracles in his hand. There will be light and no darkness. May the Lord hasten this: and happy is he who will see it and will reach [that time]." There is no mention here of resurrection, or the day of judgment. We need not conclude, therefore, as does M. Gaster, that our author represents here "the Messianic idea in its embryonic stage." The Samaritans consistently refused to accept either the Jewish or the Christian interpretation of the Old Testament prophecies involving anything more than national-religious liberation. As they were restricted to a biblical text which included the Pentateuch and Joshua but neither the Prophets nor the Psalms, they repudiated any expectation that fundamental transformations in the nature of man and society would accompany the advent of the Messiah. Moreover, in the periods of their military uprisings under Justus and Julian, they must have preferred to tone down any supernatural or even superhuman aspects of their messianic hope, as had the Jewish contemporaries of Bar Kocheba. Subsequently they had the less reason to depart from these moderate expectations, as opposition to anything taught by Judaism and Christianity had become to them a matter of extreme urgency for their sheer self-preservation. Fairly typical is Abu Sa'id's scholion on Num. 14:21 into which, unlike their Jewish counterparts, the Samaritans pressed a messianic interpretation: "The purport of this verse is that mankind will adopt the religion which teaches God's unity and the perfect Law. Most certainly a man empowered by God will arise through whom this will be achieved. But God knows best." Even the doctrine of resurrection, grudgingly accepted from the Jews by Baba Rabbah and Marqa, was still repudiated by many later Samaritan leaders according to the unanimous testimony of the rabbis and such students of heresies as Epiphanius and Shahrastani, separated though these were by seven centuries.[37]

Although both Jews and Samaritans now universally spoke Arabic, they emphasized more than ever before the superiority of their respective Hebrew dialects. Just as the Muslims had made of the impeccability of the Qur'an's Arabic a theological argument of major importance, so did the Samaritan chronicler Abu'l Faṭh describe Ezra's introduction of the new square characters as the most disastrous event in Jewish history. "Using this newly fabricated alphabet of twenty-seven letters," Abu'l Faṭh states, Ezra and Zerubbabel "struck out many of the verses of the Law on account of the fourth of the Ten Commandments and the reference to Mt. Gerizim and its boundaries, and they added and omitted, changed and altered" the Scriptures. Since, as we recall, the Samaritan Hexateuch has some 6,000 variants from the Masoretic text, such accusation of conscious falsification (*taḥrif*) could be argued indefinitely. On the other hand, Benjamin after his visit to Nablus where he had found 1,000 Samaritans, reported a neat homily which he had doubtless heard from some local Jews.

> Their [the Samaritans'] alphabet lacks three letters, namely He, Ḥeth and 'Ayin. The letter He is taken from Abraham our father, because they have no dignity [*hod*], the letter Ḥeth from Isaac, because they have no kindliness [*ḥesed*], the letter 'Ayin from Jacob, because they have no humility [*'anavah*]. In place of these letters they make use of the Aleph, by which we can tell that they are not of the seed of Israel, although they know the Law of Moses with the exception of these three letters.

Understandably, the Samaritans also made extensive use of Jewish defenses against the Muslim emphasis upon power, and applied to themselves those biblical passages which Jews were wont to cite in extolling their own powerlessness. "We are the children of Israel," these sectarians likewise claimed, "about us is written, 'for ye were the fewest of all peoples,' and 'the Lord hath chosen us for ever and evermore.' " To which the unnamed Jewish apologist could only reply that world-wide dispersion, making possible the carrying on of the Jewish religious mission among all peoples and the ultimate ingathering of the dispersed communities to the homeland, were necessary corollaries of the biblical prophecies; below it smallness would become self-defeating. This condition applied of course to Jews, but not to Samaritans, few of whom lived outside Palestine.[38]

Away from their stronghold in Nablus, indeed, the Samaritans lived a tenuous and more or less temporary existence, largely depending on the good will of their Jewish neighbors. The very countryside around Nablus was gradually emptied of its Samaritan population. Beginning with Harun ar-Rashid, an increasing though unplanned exchange of population led many Samaritan farmers to emigrate to neighboring districts in Palestine and even to Babylonia, while Muslim farmers and Bedouins established themselves on their lands. "By the time of Saladin," rightly observes A. N. Poliak, "the majority of the population in the district of Samaria had already become Muslim, the Samaritan peasants having in part been massacred, and in part carried away as slaves by the various belligerents." This process of urbanization continued under the Mameluks, the Samaritan majority soon being concentrated in the three communities of Nablus, Damascus and Cairo. As in the case of Jews, there is a large gap in our information concerning the Samaritan communities in Egypt which, as we recall, had already played a certain role in Jewish history there during the Graeco-Roman period. When they reappeared in the Nile Valley after the Arab conquest, they were treated by the new rulers as but an appendage of the Jewish community. From the outset they shared the Jewish cemetery in Cairo, although they maintained there, and doubtless also in other sufficiently large settlements, synagogues of their own—a clear borrowing from Diaspora Jewry. Despite occasional disputations and even outright hostility, as when Samaritan informers endangered all of Egyptian Jewry by denouncing its alleged conspiracy with the approaching Turkish armies (1517), both groups lived under the control of the Egyptian *negidim*. Even Maimonides considered them, as well as the Karaites, an integral part of the Jewish community, and, rather unhistorically, once equated them with the ancient Boethoseans.[39]

In short, as in antiquity, they owed their very survival to the Jews, with whom, notwithstanding the mutual animosities carried over from the mother country, they established a *modus vivendi* more or less satisfactory to both sides. In the long run, however, their adjustments to diaspora life were less effective than those of their Jewish neighbors, and they suffered more severely from the constant political and socioeconomic changes. Under the Turkish regime, finally, their organized communities disappeared entirely from all countries outside Palestine.

NEWER DIVISIONS

For the Jewish community these developments within a group of schismatics, long recognized as outsiders by both rabbinic law and Jewish public opinion, were far overshadowed by the new internal conflicts in its own midst. Here the top-heavy, self-governmental structure itself had serious drawbacks. Some judges abused their power, conniving with the rich and oppressing the poor under their jurisdiction. The moving charge, made by the tenth-century Karaite Sahl ben Maṣliaḥ, of criminal neglect of duties toward the poverty and disease-stricken masses by the Rabbanite authorities, and his condemnation of their extortions carried on with the aid of corrupt state officials may in part be discounted as the biased account of a harsh opponent. But we also possess a responsum by Hai Gaon in which he cursed, with characteristic vigor, those "judges of Sodom, highwaymen, and robbers" who help wealthy creditors seize the household furnishings of poor debtors (otherwise exempted by law). He even incited the inquirers to exert pressure, through public opinion, for the removal of such judges. Hai and his father also caustically disposed of those students of the Talmud who "permitted themselves to take advantage of money belonging to an *'Am ha-Areṣ"* by literally applying the vehement denunciations of this class in the Talmud. Many complaints were voiced, on the other hand, that the autonomous Jewish court failed to enforce its decision against one or another powerful financier who was protected by the government. Ibn Daud, the historian, merely reechoed an old partisan imputation when he placed the exilarch David ben Zakkai, Saadiah's opponent, on a par with the ancient "publicans" because the prince of captivity had allegedly bribed the caliph to appoint him and to countenance his abuses. In an enthusiastically religious age, using mainly a religious nomenclature, such discrepant social and political forces often resulted in sectarian divisions.[40]

Regional differences aggravated these social cleavages. The unity secured by the Palestino-Babylonian leadership in the emergency of the great Christian expansion sufficed to rally the whole people, or at least its unconverted segments, to the defense of the ancestral faith. But it could not possibly do more than gloss over the deep-rooted differences in outlook and mores between the remnants of metropolitan Jewries of Alexandria and Rome, the Jewish half-nomads of Arabia and the mountaineers of the Iranian Plateau. The talmudic rabbis had many a provocation to condemn outright entire provinces like "sick" Media or "dead," as well as impudent, Mesene. Even in the heartland of talmudic Judaism the age-old differences in local customs in the various sections of Palestine and Babylonia, and particularly those between the two countries themselves, had to be given grudging recognition. Those prevailing among the Jewries of other lands were formally ignored rather than suppressed, as were in essence all manifestations of hostility to the established rabbinic leadership in the very citadels of talmudic learning. We are vouchsafed only a few glimpses of such opposition as was voiced by the family of the Babylonian physician, Benjamin, or has been ingeniously reconstructed from stray and incidental references for the wealthy leadership of ancient Sepphoris by Büchler.[41]

During the "dark ages" immediately preceding and following the rise of Islam, these centrifugal forces must have waxed in strength and variety. Although unrecorded in the few sources extant from the crucial sixth and seventh centuries, it stands to reason that the eclipse of both the patriarchate and the exilarchate, combined with the pressures of hostile regimes, the vigorous propaganda of Christian and Zoroastrian (including Mazdakite) missionaries, and the mysterious appeal of Manichaean, Mandaean and other gnostic teachings, must have greatly undermined the traditional controls within the Jewish community. If many Jews were now ready to abandon their faith and join the new triumphant Mosque, there must have been many others who, without going the whole length of conversion, were prepared to enter all sorts of compromises with the beliefs and observances of their non-Jewish neighbors. Once again syncretistic belief or practice readily paved the way for sectarian deviation.

When practically all of world Jewry found itself united under the rule of the Caliphate, the new heterogeneous society, though ultimately serving as a melting pot, at first helped to underscore these great diversities. Even before the arrival of the Arab horsemen Jewish refugees from Yathrib and Khaibar had injected a new element into many communities of Palestine, Syria, and Babylonia. Although far from the ignorant mass they have long been reputed to be—we recall the tragic last night of the Banu Quraiẓa spent in study—these proud and warlike sons of the desert brought with them not only a variety of customs and traditions shockingly strange to the majority of coreligionists among whom they settled, but also, in many ways, a fundamentally different attitude to life. Moreover, we now know that long before the rise of Islam Ḥimyarite Jews had maintained steady contacts with Tiberian Jewry—and Tiberias now not only developed into a major focus of Palestinian Jewry's resistance against Babylonian encroachments, but also early became a center of Shiʿite agitation. It stands to reason that during the half century of Persian control over southern Arabia, some Jews from Ḥadramaut and the Yemen, including full-fledged and half converts, found their way into the great centers of the Sassanian empire. If Arabian Jews roaming through the buffer states of the Lakhmids and Ghassanids had undoubtedly been instrumental in paving the way for the spread of the new religion, if Jewish refugees from Khaibar, established in the military camp of Kufa, greatly contributed to the rise of the Kharijite and other Muslim sects which soon expanded into the Iranian Plateau, their impact on their own coreligionists must have been even more immediate.[42]

Each new province annexed to the Caliphate by the irresistible hosts of the Crescent also brought closer to one another the newly awakened segments of the Jewish people. The new facilities and speed of communication and the intensification of commercial relations, which attracted growing numbers of travelers, merchants, and students to certain focal points in the empire, strengthened these uncontrollable personal and cultural exchanges. The dazzling career of an "upstart" like Saadiah, who, born as an obscure provincial in Fayyum, within a few years assumed the spiritual leadership of the whole people, dramatized the ascendancy of the Jewish communities outside Palestine and Babylonia.

Revitalized Babylonian leadership of exilarchs and geonim undertook to unify these diverse groups under the exclusive aegis of the Babylonian Talmud. Hitherto transmitted for the most part orally from one generation of scholars to another, this monumental achievement of ancient Judaism had remained an esoteric lore even to the majority of Babylonians. Outside the two academies, only the visitors to the semiannual *kallah* assemblies had an inkling of the searching debates carried on by the Amoraim and their disciples, the barest outline of which had been handed down to posterity by faithful recorders. Now a determined effort was made to compile authoritative texts, have them distributed among the learned Jews of all lands, and, through suasion or threats, to make them, together with Scripture, the fountainhead of all Jewish religious and communal life. The same Pirqoi ben Baboi who had tried to suppress some Palestinian divergences under the flimsy excuse that they had owed their origin to anti-Jewish persecutions, also attacked with unrestrained violence those who opposed the equation of Oral and Scriptural laws. Citing older authorities, this native Palestinian student turned pan-Babylonian declaimed:

"The fool hath said in his heart, there is no God." The sages explained that there is no fool but a swine which pollutes itself with dirt and everything that smells badly. And there is no swine like the one who studies the written, but denies the oral Torah. . . . When a man studies the written Torah and fails to study the oral Torah which is the explanation of the written Torah, he is like "a fair woman that turneth aside from discretion," for he understands nothing.[43]

Such efforts at *Gleichschaltung* (if one may be allowed to use a term rendered hateful by Nazi excesses) provoked widespread reaction. We have seen how staunchly Palestinian Jewry defended its independence and how even the climactic Saadiah-Ben Meir controversy had ended in deadlock. Other countries had neither the intellectual resources nor the historic claims of the Holy Land. But, cherishing no less deeply their age-old traditions and way of life and pursuing their own diverse social and political interests, they often produced individual "rebels" who, hurling defiance at the central leadership, gathered around them groups of discontented adventurers and desperadoes and often unwittingly gave rise to new doctrines and practices. Thus arose many new "sectarian" movements. Most of these undoubtedly sank into speedy oblivion. Several, however, attracted the attention of some more influential writers by virtue of their numerical strength, picturesqueness, or mere chance, and joined the procession of heterodoxies so eagerly sought out by later historians of religion, both medieval and modern.

By far the most important of these sects was that of the Karaites, founded by 'Anan ben David (about 767). For a time even that movement was split, as we shall see, into many independent groups, which only after the tenth century became consolidated into a single sect, surviving until the present day. Recruited in part from the leading intellectual circles, this sect left behind many distinguished writings which enable us to reconstruct its story. The other sects were less fortunate. They were for the most part headed by unlearned, if religiously creative, leaders and possessed few, if any, literary documents of their own. Their very memory would have been totally obliterated were it not for the interest taken in them by their opponent Qirqisani, the eminent Karaite student of religion. Owing to Qirqisani's brief and evidently selective description—he was interested principally in those sects of which at least a remnant had survived to his day (937)—we know the bare outlines of some of these movements, their leaders and ideologies.

According to Qirqisani, only two more or less significant sects emerged under Islam before 'Anan and four after 'Anan (not including the intra-Karaite schools of Benjamin Nahawendi and Daniel al-Qumisi). The first to found a sect which long survived him was Abu 'Isa al-Isfahani, known in Hebrew as Obadiah. He started a rebellion in the turbulent days of Caliph 'Abd al-Malik (685–705). Although defeated, he was followed by an alleged disciple, Yudghan (Yehudah), surnamed the Shepherd, who likewise claimed to possess the gift of prophecy. (From other sources we learn also of Yudghan's disciple, Mushkha, who headed a group of his own.) Qirqisani still knew of 'Isawites in Damascus some two and a half centuries after the death of their founder. After 'Anan there appeared Isma'il al-'Ukbari (under Mu'tasim, 833–42), Musa al-Za'frani, also known as Abu 'Imran at-Tiflisi (said to have been Isma'il's pupil), Malik ar-Ramli, and Mishawayh al-'Ukbari. Followers of all these ninth-century sectarians, known as 'Ukbarites, Tiflisites, Ramlites (or Malikians), and Mishawayhites, still adhered to their schismatic beliefs in Qirqisani's days. There is no way of telling how many more such splinter groups operated for years or even decades without being mentioned by him. He makes no reference, for instance, to the pseudo-Messiah Severus (about 720), probably because the latter's heterodox teachings did not long survive their exponent. In all, the total number of Jewish heterodoxies under Islam probably exceeded the twenty-four sects which, according to an ancient homilist, had existed during the declining Second Commonwealth and were responsible for its downfall. Shahrastani's figure, however, of seventy-one Jewish sects is obviously exaggerated; even more so than that of seventy-three Muslim sects, quoted from an old tradition by Goldziher, or that of three hundred such heterodoxies given by Maqrizi.[44]

The Iranian Plateau, in particular, was a fertile soil for all sorts of movements, social, political, religious, and philosophical. This is true of Islam as well as of Judaism. Although Persia apparently offered less military and religious resistance to the invading Arabs than did most other Asiatic and African countries, the accumulated forces of millennia persisted beneath the surface. Persia, in fact, was the only country which, after about three centuries of linguistic assimilation, underwent a national reaction and returned to the old Persian tongue.

Zoroastrian survivals, whether overt or underground, the more readily influenced Jewish schismatics, too, as many of them doubtless believed that Zoroaster himself had been a native of Palestine, a descendant of the Hebrew patriarch Isaac, and a pupil of Baruch, Jeremiah's associate. It is no mere accident that, as indicated by such names as Nahawendi and Kumisi, the most important Karaite leaders also came from Persia. Nahawend, especially, with its large Jewish population, which, although situated in the midst of "sick" Media was largely of pure Jewish descent —even the rabbis of the Talmud had to admit it—gave birth to more than one protagonist of the Karaite schism. As pointed out by Israel Friedlaender, not only such geographic designations as Isfahani, 'Ukbari, Za'frani, Tiflisi, and Damaghani, but also the names of some heresiarchs like Yudghan, Shadakan or Sharakan, and Mushkhan are all "of undeniably Persian origin." Even 'Anan is said to have spent many years of his life in the Persian provinces before he came West to take up the struggle for succession. He is also said to have brought from there a more authentic manuscript of the Pentateuch than the one in use in Babylonia and Palestine. The leaders of the other Jewish sects, from the days of Abu 'Isa, were generally Persians. Similarly, the Shi'a, the largest sect in

Islam, resembling the Karaite sect in its origin from a strife over the legitimacy of a dynastic succession, its denunciation of the prevalent traditions and customs, and its emphasis upon an authoritative rather than popular religion, soon found its most numerous followers in the Iranian districts.[45]

NATIONAL UPSURGE

In many of the Jewish movements, messianism played a prominent part. Mohammed's success induced many individuals to feign or really to believe that they too had a call to prophesy. Sudden political transformations likewise stimulated the millennial hope. The main principle of Islam, the Muslim state, exercised a universal appeal, and even Jewish messianism was now interpreted more and more in political terms. The Messiah was to be the redeemer of the scattered people of Israel, who had to reestablish the Jewish state in Palestine. No sooner did the Arab invaders occupy the rapidly disintegrating Sassanian empire, when (in the days of the Nestorian Patriarch Mar Emmeh, 643–47), according to a Syrian chronicler,

> some Jew, native of Bet Aramaye, got up in a town named Pallughta [Pumbedita?] at the point where the waters of the Euphrates separate for the irrigation of the soil, and asserted that the Messiah had come. He gathered around him weavers, carpetmakers [?] and launderers, some four hundred men. They burned down three [Christian] sanctuaries and killed the chief of that locality. A military force, however, sent from the city of Aqula, intervened, slew them with their wives and children, and crucified their leader in his own village.

Similarly when the Visigothic regime in Spain crumbled away under the blows of a small Moorish expeditionary force, the sudden release from a century-old state of utter insecurity induced, as we shall see, a great many Spanish Jews to listen to the blandishments of a Syrian adventurer, Severus, who promised to make them miraculously "fly to the Promised Land." [46]

Few if any of these visionaries seem to have claimed Davidic descent, one of the rare constants in the multicolored story of Jewish messianic movements. Even the few extant records, stemming all from hostile quarters, indicate that they often merely announced the coming of the redeemer, pretended to be his "messengers" or, at the most, ascribed to themselves the functions of the messiah of the house of Joseph who, through his military victories, would pave the way for the advent of the final Redeemer. Their unsophisticated followers drew no such fine distinctions. Abu 'Isa, for example, seems to have claimed only to be the last of five "messengers," forerunners of the Davidic Messiah. As such he felt superior to all his prophetic predecessors, including the four "messengers" (probably Abraham, Moses, Jesus, and Mohammed). His adherents nevertheless invested him with supernatural qualities, especially since they believed, as did some of Mohammed's contemporaries, that their leader had been wholly illiterate and yet, under divine inspiration, had succeeded in writing unaided a memorable book. Harking back to an old aggadic concept of the reiterated concealment and reappearance of the messiah—this idea was doubtless interrelated with the Christian belief in the second coming of Christ and, together with it, greatly influenced the manifold Muslim sectarian teachings of the concealed and ever reappearing *Mahdi*—some " 'Isawites" still believed two centuries later that their leader had not been killed but had "entered a hole in a mountain" and, before long, would reappear to lead them to the Holy Land. Abu 'Isa's pupil, Yudghan, too, only "pretended to be a prophet; [but] his followers assert that he was the Messiah and that he did not die; they expect him to return (any moment)." [47]

Concomitant with these messianic currents there was an intensified longing for the Holy Land. Never absent from the innermost yearnings of Diaspora Jewry, love for Palestine was constantly reactivated in periods of great stress or epochal transformations. The rise of Islam, too, gave new impetus to pilgrimages and permanent settlement there by pious and learned Jews. Living a life of self-abnegation and politically rather impassive, this ever growing group of "Mourners for Zion" formed an important segment of Jerusalem's population. After the disasters which sooner or later overtook the more strictly messianic movements, the ranks of these "mourners" were swelled from both the Rabbanite and the sectarian camps. The Karaite Bible commentator, Daniel al-Qumisi, actually exhorted his brethren to return *en masse* to the

Holy City. "But if you do not come," he added, "for you are engrossed in and running after your trades, send five men from each city and provide them with a livelihood. In this manner we shall become a united people, dedicated to constant prayers to our Lord on the mountains of Jerusalem." Clearly, this call to organized action remained unheeded. Nonetheless, urgent appeals of this kind, reiterated also by Qumisi's successor, Sahl ben Maṣliaḥ, attracted many Karaites to the Holy City. Rabbanites, too, flocked to Palestine in large numbers even from distant Spain. Joseph ibn Megas of eleventh-century Lucena discussed the case of a Jew who had vowed to abstain from both meat and wine until he reached the Holy Land. The streets of Jerusalem reverberated with sectarian disputations, which merely accentuated the internal cleavages natural to a community recruited from all corners of the dispersion.[48]

Nationalist revival could well go together with greater religious tolerance, on the one hand, and with ethnic exclusivism on the other hand. Abu 'Isa, for instance, readily acknowledged both Jesus and Mohammed as the prophets for their peoples. According to Ibn Ḥazm, he even assumed that Jesus had been sent only to the children of Israel, while Mohammed served as a messenger to the children of Ishmael, just as Job had prophesied to the children of Esau, and Balaam to the children of Moab. "I have encountered," Ibn Ḥazm added, "many distinguished Jews who professed that doctrine." 'Anan, too, although claiming no prophetic gifts for himself, was ready to admit that Mohammed was sent to the Arabs by God, whereas the ordinary Rabbanite Jew, to quote Sherira Gaon and Maimonides, regarded the Arab "Messenger" as nothing but a "madman." This was not a mere political gesture on the part of these rebels, for the government, as well as the orthodox Muslim public, doubtless condemned all these opinions as subversive and running counter to Mohammed's assertion that he was "the Seal of the Prophets" (Qur'an 33:40). This objection to Abu 'Isa's attempted harmonization was, indeed, to be raised by both Qirqisani and Baqillani. Only such Muslim sectarians as the Kharidjites were prepared to accept as equals Jews and Christians subscribing to the credo (*shahada*) that "Mohammed is a messenger of Allah to the Arabs but not to us." There are indeed many subtle threads, ideological as well as political, linking the 'Isawites to the Kharidjite movement.[49]

At the same time, however, 'Anan rigidly forbade the Jews to live in the same quarter with the Gentiles, a measure rarely and always timidly suggested by a rabbi, either as a precautionary measure or for the sanctification of the Sabbath. Later, Daniel al-Qumisi and Sahl ben Maṣliaḥ bitterly censured the intimate social contacts of the Rabbanites with the Gentiles, which, the latter asserted, often went so far that Jews partook of Gentile food. In other words, Judaism became for these sectarians a purely national religion, frankly renouncing all claims to universalism.

These new national-religious emphases would have created a state of mind conducive to a revival of Sadducean teachings, even if there had been no direct vestiges of ancient Sadducean writings and oral traditions. The controversy over the existence of such literary remains in the early Muslim age has been raging for many years. It cannot be completely resolved until such time when a lucky find in a medieval *genizah* might bring forth some authentic text stemming from this sectarian group. However, the rare unanimity among the earlier medieval writers, both Rabbanite and Karaite, that the movement initiated by 'Anan was a direct offshoot of these ancient schismatics, although not conclusive proof, creates a strong presumption in favor of some such historical connection.

Nor have any valid reasons been advanced to cast serious doubt on Qirqisani's familiarity with "Zadok's" books in which the ancient heresiarch allegedly "did not adduce any proofs for anything he said, but limited himself to mere statements, excepting one thing. . . ." Another tenth-century Karaite (Ḥasan ben Mashiaḥ, or Sahl ben Maṣliaḥ) was even more explicit and in his commentary on Exodus argued against the Rabbanites by referring to "the writings of Sadducees [which] are generally known." We need not be too much concerned about the simon-pure authenticity of these letters. Most likely they contained a great many interpolations and alterations which would have made them unreliable witnesses of the ancient sectarian tradition as such. But they doubtless preserved many fundamental Sadducean and related teachings, just as many Philonic doctrines and a large variety of concepts borrowed from the pre-Christian apocalyptic literature had come down the centuries. The presence in the Cairo Genizah of copies of the "Zadokite" fragment of the ancient New Covenanter and of the Hebrew text, however altered, of Sirach; the attested withdrawal by Jews of some documents from a cave (about 800 C.E.); and the uninterrupted use of such caves as that recently found at Murabba'at in the Dead Sea wilderness, from the days of Bar Kocheba to the Muslim age—all strongly confirm the impression of the underground persistence of many unorthodox teachings throughout the first millennium. Together these remnants of ancient thought helped fructify the religious thinking of the newly receptive and religiously creative generations after the rise of Islam. Residua of outside heterodoxies, carried down through the ages by the Judeo-Christian fringe movements, must have reinforced these inner Jewish reminiscences.[50]

Many of these discussions, moreover, are vitiated by their exclusively "literary" approach. Important as it may be to ascertain the existence per se of such ancient literary remains in the earlier Middle Ages, this quest has relatively little bearing on the genesis and evolution of the medieval religious movements. Where these were influenced by heterodox traditions, the latter must have been oral and folkloristic much more than literary and canonical. We need not imagine that even the relatively few learned men among the sectarian leaders derived their inspiration or appealed to their followers by citing chapter and verse from some such older writings. Of course, they made whatever use they could of the revealed biblical sources with the aid of their own hermeneutics. But they hardly invoked other sources, unless they wished specifically to controvert certain rabbinic sayings. They and their followers must have received their main direct stimuli from heterodox teachings transmitted orally from generation to generation, from widespread and constantly intermingling folkloristic tales and superstitions, and from many unorthodox practices which they could readily observe in their respective communities.

Just as talmudic lore could be handed down orally for centuries by faithful recorders, so did the suppressed, but far from extinct, minorities doubtless find some loyal adherents to perpetuate their views through an equally unwritten chain of tradition. Suffice it for us to imagine, by way of illustration, that some overwhelming catastrophe had engulfed Palestinian Jewry before 200 C.E., or both Palestinian and Babylonian Jewry before 400 C.E., when practically none of the tannaitic or amoraic teachings had been committed to writing. Would it not have been preposterous for us to deny, on this score, the very existence of a great and ramified rabbinic Oral Law? Except for the questionable *Sefer Gezerata* mentioned in the "Scroll of Fasts," we know nothing of any ancient Sadducean *literature,* and yet we feel confident that the Sadducees possessed a rich oral tradition which remained alive for untold generations. Why should it, or similar oral traditions of lesser sects, not have been carried on for several more centuries by overt or clandestine devotees? General historic experience certainly makes it highly unlikely that such tremendous energies as had been released by the sectarian movements before 70 C.E. should have completely vanished during the period of talmudic consolidation. Many of their teachings, and even those of many Judeo-Christian sectarians, must have percolated by word of mouth into the Jewish masses, particularly in those outlying regions where the steamroller of the Palestino-Babylonian academies had not yet succeeded in leveling all overt expressions of dissent.[51]

Sooner or later all these sectarian movements, whatever their outward manifestations and sociopolitical objectives may have been, developed legal deviations from the orthodox *halakhah.* If, true to its peculiar Hellenistic Jewish origins and early evolution, Christianity always channelized its sectarian diversities into some ultimate *dogmatic* divergences, if in Islam the primarily *political* conflicts over the legitimacy of succession to the caliphate overshadowed all other issues, Jewish sectarianism became truly meaningful only when it seriously infringed upon the domain of *law.* Here again a sharp line of demarcation was drawn between overzealous extension of existing prohibitions or even their violation, however otherwise serious, which did not lead to the disruption of over-all Jewish unity, and those heterodoxies which threatened to undermine the people's ethnic foundations.

Official opinion frowned upon the former and at times adopted stringent measure to suppress them. But it never excluded such deviationists from the community of Israel. Asked about the treatment to be accorded the followers of the false messiah Severus, Naṭronai I replied:

It seems to us that those evildoers, although they have strayed into bad ways, denied the words of the sages, profaned holidays, violated [other] commandments and polluted themselves with dead carcasses and forbidden meats, ought nevertheless to be attracted, rather than repelled. As to their transgressions, such as their consumption of dead carcasses and forbidden meats or their despoiling of their marriage contracts [by disregarding the required rabbinic forms], you shall flog them before the courts, impose fines upon them—each according to his evil deeds—punish them and make them stand up in the synagogues and promise never to return to their aberrations, but you shall accept and not repulse them.

When, however, an opposing faction began tampering with the laws governing the calendar in a way entailing the celebration of holidays on other than the accepted days, such deviation could readily lead to irremediable separation. That is why when Qirqisani asked Jacob ben Ephraim the Syrian (hardly identical with Saadiah's pupil, Jacob ben Samuel) why the Rabbanites allowed intermarriage with 'Isawites but not with Karaites, the latter answered bluntly, "Because they [the 'Isawites] do not differ from us in the observance of holidays." Jacob could also have pointed to the Karaite deviations in family laws which, by threatening chaos in all Jewish family relations, even more directly menaced the ethnic consistency of the people. Orthodox Judaism, rightly observed L. M. Epstein, could afford to be relatively lenient toward other deflections from the established law. But "the moment a group subscribed to a doctrine which taught a fundamental deviation from the accepted law of marriage, it was doomed to the status of a 'sect' and was gradually eliminated from Jewish group life." [52]

Needless to say, not all legal digressions led to sectarian groupings. Even most of the Jewish "sects" listed as such by medieval students of religion, and through them also by modern historians, hardly deserve to be thus dignified. The propensity to find seventy-three sects in Islam, in order to justify a saying attributed to Mohammed by a faulty linguistic interpretation, led to many artificial distinctions between otherwise kindred movements. This tendency communicated itself also to medieval students of Jewish heterodoxies, both Muslim and Jewish. Shahrastani, as we recall, actually claimed that there existed seventy-one Jewish sects of which he described only the four best known and most widespread.[53]

MILITARY AND IDEOLOGICAL COMMOTIONS

We need not repeat here in any detail the thrice-told tale of the medieval sectarian movements. The earliest and in some respects the most important of them, apart from the Karaites, namely the interrelated movements of 'Isawites, Yudghanites or Shadghanites, and Mushkhanites, did not seriously depart from the main teachings or practices of orthodox Judaism, but merely tried to sharpen the existing provisions so as to live an even holier and more ascetic life. In fact, Abu 'Isa himself (his real name seems to have been Isaac ben Jacob but, with reference to his messianic role, he was surnamed Obadiah or servant of the Lord), held the talmudic sages in high esteem and likened them to the prophets. On the other hand, he seems to have rated the ordinary prophets far below the "messengers" or the Messiah. To be sure, to quote Qirqisani, "he prohibited divorce as do the Sadducees and the Christians. He prescribed seven daily prayers, inferring this from the saying of David [Ps. 119:164] 'Seven times a day do I praise Thee.' He also prohibited meat and intoxicating drinks, not on the authority of the Scripture, but asserting that God commanded him to do so by direct revelation." But any Rabbanite Jew could refrain from divorcing his wife, abstain from any kind of food and add as many prayers as he wished. Nor did this allegedly ignorant tailor cite any Sadducean, Christian, or other heterodox writings in support of his measures, but merely enacted them on his own authority. The Yudghanites, too, "forbade the consumption of wine and meat and increased greatly the fasts and prayers." [54]

More serious would have been Abu 'Isa's insistence, doubtless inaccurately reported by Yehudah Hadassi, on the observance of holidays in accordance with the solar year. All he may have meant to say was that, unlike the strictly lunar calendar of the Muslims with their movable holidays, the Jews observed their holidays according to the solar seasons of the year. This seems to be, indeed, the meaning of Hadassi's own admission that the 'Isawite computation agreed with that of the Rabbanites (*ke-dibrehem*). Abu 'Isa may also have theorized about the calendar in the same vein as Yudghan, namely that holidays in the dispersion were merely memorial days, rather than legally binding. But evidently neither master nor pupil ever shifted the actual days of their observance. 'Isawite conformity in this matter was indeed advanced, as we recall, by Jacob ben Ephraim as the main reason for their preferential treatment on the part of Rabbanite leadership.[55]

The messianic claims of Abu 'Isa, Yudghan, and Mushkha could be treated by the communal leaders with far greater condescension. The various miracle tales told by their followers for generations thereafter could be viewed as fairly innocuous fantasies. Abu 'Isa's alleged drawing of a circle around his camp which the attacking Muslim army was unable to penetrate, his single-handed victorious sorties, his visit, beyond the desert, to the legendary *Bene Moshe* (descendants of Moses) "to announce to them God's word," and his final withdrawal to a mountain "hole" (perhaps in some connection with the then still remembered ancient sect of *Maghariya* [Cave Men], reminiscent of the depositors of our Dead Sea scrolls) [56] from where he was to stage a comeback in a later generation—all lay in that obscure domain of uncontrollable popular beliefs and superstitions which most rabbis were prepared to dismiss with a shrug. Even his (and some Mushkhanites') acceptance of the prophetic qualities of Jesus and Mohammed, on a par with such Gentile prophets as Balaam, seemed rather harmless so long as it was not accompanied by any direct syncretistic action and did not involve any recognition of the latter's prophetic authority with respect to Jews.

All these were aberrations, to be sure, not to be indulged in by the truly orthodox. But they were not serious enough to call forth concerted action on the part of the central leadership in Babylonia. Exilarchs and geonim doubtless viewed all such movements as but ephemeral excesses of the popular mind in a period of epochal transformations, and probably expected their quick suppression by Muslim arms. In fact, all three leaders fell in battle; Abu 'Isa allegedly at the head of "hundreds of thousand" men, after reaching the vicinity of Baghdad, while Mushkha's die-hard followers at the battle of Qumm (an Arab garrison city and early Shi'ite center) had already dwindled to nineteen individuals. True, the 'Isawite sect survived these military defeats, and with remarkable tenacity persisted particularly in Damascus, that ancient home of Jewish heterodoxy. In 937, Qirqisani still found twenty 'Isawites in that Syrian city. A "small number" of Yudghanites had also survived in Isfahan. But evidently these sectarians neither separated themselves voluntarily from the Jewish people, nor were they considered a sufficient threat to general Jewish conformity to call forth their drastic excision from the main body of Jewry by the leaders of the majority.[57]

No more serious were the legal divergences introduced by Severus the Syrian a generation after Abu 'Isa (about 720). This Christian convert to Judaism seems to have been an outright adventurer. Whether or not we believe the yarn of the early Syriac chronicler Pseudo-Dionysius about Severus seducing a Jewish girl in Samaria, his chastisement by the enraged Jewish populace, and his ensuing vow of vengeance, it appears that this skilled *jongleur* presented himself to the Jews from Mesopotamia to Spain as their redeemer. His timing was excellent. The messianic expectations of the people had surged higher and higher when the Muslim conquests in Spain and southern France seemed to carry the flag of the Caliphate to the ends of the known world and the siege of Constantinople in 717–18 promised to eliminate the last bastion of resistance in the West.

Severus played his game carefully. According to a well-informed Christian chronicler of the thirteenth century, contemporaries were not sure whether he had pretended to be the Messiah in person, or only a "messenger" and forerunner of the real Redeemer. Out of ignorance or design, he introduced a number of ritualistic alleviations. His followers at least, to quote an inquiry submitted to Naṭronai I, "do not pray, do not abstain from forbidden meats or guard their wine from turning into wine of oblation [by contact with Gentiles], work on second holidays, and do not write marriage contracts in the form prescribed by our sages." All these acts, however serious, were contrary to talmudic rather than biblical law. Nor were they antinomian in principle, although antinomianism of both the messianic and the rationalist variety was not totally absent from the Jewish community of the time. In fact, the same gaon subsequently answered an inquiry concerning such a schismatic group which was "different from all other heretics in the world" inasmuch as they did not repudiate merely talmudic law, but also "denied the very core of the Torah." In this case Naṭronai decided to refuse their members readmission to the Jewish community even after due repentance, lest their children, "bastardized" because of their defiance of the biblical laws of marriage and divorce, contaminate the purity of the Jewish families. That is why, after a few years of successful financial exploitation of his credulous adherents—he himself was supposed to have admitted to the caliph that he had "made fun of the Jews"—Severus was unmasked and executed, and left behind neither a military nor a sectarian heritage. We do not hear of any armed uprisings or of permanent sectarian deviations of the kind engendered by Abu 'Isa, Yudghan, or Mushkha. Almost all of Severus' followers seem to have returned meekly to the fold, without even attempting to preserve for posterity the name of their leader.[58]

By the middle of the eighth century, with the stabilization of imperial power, the military phase of the Jewish separatist movements drew to an end. It was not to be revived until the conditions became again more propitious after the collapse of the Great Caliphate and the invasions of the Seldjuks and Crusaders. This self-imposed military restraint not only deprived Mushkha's successors of the glamor of a "holy war," but also ran counter to the deep-rooted tradition of the Messiah's warlike exploits. An old Muslim source, already cited by the tenth-century Spanish writer, Ibn 'Abd Rabbihi, ascribes to the Jews a saying, "There shall be no fighting for the sake of God, until the Messiah, the Expected One, goes forth and a herald from heaven proclaims [his arrival]." This reconciliation of actual Jewish powerlessness with high national aspirations for the future, understandably enough, appealed also (as that Muslim author suggests) to similarly disarmed Muslim sectarians. That is why, Shahrastani carefully notes, Mushkha "considered it his duty to rise against his enemies and to wage war against them," although he and his nineteen followers apparently were fully aware of the suicidal nature of their undertaking. His ninth-century successors were far more careful, and they toned down the messianic element in their preachment. Even Isma'il al-'Ukbari who, according to Qirqisani, dared coin "many sayings that are harmful, shameful, and absurd to the utmost degree," only ordered that his tomb be inscribed, "The chariot of Israel and the horsemen thereof" (II Kings 2:12)—an obvious allusion to Elijah who had long been viewed in the Aggadah as the forerunner of the Messiah.[59]

Deprived of their essential messianic appeal, the leaders of the later deviationist movements had to stress exclusively legal and ritualistic disparities. They were also encouraged therein by the evident successes of the Karaite propaganda. Among these ninth-century sectarians, the 'Ukbarites founded by Isma'il of 'Ukbara in Persia (which embraced a populous Jewish community even in the days of Benjamin of Tudela), the Tiflisites led by Abu 'Imran (Musa al-Za'frani), a native of Baghdad but resident of Tiflis in the Caucasus, and the Mishawayhites organized by Mishawayh (Mesvi), likewise of 'Ukbara—all dissented in the interpretation or reading of Scripture. Isma'il, in particular, seems to have accepted some readings from the Samaritan version, but he also allowed himself emendations based on reasoning, and generally preferred the biblical *ketib* (written form), rather than the *qeri* (readings accepted by the Masorah). All these sectarians also differed from the main body of Jewry, as well as among themselves, in basic practical problems affecting the calendar. Abu 'Imran and Mishawayh (whose "mind was always wandering") accepted the Sadducean-Karaite interpretation of "from the day after the Sabbath" (Lev. 23:15) as enforcing the observance of the Festival of Weeks on a Sunday. The 'Ukbarites and Tiflisites insisted upon starting the new moons at times a day earlier than the rest of the people, while Mishawayh "was in doubt as to how to fix the beginning of months, since he could not decide what system to adopt." On the other hand, the Mishawayhites accepted their master's interpretation that the Day of Atonement is called in Scripture the *shabbat shabbaton* (Lev. 23:32) only because it is a "double sabbath" and must always be celebrated on a Saturday. Consequently, every Passover must begin on a Thursday. One may readily envisage the confusion which was bound to arise if every group of Jews were to observe their holidays according to their private Bible exegesis. There were many debates about which animal fats were allowed for consumption. Mishawayh also enjoined his followers always to pray in the westerly direction, unless they lived in Egypt or Morocco, in which case their orientation was to be eastward toward Jerusalem. Because of the joy and satisfaction to be derived from it, he also allowed the counting of one's money on Sabbath. Another sectarian leader, Malik ar-Ramli (of Ramleh in Palestine), we recall, once proclaimed from the Temple mountain in Jerusalem that cocks used to be sacrificed there. He evidently wished to controvert in this way 'Anan's prohibition of chicken for Jewish consumption.[60]

That such debates could still be carried on, and their lessons still applied in practice during the ninth and tenth centuries, is but another illustration of the failure of the Masorites to secure universal acceptance for their final revision of the biblical texts. Similarly, the extensive divergences concerning the calendar were possible only because of the lack of a generally recognized system, half a millennium after its promulgation by Hillel II. Its absence even among the orthodox was soon to be widely dramatized by the Saadiah–Ben Meir controversy. Dogmatic divergences, on the other hand, or differences in purely historical explanations, which had little bearing on the people's unity, were safely disregarded. That Yudghan, for example, tended to subscribe to the Sadducean-Mu'tazilite doctrine of the complete freedom of will, and insisted upon an unorthodox differentiation between the literal and allegorical meaning of Scripture, is not even mentioned by any writer before Shahrastani. He was therein in excellent orthodox company, both Rabbanite and Karaite. Similarly, only Jephet ben 'Ali condemned Abu 'Imran's denial of resurrection, ascribing it entirely to the influence of some Arab sectarians and forgetting the Sadducean tradition. Only Mishawayh seems to have drawn the extreme consequence of his syncretistic teachings. According to the eleventh-century Karaite scholar Tobiah ben Moses, he not only professed Christianity—Tobiah chides him by comparing him with Matthew, John, Paul, and Luke—but also "served three deities in his old age," that is, he simultaneously professed belief in the God of Israel, Jesus, and Mohammed. Like Shabbetai Zevi's or Jacob Frank's conversions thereafter, his, too, apparently did not entail the complete loss of his Jewish following. But this act of apostasy doubtless reinforced the general attitude of aloofness on the part of Jewish leaders. Splinter groups, like the Jalutiyites who overstressed biblical anthropomorphisms, Fayyumites who excessively applied the *noṭariqon* (treatment of words as abbreviations) in their biblical exegesis, and even the Shahrashtanites who claimed that eighty verses had dropped out of the Masoretic Pentateuch, if they were more than small coteries of cranks, were not considered worthy of recording by any extant historian until Maqrizi of the fifteenth century. This Arab historian, or his Jewish or Muslim source, moreover, needed these small groupings, as well as some minor Karaite subdivisions, to round out the total number of ten Jewish "sects," other than Rabbanites and Karaites.[61]

Otherwise we might have to count among the "sectarians" all those, apparently sizable, groups of simple lawbreakers, whether out of rationalist conviction or from sheer religious indifference. In another context we shall see that these nonconformists played a greater role in the Jewish communities under medieval Islam than did all formal non-Karaite "heretics" put together. Even these "sectarians," however, undoubtedly more numerous and variegated than is reflected in the few extant sources, greatly contributed to that spiritual fermentation of which they themselves were the effect and which so deeply colored all Jewish religious creativity during the Renaissance of Islam.

REAPPEARANCE OF PSEUDO-MESSIAHS

By the tenth century the forces of Jewish sectarianism were spent. With the general stabilization of the Renaissance of Islam, concomitant with its growing political decline and economic retardation, the Jewish community, too, lost some of its creative rebelliousness and rather devoted itself to the consolidation of its socioreligious positions. The very decentralization of Jewish communal controls, which enabled each region to develop more freely along its chosen paths, rather than promoting religious disparity proved to be a cementing force of Jewish ideological unity maintained by living contacts and literary exchanges. Previously, any opposition to the recognized authority of exilarchs and geonim, as well as to officials appointed by them, generated trends going far beyond sheer disobedience in detail. Frequently the only effective protest against that overwhelming authority seemed to be an attack on its very foundations, namely Jewish law, or at least Oral Law. Now local adjustments proceeded apace with far less difficulty. Within the broader Islamic civilization, moreover, all unorthodox trends, including the formerly powerful Mu'tazilite movement, were likewise giving way to increasing conformity.

Such drying up of the heterodox mainsprings did not, however, diminish in the least the people's attachment to its Holy Land and its hope for speedy politico-religious restoration. In critical periods, particularly, that hope found expression not only in new messianic dreams and visions, but also in recurrent attempts to accelerate that end by human action. Once again ambitious or idealistic individuals, often megalomaniacs, felt the call to prophesy and to lead their people out of bondage. Although invariably discouraged by the established communal leaders and hence, willy-nilly, forced into some sort of opposition to the existing order, these new self-avowed redeemers rarely incited their followers to depart from the accepted religious practices or beliefs.

Perhaps because of the absence of ideological clashes, as well as of the limited geographic compass of most of these messianic movements, they left behind them few records. Their story had to be pieced together in recent decades from stray items of information, preserved only in the Cairo Genizah. Even our main source, Maimonides' *Epistle to Yemen,* was long available only in greatly abridged Hebrew renditions; the translators apparently considered these stories less worthy of attention. From the Arabic original of that epistle, however, written on the occasion of a messianic movement in Yemen in 1171–72, and other extant sources it appears that the preceding century belonged to the messianically most excited periods in Jewish history.[62]

As in most other public manifestations of Jewish popular frenzy, the reasons have to be sought in a combination of external and internal factors. The growing conflicts between the Muslim and Christian worlds, which resulted in the prolonged series of Christian Crusades in the direction of both the Holy Land and the Iberian Peninsula, offered a most propitious background for the long cherished expectations that the Messiah was due to come at the end of the first millennium after the fall of Jerusalem, or soon thereafter. We recollect how deeply disappointed Spanish Jewry and its leading poets were when the year 1068 had passed without the advent of the Redeemer. It is small wonder, then, that in that very period a messianic pretender appeared in a Christian city, called by Maimonides "Linon, a large center in the heart of the Frankish kingdom, which numbered more than ten thousand Jewish families." By performing the extraordinary feat of gliding "from tree to tree like a bird" he gained many votaries. But the "Franks" quickly suppressed the ensuing commotion and executed the "messiah" and many of his followers. Discounting the obviously exaggerated population estimate, the city is usually identified with Lyons in France, which had boasted of a sizeable and affluent Jewish community since Carolingian times. But it is difficult to explain why no persecution of Jews in France at that time is recorded in any other source, Jewish or Christian. Perhaps Maimonides had rather the Spanish city of Leon in mind, the messianic movement and its bloody suppression there being in some way connected with the recorded attacks of Spanish Crusaders on Jews in 1063, which were to evoke the papal intervention in the latter's behalf.[63]

When the year 1068 passed without bringing liberation, Jews began rationalizing that computation as they had done after 468. History repeated itself. Just as in antiquity the due date was extended to the entire eighty-fifth jubilee cycle, that is to 490 C.E., the belief now spread that redemption was to be expected some time during the 256th nineteen-year cycle, beginning in 4846 (1085–86). We recall the melancholy opening of Solomon bar Simson's chronicle of the tragic events during the First Crusade referring to that cycle which "we had expected to bring salvation and comfort in accordance with the prophecy of Jeremiah [31:6], but which turned to grief and sorrow." Perhaps to underscore that nexus, the chronicler emphasized that the bloodshed occurred "in the year 4856 [of Creation], 1028 of our Exile, and 11 of the 256th cycle." These world-stirring events understandably generated new messianic expectations. From the much-debated, but still very obscure, Byzantine letter published by Neubauer we learn about the impact of the arrival of the disorganized hosts of Crusaders in the Balkans on both Jews and Christians, particularly in Salonica. We are also told that the revived messianic hope aroused seventeen Khorasanian communities which, even in their political eclipse, had retained much Jewish feeling and considerable independence, to leave their homes and proceed to the "desert." There they expected to meet the descendants of the Ten Tribes who, according to old legends, were supposed to participate in the general return of Jewry to its ancestral home. Curiously, one of our correspondent's main sources of information, Tobiah ben Eliezer—if he be the Tobiah several times mentioned in the letter—alluded in his works, written in 1097 and revised a decade later, to the tragic happenings of 1096 in Germany, but made no reference whatever to any Balkan repercussions of the Crusades.[64]

The effects of the First Crusade, the conquest of Palestine by the Christians, and the destruction of many Jewish communities in Europe and Palestine were bound to evoke in many minds the picture of the wars of Gog and Magog, preliminary to the final arrival of the Messiah. Students of rabbinic leaders must also have long been impressed by the old legends summarized in Hai Gaon's prediction that "when we see Edom ruling over the land of Israel we believe that our salvation had begun, for it is written, 'And saviours shall come up on mount Zion, to judge the mount of Esau' [Ob. 21]." The urgency of that hope was further intensified in the apparently spreading belief in Muslim countries that the Messiah must come before the end of half a millennium after the appearance of Mohammed, for otherwise the *dhimmis* would forfeit their right to "protection." This belief, perhaps originating in Spain and Morocco where it is attested in the aforementioned threat of the Almoravid ruler, seems to have extended before long to eastern Islam as well. It greatly increased the anxieties of the Jewish communities under Muslim rule. That is why even enlightened Cordovan Jewry lent a willing ear to astrologers who had computed that the messianic age was to begin about 1107 C.E., or 500 A.H. This time the populace did not even wait for a self-appointed pretender to perform miracles and otherwise to prove his divine mission, but on its own "picked a pious and virtuous person by the name of Ibn Aryeh who had been instructing the people" and declared him to be the expected Redeemer. According to Maimonides, the saner leadership of the community, headed by his father Maimon, summoned Ibn Aryeh to the synagogue and flogged him for his tacit encouragement of the belief in his messiahship. "They did the same thing to the persons who assembled about him. The Jews escaped the wrath of the Gentiles only with the greatest difficulty." [65]

Although the year 1107 passed without any untoward consequences for Jewries under Islam, the new semimillennarianism seems to have persisted and even to have spread to eastern communities. Now, however, the 500-year period was interpreted to refer to solar rather than lunar years, the redemption being calculated for about 1122 C.E. We recall the decisive turn in history expected two centuries later by Sa'id ibn Ḥasan from the passage of 700 solar years. Not surprisingly, therefore, Jews in various parts of the Muslim world reacted independently, and yet almost simultaneously, to the approach of that crucial year. From Maimonides we learn of the appearance in Fez of one Moses al-Dar'i, a learned and pious Jew from Spain and former pupil of Joseph ibn Megas. Without claiming to be the Messiah himself, he predicted on the basis of dreams that the Messiah would arrive on the following Passover eve. To demonstrate the veracity of his prediction, he foretold several other forthcoming events, and they came true. For instance, he forecast a heavy rain with drops of blood for a particular autumnal Friday, seeing in it a messianic portent in accordance with Joel's prophecy (3:3). On that day, indeed, a heavy rain fell and, as Maimonides tried to explain it rationally, "the fluid that descended was red and viscous as if it were mixed with clay." Despite Maimon's opposition, Moses succeeded in persuading the people "to sell their property and contract debts to the Muslims with the promise to pay back ten dinars for one," for after Passover they all would have left the country. The ensuing fiasco and ruin of most of his adherents forced Moses to leave Morocco and proceed to Palestine, where he died in relative obscurity many years later.[66]

About that time Palestine herself witnessed a similar resurgence of messianic hopes. Here it was the turn of the Karaite community, more freely tolerated by the Latin rulers, to produce its first messianic pretender in history. The Norman proselyte Obadiah tells us about his encounter in Dan (Baniyyas) with a Karaite, Solomon ha-Kohen, who had been traveling up and down the country announcing that the Messiah would come within two and a half months, and that he would be the man "whom Israel seeks" (an unmistakable allusion to Mal. 3:1). He overruled Obadiah's objection that the Messiah was supposed to be of the house of David, rather than of the tribe of Levi, and urged him to give up his projected trip to Egypt. "I am going to Egypt," Obadiah sarcastically replied, "and I shall return with our Egyptian brethren to Jerusalem." Still another commotion of that type is recorded during the same period in Baghdad. According to a garbled story in an incomplete Genizah fragment, the Jewish masses in the declining but still magnificent Islamic metropolis became excited when the daughter of a physician, son of one Joseph, announced that she had seen Elijah and heard him announce the forthcoming liberation. The outcome was the imprisonment of Jewish leaders, who were freed only after the Caliph himself had a vision of Elijah. As usual, Jews had to pay a severe fine and, allegedly, the regulations concerning badges to be worn by *dhimmi* women were now sharpened.[67]

Apparently another independent movement arose in Kurdistan and its vicinity. Unlike other disturbances of that period, this agitation led to the revival of military ventures to secure the restoration of Jews to Palestine. Long known from a brief hearsay report by Benjamin of Tudela, this movement under the leadership of David Alroy (Al-Ro'i) attracted wide attention and was later dramatized in a novel by Benjamin Disraeli. Much fuller, though even more distorted, is the hostile account by Samau'al ibn Yaḥya al-Maghribi, who saw in this commotion and its ultimate failure an opportunity to ridicule the Jewish gullibility and, to some extent, also the Jewish messianic expectations as such.

Further information is available in a Genizah fragment published by Mann.[68]

From these often confused and contradictory accounts it appears that in the days of the powerful Egyptian vizier Al-Afdhal (Abu'l Qasim Shahanshah, died 1121), one Solomon ben Duji of Khazaria, acting in cooperation with his son Menahem and a Palestinian scribe, Ephraim ben Azariah ibn Sahalun, sent out letters to various communities announcing the forthcoming ingathering of the exiles from all lands under his own leadership. We are not informed about the practical measures he proposed to take in order to accomplish this plan. Many years later (probably about 1147), we hear again, this time from his son Menahem or David al-Ro'i or al-Roḥi (both first names are equally messianic) who, through an appeal to the Jews of Adharbaijan, assembled around him a substantial Jewish armed force. At first, it appears, the local Muslim commanders viewed that movement calmly, even benevolently. We recall that when Imad ad-Din Zangi reconquered Edessa from the Christians in 1146, thus marking in some ways the beginning of the end of the Latin Kingdom, he transplanted 300 Jewish families there to replace departing Christian Armenians. Probably Alroy and the Jews of Amadia, a strategically located fortress northeast of Mosul, whose anti-Christian feelings were especially stressed by Samau'al, readily cooperated with the Muslims against the Christian rulers of the Holy Land. But perhaps utilizing the confusion arising from Zangi's assassination soon thereafter, Alroy, by magic or trickery, took possession of Amadia. From there he may have hoped to conquer Edessa and, utilizing the unceasing hostilities between the resuscitated Muslim armies and the slowly disintegrating powers of the Crusader principalities, to fight his way through to the Holy Land. He also dispatched messengers to many communities, including that of Baghdad, to prepare the ground for this military march. Possibly going beyond their orders, the messengers instructed the Baghdad Jews on a certain night to assemble on their roof tops whence they would be miraculously flown to the Messiah. Unbelievable though this may sound to modern readers, many members of that highly sophisticated community, lent a willing ear to this unusual demand, and spent that night on their roofs awaiting the miraculous flight. The next day, of course, this much-publicized stunt became the subject of general derision. Whatever their own attitude may have been at the inception of the movement, the exilarch and the head of the academy had no choice now but to disavow it and threaten its initiators with a ban. At the same time the Persian Jews were threatened with severe retaliation by the local authorities. With their apparent cooperation, the district governor bribed David's father-in-law, who allegedly assassinated the leader in his sleep. Nonetheless the northern Jews retained the memory of Alroy in great reverence and, when Benjamin arrived there some twenty years later, they still spoke lovingly of their dead leader. According to Samau'al, "the Jews of Amadia still praise him in many assemblies, and there are people among them who view him as their expected messiah. I have seen Persian Jewish communities in Khoi, Slamas, Tabriz, and Maragha [all in northwestern Iran, not too far from Amadia], who mention his name during their highest adoration. . . . In that city [Amadia] there is a congregation professing a faith which, they claim, emanated from that swindler, Menahem." [69]

With the aid of astrological computations one could prove almost any date as the likely time for the advent of the Messiah. Because some astrologers messianically interpreted an existing stellar constellation, Yemenite Jewry was prepared to listen to the preachment of a rather simple-minded miracle worker who claimed to be the Messiah. It was this episode which induced Jacob ben Nathaniel al-Fayyumi to send his inquiry to Maimonides, the latter's *Epistle to Yemen* becoming the only truly enduring monument to that unfortunate venture. The jurist-philosopher was not surprised at either the appearance of the pseudo-messiah, whom he considered an obvious mental case, or at the latter's ignorant followers who thus found comfort in their tribulations. But he rebuked his learned questioner for failing to realize that the Redeemer must be "a very eminent prophet, more illustrious than all the prophets after Moses." He advised the communal leaders to place the pretender in chains for a while, until the Gentiles might learn that he was a demented person. "If you procrastinate until they learn of this affair of their own accord, you will most likely incur their wrath." From another epistle of the sage of Fusṭaṭ, written some twenty-two years later, we learn that his advice was not heeded.

> Finally after a year he was taken into custody, and all his adherents fled. When the Arab king who had seized him inquired, "What have you done?" he replied, "Indeed, I have done it in truth and at God's behest." When the king demanded proof, he added: "If you sever my head, I shall immediately be revived." The king exclaimed: "I do not need any better evidence than that. [If that miracle comes true] not only I, but the whole world will acknowledge the error of our ancestral faith." Whereupon they immediately killed the poor fellow. May his death be an expiation for him and for all Israel. The Jews of many localities paid a fine. Yet there still are some fools who believe in his early resurrection.

With this melancholy observation Maimonides concluded his sad narrative, to him but another testimony to the frequently irrational behavior of the uneducated masses, which could only be cured by the spread of enlightenment and the reign of reason.[70]

UNITY WITHIN DIVERSITY

In this way Judaism weathered another great internal crisis. Emerging in the sixth century weakened in numbers as well as in intellectual and spiritual strength, having lost its effective central leadership in both Palestine and Babylonia, and confronted with ever deepening sectarian struggles in its Christian and later also in its Muslim environment, the Jewish people revealed an enormous tenacity in resisting both the tremendous external pressures and the powerful centrifugal forces in its own midst. Under the impact of Mohammed's successful challenge to the existing political and religious order, there arose in the following two centuries a number of sectarian movements in Judaism, too. They were as a rule accompanied by messianic pretensions of their leaders. Conversely, when before and after that sectarian outburst some purely messianic movements emerged within the orthodox body, most of these smacked of some heterodoxy, or were driven to it by the resistance of the established leadership. Yet what is truly amazing is not the frequency of commotions of either kind, but rather their relative paucity and historical insignificance. With all the research hitherto done by modern scholars, intensely interested in any form of Jewish heterodoxy as well as in yearnings for the return to Zion, only about half a dozen non-Karaite heresiarchs and less than a score of messianic pretenders, including all the former, are known to us by name in the long and crucial period of seven centuries following the religious consolidation of the Babylonian Talmud.

With the sole exception of the Karaites, none of these movements left behind any enduring heritage. It was a lucky coincidence for modern research that, perhaps stimulated by the example set by Muslim historians of religion who had recognized that sectarian divergences touched the very core of Islam's religious and political life, Qirqisani found it necessary to describe briefly the heterodox trends apparent also in contemporary Judaism. But his own description showed how little this disparity mattered in world Jewish life during the mid-tenth century. Most of the sects enumerated by him had either disappeared or dwindled to as little as twenty members. At the same time, he did convey the idea of a great spiritual effervescence and widespread religious quests in the eastern communities, from which both Karaite and Rabbanite Judaism ultimately received many valuable stimuli. Similarly, we would have known very little about the messianic movements from Moses of Crete to the demented pretender in Yemen, were it not for Socrates' polemically inspired narrative or the equally fortuitous circumstance that the Yemenite disturbance induced a leader to question Maimonides. This inquiry stimulated the latter to offer both an exposition of his messianic doctrine and a number of illuminating illustrations from the then recent past. That section of his *Epistle,* moreover, appeared so inconsequential to his Hebrew translators and many copyists of the Arabic text, that, despite the author's extraordinary popularity, only one more or less complete copy is extant today.

At the same time the messianic *idea* played an enormous role in Judaism. Throughout the ages it remained the cynosure of all Jewish eyes, and most thinkers and poets tried to add some new little insights or new formulations to the people's undying hope. Yet the same Hai Gaon, who composed one of the most eloquent restatements of that hope, found no occasion to deal with any of its practical aspects or actual messianic movements during his long life. At least none are mentioned in the more than one thousand responsa attributed to him. Even the earlier geonim rarely dealt with contemporary sectarian or messianic trends, unless they happened to be asked, as was Naṭronai I, about the legal aspects of readmission of some such errant individuals to the orthodox fold. None of these heresiarchs or messianic pretenders, moreover, seems to have been articulate enough to leave behind writings of his own; probably because most of them were unlearned. Even Moses al-Dar'i, whom Maimonides grudgingly recognized as a man of "piety, virtue, and learning," is known to us only at second hand. We may discount the possibility, unsupported by any intimation in the sources, that some sectarian writings may once have existed but were suppressed by the official leaders, for even less than the state authorities was the Jewish community able to impose an effective book censorship upon its members. Its main weapon, the excommunication of an offender, must have proved entirely ineffectual in the case of professed dissidents, whose doctrines were in any case anathemized by the rabbis. Whenever sectarian chiefs were learned and articulate, as in the case of the Karaite authors, much of their literary heritage was transmitted to posterity. Perhaps this was, indeed, the main weakness of the other sectarian and messianic spokesmen. No one seems to have been able enduringly to influence the "people of the book," unless he, or his immediate disciples (as in the later instances of Isaac Luria or Israel Ba'al Shem Tob), made a significant and appealing literary contribution which in some way enriched the literary and intellectual patrimony of his people.[71]

Precisely because the sectarian differences mattered so little in the long run, Shahrastani, who seems to have made a genuine effort to ascertain the whereabouts and teachings of the various Jewish heterodoxies, was able to supply so little solid information. He may have allotted equal space to the 'Isawites and Yudghanites as to the 'Ananites (Karaites) and Samaritans, and called all four "the best known and most widespread" Jewish sects. But he could not conceal the fact that in his day the former were mere historical curiosities. He certainly could not even remotely itemize the seventy-one sects which, he claimed, had existed within the Jewish religion. In his summary, moreover, he admitted that all Jews, regardless of their sectarian divergence, believed in monotheism, the uniqueness of the Torah revealed to Moses, the observance of the Sabbath, and the coming of the Messiah, "the shining star, which will illumine the world." We may agree with this Muslim student of religion that, indeed, all Jews of his time, were "waiting for him and the Sabbath [which] is his day," for, as some Jews explained, the universe was to endure only for six thousand years, to be followed by the cosmic Sabbath of redemption. Notwithstanding their endless sufferings and the unceasing frustrations of all their petty messianic ventures, their unshakable faith in the ultimate coming of the Redeemer, under one guise or another, remained their perennial source of strength and endurance.

XXVI

KARAITE SCHISM

NONE of these sectarian movements achieved intellectual respectability. Hence apart from splinter groups on the Iranian Plateau and Damascus, all of them were quite ephemeral. Certainly, none exercised strong appeal on the Jewries of Babylonia, Palestine, or Egypt, which were still making Jewish history at large. The overshadowing issue of the day, the extent to which the Jewries of the far-flung empire were ready to submit to a uniform Oral Law and its authoritative interpretation by the Babylonian academies, could not be resolved by such haphazard and erratic measures. The inner divisions in the Byzantine communities had already been responsible not only for Justinian's insistence on the use by the Jewish congregations of Greek and other versions alongside of the Hebrew Bible and his threat of expulsion of those rationalistic Jews who denied resurrection, the last judgment, or the angels being created by God, but also for his sharp outlawry of the study of Oral Law (*deuterosis*). These divisions now increased in magnitude and vehemence among the disjointed communities of the vast Caliphate.

Stirred to their depths by the world-shaking rise of the new religion and empire, the Jews could not remain unimpressed by the heated controversies among their Muslim neighbors about the genuineness of certain traditions allegedly going back to Mohammed, and even about the very fundamentals of the relation between tradition and Scripture. They must have heard their neighbors quoting many such traditions with respect to the Jewish status or religious convictions, which, they knew, were mutually exclusive and, often, intrinsically false. Many a questioning mind doubtless deduced therefrom that perhaps many Jewish traditions were equally spurious. The spectacle of distinguished Muslim theologians traveling hundreds of miles in search of "genuine" traditions within a few generations after the Messenger's death, and the endless casuistic quarrels between schools and individuals as to which of the various "chains of tradition" were to be accepted and which utterly repudiated, were not lost on inquisitive Jews, too. The more impatient some of these Jewish members of the rapidly growing Arabic-speaking intelligentsia became with the slow rhythm of legal and doctrinal adjustments of their ancestral faith to the revolutionary transformations in general society and culture, the more prepared they were to throw off the shackles of a confining tradition, whose divine origin they now seriously questioned.

'ANAN

A new impetus was given to these heterodox currents when 'Anan ben David appeared on the scene. Apparently a long-time resident of some eastern province, he returned to Babylonia where he became the disciple of Yehudai Gaon, the leading scholar of the generation. As the eldest son of David, brother of the reigning exilarch Isaac, he seems to have considered himself a crown prince, with all the glamor attached to a prospective head of all Jewry. He developed certain traits of "haughtiness and fearlessness" which made him obnoxious to the ruling circles at the academies. Evidently of independent mind, he was also suspected of heretical leanings. When upon the exilarch's death a successor was to be chosen, the academies, disregarding custom, passed over 'Anan in favor of his younger, evidently more pliable, brother Ḥananiah (about 767).

'Anan's refusal to accept meekly this decision of the scholarly leaders set in motion a chain of developments which ultimately resulted in the formation of the Karaite sect. Since he refused to recognize his brother's election, despite its approval by the caliph, he was thrown into prison for insubordination. Here he was allegedly saved from impending execution by the counsel of a fellow-prisoner, the distinguished Muslim jurist, Abu Ḥanifa. This founder of one of the great schools of Muslim jurisprudence advised him to declare himself head of an independent sect. From its inception the Caliphate had learned to be tolerant of sectarian diversity. Moreover, 'Anan emphasized that one of the main differences between his point of view and that of the other Jewish leaders related to the vital question of the Jewish calendar. While the majority had chosen to follow a perpetual, astronomically computed sequence of months, he wished to revert to the original biblical form of proclaiming new moons on the basis of actual observation. This contention, we are told, struck a responsive chord in the caliph's heart, because this method corresponded to prevailing Muslim practice.[1]

Whatever one thinks of the historicity of this narrative, it gives us in a nutshell the main issues which soon began to differentiate the Karaite group from the Rabbanite majority. Beginning with the political struggle for succession—a major factor in the rise of almost all Muslim sects—it soon turned into a conflict relating to the authoritative control over the whole domain of Jewish *law*. Like Abu Ḥanifa, 'Anan may merely have intended to establish another school of jurisprudence, rather than a sect. That is why he evidently refrained from injecting any serious dogmatic deviations from orthodox Judaism. He was supposed to have written a book on the transmigration of the soul. But there is no evidence that either he or any of his followers considered this belief an article of faith sufficiently different from the general Jewish system of beliefs to create a serious schism. Nor did this problem ever assume in Jewish life the importance ascribed to it, for example, by some radical wings in the Shi'a. There were, on the other hand, many pious Rabbanite Jews who in later generations shared this belief, while an outstanding Karaite thinker like Qirqisani devoted an entire chapter in his book to arguments against it.[2]

The main issue soon became whether in all legal matters Judaism must follow the decisions made by the Palestino-Babylonian academies of the talmudic age. More, whether it must accept, without demurrer, the cumulative interpretation of these decisions by the accredited successors of those ancient academicians. Within the Jewish faith legal deviation easily turned into sectarian separation.

Calendar problems lent themselves particularly well to the drawing of a line of demarcation between the reformers and the orthodox majority. As we recall, actual observation had been universally accepted practice until the middle of the fourth century when, largely under outside pressures, Hillel II proclaimed a perpetual calendar. Even then, however, observation was not altogether abandoned, particularly in Palestine. More than a century and a half after 'Anan, we remember, the Rabbanite world was stirred to its depth by the Saadiah–Ben Meir controversy concerning the date to be set for the beginning of two months and the respective authority of the Palestinian or Babylonian leadership in making the ultimate decision. From this initial point the controversy could the more readily expand to the whole area of talmudic law, as the Talmud itself had not yet become that generally known and studied compendium of Jewish law which the geonim had just been endeavoring to make it. 'Anan must have found a good many attentive readers for his *Sefer ha-Miṣvot* (Book of Commandments), one of the first attempts of redefining the whole domain of Jewish law during the posttalmudic era. Unfortunately, only disjointed fragments of this work are now extant. It is difficult therefore to reconstruct its original compass and arrangement. But it is likely that he followed his teacher's example in grouping a number of laws together and commenting on them in some systematic order. Unlike the *Halakhot qeṣubot* attributed to Yehudai Gaon, 'Anan's legal compilation, of course, failed to invoke the testimony of talmudic sources, but reverted directly to the biblical text. By itself, however, such reversion to the Scriptural origins of each law and the quest to trace therefrom the manifold ramifications were not necessarily heterodox. Did not Aḥai of Shabḥa, Yehudai's contemporary and possibly elder colleague, likewise attempt to reformulate at least parts of the Jewish law in the form of a legal commentary on the Pentateuch? [3]

In contrast to Aḥai and other Rabbanites, however, 'Anan placed the Prophets and Hagiographa on a par with the Pentateuch. In this way he considerably broadened the base for his independent deductions. By enjoining his followers (at least according to a later tradition) to "Search well in the Torah," he may merely have voiced a variation of Ben Bag Bag's well-known saying, "Turn it [the Torah] over and over in your mind, for everything is in it." Nor was this substantially at variance with the attitude of the Muslim jurist Shafi'i, who, according to one of his outstanding followers, "forbade anyone to follow him or anyone else." But 'Anan's became a fighting slogan, calling for the return to the original sources and the total discard of talmudic accretions. It shouted defiance against any established authority, and demanded the free exercise of individual discretion in independently deriving the truth hidden in the words of Scripture.[4]

Clearly, this did not mean simple adherence to the literal sense of the biblical text. Even the ancient Sadducees and Samaritans had no longer been able to regulate their lives on the basis of the succinct and obviously incomplete summaries of ancient legal practice recorded in the Bible. 'Anan followed the logic of circumstances, rather than consciously emulating the rabbis, when they interpreted Scripture with the aid of those hermeneutic categories of thinking which were inherent in the mind of any Near Eastern reader when he tried to penetrate the full meaning of a revered text. Without the slightest compunction, he employed the more important hermeneutic rules, the *middot*, as formulated by Hillel and the school of Rabbi Ishmael. He made extensive use not only of the syllogism and the logical analogy (*qol vehomer* and *binyan ab*), but he went much further than the rabbis in utilizing the verbal analogy (*gezerah shavah*) and the hints allegedly given by the Bible through the insertion of apparently superfluous letters or words (including the preposition *et*). Whether or not he was also influenced therein by Abu Ḥanifa's predilection for the *qi'as* (analogy), he went to great lengths in using the related, though not identical, Jewish method of *heqqesh* which had, together with its Hellenistic counterpart, served as the matrix of the Muslim juristic mode.

Much has been made by modern critics of Karaism of the alleged inconsistency between the latter's universal repudiation of the rabbinic Oral Law and the necessary reliance of its teachers on rabbinic modes of interpretation. In fact, however, none of the Karaites ever claimed that one ought to restrict oneself to the literal sense of the biblical laws. Absolute literalness was hardly considered a virtue even by outright translators of Scripture from the Septuagint and the Aramaic Targumim down to the Arabic versions by Rabbanite, Karaite, or Christian authors. Neither 'Anan nor any of his early successors was at all self-conscious about using these basic and universally accepted methods of deducing more concealed lessons from the revealed texts. Later Karaites, too, spoke on the whole approvingly of the thirteen modes of R. Ishmael. The first to make any issue of it at all seems to have been Moses ben Elijah Bashyatchi of sixteenth-century Constantinople. This brilliant young scholar, long reputed to have died at the age of twenty-eight or even eighteen, not only quoted 'Anan as explicitly using at least two of these modes, but also declared on his own that "there are thirteen modes of interpreting the Torah, and we have accepted eleven of these." Naturally, deprived of the living flow of tradition, the Karaites had to try to squeeze out of the biblical texts even more practical guidance than was required by the early Pharisaic or Sadducee teachers, who had been both chronologically and topographically far less removed from the original biblical legislation and had faced far less complicated living conditions. That is why the Karaite jurists had to employ the available methodological tools much more extremely than did their Rabbanite counterparts. Hence the excessive use of, for example, the *heqqesh,* which had become a major necessity for 'Anan regardless of any stimuli he may have received from Abu Ḥanifa and other Muslims. But had not shortly before 'Anan, the Rabbanite jurist Aḥai of Shabḥa hermeneutically derived thirty-seven commandments from the narrative portions of Genesis? For the same reason the heresiarch and his successors also had to search for clues outside the Pentateuch (for example in Ezra) on a par with the Books of Moses themselves.[5]

Like many other jurists, 'Anan sometimes merely followed what he conscientiously regarded as the true interpretation of the sources. A technique of hermeneutic legal exegesis has logical sequences of its own, and 'Anan often adhered to them for no other apparent reason. In some other cases, he probably wanted to spite his opponents by advocating a particular objectionable deviation, as when he replaced the Ninth of Ab by two fast days of Ab 7 (as indeed one was to fast on the seventh day of every month) and Ab 10, enjoined his adherents to fast, rather than rejoice, during the Purim holidays, or forbade the consumption of any meat except that of deer and pigeons during Israel's life in Exile. By eliminating all *minima* of rabbinic law, he infinitely increased the destructive force of even the smallest particle of forbidden matter. He also insisted that circumcision must be performed with scissors, rather than a scalpel; otherwise the circumciser was guilty of a capital crime! 'Anan also prescribed other detailed minutiae for circumcision, without which the ritual was null and void and had to be repeated. He did not explain, however, how the main purpose, namely the removal of the *praeputium,* could be achieved on the second occasion. The doctrinaire slant of 'Anan's enactments is also illustrated by his statement, reported by Qirqisani, "that a man circumcised by a person who had not been operated upon in the same manner cannot be considered circumcised, and has to undergo a second operation." There is no record that either he or any of his immediate followers, evidently circumcised in their childhood in accordance with the Rabbanite ritual, ever submitted themselves to a new operation so as to be able to circumcise others, or that any kind of ritual accompanied the conversion of born Rabbanites to Karaism in later generations.[6]

In many cases 'Anan seems to have accepted a local custom known to him from observation, hearsay or existing literature. He listened with rapt attention to those heretical Jews whose allegorical interpretation of the biblical *le-ṭoṭafot* (frontlets; Deut. 6:8) had completely nullified the commandment of phylacteries and who had been severely chastised by a gaon, possibly Yehudai. He must have known of many more regional variations in usage and ritual, particularly in those eastern provinces where he had spent some years, than are familiar to us from the few chance records now extant. He paid special attention to those numerous differences between Palestine and Babylonia which, recognized by the very rabbis, admirably lent themselves as a proof against the authenticity of a single revealed Oral Law. He may well have taken over a good deal also from those "Sadducean" writings which, as we recall, were still circulating in his day, and which doubtless contained a great many modifications of the genuine teachings of ancient sectarians. Without much ado, he shifted, for example, the observance of the Festival of Weeks to the Sunday following the seventh Sabbath after Passover. He was apparently familiar with some Samaritan customs and perhaps even with some residua of the ancient New Covenanters and other sects.

Perhaps in consonance with them he strictly forbade the marriage between an uncle and a niece and interpreted the prohibition, "And thou shalt not take a woman to her sister . . . in her lifetime" (Lev. 18:18), as referring to a wife's niece, rather than sister. The latter was, namely, forbidden even after the wife's decease, because a woman must no more marry the widowed husband of her sister than a man may marry his brother's widow. Adhering strictly to this interpretation, 'Anan insisted that, as in the case of Boaz and Ruth, not a brother, but a more remote male relative was obliged to serve as levir. 'Anan seems also to have carefully studied whatever writings of Philo of Alexandria, or paraphrases thereof, had come down to his age. That is perhaps why so many of his legal postulates agreed with what may be reconstructed as the Philonic *halakhah* wherever the latter was at variance with the teachings of the ancient rabbis.[7]

THREE APPROACHES

In most cases, however, 'Anan, like other religious reformers, utilized the new technique to justify measures he wished to see adopted because of his particular socioreligious biases. It is not easy to reconstruct a uniform pattern from the few extant fragments of his works. Nonetheless, certain basic traits seem to color his entire approach to Jewish law and life. These may perhaps best be subsumed under the three complementary headings of religious self-abnegation, extreme nationalism, and metropolitan individualism.

Apparently not an ascetic in the usual sense, seeking mortification of the flesh as a good per se, 'Anan nevertheless heaped prohibition upon prohibition which, when pushed to their logical conclusions, became unbearable even to his most ardent followers. Apart from the aforementioned fast days, he decreed, apparently under the influence of the Muslim month of Ramadan, that a pious Jew must observe an annual seventy-day fast from the 13th of Nisan to the 23d of Sivan. There is no evidence that this ever became accepted practice in any Karaite community. More widely shared was his rigid interpretation of the Sabbath rest commandment. Because he considered fire left burning after sunset as a continuous process of the human work involved in its previous kindling, many Karaite communities were and still are plunged in total darkness every Friday night. Some of his successors merely debated the problem as to whether the extinguishing of a candle left burning accidentally was a lesser transgression than allowing it to burn to the end. All Karaites, however, at least to the end of the Middle Ages, uniformly repudiated the popular Rabbanite equation, expressed by the author of Midrash Tanḥuma perhaps in overt defiance of such ascetic trends, " 'And call the Sabbath a delight,' that is kindling a light on the Sabbath." In fact, the homilist, quoting the Mishnah, counted failure to kindle such lights among the three transgressions for which women die in childbirth.[8]

Rejecting the rabbinic doctrine of the primacy of positive over negative commandments, 'Anan also forbade circumcision on the eighth day which happened to be a Sabbath or—a purely antiquarian reference to Rabbanite Jewry though not to Samaritans —the sacrifice of the Paschal lamb on a Sabbath which happened to fall on the 14th of Nisan. In fact, he was prepared to postpone the celebration of Passover (as well as of the Feast of Tabernacles) from Saturday to Sunday. The biblical demand that unleavened bread be "bread of poverty," he interpreted to mean that it must be the "poor man's bread" and, hence, made of barley. Eating "unleavened wheat bread," he is reported as saying, "is just as [sinful as] eating leaven" (Harkavy, *Zikhron,* VIII, 72 f., 77, 132 f.).

Of course, demanding strict observation of the new moon, 'Anan completely discarded the rabbinic rule that the first day of Passover could never be a Monday, Wednesday, or Friday, but he left open the question of how one could avoid the result that the subsequent Day of Atonement would fall on a Friday or Sunday and cause much hardship to Karaite worshipers. 'Anan also gave a curious twist to the phrase, "In plowing time and in harvest thou shalt rest" (Exod. 34:21) and explained it as a prohibition of sexual intercourse on the Sabbath, defying a widespread preference among Rabbanite Jews. He also interpreted the biblical phrase of a husband and wife becoming "one flesh" (Gen. 2:24) so literally as to prohibit unions between any close relatives of a husband with any of his wife's close relations, while

Rabbanite Jewry until the present day often witnesses the marriages of two brothers to two sisters. On occasion a more literal reading of a scriptural prohibition induced ʿAnan to alleviate an existing practice. He eliminated phylacteries, though not the showfringes, and reduced the required daily services to two rather than three, largely substituting scriptural lessons and psalms for the existing liturgy. But much of that liberality was more apparent than real. When he permitted, for example, the simultaneous consumption of meat and milk, such alleviation was almost meaningless in practice because of his nearly total outlawry of meat until the rebuilding of Jerusalem. Similarly, any doubts entertained by his successors concerning the prohibition of wine touched by a Gentile were purely theoretical, since no observant ʿAnanite was supposed to imbibe any wine during the days of the Exile.[9]

The daily recitation of scriptural lessons, as well as psalms, was instituted by ʿAnan himself. He enjoined his followers to recite on every weekday the biblical section relating to the daily sacrifice at the Temple (Num. 28:2 ff.). But he omitted, of course, the daily reading of the more elaborate Mishnaic description of the sacrificial practices at the Temple, known by its initial words, *Ezehu meqoman* (Which Is the Place?), and the enumeration of the thirteen modes of interpretation by the school of R. Ishmael, which may already at that time have been inserted into some Rabbanite prayer books. On the other hand, these rabbinic passages may have owed their liturgical function precisely to the Rabbanite reaction to Karaite, or pre-Karaite, opposition to Oral Law. ʿAnan also formulated a number of new benedictions and generally ordered his adherents to pray "with fear and trepidation." Nevertheless, it is difficult to reconstruct from the few extant sources the form and content of Karaite divine services in the days of ʿAnan and his early successors. Very likely here, too, great leeway was left to individual preferences.[10]

Doubts concerning the outlawry of Gentile wine need not reflect friendliness toward Gentile nations, although ʿAnan's general attitude in this respect was so ambivalent that it became an easy target for Rabbanite accusations of duplicity. On the one hand, he accepted the Muslim type of lunar month and long-term fast period. More, according to a later tradition reported by Maqrizi (doubtless from Karaite sources), he was prepared (together with the Tiflisites and Yudghanites) to recognize the work of Jesus for Christianity, and the prophetic mission of Mohammed for Islam. Since his ardent nationalism did not tolerate the idea that Jews should ever have been enslaved by other Jews, he anticipated some of the modern discussion on the *Ḥabiru-'Ibri* problem, and contended that the "Hebrew" slave in the Bible really was a "descendant of Abraham" from issue other than Isaac or Jacob. He was thus advocating favored treatment and but temporary bondage for all Ishmaelite or Arab slaves.[11]

On the other hand, he preached total segregation of Jews from Gentiles. He forbade, for example, the consumption even of milk milked or water warmed by a Gentile. Going further than anything demanded by the Samaritans and New Covenanters, he insisted that not only should Jews stay within the confines of their quarters on Sabbath but that in cities with non-Jewish inhabitants —and there existed no all-Jewish city in his day—Jews should not leave their respective dwellings, except for such necessary walks as visits to the synagogue. Perhaps influenced by the New Covenanters' discriminating treatment of proselytes, 'Anan also demanded that new converts or slaves should be circumcised only by other converts or slaves with utensils prepared by converts or slaves, respectively. He even subscribed to the stricter of two rabbinic interpretations of Num. 15:38, which sought to discourage the preparation of showfringes by non-Jews. In a characteristic passage of his Book of Commandments he inquired about the reason why the biblical lawgiver had found it necessary to add the general injunction, "Ye shall keep my statutes" (Lev. 19:19), in connection with the specific prohibition of *kil'ayim* (mixtures of two unrelated kinds).

It is to enjoin them [he explained]: Make an effort to study the Torah and to separate yourselves from the Gentiles, just as I command you to separate *kil'ayim* from one another. It is also written, "Make confession unto the Lord . . . [and separate yourselves from the people of the land, and from the foreign women," Ezra 10:17]. He [Ezra] enjoined them in two matters: Separate yourselves from the illiterate people ['*amme ha-areṣ*] and do not live among them. Similarly if you have a wife who does not conform with your practice . . . even a father, mother, brothers or children who do not serve Heaven in a way similar to ours, we are obliged to separate ourselves from them, as it is written, "Who said to his father and his mother: ['I have not seen him'; neither did he acknowledge his brethren, nor knew he his own children," Deut. 33:9]. So long as Israel mixes with Gentiles this causes them to imitate the ways of the Gentile nations, as it is written, "But mingled themselves with the nations, [and learned their works," Ps. 106:35]. Any Jew who does not fulfill the commands of the Torah is called a Gentile, as we have explained. And it is our duty to segregate ourselves from them, and we ought to live together in one place, as it is written, "Gather My saints together unto Me" [Ps. 50:5]. And if we do it, the Merciful One distinguishes us before Him, as it is written, "And ye shall be holy unto Me [for I the Lord am holy, and have severed you from other people, that ye should be Mine," Lev. 20:26].

In short, segregation was 'Anan's remedy for the main ills: segregation from the Gentile world, segregation from the illiterate masses, and segregation from the impious in one's own community.[12]

Physical banishment and the concomitant mental anguish were also to be the main instruments of enforcement of the communal will. Going further than his Rabbanite contemporaries in the use of the anathema, 'Anan taught that any recalcitrant party refusing a summons to appear before a Jewish court of justice should be kept in complete isolation until he complied. A person guilty of a capital crime, whom an exilic court was in no position to execute, was to be boycotted by his community permanently without any chance for a reprieve—a rule adopted also by Rabbanite jurists such as Naṭronai, Palṭoi, and most clearly by Maimonides.[13]

In all this 'Anan was anything but a typical heresiarch. In fact, there is no evidence that he ever undertook to spread his views among the masses. All he seems to have attempted was to organize a number of like-minded intellectuals into a group recognizing him as the legitimate exilarch and throwing off the shackles of the much resented academic leadership. Even his extreme nationalism was not of the activist messianic kind characteristic of the other more overtly sectarian movements of the time. None of the sources records 'Anan's espousal of a military uprising or even his theoretical claim to the mantle of the Messiah. As a recognized scion of the house of David—several generations later there still circulated genealogical lists tracing his descent back in direct lineage to Rehoboam and Solomon—he was in a much better position to find believers in his messianic call than were such obscure chieftains as Abu 'Isa or Severus. But he obviously made no such claims; they probably would have appeared incongruous to the main group of his adherents among the disgruntled intellectuals of Baghdad. Convinced that Palestine could not be considered the "land of the Lord" until it was under Jewish domination, he did not even advocate the return there by pious individuals. His own ultimate settlement in the Holy Land was but a wishful invention of later Palestinian Karaites. In his day he envisaged only segregated, autonomous living in the various countries of Jewish settlement, and somewhat incongruously anticipated the thinking of modern "diaspora nationalists." [14]

His main appeal to the metropolitan intelligentsia also colored some of his other teachings. His insistence upon individual conscience and individual interpretation of Scripture must have appealed greatly to many students of the Law, in whom the rising tides of rationalism and the ceaseless debates on the meaning and validity of the Qur'anic revelation among their Arab neighbors had undermined the simple, unquestioning acceptance of traditional concepts. His own approach may have been unscientific by the standards of his day and, in many ways, even antirationalist, but there were a great many others like him in the metropolitan Jewish intellegentsia. Some of them gladly subscribed even to his extreme "biblicism," so long as it freed them from the chains of uncritical acceptance of the existing law.

If 'Anan had ever given thought to the long-range implications of his expanded doctrine of incest, he might have realized that before long his adherents living in smaller communities would find it difficult to secure mates not related to them in any of the newly prohibited degrees of consanguinity. But he apparently envisaged only a relatively small metropolitan following which would retain an ample selection within the ever growing Jewish population of a city like Baghdad. Similarly, he took cognizance of the general new attitudes toward marriage and divorce, based upon individual preference by bridegroom and bride rather than their parents, and the new position of women in the metropolitan society. He defied, therefore, not only tradition but also fairly explicit statements in the Bible, and demanded that parents should not marry off children without the latter's consent, and that both husband and wife might demand divorce on the basis of simple incompatibility. Such freedom on the part of women was unheard of in the Jewish community since the days of the Elephantine soldiers. Less radical, but likewise typical of the newly acquired status of women, was 'Anan's denial of the husband's automatic rights of inheritance of his wife's estate. All this was evidently designed to meet the desires of a few patrician ladies much more than those of the rank and file of Jewish women. It carried little appeal even to 'Anan's direct successors in the leadership of the sect.[15]

'ANANITES AND KARAITES

It is small wonder, then, that upon 'Anan's death only a small group of " 'Ananites" carried on the teachings of their master. In the first place they recognized his son, Saul (like 'Anan, a former disciple of Yehudai Gaon) as their true exilarch. Although located in the capital, the new group seems to have played but a minor role in the Jewish community. In 825, however, Saul's son, Daniel, once again contested the election of the exilarch by the heads of the academies and declared himself the only legitimate prince of the whole captivity of Israel. This dispute, as we recall, induced Caliph Al-Ma'mun to issue his memorable decree proclaiming the right of any group of unbelievers to set itself up as an independent community. This decree may indeed have widened the breach between the two groups and helped gradually to convert the 'Ananite conventicles into a permanent schism.[16]

Differences between the two groups were further sharpened by the progressive dissolution of the Caliphate and the concomitant decline of the Babylonian Jewish leadership. Under the Tulunide semi-independent rule of Palestine (868–905), especially, the descendants of Josiah, another son of Saul ben 'Anan who had in the meantime removed to Jerusalem, actually enjoyed the patronage of the new rulers. The Tulunide "governors" doubtless thus wished to undermine the authority of the Babylonian organs controlled by their enemies in Baghdad. By the beginning of the tenth century these 'Ananite "princes of captivity" had become so well entrenched in the Holy City that they could venture to cause the arrest and flagellation of the outstanding Rabbanite leader, Aaron Ben Meir. Jerusalem itself had by then become the world center of the new movement, and it was from there that its leader, Daniel al-Qumisi, issued his memorable appeal for Jewish mass immigration to the ancestral land.[17]

Spiritually, too, the movement made great strides as a result of the literary activity of Benjamin ben Moses Nahawendi (of Nihavend in Media, already called "sick" or heretical by the ancient sages; about 830–60), its outstanding theologian and, in many respects, its cofounder and chief organizer. Unlike Paul, however, Benjamin was quite critical of the founder himself. Serving as a judge in the rather difficult Iranian community of Nahawend, he had to pay heed to many practical considerations. That is perhaps why as a jurist, he was often more moderate than 'Anan, and eliminated many of the master's more extravagant interpretations. While maintaining the prohibition of keeping lights burning on the Sabbath, he granted greater freedom of movement within the city precincts and permitted sexual intercourse, as well as the performance of such positive commandments as circumcision or the sacrifice of a Paschal lamb on that day. He also allowed the consumption of fruit plucked on the Sabbath by a Gentile acting on his own initiative. With respect to circumcision, Benjamin reverted to the use of scalpels, removed the obligation of circumcising adults only on the eighth day of a month, and abolished, by way of a different interpretation of what happened in the days of Joshua, 'Anan's curious argument in favor of second operations. While maintaining the woman's right to circumcise her child, he restored the husband's hereditary right in the wife's estate. Above all, he wished to uphold the solidarity of the group and more explicitly than 'Anan insisted on the use of excommunication against Jews repairing to Gentile courts. In his desire to strengthen the authority of the Law, he went even to the curious extreme of demanding that children be made subject to all commandments as soon as they were able to speak. He was generally harsh on children. He not only restored the exclusive right of fathers and guardians to marry off even adult girls, but he also was a strong believer in severe physical chastisement of children by parents and teachers. He actually advocated a vast extension of this prerogative to include employers flogging their employees and husbands beating their wives. More, he reintroduced the ancient Israelitic debt bondage for defaulted debtors and their children. This residuum of ancient corporate responsibility had fallen into desuetude for many centuries. Benjamin, however, revived the biblical law (only limiting the seizure to "small children living in their parents' household") and applied it to the nonpayment of fines for thievery. The rabbis had long striven to delimit these biblical provisons by as literal and restrictive an interpretation as possible. The distinguished Karaite jurist of Nahawend, on the contrary, sought greatly to enlarge their scope. He expanded, for example, the biblical penalty of a fivefold return of the value of a stolen ox to all other household animals from camels to donkeys.[18]

On the other hand, at least according to later Karaite authorities, Benjamin went out of his way in protecting the rights of sons of unloved wives. Perhaps responding to the new freedom of Jewish women, he also insisted, against regnant rabbinic opinion, that a betrothed girl required no writ of divorce. Another moral victory for the deep sensitivities of his feminine contemporaries was his declaration that "levirate is obligatory only in regard to a female slave," thereby reducing to a minimum the range of these much-resented marriages. By implication he also undermined the old rabbinic prohibition of unions with unenfranchised slave girls, although he technically accepted the traditional law of prohibiting such unions until after the delivery of a formal writ of manumission in accordance with Jewish (not state) law. His views concerning the Jewish calendar were equally unconventional. He suggested a calendar reform which, in so far as we can judge from incompletely preserved fragments, would have introduced straight thirty day months except in Nisan and Tishre, for which, on account of the holidays, actual observation was to be retained.[19]

In all these demands Benjamin was anything but dogmatic, however. Even more than 'Anan he took seriously the right of each individual to interpret the Law in accordance with his own lights. He insisted that he was neither a prophet nor the son of a prophet, and that his readers were fully entitled to differ with him. In fact, no father, he insisted, had the right to censure a son for an honest difference of opinion, and each true investigator would be rewarded from Heaven even for a mistaken judgment honestly arrived at (Harkavy, *Zikhron,* p. 176). He concluded his brief treatise on civil law with the following characteristic message:

I, Benjamin ben Moses, send heartfelt greetings to all the sons of the Dispersion, together with all the saints [*ṣaddiqim,* a synonym for members of the Karaite group]. I am but dust and ashes under the soles of your feet. I have composed this small law book only for your benefit, so that you, O Men of Scripture! [this seems to be the first mention of the designation of the new sect as *ba'ale miqra* or Karaites] may pass judgments on your brothers and friends. For every law I have referred to its source in Scripture. If for some other legal cases adjudicated among, and recorded by, Rabbanites I was unable to supply the scriptural authority, I have nevertheless decided to write them down here so that you may, if you so desire, apply them in your judgments.

In some respects more significant were Benjamin's contributions to Karaite theology and Bible exegesis. Although none of his Bible commentaries is extant today, he seems to have initiated this branch of literature for both Karaites and Rabbanites, and his example was followed by almost every distinguished Karaite writer of the following few generations. His religious outlook seems to have been no less nationalistic than that of 'Anan, although he, too, obviously displayed no symptoms of messianic megalomania. In fact, when in his commentary on Daniel he came to the crucial messianic prediction in 12:11–12, he merely interpreted the word *yamin* to mean years and thus computed the date of the arrival of the Redeemer at 1012 C.E., or about a century and a half after his own time (cited in Jephet ben 'Ali's *Commentary on the Book of Daniel,* pp. 151 f. [Arabic], 86 [English]).

Benjamin was the first medieval writer, however, to concern himself with the philosophic foundations of his faith and particularly with its cosmological problems. Even in his commentary on such an intrinsically skeptical book as Ecclesiastes he was more interested in "King Solomon's" hidden, mystic intentions than in the overt meaning of many passages. There is little doubt that he was familiar with the Philonic doctrine of intermediaries. His unquestioned adherence to the word of Scripture did not prevent him from interpreting away all the biblical anthropomorphisms by stating that all the works of Creation and every revelation of God to man were performed not by the Lord Himself, but rather by an intermediary power; indeed, a succession of powers. Apparently adopting some variation of the Neo-Platonic doctrine of emanation, he stated that from the Divine there first emanated the Throne (*kisse*), then the Glory (*kabod*) and, finally, the angels (*mal'akhim*) who became the true revealers of God's will to man. With this philosophic interpretation he evidently succeeded in meeting certain theological challenges in his immediate Iranian environment. At the same time, he raised the general level of the Karaite opposition to the accepted rabbinic doctrine by making it philosophically, as well as juridically, fully respectable.[20]

CACOPHONY OF DISSENT

On 'Anan's death the Karaite community seems to have been little more than a congerie of intellectuals opposing the existing regime. It expanded slowly into East and West, in response to both the heterodox trends in the eastern provinces and the renewed self-assertion of Palestinian Jewry. Only the memorable conflict between Daniel and David ben Yehudah and the legislative as well as organizational activity of Benjamin seems to have established it on firmer foundations. Perhaps to steal the thunder from the sectarian agitators David ben Yehudah tried, as we recall, to conciliate the Palestinians by recognizing their supreme authority in regulating the calendar. Probably at no time since the extinction of the patriarchate had a Babylonian leader written a letter like that sent out by David in 835. "We always," the exilarch here declared with respect to the calendar regulation, "rely on them [the Palestinians] so that Israel shall not break asunder into independent cliques. Therefore I and the heads of the academies and the rabbis and all Israel rely on the intercalation as dispatched by the scholars [of the Holy Land]." One can still detect between the lines of the exilarch's long argument his anxiety to meet more than half way the Palestinian susceptibilities. If both months of Marḥeshvan and Kislev 4595 had been declared "full" and hence Passover fell on Thursday, the Palestinians would have been forced to celebrate the new month of Nisan two days after the moon had become visible on their horizon. The Babylonian leaders evidently realized that, as long as the unity of the Jewish people could be maintained in the observance of the new moons and holidays, the breach need not be definitive.[21]

Conversely, the Karaites and other sectarian leaders often attacked the established order precisely in this most sensitive spot, where divergences in dates would make themselves immediately felt. Although far from agreeing among themselves on the length of the months and exclusive reliance on observation, the opponents were unanimous in repudiating the accepted system and, particularly, the overwhelming control exercised in this domain by the rabbinic authorities. In this sense, Naṭronai bar Hilai was right in accusing the new group of having "become a people apart."

Not that the Karaites had wished to become an independent sect. Reversing 'Anan's segregationist policies, his successors tried to appeal to the whole people. Benjamin had already addressed his civil code "to all the sons of the Dispersion," and encouraged the preservation of many existing customs and rabbinic decisions. He also realized the great drawback of 'Anan's Book of Commandments. Written in the Aramaic lingo of the Babylonian academies, this work of technical scholarship may have appealed to some restless students in Babylonia, but it hardly could become meaningful even to the upper classes of the far-flung dispersion, especially in Benjamin's own Persian environment. We shall see that, unlike Babylonia, Palestine had increasingly abandoned the use of Aramaic as a daily language. That is why Benjamin decided to write all his books in Hebrew. His example was followed by all his Karaite successors, except those who employed the still more popular medium of Judeo-Arabic.[22]

For several generations, Karaite leaders cherished the hope that sooner or later the majority of Jews would see the light. Elijah ben Abraham, the twelfth-century author of a treatise defining the "Difference between the Karaites and Rabbanites," repudiated, on the other hand, the Rabbanite boast "that their scholars are legion, whereas there are only one, two, or three Karaite sages, and how should the few be in the possession of the truth, rather than the many?" He pointed to the fact of the Jewish minority living among the Gentile nations, the examples of Joshua and Caleb facing the other ten spies and of Ezekiel's "men that sigh and that cry" (9:4) who unhesitatingly opposed the majority of Jerusalem's population before the destruction of the First Temple. At the same time he quoted a long array of Karaite authorities who had asserted that

although the Rabbanites are mistaken with respect to most commandments, they are our brethren and members of our faith, our soul being saddened by their error. For our Creator had said to the totality of Israel because of its repudiation of idolatry alone, "So will I also be for thee" [Hosea 3:3]. How much more ought we to do so! The Lord said all that, because there always is hope that their offspring will be genuine believers.[23]

To begin with there never existed any serious disagreement between the two groups with respect to the dogmatic fundamentals of their faith. Whatever Karaism may have owed to the survivals of Sadduceeism probably had reached the generations of 'Anan and Benjamin in such an attenuated form as to make them dogmatically indistinguishable from the rest of Jewry. Just as most Samaritans had long abandoned their opposition to the Jewish doctrines of the Hereafter, so probably did the remnants of ancient Sadduceeism. The rabbinic teachings of resurrection, the messianic future, and even the compromise between Providence and free will, much as they may have become difficult philosophic problems to be debated back and forth among the scholastics, no longer were living religious issues. After all, even Islam and Christianity had long accepted these basic solutions of Pharisaic Judaism. They could be elaborated and refined in detail, but they no longer were subjects of partisan controversies.

'Anan's speculations on the transmigration of souls and Benjamin's doctrine of intermediaries were semiphilosophic niceties, which could be either accepted or rejected equally by any Rabbanite or Karaite. In fact, they were sharply repudiated by Qirqisani and the latter also by Daniel ben Moses al-Qumisi (also called Al-Damaghani from his birthplace in Tabaristan), in point of time and dignity the third-ranking teacher of the new movement. Similarly the dogmatic elaboration of the Ten Commandments, attributed to Nissi ben Nuḥ, and, on a much broader canvas, by Hadassi, could have been accepted in all its basic points by any Rabbanite Jew as well. Later Karaites, like Elijah Bashyatchi formulated a ten-point credo which bore a striking resemblance to most of the thirteen Maimonidean principles. Only Bashyatchi's sixth article relating to the obligation of every Jew to study the Bible in Hebrew had no direct equivalent in the Maimonidean formulation. But Hebrew studies, though perhaps not quite so exalted by the Rabbanites, always were an integral element of their educational system. Even this distinction was toned down by the seventeenth-century Karaite, Solomon ben Aaron of Troki, who in his apologia for Karaism written at the behest of Johann Pufendorf reformulated, among its other teachings, the "ten principles of faith according to the Karaite sages." Here he included the obligation to study Hebrew only as a part of the general doctrine concerning the truth, eternity, and unchangeability of the Torah because, as he wrote, only the reader of the original text was in a position properly to discount the biblical anthropomorphisms. No wonder, therefore, that, as time went on, the two groups moved dogmatically ever closer to each other rather than, as is usual in sectarian strife, drifting further and further apart.[24]

Occasionally we learn of more serious divergences. In his enumeration of the manifold differences, past and present, existing among various groups of his coreligionists Qirqisani tells us that

> some of the Karaites of Khorasan do not recognize the Ketib and the Qeri [the variants between the masoretic text and readings] and read (the Torah) just as it is written; some of these Karaites do so even with the (Holy) name which is written yod-hē; they assert that whoever reads it as (if it were written) alef-daleth [*Adonai*] is a heretic. Among the Karaites of Khorasan and Jibal there are some who assert that the promised Messiah had already come and passed away, also that the temple (which the Jews hope to build) is the one built by Zerubbabel and that there is going to be no other. Some of these Karaites also deny the resurrection of the dead and assert that whatever the Scripture says about it (really) means the restoration of the (Jewish) people from the captivity and humiliation. Some of the people of Bagdad assert that Enoch and Elijah died, for it is impossible that they should have ascended to heaven [I.19, 4–5, pp. 62 f.; *HUCA*, VII, 395].

But Qirqisani seems to refer here to opinions held by small minorities. Very likely these extremist speculations were restricted to small circles of scholars which failed to find their way into any of the more widely read works of the leading Karaites of the following generations.

In some respects more important were the vast differences in law and ritual which characterized the Karaite communities of the first two centuries. Rabbanite Jewry had long been fairly tolerant of theological diversity and allowed considerable leeway in beliefs and opinions so long as these did not affect the actions of the believers. Now the geonim were making a consistent and, on the whole, increasingly successful effort to level down even the regional variations which had grown up in the course of the preceding centuries. Karaism, on the other hand, essentially a protest against that enforced uniformity, for a long time allowed complete freedom of interpretation. Its teachers not only constantly repeated 'Anan's reputed advice to "search well in the Torah," but added to it the important amplification, "And do not rely on my opinion."

In fact, fewer and fewer Karaites accepted the teachings of the founder without serious reservations. The 'Ananites, Qirqisani informs us, "are now [in 937] very few in number, and their number is constantly decreasing." As late as the twelfth century Jacob ben Reuben spoke of a third "Karaite" faith, in contradistinction to both the Rabbanites and the 'Ananites. All Karaites, however, took to heart 'Anan's and Benjamin's injunctions to follow their own conscience. Apart from such individualistic emphases Karaite diversity was nurtured from those regional and sectarian differences which had reasserted themselves under the reign of Islam. The more Karaism began to unite under its aegis the chief opposition to the central controls administered by exilarchs and academies in the name of the Talmud, the more it had to absorb the enormous differences prevailing in the Jewish life of the far-flung empire. It was not accidental that some of the extreme views mentioned in our quotation from Qirqisani sprang either from the formerly Sassanian eastern provinces, or from the sophisticated and increasingly rationalistic metropolitan population of Baghdad, doubtless recruited from all over the Caliphate. Qirqisani includes in the category of "Karaites" a large number of persons professing a variety of religious beliefs and practicing an enormous variety of rites, who were adherents of neither 'Anan, Benjamin nor Daniel al-Qumisi. Sometimes the same men changed their minds from day to day. As Qirqisani resignedly declared, "it is impossible to find two of them agreeing in everything." [25]

It was difficult even for this outstanding tenth-century student of religion to establish a pattern in that maze of conflicting opinions. This difficulty has increased many times over since that time, because so few records were transmitted to posterity and still fewer are extant today. The greatest creedal and ritualistic disparities were doubtless found among the highlanders of the Iranian Plateau and further east, who had been drawn out of their centuries-old isolation by the new "Renaissance of Islam." These economically and politically flourishing, but culturally struggling Jewish communities felt most directly the impact of those nativist forces in their immediate environment which fiercely resisted the "melting pot" function of the new civilization. Most of the Jews living in the eastern provinces were not learned men. Few of them were able, even if willing, to commit to writing their teachings, however fervently they tried to spread them among their immediate associates. Certainly few of them knew Aramaic or even Hebrew well enough to compose treatises of the kind written by Benjamin of Nahawend. If they wrote anything in Persian or any other local dialect, these works very likely never reached the western communities which alone succeeded in salvaging some of their older literary heritage. Circulation of even the outstanding works of Karaite scholarship was long so limited that Qirqisani evidently never saw 'Anan's Book of Commandments or his treatise on metempsychosis, while such an omnivorous reader as Yeshu'a ben Yehudah could not secure a complete copy of Benjamin's treatise (or section of a larger work) on the prohibited degrees of consanguinity in marriage. Considering how little of these original works of the masters, 'Anan, Benjamin and Daniel, before long generally revered as the founding fathers of the new movement, has come down to us, and that a commentary on Kohelet composed in 993 by the Karaite exilarch of Jerusalem, David ben Boaz, is totally lost, we shall not be astonished that absolutely nothing of the undoubtedly meager literary output of these obscure easterners has survived to the present day.[26]

Karaism seems to have reached the acme of its diversity in the days of Abu Yusuf Ya'qub ibn Isḥaq ibn Sam'awayh al-Qirqisani, probably so styled because he was a native or resident of ancient Circesium (Qarqisiya, wrongly identified with Karkemish by Benjamin and others) in Babylonia. One of Qirqisani's younger contemporaries, Salmon ben Yeruḥim, already discussed four stages in the history of Karaism. Taking as his standard of measurement the degree of the successive generations' alleged disagreement with Rabbanite law, he wrote:

Under the fourth kingdom [the Caliphate] 'Anan arose and awakened the hearts of men and opened their eyes so that they became desirous of studying the Torah to the best of their ability. For the practice of the rabbis and their concentration on the Talmud had made them forget the Lord's Torah and the understanding of its true meanings. After him appeared Benjamin adding strength and discovering matters in which 'Anan (may the Lord have mercy on him) still followed the practice of the rabbis. After Benjamin there arose the Karaites and built additional fences for the Lord's commandment. Afterwards men arose in East and West and added further strengthening of religion and intensive study of wisdom. Leaving homes and fortunes behind and despising this-worldly enjoyments, they proceeded to settle in Jerusalem, where they now live.

Salmon was evidently unfamiliar with Benjamin's authorship of the designation "Karaites," a derivative of "Men of Scripture." Nor is his mechanical explanation of the four stages in the evolution of early Karaism borne out by the record. But, perhaps for this very reason, it the more clearly reflects the state of confusion in leading Karaite circles in the middle of the tenth century. Karaism was, indeed, at that time in danger of falling apart into an anarchical conglomeration of dissident groups and individuals, having in common only a passionate hatred of the existing law and order. Had that come to pass, it would have gone the way of all the other sectarian movements which it largely superseded. Like these diverse schismatic trends, the Karaite upheaval would have left in its wake no more than a slight ripple on the waves of the destiny of its people.[27]

WORK OF CONSOLIDATION

Among Qirqisani's and Salmon's contemporaries and early successors there arose an array of distinguished leaders whose intellectual and moral strength salvaged the movement from the growing anarchy. Realizing the danger of ultimate dissolution, a number of Karaite scholars, mainly assembled at the academy established by their recognized princes of captivity in Jerusalem, succeeded in reformulating the whole body of Karaite beliefs and practices in a fairly uniform fashion. Many descendants of 'Anan sported the combined titles of "exilarch and head of academy." Joseph ben Nuḥ (about 1,000) is said to have presided in Jerusalem over an academy of seventy disciples (this number doubtless was an imitation of the ancient Sanhedrin, and contemporary Rabbanite academies), including such eminent scholars as Joseph (Abu Ya'qub) ben Abraham al-Baṣir (because of his blindness euphemistically surnamed ha-Ro'eh, the Seer), and his disciple Yeshu'a ben Yehudah (Abu'l Faraj Furqan ibn Asad). Other eminent Karaites of Jerusalem in the crucial period from the mid-tenth century to 1099, included the controversialist (Abu'l Surri) Sahl ben Maṣliaḥ, the eminent Bible exegete Jephet ben 'Ali ha-Levi (Abu 'Ali al-Haṣan ibn 'Ali al-Baṣri), and his son Levi, as well as the noted philologist Abu'l Faraj Harun ibn al-Faraj. The distinguished lexicographer, David ben Abraham al-Fasi of Fez, Morocco, likewise seems to have settled in the Holy Land, as did his Rabbanite compatriot, the gaon Solomon ben Yehudah. So highly did the Karaites esteem settlement in the Holy City that, before long, they invented the legend that 'Anan himself had spent there the last years of his life. Already Daniel al-Qumisi spoke with condescension of the Babylonian and other foreign leaders as the "wise men of the Exile." He included in this category 'Anan, whom he counted among the "mistaken wise men" (*ha-maskilim ha-nikhshalim*). As late as the eleventh century Levi ben Jephet spoke disparagingly of "the Karaites of Babylonia and other countries remote from Palestine [who] followed the Rabbanites in matters pertaining to the calendar." In these men, as well as in Yashar ben Ḥesed (Sahl ibn Fadl) at-Tustari and a visitor from Byzantium, Tobiah ben Moses of the eleventh century, Karaism found a series of distinguished exponents who, working together rather than against one another, succeeded in introducing order and unity into this apparently irremediable chaos. In apologias defending their faith against the attacks of such opponents as Saadiah Gaon, as well as in their positive restatements of the more or less accepted doctrines in their Bible commentaries, liturgical poems, or books of commandments, they achieved a semblance of organic unity which was to outlast all subsequent storms. Even the loss of the Palestinian center as a result of the blood-letting by the Crusaders in 1099—although apparently faring better than the Rabbanites, the Karaite community of Jerusalem never fully recovered from that shock—caused no irreparable damage to that newly won unity.[28]

Beginning with Tobiah ben Moses, whose Hebrew translations of some major works of the Jerusalemite school made them accessible to Jews under Christendom (after 1041), the Karaite community of Constantinople became a center of Karaite life and learning. In Yehudah ben Elijah Hadassi (12th cent.), Aaron ben Joseph (the Elder, 13th cent.), Aaron ben Elijah (the Younger, 14th cent.), Samuel ben Moses al-Maghribi, Elijah ben Moses Bashyatchi and the latter's disciple Caleb ben Elijah Afendopolo (all 15th cent.) Karaism found codifiers, exegetes, and apologists of considerable distinction. Fortunately, many works by all these men, and their eastern predecessors, written in Hebrew or Arabic in countries of age-old literary tradition, found zealous and, on the whole, faithful preservers in manuscript and later also in printed form. These scholars often differ among themselves in many significant details. They even have the habit of frequently citing conflicting opinions without resolving for the reader the difficulty of reaching a decision. Nor did they object to the circulation of a "Work on the Differences and Agreements between the Sheikhs Abu 'Ali [Jephet ben 'Ali] and Abu'l Surri [Sahl ben Maṣliaḥ] in the Exposition of the Laws," notwithstanding the frequent taunts by Rabbanites and complaints by some of their own leaders about their internal squabbles. Yet in the aggregate they offer a body of laws and beliefs sufficiently uniform for modern students to venture some sort of generalization.[29]

The individualism preached by the masters was not fully abandoned. However, one no longer finds such emphatic assertions as had been voiced by 'Anan, that if through an independent interpretation of Scripture a believer reached a legal conclusion, however erroneous, he must, unless taught to the contrary by a fully informed scholar, strictly observe that law in defiance of the majority. Far more stress was now laid on the duty of each member to submit to the wishes of established communal authority. Antinomianism in any form was to be sharply repudiated. 'Anan's successors mainly stressed his complementary statement that anyone "bagatelizing the commandments or the Torah and asking, Who is the Lord?" was guilty of a capital crime (Harkavy, *Zikhron,* VIII, 13).

Even here, however, we shall look in vain for real consistency. On the one hand, all Karaites had to repudiate the usual Rabbanite expostulation that pious men must follow the customs of their forefathers and the words of their teachers. Sahl was particularly vehement in denouncing such uncritical emulation. Pointing to the example of Adam who should not have listened to Eve, just as Eve should have resisted the serpent's persuasive words, he cited with telling effect Zechariah's call, "Be ye not as your fathers" (1:4) and the psalmist's wish that the generation to come "might not be as their fathers, a stubborn and rebellious generation" (78:8). "It is our duty," he concluded, "to examine their ways and to measure their deeds and judgments against the words of the Torah" (Pinsker, *Lickute kadmoniot,* II, 33 f.). On the other hand, once it became an organized religion Karaism, too, could not get along without traditional customs of its own, or what it came to designate as the "burden of heritage."

A curious illustration of the ambivalence of the Karaite doctrines of authority may be seen in the leaders' contradictory attitudes to the priesthood. Beginning with 'Anan, most Karaite teachers felt obliged to harp on the biblically prescribed priestly dues. Like the Samaritans, some of them even diverted to priests the fruits of a new tree in its fourth year. They also taught that the "second tithe," which Rabbanite law had divided between consumption by the owner in Jerusalem during two successive years and distribution among the poor every third year, was a permanent impost limited to consumption at the Temple. They demanded that an additional "third tithe" be given to the poor on the third and sixth years of each Sabbatical cycle, paying no heed whatsoever to the farmer's ability to carry this crushing burden. In substance, however, everyone knew that, unlike the Samaritans who continued sacrificing their Passover lambs at Mt. Gerizim, the Karaites were merely awaiting the rebuilding of their sanctuary. Only after the Faṭimid conquest of Jerusalem in 970 were they allowed to pray at the Wailing Wall. They agreed, therefore, that priestly dues no longer literally applied in Exile, and that the priestly lineage of the contemporary *kohanim* and levites was quite dubious. 'Anan himself made it perfectly clear that, until the coming of the Messiah, Palestine itself must be considered an exilic land. Sahl ben Maṣliaḥ accused the ancient Rabbanites of wholesale destruction of the genealogical records proving priestly descent. They had done it, he asserted, "in order that the various segments of the population mix with one another and that no person enjoy a privileged position before the others on account of his descent." Sahl, and after him Samuel al-Maghribi, did not mean to denounce these underlying democratic motives so much as the alleged willful nullification of the intentions of the biblical lawgiver. Daniel al-Qumisi, on the contrary, objected to the entire system of gifts to the contemporary priesthood and declared that both donor and recipient were guilty of misappropriation and robbery.[30]

Karaite leadership conceded, however, with almost complete unanimity, the preservation of authentic family records proving the Davidic descent of the exilarchic family. After all, on the authenticity of these records rested the claim of the Karaite *nesi'im* in the Holy Land to the title of "princes of the whole diaspora of Israel." True, die-hard dissenters like Salmon ben Yeruḥim denied this very historic basis of the exilarchate. In one of his vitriolic attacks on Rabbanism Salmon explained the Psalmist's complaint, "I have gone astray like a lost sheep" (119:176), by saying that "Israel's misfortune from beginning to end stemmed from its shepherds. That is why the 'people of the book' have rebelled against rabbinic leadership and took upon themselves not to have a chief [*ra'is*] during the period of Exile." The majority of the Jerusalem leaders, however, the more readily recognized their own "princes," as their livelihood largely depended on the voluntary contributions collected in good Rabbanite fashion from all Karaite communities for the maintenance of their princely dynasty and its associated academy. Salmon's younger contemporary, Jephet ben 'Ali, went so far as to declare the cursing of king and prince (*nasi*) a capital crime, which some of his successors extended to the cursing of any righteous judge (Hadassi), or of any chief of clan or family (Al-Maghribi).[31]

Interterritorial Karaite support for the Jerusalem academy accrued, like its Rabbanite counterpart, to the direct benefit of the diaspora communities as well. It not only helped cement the unity of the people and promote constant cultural exchanges, but it also brought to the Holy City eager students from many lands. At Joseph al-Baṣir's and Yeshu'a ben Yehudah's school, pupils from Spain and Byzantium met colleagues hailing from Babylonia and other lands. Some disgruntled foreign students, like Tobiah ben Moses, may have complained of not having received their due share of the incoming alms and returned home. But even they enriched their native lands with the new knowledge they had acquired in Palestine. Certainly the return to Constantinople of Tobiah, by that time a well-trained scholar steeped in the methods of Karaite scholarship in the Holy Land, was highly instrumental in developing there the new center of Karaite life and learning. Even the sudden eclipse of the old center, however, by no means abrogated the Karaite practice of following hereditary leaders. In nineteenth-century Crimea the Karaite communities still bowed in reverence to their hereditary "princes." [32]

Noble descent and wealth, as well as learning, played a great role also in the selection of local elders. No matter what appeal Karaism in its formative period may have had to members of the lower classes, and regardless of the number of underprivileged who may have joined the new movement directly or through the mediation of the more extreme messianic sects (the extent of both still is highly problematic), its communal leadership was recruited from the same classes as was that of its Rabbanite adversaries. Perhaps the most telling expression of dominant Karaite opinion is found in Samuel al-Maghribi's chapter on the Duties of Priests and Judges. As in other areas, this fifteenth-century compiler merely summarized long-accepted views. Contrasting the extinction of levitical functions in Exile with the perpetuity of judges and officers "whose appointment is incumbent upon us at all times and in every place," Samuel discussed the required qualifications of these officials in the light of the biblical injunction (Exod. 18:21):

"Thou shalt provide out of all the people able men, such as fear God, men of truth, hating unjust gain." The term, "able," comprises three attributes: first is wisdom, second wealth, and third strength, for the following reasons: If a judge is not wise, he does not know how to secure justice. If he is poor, his soul is preoccupied with his poverty, as it is written, "The ruin of the poor is their poverty" [Prov. 10:15]. Nor do people trust his [a poor man's] aversion to the acceptance of bribes, whereby justice suffers. If he [the judge] possesses no strength, he feels oppressed and has no patience to study each legal case with the necessary thoroughness. . . . By "hating unjust gain" are meant those who, by nature, despise bribery, rather than those who acquire this attitude because of existing regulations; "hating" depends on one's heart.

To these requirements Samuel added one derived from the biblical selection of men "known among your tribes" (Deut. 1:13). This means, Samuel explained, that "they must be exalted by their position, which includes their being exalted through their clan and their ancestry." Catching some of the old sectarian spirit of intolerance which 'Anan had already shared with the New Covenanters, this fifteenth-century Egyptian codifier insisted upon the total exclusion of proselytes from such local offices, on a par with their exclusion from royal office or the prophetic call.[33]

Social justice as such was never a major issue between Karaites and Rabbanites. The former took over from Rabbanism all the principles of social ethics almost intact. Hence the occasional attacks of Karaite polemists on Rabbanite oppression of the poor and illiterate, such as we have cited above, were aimed not at Rabbanite law generally or in specific details, but rather at the alleged widespread neglect of that law. Jephet ben 'Ali spoke with equal contempt of the uneducated masses and of the exploiting upper classes or the mercenary teachers. He contrasted all these three groups with the small band of devoted Karaite scholars who taught their pupils without remuneration. Even Sahl ben Maṣliaḥ's eloquent exhortation against the dictatorial and oppressive methods of rabbinic leadership which forced poverty-stricken taxpayers to borrow money on usury to satisfy the fiscal extortions, essentially assailed only the abuses of Rabbanite law and, at worst, its inefficacy in stemming such abuses. Similarly Sahl's (?) dire predictions of the fate awaiting stubborn sinners who rely "on the silver and gold they had gathered from their robberies, extortions, and false oaths" could have been uttered with equal abandon by any Rabbanite preacher. Certainly Sahl's fervor had its full counterparts in some of the Midrashim compiled in the Muslim era. Nor is this issue anywhere played up by the other Karaite writers, much as the latter may occasionally point to their own poverty, resulting mainly from their renunciation of worldly goods. Hadassi voiced the regnant opinion when, in reiterating the old biblical-rabbinic prohibition of despoiling the rich as well as the poor of their property, he exclaimed: "The poor and the rich are like one before thy God, so shall they be before thee." [34]

More, there is not the slightest evidence that the Karaite leaders tried to remedy these social evils by appropriate new legislation. It certainly was cold comfort for the poor that Jephet demanded a low standard of life for all. He computed from Hosea 3:2 that any man ought to be satisfied with an income of one fifth of a drachma (some 7 cents) a day and the consumption of "two loaves of barley bread; one for breakfast and one for supper . . . with no spice, no beverage, and no sweetmeat." Such sporadic modifications of the existing law as 'Anan's insistence on unleavened bread made of barley, permissible also under Rabbanite law and, in any case, speedily abandoned by 'Anan's successors, or even the permission to distribute charity on Sabbath, hardly facilitated the struggle for subsistence on the part of the masses. This struggle, often very bitter, was, on the contrary, far more seriously hindered by the excessively rigid ascetic demands of most other Karaite laws. A few extremists denounced economic endeavor as such. A Karaite Bible commentator (Qumisi?) complained of the "men of Exile" (Babylonians) who derived encouragement for commerce from the Psalmist's assertion, "When thou eatest the labour of thy hands, happy shalt thou be" (128:2). "They did not know," he exclaimed, "that 'labour of thy hands' means the practicing of the Lord's commandments." Some forms of Karaite asceticism actually led to outright discrimination against working people by Karaite interpreters of the law, for which we shall find no parallel whatsoever in the rabbinic codes. For example, Qumisi, or one of his disciples, proposed a most rigid interpretation of the biblical marriage impediment for priests, "They shall not take a woman that is a harlot; or profaned" (Lev. 21:7). A harlot, in that author's opinion, was any woman who *married* without her father's consent and, hence, without a previous betrothal, while one "who is known to walk into the markets and streets without covering her face" was profaned. He also demanded death by burning for a priest's daughter who, even if neither married nor betrothed, had been found guilty of fornication. According to Samuel al-Maghribi, this prohibition included not only any unmarried girl, even if seduced by her own fiancé ('Anan's son, Saul, had already included illicit relations with unmarried girls in the category of "adultery" outlawed by the Ten Commandments), but also any woman guilty merely of frequently associating and gossiping with men. Entire classes of working girls, such as hairdressers, shopgirls, midwives, and even domestic servants, were in his opinion "profaned" in terms of the biblical prohibition. This contrasted with Maimonides' eloquent injunction to give preference to fellow Jews in domestic employment, so that "the descendants of Abraham, Isaac, and Jacob shall derive the benefit of one's fortune." [35]

LEGALISTIC RIGOR

Combining ascetic fervor with literal biblicism, the early Karaite leaders were also prepared to cancel the humanitarian evolution of the preceding millennium and to restore the death penalty to its ancient position. Not only outright antinomianism, blasphemy, or even *lèse-majesté* against prince and chieftain were punishable by death, but also the merely inappropriate mention of the divine name or any form of perjury. Generally reverting to the biblical *lex talionis,* the Karaites demanded an eye for an eye in lieu of the Pharisaic-rabbinic fine. Murder or even manslaughter had to be avenged by the death of the criminal, and Benjamin specifically enjoined the blood avengers not to forgive even an accidental slayer. Any violence whatsoever done to parents was to be punished by stoning. The same penalty was also demanded for adultery (in its narrower sense) which, according to many Karaite authorities even if less strict than Saul ben 'Anan, was committed by any betrothed girl before her marriage as well as any divorcée or widow. In the case of death inflicted by a forewarned owner of a goring ox, the blood avengers of the victim were to be given the choice between the owner's ransom or death. Qirqisani sharply censured the Rabbanites for "explicitly contradicting the holy text" (Exod., 21:29) in not requiring the owner's execution. The biblical *karet* (premature death), which rabbinic law had long removed from the jurisdiction of the earthly courts, was interpreted by the Karaites as a regular death penalty. Beginning with Benjamin, they also greatly relaxed the rules of evidence wherewith rabbinic law had tried to hedge the conviction of criminals. A plea of guilty was now accepted as sufficient evidence for a death sentence. A husband's accusation of lack of virginity created the presumption of the bride's adultery after the betrothal which, unless disproved by her, made her liable to the extreme penalty.[36]

True, all this was largely academic, for no more than Rabbanite Jewry did any eastern Karaite community retain genuine capital jurisdiction. But in Spain, for instance, where Jews enjoyed vast judicial autonomy, Karaites, too, although themselves weak and generally oppressed by the Rabbanites, may have been given the right to execute informers. Their jurists had long claimed that anyone causing a man's death through informing was guilty of murder. Moreover, even the total and irrevocable exclusion from the community, already demanded by 'Anan as a substitute for physical execution, could, under the confining conditions of the small Karaite communities, cause hardships which the offender might consider worse than death. At the same time, the way out through suicide was barred by the teaching of Qirqisani and others that self-inflicted death was as great a sin as murder.[37]

Severity was also the keynote of other Karaite regulations governing the relations between the sexes. From Benjamin on, Karaite law insisted upon the dismissal by her husband of any raped woman, despite her obvious innocence. Levi ben Jephet deprived her even of any formal writ of divorce and the concomitant marriage settlement. The freedom of divorce demanded by 'Anan for both mates was retained by Benjamin and his successors only for the husband, Benjamin declaring pointedly, "Divorce is in the hands of men, not women." Only a few of the later jurists restricted this right to the dismissal of a wife in whom the husband had detected some physical blemish, while still fewer considered only religious nonconformity as a sufficient defect. To make sure that marriages would receive the necessary publicity, 'Anan insisted that weddings take place in the presence of ten adult male Jews, a practice half-heartedly adopted by Rabbanite Jewry as well. Similarly, formal presentation of writs of divorce in courts of justice, never made obligatory by Rabbanite law, was converted by Benjamin into a legal requirement.[38]

Sex morality and sexual restraints were likewise pushed by the Karaites to remarkable extremes. Qirqisani sharply attacked the Rabbanite permission for a man who had "secluded himself" with an unmarried girl to marry her, and singled out some "immoral" *aggadot* and strange local customs for public ridicule. For example, he cited with disdain the talmudic advice to a man overcome with irresistible passion to satisfy his desires under some guise in a distant place "lest he publicly desecrate the name of Heaven." The bride's virginity always remained a major issue with the Karaites. Riding roughshod over the more delicate compunctions of sophisticated authors like Aaron ben Elijah, leaders and public alike took literally (as had the Sadducees and such rabbis as R. Eliezer ben Jacob?) the Deuteronomist's provision, "And they shall spread the garment before the elders of the city" (22:17). Even in modern times they employed at each wedding of a virgin two "best men," whose duty it was on the following morning to place the bridal sheet before the judges.[39]

Best known is the rigidity of Karaite law with respect to the prohibition of incest. Based upon the aforementioned principle, introduced by 'Anan, whereby relatives of the husband automatically became the wife's relatives, too, the later Karaites began multiplying prohibited degrees until the selection of mates in the small and often interrelated Karaite communities became well-nigh impossible. Before long the Karaite teachers themselves, beginning with David ben Boaz and Joseph al-Baṣir, objected to this type of staggered relationships (*rikkub 'al rikkub*). Joseph reduced the prohibited degrees to five, while Yeshu'a ben Yehudah proclaimed the general principle, "One must not apply the *heqqesh* to marital impediments" (*En heqqesh ba'arayot*). But at all times the Karaite doctrine of incest remained a complex body of regulations, exceptions thereto, and exceptions to exceptions. Samuel al-Maghribi had to devote an entire section in his code to the laws of incest which, he admitted, "were very difficult, because all Jews have agreed to outlaw more than is expressly prohibited in the Torah." [40]

Few of these regulations had an outright antifeminist bias. On the contrary, early Karaite law, following 'Anan's example, was prepared to liberalize further the existing Rabbanite provisions concerning the rights of women, which, as we recall, had already compared favorably with the latter's treatment in the contemporary non-Jewish communities. Defying biblical precedents, David ben Boaz (possibly harking back to Sadducean teachings) demanded absolute equality of daughter and son in the inheritance of their father's estate, while others argued that the biblical preference for male heirs be restricted to Palestine. Daniel al-Qumisi gave daughters the right to one third of the estate, agreeing with similar postulates of some Muslim jurists. He also insisted on the reversion of childless women's estates to their families as against the Rabbanite preference for the exclusive hereditary rights of husbands. The conservatism of the majority, however, reasserted itself also in this domain and, before long, prevailing Karaite opinion, led by Jephet and his son Levi, reverted to the denial of feminine hereditary rights in the presence of sons or their descendants. There seem to have been even fewer Karaite than Rabbanite businesswomen in medieval society; the widow of Ibn al-Taras, the feminine leader and "teacher" of the eleventh-century Karaite community in Spain, was but a rare exception. Moreover, like her husband, she may have been a converted Rabbanite who, while in Jerusalem, had come under the spell of the distinguished Karaite Bible exegete and philosopher, Yeshu'a ben Yehudah.[41]

Nor did regnant Karaite law relax the rigidity of 'Anan's provisions for the Sabbath and holiday rest. More than any other domain of the law, Sabbath observance and calendar regulations lent themselves to extremes of individual and group interpretation in the early, creative stages of that sectarian upheaval. These differences not only outweighed all others in the recollection of Qirqisani, but they seem indeed to have occupied the minds of men far more than any other aspect of social and religious life. To quote only a selection from Qirqisani's record,

> Some of them forbid ablutions from impurity during the Sabbath, others do not allow washing the face during the Sabbath. Some of them forbid one to bring in trays (with food) or to make the bed on the Sabbath; . . . Others allow the bringing in of trays . . . but forbid one to remove them. Some of them do not allow keeping food hot until the approach of the Sabbath, but let it get cold before the Sabbath comes in; they assert that if it is left hot some (internal) changes, expansion and contraction, take place in it during the Sabbath; this is the opinion of some of the people of Tustar. . . . Some of them think that it is unlawful to go out of one's dwelling during the Sabbath, others think it is unlawful to remove (anything) from one place to another, . . . even if there is no separation or distance between the two places. . . . Some of them follow 'Anan in prohibiting circumcision on the Sabbath, although most of them allow it. . . . Some of them allow one to read on the Sabbath [also] any writing other than Hebrew, others forbid it. . . . Some of them assert that if Passover falls on a Sabbath night the feast should be transferred to the next month. . . . Strangely enough [there are some who] allow, in fact they require, working and moving about during the Sabbath and forbid any recreation and rest.

Compared with this kaleidoscopic variety of observances among the Karaites themselves, the few features of the Rabbanite Sabbath, such as the *'erub,* keeping food hot and other minor chores, as well as sexual intercourse, found objectionable by this Karaite apologist, pale into insignificance. In time, however, these Karaite vagaries gave way to calmer and more uniform behavior, and Karaite Sabbath observance, except for the kindling of lights, differed less and less from that of the Rabbanites, particularly those following the Palestinian ritual. In the later Middle Ages even the dark Friday nights were gradually abandoned in most European communities.[42]

Curiously, the fundamental distinction between the Rabbanite and Karaite Sabbath is mentioned only tangentially by the Karaite controversialists. With talmudic Jewry the Sabbath was first and foremost a day of gladness, both spiritual and material. Hence the rabbis not only insisted on much illumination of homes and synagogues, but also on celebrating the joyous festival with a blessing on a cup of wine. The *qiddush* ceremony became so important for them that, although primarily designed for the home, it was also performed during the Friday evening synagogue services for the benefit of travelers and homeless persons. Understandably, this custom evoked the ire of the Karaite ascetics who wished to outlaw all use of intoxicating beverages. Salmon ben Yeruḥim voiced a widespread grievance when he attacked Saadiah's "lightheadedness," because "this inebriate drinks during the very time of prayer." Some Karaites, like Ibn Saqawaihi, opposed even the offering of charitable pledges (as were frequent in Rabbanite congregations during the recitation of the Scriptural lesson) or mere conversation on the Sabbath. The Rabbanites also tried to make their Sabbath meals as palatable as was consistent with Sabbath rest observance, and insisted that one must not fast on that day except if it happened to coincide with the Day of Atonement. Rejecting certain ascetic trends in talmudic Jewry itself, which wished to encourage fasting at least on the "Sabbath of Repentance" after the New Year's festival (first definitely forbidden by Yehudai Gaon), the majority of rabbis peremptorily postponed even the stated fast days from Saturday to Sunday. To the Karaites this was both an unwarranted human interference with the calendar set by God's movement of celestial bodies, and a profanation of the holiday itself. 'Anan, Daniel and, still more insistently, Hadassi demanded the observance of the Day of Atonement, not as a solemn yet serene festival, but as a regular day of mourning with sackcloth and ashes. As an early Karaite exegete remarked, "Today our holidays are [dedicated to] mourning and weeping, not joy. Happy is he who assiduously devotes his holidays to fasting, prayer, and study, not to the preparation of food." The Karaite Sabbaths and holidays became indeed those bleak and somber festivals which alone, in the leaders' opinion, were fitting for a people living the unregenerate life of exiles.[43]

The manifold variations in the celebration of other Karaite holidays, especially Passover, were likewise gradually reduced to a common denominator. After Qirqisani, one no longer hears suggestions of postponing the Passover feast for a month. In fact, forgetful of the extent to which their own schism had originally been nurtured by the variations in local customs, the Karaites joyfully derided the numerous regional divergences in Rabbanite holiday observance and other rituals. The same Qirqisani who was overwhelmed by the enormous diversity of customs among Karaite groups, nevertheless relished a contemporary Rabbanite publication concerning some fifty ritualistic differences between Babylonia and Palestine. Listing only the more important differences, he readily exaggerated their consequences in rabbinic law. For example, mentioning the two successive days observed in Babylonia for each festival except the Day of Atonement, in contrast to the one day alone celebrated in Palestine, he added, "Thus, in the opinion of the people of Babylonia the people of Syria profane the holidays and transgress the commandment 'Thou shalt not diminish' [from it], whereas in the opinion of the people of Syria the people of Babylonia observe feasts not enjoined by God and transgress His commandment 'Thou shalt not add thereto.' " Of course, this biblical verse (Deut. 13:1), a standard weapon in the armory of the Karaite warriors against Oral Law, was never invoked in this context by the Rabbanites of the two countries who had long learned to respect their minor disagreements.[44]

All Karaites continued, however, to set their holidays by the observation of the moon, rather than through use of astronomic calculations. Leap years were set in accordance with the actual outcropping of spring vegetation. While 'Anan seems to have wavered between signs of such outcroppings in Babylonia or Palestine, the shift of the Karaite center to Jerusalem made the entire Karaite world dependent on the cycles in the plant life of the Holy Land and, more specifically, around Ramleh. Many Karaite leaders echoed Qumisi's denunciation of astronomic computations as the "calculation of sorcerers," which they put on a par with the soothsayers' art of the ancient Chaldean astral religion, so vigorously combated by the Israelitic prophets. They also uniformly rejected Ḥanukkah, because it was nowhere mentioned in Scripture, but rather inconsistently adopted a new series of prescribed fast days, although 'Anan's suggestion of a Ramadan-like seventy-day annual fast elicited little enthusiasm among his followers.[45]

Apart from the dates of holidays, however, and other details, divergences from Rabbanite law diminished in the course of time —here, too, running counter to the usual progressive widening of sectarian cleavages. Qirqisani himself admitted that some Karaites followed "the exilarch" in observing a second day of Passover and the Feast of Tabernacles. An eleventh-century Rabbanite correspondent from Constantinople (?), to be sure, bitterly complained that the Karaites "quarreled with us" and that they "desecrated the divine festivals" by celebrating both Passover and the New Year a month late, because of the late ripening of Palestinian barley that year. But in a responsum sent by Jerusalem's Karaite elders to Tobiah ben Moses the Karaite communities were allowed, in case of serious doubt, to follow the existing (Rabbanite) computations. Samuel al-Maghribi finally suggested that the entire method of setting the annual calendar in accordance with the observation of barley-ripening applied only to Palestine and such adjoining cities as Cairo or Damascus, but that in more distant lands one was to follow the nineteen-year cycle of "Jehoiachin." We also recall how early the successors of 'Anan abandoned his insistence on unleavened bread made of barley and allowed the use of four other cereals provided in the Talmud. So overwhelming was the impact of the Rabbanite majority not only on the beliefs, but also on the practices of these "heretics." Only when in later centuries the Crimea became a major center of Karaism, did the ensuing cultural and linguistic separation from the mainstream of world Jewry (these Karaites developed a Tartar dialect of their own, the so-called Karaimic tongue) create a really different "people," as Naṭronai bar Hilai had prematurely termed them at the end of the ninth century.[46]

Understandably, some of the greatest and most permanent deviations occurred in the Karaite synagogues and their liturgy. Here, too, early Karaism was not of one mind. If 'Anan had tried with all the means at his disposal to make of the synagogue a replica of the ancient Temple, his successors, and especially Qumisi, wished to draw the sharpest possible line of demarcation between these two houses of worship. Qumisi bitterly attacked the Rabbanites precisely because they built arks into their synagogues, bowed before them, used candles and spices—all of which practices were, in his opinion, too closely modeled after the Temple ritual (see Mann, *Texts and Studies,* II, 50 f.). He did not realize that he thus merely echoed an old anti-Jewish accusation voiced by Aphraates and Chrysostom against the placement of arks in synagogues, just as six centuries later a Yemenite compiler of aggadic statements unwittingly gave vent to similar heterodox sentiments (see Lieberman, *Midreshe Teman,* pp. 24 f.).

Many of the prayers recited in the synagogues likewise lent themselves to attack by sectarians not tied by reverence to age-old traditions. They could the more readily discard some of the Rabbanite prayers, as the prayer book still was in its formative stage in the days of 'Anan and his early successors. The manifold differences in local customs between the synagogues of Palestine and Babylonia (and those in neighboring lands which depended on either) were greater in this than in any other domain. There is no way of knowing what the liturgy of the eastern and other peripheral provinces was before the prayer books then being prepared by Amram and Ṣemaḥ, or Saadiah, took hold in the various communities and established a measure of liturgical uniformity at least within large segments of Rabbanite Jewry.

At any rate, starting afresh, the Karaites repudiated both the established general liturgical order and most individual prayers. They reduced the three daily assemblies to an evening and a morning service alone. On the other hand, on holidays they added additional (*musaf*) services and made them cumulative. On a New Year's day falling on a Sabbath they were prepared to recite three such additional groups of prayers, one each for the Sabbath, the New Moon and the New Year. They accepted the biblical *Shema'* and placed this proclamation of God's unity at the beginning of the services. But the *'Amidah* and other prayers of postbiblical origin they replaced by Psalms and varying combinations of biblical quotations. They allowed each individual, particularly if he was "wise and understanding," to add prayers of his own. They also introduced daily readings of Scriptural lessons.[47]

At the same time, some Rabbanite liturgical practices, often originating from temporary exigencies or obscure folkloristic preoccupations, were particularly welcome targets for Karaite reformers. For example, the *Kol nidre* prayer of the Day of Atonement, at that time evidently of recent origin and designed to allay the obsessive fears of persons afraid of unconsciously breaking vows, doubtless was the more readily rejected by the Karaites as they repudiated the very principle of public dissolution of vows. Benjamin even hedged about the explicit biblical authorization for fathers or husbands to dissolve vows rashly made by women by allowing annulments only on the first day. Many *piyyuṭim,* which did not enjoy uncontested popularity even within the Rabbanite world, could easily be denounced on linguistic as well as on theological grounds, not to speak of such a clearly superstitious performance as the *kapparot* ceremony, whereby the sinner tried to delegate his sins to a sacrificial animal, obviously a residuum of ancient folklore rejected by many geonim themselves. Like the gross anthropomorphisms of the popular mystical literature of the day, this custom became a fit object of derision for Karaite apologists. Before long, however, the Karaite prayer book not only became equally standardized, but it also included liturgical poems resembling *piyyuṭim.* A codifier like Samuel al-Maghribi himself allegedly composed no less than a thousand religious poems.[48]

All these innovations were far overshadowed in practice by the new legislation in the domain of dietary laws and ritual purity, since these regulations deeply affected the daily life of the people. We recall 'Anan's outlawry of most meats and all intoxicating drinks. To uphold the prohibition of fowl, except pigeons, Qumisi devised a philological rationale. Being unable, he contended, to identify exactly the names of the permissible birds in the Bible, we would better play safe in refraining from the consumption of all except those of which we are absolutely sure, namely pigeons. Because of similarly excessive conscientious scruples, many Karaites forbade the consumption of eggs and, possibly, of honey, which at times contained particles of the bees. Eating either of those foodstuffs would, in their opinion, violate the prohibition of *eber min ha-ḥai* (limb of a living animal). Together with the comprehensive Karaite definitions of forbidden fats, different forms of slaughtering, differences in priestly tithes, and a multitudeof other legalistic minutiae, these scruples all but eliminated simple conviviality between ordinary Rabbanites and Karaites.[49]

Even a tighter wall of separation must have been erected by the

Karaite laws of purity. Restoring and expanding most of the Old Testament taboos, the later Karaites (surpassing 'Anan in severity) not only declared lepers and gonorrhea patients themselves impure, but also all those who were in any direct contact with them. More, touching a dead body, even during the necessary funeral rites, lying in the bed of a menstruating woman, indulging in sex relations, and the like, generated, in their opinion, a chain reaction which shut off an untold number of persons from the ordinary pursuits of life. While conceding a wide variety of interpretations, regnant Karaite opinion held that an impure person was not allowed to pray, for prayer substituted for ancient sacrifices whose performance in a state of impurity had been specifically prohibited by Scripture. This was all in line with Benjamin's declaration that "all biblical commandments which we are at all capable of fulfilling, must be fulfilled" (Harkavy, *Zikhron,* p. 183).

In their attacks on the majority, Karaite leaders also frequently censured the allegedly unforgivable Rabbanite lack of cleanliness during synagogue attendance. Hadassi's aside is typical of numerous such outbursts. "Even in their prayers," he wrote, "they [the Rabbanites] wear shoes abominably dirtied from the blood of pigs and reptiles and from refuse, and their bodies are impure from their excretions without washing." One is reminded in this context of the ancient controversy between the Pharisees and the Hemerobaptists. The constant preoccupation of the Karaite jurists with the laws of purity explains also the disproportionately large space assigned to these laws in most Karaite law books. A twelfth-century Rabbanite controversialist, wishing to point up the differences of opinion among the Karaites themselves, enumerated five legal distinctions (mnemotechnically summarized by Hebrew terms beginning with the letter *mim*) in which 'Anan's successors disagreed with the views of the founder. Among these no less than two were concerned with the contemporary application of the laws concerning the impurity of dead bodies and lepers. Rabbanite Jewry, as a whole, though itself far from completely freed of these ancient restrictions, must have been appalled by the sight of the numerous temporary outcasts in the Karaite community, segregated from their coreligionists, even their families, because of some such "impurity." One can readily imagine the psychological effects of such segregation upon these outcasts themselves, who were not only shunned by their fellow-men, but had to be constantly on guard lest they communicate their impurity to other persons or objects. No system could have been more conducive to increasing immeasurably the greyness and joylessness of Karaite life. An anti-Karaite Bible commentator was certainly right in speaking of it in Jobian terms, "Their harp is turned to mourning, and their organ unto the voice of them that weep." [50]

APPEALS TO HISTORY

No Jewish sectarian movement, whatever its peculiar origins, could long persist without trying to justify its brand of historical monotheism by past experiences. In itself Karaism was as unhistorical a movement, its leaders as unhistorically minded, as any comparable group in Jewish history. Beginning with a rupture with the historic tradition of their people, these teachers long persisted in defying the authority even of their own predecessors and in looking for the resolution of all difficulties in their individual resources. Sharing with all medieval Jewry the belief that the teachings of the masters, and not their lives were important, they allowed the biographical data of even their greatest scholars to sink into oblivion; only the bare outlines of a few could be pieced together by modern scholars after most painstaking research. The works of the masters fared somewhat better. But not until the general awakening of historical interests among the Karaites, too, in the nineteenth century did many of their classics appear in print. Nevertheless, sooner or later they had to look for justification in some sort of historical reconstruction.

The basic principle of the new heterodoxy, the denial of tradition as incorporated in the Oral Law, was more easily postulated than applied in practice. Life had progressed and changed greatly since the days of the Sadducees who, even in their time, had found it very difficult to dispense entirely with the accepted folkways which had developed by the side of, and after, the legislation of the Pentateuch. The Karaites were helped but little by the addition of Prophets and Hagiographa to their concept of Torah. The latest of these writings were separated from the realities of Karaite life by a millennium of dramatic and far-reaching changes. The most extensive use of rabbinic modes of hermeneutic interpretation, and the broadest expansion of the *heqqesh* type of analogy, did not suffice to fill the gap.

Before long the Karaite leaders bowed to the inevitable and readmitted much of the traditional lore. They did it first under the guise of adaptation of the widely accepted Muslim principle of *idjma'* (common consent). Since the sheer understanding of biblical terminology depended on what all Jews had long agreed it to mean—how could one possibly guess the pronunciation of the divine name in the Bible without the aid of a tradition transmitted from generation to generation? asked a Rabbanite polemist —it was not too difficult for Karaite teachers to argue that wherever all Jews agreed on a legal application, this must have been the intent of the Lawgiver. Hadassi succinctly summarized the debate which had been going on in Karaite circles in the preceding two or three centuries:

> Sahl ben Maṣliaḥ Abu'l-Surri ha-Kohen put them [the modes of interpretation] under four headings. [He said:] The Torah grows through the instrumentality of Reason, Scripture, Analogy, and Community [common consent]. In Analogy [*heqqesh*], indeed, are included all the modes, for by drawing analogies from one another the power of the Torah becomes manifest. Sa'id [Levi] ben Jephet ha-Levi put them under three headings: Scripture, Analogy, and Community, but not Reason, for . . . the Torah forbids matters permitted by Reason and permits matters forbidden by Reason. . . . There also are some who concede Scripture and Analogy, but do not recognize the Community and its burden of heritage. . . . There also is one who admits Scripture and Community, but denies Analogy, and that is Joseph ben Nuḥ.

In time this element of common consent, which already here appears under the two designations of *'edah* and *qibbuṣ,* came to be known under the franker terms of *ha'ataqah* (transmission) or *sebel yerushah* (burden of heritage). Hadassi himself equates the latter two terms with *'edah* and even with the peculiarly Rabbanite *qabbalah;* "all four terms have but one meaning." The only reservation with respect to the validity of such traditions made by Tobiah ben Moses was that they must have some support in Scripture. But, added the Byzantine translator, "those claiming that there exists a [genuine] tradition without Scriptural support, do it only because their minds are too weak to find the derivation from biblical law." Later Karaites of the rank of Elijah Bashyatchi, to whom we owe the citation from Tobiah, defined the rule more sharply, namely "that every tradition which does not contradict Scripture, does not add to what is written in Scripture, is shared by all Israel, and has some backing from Scripture, is called *ha'ataqah,* and is accepted by us." [51]

It is small wonder, then, that the leading Karaites found it necessary to study the Talmud, if at times only for the purpose of detecting in it fit targets for disagreement and attack. Not only 'Anan, but also Benjamin and many of their successors were trained students of talmudic letters. Salmon ben Yeruḥim's aforementioned reconstruction of the evolution of Karaism up to his time as four stages of progressive deviation from talmudic tradition, is controverted by the fact that some of 'Anan's most extreme innovations had been rejected by Benjamin and his disciples in favor of the talmudic usage. Of course, the latter did not hesitate to introduce innovations of their own. But they hardly ever surpassed the founder in his reformatory anti-Rabbanite zeal. Many undoubtedly agreed with Nissi ben Nuḥ's purported enumeration of the qualifications needed by a thorough student of Scripture. Among these the last, but not the least, requirement was that "he be erudite in Mishnah, Talmud, and Halakhot, and study the Tosafot [Toseftot?] and Aggadot." Joseph ben Nuḥ, too, doubtless taught rabbinic lore to his disciples at the Jerusalem academy modeled after the Rabbanite schools of higher learning. Ultimately Aaron ben Joseph and still more sharply, Bashyatchi, claimed with abandon that "most of the Mishnah and Talmud are words of our [Karaite] ancestors." [52]

Needless to say that Karaite attitudes to talmudic literature were neither uniform nor even consistent with the same persons and that most early Karaite sages referred to it only for purposes of polemical distortion. The mysterious Ibn Saqawaihi composed a special Book of Shameful Things, analyzing the major areas of Jewish law in which, in his opinion, the rabbis had been in error from the outset, and others in which the later rabbinate unjustly abandoned a correct position taken by its predecessors.

To be valid among intelligent students, such criticism had to be buttressed by extensive quotations from the Talmud and later rabbinic writings. Similarly, Qirqisani, as we recall, often tried to refute the Rabbanites by citing their own authorities. Sahl ben Maṣliaḥ, too, assailed the "shamelessness" of Rabbanites, "who contend that there is an Oral Law beside the Five Books of Moses. And yet it is written plainly in their Priestly Lore that the Torah is interpreted through the thirteen modes," and that hence all law really must be deduced by men through such hermeneutics. More, in his famous satirical exhortation Sahl boasted of having studied the older, or rabbinic, literature more intensively than many of those who prided themselves of its possession.[53]

Negativism of this kind, particularly if weakened by inner inconsistencies, did not suffice to supply the Karaites with a satisfactory historical rationale. Quite early, therefore, their leaders began to retell the entire history of the Jewish people in a fashion making them the sole legitimate heirs of ancient Israel's prophets and lawgivers and stamping the Rabbanite majority as heretics. As early as 937, Qirqisani presented a comprehensive theory of the historical evolution of the Jewish religion and its sects, admittedly based not only on written sources (he often referred in particular to David al-Muqammiṣ), but also on what he had heard in scholarly assemblies and elsewhere. According to this theory, Jeroboam I was the first schismatic in Jewish history. Without departing from the basic principles of the Mosaic religion, he introduced certain ritualistic innovations, only a few of which are recorded in Scripture. These "licentious customs" developed in Judah, as well as in Israel. When the Jews went into Exile, "they spread all over the world transmitting them [these customs] down to the present time." After Jeroboam came the Samaritans, and after them the "chiefs of the Assembly," that is the Rabbanites. Beginning with Simon the Righteous, these chiefs confirmed Jeroboam's customs, "defended them by argumentation, and composed the Mishnah and other books in explanation of them." Persons disagreeing with them (even their own leaders such as R. Gamaliel and R. Eliezer ben Hyrcanus) were severely persecuted. After them came the Sadducees. Zadok, who had "discovered part of the truth," attacked the Rabbanites in books. After the appearance of several other sectarian leaders, including Jesus, there finally arose the exilarch 'Anan who "was the first to explain the whole truth about the laws" (1.2, pp. 6, 13; *HUCA*, VII, 322 ff., 328 f.).

Later Karaites disagreed with, or even completely forgot, some important elements of this historical reconstruction. But in substance they were unanimous in classifying the Rabbanites among the followers of Jeroboam, although rather inconsistently they traced the formal beginnings of the Rabbanite schism to the conflict between Alexander Jannaeus and the Pharisees, led by Simon ben Shetaḥ and Judah ben Ṭabbai. They were not even sure who of the latter two was the Rabbanite heresiarch. In any case, they believed that the Karaites had persevered as a minority, often clandestinely observing the correct rituals, from the days of the First Commonwealth, and Ezekiel had them in mind when he spoke of "the men that sigh and that cry for all the abominations that are done in the midst" of Jerusalem (9:4). According to some early Karaite authors, these submerged groups finally raised their heads during the Second Commonwealth under the names of Sadducees and Boethuseans, the latter contributing in particular the Sunday celebration of Pentecost. Later Karaites, however, sharply repudiated this association of their sect with the much-hated Sadduceans, a nexus almost universally postulated by their Rabbanite opponents. They preferred to believe, therefore, with Yehudah Halevi, that the Sadducees who had denied resurrection were just another group of *minim* (heretics), while their own spiritual ancestry went back to a revered ancient sage like Judah ben Ṭabbai, or even Shammai. They also explained the different customs of Babylonian and Palestinian Rabbanites by the controversies between Hillel, the Babylonian, and the Palestinian Shammai. Some Karaites, finally, began invoking the testimony of ancient sectarian writings found in caves, evoking a Rabbanite retort that " 'Anan the heretic and his associates wrote tracts containing heresies and falsehoods and hid them in the ground. They then unearthed them and claimed: 'This is what we found in ancient writings.' " [54]

In any case, according to the Karaites, the wickedness of the ancient Rabbanites reached its height during the corrupt Maccabean regime. However deeply imbued they may have been with the ideal of national independence, the Karaite authors had nothing but words of condemnation for the Hasmonean dynasty, the great national liberators. They so greatly resented any Jewish holiday unrecorded in the Bible that, together with Ḥanukkah, they condemned its originators, the Maccabeans, and rather utilized Josephus' descriptions (in whatever form these were accessible to them) of the ultimate corruption which had brought about the downfall of the Maccabean rule. They did not deny Rabbanite contentions that the Mishnah had been the work of many generations—according to Saadiah it required 510 years for its completion—but they either replied that the Rabbanites concentrated in Palestine had no right to impose their Mishnah on the majority of world Jewry then living in other lands, or saw in this very fact proof that that compilation by R. Judah the Patriarch was *not* the repository of an Oral Law revealed by God to Moses. A single revelation could not possibly have required, they contended, such a long time to compile.[55]

Before long, the Karaite leaders were prepared to deny the very facts of the Jewish past summarized in the Rabbanite *Seder 'olam rabbah,* although they were at a complete loss of substituting for it any new total reconstruction of Jewish history. About 1145 Jephet ben Sa'id (Jephet ben 'Ali's grandson) compiled a "chain of tradition" from Moses to his own day, but his outline was too skeletal and too dependent on Rabbanite sources to serve in any way as a valid substitute. He and his confrères were even forced to make extensive use of the much less venerable *Seder 'olam zuṭa*. The genealogical claims of their own exilarchic family were essentially based on the very latest accretions to this rather dubious chronicle.[56]

Not that there existed complete unanimity in regard to the leadership of that family itself. In the early, anarchical period of Karaite history, there were some who ventured to speak slightingly of the founder himself. We recall that already in the days of Benjamin a sharp line of demarcation was drawn between the 'Ananites and the real "Men of Scripture." Daniel al-Qumisi, who had started as an admirer of 'Anan and had called him *rosh ha-maskilim* (chief of the enlightened men, a preferred designation for Karaite scholars), later changed his tune and styled the exilarch the *rosh ha-kesilim* (chief of fools). Soon, however, Daniel's own community of Jerusalem realized the need for a common hero to whom the dispersed groups of Karaites could look up as the symbol of their unity and legitimacy. Under the lead of 'Anan's descendents, the Karaite exilarchs of the Holy City, there grew the legend of 'Anan's settlement in Jerusalem at the head of a group of "Mourners for Zion." Here he allegedly built a synagogue which, called after him, became a major center of attraction to pious pilgrims from other lands. Ultimately, a prayer for 'Anan was inserted in the Karaite prayer book—the highest honor at the disposal of any wing of medieval Jewry.[57]

DETERMINED MINORITY

On the whole, the Karaites thus absorbed the predominant political tendencies. Not only did their movement start from a merely political quarrel over succession in office, but it appears that in more than one respect they resembled the ancient Sadducees. They, too, were representatives of the richest and best educated classes of Jewry. Of course, under the changed economic structure of the Jewish people, few of them were landowners or farmers; fewer, in fact, than was warranted by the declining role of agriculture in the total Jewish economy. The agricultural laws, which occupy so much space in the Bible, are given but scant attention in the Karaite law books; they certainly are treated much less frequently and with less attention to detail than in the contemporary geonic responsa. But at least some Karaite leaders (including 'Anan and his children, as well as Benjamin) evidently belonged to the wealthier members of urban communities, although when they became imbued with the ascetic ideals of their sect, quite a few "abandoned their fortunes and their homes, and despised this-worldly enjoyments" (Salmon, quoted by Pinsker in *Lickute kadmoniot,* I, 22).

At times a closely knit Karaite community, resembling therein such other sectarian minorities as the Quakers, achieved disproportionate economic success. Already in eleventh-century Cairo we hear of "distinguished merchants" among the Karaites and of the latter's reliance on "their dignitaries, scribes, capitalists and those close to the government." The leading bankers-statesmen, sons of Sahl at-Tustari, probably were of the Karaite persuasion. A Genizah fragment of the eleventh century showed equal fiscal contributions by the Karaite and Rabbanite communities. In 1488, Bartenora actually found that both the Samaritan and Karaite minorities there far outstripped the Rabbanite majority in wealth. In Constantinople, too, zealous Rabbanites bitterly complained of the usury exacted from them by Karaite money-lenders and of the treatment of Rabbanite domestics by Karaite employers. Especially in the early stages of their movement, moreover, the Karaites seem to have recruited their main following from among the better educated, and yet dissatisfied, groups on whom recourse to the private reasoning powers and individual interpretation of Scripture exercised great appeal. Like the Sadducees, they developed strong nationalist tendencies in the direction of political independence. Not by mere chance was that beautiful group of "Mourners for Zion and Jerusalem" to a large extent constituted of Karaites, who left their safe abodes and turned to Palestine, where they lived in poverty and renunciation of worldly pleasures.[58]

True, unlike their Sadducean forerunners, the Karaites could not think of raising their hands against the overwhelming power of the Caliphate. They could but dream, and their dreams assumed at times a mystic coloring. Not in the sense of the contemporary mystic writings of the type of the *She'ur Qomah* (Measure of God's Stature) which, because of their crude anthropomorphisms, became choice targets for Karaite barbs. Karaites also objected to the Rabbanite practice of visiting the graves of ancestors and of distinguished rabbis. An eleventh-century Karaite author blandly asserted, "Know that there are no demons in the world." All such "superstitious" beliefs and practices, nurtured from the folklore of the masses and treated with forbearance by Rabbanite leaders, were haughtily dismissed by the Karaite intellectuals. Attacks on Rabbanite anthropomorphisms, despite the latter's support by the literal meaning of many biblical passages, became so stereotyped that even Saadiah, himself an ardent champion of the doctrine of God's incorporeality, did not escape their brunt. In one of his tirades against the gaon, Salmon exposed to ridicule a number of anthropomorphic legends included in the Midrash and books like the *Otiot de-R. 'Aqiba,* and exclaimed, "If Gentiles should learn of the extent of these abominations which we have described, they would throw stones at us, and heap derision and contempt upon us. . . . And you claim that the Karaites are new, while the ancient rabbis are saints. If authors of such abominations are saintly, then Sisera, Haman, and their ilk must enjoy great bliss in Paradise." [59]

Nevertheless some of the Karaites themselves indulged in such escapes into supernatural speculations as 'Anan's doctrine of the transmigration of souls, or Benjamin's lucubrations about the divine government of the world through intermediary "angels." If Qumisi rejected the latter doctrine, it was not because of an excess of rationalism. In fact, he surpassed even 'Anan himself in his opposition to science. We recall his objection to the astronomic foundations of the Rabbanite calendar. Nor did he in any way mitigate 'Anan's general aversion to medicine and particularly to medical treatment on the Sabbath. Taking literally such biblical phrases as "I am the Lord that healeth thee" (Exod. 15:26), and the Chronicler's censure of King Asa because "in his disease he sought not to the Lord, but to the physicians" (II Chron. 16:12), many 'Ananites roundly rejected medical treatment of any kind. Qirqisani, to whom we owe this information, also singled out Qumisi for censure for his inconsistency in employing rigorous logical reasoning to the interpretation of Scripture and yet being "dissatisfied with rationalism to such an extent that he reviles both it and its devotees many times in his works." Salmon ben Yeruḥim likewise cursed those among his coreligionists who studied modern Arab rationalist philosophy and declared even preoccupation with Euclidian mathematics as more than useless. All these facts are given, he said, in the Bible with perfect certainty, whereas human computations are advanced by some scientists only in order to be demolished by others.[60]

Qirqisani's own position, to be sure, was that "intellect is the foundation upon which every doctrine should be built, and that all knowledge should be derived by means of reason only." He even gave a purely psycho-physiological explanation to dreams, whose divinatory functions are so frequently stressed in Scripture. But only few among the early Karaites, and none among their later successors, dared to follow the Sadducean example and to deny physical resurrection, or to reinterpret it in the sense of Israel's future deliverance from Exile. In view of their extreme nationalism, the early Karaite authors gave even freer rein to messianic speculations than did their Rabbanite contemporaries. In his Bible commentaries Jephet ben 'Ali so frequently expatiated on the scriptural allusions, overt or hidden, to the coming of the Redeemer and gave them such a contemporary coloring that, as we recollect, a later Karaite author felt prompted to circulate a collection of these passages under the expressive title, *Sharḥ al-'atidot* (Elucidation of Things to Come). Ever since the days of 'Anan, moreover, the Karaites included a reference to Zion almost in every benediction. Long before Yehudah Halevi, their poets, including Jephet, composed Zionide elegies. "Your Holy House," Jephet lamented, "is in the hands of strangers, yet you are far away." Menahem ben Michael's moving poem beginning, "Zion weeps over her children, precious as gold" (included in the Karaite prayer book) seems likewise to have been written independently of Halevi. Deep conviction, and not mere partisan bias, thus inspired the endlessly reiterated Karaite declarations that the loss of Jewish independence had come because of divine anger over Rabbanite sins, and only a return to the proper teachings of Scripture would usher in the days of the Messiah. There was little room, however, in the sophisticated Karaite communities for false messiahs. None of the great Karaite leaders anywhere intimated that he himself may have been selected by God as an instrument of divine redemption. We know of only one Karaite messianic pretender, Solomon ha-Kohen (about 1121), but he was characteristically mentioned by Obadiah, the Norman proselyte, rather than by a Karaite author. Obviously inspired by the sudden catastrophe which had overcome the Karaite center in Jerusalem in 1099 and by some fears about the approaching end of the fifth solar century since the Hejira, this false messiah seems to have remained a solitary exception in Karaite history.

Ultimately, some Karaites toned down the messianic hope altogether. Not only did Aaron ben Elijah pass it over in silence in his philosophic treatise, but the fourteenth-century Cairo judge, Israel ben Samuel ha-Ma'arabi, failed to include it in the six articles of faith formulated by him. Nor is it mentioned in the modern Karaite catechism published in Cairo.[61]

All Karaites, of course, like the Sadducees before them, denounced more or less radically the historical flow of tradition. Borrowing the terminology from related Muslim controversies, they uniformly emphasized reliance on individual reasoning (*idjtihad*), in contrast to the Rabbanite subservience to earlier authorities (*taqlid*). Centuries after the extinction of Sadduceeism, their state ideal brought them to another rejection of the oral law, and they focalized all their energies around the study of the written law. It was also a necessary consequence that each important Karaite leader, 'Anan, Benjamin, Qumisi, Qirqisani, and others, wrote his own Book of Commandments in trying to construct a *final* codification of the law.

History, which had crushed the Sadducees, however, could still less be reversed now. Unlike the Sadducees who, however tenuously at times, controlled the powers of a state, the Karaites from the beginning were only an opposition party against the powers that were. Opposed to almost everybody else, to Muslims, Christians, and Samaritans, as well as to the majority of their fellow Jews, and at no time commanding a substantial following outside the few large urban centers, they found their salvation willy-nilly in some form of segregated living, which their founder had recommended to them from the outset for purely religious reasons.

Karaite contacts with the Samaritans seem to have been few and far between. Even during the two centuries when Jerusalem was the world center of the new movement and its chief exponents lived in fairly close geographic proximity with these oldest Jewish sectarians, there seem to have been few personal relations between them. Extreme Samaritan xenophobia combined with the Karaite acceptance of the biblical condemnation of the Samaritan schism to establish an almost water-tight separation. Qirqisani, himself a non-Palestinian and familiar with Samaritan life only through reading or hearsay, gave the clearest, if brief, description of Samaritan customs to reach us from any medieval non-Samaritan pen.

> The Samaritans [he wrote] do not recognize any prophet except Moses and Joshua and do not acknowledge any book of prophecy except the Torah and the book of Joshua. They do not recognize the sanctity of Jerusalem and their prayer is (directed) towards Shiloh [Gerizim]. They offer sacrifices down to the present day. They have a priest who does not mix among them and does not intermarry with them [their laymen], according to what we have been told. They do not mix with, nor come near to, any person (of another faith), and if any person who is not one of them comes near to them they wash themselves.

Even this keen student of the history of Jewish sects, however, evidently knew about the origins of Samaritanism only what he had read in the Bible. He knew the existence of a Dosithean offshoot, but he was uncertain which of the two groups denied resurrection. He seems to have heard of, rather than seen, the Samaritan Bible, although he quoted some of its "alterations," and assumed that Isma'il al-'Ukbari may have borrowed from it some of his readings. Later Karaites like Hadassi essentially repeated Qirqisani's statements. Hence the imputation of manifold Karaite borrowings from Samaritanism, often repeated since the days of Estori Farḥi (14th cent.) and made by Geiger an integral element of his revolutionary theory concerning the growth of the Old Testament canon, as well as the opposite suggestion, made by some modern scholars, that the medieval Samaritans borrowed heavily from Karaism, have little to commend them.[62]

Somewhat more friendly were the relations between Karaites and Christians, not only in Christian lands, such as Byzantium or Poland, where many of them came to live, but also in their original habitat under Islam. Shahrastani and Maqrizi undoubtedly heard from Karaite sources that 'Anan himself had spoken reverently of Jesus. The 'Ananites, Shahrastani reported, "consider 'Isa [Jesus] right in his exhortations and precepts. They declare that he had in no way contradicted the Torah, but rather confirmed it and appealed to all humanity to observe it. He had belonged to the children of Israel who lived according to the Torah and had paid homage to Moses. They do not recognize, however, his prophecy and mission." Qirqisani, too, wrote with considerable sympathy of Jesus as a rebel against the Rabbanite majority of his day, and even calmly described the Christian deviations from Judaism initiated by Paul. He also had high words of praise for a contemporary Christian bishop with whom he seems to have had friendly debates on religious issues. This did not prevent him from writing a polemical chapter against Christianity and censuring Abu 'Isa for his excessive recognition of Jesus' prophetic message. Occasionally he attacked the "nonsense and insolence" of Christian exegetes or declared that the Rabbanites "surpass in nonsense and lying even the Christians." Ben Mashiaḥ likewise had a debate with the Christian physician, Abu 'Ali 'Isa ibn Zar'a of Baghdad, probably after 997 when the latter published an anti-Jewish tract.[63]

More complex were the relationships with Islam. From the outset the new movement had to proceed gingerly, lest it antagonize the Muslim rulers on whose recognition as an independent Jewish sect its entire status depended. Only thus could its adherents appear as part and parcel of the Jewish "people of the book" entitled to governmental toleration, and yet as an entity separate enough to develop freely its religious institutions even against the will of the autonomous organs of that people. That is why Rabbanites often accuse their "heretical" opponents of overstressing their affinities to Muslim practices as a conscious stratagem to captivate the benevolence of the dominant classes. At the same time, Karaite xenophobia generally far exceeded that of the Jewish majority—an ambivalence frequently mirrored in the Karaite sources.

Karaite leaders could easily point out to their Muslim neighbors the similarity of their respective calendars. The Karaite *nesi'im* of the Holy Land could also use to best advantage the existing antagonisms between the Tulunid and, later, the Faṭimid rulers of Palestine and the caliphs of Baghdad. In their zeal to undermine the authority of the Rabbanite exilarchate these heterodox leaders were even prepared to support their archenemy, Saadiah, in his struggle against David ben Zakkai.

Intellectually, too, they could pay passing recognition to the prophetic merits of Mohammed without abandoning their own point of view. Since the Messenger of Islam had not arisen within the Jewish community, Qirqisani saw no need of discussing his work per se. Unlike Jesus, therefore, who is listed and refuted alongside of other Jewish sectarian leaders, Mohammed and his message, as well as Islam's generally anti-Jewish polemics, are only treated tangentially in connection with Abu 'Isa's syncretistic leanings. To be sure, Qirqisani mentions a book he had written against some "modernists" among the Muslim theologians and their interpretation of Mohammed's citations from the Bible. But this treatise hardly deviated from the typical, more or less cautious, Jewish and Christian apologias against the dominant faith. In a homily on Zechariah's prophecy, "And I took my staff, Graciousness" (11:10), Sahl ben Maṣliaḥ explained this verse as referring to Gentile domination, one of the two staffs which God had placed over his people. "It is called Graciousness," Sahl added, "in recognition of the nations not having despoiled the law and mores kept by Israel." Nor were Yeshu'a ben Yehudah's contemporaries alone in their feeling of gratitude for Muslim toleration which had made it possible for them to reside in Jerusalem in peace and security.[64]

If Sahl thus generously acknowledged the indebtedness of the Jewish people to the Muslim policy of limited toleration, he nevertheless wound up by quoting Zechariah's continuation, "And cut it asunder," together with the vindictive finale, "Then I cut asunder mine other staff, even Binders, that the brotherhood between Judah and Israel might be broken" (11:14). These passages referred, in Sahl's opinion, to the end of days when Israel and Judah, that is, Rabbanite and Karaite Jewry, would be reunited after the "cutting asunder" of both Graciousness, or Gentile domination, and Binders, or the reign of the two academies. This peroration is fairly typical of other Karaite attacks on the dominant religion which, incidentally, for the sake of security, were usually written in Hebrew even within an Arabic context. Many Karaite teachers, such as Jephet ben 'Ali readily adopted the scathing Rabbanite designation of Mohammed as a "madman," although many others, like Salmon ben Yeruḥim, saw in the successes of Christianity and Islam principally a sign of the inscrutable divine guidance of history. Salmon interpreted, for instance, Isaiah's vision of the watchman who "seeth a troop, horsemen by pairs, a troop of asses, a troop of camels" (21:7) as relating to Jesus who was riding on a donkey and the pre-Islamic Arabs who were wont to sacrifice camels on their holidays.[65]

Curiously, in the same exhortation Sahl sharply attacked the Rabbanites for their intimate social and business relations with the Gentiles, which, in his opinion, were bound to lead to manifold violations of ritual law. Segregation, from the outset preached by 'Anan, could the more readily remain the keynote of Karaite law and exegesis, as these Jerusalem ascetics evinced little interest in the cost of living or the ways of earning it. Qumisi repudiated even such a purely theoretical Rabbanite liberality as the permission to accept Temple sacrifices from Gentiles, notwithstanding the precedents established by ancient Persian (and Roman) monarchs and recorded in Scripture. Most of all, Gentile courts had to be shunned, even Rabbanite bridegrooms often being forced to insert a pertinent clause into their very marriage contracts with Karaite women.[66]

Marriage contracts were also used to safeguard religious conformity and, most remarkably, religious freedom. This was particularly important in the occasional instances of intermarriage between Rabbanites and Karaites. If we may draw any conclusions at all from the few chance records now extant, there seem to have been more cases of unions between Rabbanite husbands and Karaite wives than vice versa. In both cases the bridegroom often had to promise that he would not force the bride to violate her ceremonial laws. We have the text of a noteworthy marriage contract concluded, in 1082, by the Rabbanite Nasi David, son of the distinguished Palestinian leader, Daniel ben Azariah, with Nasiah, daughter of the wealthy Karaite Moses ha-Kohen of Fusṭaṭ. In one stipulation the bridegroom "took upon himself not to force his wife Nasiah to sit with him [in a room lit by] a Sabbath candle, to eat fat tail, or to desecrate her holidays, under the condition that she would observe his holidays with him." Other bridegrooms of lesser standing seem to have been more specific. In a contract signed in the early eleventh century in Fusṭaṭ, the bridegroom promised,

> not to bring into the house in which she lives as his wife fat tail, kidneys, the large lobe of the liver, the meat of a pregnant animal, or Gentile bread, wine or refuse [?]. He will not kindle lights on Sabbath evenings, nor burn a fire in his house on Sabbath days, nor sleep with her on Sabbaths and holidays the way he sleeps on weekdays [engage in sexual intercourse], and will not force her to desecrate the holidays of the Lord of Hosts based on the observation of the moon and the arrival of spring in Palestine.

This seems to have been the more standardized form. Conversely, we read in a "contract drawn up in Rabbanite style" by a Karaite bridegroom at Fusṭaṭ in 1052, that he would not "make her [his wife] desecrate the Lord's holidays as kept by the Rabbanites." The document is regrettably cut off at this dramatic point, so that we learn neither of additional safeguards, nor of sanctions placed on their violation.[67]

Not that intermarriage between the two groups was either frequent or in any way encouraged by the leaders. The geonic sources maintained a remarkable silence on the subject. But Maimonides, even in his most tolerant period as unofficial leader of all Egyptian Jewry, could not refrain from stating that "Karaite divorces have no validity whatsoever in our law, for they [the Karaites] do not believe in our customs relating to marriage and divorce." He undoubtedly realized that he thereby cast a shadow of illegitimacy on the offspring of Karaite divorcées, which was but slightly mitigated by the fact that, as we recall, some extremists among the Karaites opposed any kind of sex relations with divorced women in the lifetime of their husbands. If consistently interpreted in terms of the long-accepted rabbinic law, children from such invalid, and hence "adulterous," unions would be classified as "bastards" in the technical sense and as such barred, together with all their descendants, from unions with Rabbanites. Neither Maimonides nor his son, Abraham, seems ever to have drawn this conclusion. Under the administration of Maimonides' great-grandson, Abraham ben David, we are told two centuries later, there occurred a mass conversion of Karaites in 1312–13, followed by numerous marriages between these newcomers and scions of the most distinguished Rabbanite families in Egypt. In other countries, however, separation was far more complete. In Damascus, for instance, Benjamin of Tudela observed that there was no intermarriage among Rabbanites, Karaites, and Samaritans. Even in Constantinople, where their social relations were to become most intimate, he noticed "a fence" [*meḥiṣah*] between the two groups. Ultimately, after extended debates among leading rabbis of the fifteenth and sixteenth centuries, total separation became accepted law. There was no disagreement on this score between Karo and Isserles, the two main codifiers of sixteenth-century Jewry. This prohibition is still enforced by the rabbinic courts in Israel today.[68]

On the Karaite side, the more liberal attitude long prevailed. Doubtless cognizant of their minority status and the frequent inability of individual coreligionists to find mates in the small Karaite communities, the leaders refrained from placing a formal ban on such outside unions, although an outright prohibition would have been perfectly in keeping with the general segregationist ideals of their sect. Sahl ben Maṣliaḥ removed, in fact, the main legal basis for total exclusion by seemingly interpreting, as did Philo, the biblical prohibition, "A bastard shall not enter into the assembly of the Lord" (Deut. 23:3), as relating to religious assemblies and social gatherings, but not to marital unions. Even strict Hadassi demanded only that a Karaite marrying the offspring of adulterous, incestuous, and denominationally mixed relations, "record that blemish and genealogical defect in the marriage contract as a warning for the generations to come." Only belatedly and evidently as a reaction to Rabbanite intransigence, do we find a Karaite author, Solomon ben Abraham of Troki, Lithuania, invoking 'Anan's authority for a total outlawry of marriages with Rabbanites (1737). Even here, however, there is no indication that this prohibition was to apply also to Rabbanite converts.[69]

KARAITE PROPAGANDA

Apart from the biological factors, Karaite missionary efforts doubtless contributed to this moderation. The sectarian teachers seem to have objected to the intermarriage of a Karaite woman even less than to that of a Karaite man. Once the wife secured in her marriage contract complete liberty of conscience and freedom of worship at her home, they knew that she would serve, even unwittingly, as an agent of religious conversion. Since she was in charge of the household, her food habits and holiday observance were the more likely to prevail as her law was as a rule more rigid. The husband could partake of her food more readily than she could partake of his. Moreover, few husbands could afford to employ housekeepers to prepare for them their food in Rabbanite fashion, even if they were willing to indulge in the luxury of a double menage.

Missionary aims colored Karaite behavior in many other areas as well. Reversing the extreme isolationism preached by 'Anan, his successors, particularly during the Karaite "golden age" between 900 and 1050, embarked on a large-scale conversionist enterprise. True, their missionary efforts were restricted to the Jewish people. Their extreme nationalism would have accentuated the now traditional aversion of the leading Jewish circles to converting Gentiles even if they had not faced insurmountable legal obstacles, since conversion from one "protected" faith to another was severely outlawed.

At times the very right of missionizing among Rabbanite Jews was seriously questioned. The answer largely depended on the definition of Karaism as a Jewish sect, in which case conversion meant merely the transfer from one permissible branch of Judaism to another, or as an independent "protected" religion. The problem was highlighted later by a bitter controversy, provoked by the arrival in the Egyptian capital of twenty-one Marranos from Toledo who wished to join the Karaite celebration of the High Holidays. This controversy elicited, in 1465, contradictory legal opinions by the local qadhis of the four Muslim schools of jurisprudence. The Shafi'ite High Qadhi declared that "if they [Rabbanites and Karaites] do differ as regards the maxims of faith to such an extent that each party considers the other heretic, then anyone who desires to change his belief can only become a Muslim." On the other hand, the second-ranking qadhi of the same school unequivocally stated, "There can be no objection raised either way, because the Jews form one community as regards the principles of faith." The representatives of the three other schools concurred in the latter view, which ultimately prevailed after the personal intervention of the fairly tolerant Mameluk sultan, Al-Malik az-Zahir Khoshkadem (1461–67). On the whole, however,

Karaite missionaries seem to have encountered few legal difficulties in spreading their gospel among their fellow Jews.[70]

For the most part the Karaite propagandists sought to achieve their aims by working within the Jewish communities. They not only used personal suasion on individuals with whom they came in contact, but often went out into streets and synagogues to present their case to the Jewish public at large. An outstanding apologist like Sahl ben Maṣliaḥ undertook a regular missionary journey from Jerusalem to Baghdad, the very center of Rabbanite orthodoxy. Defying Rabbanite bans, Sahl and his fellow preachers seem to have gained easy access to synagogues. Curiously, they even complained that the Rabbanites introduced the Sabbath illumination of their houses of worship for no other reason than to keep out Karaite speakers to whom Sabbath lights were an abomination. Ben Mashiaḥ and others challenged such leading Rabbanites as Saadiah to public debates. They also appealed to the broader reading public in pamphlets in which they combined more or less plausible arguments in favor of their interpretation of Scripture with sharp, often personal, attacks on the immorality and social inequities of the ruling circles, and with dire predictions of the fate in store for recalcitrant listeners. As the difficult, technically irreproachable but highly sophisticated, style of these outpourings indicates, they addressed themselves principally to the intellectual élite. Above all, they disclaimed all separatist intentions. Salmon ben Yeruḥim invited Saadiah, "If you have no reply to the truth, join my community." Typical of most of these harangues is one of the concluding passages of Sahl's oft-quoted exhortations:

The days of reckoning on the nations have arrived [he wrote at the height of the imperial anarchy in the middle of the tenth century] and the time of Israel's redemption is approaching. May the Lord hasten for us the time when we shall be freed from the Two Women [the two academies according to his homiletical interpretation of Zech. 5:9] and the Messiah son of King David (may he rest in peace) will reign over us as it is written, "Behold, thy king cometh unto thee" (Zech. 9:9). And now, O brethren! do not harden your hearts against us, but listen to us. Come search our ways and examine our teachings. Perhaps the Lord will send a remedy for our affliction, take pity on our remnant and help us, so that we may be among those who succeed and not among those who falter. Amen.

At that time the Karaites deserved indeed the designation of "Callers" or evangelists, as some of them seem to have explained later the meaning of their name to Maqrizi.[71]

This fervor, however, spent itself rather quickly. The polemical element, to be sure, always remained an integral part of the Karaite movement. As protestants against the established order, its leaders necessarily had to attack that order and to state, even overstate, their differing point of view. At times, they understandably created even imaginary targets in order the more effectively to demolish them. This tendency, characteristic of many reformatory trends, colored practically all Karaite writings in the early "Sturm and Drang" period of their movement. From the eleventh century on, however, Karaite leaders, yielding to the implacable resistance of the Jewish masses and their authoritative teachers, greatly toned down their propagandistic endeavors. It was to some extent a testimony to the inner consolidation and growing feeling of security of their movement that now their polemical outbursts receded, while their positive contributions to Bible exegesis, law, and theology became more focal. Giving up the hope of a speedy natural conquest of the whole people, the Karaite sect increasingly retreated into its inner self.

How effective was the Karaite mission in its heydey? There is no way of ascertaining that movement's numerical growth during the crucial three centuries after 'Anan. It probably would have been extremely difficult even for Qirqisani to quote definite figures. We certainly cannot subscribe to his broad definition of Karaism as the sum total of almost all contemporary dissenters from the Rabbanite majority, except for the outright heretics like the Yudghanites or Mishawayhites, although most of these sectarian currents, in so far as they did not run completely dry, seem ultimately to have flowed into the broader stream of Karaism. Moreover, as we learn from Sahl himself, there were in the tenth century many half-converts who "celebrated two holidays, one according to the observation of the moon, the other according to their previous practice" (Pinsker, *Lickute kadmoniot,* II, 33). We shall see that even such distinguished men of letters as the Ben-Asher family, or Yehudah ibn Quraish, occupied a twilight position between the two groups. How could even contemporaries estimate, with any degree of approximation, the number of such compromisers, public or secretive?

At no time, it appears, however, were the Karaites really successful in attracting a mass following. In no medieval community did they outnumber the Rabbanites, unless it was in such new settlements as the Crimea. Ibn Ḥazm, the eleventh-century student of sectarianism, knew of their presence only in Iraq, Palestine, Egypt, and Spain. In his native Spain, moreover, he found Karaites only in the two cities of Toledo and Talavera. A century later their harsh enemy, Ibn Daud, mentioned that they had been restricted to only one city in Castile. After 1178 they seem to have totally disappeared from the Iberian Peninsula.[72]

Significantly three of the four countries mentioned by Ibn Ḥazm were under the domination of rival caliphs, who certainly had no interest in helping the Rabbanite authorities in Babylonia to reestablish their unitarian control over the Jewish communities. In fact, although 'Anan's schism originated in Babylonia, its progress in this focal center of Jewish and Arab life was painfully slow. Nor did Sahl's missionary journey substantially increase the number of the Baghdad devotees who always remained but a small and struggling minority of the tolerated "people of the book." In Palestine, too, we recall, the Karaite center never was very large. Qumisi and others spoke of sixty Karaite "Mourners for Zion" (despite its allusion to Cant. 3:7, this figure probably represented a significant segment of the Karaite community of the Holy City in the ninth and early tenth centuries). Later on their number grew substantially, and by 1024 they successfully challenged the Rabbanite supremacy, securing a favorable decree from Caliph Az-Zahir. Obviously, the Rabbanites protested, and ultimately they obtained another decree from the Caliph, enjoining the two communities not to "interfere with one another; and that everyone who belonged to one of the two denominations should be enabled to live according to the customary traditions of his religion." But this wave of prosperity was of short duration. After the First Crusade, neighboring Damascus was a major center of Jewish life, and yet on his arrival there in the 1160's Benjamin of Tudela found 3,000 Rabbanites and 400 Samaritans, but only 100 (or 200) Karaites. Even in Egypt, where the Karaites reached the acme of their power and influence and where Genizah records flow more freely, the scarcity and smallness of the Karaite communities is borne out by all the sources, native as well as those stemming from visitors. Certainly the 150 Karaite (among 700 Jewish) families of Cairo in 1488 impressed Bartenora by their relative economic prosperity and the very fact of their sectarianism much more than by their number.[73]

The Karaite ratio in the Jewish population was highest in Constantinople, where Benjamin found some 500 Karaites living side by side with 2,000 Rabbanites. Assuming that Benjamin had in mind families rather than individuals, it is truly remarkable that this community, first recorded about 970, had grown within two centuries into a population of some 3,000 souls. Under the leadership of Hadassi (who had completed his important, though awkwardly written, encyclopedic law book in 1148, less than twenty years before Benjamin's visit), it had developed into a new world center of Karaism. Perhaps harking back to some residua of those Jewish opponents of Oral Law who had elicited Justinian's harsh prohibition of the Jewish *deuterosis,* this sect must have enjoyed a modicum of good will on the part of the Byzantine rulers, the hereditary enemies of the Caliphate of Baghdad. At the same time, no Karaite communities succeeded in establishing themselves anywhere in the Christian West, not even in Spain or Sicily after their reconquest by the Christians. With some exaggeration Ibn Daud claimed that, while Rabbanites inhabited the entire Mediterranean world, there were only a few Karaites in Palestine, Egypt, and the Algerian oasis of Warjalan (Ouargela). This statement is reemphasized more than two centuries later by Simon bar Ṣemaḥ Duran. In short, Solomon ben Aaron of Troki's melancholy observation, occasioned by his survey of Karaite life for the benefit of Johann Pufendorf, might have been anticipated by almost any medieval Karaite apologist in a Western country. "The Rabbanites are known," Solomon commented, "to the ends of the earth and distant seas, whereas the Karaites are merely mentioned by name in some scholarly works." [74]

Even in the countries of their settlement these sectarians seem to have been limited to a few major urban centers. We have already noted the lack of interest in agricultural problems on the part of Karaite leadership. The extant records, admittedly few and one-sided, mention nothing of early Karaite settlements in rural districts, or even in the numerous small towns with their manifold semirural occupational features. We hear of Karaite scholars, traders (including big merchants), and later on craftsmen, but hardly of any farmers. In Palestine they were settled in Jerusalem and Ramleh, but apparently not in most of the other towns still inhabited by Jews. Their Cairo community seems to have far outnumbered the combined population of their sporadically recorded settlements in the Egyptian provinces. From Constantinople they probably expanded into some other Balkan cities, but remarkably there was not a single Karaite in Salonica, the second-largest Jewish community in the Ottoman Empire, during the early sixteenth century, according to the testimony of its rabbi, Solomon Cohen.[75]

We must bear in mind, however, that apart from their meagerness these statistical data do not suffice to indicate fully the actual successes or failures of the Karaite mission because of the tenuous nature of Karaite allegiance in the early centuries. There must have been many Karaites or Karaite sympathizers living outside these major urban centers who attended Rabbanite synagogues and participated in the general life of the Jewish community while adhering to Karaite beliefs and observing Karaite rituals as well as they could. Those half-hearted Karaites censured by Sahl for their observance of both the Karaite and the Rabbanite holidays must have been particularly numerous in smaller communities. There must also have existed great regional variations on this score. While in the Babylonian heartland of talmudic Judaism, entire Karaite communities, according to Levi ben Jephet's admission, followed the Rabbanite calendar based on astronomic computation, in the more isolated Byzantine communities as late as the days of Aaron ben Elijah many Rabbanite groups, perhaps unthinkingly, observed on the contrary the Karaite festivals. More importantly, transition from one group to another was extremely simple. For a long time, transfer from a Karaite to a Rabbanite congregation or vice versa, even where both existed side by side, appears to have been no more difficult than is change of membership from a Reform to a Conservative or an Orthodox congregation today. In most cases one hardly required even verbal "repentance," occasional Rabbanite demands to the contrary. Only in fifteenth-century Egypt do we hear of a formal ceremony of readmission to the Rabbanite community. "If Karaites," we are told by Rabbi Jacob Castro, "wish to accept the Oral Law and live like other faithful Israelites, we customarily make them swear on a scroll of law before the court that they would fulfill all the requirements of the sages on a par with the Rabbanites. There is no danger of their relapse, for the Karaites do not recognize any absolution of oaths and, hence, even against their will they must adhere to the end of their lives to the belief in Oral Law." The very casuistry of Castro's argumentation indicates that this had not been a well-established and widespread practice even in that late period of far more advanced segregation between the two groups. In the earlier centuries those Rabbanites who, according to Tobiah ben Moses, had become disgusted with some anthropomorphic *aggadot,* "gave up their faith and turned Karaites," doubtless did it without any formal ceremony of induction into the new community.[76]

For this reason, despite bans and counterbans, it was easy for members of the two communities to interfere quite actively in each other's communal affairs. No sooner, we recall, did Nathan ben Abraham arrive from North Africa in 1039 to serve as the second-highest officer (*Ab*) of Jerusalem's Rabbanite academy, than he began campaigning against his chief, Solomon ben Yehudah, by paying numerous visits and otherwise trying to curry favor with the constituents, including Karaites. Evidently Karaite support appeared important even in such strictly internal affairs as the management of a Rabbanite academy. In the ensuing controversy, moreover, the Jews of Damascus (apparently again recruited from both groups) voted in favor of Nathan. There was, in fact, a great celebration at the reading of the Scroll of Esther in the Damascus synagogue in which some two hundred Karaites, as well as non-Jews, participated. A philosopher like Ibn Kammuna could serve as official *mufti* of both groups in the thirteenth century and write a treatise analyzing and, in some respects, defending both points of view. In Egypt it became customary for the *nagid* to serve as the official spokesman of both communities before the governmental authorities. Only with European ascendancy in the late Middle Ages and early modern times did the implacability of Spanish Jewry and Ashkenazic Jewry's total unfamiliarity with Karaite beliefs and rituals finally erect that wall of separation which found its extreme expression in the sharply endogamous provisions of Karo and Isserles.[77]

RABBANITE REACTIONS

Under these circumstances, Rabbanite leadership evinced little concern about the rise of the new schism. The idea that the rise of Karaism shook the Jewish community to its foundation, and that the great danger of a complete breakdown was averted only by the intervention of the militant and superlatively gifted Saadiah Gaon, is part of a scholarly mythology which has grown up since the days of Pinsker and Graetz. Blinded by the flashes of light thrown on the theretofore obscure Karaite history by newly discovered documents, spurious as well as genuine, the generation of scholars living between 1850 and 1880 proceeded to rewrite in a "pan-Karaite" vein the entire cultural history of the Jewish people in the crucial centuries after the rise of Islam. Before long all the revolutionary discoveries of that period in Hebrew philology, Bible exegesis, and philosophy were ascribed to Karaites or, at best, to Rabbanites reacting to the rise of the new sect. These exaggerations of literary history have, as we shall see, been effectively disproved by more recent painstaking research, which, at times, went to the opposite extreme of denying even some indubitable pioneering merits of Karaite authors. But there remained the residual conviction of the great impact of Karaite propaganda on all Jewish life and letters of the period. This view, too, requires considerable qualification.

For a long time after the rise of the new sect Rabbanite leaders remained totally silent. At the most, if we are to believe the exaggerated complaints of Karaite controversialists, they repeatedly excommunicated the new movement. But excommunication, in both its lighter and severer forms, was the commonplace instrument of law enforcement readily wielded by the Jewish authorities on much slighter provocations. Courts banished any number of recalcitrant debtors or persons who failed to obey a summons. Saadiah was by no means an exception when, in replying to an inquirer, he declared a certain marriage null and void. "We immediately excommunicate the couple," he added, "until [the bridegroom] leaves [the bride's] house. We do the same to all persons who were present at this [unlawful] wedding of a married woman and permitted it to happen. They are all subject to excommunication, even if they be scholars like Shela." Heretics, too, in so far as they deviated from accepted practices, were formally banished from the community until they repented.[78]

The first Rabbanite leader to react, more or less publicly, to the Karaite schism was Naṭronai bar Hilai Gaon who headed the academy of Sura about a century after 'Anan. In his answer to some unknown inquirers he briefly explained that 'Anan had instigated his followers to ridicule the words of the talmudic sages and promised them, "I shall prepare for you a Talmud of my own." Curiously, the gaon did not even bother to secure a copy of 'Anan's Book of Commandments, about which he had only heard from another academy official, Eleazar, who had come to Sura from Lucena in Spain. The only remedy he suggested was that these heretics "be banished, not allowed to pray with Jews in the synagogue and be segregated until they mend their ways and pledge themselves to observe the customs of the two academies" (Amram Gaon, *Seder,* II, 206 f.).

From Qirqisani, but not from any Rabbanite source, we also learn about a curious action taken by another gaon, Hai ben David of Pumbedita (890–97). The gaon, we are told, together with his father translated 'Anan's work into Hebrew or Arabic (according to Joseph al-Baṣir's version) and found "nothing of which they could not trace the source in the doctrine of the Rabbanites." They identified even two remaining minor divergences as stemming from "the elegies of Yannai," a leading seventh-century poet. If true, this story would only seem to indicate that the academy wished to have at its disposal a record, in Hebrew or Arabic, of 'Anan's legislation, which would show the Jewish intellectuals in other countries that 'Anan utterly lacked originality. This contention is, in part, historically justifiable, if by the term "Rabbanites" we understand all Jews, including some questioners of the established order, in the days before 'Anan. That this geonic memorandum was never intended for widespread circulation is intimated by Qirqisani himself who admits to never having seen a copy.[79]

Even Saadiah was not particularly alarmed. Although both the quantity and quality of Karaite polemics had greatly increased in the intervening years, this born controversialist, who was always spoiling for a fight, gave the public struggle against Karaism a low priority. The rapid deterioration in the imperial situation, we recall, had induced this great gaon to dream of the reunification of world Jewry under his own leadership. Among the forces of dissolution, he undoubtedly realized, were also the various sectarian movements. But he personally felt far more the menace of religious indifferentism and, within the Jewish communal structure, the threat of those centrifugal forces of regional independence which had become unmanageable by the weakened exilarchate.

Although at the age of twenty-three he composed a treatise against 'Anan and in subsequent years added at least two other polemical tracts, he apparently did it only to have the replies ready at hand in case of need. Personally he not only refused to debate controversial issues with leading Karaites—he was allegedly challenged to such a debate by Ben Mashiaḥ—but he never circulated copies of his treatises outside a small circle of associates. According to Sahl ben Maṣliaḥ, none of his anti-Karaite writings "came out from under his hands in his lifetime, but one came into Ben Mashiaḥ's possession." Such private circulation, rather than, as some modern scholars suggested, wholesale destruction of all then extant copies by Karaites, accounts also for their almost total disappearance in the later Middle Ages. Certainly willful destruction by enemies would have rather whetted the appetites of Rabbanite readers for such literature and vastly increased its circulation. As it is, only some of Saadiah's contemporaries and immediate successors, chiefly among the Karaite controversialists who indulged in vicious attacks on this "archfoe of Karaism," were directly acquainted with those polemical essays. Later writers, even among his Karaite opponents, seem to know his arguments largely from second hand. Almost all of Saadiah's anti-Karaite writings, moreover, seem to antedate his ascension to the gaonate. As soon as he became the official head of the academy, he not only moderated his attack on this small but influential segment of the Jewish community, but ultimately, in the great stress of his conflict with the exilarch, even welcomed the support of the Karaite chieftains in Jerusalem.[80]

Intellectually, to be sure, the Karaite challenge could not be quite so easily dismissed. The other heresies, unsupported by learned arguments from Scripture and philosophic reason, could be ignored as a "lunatic fringe." But the energies generated by the debates raised by scholars of the rank of 'Anan, Benjamin, Qumisi, Qirqisani, and some of the younger men living in Saadiah's time who were to reach eminence in the following decades, added greatly to that intellectual ferment of which the gaon himself was in many ways the outstanding product and to which he constantly responded. In the area of biblical research, in particular, the commentaries by Nahawendi, Qumisi, and probably many others whose works and even names are no longer known to us, had made novel and significant contributions. Their methods and basic approaches were totally at variance with the traditional hermeneutic interpretation of the talmudic sages, which no longer satisfied the scholarly tastes of the new generations. Like these men reacting also to the more "modern" exegesis of the Qur'an among the Muslims, Saadiah himself had much too much in common with them to gloss over completely their novel approaches or even some of their detailed interpretations. That is why, however little he thought of the Karaite "peril" in terms of Jewish communal coexistence and unity, he had to pay considerable attention to these predecessors' exegetical efforts. For the benefit of his own disciples and followers he had to answer, at least obliquely, some of the searching questions raised by these "heretical" interpreters, free from the bounds of rabbinic tradition. He had to justify, for example, the rabbinic interpretation of "on the morrow after the Sabbath" (in Lev. 23:11, 15) as referring not to a Sunday, but to any day after the first day of Passover. This rabbinic interpretation had been under attack by almost all heterodox groups beginning with the ancient Sadducees. If God had wished, Qirqisani observed, that the Festival of Weeks should always "fall on the same day of the month as do the other holidays, Scripture would have stated it expressly, as it did with respect to the other holidays." More generally, the dates of Jewish festivals, based upon an astronomic computation, were questioned as running counter to the ancient method of direct observation of the movements of the moon, which was now buttressed by its renewal among the Muslim majority. In his fervor, as we recall, Saadiah went so far as to try to find biblical support for the astronomic computation and to claim that it had already been enjoined by Moses on Sinai. These examples could readily be multiplied. But we must not be misled by these frequent intellectual exercises, even acrobatics, into believing that the gaon, or any other leading Rabbanite of that period, considered the Karaite movement as such a serious threat to the Jewish community or even to the traditional religious forms and way of life.[81]

While to Karaites Saadiah's name always conjured associations of unreasoning hatred, his own successors in the gaonate never referred to this phase of his public activity. In fact, Sherira included in his *Epistle* only a passing reference to the appearance of 'Anan. His son Hai and the latter's father-in-law, Samuel ben Ḥofni, the last of the distinguished Babylonian teachers of world Jewry, mentioned Karaism but casually and without any signs of fear or anger.

Even in Palestine and Egypt, where the rise of an intellectually as well as politically influential group of Karaites might have caused alarm to the Rabbanite community, the latter's leadership maintained on the whole its *sang froid*. True, there were extremists on both sides. Ben Meir, as we recall, had occasion bitterly to complain of his and his ancestors' persecutions at the hand of Karaites. But we cannot now ascertain how many of these difficulties were of the Rabbanites' own making. Certainly, the long practice of pronouncing from Mt. Olivet on every Feast of Tabernacles, a formal ban against the violators of the milk-and-meat prohibition, was a grave Rabbanite provocation. This excommunication was accompanied by the customary maledictions against the transgressors, and it was recited loudly within the earshot of Karaite worshipers. Even when, to establish peace, Caliph

Az-Zahir formally forbade these bans, some fanatics insisted on defying the governmental order and suffered severe retribution. The Rabbanites had such a preponderant majority that, through sheer weight of numbers, they were able to force the Karaites to keep shops closed on Rabbanite holidays and, despite obvious religious scruples, to buy in Rabbanite butcher shops whatever little meat they felt entitled to consume in Jerusalem. Only after strenuous efforts by the Karaite grandees in Cairo did their Jerusalem coreligionists secure the necessary freedoms, in which they were curiously aided by conciliatory policies of the outstanding Rabbanite gaon, Solomon ben Yehudah (about 1025–51). In a remarkable letter the gaon actually wished the Karaite chief in the Holy City, of whom he speaks with great respect, full success on his political mission to Cairo, which probably had something to do with curbing the Jerusalem extremists on both sides. About the same time the elders of a Palestinian community, doubtless predominantly Rabbanite, unconcernedly addressed themselves to the two communities, Rabbanite and Karaite, in Cairo and requested, in particular, the intervention of "our elders, the elders of the Karaites." [82]

By the time of Maimonides matters had settled in a somewhat more definitive groove. In his earlier writings the great jurist-philosopher revealed some of the animus prevailing in his original Spanish habitat. In his *Commentary* on the Mishnah (Ḥullin 1.2) he not only excluded the contemporary heretics (with an unmistakable reference to the Karaites) from the category of apostates whose slaughtering, according to the talmudic sages, did not disqualify the meat for use by pious Jews, but also added:

> Know that we possess a tradition from our teachers, transmitted as a matter of public knowledge from generation to generation, that the rule that capital punishment is not to be imposed in the days of Exile applies only to a Jew committing a capital crime. Heretics, Sadducees and Boethoseans, however, are punished by us in accordance with the severity of their evil deeds, so that they may not corrupt Israel and cause it to lose its faith. This norm has already been put into practice on many occasions in all western lands.

Ironically, Maimonides here quoted another tradition from his teachers, whereby Jews guilty of capital crimes were irrevocably banished from the community—a tradition which, as we remember, may have originated with 'Anan.

In Egypt, however, confronted with the realities of closer Karaite-Rabbanite relations, the sage of Fusṭaṭ increasingly toned down his animosity. Although he resented Karaite influences on his coreligionists, for instance with respect to laws of purity, he only placed these sectarians on a par with the Samaritans, whose rejection had been hedged about in the Talmud with many qualifications. While insisting that Karaite writs of divorce were not valid even for Karaites, he denied that the latter were "heretics" (*minim*), in the technical meaning of that term. On the contrary, in a much-quoted responsum he urged a correspondent to treat them with great moderation and respect: "One ought to inquire about their well-being even by visiting their homes, to circumcise their sons even on the Sabbath, to bury their dead, and to comfort their mourners," provided only that they refrain from speaking slightingly of the rabbis of that and the former generations. This more tolerant policy was pursued by Maimonides' son Abraham, officiating as *nagid* of all Egyptian Jewry. Always stressing the basic difference in the two groups' attitude to Oral Law, Abraham nevertheless advised his correspondents to believe a pious Karaite's assurance under oath that he had not employed a Gentile in the preparation or the transportation of wine.[83]

Some of that aloofness of Rabbanite leadership undoubtedly stemmed from the traditional Jewish policy of ignoring sectarian trends. But its persistence over a period of centuries can be explained only by the absence of any real sense of danger. A mere comparison with the reactions of talmudic Judaism to the rise of Christianity shows how relatively little the rhythm of Jewish life was affected by the presence in some communities of a Karaite minority.

Minor modifications did take place, however. True, repeated assertions of Karaite apologists to the contrary, the number of direct borrowings of Karaite practices even by Palestinian Rabbanites was exceedingly small. In most cases, it seems, the Karaites claimed as their own some ancient Palestinian customs which, for some reason, had not been recorded in the rabbinic literature. Yet some relatively minor new observances and teachings, or somewhat novel emphases, imperceptibly crept into Rabbanite life which find their best explanation in the acceptance or, more frequently, in the rejection of these sectarian teachings.

Extreme Karaite nationalism and the call for the return to the Holy Land may well have added force to the Rabbanite efforts to strengthen the supremacy of Babylonia's central authorities. Rabbanite homilists now had their field day in extolling the greatness of the Babylonian academies and, more generally, of the Oral Law expounded there. Commenting on the concluding verse of the Song of Songs, one preacher declaimed: " 'Upon the mountains of spices,' this refers to the two academies and demonstrates to you that the Divine presence [*shekhinah*] departed from Jerusalem and stayed in Babylonia." Another medieval homilist went back to the days before the Sinaitic revelation. The Gentile nations, he contended, had been fully prepared to accept the totality of the Written Law, but refused to submit to the endless legal minutiae included in the Oral Law. Hence they were rejected by the Lord. One did not have to strain one's imagination thus to equate the Karaite position with the "audacity" of these Gentile deniers of the oral tradition. Harping on this theme of the Lord's Covenant with Israel only on account of the latter's acceptance of the Oral Law, another rabbi stole the thunder of the Karaite ascetics. "You will not find," he exclaimed, "the Oral Law among persons seeking worldly pleasures, lust, honor, and greatness of this world, but only among those who are sacrificing their lives in its behalf, as it is written, 'This is the law: when a man dieth in a tent [Num. 19:14].' " If Karaites pointed an accusing finger at contradictory judgments rendered by the two academies and cited them as proof that neither was in possession of genuine traditions, the Rabbanite leaders countered, as we recollect, by demanding that inquiries be addressed to only one of them, thus forestalling a possible divergence in replies.[84]

Opposition to Karaism also led to the reaffirmation and further elaboration of talmudic law. Pirqoi ben Baboi, the most radical champion of Babylonian hegemony, seems to betray some such influence in his tacit repudiation of 'Anan's prohibition of administering medical treatment on the Sabbath. The Karaites prohibited the kindling of fire on the Sabbath for the benefit of a childbearing woman, even if her life be thereby jeopardized.

Why should we profane the Sabbath for her sake [asked Hadassi], when we have seen so many women in childbed without a candle or fire who notwithstanding severe labor pains were saved by the grace of God? . . . Moreover, if we profane the Sabbath and the woman happens to die, we will not have rescued her, but merely sinned to our God and desecrated the day of his holiness [*Eshkol*, fol. 73a].

Contrast with this the (perhaps polemically) pointed statement of Pirqoi ben Baboi,

Even in doubtful cases danger to life abrogates all negative commandments in the Torah, including Sabbath rest. . . . The Holy One, blessed be He, has not given commandments to kill Israel, but the Torah and the commandments are life to Israel, life both in this world and in the world to come. Indeed, not one commandment whose performance is dangerous has God enjoined upon Israel [Ginzberg, *Ginze Schechter*, I, 19 f.].

Nonetheless, a few Karaite customs (for example, standing up all night on the Day of Atonement) imperceptibly crept into the life of Rabbanite Jewry. Out of the very anti-Karaite mood arose some new observances which soon became sanctified. For instance, a special benediction was now introduced for the lighting of candles on the Sabbath, while the Talmud had intimated that one does not have to make a benediction at an obligatory performance. The Rabbanites insisted upon the presentation of a symbolic ring to the bride as a prerequisite of marriage, instead of the payment of the actual biblical *mohar* as demanded by the Karaites. To make sure that the masses not be misled by the Karaite insistence on the daytime counting of the *sefirah* during the seven weeks between Passover and the Festival of Weeks, Simon Qayyara, followed by Saadiah, declared that if one forgot to count it on the first evening, one could no longer count it during that year. We possess the testimony of Simon bar Ṣemaḥ Duran (fifteenth century) that, out of spite, the Rabbanites began calling each other "Rabbi," an honorific title originally reserved for those officially "ordained" in Palestine. Rabbanite Jewry has ever since adorned with this title the first names of all its orthodox members.

Simon Qayyara even ventured to count the festivals of Ḥanukkah and Purim among the 613 Mosaic commandments—obviously an overzealous anti-Karaite move, in defense of which many medieval rabbis, such as Naḥmanides, vainly sharpened their wits. In another unguarded *pronunciamento,* we recollect, Sherira exclaimed, "Whosoever disapproves of one word of the geonim is like one who attacks God and the Torah!" [85]

PERMANENT GAINS

Bitterness generated by this controversy undoubtedly had many unpleasant features. It helped, nevertheless, to stir popular interest in the various aspects of the conflict—theological, scientific, and political. In the long run, it mattered little that the leading Karaites vilified their rabbinic adversaries in most scurrilous terms, often casting aspersions on the descent or personal character of their opponents. Even when they denounced the Rabbanites before the governments or Gentile public opinion, the harm done was much less than the ultimate gain. Hadassi may have anticipated Eisenmenger in collecting all the acrimonious passages of the Talmud concerning the 'Am ha-Areṣ; other Karaites may have exposed to public ridicule the anthropomorphic passages in talmudic literature; still others, like Salmon ben Yeruḥim, may have contended that the Rabbanites had given up the Ten Commandments. Yet the final effect was only to evoke a rabbinical reformulation of the old ideas in conformity with the demands of the new age. The story told by Ibn al-Hiti about Saadiah attending Salmon's funeral in Aleppo "with his garments torn, girded with a rope and barefoot" (G. Margoliouth in *JQR,* [o.s.] IX, 441) is indubitably apocryphal. But Saadiah's alleged statement on this occasion, "We both derived much profit from our controversies," though likewise spurious, well mirrors the historic realities. Out of the controversy grew an important polemical literature, and many new impulses were given to literary activity in the whole range of Jewish studies. The Rabbanites, too, used harsh terms. The pig, the most obnoxious animal in Jewish zoology, was drawn into the controversy to such an extent that it often was unnecessary to name the opposing party. But in the last analysis the rabbis were forced to evolve ever new arguments in the defense of their traditions, and thus to reconsider their own position.

Taken as a whole, the social forces behind Karaism sufficed to disrupt the unity of Israel for a time, but they could not destroy it permanently. Unlike Pauline Christianity, the Karaite movement never preached separation from the mother religion. In their very polemics its leaders prayed, as did Salmon, that the Lord "may restore the tents of Judah and Israel to their pristine glory, so that they become united. No longer shall they be divided into two nations, but they shall become one nation, the Chosen People" (*Milḥamot,* p. 131). Resembling far more the Samaritan schism, the Karaite movement became separated from the main body of Jewry not as a result of any conscious designs of its own, but rather because of the growing intransigence of the majority.

Like its Samaritan predecessors, too, the Karaite sect, with its static and alien modifications, was so wholly dependent on temporary conditions that, when these passed, it lost ground from generation to generation. Once its moderate expansion was checked in the eleventh century, its influence waned, even among its own adherents. If we are to believe a twelfth-century convert, Samau'al ibn Yaḥya, the majority of Karaites abandoned Judaism altogether and adopted Islam. Outside the Muslim and Byzantine environments, Karaism never acclimatized itself in any degree, and the Karaite settlements of Troki or Halicz were but islands within the sea of European Judaism. Ultimately excluded more rigidly than Gentiles from the connubium with Jews, unable and unwilling to establish far-reaching contacts with the non-Jewish world, the Karaites gradually sank to a position of minor significance in the history of their people.

NOTES

ABBREVIATIONS

AHR	American Historical Review
Abrahams Mem. Vol.	Jewish Studies in Memory of Israel Abrahams. New York, 1927.
Baron Jub. Vol.	Essays on Jewish Life and Thought. Presented in honor of Salo Wittmayer Baron. New York, 1958.
b.	Babylonian Talmud
B.B.	Baba Batra (talmudic tractate)
BIES	Bulletin of the Israel Exploration Society
BJPES	Bulletin (*Yediot*) of the Jewish Palestine Exploration Society
BJRL	Bulletin of the John Rylands Library, Manchester
Blau Mem. Vol.	Zikhron Yehudah. Tanulmanyok Blau Lajos. Budapest, 1938.
B.M.	Baba Meṣiah (talmudic tractate)
B.Q.	Baba Qamma
BSOAS	Bulletin of the School of Oriental and African Studies (University of London)
CSCO	Corpus Scriptorum christianorum orientalium
EI	Encyclopaedia of Islam
EJ	Encyclopaedia Judaica
Essays Hertz	Essays in honour of J. H. Hertz. London, 1942.
Festschrift Harkavy	Festschrift zu Ehren des Dr. A. Harkavy. St. Petersburg, 1908.
Festschrift Kaminka	Festschrift für Armand Kaminka. Vienna, 1937.
GK	Ginze Kedem
Goldziher Mem. Vol.	Ignace Goldziher Memorial Volume. 2 vols. Budapest, 1946–55.
GS	Gesammelte Schriften
Ḥ.M.	Ḥoshen Mishpaṭ (sections of Jacob ben Asher's *Ṭurim* and Joseph Karo's *Shulḥan 'Arukh*)
HTR	Harvard Theological Review
HUCA	Hebrew Union College Annual
IC	Islamic Culture

j.	Palestinian Talmud
JA	Journal asiatique
JAOS	Journal of the American Oriental Society
JBL	Journal of Biblical Literature and Exegesis
JJGL	Jahrbuch für jüdische Geschichte und Literatur
JJS	Journal of Jewish Studies
JPOS	Journal of the Palestine Oriental Society
JQR	Jewish Quarterly Review (new series, unless otherwise stated)
JRAS	Journal of the Royal Asiatic Society
JSS	Jewish Social Studies
Kohut Mem. Vol.	Jewish Studies in Memory of George A. Kohut. New York, 1935.
KS	Kirjath Sepher, Quarterly Bibliographical Review
Löw Mem. Vol.	Semitic Studies in Memory of Immanuel Löw. Budapest, 1947.
M.	Mishnah
Magnes Anniv. Book	Magnes Anniversary Book. By Staff of the Hebrew University. Jerusalem, 1938.
MGH	Monumenta Germaniae Historica
MGWJ	Monatsschrift für Geschichte und Wissenschaft des Judentums
MJC	Mediaeval Jewish Chronicles, ed. by A. Neubauer
M.T.	Moses ben Maimon's Mishneh Torah (Code)
MW	Moslem World
MWJ	Magazin für die Wissenschaft des Judentums
O.Ḥ.	Oraḥ Ḥayyim (sections of Jacob ben Asher's *Ṭurim* and Joseph Karo's *Shulḥan 'Arukh*)
OLZ	Orientalistische Literaturzeitung
PAAJR	Proceedings of the American Academy for Jewish Research
PG	Patrologiae cursus completus, series Graeca
PL	Patrologiae cursus completus, series Latina
Poznanski Mem. Vol.	Livre d'hommage à la mémoire du Samuel Poznanski. Warsaw, 1927.
r.	Midrash Rabbah (Gen. r. = Bereshit rabbah; Lam. r. = Ekhah rabbati, etc.)
Rashi Anniv. Vol.	American Academy for Jewish Research, Texts and Studies, Vol. I. Rashi Anniversary Volume, New York, 1941.
RB	Revue biblique (includes wartime *Vivre et Penser*)
REJ	Revue des études juives
Resp.	Responsa (*Teshubot* or *She'elot u-teshubot*)

RH	Revue historique
R.H.	Rosh ha-Shanah (talmudic tractate)
RHC	Recueil des historiens des croisades
RHDO	Revue d'histoire du droit oriental
RHPR	Revue d'histoire et de philosophie religieuses
RHR	Revue d'histoire des religions
RMAL	Revue du moyen âge latin
RSO	Rivista di studi orientali
Saadia Anniv. Vol.	American Academy for Jewish Research. Texts and Studies, Vol. II. Saadia Anniversary Volume. New York, 1943.
SB	Sitzungsberichte der Akademie der Wissenschaften (identified by city: e.g., *SB* Berlin, Heidelberg, Vienna)
Schwarz Festschrift	Festschrift Adolf Schwarz. Berlin, 1917.
Shorter EI	Shorter Encyclopaedia of Islam, ed. by H. A. R. Gibb and J. H. Kramers. Leiden, 1953.
T.	Tosefta. Ed. by M. S. Zuckermandel
TZ	Theologische Zeitschrift (Basel, 1945–)
Vienna Seminary Mem. Vol.	Sefer ha-Zikkaron le-bet ha-midrash le-rabbanim. Jerusalem, 1946.
VT	Vetus Testamentum
YB	Yivo Bleter
Y.D.	Yoreh de'ah (sections of Jacob ben Asher's *Ṭurim* and Joseph Karo's *Shulḥan 'Arukh*)
Yearbook CCAR	Yearbook of the Central Conference of American Rabbis
ZDMG	Zeitschrift der Deutschen Morgenländischen Gesellschaft
ZNW	Zeitschrift für die neutestamentliche Wissenschaft und die Kunde der älteren Kirche

NOTES

CHAPTER XXIII: COMMUNAL CONTROLS

1. Saadiah's Hebrew "Letter," published by B. Revel in *Debir,* I, 186; his *Book of Beliefs and Opinions,* III.7, ed. by Landauer, p. 128; in Ibn Tibbon's Hebrew trans., p. 66; in S. Rosenblatt's English trans. p. 158; his responsum reproduced in J. Müller's edition of his Treatise on Inheritance and other legal works in *Oeuvres complètes,* IX, 114 f. No. 24; Mann's *Texts and Studies,* I, 556 No. IV; Sheshna's decision in *Sha'are teshubah* (Responsa of the Geonim), No. 195. Cf. also the sources cited by W. Leiter in the introduction to his ed. of the latter work, p. 15; and on Sheshna's authorship of this enactment, J. Mann's "Responsa of the Babylonian Geonim as a Source of Jewish History," *JQR,* X, 124 n. 184. One must bear in mind that not only were Jewish parties apprehensive of being discriminated against in Muslim courts—the generally prevailing double standard of morals in dealing with coreligionists as against outsiders fully justified these fears—but they also generally held the Muslim judges' professional ethics in very low esteem. Hai Gaon's friendly, but condescending, words about the Baghdad judiciary placed in even bolder relief his condemnation of other Muslim courts. Cf. E. Tyan's *Histoire de l'organisation judiciaire en pays d'Islam,* I, 428 ff.; the sources cited by S. Assaf in his *Teshubot ha-geonim,* 1942, pp. 19, 21 f., 75 f.; and his lectures on *Tequfat ha-geonim ve-sifruta* (The Geonic Period and Its Literature), pp. 20 f. These themes are so fundamental to the entire inner life of medieval Jewry that they will recur here in different contexts with many variations.

2. Nathan the Babylonian's Report, in *MJC,* II, 85; A. Mingana's ed. and English trans. of "A Charter of Protection Granted to the Nestorian Church in A.D. 1138, by Muktafi II, Caliph of Baghdad," *BJRL,* X, 132 f. (the last two plates of the Arabic text). A decree issued in 1208–9 by Caliph An-Naṣir bidin Allahi in favor of the Baghdad gaon Daniel ben Eleazar ben Hibbat-Allah (Natanel), was far narrower in scope and can hardly be used for the reconstruction of a decree addressed to an exilarch. Cf. the Arabic text with a German trans., cited from Ibn as-Sa'i's report, by S. Poznanski in his *Babylonische Geonim im nachgaonäischen Zeitalter,* pp. 37 ff.; and *infra,* nn. 7, 23. Another text of a decree for a *catholicos* was published by A. von Kremer in the second of his "Zwei arabische Urkunden," *ZDMG,* VII, 215–23 (with an abridged German trans.); and revised with an English summary, by H. F. Amedroz in his "Tales of Official Life from the 'Tadhkira' of Ibn Hamdun, etc.," *JRAS,* 1908, pp. 447 ff., 467 ff. On the impact of the sectarian divisions on Jewish self-government, see *infra,* n. 6; Chaps. XXV, n. 52, and XXVI, nn. 78 ff. Prayers for the reigning monarch, mentioned in the concluding paragraph of the Nestorian charter, had become a major test of political loyalty both in the Byzantine and Muslim empires. It is therefore more than probable that Jews, too, were required by law to include such "invocations" in their services.

They must have complied the more readily as they may have been in some measure coresponsible for the introduction of this entire liturgical innovation. Cf. *infra,* Chap. XXXI; and, more generally, N. Edelby's detailed juridical analysis of "L'Autonomie législative des Chrétiens en terre d'Islam," *RHDO,* V, 307–52, which applies largely to the Islamic world's Jewish minorities as well.

3. Ibn Lahi'a, quoted by Goldziher in "Renseignements de source musulmane . . . ," *REJ,* VIII, 124 f.; S. Pinès edition of an excerpt from Al-Qasim ibn Ibrahim's work written between 834 and 860 in "Une Notice sur le Rech Galuta chez un écrivain arabe du IXe siècle," *ibid.,* C bis, 71–73; A. S. Tritton's *Caliphs,* pp. 78 ff. On the generally good life expectancy of Jewish leaders of that period otherwise filled with political assassinations, see *supra,* Chap. XVIII, n. 2. Perhaps in answer to the taunts of Jewish controversialists, some Arabs invented the yarn that the demise of Abu Bakr, the first caliph and the only one among the first four rulers to die a natural death, had been caused by Jews. According to a report of the poet Harit ibn Malik, Jews had mixed some poison into the meats served to Abu Bakr. "That poison did not take effect until after the passage of a year, and killed the caliph after an illness of fifteen days." Cf. Mas'udi, *Prairies d'or,* ed. and trans. by Barbier de Meynard and Pavet de Courteille, IV, 183 f.

4. Barhebraeus, *Chronicon ecclesiasticum,* II.50, ed. by Abbeloos and Lamy, III, 275 (with the editors' note thereon); Michael Syrus, *Chronique,* ed. by J. B. Chabot, III, 519 (Syriac), 68 f. (French); Isidore of Seville, *Adversus Judaeos,* I.8.2, in *PL,* LXXXIII, 464; Ḥisdai's letter, ed. by E. N. Adler in "The Installation of the Egyptian Nagid," *JQR,* [o.s.] IX, 717–20; Daniel b. Ḥisdai's epistle in S. Assaf's "Letters of R. Samuel ben 'Ali and his Contemporaries" (Hebrew), *Tarbiz,* I, Part 3, p. 75; Nissim of Marseilles, *Ma'ase nissim,* cited by J. H. Schorr in his "R. Nissim bar Moses of Marseilles" (Hebrew), *Hechaluz,* VII, 110. The apologetic import of the existence of an exilarchate for the Jews in the Christian world is also evident in Jacob bar Elijah's *Iggeret* (Polemical Letter) against Fra Pablo which, even in the late thirteenth century, still extolled the contemporary exilarch, Samuel, "who is of the house of David, a foremost leader and one of the royal councillors and dignitaries of state." Cf. J. Kobak's edition of that letter in *Jeschurun,* VI, Hebrew section, p. 29; and, on its date, J. Mann's "On the Time and Place of R. Jacob b. Elijah" (Hebrew), *'Alim,* I, 75–77 (a reply to A. Z. Schwarz). Cf. also *supra,* Chap. XVI, n. 47; Mann's *Jews in Egypt,* I, 253 (discussing Ḥisdai's identity and background, though somewhat unduly minimizing the meaning of the phrase here quoted); his *Texts and Studies,* I, 230 n. 63, restoring the text of a line (fol. 3 recto, l. 15) in Daniel ben Ḥisdai's letter (in Assaf's ed., Part 3, p. 69) to read that the writer designated himself "king on earth by the grace of God"; and, *infra,* n. 47. A careful chronological survey of the succession of exilarchs till the Mongolian conquests is given by A. D. Goode in "The Exilarchate in the Eastern Caliphate, 637–1258," *JQR,* XXXI, 149–69. Some further aspects of the exilarchate and the medieval sources relating thereto are discussed in my *Jewish Community,* I, 173 ff.; III, 39 ff. Cf. also *supra,* Vol. II, pp. 195 ff., 403.

5. Sherira, *Iggeret,* ed. by Lewin, pp. 92 f.; and the editor's supplement thereto, pp. xv ff.; Abraham ibn Daud's Chronicle, in *MJC,* I, 62. See *supra,* Chap. XVII, n. 20. Cf. the eight versions of the Bustanai story reproduced and analyzed by

H. Tykocinski in his "Bustanai, the Exilarch" (Hebrew), *Debir,* I, 145–79; and the additional text published from an Adler MS by A. Marx in "Der arabische Bustanai-Bericht und Nathan ha-Babli," *Poznanski Mem. Vol.,* pp. 76–81. Partisan bias often colored even the identification of the descendants of the Persian princess. It was almost generally agreed that her line had come to power in the middle of the eighth century and that hence, for instance, David ben Zakkai belonged to her progeny. Nevertheless Khalaf-Aaron ibn Sarjado, one of David's leading partisans in the struggle with Saadiah, endeavored to shift the blemish to Saadiah's adherents from the house of Boaz. By indirection Ibn Sarjado thus tried to whitewash the reigning exilarch, although the same reasoning could of course be used also in favor of David's brother and rival, Josiah-Ḥasan. Cf. the rather corrupt text in Harkavy's *Zikhron,* V, 227; and Mann's *Texts and Studies,* I, 335 n. 21. Here (pp. 334 f.) Mann has also identified Nathan ben Abraham, the pretender to the gaonate of Palestine, as the author of one of the Bustanai accounts. See *infra,* n. 36; and Chaps. XXV, n. 3 (some messianic aspects of the Bustanai story); XXVIII, nn. 60–61 (the earlier genealogy and the exilarchic branch in Palestine).

6. Barhebraeus, *Chronicon ecclesiasticum,* I, 365 ff.; Denys of Tell-Mahré, *Chronique,* IV, ed. by J. B. Chabot, pp. xii, xx ff.; Samuel ben 'Ali's "Letters," ed. by Assaf in *Tarbiz,* I, Part 2, pp. 66 f. Curiously, this major menace to Jewish unity found few echoes in contemporary Jewish letters. Mainly concerned with the story of the academic leaders, Sherira Gaon merely mentioned that "in the middle of the Muslim regime in the days of David ben Yehudah the Prince, they [the exilarchs] were deprived of their governmental authority," and that hence the heads of the Pumbedita academy ceased attending the convocations at the exilarchic court. Cf. his *Iggeret,* p. 93 (French recension; the Spanish version mistakenly substituted the name of the better known exilarch, David ben Zakkai, for ben Yehudah). Like the even more pointed contention by Samuel ben 'Ali, this statement reflects the bias of the geonic party, and hence is not necessarily an exact reflection of Al-Ma'mun's original enactment, and of its subsequent full or partial reversal. Nevertheless, because of their great authority, the word of these geonim has generally been accepted without demurrer by Jewish scholars, including F. Lazarus in his otherwise meritorious essay, "Neue Beiträge zur Geschichte des Exilarchats," *MGWJ,* LXXVIII, 279–88.

7. The story of 'Uqba's deposition and the bankers' role in these internal struggles still is full of obscurities. Our main rapporteur, Nathan the Babylonian (in *MJC,* II, 78 f.; and in the Arabic original, ed. by Friedlaender in *JQR,* [o.s.] XVII, 753 ff.) is controverted in many significant, though secondary, details by Sherira (in his *Iggeret,* Lewin ed., pp. 119 f.). Neither author was a contemporary of these events, and all efforts at reconciling their reports have proved futile. But the weight of evidence favors Nathan. See my reconstruction of these events in "Saadia's Communal Activities," *Saadia Anniv. Vol.,* pp. 25 ff. On Neṭira and his banking associates, see also *supra,* Chaps. XVIII, n. 36; XXII, n. 65. Ultimately, a *jahbadh* (banker-contractor) of the Imperial Cabinet, Abu Tahir ibn Shibr, became the recognized *rais al-yahud,* a title formerly reserved for the exilarch. Cf. Ibn as-Sa'i al-Khazin, *K. al-Djami' al-muktasar* (Annales et biographies), ed. by Mustafa Jawad and P. Anastase-Marie de St. Elie (about Abu Tahir's son, Abu Ghalib, who served as Chief of Money), cited in C. Cahen's review of D. S. Sassoon's *History of the*

Jews in Baghdad in *RH,* CCVIII, 307 ff. The "Panegyrics in Honour of a Baghdad Dignitary from the Kaufmann Geniza," recently published, from three MSS, by A. Scheiber in the Budapest Academy's *Acta orientalia,* III, 107–33 (also in Hebrew in *Zion,* XVIII, 6–13, with "Notes and Supplements" by M. Zulay, pp. 13–14), likewise extolled one of the wealthy bankers, rather than a member of the exilarchic family. Incidentally, this grandee owned a private synagogue, at which the distinguished cantor, Nahum ben Joseph al-Baradani seems to have served as reader, perhaps until his departure for Kairuwan in 996. Such exaltation of wealthy patrons is not surprising, since even poets of the rank of Yehudah al-Ḥarizi had to resort to this means of securing a living. See *supra,* Chap. XXII, n. 86; and *infra,* Chap. XXXII. Of course, exilarchs, too, even if not necessarily serving as generous patrons of belles-lettres, sometimes became the subjects of such adulatory poems. One such *yoṣer* (liturgical poem intended for recitation during morning services) in honor of an exilarch has likewise been published by A. Scheiber from the Kaufmann collection in a Hebrew essay in *Sinai,* XVI, No. 198, pp. 238–43. Scheiber's suggestion that this poem was addressed to David ben Zakkai, Saadiah's well-known opponent, still awaits confirmation.

8. Samuel ben 'Ali's letter, ed. by Assaf in *Tarbiz,* I, Part 2, pp. 65 ff.; *infra,* n. 49; Benjamin's *Massa'ot,* pp. 40 f. (Hebrew), 39 f. (English)—with reference to Gen. 49:10; Maimonides' well-known letter of 1190 (rather than 1191) to his pupil, Joseph ben Yehudah ibn Shime'on in *Iggerot ha-Rambam* (Epistles from and to Moses b. Maimon), ed. by D. Z. Baneth, Part I, pp. 64 f. Baneth denies both the long-accepted identity of Ibn Shime'on with Joseph ben Yehudah ibn 'Aqnin, another distinguished contemporary, and Z. Diesendruck's theory that this letter was a composite work compiled by early editors from seven or more distinct fragments of epistles written by the philosopher at different times. Cf. *ibid.,* pp. 1, 33 ff., and Diesendruck's "On the Date of the Completion of the Moreh Nebukim," *HUCA,* XII–XIII, 461–97. On the authenticity of this letter, ingeniously, but far from conclusively, impugned by J. L. Teicher (in his "Maimonides' Letter to Joseph ben Jehudah—A Literary Forgery," *JJS,* I, 35–54), cf. *infra,* Chap. XXXIV. More recently, A. S. Halkin has successfully defended both its authenticity and Diesendruck's "fragmentary" theory on the basis of a letter written by a contemporary of Abraham Maimuni. Cf. Halkin's "In Defense of Maimonides' Code" (Hebrew), *Tarbiz,* XXV, 413–28. In another context, Maimonides also restated sharply the talmudic insistence on the universal validity of an authorization given to a judge by a Babylonian exilarch, as against the merely regional range of such an authorization by a Palestinian academy. Cf. his *Commentary* on M. Bekhorot IV.4. Hezekiah's regime as both exilarch and gaon from 1038 to 1058, rather than 1040, has plausibly been suggested by Poznanski (by substituting *kaf* for *bet* in Ibn Daud's chronicle), and accepted by Mann in "The Exilarchic Office in Babylonia and Its Ramifications at the End of the Geonic Period," *Poznanski Mem. Vol.,* Hebrew section, pp. 21 f. Cf. also *supra,* Chap. XVIII, n. 2. A small ray of light on the obscure period after Hezekiah's death in 1058 (see Mann, p. 23) was thrown by a brief entry in Abu 'Ali al-Ḥanbali's Diary, dated February 13, 1069. He had heard, Al-Ḥanbali reports, "that discussion has risen to its highest point among the Jews [of Baghdad]; and that they wanted to appoint one particular son among the sons of David, but that Ibn Fadhlan opposed them and wanted to appoint someone else." Cf. G. Makdisi,

"Autograph Diary of an Eleventh-Century Historian of Baghdad," *BSOAS,* XIX, 25 (Arabic), 43 (English).

9. Nathan the Babylonian, *loc. cit.;* Al-Qasim, cited by Pinès in *REJ,* C bis, 71 f.; 'Amr ibn Baḥr al-Jaḥiẓ' *K. al-Hayawan* (Book of Animals), IV, 9; previously cited, together with Ibn Ḥazm, from manuscripts by I. Goldziher in *REJ,* VIII, 122, 125; Al-Biruni's *K. al-Athar al-bakiya* (Chronology of Ancient Nations), English trans. by E. Sachau, p. 19. On the latter's fairly reliable Jewish informants, cf. *infra,* Chap. XXXV. As we shall presently see, flogging was rather frequently imposed even by local Jewish courts. Cf. also W. J. Fischel's brief survey of "The 'Resh Galuta' in Arabic Literature" (Hebrew), *Magnes Anniv. Book,* pp. 181–87. Most Arab writers reflected, however, personal wishes and popular superstitions (including such queer beliefs as that each exilarch's long hands touched his knees) much more than legal theory or practice.

10. Nathan the Babylonian's Report, in *MJC,* II, 86 f.; *supra,* Vol. II, pp. 271, 420 n. 47. Muslims, too, often evinced preference for entrusting the leadership of an academy to members of the same family. As pointed out by A. S. Tritton, all teachers of one school for 160 years were descendants of the founder. In another academy the offspring of an early teacher held office, with but one interruption, for more than 200 years. Cf. Tritton's "Muslim Education in the Middle Ages (circa 600–800 A.H.)," *MW,* XLIII, 91. A good chronological list of all known geonim has been compiled by S. Assaf in his "Geonim," *EJ,* VII, 275 ff. To the end of the tenth century this chronology largely stands and falls with the dependability of our main source, Sherira's *Iggeret,* which is based, in part, on records preserved in the Pumbedita academy. Its evident occasional inaccuracies need not shake our confidence in the Epistle's general trustworthiness. Cf. my remarks in *Saadia Anniv. Vol.,* pp. 25 n. 41, 32 n. 53; and *infra,* Chap. XXVIII, n. 66. Cf. also S. Eppenstein's "Beiträge zur Geschichte und Literatur im gaonäischen Zeitalter," *MGWJ,* LII–LVII; and Assaf's *Tequfat ha-geonim, passim.*

11. J. Kaplan in *The Redaction of the Babylonian Talmud,* p. 321; Sherira's *Iggeret,* p. 105. Because of the ambiguities in Sherira's narrative and its underlying sources, modern scholars have differed widely in their interpretation of these early events. Cf., however, the felicitous, though partial, reconstruction of the major conflicts in L. Ginzberg, *Geonica,* I, 14 ff. The long and heatedly debated problems of transition from the "Saboraic" to the "geonic" periods are of greater importance for the history of Jewish law and letters than for that of Jewish self-government. They will, therefore, be more fully discussed *infra,* Chap. XXVII.

12. Sherira's *Iggeret,* ed. by Lewin, pp. 104 ff., 109 ff.; Samuel ben 'Ali's letter, cited *supra,* n. 6. On the jurisdictional divisions of the two academies and the early supremacy of Sura, see especially Nathan the Babylonian's Report, in *MJC,* II, 78 ff. Neither the date when, nor the extent to which, judgments of exilarchic courts required geonic confirmation is clear. Both known cases relate to Saadiah and David ben Zakkai and contain many ambiguities. In one instance (recorded in *Teshubot ha-geonim,* ed. by Harkavy, pp. 276 f. No. 555, 389; Saadiah's *Oeuvres,* IX, 119 f. No. 32) Saadiah was merely approached with a text of the exilarchic

judgment, asked to confirm its authenticity, and "after certification to decide what the law is" in the litigation. Here evidently the gaon was not asked to approve the original judgment, but to adjudicate on the basis of its authenticity, a *new* controversy which had arisen among the parties. The more famous case of the inheritance which became the starting point of the great conflict between the two men (see *infra,* n. 21) is told by Nathan with more dramatic flavor than precision. But it is not at all impossible that, while the deceased person had belonged to the exilarch's district, his large holdings were scattered through the provinces under geonic jurisdiction as well. Perhaps only for that reason was confirmation of the judgment by both geonim required. This matter awaits further elucidation which, in the light of the endless debates on this score, may be expected only from the discovery of some new sources.

13. Ibn Daud's Chronicle, in *MJC,* I, 74. The names of the communities to whom Saadiah had addressed the letter are partly misspelled. Perhaps Bajjan stands for Beja, and Kalsana for Calatayud. These were indeed major cities in Muslim Spain, and were often recorded by Arab geographers alongside the other localities here mentioned (except Lucena) as capitals of important Spanish subdivisions. Cf. Lévi-Provençal's data in *L'Espagne musulmane,* pp. 116 f. Of course, the great Jewish center of Lucena could not be omitted. Similarly, the emphasis on Merida being a great city seems awkward. Certainly Cordova and some of the others mentioned earlier were larger. Possibly, Saadiah concluded his address by using the term *medinah* in the meaning of country, and referred to the rest of Spain and the countries in its vicinity, whereas the copyist or the translator (if the letter was originally written in Arabic) reproduced it in the narrower sense of city. On the capital jurisdiction of Spanish Jewry, see *infra,* n. 52. See also *infra* Chap. XXVII, where some other aspects of Jewish judicial autonomy will also become clearer in the light of the general evolution of Jewish law; and N. Edelby's aforementioned essay in *RHDO,* V, 307 ff.

14. Cf. the extensive debates reproduced in Lewin, *Otzar ha-gaonim,* VIII, 124 f. Nos. 312–19; and the description in *Teshubot ha-geonim,* ed. by Harkavy, pp. 233 f. No. 440, with the editor's comments thereon, p. 384. Cf. also the comprehensive analysis of the two types of flagellation in A. Aptowitzer's Hebrew essay, "*Malqot* and *Makkat mardut,*" *Ha-Mishpaṭ ha-'ibri,* V, 33–104; and, more generally, S. Assaf's brief survey of *Bate ha-din ve-sidrehem* (Jewish Courts and Their Organization since the Conclusion of the Talmud). Additional bibliographical items are listed by P. Dickstein (Dikshtayn) in his *Dine 'Oneshin* (Criminal Law with Special Reference to Jewish Law and to the Law of Palestine), pp. 28 ff.

15. Maimonides, *Commentary* on M. Ḥullin, I.2; Naṭronai's resp. reproduced in Lewin, *Otzar ha-gaonim,* VIII, 106 f. No. 275; that by Palṭoi in *Sha'are ṣedeq,* v.4.14, fol. 75a; *infra,* Chap. XXVI, n. 13; Jaḥiẓ, *loc. cit.* (*supra,* n. 9); the anonymous Hebrew poem published by S. Schechter in his edition of "The Oldest Collection of Bible Difficulties, by a Jew," *JQR,* [o.s.] XIII, 365. The substitution of capital punishment by an irrevocable ban was also advocated by the Karaite, 'Anan. See *infra,* Chap. XXVI, n. 13. In his *Texts and Studies,* II, 58 ff., 97 ff., J. Mann has made a case for identifying the anonymous poet with one 'Ali ben Israel Alluf, an anti-Karaite controversialist (about 1066). As a wanderer from the vicinity of

Khorasan to Palestine, 'Ali had ample opportunity to observe the dismal effects of an excommunication in many communities. Cf. also *infra,* n. 55. Interesting formularies for bans, as well as their revocation, are communicated from a Montefiore MS and discussed on the basis of other geonic sources by V. Aptowitzer in his "Formularies of Decrees and Documents from a Gaonic Court," *JQR,* IV, 26 ff., 41 ff. The story told by Yehudah he-Ḥasid about a repentant murderer in the days of Hai Gaon who considered flogging and other tortures insufficient expiation (*Sefer Ḥasidim,* ed. by J. Wistinetzki, p. 169 No. 630), has all the earmarks of a folkloristic tale. Its connection with Hai Gaon's alleged annual visit to Jerusalem brands it unhistorical.

16. *Sefer ha-Ma'asim,* ed. by J. Mann in *Tarbiz,* I, Part 3, p. 12; Ṣemaḥ Gaon's resp. in the version quoted in *Sefer ha-Yishub,* II, 88 No. 9. On the complex and ramified problems of medieval Jewish criminal laws and procedures, cf. S. Assaf's *Ha-'Oneshin aḥare ḥatimat ha-Talmud* (Criminal Jurisdiction since the Conclusion of the Talmud); D. M. Shohet's dissertation, *The Jewish Court in the Middle Ages;* my *Jewish Community,* II, 220 ff.; III, 177 ff., and other literature cited there.

17. Qur'an 2:176; H. Lammens's *Islam,* p. 66. This *ḥadith* is clearly an invention of the first century after Mohammed to satisfy the parallel interests of the state and the masses of unbelievers. Cf. the data assembled by M. Schreiner in his "Notes sur les Juifs dans l'Islam," *REJ,* XXIX, 208 ff.; and Mez in his *Renaissance,* pp. 33 f., 112 f. According to both Malik and Shafi'i, a Muslim could not even inherit the estate of his apostate father. Opinions were more divided on the inheritance rights of Jews from Christians and vice versa, the Malikite school denying, Shafi'ites and Ḥanifites affirming them. Cf. the sources cited by Edelby in *RHDO,* V, 339 ff. This renunciation by Muslim legislators of the claims of converts to Islam is the more remarkable as, for certain internal purposes, Jewish legal theory treated apostates as Jews. Supported by local custom, R. Yehudai Gaon tried to free a childless widow from depending on the *ḥaliṣah* by a converted brother-in-law, at least if that levir had already been converted at the time of her marriage to his brother. But Yehudai was controverted by Sherira, Maimonides and others. Cf. *M.T.,* Yibbum, 1.6, with reference to M. Yebamot, 11.5; b. 22a; Ibn Gaon's comments thereon; Ginzberg's *Ginze Schechter,* II, 167 f., 172; and Lewin's *Otzar ha-gaonim,* VII, 33 ff. The treatment of converts must have been a doubly "burning" issue during the early expansion of Islam, and the Palestinian *Sefer ha-Ma'asim* generally proved as intransigent on this score as did the later geonim.

18. Ketubot 106a; *Teshubot ha-geonim,* ed. by Harkavy, pp. 105 f. No. 225; Nathan's Report, in *MJC,* II, 83 ff., 86; Sherira's *Iggeret,* ed. by Lewin, pp. 91 f. Sura's early preeminence is also illustrated by the large number of inquiries addressed to it before Sherira's days. Its responsa from that period now extant outnumber those of Pumbedita by four to one, according to Assaf's *Tequfat ha-geonim,* p. 49. Under Sherira and Hai the supremacy of Pumbedita also in this sphere was uncontested. The known replies sent out by father and son exceed in number those of all other geonim combined. Sura's inferiority in the early eleventh century is also clearly reflected in its gaon, Samuel ben Ḥofni's letter to a Kairuwan correspondent, Joseph ben Berakhiah, informing him that he and Sherira had some years before reached an agreement that thenceforth all general gifts should be equally divided between

the two academies. This agreement was obviously now regarded as a concession on Pumbedita's part. Cf. the text reedited by B. M. Lewin in *GK,* II, 19–21; and Mann's comments thereon and on another letter by the gaon in his *Texts and Studies,* I, 148 f., 157 ff. Cf. also Ginzberg's *Geonica,* I, 37 ff.

19. *Teshubot ha-geonim,* ed. by J. Musafiah, No. 56 (this important older collection has often been quoted not under its editor's name, but rather under that of its place of publication, Lyck). On the *kallah* assemblies and their ancient origin, cf. *supra,* Vol. II, pp. 247, 276 f., 421 n. 52. In Babylonia, the seven rows of ten members each were presided over by seven "heads of the *kallah,*" an office derived from those semiannual gatherings. The Palestinian academies had no such officials, because Palestine never indulged in these regular convocations. Their officers, other than the chairmen and vice-chairmen, carried the rather colorless designations of Third, Fourth, or Fifth. Cf. S. Poznanski's careful Hebrew study of the "*Allufim* or *Rashe kallot,*" in his *'Inyanim shonim* (Studien zur gaonäischen Epoche), pp. 45 ff. (reprinted from *Hakedem,* Vol. II); and, on the Palestinian academies, Mann's *Jews in Egypt,* I, 272 ff. Mann quotes here several contemporary literary works, revealing their authors' pride in the splendor and authority of the academies. These descriptions could, with minor variations, apply also to the Babylonian schools.

20. *Teshubot ha-geonim,* ed. by Harkavy, pp. 80 f. No. 180; B. M. Lewin's *Otzar ha-gaonim,* IV, Part 3, pp. 24, 80. Cf. W. Heffening's brief summary, "Ta'zir," *Shorter EI,* pp. 589 f.; Maimonides' sweeping declaration, cited *supra,* Chap. XXII, n. 92; and *infra,* n. 80. In his graphic description of the Babylonian academies (*MJC,* I, 87 f.), Nathan also emphasized the general preference for recruiting new members of the academies from among the sons of retiring elders. Such hereditary preference must have somewhat restricted the choice of exilarchs or geonim in the appointment of local judges as well, especially since local Muslim *qadhis* likewise enjoyed more or less hereditary tenures. Cf. Tyan's *Histoire de l'organisation,* I, 462 ff. On the geonic "supreme courts," see especially the instances quoted by V. Aptowitzer in "Formularies of Decrees and Documents from a Gaonic Court." *JQR,* IV, 35 ff.; and by Ginzberg in *Ginze Schechter,* II, 47 f., 292, 297. A gaon's interesting intervention in a case "decided against the law and through error" by a local court in Kairuwan, is recorded in a ninth-century responsum by either Naḥshon bar Zadok of Sura, or Ṣemaḥ bar Palṭoi of Pumbedita. Cf. the text in Assaf's *Teshubot ha-geonim,* 1928, pp. 23 f. No. 69, and his comments thereon, pp. 3, 24 n. 11. Cf. also *infra,* Chap. XXVII, n. 7.

21. A. E. Harkavy, *Zikhron la-rishonim,* V, 155, 164, 229, 232; Berakhot 17b, 61b. Cf. various other sources discussed by M. Auerbach in "Der Streit zwischen Saadja Gaon und dem Exilarchen David ben Sakkai," *Jüdische Studien Josef Wohlgemuth . . . gewidmet,* pp. 1–30; and by me in *Saadia Anniv. Vol.,* pp. 57 ff., 62 ff. The immediate issue was Saadiah's refusal to countersign a decision by the exilarchic court in the settlement of a wealthy estate, although Kohen Zedek of Pumbedita had no such compunctions. We are not told what the specific legal problems were, but Saadiah, who had previously written a special "Treatise on Inheritances" (see *infra,* Chap. XXVII, n. 75), probably found some legal flaws in the exilarchic decision. Since large amounts were involved (the legal fee alone of some 10 percent

amounted to 700 dinars or $2,800) Saadiah's behavior led to an overt break, in which the whole Jewish community became involved. Divisions of estates were a particularly sensitive area, as everyone knew how frequently *qadhis* got rich from fees in such litigations. Cf. Tyan's *Histoire de l'organisation,* I, 438. The conflict had wide repercussions also outside Jewish circles, led to governmental interventions, largely favoring the legitimate exilarch against his brother, the counter-exilarch, and was briefly recorded by Mas'udi. Of the numerous pamphlets published by both sides only those favoring Saadiah have been largely preserved, whereas the exilarchic side was presented only by intemperate outbursts by Aaron (Khalaf) ibn Sarjado, later circulated by Saadiah's Karaite enemies. Cf. the material assembled by Harkavy in his *Zikhron la-rishonim,* V; and "A New Fragment from the *Sefer ha-Galui* of Saadiah Gaon," ed. by S. M. Stern in his Hebrew essay in *Melilah,* V, 133-47. It was doubly welcome therefore that M. Zucker has recently published Mubashshir ben Nissi ha-Levi's *K. Istidrak* (A Critique Against the Writings of R. Saadya Gaon) which, written during or shortly after the controversy, helps redress the balance. The date of Mubashshir's pamphlet largely depends on our dating of the respective section of Saadiah's main philosophic work, cited in it. Cf. *infra,* Chap. XXXIV; and the textual corrections suggested by L. Nemoy in his review of Zucker's ed. in *JQR,* XLVI, 198–202. Because of the gaon's great authority, and possibly also because of their own pro-rabbinic bias, most medieval and modern scholars uncritically took sides with Saadiah. Typical of most later writers is the brief dismissal of the controversy in Ibn Daud's chronicle (*MJC,* I, 65), "for these princes of captivity were not men of truth, and were purchasing their posts from the kings like publicans." In retrospect it appears that Saadiah's insatiable ambition, nurtured by his friendship with influential Baghdad Jewish bankers, was the main cause of a conflict which threatened to engulf the self-governing institutions of Babylonian Jewry, and undoubtedly led to the weakening of them all.

22. Mann, *Texts and Studies,* I, 564; Lewin, *Otzar ha-gaonim,* VIII, 133 f. No. 341; Maimonides' *Treatise on Resurrection,* ed. by J. Finkel in *PAAJR,* IX, 64 ff.; and the letter to Joseph ibn Shime'on in his *Iggerot,* ed. by Baneth, pp. 66 f. Cf. also *supra,* n. 8; and Finkel's comparative study of the Maimonidean treatise in *Essays on Maimonides,* ed. by me, pp. 93–121. It may be noted, in passing, that we owe the preservation of Naḥshon's responsum to a Karaite apologist, interested in it precisely because it reflected the disagreements in Rabbanite tradition.

23. *Teshubot geone mizraḥ u-ma'arab,* ed. by J. Müller, fols. 22b No. 90, 24a No. 94, 25a No. 96; *Ḥemdah genuzah* (geonic responsa), fols. 1a No. 1, 7b No. 37. As we shall see, these exorbitant claims were more fully accepted by later generations of rabbis, particularly in the West, than by Eastern contemporaries. Cf. *infra,* Chap. XXVII.

24. Saadiah Gaon's "Letter," ed. by D. (B.) Revel in *Debir,* I, 180–88, with the interpretation thereof by J. N. Epstein, *ibid.,* pp. 189 f.; and by me in *Saadiah Anniv. Vol.* pp. 54 f.; that by Nehemiah Gaon of 962, published by A. Cowley in his "Bodleian Geniza Fragments," *JQR,* [o.s.] XIX, 105 f.; and that by Sherira, reconstructed from several fragments by J. Mann in his *Texts and Studies,* I, 105. Obviously local needs of the communities sometimes interfered with the regular dispatch of donations to the two academies. Even the "Babylonian" congregation

in Fusṭaṭ, specifically named after the Pumbedita academy, apologized (some time before 1032) for the delay in forwarding its contribution because it had to defray much money for the reconstruction of its synagogue (previously destroyed by Al-Ḥakim), and for the redemption of captives. Cf. Mann's *Texts,* I, 136 ff.; and *supra,* n. 17.

25. 'Abd ar-Razzaq ibn al-Fuwaiti, cited by W. Fischel in his *Jews in the Economic and Political Life of Mediaeval Islam,* p. 131, and Poznanski's *Babylonische Geonim,* pp. 46 ff. A similar earlier decree (of 1208), previously cited from MS by Goldziher and Poznanski (see *supra,* n. 2), is now available in Ibn as-Sa'i's *K. al-Djami' al-mukhtaṣar,* pp. 266 ff. Cf. also *supra,* Chap. XVIII, n. 53; and C. Cahen's review of Sassoon in *RH,* CCVIII, 307 f. On Samuel ben Ḥofni's demise in 1013, his succession in Sura by Saadiah Gaon's aged son, Dosa (1013–17) and by his own son Israel (1017–34), see S. Poznanski's Hebrew biography of *R. Dosa barab Saadiah Gaon;* and Assaf's *Tequfat ha-geonim,* p. 50.

26. Cf. Ṣemaḥ's responsum in A. Epstein, *Eldad ha-Dani,* pp. 8, 20 f.; Saadiah Gaon's *Sefer ha-Galui* (Book of the Exiled), cited by an anonymous Karaite controversialist, in Harkavy, *Zikhron,* V, 194 f. The custom of including the names of the exilarchs and geonim in office during services in all Babylonian synagogues is indeed recorded in "Ancient Fragments from the Holiday Prayer Book at the Academy of Pumbedita" (Hebrew), ed. by B. M. Lewin in *GK,* III, 51–56 (in Pumbedita it was customary to mention the local gaon ahead of his Sura colleague). See also *supra,* n. 7. On the more general prayer, *Yequm purqan,* in behalf of the academies and exilarchs, as well as the prayers for the reigning monarchs of each country, see *infra,* Chap. XXXI, n. 2. Most of our information about the relations between Palestine and Babylonia is of fairly recent origin. The previously known references in the responsa were assembled by S. Assaf in his "Palestine in the Responsa of the Babylonian Geonim" (Hebrew), *Ṣiyyon,* I, 21–30. Most illuminating is L. Ginzberg's excursus on Pirqoi ben Baboi, in his *Ginze Schechter,* II, 504–73, 638–40. As to the proper name Pirqoi, cf. J. N. Epstein's "In the Light of the Genizah" (Hebrew), *Tarbiz,* II, 411 f. Cf. also B. M. Lewin's "Genizah Fragments, I, Chapters of Ben Baboi" (Hebrew), *ibid.,* 383–410. Ginzberg's theory is substantially correct, despite Mann's strictures in his *Texts and Studies,* I, 64 n. 2; and V. Aptowitzer's somewhat tangential reservations in his "Untersuchungen zur gaonäischen Literatur," *HUCA,* VIII–IX, 415 f.

27. Amram's *Seder* (Prayer Book), XXI, ed. by A. L. Frumkin, I, 201; ed. by D. Hedegard, pp. 21 f. (Hebrew), 54 f. (English; on the date and authorship of this important geonic compilation, see *infra,* Chap. XXXI); Lewin's *Otzar ha-gaonim,* V, 62; and other sources cited in his edition of *Otzar ḥilluf minhagim* (Thesaurus of Halachic Differences between the Palestinian and Babylonian Schools), I, 1 ff., 98 f. Cf. also M. Margulies's edition of *Ha-Ḥilluqim she-ben anshe mizraḥ u-bene Ereṣ Yisrael* (Differences between Babylonian and Palestinian Jews), pp. 91 ff. Byzantine outlawry of the two prayers is recorded only in an obscure Hebrew document published by Ginzberg in his *Geonica,* II, 50 f. Mann's suggestion (in *Jews in Egypt,* I, 42) that it was enacted by Heraclius after his reconquest of Palestine in 629, is very dubious. There is no evidence for that emperor's inter-

ference in internal Jewish affairs, although he severely punished the Jerusalem community for its part in the Persian occupation and later tried forcibly to convert all his Jewish subjects to Christianity. Such a law would have been much more in line with Justinian's *Novella* 146, and his prohibition for Jews to celebrate Passover before the Christian Easter. Cf. *supra,* Chap. XVI, nn. 10–11 and 28; and *infra,* n. 66; and, more generally, G. Ferrari delle Spade's aforementioned study of the "Giurisdizione speciale ebraica nell' Impero romano-cristiano," in his *Scritti giuridici,* III, 279–304. The geonim also drew a sharp line of demarcation between Babylonian and other (for instance, African) Jews. If one of the latter lives in Palestine, they taught, for over a year and marries a Palestinian woman, he is subject only to the rules and regulations affecting Palestine, even though he intends eventually to return to his native land. But a Babylonian residing for many years in Palestine must still adhere to the more rigid observances of either country, because he comes from the land of "the two academies." Cf. J. Müller's ed. of *Teshubot geone mizraḥ u-ma'arab,* fol. 12a No. 39 (Müller tentatively attributes this responsum to Kohen Zedek).

28. Midrash Agur, appended to *The Mishnah of Rabbi Eliezer,* ed. by H. G. Enelow, Hebrew text, p. 50. On the date of this midrash, see *infra,* Chap. XXVIII, n. 8. As a matter of fact, other countries did not blindly follow the Palestinian practice, and the insertion of prayers for rain in the silent prayer (*'Amidah*) in the winter months, and for dew in the summer, has revealed many regional variations persisting to the present day. See the data briefly summarized by I. Elbogen in *Der jüdische Gottesdienst,* 3d ed., pp. 44, 138, 214 f., 439, 518 f.

29. Assaf's ed. of *Teshubot ha-geonim,* 1928, p. 31 No. 78; Ginzberg, *Ginze Schechter,* II, 11, 38, 632; Maimonides' *M.T.* Sheluḥin III.7, and the commentaries thereon; as well as other sources cited by H. Tykocinski in *Die gaonäischen Verordnungen,* pp. 117 ff. The latter author unduly minimizes the differences on this score between the two Babylonian academies, strongly emphasized by Ginzberg. But he rightly asserts that the Pumbedita geonim likewise agreed on the legitimacy of using the ideal claim of four Palestinian ells for letters of authorization, even if he is forced to emend the text of a crucial responsum by Hai Gaon, reproduced in *Teshubot ha-geonim,* ed. by Harkavy, pp. 90 ff. Nos. 199–200. Neither were Maimonides' reservations dictated by any anti-Palestinian feelings, but rather by such purely formal considerations as the absence of that institution in talmudic law and the vagueness of a general claim to four ells unspecified as to location and boundaries. Probably similar objections motivated the switch from four ells in Palestine to four ells in space surrounding every individual by the author of the responsum cited by Rashi in his *Pardes,* ed. by Ehrenreich, pp. 113 f. Tykocinski's assumption (pp. 123 f.) that, because this responsum appears in Rashi's work in conjunction with geonic responsa (especially Hai's), it, too, must be of geonic provenance, appears unlikely. A Babylonian gaon would hardly have used the term, *rabbotenu* (our teachers), for his geonic predecessors who had introduced that innovation, nor would his theory of air space have remained without a parallel in other geonic writings. This theory definitely suggests an attempted compromise between strict adherence to talmudic precedents and the general reverence toward geonic teachers, which characterized the Franco-German schools of that period. See *infra,* Chap. XXVII, n. 18.

30. J. Mann, *Jews in Egypt,* I, 148 ff., 167–71; II, 170 ff., 194, 202 f.; his "Genizah Fragments of the Palestinian Order of Service," *HUCA,* II, 269 ff.; and his *Texts and Studies,* I, 416 f.; and *infra,* n. 60. The great prestige of the Maimonidean codification of the laws governing liturgy is documented in I. Elbogen's analysis of "Der Ritus im Mischne Thora" in Jakob Guttmann *et al., Moses ben Maimon,* I, 319–31. On the daily recitation of the Decalogue and later discussions thereon, see Mann's *Jews in Egypt,* I, 223; my *Jewish Community,* III, 21 f.; and *supra,* Vol. II, 134 f., 380 n. 7.

31. Alfasi on Beṣah 5a No. 849; Zeraḥiah ha-Levi's comments thereon in his *Sefer ha-Ma'or* (Book of Light), *ibid.;* other sources cited in B. M. Lewin's *Otzar ḥilluf minhagim,* pp. 81 ff. See also M. Margulies's observation in his ed. of *Ha-Ḥilluqim,* pp. 34 f., 55, 87 No. 41, 161 ff. On Alfasi's unmatched reputation, see *infra,* Chap. XXVII, n. 102. Of course, the discontinuation of celebration of the New Moon by observation, now appropriated by the Karaites, and the reliance on astronomic computations, had removed all doubts concerning the accuracy of dates. The observance of a second day now became a mere ceremonial compliance with custom.

32. Lewin, *Otzar ḥilluf,* pp. 52 ff., 77 f.; Margulies, *Ha-Ḥilluqim,* pp. 86 No. 38, 158. Lewin's attempt to explain the difference in the preferred wedding days (as well as that concerning absolute abstention from work on half-holidays, *Otzar ḥilluf,* pp. 78 ff.) by the greater poverty of Babylonian Jewry, is unsupported by any historical evidence for either the talmudic or the geonic period. While the masses of the population in both countries undoubtedly suffered from much misery and squalor in all but exceptionally prosperous periods, it appears that in peacetime the Babylonian farmers and city dwellers usually benefited more fully from their country's rich natural resources. They probably also suffered somewhat less from the exactions of rapacious governors because of the proximity of the central administrative organs. Cf. also the ritualistic reasons advanced by Margulies, *loc. cit.;* and the geonic as well as European sources cited in Lewin's *Otzar ha-gaonim,* VIII, 9 No. 22.

33. Maimonides' letter to Phineas ben Meshullam of Alexandria in *Qobeṣ teshubot ha-Rambam* (Collection of Responsa and Epistles), ed. by Lichtenberg, I, fol. 25b; and other sources cited by Lewin, *Otzar ḥilluf,* pp. 23 ff. Cf. also more generally, H. S. Halevi's essay on "Jewish Family Life in the Geonic Period" (Hebrew), *Ha-Hed,* X, Part 10, pp. 17–24; Part 11, pp. 15–22. Only a few hints could be given here; a few other data will be discussed *infra,* Chap. XXVII. A fuller monograph on the historical and sociological background of these and other differences between Babylonian and Palestinian customs would be highly rewarding.

34. Saadiah's inquiry addressed from Palestine to Yehudah bar Samuel Gaon of Pumbedita and reported by the latter's grandson, Sherira, in a resp. published by J. Mann in his "Gaonic Studies," *HUCA,* Jub. Vol., pp. 237 ff., 241, 248; and Saadiah's letter to three Egyptian rabbis, ed. by H. Hirschfeld in "The Arabic Portion of the Cairo Genizah," *JQR,* [o.s.] XVI, 292, 296 f. The astronomic and mathematical aspects of this controversy, and Saadiah's radical stand in it will become clearer in connection with the general scientific progress among the Arab and Jewish scholars

of the period, discussed *infra,* Chap. XXXV. Cf. especially M. D. (U.) Cassuto's Hebrew essay on "What Was the Difference of Opinion between R. Saadiah Gaon and Ben Meir?" in *Rav Saadya Gaon,* ed. by Fishman, pp. 333–64; and the literature cited in note 35.

35. Sahl ben Maṣliaḥ in S. Pinsker, *Lickute kadmoniot* (Zur Geschichte des Karaismus und der karäischen Literatur), II, 36; Mann, *Jews in Egypt,* I, 52 ff., II, 42; Elijah bar Shinaya of Nisibis in F. Baethgen, *Fragmente syrischer und arabischer Historiker,* pp. 84, 141; the Scroll of Abiathar in S. Schechter's edition of *Saadyana,* pp. 102 f.; Saadiah's *Siddur,* p. 37 n. 6, and S. Assaf's introduction thereto, p. 25; and *infra,* Chap. XXVII, n. 144. Cf., however, *infra,* Chap. XXVI, n. 21. Most of the older sources are reprinted and carefully analyzed by H. Y. Bornstein in "The Conflict between R. Saadiah Gaon and Ben Meir with Respect to Setting the Years 4682–4684" (Hebrew), *Sefer ha-Yobel . . . Nahum Sokolow* (Jubilee Volume), pp. 19–189. More recent data are discussed in *Saadia Anniv. Vol.,* pp. 36 ff. and in S. Bialoblocki's biographical sketch of "Rab Saadiah Gaon" (Hebrew), *Keneset,* VIII, 160–209, especially pp. 163 ff., 183 ff. It should be noted, however, that the ambitious exilarch, Daniel ben Ḥisdai, categorically asserted in 1161 that "no one, not even the prince of his generation and unmatched leader of the day, had any longer the right to intercalate years or to change anything in the established laws of intercalation." Cf. his letter, ed. by Assaf in appendix II to his ed. of "Letters of R. Samuel ben 'Ali" in *Tarbiz,* I, Part 3, p. 70; and Mann's careful analysis thereof in his *Texts and Studies,* I, 230 ff.

36. Mann, *Jews in Egypt,* I, 55 n. 1; Ibn Daud's Chronicle, in *MJC,* I, 63; Sherira's *Iggeret,* p. 103. A contemporary chronicle, the *Seder 'olam zuṭa* (in *MJC,* II, 76 f.), has preserved the names of ten generations of descendants of Mar Zuṭra down to R. Phineas, possibly identical with the poet and Masorite by that name. No dates are given, however, nor is there any clear indication as to whether they served as heads of the academy in an unbroken chain. If the names here recorded are for the most part those of oldest sons, the average generation hardly exceeded twenty-five years in duration. Hence this list would bring our story down only to the middle of the eighth century, or the period of R. Aḥai's settlement in Palestine. But this probably is a mere coincidence. Cf. Mann's *Jews in Egypt,* I, 58 n. 1; and *supra,* Vol. II, pp. 182, 399. Nothing else is known about these earlier leaders, except that they most likely were members of the famous school of Tiberian Masorites. See *infra,* Chap. XXIX, n. 14. Unless there is a gap in the enumeration of Mar Zuṭra's progeny (a frequent occurrence in older genealogical lists), we would have an interval of perhaps a century between its last recorded member and the appearance of one Moses, followed by Meir I, possibly both ancestors of Aaron Ben Meir. Aaron, it should be noted, claimed descent from Judah the Patriarch and the house of Hillel, rather than of Mar Zuṭra's family of Babylonian exilarchs. But we know nothing about when and how this transfer of authority from one of these "Davidic" families to the other took place, nor how soon after the relaxation of the ban on Jewish residence in Jerusalem by the Muslim regime, the academy was allowed to move its headquarters to the Holy City. According to Barhebraeus' aforementioned report about the controversy between David ben Yehudah and Daniel, the "Tiberians" sided with David. This may be an indication that in 825 the academy still had its main seat in Tiberias, although a branch may have been

established in Jerusalem, just as later a branch of the Jerusalem academy functioned in the administrative capital of Ramleh. Cf. also the extensive genealogical reconstructions, some of them quite daring but heretofore the most complete, in Mann's *Jews in Egypt,* II, 43 ff. On the Karaite patriarchs and scholars, cf. *infra,* Chap. XXVI, nn. 17 and 28.

37. Josiah's letter of solicitation was published by Mann in his *Jews in Egypt,* II, 69 f. Cf. also *ibid.,* I, 38 f., 71 ff.; II, 39 f. Not surprisingly, it took the Palestinian academy some time before it developed a following similar to that of the Babylonian schools. Apart from their general attachment to Babylonia and to Hai Gaon personally, the Kairuwan leaders especially must have found the Jerusalem appeal rather burdensome in view of the unsettled conditions in their own country. We hear, therefore, only of a shipment of 10 dinars for Jerusalem, in addition to 200 dinars dispatched to Fusṭaṭ for the benefit of the Baghdad school. Cf. the first of the "Letters from Kairuwan and Alexandria to R. Joseph ibn 'Ukal," published in Arabic with a Hebrew translation and introduction by S. Assaf in *Tarbiz,* XX, 180, 183. This gift for the Jerusalem academy, incidentally, reinforces Assaf's assumption that the Kairuwan letters were written about 1020, that is after Al-Ḥakim's suspension of the state subsidy for the Jewish school. Generally Mann's discoveries and analyses of pertinent Genizah materials in both his *Jews in Egypt,* Vols. I–II, *passim;* and his *Texts and Studies,* I, 309–56, still furnish the fullest information on the communal life of Palestinian Jewry during the eleventh century. Utilizing largely the same data, S. Assaf succeeded in presenting a brief but lucid picture of the developments at the Jerusalem academy in his introduction to *Sefer ha-Yishub,* II, xxxv ff., further documented through some informative excerpts, *ibid.,* pp. 89 ff.

38. Cf. Solomon's pathetic letter, published by Mann in his *Texts and Studies,* II, 337 ff.; and a description of the whole controversy *ibid.,* pp. 323 ff. The compromise agreement signed by the contesting parties and published in Gottheil and Worrell's *Fragments from the Cairo Genizah,* pp. 197 ff., sheared Nathan of almost all independent authority, but promised him the usual advancement, that is, succession to the geonic office after Solomon's demise. On the other hand, it safeguarded the rights of the "Third," "Fourth," and "Fifth" ranking officials that "each one of them be raised to the rank to which he is entitled," and not passed over by the prospective gaon in favor of personal friends, including those whose previous appointment by Nathan had been nullified by the agreement. Yet within less than ten years, the very gaonate was entrusted to an outsider.

39. "Scroll of Abiathar," published in S. Schechter's *Saadyana,* No. xxxviii, p. 88; Mann's *Jews in Egypt,* I, 178 ff.; II, 215 ff. According to Abiathar, Daniel had secured his appointment through the combined efforts of the "Babylonians," Karaites, and governmental officials, who allegedly had even sent policemen to disturb congregational services of the opposition. But Abiathar, though an eye-witness, is not unbiased. As nephew and son of two of Daniel's leading rivals, who only reluctantly reached an agreement with the intruder by successively occupying the vice-presidency, he had every reason to resent Daniel's usurpation of power. Cf. the felicitous reconstruction, with the aid of two additional Genizah fragments, of "The Struggle between Daniel ben Azariah and Joseph ha-Kohen for the Geonic

Office in Palestine" by J. Braslavsky in his Hebrew essay in *Ha-Kinnus* (World Congress of Jewish Culture), I, 407–16.

40. Schechter, *Saadyana*, pp. 113 f. No. xlii; Mann, *Jews in Egypt*, II, 216. The concluding sentence in Joseph's pledge bears some resemblance to the *excommunicatio latae sententiae* of canon law. Although in the case of violation of his pledge, Joseph could not be treated by his fellow citizens as a man living under a ban unless such were formally pronounced by a court, in his own conscience, as well as in the esteem of informed acquaintances, he would be living under a cloud. Moreover, if he died without being absolved, he would face retribution in the Hereafter. The implications of such unproclaimed bans in Jewish law bear further investigation.

41. "Lettre du Gaon Hai à Sahlân b. Abraham de Fostât" (of 1038) published by B. Chapira in *REJ*, LXXXII, 328 ff.; Mann, *Texts and Studies*, II, 233 n. 69, 255, 395 n. 6 (revising his views on the nature and chronology of David ben Daniel's activities); Daniel ben Ḥisdai's aforementioned letter, ed. by Assaf in *Tarbiz*, I, Part 3, pp. 69–73, with Assaf's comments thereon, *ibid.*, Part 1, p. 117, and those by Mann in his *Texts*, I, 230 n. 63. The pointed omission of the title *gaon* in Hai's letter is the less astonishing, as the Sura geonim had long refused to apply that title in their communications to Hai's own illustrious predecessors of Pumbedita. But Hai's inquiry from Sahlan about Solomon's situation "and what rank he occupies" is truly amazing, since by 1038 Solomon had presided over the Jerusalem academy for some eleven years. Perhaps Nathan ben Abraham's uprising had raised these doubts in Babylonia.

42. The appeal to the caliph, published from an Adler MS and translated into English by S. D. Goitein in his "Congregation versus Community," *JQR*, XLIV, 291–304; with additional remarks in his "Petitions to Fatimid Caliphs from the Cairo Genizah," *ibid.*, XLV, 30 ff. Unfortunately, this important document is undated, and since neither writer nor recipient are named, there is no further way of reconstructing its chronology. Whatever minor comfort one might derive from the meager paleographic aids for Hebrew writings of that period, is absent here since the extant copy is written in a childish hand at a later date, perhaps merely as an exercise in copying official documents. The only name given, that of Joseph, head of the "Babylonian" congregation, can not easily be identified. Nevertheless, historically the period of Elijah and Abiathar seems to offer the best foil for this quarrel. Although a public controversy after the death of Daniel ben Azariah was staved off by the obvious immaturity of his sons, the contemporary exilarch's refusal to recognize Elijah's succession, and the subsequent establishment in Fusṭaṭ of another academy by Daniel's son David, must have created the most propitious background for the attempts of the "Babylonian" congregation in Jerusalem to seek independent control over the distribution of the charitable funds arriving from Egypt. If this hypothesis should prove correct, one might perhaps identify our Joseph with Joseph ben Samuel to whom the Jerusalem leader, Baruch ben Isaac, addressed a letter in 1094. Cf. the text in Mann's *Jews in Egypt*, II, 235 f. From the tenor of that letter it appears that Joseph had left Palestine not long before, and that the fate of his former colleagues at the academy in Jerusalem still was of deep interest to him. It may not be too venturesome to assert that he had

taken a part in David ben Daniel's attempt to dominate Palestinian life from Fusṭaṭ after 1078. While in Fusṭaṭ he signed two documents, in 1081 and 1085, the latter jointly with David. But after David's downfall in 1092 (see *infra,* n. 49), he became convinced of the futility of his previous communal ambitions, and advised his friend, Baruch, not to spend too much time on communal affairs, but rather use it more profitably for study. Cf. Mann's *Jews in Egypt,* I, 192 n. 1, 198 f.

43. Schechter, *Saadyana,* p. 89. The narrator's pride in this burial place and its very selection are not surprising, since the populace was then viewing R. Jose's grave with special awe and reverence. In his attack on Rabbanite practices, the tenth-century Karaite, Sahl ben Maṣliaḥ, denounced the popular vestiges of Jewish *weli* worship as an imitation of idolaters: "They [Rabbanite pilgrims] sit among graves of saintly persons," he claimed, "and spend nights among tombstones, while they seek favors from dead men, saying, 'O Jose the Galilean, grant me a cure!' or 'Vouchsafe me a child!'" Cf. the text of Sahl's "Epistle" in S. Pinsker's *Lickute kadmoniot,* II, 32; and in L. Nemoy's English trans. in his *Karaite Anthology,* p. 115. On Dalata, located north of Safed and the discovery there of remains of an ancient synagogue, see J. Braslavsky's study of "The Synagogue Remains at Kefr Dalâtā" (Hebrew), *BJPES,* II, 14–20; S. Klein's *Toledot ha-yishub ha-yehudi be-Ereṣ Yisrael* (History of the Jewish Settlement in Palestine), pp. 32, 105 f., 145 f.; and his *Ereṣ ha-Galil* (Galilee), pp. 133, 164. These archaeological finds have weakened the doubts, previously voiced, about the authenticity of the medieval tradition concerning the location of R. Jose's tomb.

44. Schechter, *Saadyana,* p. 89. This reconstruction is presented here with considerable diffidence, for our main source of information, the Scroll of Abiathar, was written by David's outspoken opponent. Cf. the story as retold by Mann in his *Jews in Egypt,* I, 185 ff.; with numerous important corrections in his *Texts and Studies,* especially I, 231 ff., 395 n. 6; II, 157 f. Abiathar's silence in regard to the Karaite allegiance of David's second wife may perhaps be explained by his wish not to antagonize influential Karaites in his own community, and also by his desire to depict primarily David's black ingratitude toward his two successive fathers-in-law, to whom the young exilarch had owed so much.

45. Joseph ben Isaac Sambari's "Chronicle," in the excerpts (*Liqquṭim*) published by Neubauer in *MJC,* I, 115 f.; more briefly and soberly narrated in David ibn abi Zimra's *Resp.,* III, No. 509 (Sudzilkov ed., fol. 20c); Mann's *Jews in Egypt,* I, 172 ff.; II, 205 f.; his *Texts and Studies,* I, 394 ff. The date of Shem Tob's appearance, and even of the letter recording it, is uncertain. While Mann believes that both date from the eleventh century, S. Assaf suggested, without further proof, that they belong to an earlier period. See his note in *Sefer ha-Yishub,* II, 89 No. 13.

The story that the highest office of Egyptian Jewry owed its origin to the suggestion by a Baghdad princess is demonstrably unhistorical. See especially the arguments presented by D. Neustadt in his generally plausible analysis of "Some Problems Concerning the 'Negidut' in Egypt during the Middle Ages" (Hebrew), *Zion,* IV, 126–49. Neustadt goes too far, however, in denying altogether the Egyptian caliphs' preference for an independent governing organ of Egyptian Jewry, akin to that existing in Baghdad under the control of their rivals (pp. 143 ff.). The argument from the silence on this score of the contemporary Arab chroniclers, while other Arab writers stressed that point in connection with the Caliphate of Cordova (see *infra,* n. 57), is the less conclusive, as the Egyptian authors have generally furnished but little information about the political status of Jews. They evinced, naturally enough, even less interest in internal Jewish affairs. Nor are the occasional interventions of Babylonian Jewish authorities in the congregational disputes in Fusṭaṭ, especially in the later, less tense period of Faṭimid-'Abbasid relations, proof of the Egyptian administration's total indifference toward the foreign entanglements of its Jewish "protégés." It certainly resented the exercise by any foreign dignitary, and particularly one residing in Baghdad, of the prerogative of appointing local judges or collecting governmental, as well as communal, taxes. In fact, David ben Daniel's rapid success in overthrowing Meborakh and his strongly entrenched faction may have been owing to his persuasive plea that, as member of the exilarchic line ousted from office by less legitimate relatives some sixty years before, he might more effectively outweigh the Baghdad influence than could a mere layman like Meborakh. Perhaps only his personal defects caused his downfall. With him failed the entire ambitious scheme to establish, with governmental support, a regular competing exilarchate on the shores of the Nile.

46. Cf. J. Mann's "Abraham b. Nathan (Abū Isḥak Ibrahim b. 'Aṭa), Nagid of Kairowan," *JQR,* XI, 429–32; his *Texts and Studies,* I, 69 n. 16, 113 n. 96, 150, 162, 180, 183 f., 329 n. 7; Assaf's *Mi-Sifrut ha-geonim,* pp. 121 f.; his ed. of the Kairuwan letters in *Tarbiz,* XX, 177 ff. (despite its natural overstatements, the second letter bears particularly eloquent testimony for the community's sense of bereavement after the death of Ibn 'Aṭa); and more generally, S. Poznanski's older study of *Anshe Kairuwan* (Men of Kairuwan; in *Festschrift Harkavy,* Hebrew section, pp. 175–220); and A. I. Laredo's brief review of "Les Académies rabbiniques nord-africaines et le transfert de la culture hébraïque d'Orient en Occident au moyen âge," *Al-'Adwatana* (Tangiers), I, 3–11. Mann has suggested (in *Texts,* I, 116, 129) that, because in his poem addressed to the academician Yehudah ben Joseph in Kairuwan Hai Gaon referred to Yehudah's father as "our patron, lord of his people and its leader," Joseph might be considered as Abraham ibn 'Aṭa's predecessor in the office of Kairuwan *nagid.* This hypothesis, however, depends not only on the equivocal interpretation of the term *salar,* equated by Bacher with a Persian loan word meaning leader (one would expect *salaro,* rather than *salarah*), but such flowery terminology could well have applied also to any distinguished citizen holding no office. More intriguing is the problem of what happened to 'Uqba's progeny and the reasons why no successor is recorded until the eleventh-century *negidim.* Interested only in the ritualistic aspects of 'Uqba's honors at the synagogue, Abraham of Lunel failed to extract more information from his source which, if Poznanski is right, was none other than some work by Nissim bar Jacob himself. Cf. his *Anshe Kairuwan,* No. 42 (in *Festschrift Harkavy,* p. 219). See also *infra,* n. 62; and on Eldad the Danite's early appearance in Kairuwan and the ensuing correspondence with Babylonia, *supra,* Chap. XVII, n. 53.

47. Our main source, *The Chronicle of Aḥimaaz,* is not only vague in many significant details, but mixes history with legend in an almost indistinguishable blend. Cf. especially the text ed. by M. Salzman, pp. 16 ff. (Hebrew), 88 ff. (English); ed. by B. Klar, pp. 38 ff., with the latter's comments thereon, pp. 168 ff. On the various

attempts at identifying Palṭiel with Jauhar (first suggested by De Goeje), or Ibn Killis (proposed by D. Kaufmann and others), although both these men were Muslims while Palṭiel lived and died a Jew, see Neustadt's observations in *Zion,* IV, 135 ff.

48. Aḥimaaz' two mentions of the term *nagid* (Salzman, pp. 20, 22, 95, 99; Klar, pp. 45, 48) do not give the impression of its being used in the technical sense. Only in connection with the statesman's demise, he is called *ha-menagged* (the ruler, an awkward variant of *nagid*), if we accept that emendation of the senseless *ha-menaggen* (singer) in some manuscripts (Salzman, p. 21). But probably the reading was simply *ha-magen* (the shield, as in Klar's text, pp. 46 f.), that is, the protector of Jews through all the provinces of the Faṭimid empire. Palṭiel certainly could have earned that epithet without ever holding any formal office.

49. Mann, *Jews in Egypt,* I, 218, 254 f., subsequently corrected by him through the elimination of the alleged intervening links of Samuel ben Palṭiel and his son, Joseph (the pertinent documents refer, in fact, to the *negidim* of Granada bearing those names; see *infra,* n. 54); his *Texts and Studies,* I, 255 ff., 394 ff., II, 137 f.; and the aforementioned document, ed. by Assaf in *BJPES,* XII, 116 ff. (apparently dating from 1140–45). Cf. also S. Abramson's reconstruction from various fragments of "Yehudah Halevi's Letter about His Emigration to Palestine" (Hebrew), *KS,* XXIX, 133–44. This letter, addressed to Samuel ben Ḥananiah, is supplemented by several poems written by Halevi in honor of the *nagid* and his two sons. Mann denies that the installation of the Egyptian *nagid* "with the authorization of our lord, head of the dispersion, under the sceptre of whose kingdom we and all Israel live" (cf. the aforementioned text published by E. N. Adler in *JQR,* [o.s.] IX, 717 ff.), referred to the Babylonian exilarch Daniel ben Ḥisdai, because the request for such an authorization would have been a flagrant violation of the Faṭimid efforts to secure the independence of their Jewish subjects. For this reason Mann rather assumes that the authorization had been obtained from the Karaite *nasi* in Jerusalem for a Karaite chief in Egypt. Cf. *supra,* n. 4; and, on the *nagid's* general control also over the Samaritan and Karaite communities in Egypt, *infra,* Chaps. XXV, n. 39; and XXVI, n. 77. This argument overstresses the government's watchfulness over Jewish affairs and the 'Abbasid-Faṭimid enmity at the beginning of the twelfth century. In fact, our *nagid* expressly claims that he had been appointed to office by the king and confirmed by the exilarch, who had previously designated him as a ranking candidate. Even the reference here to the "Palestinian" gaon offers no help for dating our ceremony, as it could apply equally well to one residing in Tyre or Damascus. It is quite possible, nevertheless, that our document records the installation of Samuel ben Ḥananiah and his confirmation in the office of *nagid* by Exilarch Ḥisdai ben David in 1140. Cf. the exact replica of the title given to our Ḥisdai in S. Assaf's text of "Blessings for Exilarch Ḥisdai ben David" (Hebrew), *GK,* IV, 63 f.

50. David ibn Abi Zimra's *Resp.,* II, No. 622; Mann's *Texts and Studies,* I, 416 ff. Cf. also the numerous biographies of Maimonides, listed *infra,* Chap. XXVII, n. 117; A. Ovadiah's Hebrew biographical sketch, "Abraham Maimuni," in *Sinai,* I, Nos. 7–8, pp. 81–101; A. H. Freimann's "On the Genealogy of the Maimonidean Family" (Hebrew), *Alummah,* I, 9–32, 157–58; *infra,* Chap. XXVII, n. 65; and Neustadt's

observations in *Zion,* IV. Neustadt's more recent attempt to revive the issue of Maimonides' occupancy of the office of *nagid,* because he is called *rais al-yahud* (chief of Jews) by Ibn al-Qifṭi and Barhebraeus (cf. Neustadt's Hebrew note, "On Maimonides' Title of 'Nagid,'" *Zion,* XI, 147–48), has not proved successful, although even Yemenite Jewry saw in Maimonides the recognized leader of the Egyptian community. He was styled *al-rais* also by the contemporary writer of a Yemenite epistle, describing the dangers which had threatened the local communities as a result of the political upheaval in 1201–2. Cf. the Arabic text and Hebrew translation (lines 28, 35) of "A Letter from Yemen Dated 1202" (Hebrew) published by D. H. Baneth in *Tarbiz,* XX, 205–14. See also *infra,* n. 58. The data relating to the "patriarch" Yehudah ben Josiah are assembled in Mann's *Texts and Studies,* I, 396 ff.; and E. Ashtor-Strauss's observations on the communal developments under Saladin in his "Saladin and the Jews," *HUCA,* XXVII, 307 f., 313 ff.

51. Petaḥiah of Ratisbon's *Sibbub,* ed. by Grünhut, p. 5; ed. by Benisch, pp. 8 ff.; Yehudah al-Ḥarizi's *Taḥkemoni,* XLVI.8, ed. by Lagarde, p. 176; ed. by Toporowski, p. 365; and other data assembled by Mann in *Poznanski Mem. Vol.,* Hebrew section, pp. 26 f. Samuel's personal insufficiency did not prevent Maimonides from paying him the accustomed homage due to a reigning exilarch (see *supra,* n. 8). In Mosul the mania for titles and exaggerating tributes reached a new high. Our Samuel's ancestor, Zakkai ben Joseph, was once extolled as "our prince, our king, our lord, our prince, who all his life was the pride and crown of our heads, the great prince, the prince of the dispersed communities of all Israel." See the Genizah excerpt summarized in B. Halper's "Descriptive Catalogue of Genizah Fragments in Philadelphia," *JQR,* XIV, 559, No. 462; and cited by Mann in *Poznanski Mem. Vol.,* p. 20.

52. Benjamin's *Massa'ot,* ed. and trans. by Adler, pp. 47 (Hebrew), 48 (English); and Mann's reconstruction of the genealogy of the exilarchic family in *Poznanski Mem. Vol.,* pp. 29 ff. Cf. also S. D. Goitein's study of "The Jewry of Yemen between the Gaonate of Egypt and the Exilarchate of Baghdad" (Hebrew), *Sinai,* XXXIII, No. 198, pp. 225–37 (publishing two Genizah fragments and stressing the impact of economic factors on Yemen's dependence on Egypt). There is no clear evidence for the presence of a permanent exilarchic branch in Aleppo, although as late as 1471, a local grandee, Joseph ben Zedekiah, not only styled himself "prince," but also recorded an abridged genealogy leading back to David ben Zakkai. Cf. S. Poznanski's *Babylonische Geonim,* p. 125. In time many of these "princely" titles in both East and West entirely lost their official meaning and often served merely to satisfy inflated ambitions of wealthy individuals. See *infra,* n. 61.

53. Ibn Daud's Chronicle in *MJC,* I, 70 ff. The dates of Ibn Jau's rise and fall are clarified in Graetz's *Dibre yeme Yisrael,* III, 370, with S. P. Rabbinowitz's important note 2 thereon. On the importance of Spanish silk manufacture and the intricate *tiraz* weaving see *supra,* Chap. XXII, n. 20.

54. Ibn Daud, *MJC,* I, 72, uses the term "ordained" for Samuel's elevation to the office of *nagid,* connoting the conferral of that title by Jewish authorities. But in his story he connects it only with Badis' succession to the throne of Granada in

that year, and the flight to Seville of three Jewish grandees, who had sided with Badis' brother. The general impression is that, after seven years at court, Samuel was now rewarded for his services with the supreme management of Jewish communal affairs. Perhaps following the royal appointment Samuel secured some confirmation of his authority from either Hai Gaon, with whom he frequently corresponded through the mediation of Nissim bar Jacob, or from the Palestinian academy with which he maintained friendly contacts during all his tenure of office. One of these eastern academies must also have awarded him the title, *rosh ha-seder* (head of a section of the academy). He was thus addressed in a letter from 'Ali ben Amram, head of the "Palestinian" congregation in Fusṭaṭ, where he was also more pointedly called "*nagid* of the dispersion and *nasi* of the chosen people." See Mann, *Texts and Studies,* I, 205 n. 7, 386 n. 2; *Sefer ha-Yishub,* II, 22 No. 33, 92 No. 12, 113 No. 16; J. Schirmann's observations in "Samuel Hannagid," *JSS,* XIII, 112 ff.

55. Joseph ibn Abitur's letter to Samuel ben Joseph ha-Kohen, the gaon in Jerusalem, in A. Marmorstein's review of Samuel Poznanski's *Babylonische Geonim* in *REJ,* LXX, 104, with J. Mann's corrections, *ibid.,* LXXI, 110–12; Maimonides' *Commentary* on M. Ḥullin, 1.2; Ibn Daud's Chronicle, in *MJC,* I, 79 (on Ferrizuel, see *supra,* Chap. XX, n. 44); and, more generally, J. Mann's "Historical Sketch of 'Capital Punishment in Our Time'" (Hebrew), *Ve-zot li-Yehudah* (Dissertationes hebraicae) in honor of Ludwig Blau, ed. by S. Hevesi *et al.,* pp. 200–208. See also *supra,* n. 15. Mann correctly points out the exceptional nature of Spanish Jewry's right to execute criminals, which ran counter to both the general state legislation under Islam and Christendom and the then prevailing Jewish law. But he is at a loss to explain the reason. However, the capital jurisdiction of Spanish Christians, equally an exception from the existing Muslim law in other lands, was delimited only to the extent that approval by the local *qadhi* was expected. Cf. Count W. W. Baudissin's *Eulogius und Alvar,* p. 13 n. 6. Certainly, Spain's exposed position on the frontier between the two worlds and the presence of a Christian majority, or at least substantial minority, in the population justified some such exceptional treatment, of which the Jews became indirect beneficiaries. They continued to enjoy that privilege also under the later Christian regimes. See my *Jewish Community,* II, 221 ff.

56. Ibn Daud's Chronicle, in *MJC,* I, 67 ff.; Sherira's *Iggeret,* p. 104; Yehudah bar Barzillai's *Sefer ha-'Ittim,* ed. by J. Schor, p. 267 (cf. also the editor's intro. thereto, pp. xi f.); his *Perush Sefer Yeṣirah* (Commentary on Yeṣirah), ed. by S. J. Halberstam, p. 103; Ginzberg's *Geonica,* I, 16 ff.; and M. Auerbach's careful analysis of *Die Erzählung von den vier Gefangenen;* and W. Jawitz's excursus in his *Toledot Yisrael,* X, 238 ff. On the proper spelling of the name of Exilarch Naṭronai's father, variously recorded in the sources, cf. Ginzberg, p. 17 n. 1. The sources concerning Ḥushiel are particularly confusing; they have even given rise to the highly improbable theory that there were two different Ḥushiels living in Kairuwan at the same time. See *infra,* Chap. XXVII, n. 50. Although departing from Bari, our four scholars may have been Babylonians sent to Italy to collect funds. A similar shipment of contributions collected in the Italian communities for the benefit of the eastern academies is, indeed, recorded to have fallen into the hands of pirates. On the general impact of Mediterranean piracy as well as that of the eastern immi-

grants in Spain, see the literature listed *supra,* Chap. XXII, n. 47; and *infra,* Chap. XXX, nn. 19 and 21.

57. Ibn Daud, *loc. cit.;* Abu Qasim ibn Sa'id's *K. Tabaqat al-'Umam* in the excerpt translated by J. Finkel in *JQR,* XVIII, 51; Abraham Maimonides' *Resp.,* pp. 13 ff. No. 4. Political divisions were primarily responsible also for the relative absence of direct exilarchic, and even geonic, authority over Jews in Christian lands. Yet their influence must not be exaggerated; it was but one of many divisive factors.

58. Abraham Maimonides' *Resp.,* p. 19. Cf. also his father's testimony (in *Commentary* on M. Bekhorot, IV.4): "I have seen in Palestine men called *ḥaberim* (scholars), and in other places men may be styled heads of academies, while they are not even freshmen students." A great many honorary titles in use in the Faṭimid empire have been culled from the Genizah by Mann in his *Jews in Egypt,* I, 259 ff. In this respect Jews merely emulated their Muslim neighbors among whom "the craving for titles and use of involved phraseology in official documents . . . began in the 4th/10th century and has continued to this day." Cf. Mez, *Renaissance,* pp. 86 f.

59. Hai's aforementioned letter to Shalal ben Abraham of Fusṭaṭ, ed. by Chapira in *REJ,* LXXXII, 327 ff.; those by Solomon ben Yehudah addressed to Ephraim ben Shemariah (?), in Mann's *Jews in Egypt,* I, 115; II, 125 f.; and by Nissim bar Jacob to Hai in Mann's *Texts and Studies,* I, 137, 142 ff.; Assaf's *Mi-Sifrut ha-geonim,* pp. 160 f.; Samuel ibn Nagrela's poem, *Ha-be-mavet peliliah* (Is There Escape from Death?) in his *Diwan,* ed. by D. S. Sassoon, pp. 11 ff. No. xi; ed. by A. M. Habermann, II, 128 ff. No. 22; Solomon ibn Gabirol's elegies *Bekhu 'ammi* (Let My People Cry), *Ha-lo tibku* (The Masses of the Dispersion Will You not Bewail?), and *Mi yaḥabosh* (Who Will Tie the Wreath of Jesse's Son?), in his *Shire* (Poems), ed. by H. N. Bialik and J. H. Rawnitzky, I, 88 ff.; and the Yemenite homage to Maimonides still recorded by J. Saphir in his *Eben Sapir* (Travelogue), I, 15, fol. 53ab. The nexus between that homage and the expectation that the scepter would not depart from Judah was facilitated by the widespread belief in Maimonides' Davidic ancestry. Cf. A. H. Freimann's remarks in *Alummah,* I, 10. The memory of Hai's greatness persisted, however, for generations. Two centuries later Naḥmanides still spoke of the gaon's authority as being "equal to that of the majority of the Sanhedrin." Cf. Lewin's *Otzar ha-gaonim,* VIII, 150 n. 2. Cf. also *supra,* n. 50; Mann's *Texts and Studies,* I, 118 ff., 136 ff.; A. Ovadiah's Hebrew sketch of "The Life of R. Hai Gaon," in *Sinai,* I, Nos. 11–13, pp. 549–91; other essays in that special number issued on the nine-hundredth anniversary of the gaon's death; and, on the relations between the Palestinian academies and Jewish communities in other countries, S. Assaf's summary in the introduction to *Sefer ha-Yishub,* II, 40 ff., 42 ff.

60. Ben Meir's letter, ed. by Bornstein in *Sefer ha-Yobel . . . Nahum Sokolow,* pp. 62 ff.; and the eleventh-century letter published by Assaf and reproduced in *Sefer ha-Yishub,* II, 1. The designation of Jerusalem as God's sanctuary (*miqdash*) is obviously a retranslation into Hebrew of the Arabic Al-Quds. On the "memorizers" called here *meshannenim,* while in Babylonia they were usually designated *tannaim,*

see *infra,* Chap. XXVII, n. 19. To be sure, even the more authoritarian Babylonian academies were wont to address letters not only in behalf of their heads but also of other officials. Cf. the examples cited by Bornstein in his note 11; these could readily be multiplied. But the noteworthy difference was the express Palestinian addition of judges, elders, and the rest of the community outside the ranks of academic membership.

61. Nathan's Report, in *MJC,* II, 85; Benjamin's *Massa'ot,* pp. 32, 39 (Hebrew), 31, 39 (English); Al-Ḥarizi's *Taḥkemoni, supra,* n. 51. The ancient antecedents of these city councils, including the "ten men of leisure," were discussed *supra,* Vol. II, pp. 201, 404 n. 34. Neither the electoral procedures nor the duration of offices is indicated in the sources. Even the formula for the so-called writ of appointment, communicated by Yehudah bar Barzillai, is hardly of any help for the Eastern communities. For the suggestion of modern scholars, including Mann (in his *Jews in Egypt,* I, 262), that the Barcelona rabbi copied here a text originally included in Saadiah's "Book of Deeds," has little support in the general situation. On Jewish officials in charge of merchants and bazaars, see *supra,* Chaps. XX, nn. 32 and 45; XXII, nn. 36–37; and S. D. Goitein's *Jews and Arabs,* pp. 118 f.

62. The Kairuwan letter referring to one Shabbetai ben Hodayah (or Yehudah) ben Amittai is reproduced in the Appendix facsimile 5 of the *Catalogue of Hebrew Manuscripts in the Collection of Elkan Nathan Adler.* Cf. Mann's *Texts and Studies,* I, 47. In the medieval Spanish sources, to be sure, we come across a great many dignitaries bearing titles like *nagid* or *nasi.* But by that time these designations became purely honorific, and often corresponded to no particular offices. Even in the East many high-sounding titles no longer bore any relation to the holder's official position and status, bearing out Maimonides' and his son's aforementioned strictures. It is questionable, for instance, whether the Samuel grandiloquently referred to in a poem by Eleazar ben Jacob ha-Babli as the *negid 'am el ve-kheter ha-neṣibim* (prince of God's people and the crown of lords) was in any way in formal charge of Jewish communal affairs. Cf. Eleazar's *Diwan,* p. 89 No. 206; and the excerpts previously communicated by Mann in his *Texts,* I, 281 No. 21 line 24, 303 No. 54.

63. Geonic responsum in *Ḥemdah genuzah,* fol. 3a No. 15; and other examples cited by Assaf in *Tequfat ha-geonim,* p. 64. Maimonides sometimes justified his opposition to geonic innovations either by stressing the frequent differences of opinion between the older and more recent geonim, or else by alleging that the latter had wrongly interpreted talmudic law only because they had before them some faulty versions of the talmudic text. At times he explained them as stemming from Babylonian customs which diverged from those of other countries; as such they were not to be followed elsewhere. Cf., e.g., his *M.T.* Ishshut VI.14; XI.13; XIV.14. But frequently he did not even search for such excuses, but repudiated the geonic authority on purely logical or exegetical grounds. Cf. the data assembled by A. Schwarz in "Das Verhältnis Maimuni's zu den Gaonen" in *Moses ben Maimon,* ed. by Jakob Guttmann *et al.,* I, 332–410. This independence was not shared by most of Maimonides' contemporaries and immediate successors, however, who placed geonic teachings almost on a par with those of the talmudic sages. See *infra,* Chap. XXVII, n. 25.

64. Assaf's ed. of Samuel's letters in *Tarbiz,* I, Part 2, pp. 61 f. It should be noted that even the ceremony of the "redemption of the first-born son" had still retained some of its ancient implications in the exchange of ritualistic formulas between the redeeming father and the priest. Cf. the texts cited in B. M. Lewin's *Otzar ha-gaonim,* III, Part 2, pp. 130 ff. Nos. 341–42 (on Pesaḥim 121b; essentially repeated in Jacob ben Asher's *Ṭurim,* and Isserles' note on Karo's *Shulḥan 'Arukh,* O. Ḥ. 305, 10). There was only some debate concerning the contemporary equivalent of the required "ransom" money of five shekels. While one gaon computed it at 28 7/12 Arabic dirhems, another geonic teacher figured out that it was equal to 32½ dirhems. Cf. the data in Lewin's *Otzar ha-gaonim,* IX, 12 ff., especially Nos. 37–38 (on Qiddushin 8a). There were enough complex problems connected with this entire ancient ceremonial as it affected both men and animals to require ultimate decisions by a specially authorized scholar like our Zechariah.

The characteristic distinction here between the *ḥazzan* and the leader in services or the "messenger of the people," bears out the contention of the later Arab chronicler, Al-Qalqashandi, that the eastern communities had two officials: a mere reader of prayers, and the *ḥazzan* who, comparable to the Muslim *imam,* "must be well versed in preaching. He ascends the *minbar* [pulpit] and exhorts them." Cf. the excerpts quoted from a Cairo MS and translated into English by R. J. H. Gottheil in "An Eleventh-Century Document concerning a Cairo Synagogue," *JQR,* [o.s.] XIX, 500, 527 f. Some larger communities seem to have employed also a regional "grand *ḥazzan*" or "supervisor over the readers." Cf. Hai's letter probably addressed to Jacob bar Nissim in Kairuwan, and published in Mann, *Texts and Studies,* I, 122. Cf. also Mann's comments *ibid.,* pp. 113, 151 ff.; my *Jewish Community,* esp. II, 100 ff., and III, 135 ff.; *supra,* n. 7; and *infra,* Chap. XXXI.

65. *The Chronicle of Ahimaaz,* ed. by Salzman, pp. 5 f. (Hebrew), 67 ff. (English); ed. by Klar, pp. 18 f.; Ibn Daud's Chronicle, in *MJC,* I, 68; Ibn Abitur's interesting, though poorly preserved, letter in Assaf's *Meqorot,* p. 118. The story of Moses' elevation in Cordova has all the earmarks of a typical folk tale about a career "from rags to riches"; it echoes especially the talmudic narrative concerning Hillel's rise to the presidency of the ancient Sanhedrin. Yet the fact that the populace regarded such a transition far from implausible, reveals the extent to which learning enjoyed universal appreciation. Certainly travelers like Benjamin or Petaḥiah could undertake their arduous journeys only because they were assured hospitable reception by responsive groups of coreligionists. Joseph Qimḥi was not grossly exaggerating when, in his apologetic work, he claimed that "whenever a Jew visits with a fellow Jew for a day or two, or even for many days, he is not charged by his host for his food and lodging. Thus the Jews all over the world behave toward their coreligionists with the attribute of mercy." Cf. his *Sefer ha-Berit* (An Apologetic Treatise), reprinted in J. D. Eisenstein's *Oẓar wikuḥim* (A Collection of Polemics and Disputations), p. 67b.

66. On the meaning and impact of Justinian's significant *Novella* 146, see *supra,* n. 27; Chap. XVI, n. 11; and *infra,* Chaps. XXIX, n. 32; XXXI, *passim.* Characteristically, only the elders of Constantinople were addressed here, although Palestine with its leading academy of Tiberias still was a part of the Empire. The separation of the authority over "affairs relating to Heaven" from the "affairs of the city" in an ancient Babylonian community is mentioned in Quiddushin 76b. But

this sharp division seems to have resulted from a local controversy and was not typical of other localities. On the councils of elders found in most ancient Mediterranean communities, see my *Jewish Community,* I, 95 ff., 133 ff.; III, 17 f., 25 ff.

67. Benjamin's *Massa'ot,* pp. 11 ff. (Hebrew), 10 ff. (English), with some significant manuscript variants registered by Adler especially in connection with the title *ha-rab ha-gadol* (great or chief rabbi). On the Karaite communities, see Z. Ankori's dissertation, *Karaites in Byzantium: the Formative Years* (970–1100); and *infra,* Chap. XXVI, n. 75. Only in the relatively small community of Harmilos did, according to Benjamin, the three Jewish chiefs carry separate titles of rabbi, warden (*parnas*), and leading man (*rosh*). On the basis of this brief reference, S. Krauss built up a theory that the three men headed three separate congregations: the rabbi administered the affairs of Venetian, Pisan, and Genoese Jews, the warden took care of other foreigners, and only the leading man represented the native Greeks. See his *Studien zur byzantinisch-jüdischen Geschichte,* p. 88. This is altogether unlikely. There is neither evidence for the existence of a sufficient number of Italian and other Jewish foreigners in the city (Venice alone among the three Italian cities here mentioned had at that time a small Jewish population which could hardly have sent a colony to Harmilos; see *supra,* Chap. XX, n. 26), nor that the division of functions among the three leaders ran along congregational lines. Certainly all Jews of the community required the expert services of a "rabbi." Probably here, as in most other communities, the particular communal and congregational titles of individual officers were interchangeable and owed their origin to accidental causes. See my remarks in *The Jewish Community,* I, 161 f.

68. The text of the Bari responsum and the names of its signatories were reproduced in Meir ha-Kohen's *Haggahot Maimoniot* on *M.T.* Ishshut XXII.14 No. 9. Only a few of these names have thus far been identified. Cf. J. Starr's *Jews in the Byzantine Empire,* pp. 172 f. No. 120. A considerable number of "honorary" witnesses appear also in a nuptial agreement issued in Damascus in 933. In another, written in North African Barqa in 990, no less than thirty-six men appended their signatures. Cf. the texts published by Assaf in his *Meqorot,* pp. 64 ff.; and in his edition of Hai Gaon's *Sefer ha-Sheṭarot* (Book of Deeds), pp. 53 ff.

69. *The Chronicle of Ahimaaz,* ed. by Salzman, pp. 3 ff., 10, 12 (Hebrew), 63, 67 f., 76, 180 f. (English); ed. by Klar, pp. 13 ff., 17 f., 26, 30. The extension of Jewish jurisdiction to capital punishment has legitimately been doubted by many scholars, including Klar (p. 161), and Starr in *Byzantine Empire,* pp. 38 f. In the form here presented, however, namely by action by an aroused populace, there occurred no serious breach of the existing jurisdictional limitations. It is possible, though otherwise unattested, that in the parts of Italy occupied by Muslims, Jews had been granted for the same reasons as in Spain the right to execute criminals. See *supra,* n. 55. In that case Aḥimaaz may merely have confused the area of that jurisdictional latitude. Nor is the identity of Aaron of Baghdad altogether clear, but it is more probable that he settled in a Muslim-dominated city. Ever since A. Neubauer's study of "Abou Ahron, le Babylonien," in *REJ,* XXIII, 230–37, scholars have connected with this report by Aḥimaaz a statement by Eleazar bar Yehudah of Worms in his Commentary on Prayers (cf. the excerpt reprinted in Klar's ed. p. 57). Here the famous German kabbalist attributed the beginnings of Italo-German mysticism

to the arrival from the East of Abu Aaron, son of "R. Samuel the *Nasi*." To be sure, no exilarch by that name has been safely identified in any reliable record. Nor is Abu Aaron quite the same as Aaron. According to Arabic usage, Abu Aaron may actually have had the name of Eleazar. But the tradition that eastern mysticism had been transplanted to Central Europe by a member of the exilarchic family who, like Naṭronai before and 'Uqba after him, had been forced out of his home by one of the constant internal squabbles in Babylonia, seems to reflect a sound historical recollection. Cf. also *infra,* Chap. XXXIII.

70. Manuel's decree in Zépos and Zépos, *Jus graecoromanum,* I, 426 f.; Starr, *Jews in the Byzantine Empire,* pp. 122 f. No. 172; Maimonides' letter to Phineas ben Meshullam of Alexandria in his *Qobeṣ,* I, 26c No. 140. Cf. *supra,* Chap. XIX, n. 53. Needless to say, Jews even in Byzantium still could voluntarily submit to adjudication by their own courts. Cases like that recorded by Aḥimaaz with respect to Ḥananel ben Palṭiel could also occur in the rest of the Empire. Ḥananel had secured from the imperial government a permit to recover the possessions he had lost during the Muslim raid on Oria. But while trying to recoup some objects he had identified in Bari, he ran up against the talmudic provision allowing purchasers of war booty from Gentiles to retain their acquisitions. Without invoking the aid of Byzantine authorities, Ḥananel merely argued before the Jewish court that in this case "the law of the kingdom is law," and that hence the royal permit should supersede the talmudic restriction. The litigation ultimately ended, as did most transactions before Jewish courts, in a compromise settlement. Cf. Aḥimaaz' *Chronicle,* ed. by Salzman, pp. 18 f. (Hebrew), 91 f. (English); ed. by Klar, pp. 41 f., with his notes thereon, pp. 171 f.

71. Samuel ibn Nagrela's epistle, cited by N. N. Coronel in his *Zekher natan* (liturgical-halakhic handbook for travelers), fol. 134a. The Spaniards had succeeded in persuading even the Babylonian sages of the righteousness of their claim. Writing in 953, perhaps under the impact of the desolate conditions in the eastern Caliphate, a Pumbedita leader sweepingly declared that "learning has been found in Spain from time immemorial to the present," and cited an old legend relating to Alexander the Great and "Sefarad" as an illustration of the presence there of "scholars since the First Exile." Cf. the fragment published by A. Cowley in his "Bodleian Geniza Fragments," *JQR,* [o.s.] XVIII, 401; A. Marx's "Notes" thereon, *ibid.,* pp. 768–71; and other data cited by Eppenstein in his "Beiträge, V," *MGWJ,* LVI, 83 f. Cf. also *supra,* Chaps. XVI, n. 41; XX, n. 31.

72. Jacob Tam's statement quoted in Meir bar Baruch's *Resp.,* Cremona ed., 1557, fol. 39b No. 108; his comment in *Tosafot* on Shabbat 49a *s.v. Ke-Elisha;* Isaac bar Moses' *Sefer Or zaru'a,* II, Nos. 34, 43 (pp. 16 ff.), 275; Jacob bar Yequtiel's report in *MWJ,* Hebrew section, III, 48; and other sources cited by M. Güdemann in his *Geschichte des Erziehungswesens und der Cultur der abendländischen Juden während des Mittelalters und der neueren Zeit,* I, 256 f.; L. Rabinowitz in *The Social Life of the Jews in Northern France,* pp. 174 ff.; and my *Jewish Community,* III, 123 f. n. 16. Cf. also *infra,* Chap. XXVII, nn. 151 ff. In this context Meir bar Baruch stressed the great importance of the commandment of door-post inscriptions. "If people knew," he declared, "the advantages of having a *mezuzah* on the door, they would not transgress this commandment; for I am convinced that no demon can

harm a house properly provided with *mezuzot*." He himself had, therefore, fastened no less than twently-four small scrolls on the doors of the various chambers in his house. Cf. I. A. Agus's trans. in his *Rabbi Meir of Rothenburg*, I, 264 f. No. 213; the report by Meir's pupil Asher ben Yeḥiel in his *Halakhot*, Mezuzah VIII (Vilna ed., tractate Menaḥot, fol. 116ab); and E. Urbach's *Ba'ale ha-tosafot*, pp. 223, 386, 411. This very overemphasis indicates, however, that even in thirteenth-century Germany door-posts were not yet universally provided with inscriptions. "On the History of the Commandment concerning Phylacteries and Its Neglect," see esp. N. S. Greenspan's pertinent Hebrew essay in *Ozar Hachaim*, IV, 159–64; with supplementary notes by Z. D. Grünberger *ibid.*, V, 71–72. Despite the latter's apologetic efforts, Greenspan's data conclusively prove the widespread neglect of phylacteries even in the East during both the talmudic and the geonic periods. Following the long-accepted pattern, Hai Gaon blamed such partial neglect in Palestine and its rationalization by R. Yannai (in Shabbat 49a) on Roman persecutions. Yet the Western carelessness and the conflicting views among rabbis as late as the thirteenth century (including the well-known formal distinctions between Rashi's and Jacob Tam's phylacteries) show the deep roots of that neglect and the absence of any solid and generally accepted tradition.

73. Benjamin's *Massa'ot*, pp. 6 f. (Hebrew), 5 f. (English); Isaac ben Moses' *Sefer Or zaru'a*, II, No. 275, fol. 126b; Nathan ben Yeḥiel's aforementioned poem, *Neder Nadarti*, reproduced in his *'Arukh ha-shalem*, ed. by Kohut, VIII, 301; and *supra*, Chap. XX, nn. 4 and 12. Perhaps Benjamin's designations disregarded the local titles in favor of those in more common use. His "rabbi" may have corresponded to the *nasi*, and his "head of the academy" to the *gaon* (assisted by a *resh kallah*) of the earlier sources. Cf. Vogelstein and Rieger, *Geschichte der Juden in Rom*, I, 220, where, however, the *resh kallah* is equated with head of the community. Cf. also Poznanski's *Babylonische Geonim*, pp. 106 ff., supplying a fairly lengthy list of early rabbis (including the three Roman leaders mentioned in the text) who were given the title *gaon* by admiring contemporaries or a grateful posterity.

74. Mordecai bar Hillel's *Halakhot* on B.M. Nos. 457–58; and B.B. Nos. 480, 482, 488 (Cracow ed., 1598, fol. 64cd); and Eliezer ha-Levi's *Sefer Rabiah*, ed. by Aptowitzer, II, 317 No. 590 (on Megillah 26a). Cf. also *supra*, n. 67; and M. Frank's *Qehillot Ashkenaz* (The Jewish Communities and Their Courts in Germany from the Twelfth to the End of the Fifteenth Century), pp. 2 f.

75. In "The Judaeo-Latin Inscription of Merida," *Sefarad*, VIII, 391–96, C. Roth has pointed out that the use of the form *ribbi*, rather than *rabbi*, indicates that community's close connections with Palestine. Cf. *supra*, Vol. II, p. 419 n. 44. It stands to reason that Spanish areas under Byzantine domination followed the leadership of the Palestinian center, as long as both were included in the same empire. Only after Spain's occupation by the Moors was there an incentive to adopt Babylonian patterns. Spanish Jewry's subsequent contacts with the Babylonian academies, reinforced by numerous Babylonian immigrants and returning Spanish students and visitors in the East, must have played into the hands of such spokesmen of Babylonian supremacy as Pirqoi ben Baboi, especially with respect to legal and ritualistic conformity. Cf. also A. I. Laredo and David Gonzalo's analysis of "El Nombre de 'Sefierad.' Sobre la etimologia de la voz 'Sefarad,' " *Sefarad*, IV, 349–63;

supra, nn. 30 ff.; and Chap. XIX, n. 53 (on the Kalonymids and the terms Ashkenaz and Sefarad); and *infra,* Chaps. XXVII, nn. 24–25; XXX, nn. 19, 21.

76. B. Altmann's "Studies," *PAAJR,* X, 67, 97 f., with reference to the privileges in Aronius, *Regesten,* pp. 71 ff. Nos. 170–71; and *supra,* Chap. XX, nn. 86 and 96. The pioneering services rendered to the nascent European cities by Jews as bearers of an old communal tradition in its constant adaptation to new environments are emphasized in Y. Baer's searching analysis of "The Origins of Jewish Communal Organization in the Middle Ages" (Hebrew), *Zion,* XV, 1–41. Another illustration of such Jewish influence was adduced by I. A. Agus from "The Rights and Immunities of the Minority," *JQR,* XLV, 120–29; and more broadly in his "Self-Government of the Jewish Community in the Middle Ages" (Hebrew), *Talpioth,* V, 176–95, 637–48; VI, 305–20. Neither author, to be sure, pays sufficient attention to the considerable measure of continuity from ancient times preserved after the barbarian migrations and Muslim invasions by many Italian, southern French, and even northern Spanish cities. Nevertheless they are right in assuming that certain constitutional forms were borrowed by the Christian burghers in the newly arisen northern cities from their immediate Jewish neighbors, rather than from their more distant southern coreligionists. Some ingredients of Mediterranean city life itself may have become familiar to the northern bourgeoisie through Jewish mediation. Of course, such relationships are never one-sided. Jewish community organization, too, undoubtedly received many impulses from the struggle of the southern, and later also the northern, municipalities for full autonomy, a struggle which had led to the early establishment of the sovereign Italian city republics. Precisely because of the paucity of Jewish and general municipal sources of that period and the numerous divergent theories concerning the rise of the medieval city in various parts of Europe, the interrelations between the Jewish communal and the general municipal evolution in those crucial centuries from the eighth to the eleventh would deserve much fuller monographic treatment.

77. John's two related decrees of 1199, reprinted in H. P. Stokes, *Studies in Anglo-Jewish History,* pp. 243 f.; in J. Jacobs's English trans. in *The Jews of Angevin England,* pp. 202 ff.; Baer, *Juden im christlichen Spanien,* I, 113 ff. No. 104 (citing the decree of 1257); Ibn Adret's *Resp.,* I, No. 729, Lwów ed., fol. 72b; *supra,* Chap. XX, n. 64 (Carolingian *magister*); and, more generally, my *Jewish Community,* I, 283 ff.; III, 65 ff. In his *Studies,* pp. 23 ff., Canon Stokes submitted the entire extant evidence concerning "The Arch-Presbyter" of medieval English Jewry to careful scrutiny; he also reviewed the numerous earlier discussions on this complicated subject, which, in part, went back to the pre-Cromwellian era. The initiative to the establishment of such a central office obviously came from the king, rather than from the Jewish communities, which had little choice but to accept the royal appointment. In Spain, too, Jews submitted more or less peaceably to the royal will. On the relations of the larger communities to their "dependencies," see *infra,* n. 84.

78. See the texts and introductions in L. Finkelstein's *Jewish Self-Government in the Middle Ages,* pp. 20 ff., 111 ff., 139, 142, 148 f.; with some variants published from a Budapest MS by A. N. Z. (E.) Roth in "The Ban of Interrupting Prayers and A New Recension of R. Gershom's Ordinances" (Hebrew), *Zion,* XIX, 60 ff.; the addi-

tional sources and observations cited by S. Eidelberg and I. Elfenbein in their introductions and notes to their respective editions of *Teshubot* by Gershom bar Yehudah and Rashi; and my remarks in *Rashi Anniv. Vol.*, pp. 55 ff. Gershom's original ordinances have long been debated. In their present form they undoubtedly are compilations by later generations of rabbis who lumped together older regulations stemming from various quarters and periods and placed on them the additional authority of a widely revered name. There is indeed reason to believe that Simson of Sens, mentioned in a responsum (No. 13) by the fifteenth-century rabbi of Padua Meir Katzenellenbogen as the author of one of these ordinances, was among the early compilers of such a set of older regulations. Cf. Finkelstein, p. 142 n. 2; his "Zu den Takkanot des Rabbenu Gerschom," *MGWJ*, LXXIV, 23–31; F. Baer's review of Finkelstein's volume *ibid.*, LXXI, 395; and his "Nachwort" to Finkelstein's essay *ibid.*, LXXIV, 31–34. Baer slightly expanded this view also in his remarks in *Zion*, XV, 37 f. See also *infra*, Chap. XXVII, n. 161.

79. Finkelstein, *Jewish Self-Government*, pp. 41 ff., 150 ff., 155; Joseph Tob 'Elem's reply cited by Meir bar Baruch in his *Resp.*, Prague ed., No. 940; and my observations in *Rashi Anniv. Vol.*, pp. 57 f. On the important provincial councils of the Church, which met in Troyes in the twelfth century, see T. Boutiot's *Histoire de la ville de Troyes et de la Champagne méridionale*, I, 180 f., 195 ff. Remarkably, the resolutions adopted at the Troyes synod or synods are signed, in the later reproductions accessible to us, by only four and three rabbis respectively, namely by Jacob Tam, his brother Samuel, and his disciples. Doubtless many other leaders attended the sessions, though some communities may merely have assented later. The report relating to the participation of Eliezer bar Nathan of Mayence and Eliezer bar Samson of Cologne is preserved in but a single dubious text. Even self-assertive Jacob Tam would surely have preferred scholars of that rank to appear as cosigners to forestall resistance from any quarter. One need but recall the reverence for Eliezer bar Nathan, humbly expressed by Jacob's elder brother Samuel, in the letter reproduced in Eliezer's *Eben ha-Ezer*, No. 1240, Prague ed., fol. 143d. As a matter of fact, no German community is mentioned in the record; the representation consisted entirely of Jewries subject to the suzerainty of the king of France, including those of Normandy, Anjou, and Poitou (not the city of Poitiers only), who paid homage directly to Henry II of England. None came from southern France. Narbonne is mentioned only as a model for the adoption of one regulation, while not even Lyons sent representatives, unless we were to read Lyons instead of Melun, a reading rightly rejected by H. Gross in his *Gallia judaica*, p. 352.

80. Cf. the interesting differences of opinion expressed by Jacob Tam, Eliezer bar Joel ha-Levi, and others cited by Baer in *Zion*, XV, 39 ff.; and by Agus in *JQR*, XLV, 120 ff. (with fuller documentation in his Hebrew essay in *Talpioth*, V, 637 ff.). They reveal a progressive stiffening of the rabbinic attitude toward recalcitrant individuals and groups even in regard to fiscal contributions. In fact, few rabbis would have opposed the general principle so broadly restated by Maimonides (see *supra*, Chap. XXII, n. 92) concerning the latitude of authoritative courts to dispose even of the private property of individuals for the good of the whole community. Juridically, this vast amount of discretion was justified by the old rabbinic principle of *hefqer bet-din hefqer* (the court's right of expropriation). Cf. I. E. Herzog's analysis of "The Law of Expropriation as a Basis for Rabbinic Ordinances"

(Hebrew), *Talpioth,* VI, 637–54. Largely consisting of expertly learned men, the boards of the Western communities were often equated in both Jewish law and the royal privileges with such recognized tribunals. Cf. the data assembled by Frank in his *Qehillot,* pp. 1 ff.

81. Assaf's ed. of *Teshubot ha-geonim,* 1942, pp. 105, 108 (cf. also his ed. of *Teshubot,* 1928, pp. 2 ff., 27 No. 75); Gershom's ordinance, modified by those of the Rhine communities of the early thirteenth century, in Finkelstein, *Jewish Self-Government,* pp. 15 ff., 119 f., 128 ff., 228, 243; *supra,* Chap. XVIII, n. 17; and other data assembled in my *Jewish Community,* II, 32 ff.; III, 112 n. 28; and in A. N. Z. Roth's essay in *Zion,* XIX, 57 ff. (the stricture *ibid.,* p. 58 n. 12 is pointless; the author should have realized that he used but a new 1945 impression of *The Jewish Community,* published in 1942). Some of these restrictions were waived in favor of orphans and widows. In a qualification of the Rhenish resolutions preserved in a later MS, these most defenseless plaintiffs were allowed "to close the synagogue even in making their first complaint, until justice is done." Cited by Finkelstein, p. 243 n. 1. Of a somewhat different order was the interruption of prayers after the recitation of Scripture during the morning services on Mondays and Thursdays for the purpose of administering solemn oaths in public. Such a practice is recorded in the eastern communities in the days of Hai Gaon. Cf. Lewin, *Otzar ha-gaonim,* VIII, 294 f. No. 693.

82. The early medieval sources are just as silent about the procedures employed in the election of Jewish communal officers as were the ancient writers. See *supra,* Vol. II, pp. 201 f. Only in the later Middle Ages did certain regulations and practices begin to crystallize and, though often still very cumbersome, to find their way into communal statutes, rabbinic responsa, and other contemporary records. Cf. the illustrations furnished in my *Jewish Community,* II, 35 ff.; III, 113 ff. The bewildering variety of these constitutional experiments and their frequent inner inconsistencies are further proof that there had existed no uniform, deep-rooted tradition, but that each community pursued its own course in accordance with its local needs or whims.

83. Gershom's and Rashi's *Commentaries* on the rather equivocal and hence much-debated statement of the Babylonian teacher R. Huna bar R. Joshua in B.B. 21b; the French inquiry of 1130 published by S. D. Luzzatto in "A Responsum of Roman Scholars to Those of Paris" (Hebrew), *Bet ha-oṣar,* I, fol. 57a, and briefly referred to in Mordecai bar Hillel's *Halakhot* on B.B. No. 517; Jacob Tam's statement communicated by his disciple, Eliezer of Orléans and cited by Moses bar Ḥisdai in Isaac bar Moses' *Or zaru'a,* I, No. 115 (Zhitomir ed., p. 41b); and Isaac of Dampierre's decision recorded by Mordecai, *loc. cit.* On the extent to which the existing versions of Gershom's commentary on the Talmud correctly reproduce his views, cf. *infra,* Chap. XXVII, n. 52. Understandably, this latitude led to an enormous diversity of local practices, only few of which were recorded, more or less incidentally, in the contemporary rabbinic letters. It has also created considerable confusion in the minds of modern investigators who, clinging to the usual halakhic categories and paying no heed to the great diversity of contemporary historic backgrounds, were unable to give a coherent explanation to the essentially disparate source material. Cf. my remarks in *Rashi Anniv. Vol.,* pp. 62 ff.; L. Rabinowitz's detailed study of *The Ḥerem Hayyishub,* especially pp. 54 ff., 80 ff.; S. Zeitlin's

critique thereof in *JQR,* XXXVII, 427–31; and other literature cited *supra,* Chap. XXII, n. 45.

84. Finkelstein, *Jewish Self-Government,* pp. 153 ff. The seven elders, or more literally, "best men" of the city are a standardized talmudic designation of the municipal, and later communal councils, with little bearing on their actual number. See *supra,* n. 74. By further providing that wherever no local elders were available those of the neighboring communities should intervene, the synod tried to protect also the autonomy of the scattered small settlements, while recognizing the authority of leaders of major communities over the adjacent lesser groups. This relationship between the main community and its dependencies was to be fully developed and formalized in the more populous areas of Jewish settlement in later medieval Spain and early modern Poland.

85. Many illustrations of this up-hill struggle have been cited *supra,* Chap. XX, and in various other connections. Cf. also my *Jewish Community,* especially Chaps. VII–VIII; S. Zeitlin's brief analysis of "The Opposition to the Spiritual Leaders Appointed by the Government," *JQR,* XXXI, 287–300 (illustrated by the French chief rabbinate of the fourteenth century); and *infra,* Chap. XXVII, nn. 158 ff.

86. Maimonides, *M.T.* Melakhim I.1–2; Sanhedrin I.1–2, with reference to Sanhedrin 7b, 16b, 20b; his *Guide,* I.72 (English, p. 118); Saadiah's *Commentary* on Prov. 28:2, in his *Oeuvres,* VI, 167; Baḥya's *Duties of the Heart,* IV.4–5, ed. by Yahuda, pp. 201, 219 (in Ibn Tibbon's Hebrew trans. ed. by Zifroni, pp. 133, 146; ed. and trans. into English by M. Hyamson, III, 26 f., 42 f.); Abraham Maimonides, *High Ways to Perfection,* ed. and trans. by S. Rosenblatt, II, 48 f. Cf. L. Strauss's "Quelques remarques sur la science politique de Maïmonide et de Fârâbi," *REJ,* C bis, 1–37; E. Rosenthal's "Maimonides' Conception of State and Society," in *Moses Maimonides,* ed. by I. Epstein, pp. 189–206; F. Elias de Tejada's analysis of "Las Doctrinas politicas de Baḥya ibn Paquda," *Sefarad,* VIII, 23–47. The political theories of these medieval philosophers, with their frequently doctrinaire slant, can be fully understood only in connection with their general social, ethical, and legal philosophies. Cf. *supra,* Chap. XXII, and *infra,* Chaps. XXVII and XXXIV. In his brief Hebrew essay on "The Relations to Government in Islam and in Judaism: a General Outline," *Tarbiz,* XIX, 153–59, S. D. Goitein has raised more questions than he was able to answer. The present writer's plans to complement his studies of Maimonides' historical outlook and economic views by a similar detailed analysis of the jurist-philosopher's political theories against the background of both the talmudic sources and the contemporary adjustments under Islam, also still awaits realization. In any case, these general theories of state and society had but an indirect bearing on the rabbis' views of Jewish community life which they considered but part and parcel of rabbinic law with only such modifications as were imposed by the realities of exile. See *infra,* n. 93.

87. *Midrash ha-Gadol,* on Toledot, XXVII, ed. by S. Schechter, col. 412; ed. by M. Margulies, p. 458 (the date of that late medieval compilation and its relationship to the Maimonidean thought and phrasing will be discussed in a later volume); Maimonides' letter to his pupil Joseph ben Yehudah in his *Iggerot,* ed. by D. Z. (H.)

Baneth, No. vi; his *Sefer ha-Miṣvot* (Book of Commandments), Prohib. 316, ed. by M. Bloch, pp. 313 f. (in Moses ibn Tibbon's Hebrew trans., ed. by C. Heller, p. 128); *supra*, n. 50; Saadiah's *Beliefs*, x.17, p. 315 (Hebrew, p. 154 f.; English, p. 400); and, more generally, A. Ehrenfeld's dissertation, *Der Pflichtbegriff in der Ethik des Judentums*, especially pp. 50 ff. Although greatly overstressing the comparison between the rabbinic and Kantian doctrines of duty, this thesis offers stimulating insights. In Maimonides' division between royal (*sultaniya*) and "spiritual-legislative" (*sha'ariya*) authorities, supplemented by the philosopher's conception that a king is required to "strengthen and support the authority of the judges" (*Guide*, iii.41; English, p. 347), C. Neubauer sees an adumbration of the modern division of executive, legislative and judicial powers. See *Das Wesen des Gesetzes in der Philosophie des Maimonides*, p. 101 n. 174. This is far-fetched. In Maimonides' time the judges were largely the arm of either the royal (executive and legislative) or the spiritual (legislative and judicial) powers. Many of these teachings had already been developed in the talmudic age under the combined impact of the Roman Empire's administrative and fiscal pressures, the Jews' struggle for autonomous living, and the popular Graeco-Roman philosophies of government into which had trickled down some of the theoretical speculations of the more advanced political thinkers of the Hellenistic age.

88. Maimonides, *M.T.* Melakhim i.3–7, with reference to Sifre on Deut. No. 157, ed. by Friedmann, fol. 105ab (ed. by Finkelstein, p. 209, also listing further sources); T. Sanhedrin iv, *passim*, ed. by Zuckermandel, pp. 420 ff.; Qiddushin 82a; Ketubot 103b; and many other talmudic sources.

89. Harkavy, *Zikhron*, V, 225 ff., 233; other sources cited by me in *Saadia Anniv. Vol.*, p. 20 n. 25; Sherira's *Iggeret*, pp. 116 f.; and *supra*, n. 21. The exclusion of artisans or even of women from public office did not completely bar them from intellectual pursuits, however. We hear of a learned daughter of Samuel ben 'Ali who was allowed to teach men. Following the example set by R. Meir's wife, Beruriah, she remained invisible to her pupils by giving instruction through a window. Cf. Petaḥiah's *Sibbub*, ed. by Grünhut, pp. 9 f.; English trans. by Benisch, p. 19; Eleazar ben Jacob ha-Babli's three elegies on her death in his *Diwan*, ed. by H. Brody, pp. 7 ff. Nos. 6, 10, 11; and *supra*, Vol. II, pp. 239, 275. On her husband, Zekhariah ben Berekhel, her father's lieutenant and successor, see Assaf's observations in the introduction to his edition of Samuel's letters in *Tarbiz*, I, Part 1, pp. 108 f. The position of the medieval Jewish woman, and her role in communal affairs, education, and synagogue, will become clearer in connection with the general social and educational developments of the later Middle Ages.

90. *Teshubot ha-geonim*, ed. by Harkavy, No. 537; Maimonides, *M.T.* Talmud torah vi.10; his *Commentary* on M. Abot iv.5; Abu Yusuf's *K. al-Kharaj*, pp. 70 (Arabic), 188 (French); and *supra*, Vol. II, pp. 243 f., 277 f., 413 n. 25. Maimonides' condemnation of professional scholars was completely unrealistic in the twelfth century. His most devoted disciple, Joseph ben Yehudah ibn 'Aqnin, in commenting on the passage in the "Sayings of the Fathers" protested vigorously against these doctrinaire teachings of the "luminary of the generation." Cf. his *Sefer Musar* (Book of Ethics; a commentary on Abot), ed. by W. Bacher, pp. 117 ff.

91. Asher ben Yehiel's *Resp.*, xv.7; Meir bar Baruch's *Resp.*, Prague ed., No. 716; and other sources discussed by Joseph Karo in his *Bet Yosef* (Commentary) on Jacob ben Asher's *Ṭurim* Y.D. 243; and Ḥ.M. 163. Possibly the example set by the Jewish communities affected also the tax immunities of Western Christian scholars. Originally, practically all Christian scholars were clerics, and as such enjoyed the immunities of their calling. But with the gradual rise of a lay intelligentsia, the problem of tax exemption began looming larger and larger. Surviving memories of the ancient Graeco-Roman privileges for scholars, in themselves doubtless interrelated with the favored treatment of the ancient rabbis by the Jewish communities acting in concurrence with Roman and Persian authorities, may well have been reinforced by the observation of contemporary Jewish communal practices. Cf. P. Kibre, "Scholarly Privileges: Their Roman Origins and Medieval Expression," *AHR*, LIX, 543–67.

Of a different order were the tax immunities granted by kings to their Jewish favorites. These privileges were bitterly fought by the Jewish communities, and kings had to forbid communal sanctions against their protégés. In a privilege granted to one Vitalis, son of David Abnadean and his family in 1210, Pedro II of Aragon specifically enjoined the community to refrain from placing any member of that family under a ban, nor to "dismiss on their account a synagogue service, to eject them therefrom, to desist from prayer, to pray separately, or to remain silent in the synagogue." Cf. Baer, *Juden im christlichen Spanien*, I, Part 1, p. 67 No. 74; *supra*, Chap. XX, n. 48; and my *Jewish Community*, II, 13 ff.; III, 103 n. 9.

92. Maimonides, *M.T.* Melakhim iv.1, with reference to Sanhedrin 20b–21a; Thomas Aquinas, *De regimine Judaeorum ad ducissam Brabantiae* in his *Opera omnia*, Parma ed. (or the recent New York reimpression thereof), XVI, 292–94; with H. Pirenne's comments thereon in "La Duchesse Aleyde de Brabant et le 'De regimine Judaeorum' de Saint Thomas d'Aquin," *Bulletin de l'Académie royale de Belgique*, Classe de lettres, 5th ser., XIV, 43–55; Jacob Tam's resp. in Agus's ed. of *Teshubot ba'ale ha-tosafot*, pp. 58 ff. No. 12 (with the editor's comments, *ibid.*, pp. 16 f.; also more fully in Isaac bar Aaron's responsum, *ibid.*, pp. 249 ff. No. 130); other statements cited by Urbach in his *Ba'ale ha-tosafot*, pp. 58 f., 269; Meir bar Baruch's *Resp.*, Prague ed., No. 134; and *supra*, Chap. XX, n. 82. Remarkably, the primacy of the law of the kingdom was not to be invoked by Jewish kings. As explained by Nissim Gerondi, in the name of the Tosafot, this maxim "applies only to a Gentile king, for the land is his and he may threaten them [the Jews] with expulsion, if they fail to keep his commandments; but not to Jewish kings, since all of Israel are partners in the land of Israel." *Commentary* on Nedarim 28a *s.v. Be-mokhes ha-'omed.*

93. Maimonides' *Guide*, ii.39 end (English, p. 232); his *Epistle to Yemen*, ed. by A. S. Halkin, pp. 16 ff. (Arabic and Hebrew), iv (English). The centrality of law in Jewish life and the medieval rationalizations thereof will be more fully discussed *infra*, Chap. XXVII. The ramified problems of the "law of the kingdom," so crucial for the entire history of Judeo-Gentile symbiosis in the dispersion, have not yet received their merited comprehensive juridical, historical, and sociological treatment. In addition to the older brief sketches by L. Löw, "Dina de-Malekhuta dina. Ein Beitrag zur jüdischen Rechtsgeschichte" (1862), reprinted in his *GS*, ed. by I. Löw, III, 347–58; D. M. Shohet's dissertation, *The Jewish Court*, pp. 95 ff.; cf.

A. N. Z. Roth's Hebrew essay, "The Law of the Kingdom Is Law," *Ha-Soqer,* V, 110–25 (with additional notes by D. S. Löwinger *ibid.,* p. 126); and H. Y. (L.) Roth's lecture, *Dina de-malkhuta.*

94. See *supra,* Chaps. XVIII, n. 29; XX, nn. 32, 42 and 96. The institution of the ghetto and its meaning for Jewish history will become clearer in its later medieval and early modern phases, when it turned from a voluntary into a legally enforceable means of segregation and, hence, became the subject of much legislation and debate.

95. Yoma 67b. In Rashi's interpretation the term "Satan" stands here for the individual's own "evil spirit." Cf. Maimonides' paraphrase of that expressive tannaitic statement in his *Eight Chapters,* VI, ed. by J. I. Gorfinkle, pp. 37 (Hebrew), 78 (English). Curiously, Maimonides deviates here from the tannaitic illustrations of the contrast between the rational laws, which all men were ready to accept, and the irrational "statutes" imposed on Israel by God's inscrutable will. The prohibition of incest, counted among the former in the original source, is shifted by Maimonides to the irrational category. Perhaps the sage of Fusṭaṭ was impressed by the ancient tradition of incestuous marriages in Hellenistic Egypt and some indubitable vestiges thereof in contemporary Zoroastrianism. He did not classify, therefore, unions among close relatives among the practices rationally rejected by all men. Cf. *supra,* Vol. II, pp. 229 ff., 411 n. 15.

CHAPTER XXIV: SOCIORELIGIOUS CONTROVERSIES

1. Al-Ḥumaidi, cited from an Oxford MS by R. Dozy in his review of E. Renan's *Averroës et Averroisme, JA,* 5th ser., II, 93; other data mentioned in his *Histoire des Musulmans d'Espagne,* new ed., II, 127 n. 5; and in A. von Kremer's *Geschichte der herrschenden Ideen des Islams,* p. 241; 'Abd al-Gabbar, cited by M. Horten in *Die philosophischen Systeme der spekulativen Theologen im Islam,* p. 382; I. Goldziher's "Ueber muhammedanische Polemik gegen Ahl al-Kitab," *ZDMG,* XXXII, 341. Cf. also A. Guillaume's discussion of Bishop Theodore Abu Qurra's report on "A Debate between Christian and Moslem Doctors," *Centenary Supplement to JRAS,* 1924, pp. 233–44 (defends its authenticity). Although the earliest recorded disputation allegedly goes back to Mohammed's colloquy with a Jew, 'Abd-Allah ibn as-Salam, which ended in the latter's conversion, there probably were many more such public debates between Muslims and Christians than between Muslims and Jews. We possess, indeed, no early Hebrew or Judeo-Arabic counterpart to the Syriac reports concerning the disputations held between John I, Monophysite patriarch of Antioch, and the conquering Arab generals in 639, or between Patriarch Timothy and Muslim apologists before Caliph Mahdi in 783. Cf. Steinschneider's *Polemische und apologetische Literatur in arabischer Sprache,* pp. 110 ff., 146 No. 123b and *passim;* F. Nau's ed. of "Un Colloque du Patriarche Jean avec l'Emir des Agaréens," *JA,* 11th ser., V, 225 ff.; A. Mingana's introduction to his translation of 'Ali aṭ-Ṭabari's *K. ad-Din we-ad-daula* under the title *Book of Religion and Empire,* pp. vi ff.; and *infra,* Chap. XXIX, n. 39. We get only occasional glimpses, as in the story told about Abu'l-Hudhail (about 849), whose quick repartee allegedly silenced a Jew who had previously overcome all the other Baṣran theologians with his dialectic. Cf. A. S. Tritton's "Theology in the Making," *JRAS,* 1945, p. 82. According to Mas'udi, Jewish authors (probably including Saadiah Gaon) often disputed creedal problems with Muslim scholars, including himself. Cf. his *K. at-Tanbiḥ,* ed. by De Goeje, p. 113; in Carra de Vaux's French trans., p. 160. Such appearances may perhaps help to explain the Vizier's general friendliness toward the gaon. Cf. H. Malter's biography, *Saadia Gaon,* pp. 117, 124. But nothing is known about Saadiah's part in these debates, except for what might indirectly be divined from his apologetic teachings scattered in his numerous works. On the whole we must therefore rely upon much later samples of actual controversies. Cf., for instance, M. Perlmann's summary of "A Late Muslim Jewish Disputation," *PAAJR,* XII, 51–58. Although held in 1796 and described nine years later, it probably was fairly typical of similar discussions in earlier periods as well. Chronologically much closer are the Muslim apologists analyzed by Perlmann in his studies quoted in our next notes, but many of these, too, wrote after 1200.

It is not quite so surprising, therefore, that, despite Steinschneider's pioneering efforts in this field, which culminated in the publication of his remarkable bibliographical work in 1877 (cf. Goldziher's comments in *ZDMG,* XXXII, 341–87), the study of Judeo-Muslim religious and political controversies still is in its early stages.

The Jewish side, in particular, in the controversy with either Muslims or Christians has never been made the subject of searching investigation. The period here under review has been particularly neglected with respect to both the preservation of primary sources and their scholarly interpretation. Even O. S. Rankin's posthumous *Jewish Religious Polemic of Early and Later Centuries* offers translations and analyses of but a few documents, mostly dating from the later periods. Cf. *infra,* nn. 38 and 56.

2. See Mas'udi, *K. at-Tanbiḥ,* I, 156, 200 ff.; in Carra de Vaux's French translation; Abu Bakr al-Baqillani, *K. aṭ-Ṭamhid* (Guide to Confuting the Various Heretics and Unbelievers), published in 1947; Saadiah's *K. al-Amanaṭ* and Qirqisani's *K. al-Anwar* will be more fully discussed in later chapters, particularly XXV–XXVI and XXXIV. Al-Baqillani's anti-Jewish polemics are analyzed by R. Brunschvig in "L'Argumentation d'un théologien musulman du Xe siècle contre le Judaïsme," *Homenaje a Millás-Vallicrosa,* I, 225–41. On the meaning of the term *sham'atiyya,* see *ibid.,* p. 226 n. 4. Islam continued here, on another plane, the old Judeo-Christian controversy. Following well-established patristic patterns, John of Damascus included a large chapter, "On Heresies," in his major work of Christian dogmatics, *Pegè gnóseos* (Fountain of Knowledge). Cf. the text in *PG,* XCIV, 677 ff.; and C. Güterbock's brief survey of *Der Islam im Lichte der byzantinischen Polemik.* Such chapters continued to be in vogue among both Christian and Muslim writers. Before long some of the latter devoted entire works to comparative studies. We shall have frequent occasion to quote such outstanding early students of comparative religion as Abu Manṣur al-Baghdadi, Ibn Ḥazm, and Shahrastani. Although writing in a far less detached vein than did, for example, Al-Biruni in his distinguished book on India, these authors have preserved much pertinent information also about internal Jewish controversies. See *infra,* Chap. XXV.

3. See the sources cited by Fischel in *Magnes Anniv. Book,* pp. 186 f. From street debates popular denunciations found their way into literature and vice versa. If Christians were accused of alcoholism and their nuns of easy virtue, and if the Sabeans were said to be pitiless toward their own coreligionists, Jews were supposed to emanate a specific odor—an accusation often repeated later in Christian lands. Cf. the data cited in Mez, *Renaissance,* p. 50. In retaliation some Jews, especially in Christian countries, compared the black-clad Arabs with the demonic spirits inhabiting outhouses. Cf. M. Steinschneider, *Polemische und apologetische Literatur,* p. 250 n. 18; and *supra,* Chap. XVIII, n. 22. The more scholarly writers in all camps, however, rarely resorted to these vulgar arguments.

4. See Simon bar Ṣemaḥ Duran, *Qeshet u-magen* (Bow and Shield; an apologetic treatise written in Algiers in 1423); and Steinschneider's numerous corrections thereof in the notes to his edition; Ibn Ḥazm, *K. al-Fiṣal* [or *Faṣl*] *fi-al-milal w'al-alwā w'an-niḥal* (Book of Decisions on Religions, Opinions, and Sects), and M. Asín Palacios's annotated Spanish translation of books I–VI thereof in his *Abenházam de Cordoba* (I, 267 n. 310 states reasons for his preference of spelling the title *Fiṣal,* rather than *Faṣl*); Samau'al ibn Yaḥya ibn 'Abbas al-Maghribi, *Badhl al-majhud fi Ifḥam al-Yahud* (The Silencing of the Jews; the Cairo 1939 publication includes a Risala [Missive] by a later convert, Israel ben Samuel of Jerusalem; this volume

was, however, not accessible to me). Cf. the excerpts cited from MS and annotated by M. Schreiner in *MGWJ,* XLII; M. Perlmann's "'Abd al-Ḥaḳḳ al-Islami: A Jewish Convert," *JQR,* XXXI, 171–91; 'Ali aṭ-Ṭabari's *Book of Religion and Empire,* trans. Mingana; M. Bouyges's "Nos informations sur 'Aliy . . . aṭ-Ṭabariy," *Mélanges de l'Université St. Joseph, Beyrouth,* XXVIII, 84; and, more generally, M. Schreiner's comprehensive analysis, "Zur Geschichte der Polemik zwischen Juden und Muhammedanern," *ZDMG,* XLII, 591–675. Cf. also I. di Matteo's study of "Le Pretese contraddizioni della S. Scrittura secondo Ibn Hazm," *Bessarione,* XXXIX, 77–127 (was to be continued); E. Algermissen's analysis of *Die Pentateuchzitate Ibn Hazms* (with particular reference to their similarity, or dissimilarity, with Saadiah's Arabic translation of Scripture); and, more generally, the extensive materials assembled in E. Fritsch's careful dissertation, *Islam und Christentum im Mittelalter.*

The general ignorance of Hebrew among Arab writers and their reliance on Arabic Old Testament versions by Jews and Christians is evident from every page of their writings. But only in the early, more moderate, phase of anti-*dhimmi* polemics did such authors as *Ṭabari* and *Jaḥiẓ* make allowances for the possibility that some objectionable passages may have been traceable to mistakes by translators. Cf. Fritsch, *Islam,* pp. 57 f.; and the data reviewed by D. S. Margoliouth in "On 'The Book of Religion and Empire' by 'Ali b. Rabban Al-Ṭabari," *Proceedings of the British Academy,* XVI, 165–82; G. Vajda in "Some Citations from the Book of Psalms by 'Ali aṭ-Ṭabari" (Hungarian), *Blau Mem. Vol.,* pp. 295–98; F. Taeschner in "Die alttestamentlichen Bibelzitate vor allem aus dem Pentateuch, in Aṭ-Ṭabarī's Kitāb aḍ-ḍin wad-daula, und ihre Bedeutung für die Frage nach der Echtheit dieser Schrift," *Oriens christianus,* XXXI, 23–39; and W. Hoenerbach in *"Isaias* bei Ṭabarî," *Alttestamentliche Studien Friedrich Nötscher gewidmet,* pp. 98–119 (referring to Abu Jafar aṭ-Ṭabari, who had discussed the legendary story of the prophet in both his Commentary and his History). Of more general interest are P. Kraus's "Hebräische und syrische Zitate in ismā'ilitischen Schriften," *Der Islam,* XIX, 243–63 (with special reference to Aḥmad al-Kirmani, who lived in Egypt under Al-Ḥakim and who may actually have himself acquired a smattering of Hebrew); W. Ivanow's "Noms bibliques dans la mythologie ismaélienne," *JA,* CCXXXVII, 249–55 (adding to G. Vajda's "Melchisédec," *ibid.,* CCXXXIV, 173–83); R. Edelmann's study, "On the Arabic Versions of the Pentateuch," *Studia orientalia Joanni Pedersen . . . dicata,* pp. 71–75 (or his corresponding Hebrew article in *Melilah,* V, 45–50); C. Peters's "Psalm 149 in Zitaten islamischer Autoren," *Biblica,* XXI, 138–51; and particularly his "Grundsätzliche Bemerkungen zur Frage der arabischen Bibeltexte," *RSO,* XX, 129–43. Cf. also E. Strauss's *Toledot ha-Yehudim be-Miṣrayim ve-Suriah,* I, 357 ff.; and an extensive commentary probably written by an orthodox Copt about 1150, fully analyzed by G. Graf in "Ein arabischer Pentateuchkommentar des 12. Jahrhunderts," *Biblica,* XXIII, 113–38. Of course, some mistakes of the Muslim polemists may have been owing to faulty copies at their disposal, or to sectarian interpretations of Scripture, Jewish or Christian, since lost. In "The Version of the Gospels Used in Medina *circa* 700 A.D.," *Al-Andalus,* XV, 289–96, A. Guillaume has shown that even a quotation, which can now be traced back to a Palestinian Syriac Lectionary, greatly differs from the Peshiṭṭa and other Syriac texts and shows strong influences of Jewish Aramaic (pp. 292 ff.). Similar variants in the Syriac translation of the Old Testament are even more likely, as certain formulations available in the Jewish Aramaic versions may well have appealed particularly to unorthodox readers of all three faiths on exegetical or theological grounds. See *infra,* Chap. XXIX. Of more than passing interest are also "Some Contemporary Moslem Interpretations of the Bible," discussed by C. S. Braden in *Crozer Quarterly,* XXII, 246–59 (chiefly from Ahmadiya sources).

Curiously, Qur'an verses transliterated into Hebrew script have been found in several manuscripts. Cf. E. Rödiger, "Ueber ein Koran-Fragment in hebräischer Schrift," *ZDMG,* XIV, 485–89; with M. Steinschneider's note thereon in his *Hebräische Bibliographie,* III, 113; and E. Mainz's "Koranverse in hebräischer Schrift," *Der Islam,* XXI, 229. On the other hand, we have no Jewish counterpart to the Christian polemist, Paul ar-Rahib, bishop of Sidon, who used the Qur'an itself as testimony for the truth of Christianity. His *Risala* (Missive to One of the Muslims), ed. by L. Cheikho in his *Vingt traités théologiques,* 2d ed., pp. 15–26, enjoyed considerable vogue among Eastern Christians and evoked a reply by Aḥmad al-Qarafi. Cf. Fritsch, *Islam und Christentum,* pp. 20 ff.; and *infra,* n. 6.

5. Cf. 'Abd al-Ḥaqq's statement, cited by M. Perlmann in *JQR,* XXXI, 181 f. (with reference to Gen. 1:16, 2:8, 12:2); and E. Strauss's succinct review of the main Scriptural arguments of Muslim controversialists in the sequence of biblical verses, in his "Methods of Muslim Polemics" (Hebrew), *Vienna Mem. Vol.,* pp. 182–97. The Hebrew Scriptures supposedly alluded also to Islam's holy city of Mecca. Abraham's journey "toward the South" (*ha-negbah;* Gen. 12:9) was identified by 'Abd al-Ḥaqq with a journey to Mekkah, because both words have in Hebrew the numerical equivalent of 65. We must bear in mind, however, that 'Abd al-Ḥaqq lived in the fourteenth century, when *gemaṭrias* were greatly in vogue in Jewish exegetical literature, producing such prodigious feats of "arithmetical interpretation," as the biblical commentaries of the great jurist, Jacob ben Asher. See O. Goldberg's brief analysis of "Zur Einleitung in den Baal ha-Turim; die Zahlenmystik eines grossen Talmudisten," *Revue juive,* IX, 239–43. Clearly, such arguments could not readily be employed by born Muslims who were far less proficient in the Hebrew language.

6. 'Abd al-Ḥaqq, cited by Perlmann, *JQR,* XXXI, 180; Ṭabari's *Book of Religion and Empire,* trans. Mingana, pp. 85 ff.; Samau'al al-Maghribi's *Ifḥam,* cited by Schreiner in *MGWJ,* XLII, 176, with reference to Deut. 18:15–19; Maimonides' *Epistle to Yemen,* ed. by A. S. Halkin, pp. 16 ff. (Arabic and Hebrew), iv f. (English). Cf. E. Strauss's observations in *Vienna Mem. Vol.,* pp. 191 f.; M. Perlmann's "Ibn Qayyim and Samau'al al-Maghribi," *Journal of Jewish Bibliography,* III, 71–74. The symbolism of the "little horn" doubtless reminded both Jews and Muslims of the designation *Du'l Qarnayim* given to Alexander the Great and also to a Yemenite ruler As-Sa'b about a century before the *hejira.* Cf. Qur'an 18:82; A. Abel's comments thereon in his "Dû l'Qarnayim, prophète de l'universalité," *Annuaire,* XI, 5–18; the poetic references interpreted by M. M. Bravmann in his "On the Spiritual Background of Islam and the History of Its Principal Concepts," *Muséon,* LXIV, 327 f. (or in its previous Hebrew garb in *Tarbiz,* XVIII, 71 f.); and related Judeo-Muslim legends. Cf. also I. Lichtenstadter's "Origin and Interpretation of Some Qur'ānic Symbols," *Studi Orientalistici in onore di Giorgio Levi della Vida,* II, 62 ff. In the thirteenth century a Malikite scholar, Aḥmad aṣ-Ṣinhaji al-Qarafi compiled a list of fifty-one scriptural passages allegedly supporting the Muslim view. The progress of Muslim apologetics is illustrated here by the fact that only the first seven verses are found in the Pentateuch, the following eleven come from the

paraclete references in the New Testament, while fully thirty-three are cited from the Prophets, Psalms, and Daniel. See the brief summaries by Goldziher in *ZDMG,* XXXII, 376 ff., and Strauss in *Vienna Mem. Vol.,* pp. 184 ff.

7. Qur'an 4:84, 8:144, 158, etc.; Baqillani's *Aṭ-Ṭamhid,* pp. 118 ff. As pointed out by Brunschvig (in *Homenaje a Millás,* p. 229), Baqillani had written an entire work on the beauties of the Qur'an (*K. I'jaz al-Qur'an*)—one of the numerous works of that kind then produced by Arab philologists. Cf. also M. B. Alavi's "Inimitability of the Qur'an," *IC,* XXIV, 1–15 (summarizing no less than forty-four reasons adduced by early Muslim teachers). These qualities were supposed not only to insure the superiority of the Arabic language over all other existing tongues, but also to be the ultimate proof of the Qur'an's authenticity which, as Baqillani boasted, was not denied even by unbelievers. On the other hand, Samau'al ibn Yaḥya claimed that, despite their living for centuries in an Arab environment, Jews were unable to understand the fine points in the Qur'an and to distinguish between a beautiful phrase and a corrupt expression. Cf. his *Ifḥam,* in Schreiner's translation, in *MGWJ,* XLII, 253; and, more generally, *infra,* n. 13; and Chaps. XXIX and XXX.

8. Ibn Ḥazm's *K. al-Fiṣal* (or *Faṣl*), xv.1 ff., I, 116 ff., 122 f., 127 f., 150, etc. (in Asín Palacios's trans., II, 238 ff., 250 f., 255 f., 288, etc.). These arguments have frequently been analyzed, since I. Goldziher first examined in some detail these "Proben muhammedanischer Polemik gegen den Talmud" in *Jeschurun,* ed. by J. Kobak, VIII, 76 ff.; and in his essay in *ZDMG,* XXXII, 341 ff. More recently the Spanish-Arab philosopher's lucubrations have been reviewed anew, in particular in connection with his sharp attack on Samuel ibn Nagrela's critique of the Qur'an known to him only from second hand. Excerpts from Ibn Ḥazm's polemical pamphlet, entitled *Radd* (Refutation by Abu Muhammad ibn Ḥazm of Ibn al-Nagrila, the Jew, May Allah Curse Him) were published, with detailed comments, by E. García Gómez in his "Polemica religiosa entre Ibn Ḥazm e Ibn al-Nagrila," *Al-Andalus,* IV, 1–28. Cf. also Ibn Ḥazm's *K. al Fiṣal,* xv.20.36, I, 135, 152 (in Asin Palacios's translation II, 267, 291). To judge from the Muslim thinker's ill-tempered personal attacks, Samuel must have been a formidable opponent. This is also borne out by the Jewish "prince's" extant works, as well as by Ibn Sa'id's remark that Samuel's "mastery of the Talmud and his skill for its vindication were such as none of his predecessors in Spain had ever displayed." Cf. Ibn Sa'id's *K. Tabakat al-Umam* (Catégories des Nations), p. 160 (in J. Finkel's translation in *JQR,* XVIII, 54); and M. Perlmann's "Eleventh-Century Andalusian Authors on the Jews of Granada," *PAAJR,* XVIII, 269–90. Incidentally, Ibn Ḥazm's belligerent temperament came to the fore also in his disparagement of Kairuwan and other countries as compared with the glories of his native Spain. Cf. the excerpt from his *Risala fi fadhl al-Andalus* (Missive in Praise of Andalusia), in C. Pellat's "Ibn Ḥazm, bibliographe et apologiste de l'Espagne musulmane," *Al-Andalus,* XIX, 53–102.

9. See I. Goldziher's "Sa'id b. Hasan d'Alexandrie," *REJ,* XXX, 15. On this running thread of Muslim accusations, see I. di Matteo's comprehensive analysis of "Il 'Taḥrif' od alterazione della Bibbia secondo i Musulmani," *Bessarione,* XXXVIII, 64–111, 223–60. Cf. also H. Hirschfeld's "Mohammedan Criticism of the Bible," *JQR,* [o.s.] XIII, 222–40; and the related early Christian-Muslim controversies, such as the exchange of "Missives" between 'Abd Allah ibn Isma'il al-Ḥashimi and the Christian, 'Abd al-Masiḥ ibn Isḥaq al-Kindi, ed. by A. Tien, with W. Muir's

English translation entitled *The Apology of Al-Kindy Written at the Court of Al-Mamun . . . in Defence of Christianity against Islam* (cf. also J. Muñoz Sendino's edition of a medieval Latin translation of Al-Kindi's *Apologia del Cristianismo*); I. S. Allouche's analysis of "Un Traité de polémique christiano-musulmane au IXe siècle," *Hespéris,* XXVI, 123–55 (with a French translation of many excerpts), referring to Al-Jaḥiẓ' controversial tract *K. ar-Radd 'alā an-Naṣārā* (Reply to Christians), in part ed. by J. Finkel; and, more generally, E. Fritsch's *Islam und Christentum.*

10. Ṭabari's *Book of Religion and Empire,* p. 4; C. Peters's "Grundsätzliche Bemerkungen," in *RSO,* XX, 135 f. Ṭabari's apologetic work was in many respects the fountainhead of Muslim polemics against both Christianity and Judaism. Later controversialists often knew the Bible simply from his citations. This may already have been the case of Jaḥiẓ, writing in 869. Certainly the example adduced by Allouche (*Hespéris,* XXVI, 145) from Jaḥiẓ' observations on Isa. 42:10 as indicating his knowledge of Hebrew rather proves the opposite. We must bear in mind, however, that even Ṭabari could not use the original Hebrew or Greek, but at best consulted a Syriac translation related to the Peshiṭṭa. At times he simply used existing Arabic versions. After carefully analyzing Ṭabari's biblical citations and comparing them with those in the writings of Mawardi, Qarafi, and Ibn Qayyim, F. Taeschner came to the conclusion that they all went back to a common prototype diverging from both the masoretic and the Peshiṭṭa texts. Cf. his observations in *Oriens christianus,* XXXI, 32 f. Cf. also M. Bouyges's more recent critique in *Mélanges* of the Université St. Joseph, XXVIII, 102 ff., arguing against the authenticity of Ṭabari's tract and placing it at a much later date. However, most of these arguments are far from cogent, and they hardly invalidate the affirmative proof discussed by the other scholars mentioned by Bouyges himself.

11. A. S. Halkin's ed. and trans. of "The Scholia to Numbers and Deuteronomy in the Samaritan-Arabic Pentateuch," *JQR,* XXXIV, 49 f., 59; Ibn Qayyim ibn al-Jauziya's *K. Hidayat al-ḥayara* (Guide for the Confused; about Answers to Refute Jews and Christians), cited by Goldziher in *ZDMG,* XXXII, 373; Perlmann's observations in *Journal of Jewish Bibliography,* III, 71 ff. (pointing out Ibn Qayyim's constant dependence on Samau'al ibn Yaḥya); and Sa'd ibn Manṣur ibn Kammuna cited by D. H. Baneth in his "Ibn Kammuna," *MGWJ,* LXIX, 303.

12. Samau'al ibn Yaḥya's *Ifḥam,* cited by Schreiner in *MGWJ,* XLII, 221 f.; Baqillani, *Tamhid,* pp. 114 ff., 131 ff. Cf. the summaries by E. Strauss in *Vienna Mem. Vol.,* pp. 186 f.; and Brunschvig in *Homenaje a Millás,* pp. 230 f. Mas'udi (in his *Kitab Muruj adh-dhahab,* II, 390) and Ibn Ḥazm (in his *Kitab al-Fiṣal,* xv.18–20, I, 133 ff., in Asín Palacios's trans., II, 263 ff.) made much of the Lot story. Here, too, the Muslim controversialists needed but refer to questions long debated by Jewish sectarians or extreme rationalists of the kind of Ḥivi ha-Balkhi. Partly because it was so deeply enmeshed in these religious controversies, the problem of miracles, including the supernatural endowment of genuine versus false prophets and their historical attestation, loomed very large in all works of contemporary philosophy or religion. See *infra,* Chaps. XXIX, XXXIV.

13. Deut. r. VIII.6 (on 30:13); *supra,* Vol. II, pp. 138 ff.; Saadiah's *Beliefs and Opinions,* III.7, ed. by Landauer, pp. 128 ff.; in Ibn Tibbon's Hebrew trans., pp.

66 f.; in Rosenblatt's English trans., pp. 157 ff., with reference to Jer. 31:35–36 and Exod. 31:16 (the Muslim objectors quoting Exod. 21:6); T. Roebuck's *Collection of Proverbs and Proverbial Phrases in the Persian and Hindoostanee Language,* I, 249 No. 1164, 287 No. 1396, with L. Dukes's comment thereon in "Ein persisches Sprichwort," *Literaturblatt des Orients,* 1850, p. 416; Goldziher's report in *ZDMG,* XXXII, 342 n. 1; Halevi's *K. al-Khazari,* I, 86–89, ed. by Hirschfeld, pp. 38 ff.; in his English trans., pp. 60 ff. On the prayer *Yismaḥ Mosheh* (Let Moses Rejoice), see *infra,* Chap. XXXI. Incidentally, it should be noted that the argument from the attestation of the Jewish revelation by 600,000 Hebrews had also been advanced by Nicetas the philosopher in his *Anatropé* (Confutatio falsi libri quem scripsit Mohamedes Arabus), in *PG,* CV, 705.

Almost all early Jewish philosophers took a stand on the subject of abrogation. David al-Muqammiṣ preceding, and Samuel ben Ḥofni Gaon following Saadiah repudiated this doctrine as well as that of the purported supernatural "inimitability" of the Qur'an. Moses ibn Ezra mentioned in this connection Samuel's treatise on "Abrogation of the Torah." This is at least Steinschneider's reading and interpretation of the passage in Ibn Ezra's *K. al-Muḥadhara w'al-mudhakara* (Book of Discussion and Remembrance), in the excerpt published by him from an Arabic MS in *Polemische Literatur,* pp. 102 f. No. 79. In his Hebrew trans. of that famous treatise on the Hebrew *ars poetica,* entitled *Shirat Yisrael* (The Poetry of Israel), pp. 52 f., however, B. Z. Halper prefers a reading of Samuel's title which means "Duties of the Torah." Although the latter variant seems to be borne out by the continuation, "Its Roots and Ramifications," this controversy will probably not be fully resolved until perhaps a lucky discovery of Samuel's text may show whether the gaon concerned himself primarily with a positive review of the laws of the Torah, or with their defense against Muslim polemists.

14. Maimonides' *Epistle to Yemen,* ed. by A. S. Halkin, pp. 38 ff. (Arabic and Hebrew), viii (English). Cf. also the editor's introduction, pp. xv ff.; and, on the general Maimonidean approaches to Bible criticism, W. Bacher's detailed analysis, *Bibelexegese Moses Maimuni's.* Cf. also *infra,* Chap. XXIX.

15. Cf. Fahr ad-Din ar-Razi's and the convert Ar-Raqili's arguments cited by Schreiner in *ZDMG,* XLII, 647 f.; and by M. Zucker in his "Studies in the History of Religious Disputations between Judaism and Islam" in *Festschrift Kaminka,* Hebrew section, pp. 34 f.; Al-Ilbiri's poem in A. R. Nykl's *Mukhtarat* (Selections from Hispano-Arabic Poetry), p. 142; and *infra,* note 19. The Jewish argument that abrogation of God's commandments "would imply that He changes His mind and regrets His [previous] utterances" was answered by Shahrastani with the equally standardized Muslim contentions of the changeability of all laws under changing circumstances, and of the historic record showing that pre-Mosaic laws had been changed by the divine revelation to Moses. Cf. Shahrastani's *Kitāb Nihāyatu'l-Iqdām fi 'ilmi 'l-Kalām,* ed. by A. Guillaume, I, 499 ff. (Arabic), 158 f. (English). Cf. *infra,* n. 19; the anonymous *fatwa* of 1453, cited in Steinschneider's *Polemische Literatur,* pp. 150 ff. No. 131, and related materials *ibid.,* pp. 56 f. No. 37b, 397 ff. Muslim criticisms of the Jewish permission, even encouragement, of marriages between an uncle and a niece may have further stimulated the Samaritan and Karaite outlawry of this practice, but they did not create it. The thirteenth-century Rabbanite author Estori ben Moses ha-Parḥi (Farḥi) readily blamed these sectarians

for blindly following the Gentiles. Cf. his *Kaftor va-feraḥ* (Knop and Flower; on Palestine topography and laws), v end, Venice ed., 1549, fol. 20b; and L. Zunz's observations thereon in his "On the Geography of Palestine from Jewish Sources" appended to Asher's edition of Benjamin of Tudela's *Massa'ot,* II, 447. In fact, opposition to such marriages in sectarian circles antedates the Christian era. Cf. *supra,* Vol. II, pp. 230, 411 n. 14, and the literature listed there.

16. Saadiah's *Beliefs and Opinions,* III.7, pp. 131 (Arabic), 71 f. (Hebrew), 162 (English); Samau'al ibn Yaḥya's *Ifḥam,* cited by Schreiner in *MGWJ,* XLII, 170 f.; *Otiot de-Rabbi 'Aqiba* (Letters of R. 'Aqiba), VI, ed. by A. Jellinek in his *Bet ha-Midrasch,* III, 26 f.; ed. by J. D. Eisenstein in his *Ozar ha-Midrashim* (A Library of Two Hundred Minor Midrashim), p. 414, with reference to Ps. 135:4 and Isa. 40:27. This forced reasoning of Jacob's failure to receive the Torah, in lieu of the more frequent explanation that it was a retribution for his marrying two sisters, may perhaps be accounted for by Muslim polemics. Ibn Ḥazm, Qarafi, and others followed ancient polemists in citing the later outlawry of such marriages as an instance of the divine abrogation of older laws. Cf. the sources cited by Strauss in *Vienna Seminary Mem. Vol.,* p. 187; and on other, rather fanciful, explanations of Jacob's marriage, L. Ginzberg's data in *Legends of the Jews,* V, 295 n. 167. Of course, Saadiah could have answered that the Torah merely forbade here a practice previously permitted by law. The gaon himself had to admit, however, that in certain cases such outlawry did not wholly eliminate existing practices and that, for instance, sacrifices and circumcision must be performed also on Sabbaths. He merely pleaded that their historic priority accounted also for their continued legal precedence. These arguments by the great gaon were often repeated, with many variations in detail, by Jewish apologists down to the most recent times. As late as 1796, Jewish debaters elaborated Saadiah's main doctrine by saying, "A command may be changed to suit the times; but that is not so in the case of a prohibition. A command is followed by reward, a prohibition is to ward off punishment." Cf. text and translation by Perlmann in *PAAJR,* XII, 55, 58 (g).

17. Tritton, *Caliphs,* pp. 128 f.; the Karaite Jefeth ben 'Ali's Commentary on Isa. 47:9, cited by S. Pinsker in his *Lickute kadmoniot* (Zur Geschichte des Karaismus und der karäischen Literatur), I, 158 n.; Hosea 9:7; "An Early Theologico-Polemical Work," ed. by J. Mann in *HUCA,* XII–XIII, 434, 441 f.; and many other sources cited by Steinschneider in his *Polemische Literatur,* pp. 248 ff. The mispronunciation *qalon* for Qur'an seems to have become so standardized that the three Hebrew translators of Maimonides' *Epistle to Yemen* uniformly used it in reproducing the author's apparently correct Arabic term. A. S. Halkin's suggestion that the original had already contained that misspelling is far from conclusive. Cf. his comments on his edition of those texts, pp. 14 f. n. 16, 38 n. 52.

18. Saadiah's *Beliefs and Opinions,* III.4, pp. 122 f. (Arabic), 62 f. (Hebrew), 149 f. (English); Pinsker, *Lickute kadmoniot,* II, 95; Maimonides, *Commentary* on M.R.H. II.6. Saadiah's extremism on this score naturally served as a ready target for his Karaite opponents. Cf. *infra,* Chap. XXVI, nn. 80 ff.

19. A. S. Tritton, "Foreign Influences on Muslim Theology," *BSOAS,* X, 837; Ibn Ḥazm's *Radd* (Refutation) in the excerpts published by E. García Gómez in

Al-Andalus, IV, 24 ff., and in M. Perlmann's translation in *PAAJR,* XVIII, 280 ff. (with a slight variant at the end of the quotation); Al-Ilbiri's poem in A. R. Nykl's *Mukhtarat,* pp. 141 ff., with Nykl's partial translation thereof in his *Hispano-Arabic Poetry and Its Relations with the Old Provençal Troubadours,* pp. 197 ff. It should be noted, however, that Al-Ilbiri was expelled from Granada because of these bloodthirsty attacks, and that another contemporary poet, Al-Munfatil, not only praised the Jews greatly but intimated that he secretly preferred Judaism. Cf. *supra,* Chap. XVIII, n. 41; and H. Pérès's observations in *La Poésie andalouse en arabe classique au XIe siècle,* pp. 269 f. Cf. also E. Lévi-Provençal's *Peninsule iberique,* p. 38 n. 5. Curiously, because of his dabbling in comparative religion, Ibn Ḥazm, like Shahrastani, was accused of lack of orthodoxy by more fanatical coreligionists. The same Istanbul MS from which García Gómez published Ibn Ḥazm's pamphlet against Samuel ha-Nagid also includes in the immediate sequel (fols. 163–67) his sharp reply to one such assailant. Cf. M. Asín Palacios's description of "Un Códice inexplorado del Cordobés Ibn Ḥazm," *Al-Andalus,* II, 13 ff.

20. Attacks on *dhimmi* officeholders are listed in Steinschneider's *Polemische Literatur,* pp. 55 f. No. 36 (dated 1504); 102 No. 78b (undatable); 104 f. No. 82 (fourteenth cent.); 393 f. No. 14b (about 1200); those on alleged Christian arson, *ibid.,* pp. 66 f. No. 55; 72 No. 59 (both relating to 1340); that concerning blasphemies against Mohammed, *ibid.,* pp. 59 f. No. 40 (1519; cf. Goldziher's correction in *ZDMG,* XXXII, 382); and Al-Jaubari's "Uncovering of Secrets," parts of which had been published by Steinschneider himself (as well as De Goeje), *ibid.,* pp. 188 ff. Cf. Steinschneider's "Ǵauberi's 'entdeckte Geheimnisse' eine Quelle für orientalische Sittenschilderung," *ZDMG,* XIX, 562–72; and M. J. De Goeje's "Ǵaubari's 'entdeckte Geheimnisse,'" *ibid.,* XX, 485–510. Cf. also M. Perlmann's "Notes on Anti-Christian Propaganda" in *BSOAS,* X, 843 ff.; E. Strauss's *Toledot,* 336 ff.; and on the adulteration of drugs, *infra,* Chap. XXXVI.

21. See the eleventh-century convert Abu 'Ali Yaḥya ibn Jazla's polemical "missive," described in Steinschneider's *Polemische Literatur,* pp. 57 f. No. 39, with A. Miller's comment thereon in his letter to Dr. Steinschneider in *ZDMG,* XXXII, 389; W. J. Fischel's quotation from Al-Asqalani's biographical work in "Ueber Raschid ad-Daulas jüdischen Ursprung," *MGWJ,* LXXXI, 152; his *Jews in . . . Mediaeval Islam,* pp. 119 ff.; and *supra,* Chap. XVIII, n. 31. Interesting data on medieval Jewish apothecaries (mainly from Western sources) have been assembled by L. Glesinger in his "Beiträge zur Geschichte der Pharmazie bei den Juden," *MGWJ,* LXXXII, 111–30, 417–22. On the relation between medicine and magic arts among both Jews and Muslims, and the generally mixed Muslim attitude toward the use of *dhimmi* physicians, cf. *infra,* Chaps. XXXIII and XXXVI.

Nor were attacks on the *dhimmi* physique altogether lacking. Versatile Al-Jaḥiz included the following gem in his polemical essay: "Why the Christians, ugly as they are, are physically less repulsive than the Jews may be explained by the fact that the Jews, by not intermarrying, have intensified the offensiveness of their features." Pointing out that in the animal kingdom, too, inbreeding leads to deterioration in quality, this ninth-century polyhistor triumphantly exclaimed, "The Jewish race therefore has been denied high mental qualities, sound physique, and superior lactation." Cf. his *Risala,* trans. by J. Finkel in *JAOS,* XLVII, 328. See also *supra,* n. 3.

22. Al-Ḥaqq's excerpt cited by Perlmann in *JQR,* XXXI, 177; I. Goldziher's "Sa'id b. Hasan d'Alexandrie," *REJ,* XXX, 10, 19 f.; S. A. Weston's ed. of "The Kitab Masâlik an-Naẓar of Sa'id ibn Ḥasan of Alexandria," *JAOS,* XXIV, 357 f., 382 f. Samau'al ibn Yaḥya was the exception among converts to praise the Muslim toleration of *dhimmis.* In his endeavor to explain the alleged Jewish misreadings of the Bible not as a result of conscious falsification but of mistakes which with the passage of time had unavoidably crept into it, he developed an interesting historical theory about the anti-Jewish persecutions of previous ages. "The older a people," he wrote, "and the more manifold the nations which successively humble and oppress it, the more disinclined it becomes to cultivate the history of past ages." Chaldeans and Babylonians, Persians, Greeks, and Christians had all persecuted the Jews, tried to uproot them, and destroyed their cities and books. Only Islam had extended to them its protection. In this way Samau'al even offered, as we shall see, an historical interpretation for certain liturgical peculiarities of Jewish worship. Cf. his *Ifḥam,* in Schreiner's text and translation in *MGWJ,* XLII, 219 f.; and *infra,* Chap. XXXI.

23. Al-Qarafi, cited by Fritsch in his *Islam und Christentum,* p. 22. Sa'id did not indicate the procedure for such censorship of manuscripts. But he probably had in mind methods analogous to those described, mainly on the basis of the Church's treatment of books according to Niger, by G. B. Flahiff in his "Ecclesiastical Censorship of Books in the Twelfth Century," *Mediaeval Studies,* IV, 1–22. One could not censor a treatise before it was written. Nor was it easy to discourage copyists from reproducing, severally or collectively, any book they wished to possess. Censorship *post factum* had long been practiced, and many books, even by orthodox Muslims like Ghazzali, suffered from burning by overzealous state officials. Any Jewish attack on Mohammed or the Qur'an, moreover, verbally or in writing, automatically fell under the classification of blasphemy and was punishable by death. Cf. *supra,* Chap. XVIII, n. 15. Clearly, the Hebrew alphabet was no safeguard against denunciations by Jewish informers or converts to Islam. However, Muslim surveillance was generally lax, and Jewish apologists frequently could speak their minds without too much fear of retribution. Cf. also *supra,* n. 4; and *infra,* Chap. XXXIV.

24. Aṭ-Ṭabari's *Book of Religion and Empire,* trans. Mingana, p. 58; Ibn Ḥazm's *K. al-Fiṣal,* xv.47, I, 163 (Asín Palacios's translation II, 306 f.); his *Radd,* cited by García Gómez in *Al-Andalus,* IV, 19; Samau'al ibn Yaḥya's *Ifḥam,* in the excerpts and their German summary by Schreiner in *MGWJ,* XLII, 176 ff. According to Abu'l Fatḥ ash-Shahrastani, some Jews partially conceded the Muslim claim and affirmed that God had promised Abraham to give his son Ishmael "dominion only, but not prophecy and religious mission." To which Shahrastani countered that, if it is to be just, dominion must be based on truth, and that hence Islam is the true faith. Cf. his *K. al-Milal w'al-niḥal* (Book of Religious and Philosophical Sects), 1.2.1.1, ed. by W. Cureton, p. 164, and in T. Haarbrücker's German trans. entitled *Religionspartheien und Philosophenschulen,* I, 250.

25. Samau'al's *Ifḥam,* quoted by Schreiner in *MGWJ,* XLII, 254 ff., 259 f., 407 ff. The statements here quoted were elaborated in a chapter entitled, "The Cause Why They [the Jews] Constantly Increase Their Burden," which tried to explain one aspect of the alleged falsification of the Torah by rabbinic Judaism. Yet Samau'al

did not spare the Karaites, despite their professed rigid adherence to biblical law. On the contrary, harping on the Karaite quest for individual investigation of Scripture, he accused these sectarians of attributing nothing to God or the prophets, but all to their own researches. Cf. *infra,* Chap. XXVI, n. 4. Obviously, these arguments, however ingenious, reflected internal Jewish controversies much more than conflicts between Judaism and Islam, and made little impression on later Muslim controversialists.

26. Saadiah's *Beliefs and Opinions,* III.10, end, pp. 145 (Arabic), 74 (Hebrew), 179 (English); Mann's text in *HUCA,* XII–XIII, 444. In another connection the anonymous apologist repeated that "not in vain has God dispersed them over the whole earth, and not because of their evil ways has he ousted them from their land" (*ibid.,* p. 453), alluding to a theory of the Exile which he was going to expound, but which regrettably has not come down to us. Among his predecessors he must have had particularly Saadiah in mind, since he frequently echoed the gaon's views and even individual phrases. Cf. especially Saadiah's rhetoric in his letter, ed. by Revel in *Debir,* I.

27. Halevi's *Al-Khazari,* II.36, ed. by Hirschfeld, p. 102 (in his English trans. p. 109); Pascal's *Pensées* (Everyman's Library), p. 165 (a variant of W. F. Trotter's awkward trans.). On the background and meaning of Halevi's "Answer to an Historic Challenge," see my remarks in *JSS,* III, 243–72; and on the specific impact of the sufferings during the Crusades, *supra,* Chap. XXI, nn. 65 ff. Although Pascal seems to have had few contacts with contemporary Jews, he was deeply impressed by the Jewish outlook. " 'The Jews,' " rightly observes F. Lovsky, "play an essential role in Pascal's thought: an historical role, a theological role, and above all an apologetic role." Cf. his "Pascal et les Juifs," *Cahiers sioniens,* V, 355–66. Understandably, Jacob's blessing that "the scepter shall not depart from Judah" and its deep messianic implications for Jesus, played a far lesser role in the Judeo-Muslim controversy. At best Jewish debaters could emphasize the superiority of the exilarchic dynasty with its seventy generations of Davidic descendants over the short-lived families of usurpers on the Muslim thrones. To which Ibn Ḥazm obliquely replied by casting aspersions on the exilarchs' tainted ancestry, which had arisen from the forbidden unions between Judah and Tamar, and between David and Bathsheba. Cf. his *Radd,* ed. by García Gómez in *Al-Andalus,* IV, 18 f.; his *K. al-Fiṣal,* XV.31, I, 145 ff.; in Asín's trans. II, 280 ff.; *supra,* Chap. XXIII, n. 3; and *infra,* n. 41.

28. Ibn Kammuna, cited by D. H. Baneth in *MGWJ,* LXIX, 305; Ibn Ḥazm's *K. al-Fiṣal,* V, I, 24 ff.; in Asín Palacios's trans. II, 115 ff. Cf. also the English trans. of some excerpts in M. Perlmann's "Ibn Ḥazm on the Equivalence of Proofs," *JQR,* XL, 280, 282. Of course, neither Ibn Ḥazm nor any other Muslim apologist deigned to name those Jewish skeptics or deists who, for the sake of convenience, preferred to join the dominant religion.

29. I. Goldziher, "Ibn Hûd, the Mohammedan Mystic, and the Jews of Damascus," *JQR,* [o.s.] VI, 218–20; Abu'l 'Ala al-Ma'arri, *Diwan al-Luzumiyyat* (Collection of Poems Rhymed in Two Consonants), II, 201; Abu Tahir, cited by Nizam al-Mulk in his *Siyasat nama* (Siasset Naméh or Book of Government), XLVII, ed. by C. Shefer, p. 197 (in Shefer's French trans., p. 288). In another poem, Al-Ma'arri spoke slight-

ingly. "Religion is a maiden veiled in prayer, / Whose bridal gifts and dowry those who care / Can buy in the Mutakallim's shop of words, / But I for such a dirham cannot spare." See the English trans. by A. Rihani in *The Luzumiyyat of Abu'l-Ala,* p. 48 No. xxxi. See also D. S. Margoliouth's ed. of *The Letters of Abu'l 'Ala of Ma'arrat al-Nu'man* (especially pp. xxxi, 65 ff. No. xxiv, 152 about the poet's relations to Ṣadaqa ibn Yusuf, a converted Jew who was to serve as vizier to Caliph al-Mustansir); A. Fischer's "Abu 'Ala al-Ma'arri und das Buch 'De tribus impostoribus,' " *Die Welt des Orients,* V, 418–20; L. Massignon's earlier study of "La Légende 'De tribus impostoribus' et ses origines islamiques," *RHR,* LXXXII, 74–78, and more generally, G. Vajda's comprehensive survey of "Les Zindiqs en pays d'Islam au début de la période abbaside," *RSO,* XVII, 173–229. While officially *zindiqs* were equated with Manichaeans, Vajda rightly identifies them by the following criteria: "neglect of principal religious duties (prayer, fast, pilgrimage); pretensions to surpass the literary beauty of the Qur'an; equivocal attitude toward the doctrine of the unity of God; doubts concerning anything unperceived by the senses" (p. 221). Clearly, only the third criterion was directly related to the Manichaean credo. In all other respects, the term covered a multitude of skeptics and unbelievers who could thus more readily be subjected to governmental persecutions such as occurred under Caliph Mahdi (780–87). In his alleged reply to a Christian monk, a Muslim king of Saragossa also emphasized the great variety of religious and philosophic opinions. "There is no sect or religion which does not assert that its souls are enlightened by what it teaches and rejoice in what it believes." Cf. D. M. Dunlop's analysis and translation of that correspondence in "A Christian Mission to Muslim Spain in the 11th Century," *Al-Andalus,* XVII, 266 ff. Sometimes skepticism took on an antinomian tinge, equally detrimental to Islam and Judaism. Ibn Ḥazm, for instance, composed a special pamphlet combating the view of a Kairuwanese heretic that faith excludes works and that what really matters is mental adherence to the word of God. Cf. Asín Palacios, *Abenházam,* I, 264 f. On Ar-Rawandi, his allegedly Jewish father and other Jewish connections, see *infra,* Chaps. XXIX, n. 87; XXXIV. Western free thought which, not without Muslim influences, became a power only in the thirteenth century, and the book "De tribus impostoribus," heatedly attributed to and as heatedly denied by the enlightened Emperor Frederick II, will be analyzed here in their later medieval Jewish connections.

30. Saadiah's *Beliefs and Opinions,* Intro. 7, 1.3, pp. 28, 67 ff. (Arabic), 14, 35 f. (Hebrew), 35, 80 ff. (English). True, *kofrim* (deniers of religious truths) are occasionally mentioned in the rabbinic sources of that period, but Jewish communal action, if any, was largely limited to stamping out the *minim* (heretics). Although most contemporaries were not particularly precise in using either of these terms, which to them were interchangeable, skepticism served more as a gadfly for philosophic speculation than as incentive for communal suppression. Cf. *infra,* Chap. XXXIV.

31. Mardan Farukh's *Šikand-Gumānīk Vičar* (La Solution décisive de doutes), ed. with a French trans. and commentary by P. J. de Menasce, pp. 175 ff. This important Pehlevi work by the otherwise unknown author has long been accessible to Western scholars in E. W. West's English translation of *Pehlavi Texts,* Vol. III (The Sacred Books of the East, Vol. XXIV). The chapters relating to Judaism have also been translated into French and provided with notes by J. Darmesteter in his

"Textes pehlevis relatifs au Judaïsm," *REJ,* XVIII, 1–15; XIX, 41–56. They were further interpreted by L. H. Gray in several concise essays, including "The Jews in Pahlavi Literature," *Jewish Encyclopedia,* IX, 462–65. Cf. also some pertinent remarks in A. Marmorstein's "Iranische und jüdische Religion," *ZNW,* XXVI, 231–42; and other literature cited *supra,* Vol. II, pp. 404 n. 36, 435 n. 31.

32. Mardan Farukh, *loc. cit.,* with reference to Gen. 3:9 ff., 18:1 ff., cited here in a variant from West's awkward translation, pp. 220 f., 228 f.; Menasce's rendition, pp. 192 f., 200 f., reads far more smoothly. These problems agitated also Jewish scholars of the period, especially in areas close to Zoroastrian or Manichaean influence. See *infra,* Chap. XXIX, nn. 88 ff.

33. Saadiah's *Beliefs and Opinions,* I, Intro., II.2, pp. 31, 81 f. (Arabic), 15 f., 42 f. (Hebrew), 39, 96 f. (English). On the Marcionite brand of anti-Judaism, cf. *supra,* Vol. II, pp. 67 f., 394 n. 50. See also *infra,* Chaps. XXIX, n. 93; XXXIV.

34. Jaḥiẓ' *Risala,* trans. by Finkel in *JAOS,* XLVII, 323. On the Jewish role in, and attitude toward, the sectarian clashes in Islam and Christianity, see *supra,* Chaps. XVI, n. 1; XIX, nn. 5 and 25 (here also on the meaning of *majus*); XXI, n. 54; and *infra,* n. 69. This extremely complex subject, often hidden behind the veil of secrecy consciously thrown on it by the sectarians themselves, and further confused by the ever ready application of the epithet "Jewish" to all religious antagonists, will be somewhat more fully clarified in connection with the better known sectarian conflicts in later medieval Europe.

35. John of Damascus in his main work, *Pegé gnóseos,* Intro., end, in *PG,* XCIV, 525 f.; Trullan synod, canon 19 in Mansi, *Collectio,* XI, 951 f.; and Hefele, *Histoire,* III, 566 (English, trans. by Clark, V, 227). Cf. also other examples cited by A. Ehrhard in K. Krumbacher *Geschichte der byzantinischen Literatur,* p. 39. In time, the apologetic literature became extremely large and ramified. See the large and yet incomplete list in A. C. McGiffert's introduction to his edition of a *Dialogue between a Christian and a Jew entitled Amphibolé,* pp. 12 ff., with supplements from MSS by Ehrhard in Krumbacher, p. 51. Additional materials have, of course, come to light since. Because of that plethora of readily available data, later writers were prone to refer only to their latest predecessors. They entirely forgot the true originators of certain doctrines and arguments in the early apostolic and patristic periods. Euthymios Zigabenos, a leading later controversialist, mentioned almost no pre-Nicean writers in his extensive *Panoplia dogmatica* (Dogmatic Suit of Armor), allegedly written on the initiative of Emperor Alexis Comnenus (1081–1118). Cf. J. Wickert's analysis of "Die Panoplia dogmatica des Euthymios Zigabenos," *Oriens christianus,* VIII, 278–388. The ceaseless flow of repetitive arguments is well illustrated by M. Brok's discussion of "Un Soi-disant fragment du traité contre les Juifs de Théodoret de Cyr," *Revue d'histoire ecclésiastique,* XL, 487–507. Although this fifth-century bishop of Cyrrhus had frequent occasion to combat the Jews of Syria (see for instance, his epistle CXIII to Pope Leo, in *PG,* LXXXIII, 1316) these particular nine questions seem not to stem from his pen, but to have been merely a part of a general collection of dogmatic essays. On the other hand, one need not draw too sharp a distinction between doctrinal and apologetic writings. Cf. B. Blumenkranz and J. Châtillon's pertinent observations in their "De la

polémique antijuive à la catechèse chrétienne," *Recherches de théologie ancienne et médiévale,* XXIII, 40–60.

36. Saadiah's *Beliefs and Opinions,* II.5, VIII.9, pp. 86 f., 252 f. (Arabic), 45 f., 128 f. (Hebrew), 103 ff., 319 ff. (English); Qirqisani's *K. al-Anwar,* I.2.9; III.16, ed. by L. Nemoy, I, 12; II, 301 ff.; and in Nemoy's English trans. in *HUCA,* VII, 327, 364 ff.; Halevi's *K. al-Khazari,* I.4–5, IV.11, ed. by Hirschfeld, pp. 8 ff., 250 ff.; in the English trans., pp. 39 ff., 216 f.; Maimonides' *Epistle to Yemen,* ed. by Halkin, pp. 12 ff. (Arabic and Hebrew), iii f. (English); Joseph ben Isaac Qimḥi's *Sefer ha-Berit* (Book of the Covenant: a Debate between a Believer and a Heretic), reprinted in J. D. Eistenstein's compilation *Oẓar Wikuḥim* (A Collection of Polemics and Disputations), pp. 66 ff.; and *infra,* n. 60. On the religious disputations in Sassanian Persia and the Great Caliphate, as well as the Jewish reluctance to participate in them, see E. Bratke's ed. of *Das sogenannte Religionsgespräch am Hof der Sasaniden* (although a piece of fiction, this fifth- or sixth-century account contains kernels of historic truth); *supra,* Vol. II, p. 133; and Chaps. XVI, n. 66; XVII, n. 17; XVIII, n. 45.

37. Gregentius' *Dialexis* (Disputation with the Jew Herban), in *PG,* LXXXVI, 621–784, especially cols. 777 ff.; the Slavonic translation discussed by Ehrhard in Krumbacher's *Geschichte,* p. 59; A. L. Williams' summary in his *Adversus Judaeos,* pp. 141 ff.; H. Z. Hirschberg's comments in his *Yisrael ba-'Arab,* pp. 109, 293 n. 35. The latter assumes that the dialogues took place after the defeat and death of Dhu-Nuwas in 525. But, in that case, there probably would have been some reference to that king's persecution of the Najran Christians. See *supra,* Chap. XVI, n. 83.

Another remarkable debate in a country subjected to intensive Christian mission is recorded in connection with Methodius' journey to Moravia. Unfortunately, the report in the apostle's Slavonic *Prolog Vita* is so garbled and so overlaid with an attempted equation of the Jewish debaters with the rebellious faction of Korah and with Zimri, caught by Phineas fornicating with a Moabite woman (Num. 16 and 25), that it is difficult to isolate therein the historical kernel of truth. When a certain Zambrii, we are told, "a Khazar by origin and a heretic in belief," opposed Methodius, the Moravian duke convoked an assembly attended by two thousand (!) Jews, but Methodius "as an agile fighter, armed with the words of the prophets and apostles, shot, like a glorious warrior, at both sides—the Jews and the heretics—not missing once." Here, too, a miracle intervened: Zambrii "clave asunder," while the other debaters were either swallowed up by the earth like Korah, or burned by fire. Cf. R. Jakobson's "Minor Native Sources for the Early History of the Slavic Church," *Harvard Slavic Studies,* II, 65.

38. None of these tracts came to fuller public notice until after the publication, in 1710, of the two treatises by the Qimḥis, father and son, in a collection of Jewish apologetic tracts entitled *Milḥement ḥobah* (War of Duty). The Hungarian proselytes are cited by Tosafists and other contemporary rabbis, who themselves often indulged in polemical asides. See the material assembled by E. Urbach in his "Etudes sur la littérature polémique au moyen-âge," *REJ,* C, 49–77, especially pp. 72 ff. Many more arguments on both sides can be reconstructed from the richer polemical literature of the thirteenth century, including the aforementioned apologetic treatise by Meir bar Simon of Narbonne, bearing the characteristic title, *Milḥemet miṣvah* (Obligatory

War), written about 1245, as a result of a public disputation. Cf. H. Gross's detailed analysis in his "Meir b. Simon und seine Schrift Milchemeth Mizwa," *MGWJ*, XXX, 295–305, 444–52, 554–69; his *Gallia judaica*, pp. 423 ff.; and *supra*, Chap. XX, n. 58. Because of the intrinsic repetitiveness of these writings, however, it is rarely possible to date a controversial pamphlet on the basis of internal evidence. For example, David Qimḥi's alleged authorship of an anonymous tract, first published by A. Marmorstein in his "David Kimhi apologiste. Un fragment perdu dans son commentaire des Psaumes," *REJ*, LXVI, 246–51, has effectively been disproved by N. Porges in "Sur un fragment de polémique anti-chrétienne," *ibid.*, LXVII, 128–31. Porges's suggestion that the author used Profiat Duran's polemical treatise of 1397, was reinforced by D. Camerini's comparison with four De Rossi MSS of Profiat's work. Cf. "L'Origine du fragment de polémique antichrétienne publié dans la Revue," *ibid.*, pp. 292–94. Yet the relative frankness without bitterness of that author's argumentation would have been even more reminiscent of the days of the Qimḥis or of Joseph ben Nathan the Zealot of thirteenth-century France than of the tense atmosphere prevailing in Spain after 1391. Perhaps pseudo-Qimḥi and Profiat used the same older source. An interesting attempt to reconstruct "Die jüdischen Beweisgründe im Religionsgespräch mit den Christen in den christlich-lateinischen Sonderschriften des 5. bis 11. Jahrhunderts," was made by B. Blumenkranz in *TZ*, IV, 119–47. Although realizing the precariousness of restoring views exclusively reported by opponents, Blumenkranz was able to supply some of the missing links in Jewsh apologetics, especially in the then altogether barren West.

39. Hermann of Scheda's *Opusculum de sua conversione*, in *PL*, CLXX, 803–46; and its analysis by R. Seeberg in his *Hermann von Scheda, ein jüdischer Proselyt des 12. Jahrhunderts;* Caesarius of Heisterbach, *Dialogus miraculorum*, II.25, ed. by J. Strange, I, 95 ff.; in the English trans. by H. von E. Scott and C. C. Swinton Bland, I, 107 ff. Cf. the critical analyses by Aronius in his *Regesten*, pp. 184 ff. No. 414; and J. Stengers in *Les Juifs dans les Pays Bas*, pp. 13, 94 f. nn. 32–34. Converts to Christianity are frequently mentioned in the "Book of the Pious" and other contemporary writings. Private discussions, like those between the episcopal steward and the Jewish visitor, must have been commonplace enough for Rupert of Deutz (possibly under the impression of his debate with Judas-Hermann) to prepare an apologetic handbook for the uninitiated, so that they might the more effectively counter Jewish arguments. Cf. his *Annulus sive Dialogus inter christianum et Judaeum*, in *PL*, CLXX, 559–610; and his related tract, *De glorificatione trinitatis et processione Sancti Spiritus*, *ibid.*, CLXIX, 13–202, with Aronius's comments thereon in his *Regesten*, pp. 103 ff. Nos. 223, 225.

Such missionary success stories, real or fictitious, frequently accompany the reports about Judeo-Christian debates. Even under Islam Jewish conversions to Christianity and vice versa occurred from time to time, despite the rigid governmental outlawry. Cf. *supra*, Chap. XVIII, n. 45. Much of this material is unpublished, however. The story, for instance, of the alleged conversion of a Jew, Imram, after his unsuccessful disputation with two monks in 958–59, is told in a lengthy version of some 100 folios, extant in several MSS. Cf. Steinschneider's *Polemische Literatur*, pp. 157 ff. Nos. 136, 141. See also, more generally, P. Browe's comprehensive study of *Die Judenmission im Mittelalter und die Päpste;* his related analysis of "Die kirchenrechtliche Stellung der getauften Juden und ihrer Nachkommen," *Archiv für katholisches Kirchenrecht*, CXXI, 3–22, 165–91; and R. E. Sullivan's "Early Medieval

Missionary Activity: a Comparative Study of Eastern and Western Methods," *Church History,* XXIII, 17–35 (both dealing chiefly with later periods).

40. Giraldus Cambrensis' *Speculum ecclesiae,* III.1, in his *Opera,* ed. by J. S. Brewer *et al.,* IV, 139 ff.; Jacobs, *Angevin England,* pp. 283 ff.; C. Roth's *Jews in England,* p. 41; and F. W. Maitland's juridical study, "The Deacon and the Jewess; or, Apostasy and the Common Law" (1888), reprinted in *The Collected Papers,* ed. by H. A. L. Fisher, I, 385–406. On Raymond of Sens, see Glaber's *Historiae sui temporis,* III.6, in *PL,* CXLII, 656; E. Pognon's comments on his translation thereof in *L'An mille,* pp. 93 ff., 273 nn. 101-3; and *supra,* Chap. XX, nn. 69 and 74–75; XXI, nn. 12–13. Possibly in this connection, Fulbert of Chartres, who supported the king against the judaizing count, delivered his three anti-Jewish sermons, which subsequently circulated as an independent tract. Cf. his epistle to counts Gualerannus and Gualterius, in *PL,* CXLI, 211; his *Tractatus contra Judaeos, ibid.,* cols. 305 ff.; and B. Blumenkranz's comments thereon in *RMAL,* VIII, 51–54.

41. To the literature cited *supra,* Chap. XVI, nn. 47, 55–56 and 66, one may add Isidore of Seville's *Liber de variis quaestionibus adversus Judaeos seu ceteros infideles,* ed. by A. C. Vega and A. E. Anspach (previously published by E. Martène and U. Durand in their *Thesaurus novus anecdotorum,* V, 401–594, but there wrongly attributed to Raban Maur, despite the editors' compunctions about its authenticity); as well as the imaginary *Dialogue de Saint-Julien et son disciple; poème anglonorman du XIIIe siècle,* ed. by A. Bonjour (largely a poetic paraphrase of Julian of Toledo's *Prognosticon futuri saeculi,* in *PL,* XCVI, 453–524). The lack of contacts with professing Jews on the part of these Spanish prelates is the less surprising as even under the more liberal Muslim regime monks gloried in refusing to talk to Jews. See *supra,* Chap. XVIII, n. 45. While embarking in Spain on his anti-Jewish and anti-Muslim crusade, Peter of Cluny felt strongly the need of becoming acquainted with the rudiments of both Talmud and Qur'an. But he derived all his information from converts, such as Petrus Alphonsi, rather than from close observation of Jewish and Muslim life. Cf. U. Monneret de Villard's remarks in *Lo Studio dell'Islam in Europa nell XII e nel XIII secolo,* pp. 9 ff., 17; and *supra,* Chap. XXI, n. 43. Cf. also I. Loeb's older but still informative survey of "La Controverse religieuse entre les chrétiens et les juifs au moyen âge en France et en Espagne," *RHR,* XVII, 311–37; XVIII, 133–56; P. Browe's brief list of anti-Jewish tracts from 614 to 1567 in *Die Judenmission,* pp. 99 ff.; and B. Blumenkranz's more recent detailed chronological review of "Les Auteurs chrétiens latins du moyen âge sur les juifs and le judaïsme," *REJ,* CIX, 3–67; CXI, 5–61; CXIII, 5–36; CXIV, 33–85 (to be continued).

42. Alcuin's *Epistolae,* CI (CLXXII), in *PL,* C, 314 (*MGH,* Epistulae, IV, 285; he had only "heard" that that debate was recorded; cf. *supra,* Chap. XX, n. 56); Gilbert Crispin's *Disputatio Judaei cum christiano de fide christiana,* in *PL,* CLIX, 1003–36; and in B. Blumenkranz's new critical ed. in *Stromata patristica et mediaevalia,* III. St. Anselm of Canterbury's *Cur Deus homo,* in *PL,* CLVIII, 359–432; and in his *Opera omnia,* ed. by F. S. Schmitt, II, 37–133. The identity of Crispin's interlocutor with Simon he-Ḥasid (the Pious) of Treves was suggested by J. Jacobs in his *Angevin England,* pp. 253 f., with reference to Israel Lévi's study of "Controverse entre un Juif et un chrétien au XIe siècle," *REJ,* V, 238–45. Nothing has come

to light since either to confirm or to deny that hypothesis. Cf. also Blumenkranz's earlier analytical study of "La 'Disputatio Judaei cum christiano' de Gilbert Crispin, abbé de Westminster," *RMAL,* IV, 237–52, with Cardinal G. Mercati's note thereon, *ibid.,* V, 149–50 (pointing out the relation between Crispin and Hugo of St. Victor); R. W. Southern's "St. Anselm and Gilbert Crispin, Abbot of Westminster," *Mediaeval and Renaissance Studies,* III, 78–115, showing the impact of Anselm of Canterbury's teaching on the younger churchman and the stimulus given to Anselm's thought by the problems posed by the Jewish questioner (on Anselm's own efforts to secure support for the Jewish convert Robert and his family, cf. his *Epistulae,* III, No. cxvii, in *PL,* CLIX, 153 f.; ed. by Schmitt, Nos. 380–81, in *Opera,* V, 323 f.; Jacobs, *Angevin England,* p. 12) and, by way of contrast, Crispin's *Disputatio cum Gentili,* recently published by C. C. J. Webb in his "Gilbert Crispin, Abbot of Westminster: Dispute of a Christian with a Heathen Touching the Faith of Christ," *Mediaeval and Renaissance Studies,* III, 55–77. St. Anselm's indebtedness to the Jewish debater had found an even more radical exponent in P. G. van der Plaas, whose essay on "Des hl. Anselm 'Cur Deus Homo' auf dem Boden der jüdisch-christlichen Polemik des Mittelalters," *Divus Thomas,* VII, 446–67; VIII, 18–32, had evoked considerable dissent among students of medieval scholasticism. See the studies cited by Southern, p. 93 n. 1. On "The Disputation of Barcelona (1263)," which essentially belongs to the more outspoken controversies of the later Middle Ages, see C. Roth's essay in *HTR,* XLIII, 117–44; and O. S. Rankin's *Jewish Religious Polemic,* pp. 157 ff. See also R. W. Hunt's analysis of "The Disputation of Peter of Cornwall against Symon the Jew," in *Studies in Medieval History Presented to Frederick Maurice Powicke,* pp. 143–56 (also publishing from a Bodleian MS the prologue to this vast polemical tract completed in 1208); Guillaume de Champaux' *Dialogus inter christianum et Judaeum de fide catholica,* in *PL,* CLXIII, 1045–72, speaking of Judaism in harsher terms than Crispin, whose dialogue he may have emulated; and, more broadly, R. M. Ames's aforementioned dissertation on "The Debate between the Church and the Synagogue in the Literature of Anglo-Saxon and Mediaeval England."

43. Petrus' *Dialogus* in *PL,* CLVII, 535–672. Although, according to A. L. Williams a Cambridge MS he had consulted seems to differ but little from the Migne edition, an extant Catalan translation indicates the presence of important variants in the early versions. Cf. J. Ainaud de Lesarte's analysis of "Una Versión catalan desconocida de los 'Dialogi' de Pedro Alfonso," *Sefarad,* III, 359–76. On Petrus' influence on the later English controversialists, including Peter of Cornwall who quoted also his as yet unidentified work, *Humanum proficuum,* see R. H. Hunt's observations in *Studies . . . Powicke,* pp. 148 ff. The identity of Petrus Toletanus, Peter of Cluny's active collaborator in 1141, with Petrus Alphonsi is discussed by Monneret de Villard in *Lo Studio dell' Islam,* pp. 9 ff., 14. But the likelihood of Petrus' living in Spain to the age of seventy-nine is rather remote, while the name Peter is too common for drawing any definite conclusions. On Petrus' scientific contributions, cf. *infra,* Chap. XXXV.

44. As H. Pflaum observed, much of the medieval drama was permeated with apologetic and conversionist motifs. Cf. his related studies of "Les Scènes des Juifs dans la littérature dramatique du moyen âge," *REJ,* LXXXIX, 111–34; "Poems on Religious Disputations in the Middle Ages" (Hebrew), *Tarbiz,* II, 443–76; and, with some repetition, *Die religiöse Disputation in der europäischen Dichtung des Mit-*

telalters, Vol. I. The same spirit of religious altercation penetrated also some of the medieval romances, including the twelfth-century and later paraphrases of the ancient Grail sagas. Not surprisingly, they were combined here with the glorification of the knightly crusading spirit. See the interesting materials analyzed by M. Schlauch in "The Allegory of Church and Synagogue," *Speculum,* XIV, 448–64. Cf. also B. Blumenkranz's "Juden und Jüdisches in christlichen Wundererzählungen. Ein unbekanntes Gebiet religiöser Polemik," *TZ,* X, 417–46; and, more generally, the dissertations by M. Lifschitz-Golden, *Les Juifs dans la littérature française du moyen âge (mystères, miracles, chroniques)*, pithily concluding: "in the mysteries, Jews stand up against Christ; in the miracle plays—Mary stands up against the Jews" (p. 7); S. Resnick, *The Jews as Portrayed in Early Spanish Literature,* summarized in an article under this title in *Hispania,* XXXIV, 54–58 (apart from the episode with the two Jewish moneylenders in the *Cid,* mentioned *supra,* Chap. XX, n. 31, discusses publications after 1200); A. Portnoy, *Los Judios en la literatura española medieval;* and Ames, "Debate between Church and Synagogue." The apparent Byzantine prototypes of that literature would merit further examination. Historical dramas reaching back to ancient Alexandrine models, including Ezechielos' *Exagogé,* were often used there for sectarian polemics. The staging of such plays in the cathedral of St. Sophia during major holidays, which was to annoy the Western visitor Liutprand, must have lent them much solemnity and exerted great influence on the masses of worshipers. Regrettably, however, but few of these Eastern dramas, whether intended for theatrical presentation or merely written as literary pieces, have been preserved. Cf. Krumbacher's *Geschichte,* pp. 644 ff., 746 ff.; and the more recent literature on the Byzantine drama listed in C. J. Stratman's *Bibliography of Medieval Drama,* pp. 264 f. Cf. also *infra,* Chap. XXXI.

45. Cf. *supra,* Vol. II, pp. 130 ff., 379 ff.; and M. Simon's *Verus Israel,* pp. 203 ff. Stressing the popularity of arguments derived from the expansion of Christianity, B. Blumenkranz observed that the absence of such arguments from a polemical tract makes it suspect of either having been written by a heretic, like the Arian bishop Maximinus, or in a Muslim country like the letters of Paul Alvarus. Cf. *RMAL,* X, 19 f. Interesting variants on the theme of the Roman conquest of Jerusalem and the Jewish dispersion as a sign of divine anger over the Jewish rejection of Jesus, and of the latter's position in the Jewish community, were found in Byzantine tracts of the sixth or seventh centuries as summarized, from a Turin MS since burned, by F. Cumont in his "Reliquiae taurinienses," *Bulletins* of the Academie r. de Belgique, Classe de lettres, 1904, pp. 92 ff. One tract, included in this collection of anti-Jewish polemics, is devoted to an altercation between a Jew, Theodosius, and a Christian, Philip. It tells the amazing story of Jesus' election to the high-priesthood in Jerusalem, and the ensuing embarrassment of the priestly registrars when they found that they could enter the name of the high-priest-elect's mother, but not that of his father. On the ancient topic of God's rejection of Jews because of their repudiation of Jesus' messiahship and, hence, also the Jews' own testimony for the truth of Christianity, cf. *supra,* Vol. II, pp. 132 f., 166 f.; and the sources discussed by B. Blumenkranz in *Die Judenpredigt Augustins,* pp. 167 ff., 175 ff. Cf. also *infra,* Chap. XXV, n. 9.

46. Muslim theologians, answered by the ninth-century Byzantine controversialist, Nicetas the Philosopher in his *Anatropé,* XLVIII, in *PG,* CV, 733 f.; Qirqisani and

Maimonides, *supra,* n. 36. Cf. also other Maimonidean utterances cited by me in "The Historical Outlook," *PAAJR,* VI, 71 n. 139. In Qirqisani's fuller statement (III.16, ed. by Nemoy, III, 301 ff.) we learn that opinions among Karaites were more sharply divided. Benjamin Nahawendi counted Jesus among the five major Jewish "false prophets." But other Karaites, evidently guided by their anti-Rabbanite spite, were ready to concede that he had been a righteous man and taught similarly to Zadok and 'Anan, "but the Rabbanites went after him until they killed him, just as they sought also to kill 'Anan, although they could not do it. This is their way with everyone who attempts to oppose them." This comparison must have appeared the more plausible to some Karaites, as 'Anan's difficulties had likewise arisen from the Rabbanite denunciation of his "rebellion" to the state authorities. See *infra,* Chap. XXVI, n. 1. This ambivalent attitude of medieval Jewry with respect to its ancestors' responsibility—European Jews evidently preferred to shift the "guilt" to Emperor Tiberius and his henchmen—was pointed out by Agobard in his *De judaicis superstitionibus,* in *PL,* CIV, 87 f.; *MGH,* Epistulae, V, 190.

47. Qarafi and other Muslim authors cited in Fritsch's *Islam,* pp. 49 ff. Cf. also the later medieval sources cited by Halkin in his edition of the Maimonidean *Epistle, supra,* n. 36. On the relations between Jesus and his alleged teacher, R. Joshua ben Peraḥiah, see *supra,* Vol. II, pp. 148, 387 f. n. 27. Even Abraham bar Ḥiyya, though writing in a Christian environment and often associating with Christian scholars (see *infra,* Chap. XXXV), ascribed Jesus' death to "his own sin and transgression." See his *Megillat ha-Megalleh,* ed. by A. Poznanski, p. 136. In the light of this widespread acceptance of the alleged ancient chronology, the concluding statement here quoted from Maimonides' *Epistle* must be related to Jesus, rather than Mani, as has been suggested (see my remarks in *PAAJR,* VI, 9 f., 72). The surprising absence of any reference to Mani on the part of either Qirqisani, Saadiah, or Maimonides may perhaps be explained by their general feeling that Manichaeism was not a distinct religion, but rather a mere subdivision of dualistic Zoroastrianism, as well as a sectarian trend within both Islam and Christianity. See *supra,* n. 29. Cf. also the summary of Jewish arguments presented by Blumenkranz in *TZ,* IV, 134 ff.

48. Saadiah's *Beliefs and Opinions,* VIII.9, pp. 254 (Arabic), 129 (Hebrew), 322 (English); and *supra,* Vols. I, pp. 386 n. 44; II, 139 f. The Jewish argument that the universe still was in its fifth, rather than sixth and final, eon was also presented by the adversary reported in Julian of Toledo's *De comprobatione aetatis sextae* (dedication to King Ervig and I.1, in PL, XCVI, 538 f., 541), to the combating of whom this entire chronological treatise was devoted. These messianic passages and the chronological computation based on them played a tremendous role not only in the Judeo-Christian controversy but also in the internal Jewish messianic movements. See *infra,* Chaps. XXV, n. 23; and XXXV.

49. Petrus Alphonsi's *Dialogus,* VI, in *PL,* CLVII, 608 ff., with reference to Mark 15:34; and A. L. Williams's comments thereon in his *Adversus Judaeos,* pp. 235 f., referring also to the *Zohar* on *Aḥare mot,* III, 65a; and on *Shelaḥ lekha,* fol. 162a (English trans. by M. Simon and H. Sperling, V, 55 f., 232; and more sharply in J. de Pauly's French trans., V, 178 f., 417 f. with his note thereon, VI, 425 ff.). Some of these arguments are cited by Saadiah, but they can easily be documented also

from Christian sources. Cf. the gaon's *Beliefs and Opinions,* II.4–6, pp. 84 ff. (Arabic), 44 ff. (Hebrew), 101 ff. (English). Many more Old Testament "testimonies" of this kind were used by Christian apologists from ancient times. In their medieval elaborations they were made to adumbrate even such details of the Christian tradition as Christ's passion, burial, resurrection and ascension. Cf. the passages cited by the twelfth-century Syriac apologist, Dionysius bar Salibi in *The Treatise against the Jews,* VI–VII, ed. in Syriac from a Mesopotamian manuscript by J. de Zwaan, pp. 31 ff.; and summarized by Williams, pp. 107 ff. True, an interesting non-christological interpretation of Deut. 18:15–19 was offered, for example, by the ninth-century exegete, Isho'dad of Merv, probably following Theodore of Mopsuestia. Cf. J. M. Vosté's analysis, "Le Prophète promis par Moïse d'après Mar Išo'dad de Merw (c. 850)," *Biblica,* XXX, 1–9. But, as Vosté has pointed out, Syriac Church leaders before long joined the procession of Christian exegetes who preferred to lend messianic interpretations to such Old Testament passages. In the West, collections of "testimonies" were so readily available that, in his controversy with Bodo, Paul Alvarus needed but to refer to their existence. Cf. his *Epistolae,* XIV.3; XVIII.3, in *PL,* CXXI, 480, 494; ed. by J. Madoz, pp. 215, 246. Understandably, such interpretations of the Old Testament proved particularly useful in teaching prospective converts from Judaism. Cf. R. Voeltzel's data on "Le Rôle de l'Ancient Testament dans l'instruction des catéchumènes," *RHPR,* XXXIII, 308–21 which, although principally discussing conditions today, also sheds light on some of the former less mystical propagandistic uses of the Hebrew Bible by Christians.

50. Saadiah, *loc. cit.* Christian apologists often covered up their insufficient knowledge of Hebrew by claiming that the Septuagint (or the Vulgate) contained a more authentic textual tradition than the masoretic text. This was bluntly asserted, for instance, by the Byzantine historian, Georgius Syncellus in his *Chronographia,* ed. by W. Dindorf, I, 167 ("it appears to have at one time been translated from an uncorrupted Hebrew source"). Cf. Krumbacher's *Geschichte,* pp. 123, 341; and A. B. Starratt's Harvard dissertation on "The Use of the Septuagint in the *Five Books against Heresies* by Irenaeus of Lyons" (1952), summarized in *Church History,* XXIII, 356. Starratt points out that the saint of Lyons already cited as a rule current compilations of "testimonies," rather than the Old Testament text itself. One should also bear in mind the original biblical and Judeo-Hellenistic background of the Syriac doctrine of attributes. From Philo and his Alexandrine confreres the Eastern churchmen had learned not only their general allegorical method, but also more specifically the interpretation of Abraham's vision at Mamre as relating to three divine "powers." Cf. Philo's *De Abrahamo,* XXIV.119 ff., 122, ed. by F. H. Colson, VI, 65 (God "presents to the mind which has vision the appearance sometimes of one, sometimes of three," although admitting that this "hidden meaning" open to the few does not replace the open meaning suited for the multitude); and H. A. Wolfson's comments thereon in his *Philo,* I, 202 f., 380 f.; II, 157 ff. Petrus Alphonsi, well informed about the eastern controversies, seems to have been one of the first Western thinkers vigorously to stress the three attributes of *substantia, sapientia,* and *voluntas* as the *tres personae* in God. Cf. his *Dialogus,* VI, in *PL,* CLVII, 606. In contrast thereto, the thirteenth-century author of the French *Desputoison* (Disputation between a Jew and a Christian) spoke only of the three divine attributes of Power, Knowledge, and Goodness. Cf. the text published by H. Pflaum in *Tarbiz,* II, 472 f. verses 331–36 (also in *Die religiöse Disputation,* Vol. I).

On the Muslim (and Jewish) reactions, both positive and negative, to the Christian doctrine of attributes, see H. A. Wolfson's study of "The Muslim Attributes and the Christian Trinity," *HTR,* XLIX, 1–18. Cf. also *infra,* Chaps. XXIX, n. 29; and XXXIV.

51. Cf. the anonymous anti-Jewish tract, published by Millás Vallicrosa in *Sefarad,* XIII, 6, 12; Maimonides' *Commentary* on M. Sanhedrin x. Intro. Principle 8, Holzer ed., pp. 26 f. Cf. the new Hebrew trans. from the Arabic by M. Gottlieb, pp. 52, 99 n. 74; and Maimonides' *Guide,* III.50 beg. (in Friedlaender's trans., pp. 380 f.). It is barely possible that our Spanish author followed here a mere literary reminiscence. According to St. Jerome (*De viris illustribus,* LXX, in *PL,* XXIII, 717 ff.), Novatian had already written *De cibis judaicis, de pascha, de sabbato, de circumcisione,* of which only the former is published in *PL,* III, 953–64. But it appears more likely that the medieval controversialist had personally observed some such distinctions between severe and light commandments among the Jews of the Iberian Peninsula. Although possessing little halakhic sanction, disproportionate emphasis on the Sabbath and circumcision had already been observed by the ancient teacher, R. Simon ben Gamaliel, or Eleazar. Cf. Sifre on Deut. 76, ed. by Friedmann, fol. 90b (ed. by Finkelstein, p. 141); Shabbat 130a; and *supra,* Vol. II, pp. 216 f. There is less evidence for the glorification of Passover over and above the other holidays, although in the daily life of Spanish Jewry, as in that of some modern communities, the commandment relating to unleavened bread may have been treated with particular reverence. From Jewish informants our apologist must also have derived the strange theory concerning the original purpose of circumcision to distinguish Jewish from non-Jewish corpses on the battlefields, in support of which he cited several scriptural passages from Joshua (5:4) and the apocryphal book, Tobit. Cf. *Sefarad,* XIII, 15. As suggested by the editor, this explanation may have been derived from some obscure aggadic collection, such as were current in medieval Spain. See *infra,* n. 53, and Chap. XXVIII, nn. 23–24.

52. A. Guillaume's summary in *Centenary Supplement to JRAS,* 1924, 238; A. Jeffery's "Gregory of Tathew's 'Contra Mohammedanos,'" *MW,* XXXII, 219–35; the anonymous tract, ed. by Millás in *Sefarad,* XIII, 6, 12 f. Following Ibn Ḥazm, Qarafi blamed the Christian abrogation of circumcision on Paul, and waxed rhetorical on the physiological, moral, and religious virtues of the ancient ritual. Cf. Fritsch's *Islam,* p. 144. The tale of the sewer seems to have been quite popular in the Middle Ages. It appeared among others in the Appendix to the *Gesta Romanorum,* ed. by H. Oesterley, p. 633, the editor listing fourteen parallel sources (p. 745). As in his other tales the author of the *Gesta* gave the story an allegorical turn, and claimed that the Jew in the sewer symbolized man in the gutter of sin, who suffers divine retribution in the Hereafter.

53. Saint Caesarius of Arles, *Sermones,* LXXIV, ed. by G. Morin, I, 308 f.; Agobard's *De insolentia Judaeorum,* V; and *Epistola* to Nibridius, in *PL,* CIV, 74 f., 111; in *MGH,* Epistulae, V, 183, 199 f.; John of Damascus' *De fide orthodoxa,* IV. 23, in *PG,* XCIV, 1201 ff.; the *Tratado anonimo* in *Sefarad,* XIII, 6, 12, with reference to Josh. 6:4; I Macc. 2:29 ff.; and *supra,* Vol. II, pp. 188, 400 f. n. 21. Christian resentment against Passover was nurtured by the never-ending controversies over the Easter calendar. In the story told by the Irish Saint Cummian, in 633, about an

Irish delegation spending Easter in a Roman hotel together with a Greek, a Hebrew, a Scythian, and an Egyptian, the emphasis is laid upon these Easterners favoring the Hebrew date of that holiday. But the northern Irish saw therein only an attempt at Judaizing. Cf. Cummian's *Epistola de controversia paschali,* in *PL,* LXXXVII, 969 ff.; and E. S. Duckett's *Anglo-Saxon Saints and Scholars,* pp. 11 f.

54. On the old problem of invalidation of Jewish law in the messianic age, see *supra,* Vol. II, pp. 73 f., 161 f., 298 f., 360 f. n. 25; *infra,* Chap. XXV, n. 58; and A. Diez Macho's recent discussion of "Cesarà la 'Tora' en la edad mesianica?" *Estudios biblicos,* XII, 115–58.

55. See Al-Kindi's "Apologia del Cristianesimo," ed. by José Muñoz Sendino, in *Miscellanea Comillas,* XI–XII, 410. The problem of religious laxity and the philosophic justification of religious law in general and of individual commandments in particular was of greater internal concern to the Jewish community than a matter of defense against external enemies. See *infra,* Chaps. XXVII, n. 164; XXXIV.

56. Sidonius Appollinaris' letter to Bishop Nunechius in his *Epistolae,* VIII.13, in *PL,* LVIII, 611; and *MGH,* Auct. ant., VIII, 144 f.; Alvarus' letters to Bodo in his *Epistolae,* XIV.7; XVIII.5, in *PL,* CXXI, 483, 496 f.; in a variant of C. M. Sage's English trans. in his dissertation, *Paul Albar of Cordoba: Studies on His Life and Writings,* pp. 2 f.; Isidore of Seville, *De fide catholica,* II.5, in *PL,* LXXXIII, 508 ff.; B. Blumenkranz's observation in *RMAL,* X, 25, 133; his pertinent excursus in *Die Judenpredigt Augustins,* pp. 181 ff.; and Melito of Sardis, *Clavis,* XIII, in J. B. Pitra's *Spicilegium solemense,* III, Part 1, pp. 297 f. In using the term "idolatry" for his former faith, Bodo undoubtedly echoed some objections to the Christian icons and worship of saints, which he must have heard from his new coreligionists in Spain. These objections were indeed to crop up in such later disputations as that of Abbot Crispin of Westminster. According to Blumenkranz, the Bodleian MS of that disputation contains an illustration pointing up this controversy, as does indeed another Oxford MS, still unpublished, which reproduces the so-called *Disputatio Paschalis de Roma contra Judaeos.* Cf. Blumenkranz's data in *RMAL,* IV, 242 n. 20. In his zeal of a neophyte, Bodo evidently went further than did official contemporary opinion among the leading rabbis. Certainly, Rashi spoke with much greater authority, when he emphasized that "the Gentiles of today are not well versed in idolatry." Cf. his *Teshubot,* p. 337 No. 327, with I. Elfenbein's comments thereon; and *supra,* Chaps. XIX, n. 14; XXII, n. 16. Of course, we do not have Bodo's side of the story in his own words. Blumenkranz's effort to reconstruct his letters from his opponent's replies has, by its very nature, been but partially successful. Cf. his recent essays on "Un Pamphlet juif médio-latin de polémique anti-chrétienne," *RHPR,* XXXIV, 401–13; and "Du nouveau sur Bodo-Eléazar?" *REJ,* CXII, 35–42. The latter is chiefly a critique of views espoused by A. Cabaniss in the studies cited *supra,* Chap. XX, n. 69.

57. Cf. B. W. Helfgott's ingenious demonstration of *The Doctrine of Election in Tannaitic Literature* as largely a response to the Christian challenge; A. Marmorstein's text and observations in *REJ,* LXVI, 246 f., 250 f., with reference to Matt. 22:37. On the authorship of this fragment, see *supra,* n. 38. In a similar vein, that writer analyzed fourteen other Gospel teachings, emphasizing especially the mis-

quotations of Old Testament passages in the Gospel of Matthew. Evidently, like Joseph Qimḥi, he made a careful study of the Gospels, if not of the entire New Testament. The same is true of Crispin's Jewish adversary who, according to the Abbot's own admission, was "well informed about our writings." Cf. *PL,* CLIX, 1005. Such familiarity with Christian letters seems to have been limited to outright apologists, however. The rest of the Jewish intelligentsia obviously knew Christian traditions only from second hand, for the most part from that very controversial literature, which included such crude folkloristic compilations as the *Toledot Yeshu.* Because of their unbridled denunciations of Jesus' personality and parentage, the latter could be used to advantage by the propagandistic Jew-baiters, Agobard and Amulo. Cf. especially the former's *De judaicis superstitionibus,* x, in *PL,* CIV, 86 ff.; and Amulo's *Contra Judaeos,* x, xxv, xxxix–xl, in *PL,* CXVI, 146 f., 157 f., 167 ff. Of course, the controversy over the merits of the allegorical, versus the literal, interpretation of Scripture reached back to the early period of the separation between the two faiths. Cf. *supra,* Vol. II, pp. 140, 144, 384 n. 16, 386 n. 22, 427 n. 4.

58. Cf. *supra,* Chaps. XX, n. 67; XXI, nn. 43–44; XXII, nn. 62 ff.; and, on the absence of the accusation of Jewish "usury" in the patristic letters, J. Parkes's observations in *The Conflict of the Church and the Synagogue,* pp. 192 f. Otherwise the ancient writers were unsparing in the villification of Jewish avarice and quest for pleasures. Cf. the passages cited in M. Simon's *Verus Israel,* pp. 252 f. But only since the seventh-century Toledan councils and the writings by Agobard and Amulo did the economic issue become a major bone of contention. This vigorous new line of attack is put into bolder relief by its relative insignificance not only in Muslim but also in Byzantine apologias. As late as the twelfth century, Euthymios Zigabenos, though initiating his critical review of the non-Christian and heretical sects with an attack on Judaism, limited himself to the traditional disputes over the trinitarian dogma, Jesus' messiahship, circumcision, and Jewish festivals; he had nothing to say about the Jews' allegedly obnoxious socioeconomic behavior. An interesting illustration of how a Byzantine legend about a Jewish moneylender, itself nurtured from antecedents in the Talmud (Nedarim 50a, as interpreted by "Rashi" and R. Nissim Gerondi) and Muslim letters, underwent a considerable anti-Jewish reinterpretation in its westward migration until it found its outlet in Shakespeare's Shylock, is furnished by B. N. Nelson and J. Starr in "The Legend of the Divine Surety and the Jewish Moneylender," *Annuaire,* VII, 289–338.

59. Anonymous author, ed. by A. Marmorstein, in *REJ,* LXVI, 247, 251, with reference to Ps. 15:5; Joseph Qimḥi's *Sefer ha-Berit,* in Eisenstein's *Oẓar Wikuḥim,* p. 68a; and Meir bar Simon's imaginary dialogue, cited *supra,* Chap. XXII, n. 94. The controversialist's pride in the rabbinic prohibition of the "dust of usury" mirrored the conviction of Jewish spokesmen also in Muslim lands that Jewish law opposed usury in all forms more radically than any other faith. On the opposition of Muslim jurists to this extension of the original outlawry, see Goldziher's "Mélanges judéo-arabes," *REJ,* XLIII, 4 ff. The ambivalent attitude of Christian leaders toward Jewish moneylending came to the fore in St. Bernard's aforementioned condemnation of Christian creditors for charging even "worse usuries," and the forced arguments advanced by Thomas Aquinas in his *De regimine Judaeorum* to allay the conscientious scruples of Christian rulers who, by their taxes, had become silent partners of Jewish usurers. See *supra,* Chap. XXII, nn. 62 ff.; XXIII, n. 92.

60. *Dibre ha-yamim shel Mosheh* (The Chronicle of Moses), reprinted in Jellinek's *Bet ha-Midrasch,* II, 4 (in Eisenstein's *Ozar midrashim,* p. 358b); and in O. S. Rankin's English trans. in his *Jewish Religious Polemic,* pp. 31 f. (Rankin sets that legendary story of Moses at too early a date when he considers it not "too far removed" from the second century. Cf. Zunz's *Ha-Derashot,* pp. 67, 69, 324 n. 164: ninth or tenth century); Joseph Qimḥi's *Sefer ha-Berit,* in Eisenstein's *Oẓar Wikuḥim,* pp. 70, 76 f. Curiously, Qimḥi contrasted here the miraculous preservation of the Torah during the eleven (twelve) centuries since the second fall of Jerusalem with its having been forgotten during but seventy years of the First Exile, until its restoration by Ezra. Qimḥi's contemporary, Abraham ibn Daud, adduced the very identity of the Scripture's masoretic text throughout the far-flung Jewish dispersion as incontravertible proof of its authenticity. Cf. *infra,* Chap. XXIX, n. 27. Needless to say that eleven (twelve) centuries were taken here as a round number, for only that many years had elapsed from 68–70 C.E. to the author's death. But there is no reason to deny on this score Qimḥi's authorship of the Book of the Covenant, or even of that passage where the figure 1100 could easily have been replaced by 1200 by a later copyist. Cf. however, B. Suler's "Kimchi, Josef ben Isaak," *EJ,* IX, 1240–44. On medieval Jewish serfdom, see *supra,* Chaps. XVI, nn. 52–53; XX, n. 66.

61. Julian of Toledo's *De comprobatione,* I.19–21, in *PL,* XCVI, 552 ff.; Paul Alvarus' *Epistolae,* XIV.4, in *PL,* CXXI, 480 f.; ed. by Madoz, pp. 215 f.; Christian Druthmar of Stavelot's *Expositio in Mattaeum,* LVI, in *PL,* CVI, 1456; Blumenkranz's ed. of the *Altercatio,* in *RMAL,* X, 89; and his comments thereon, pp. 142 f., 152 f. Among these writers Julian alone appears puzzling on chronological grounds. Writing toward the end of the seventh century, he had no reason to refer to Dhu-Nuwas, while the conversion of the Khazar king was not to take place until several decades later. Cf. *supra,* Chap. XIX, n. 33.

62. Cf. the ancient Christian sources assembled by Juster in his *Empire romain,* I, 45 f. n. 1, where, however, no distinction is drawn between Jewish "atheism" and "impiety." Even the former had acquired in the writings of Church Fathers a new, if often ambiguous, meaning. Cf. H. A. Wolfson's analysis in *The Philosophy of the Church Fathers,* I, 81 ff. It disappeared almost entirely from the medieval polemics, being replaced by such invectives as Jewish "blindness" and stubborn misunderstanding of the true meaning of Scripture. On the equation of Rome with the pig, see the examples cited in L. Ginzberg's *Legends,* V, 294 n. 162, and his *Ginze Schechter,* I, 262 n. 21.

Jewish rejection of pork products seems to have particularly irked Christian leaders. The ruthless Visigothic rulers attempted, we recollect, to break down the resistance of recent converts by forcing them to consume at least some such products as bacon. See *supra,* Chap. XVI, n. 15. More directly, the anonymous Spanish controversialist tried to persuade the Jews that in the messianic age they themselves would be allowed to eat pork, and that some rabbis had already permitted serving it to pregnant women. Cf. the text in *Sefarad,* XIII, 8 f., 32 f., referring to an incorrectly understood passage in Lev. r. XIII.5, ed. by Margulies, II, 295 and note 2. Cf. also L. Zunz's older essay, "*Ḥasir* aggadisch gedeuted" reprinted in his *GS,* III, 221–24. Earlier Anastasios Sinaites, or a ninth-century writer using his name, had offered an economic interpretation of the Jewish prohibition. Unlike chickens and goats, he explained, which likewise live on garbage, pigs do not yield by-products such as eggs or wool, but only meat. An Eastern legend, on the other hand, recited with glee how four hundred Tiberian rabbis, visiting Julian the Apostate, were persuaded by the impious emperor to worship idols and to gorge themselves on pork. Cf. Anastasios, *Dialogus parvus ad Judaeos,* in *PG,* LXXXIX, 1271 ff.; Parkes, *Conflict,* pp. 282, 299. The authenticity of the anti-Jewish dialogues attributed to Anastasios has been doubted by Ehrhard in Krumbacher's *Geschichte,* pp. 65 f., although his main argument from the date of 800 years since the fall of Jerusalem occurring in the text is inconclusive. The original reading may well have been revised by a ninth-century copyist. Cf. also Williams's *Adversus Judaeos,* pp. 175 ff.; T. Spačil's remarks in "La Teologia di S. Anastasio Sinaità," *Bessarione,* XXVI, 157–78; XXVII, 15–44; and *supra,* Chap. XIX, n. 1.

63. See the extensive material assembled, mainly from southern France and neighboring countries, by M. Bulard in *Le Scorpion, symbole du people juif dans l'art religieux des XIVe, XVe, XVIe siècles,* especially pp. 39 ff. On the original fairly neutral meaning of Jewish "perfidy" and its use even in the annual prayer, *Pro perfidis Judaeis,* see *infra,* n. 68. Some Christian onlookers may also have derived from that religious symbol an indirect warning against dangerous Jewish amorous approaches, since the scorpion had also served as an ancient symbol of sex. Cf. Bulard's remarks, p. 66 n. 7.

64. See the extensive documentation assembled by J. Trachtenberg in *The Devil and the Jew;* with some additional illustrations by A. Leschnitzer in *The Magic Background of Modern Antisemitism.* The complementary Muslim tradition of the Jewish *dajjal* (anti-messiah), will be mentioned *infra,* Chap. XXV, n. 70. Cf. also David Qimḥi's brief controversial tract (*Teshubot*), reprinted in Eisenstein's *Oẓar Wikuḥim,* pp. 80 f.; E. Liefmann's observations on the antisemitic implications of "Die Legende vom Antichrist und die Sage von Ahasver," *Judaica,* III, 122–56; the numerous miracle tales summarized in the literature listed *supra,* n. 44; and, more generally, B. J. Bamberger's comprehensive study of *Fallen Angels;* and *infra,* Chaps. XXXIII and XXXVI.

65. St. Ambrose's Commentary on Luke 4:27, in *PL,* XV, 1713; St. Theodoret of Cyrrhus' *Quaestiones in Leviticum,* Interr. 18, in *PG,* LXXX, 324 (even here the accusation was rather metaphorical: "Hence impure are those who enter their synagogues, as if they entered leprosy-stricken houses"; the plural is used in the Leipzig MS); J. J. Walsh in *The History of Nursing,* p. 39; and *supra,* Vols. I, pp. 189, 275; II, 249. Caesarius of Arles, too, merely reminisced about the biblical Na'aman when he declared metaphorically that, with the acceptance by the Gentile nations of the apostolic doctrine, the Jews were stricken with the "leprosy of sin." Cf. his *Sermones,* CXXIX, ed. by Morin, I, 532. On the relative rarity of leprosy even among the ancient Israelites, see A. Bloom's brief data in *La Lèpre dans l'ancienne Egypte et chez les anciens Hébreux, La lèpre dans la Bible.* Whatever resentment was now voiced against the Jews' "unproductive" occupations, as in Peter of Cluny's letter to the king, had nothing to do with their Sabbath observance. Even Agobard attacked not the Jewish Sabbath as such, but rather the weakness of the Carolingian administration in transferring the weekly fairs in Lyons from Saturday to Sunday. That the stricter Jewish Sabbath and its observance on Saturdays appealed to many,

especially sectarian Christians, has been mentioned here on various occasions. While certainly not endearing that institution to churchmen, this appeal removed all props from under the accusation of Jewish "laziness."

66. Cf. the passages cited by Simon in *Verus Israel,* pp. 250 ff.; Rashi's *Pardes,* in 'Azriel bar Yeḥiel's (?) *Haggahot Mordecai,* on Ketubot No. 286 (Vilna ed., fol. 9b; not included in the available texts of the *Pardes* itself, cf. Ehrenreich's ed., pp. 17 f.); Caesarius' *Dialogue on Miracles,* II, 23, ed. by Strange, I, 92 ff.; in the English trans. by Scott and Bland, I, 102 ff. The issue of sexual abstinence loomed larger in the West than in the East. Yet it already played a major role in Aphraates' controversy with the Jews in Sassanian Persia. According to G. Richter it was in the very focus of the Syriac Father's polemics and helped define his entire theological outlook. See his "Ueber die älteste Auseinandersetzung der syrischen Christen mit den Juden," *ZNW,* XXXV, 101–14. Cf. also Isidore of Seville's *Questiones adversus Judaeos,* XLVIII.1, in W. Martène and U. Durand's *Thesaurus novus anecdotorum,* V, 500 f. (on its authorship see *supra,* n. 39); or in Vega and Anspach's edition. This whole obscure domain of sex relations, especially among members of different faiths, will be discussed in its more familiar later medieval context. For the time being, see the few illustrations cited by me in "The Jewish Factor in Medieval Civilization," *PAAJR,* XII, 11 ff.; and *supra,* Chap. XVIII, nn. 25–26.

67. Qimḥi in Eisenstein's *Oẓar Wikuḥim,* pp. 67 f.; *Zohar* on the weekly lesson, *Balaq,* III, fol. 192b; in Simon and Sperling's English trans., V, 271 f. The sexual escapades of priests and nuns, which so prominently figured in the Muslim-Christian polemics, were to play a significant role also in the later medieval Jewish apologias by Yom Tob Lipmann Mühlhausen and others.

68. The fragment, ed. by Marmorstein in *REJ,* LXVI, 247, 251; the pseudo-Augustinian tract, cited by B. Blumenkranz in *RMAL,* V, 195; Bartholomew's *Dialogus contra Judaeos ad corrigendum et perficiendum destinatus,* cited from a Bodleian MS by R. W. Hunt in *Studies . . . Powicke,* pp. 147 f. That dialogue's subtitle obviously refers to the improvement of Christian souls. On the important doctrine of "Die Juden als Zeugen der Kirche," in the context of medieval polemics, see Blumenkranz's brief note in *TZ,* V, 396–98; Caesarius of Arles' unequivocal reference to the need of thus counteracting pagan doubters in his *Sermones,* LXXXVI, ed. by Morin, I, 355; and *supra,* Chaps. XVI, n. 34; XX, n. 3. Because of this ambivalent attitude, faithful Christians ever since ancient times were supposed to pray once a year *pro perfidis Judaeis.* In recent years, many voices were heard decrying the use of the term *perfidis* and certain derogatory instructions given to the priests in connection with its recitation. In a decree, *Maxima redemptionis nostrae mysteria,* dated November 16, 1955, the Sacred Congregation of Rites did not change the text, but altered the instructions to include the usual exhortations, "Let us pray, . . . Let us bend our knees, . . . Get up." Cf. the formula in the *Gelasian Sacramentary,* and the literature thereon cited *supra,* Vol. II, pp. 169, 395 n. 52. Cf. also J. M. Oesterreicher's additional remarks in his "Catholic Attitude Towards the Jews," *Orate Fratres,* XXIII, 385–402; P. Démann and R. Bloch, "Formation liturgique et attitude chrétienne envers les Juifs," *Cahiers sioniens,* VII, 115–78; Démann, "La Prière pour les Juifs dans le nouveau rite de la Semaine Sainte," *ibid.,* IX, 337–41. Démann also refers to the significant observations by M. Bugnini, "Una

Particolarità del Missale da Rivedere: la preghiera 'pro Judaeis' al Venerdì Santo," *Miscellanea Giulio Belvederi,* pp. 117–32; and J. Isaac's "Note sur la prière 'Oremus et pro perfidis Judaeis'" which is to appear in the Memorial Volume for Renée Bloch. Mainly oriented toward contemporary liturgical movements, these studies also shed light on the past. At the same time much more of the Christian liturgy, including its passion plays and sermons, was permeated with an anti-Jewish animus. To the examples hitherto quoted one may add a pseudo-Augustinian sermon (*Contra Judaeos, paganos et Arianos,* XI, in *PL,* XLII, 1123), repeated by Paulus Diaconus (in his *Homiliae de sanctis,* XII, in *PL,* XCV, 1470 f.), and probably from him by Peter of Cluny in the prologue to his "Treatise against the Jews" (*PL,* CLXXXIX, 507 f.). A passage from that sermon was incorporated in the Christmas liturgy of many French churches, and was often transformed into a liturgical drama with strong anti-Jewish overtones. Cf. J. Leclercq's *Pierre le Vénérable,* pp. 236 f. Cf. also *infra,* Chap. XXXI; B. Blumenkranz, "Vie et survie de la polémique antijuive," *Studia Patristica,* I, 461 ff.; and K. Sullivan, "Pro Perfidis Judaeis," *The Bridge,* II, 212–23.

69. Cf. Israel Lévi's older but still useful analysis of "Le Sacrifice d'Isaac et la mort de Jésus," *REJ,* LXIV, 160–84; LXV, 138–43 (arguing for a nexus antedating the third century, the date originally suggested by Abraham Geiger); and *supra,* Vol. II, pp. 138, 383 n. 13. On the substitution, in the Muslim tradition, of Ishmael for Isaac as the intended sacrificial victim, cf. *supra,* Chap. XVII, n. 15.

CHAPTER XXV: MESSIANISM AND SECTARIAN TRENDS

1. Cf. "Tratado anonimo," ed. by Millás Vallicrosa in *Sefarad,* XIII, 12. Elijah, in particular, appeared as the traditional harbinger of the Messiah, or even a participant in the final messianic war. After the Messiah (ben Joseph?) destroys Ammon and Moab, we are told in one apocalyptic vision, a coalition of all northern kings assembles an enormous army around Damascus, while the troops of a similar southern grand alliance are mobilized in Midian. At this critical juncture God opens the heavenly gate foı Elijah, who descends into Midian. After consulting the mystical *Sefer ha-Yashar* (Book of the Just) "of which this entire Torah is but a single verse," the Prophet causes the earth to open up and become a mass grave for the southern armies. (Needless to say, this "Book of the Just," mentioned in the Bible, is not to be confused with a very popular medieval folkloristic concoction under the same title; see *infra,* Chap. XXVIII, n. 58). Cf. *Midrash Zuṭa* on Canticles 5:2, ed. by S. Buber, pp. 30 f.; reprinted in Yehudah ibn Shemuel's *Midreshe ge'ulah,* pp. 294 ff., 300, 328 f., 428. This excellent collection of the early medieval apocalyptic writings, also provided with textual variants, bibliographies, and searching introductions, will be quoted frequently in the following notes. Many of the compiler's daring hypotheses, however, must be treated with the necessary caution. See also M. Margulies's reservations in his Hebrew review of that work in *KS,* XX, 137–39. On the more comprehensive messianic predictions included in the so-called *Sefer Eliyahu,* with its fairly identifiable hints to contemporary events during the great Perso-Byzantine wars of the early seventh century, see *supra,* Chaps. XVI, n. 23; XVII, n. 27. Cf. also G. Molin's "Elijahu, der Prophet und sein Weiterleben in den Hoffnungen des Judentums und der Christenheit," *Judaica,* VIII, 65–94; and more generally J. Brierre-Narbonne's interesting collection of messianic interpretations of Old Testament passages in the Targumim, Midrashim, and other rabbinic letters in *Les Prophéties messianiques de l'Ancien Testament dans la littérature juive en accord avec le Nouveau Testament* (arranged in the order of the biblical verses in Pentateuch, Psalms, and the Prophets, including Daniel).

2. Shabbat 33b; W. Küppers in *Das Messiasbild der spätjüdischen Apokalyptik,* p. 41. Apart from the *Sefer Eliyahu,* it is particularly the *Nistarot* (Mysteries) and *Tefillah* (Prayer) of R. Simon bar Yoḥai which have been effectively utilized for the elucidation of the obscure historical developments on the eve of, and during, the great expansion of Islam. Cf. *supra,* Chap. XVII, n. 27. As shown there in the example of R. Simon's Prayer, these apocalypses do not necessarily represent compositions of single authors or even date in their entirety from the same period. At times layers of new formulations were superimposed upon the original texts; written in precisely the same vein and in a remarkably similar style, they often appeared to later generations as parts of the original treatises. Even modern scholars were often misled into dating such tracts either by some chance remark interpolated by a later copyist or by a section whose context belongs to a chronologically different layer.

3. The text of *Sefer Zerubbabel* is now most conveniently available in Ibn Shemuel's *Midreshe,* pp. 71 ff., although in this form, somewhat arbitrarily rearranged, it is more readable than authentic. The critical reader is advised, therefore, to consult also the older versions, reproduced *ibid.,* pp. 379 ff. Because of the date, given in one version, that the redemption was due "at the completion of 990 years of Jerusalem's ruins," Graetz and others assumed that the author set the beginning of the messianic era at 1058 C.E. But apart from a certain general Jewish millennarianism, which figured that the redemption must come before the end of the first millennium since the fall of Jerusalem, no particularly significant messianic portents were recorded for that era. With more justice, A. Marx, utilizing another version containing the date 890, related this prediction to an inquiry sent by the Rhenish communities to those in Palestine concerning the signs of the approaching Messiah and placed it in 958 C.E. On the other hand, after a searching examination of that apocalyse (in his aforementioned essays in *REJ,* Vols. LXVIII–LXXI), Israel Lévi set that date aside as a later interpolation by a scribe wishing to bring the prophecy up to his own time. By identifying the recurring name Sirois with a king of Persia by that name, Lévi reinterpreted the entire tract within the context of the final stages of the Perso-Byzantine war and the rise of Islam (629–36). His argument was accepted by Ibn Shemuel who added the observation that, in the version published by Lévi from a Bodleian manuscript, the date of 990 years could relate not to the fall of Jerusalem (a second passage mentions specifically "Jerusalem's ruins"), but rather to the building of the Second Temple which, according to Jewish tradition, had lasted altogether 420 years. Subtracing these 420 years, the prediction aimed at the remaining 570 years after the fall of Jerusalem in 68 C.E., that is at the year 638. Cf. Ibn Shemuel's *Midreshe,* pp. 55 ff.; and the literature listed there and *supra,* Chap. XVI, n. 23.

Lévi's plausible date is further reinforced by another significant detail. Among the Archangel's annunciations to Zerubbabel, there is one predicting that in the year 720 from the founding of Rome that city would begin to be governed by emperors, the tenth of whom would destroy the Second Temple. "Seventy kings will rule there in all, similar in number to the seventy nations." Of course, our author does not bother to specify which monarchs he had in mind. Varying compilations of Roman and Byzantine emperors must have circulated among the Jewish, as well as the non-Jewish, populace. It is not too far-fetched an assumption that the aforementioned Hebrew list of Roman emperors, compiled in Byzantium in 967 (reproduced in *MJC,* I, 185 f.; see *supra,* Chap. XIX, n. 12) was motivated less by purely scientific curiosity than by the quest for solutions of the messianic riddle. According to that author, whose names and sequences are often quite garbled, Vespasian would indeed have been the tenth emperor after Julius Caesar, while Heraclius would have been the seventy-eighth. The author of the "Book of Zerubbabel" may either have had a different compilation at his disposal, or simply used the round number of seventy as a more portentous figure for the end of the Empire.

The connection here suggested with the internal difficulties in the exilarchic family is based upon the two versions of the Arabic story of Bustanai, published respectively by G. Margoliouth in his "Some British Museum Genizah Texts," *JQR,* [o.s.] XIV, 303–7; and E. J. Worman in "The Exilarch Bustānī," *ibid.,* [o.s.] XX, 211–15. Although clearly romanticizing, the author of that narrative is well informed about the traditions and outlook current among Bustanai's descendants. Cf. especially H. Tykocinski's comments on his translation of that account in

Debir, I, 152 ff. Of course, all such tie-ups with contemporary events must needs remain largely speculative. But they seem to offer the only chance of penetrating the studied obscurities of that branch of literature, whose ancient prototypes have been subjected to extensive and careful scrutiny by generations of competent scholars, but whose no less noteworthy early medieval specimens still are in the early stages of investigation.

4. *Sefer Ḥanokh* (The Hebrew Book of Enoch, part of the *Hekhalot* literature) in the two versions reproduced by A. Jellinek in his *Bet ha-Midrasch,* V, 179 f.; and by H. Odeberg in his ed. of *3 Enoch or the Hebrew Book of Enoch,* XXVI, pp. 44 (Hebrew), 93 f. (English). Although in its present form this apocalypse is obviously late, it is intrinsically related to the Midrash *Eleh Ezkerah* and other much older legends concerning the Ten Martyrs. Cf. the literature cited *supra,* Vol. II, p. 370 n. 9; and Chap. XXI, n. 67. Meṭaṭron and the other angelic names are discussed *infra,* Chap. XXXIII. On Archangel Michael's role as Israel's guardian angel, see S. A. Horodetzky's somewhat overdrawn distinction between the former's heavenly and Gabriel's earthly functions in his "Michael und Gabriel," *MGWJ,* LXXII, 499–506. As pointed out by Jellinek and Ibn Shemuel (pp. 3 ff.), this explanation is part and parcel of the various angelic annunciations to R. Ishmael, which form a significant element in Merkabah mysticism (related to Ezekiel's vision of the Chariot). According to another apocalypse, likewise included in that school's classical collection *Hekhalot rabbati,* R. Ishmael was allegedly shown by another angel chambers containing ledgers upon ledgers of projected tribulations for Israel. These fail to materialize, however, because every day the Israelites enter their synagogues and answer in unison, "Amen, may the great name [of the Lord] be blessed!" The rabbi was shown, on the other hand, chambers in which angels "weave garments of salvation, make vivid crowns and place in them precious stones and pearls" for all Jews, while a particularly magnificent crown, adorned by the sun, the moon, and the twelve signs of the zodiac, is destined for David, king of Israel. In the continuation of that vision the king appears in person at the head of all his descendants on the throne of Judah and is tumultuously greeted by the heavenly hosts. Cf. the text in Jellinek's reproduction in *Bet ha-Midrasch,* V, 167–69; VI, 24–26 (with his comments thereon *ibid.,* pp. xvii ff.); and in revised form in Ibn Shemuel's *Midreshe,* pp. 8 ff. Even here, however, David loses none of his human characteristics, and himself stresses the Lord's exclusive dominion by singing from his Psalms: "The Lord will reign for ever, Thy God, O Zion, unto all generations. Hallelujah" (146:10). Incidentally, it probably was in opposition to Christian assertions that some Jewish homilists, such as the author of the *Seder Eliyahu rabbah,* began emphasizing "*our* Messiah," instead of simply *the* Messiah. Cf. the observation by its editor, M. Friedmann, in his introduction, pp. vi f. This is true regardless of which date we set for the composition of that midrash; see *infra,* Chap. XXVIII, n. 7.

5. *Otot ha-mashiaḥ* (Signs of the Messiah), ed. by Jellinek in his *Bet ha-Midrasch,* II, 58–63; and by Ibn Shemuel, pp. 318 ff. Here the text is included in a substantial collection of similar prophecies, some of which seem to be of ancient origin. One published and repeatedly commented upon by A. Marmorstein has been discussed in connection with ancient messianic expectations *supra,* Vol. II, p. 397 n. 6. By specifying that the troops recruited by the Messiah ben Joseph would include soldiers from the tribes of Ephraim, Manasseh, and Gad, as well as in his description

of the tenth "sign," our author clearly controverted R. 'Aqiba's view that the ten tribes would not share in the final return, a view already rejected by 'Aqiba's own disciples. Cf. M. Sanhedrin x.3; b. 110b; and other sources discussed in Klausner's *Ha-Ra'ayon ha-meshiḥi be-Yisrael* (The Messianic Idea in Judaism from the Beginning to the Conclusion of the Mishnah), pp. 282 ff.

6. See *supra,* Chap. XVI, nn. 19, 74. The Redeemer's sufferings were, in the opinion of those visionaries, not to follow his appearance, but rather to be connected either with his birth or his subsequent life in poverty and obscurity in the city of Rome. Cf. Israel Lévi's studies of "Le Ravissement du Messie à sa naissance," *REJ,* LXXIV, 113–26; LXXV, 113–18; LXXVII, 1–11; and the legends presently to be cited. This was, of course, different from the Christian sequence. The doctrine of the Antichrist-Armilus, too, differed in many ways, as we have seen, from similar Christian teachings, which may well have been indebted to Jewish prototypes. Cf., however, the serious reservations voiced on this score by J. Klausner in *Ha-Ra'ayon ha-meshiḥi,* p. 239; *supra,* Chap. XXIV, n. 64; and *infra,* n. 8.

On the other hand, the doctrine of the two messiahs definitely had ancient Jewish antecedents. Cf. *supra,* Vol. II, p. 351 n. 1; L. H. Silberman's more recent study of "The Two 'Messiahs' of the Manual of Discipline," *VT,* V, 77–82 (denying that interpretation of 9:10–11); and other literature listed *infra,* nn. 8 and 67. It was now resented by such Jew-baiters as Amulo (*Contra Judaeos,* XII, XV, XXI–XXII, in *PL,* CXVI, 148 ff.); and utilized for polemical twists by such controversialists as Gautier de Chatillon. In the Prologue to his *Contra Judaeos,* this twelfth-century apologist claims to have forced his Jewish interlocutor to admit "that there were two messiahs, one of whom had already come, and the other was yet to come" (*PL,* CCIX, 426). These Christian objections are doubly noteworthy as some Church Fathers themselves had taught the doctrine of two messiahs, one of whom was to stem from the tribe of Levi. Cf., for instance, L. Mariès's study of "Le Messie issu de Lévi chez Hippolyte de Rome," *Recherches de science religieuse,* XXVIII, 381–96. This concept of a priestly messiah, cultivated especially under the priestly kings of the Maccabean period, was rooted in some ancient prophetic expectations of Moses himself coming back to life and redeeming his people. See A. Bentzen, *King and Messiah.* But, perhaps precisely because this expectation had become a partisan issue under the Maccabeans (see *supra,* Vol. I, pp. 397 n. 21, 400 n. 30), the idea of a levitical Messiah practically disappeared from the later rabbinic writings. It survived mainly among the Samaritans who interpreted Deut. 18:15, 18, as a promise for Moses himself "to come to life again and bring them the promised happiness." See M. Gaster, *Samaritans,* p. 91; and, more fully, A. Merx's study of *Der Messias oder Ta'eb der Samaritaner* (especially the end of the first poem, pp. 29, 32; although based on later sources, this analysis is of value also for the concepts prevailing among these sectarians before 1200); M. Haran's (Dieman?) more recent analysis of "The Concept of the 'Taheb' in the Samaritan Religion" (Hebrew), *Tarbiz,* XXIII, 107; and *infra,* n. 37.

7. The Latin text was first published by H. von Grauert in his essay, "Meister Johann von Toledo," *SB* Munich, 1901, pp. 111–325 (also discussing that prophecy's repercussions to the end of the Middle Ages); and carefully reinterpreted by F. Baer in his aforementioned study in *MGWJ,* LXX (see *supra,* Chap. XXI, n. 45). This text, with a Hebrew retranslation therefrom, is available also in Ibn Shemuel's *Midreshe,* pp. 324 f., 426 f. On Abraham bar Ḥiyya, see also *infra,* n. 23; and Chap.

XXVIII, n. 97. Certainly neither he nor his apocalyptic follower could foresee that his predictions would help arouse the passions of the Crusaders and thus indirectly contribute to the massacres of English Jewry.

8. *Midrash Konen* (Of the Correct Order) in the section describing the four world regions, including Paradise, ed. by Jellinek in *Bet ha-Midrasch,* II, 29 f.; *Seder Gan 'Eden* (Order of the Garden of Eden), *ibid.,* III, 133; with additions thereto, p. 195 No. iv; *Midrash Bereshit rabbati,* ed. by H. Albeck, p. 131; reproduced by Ibn Shemuel, pp. 20 ff., 305; the Book of Zerubbabel and some minor apocalypses, *ibid.,* pp. 75, 302 ff.; Amulo's *Contra Judaeos,* XII, in *PL,* CXVI, 148. The opening in the earth which swallowed Korah, was, according to the Aggadah, one of ten things created shortly before the onset of the first Sabbath. Cf. Pesaḥim 54a. The vision attributed to Elijah has long been known from the anti-Jewish work *Pugio fidei* by Raymond Martini, but it is now available in a slightly different version in Albeck's edition of *Bereshit rabbati,* which generally evinces many similarities with the *Pugio,* although we seem to possess only an abridged version of the work of R. Moses ha-Darshan. Cf. Albeck's intro., pp. 5 ff. On the provenance of the work and the disputed reliability of the texts preserved by Martini, a thirteenth-century Dominican monk, see *infra,* Chap. XXVIII, n. 24. Because such references to Jewish sources are absent in Martini's earlier work, *Explanatio symboli* (1258), F. Cavallera assumes that he had acquired his Hebraic knowledge in the subsequent twenty years and hence was not of Jewish origin. Cf. "*L'Explanatio symboli* de Raymond Martin O.P. (1258)," *Studia mediaevalia* in honor of Raymond Joseph Martin, p. 201 n. 1. Cf. also A. Berthier's biography of Martini in *Archivum fratrum praedicatorum,* Vol. VI, especially pp. 304 ff. Bethlehem, or perhaps a town in its vicinity, as the Messiah's birthplace, is attested, however, also by a statement of a fourth-century Palestinian Amora, R. Judan son of (or in the name of R.) Aibo, reported in j. Berakhot II.4, 5a; and Lam. r. LI, p. 36a (on Lam. 1:16), although the scene is transferred, perhaps for anti-Christian reasons, to Jerusalem by the eleventh-century author of the Midrash Lam. zuṭa. Cf. N. Wieder's dissertation, *Der Midrasch Echa Zuta,* pp. 15, 18; and S. Klein's comments on the former locality in *Sefer ha-Yishub,* I, 11 f. Cf. also Ibn Shemuel's observations, pp. 289 ff., where, however, his explanation of the chronological sequence in Elijah's vision as the result of successive additions is somewhat artificial. It would be surprising if in the original version there had been no reference to the Messiah's sojourn in Rome.

The seven preexistent things, including the name of the Messiah, are enumerated in Pesaḥim 54a and other talmudic passages. Taking their lead from Ps. 72:17, the rabbis insisted that only his "name" was eternal, and even indulged in a guessing game as to what that name might be (Sanhedrin 98b). One of them suggested, perhaps with his tongue in his cheek, that the name was Yinnon, because of the phrasing of that Psalm. More widely accepted were the names of Menaḥem or of Shiloh; in defiance of Christian attacks, the latter was recommended especially in the academy of an Amora bearing a similar name. Menaḥem (ben Hezekiah) was supported by its meaning of Comforter, the complaint voiced about his absence by the author of Lamentations (1:16), and the numerical equivalence (138) of the letters in Menaḥem with those of Ṣemaḥ (scion, that is, of the house of David), a hallowed messianic term. Hence came its extensive use in the subsequent messianic speculations. In any case, G. F. Moore's observation that "there is no trace in the tannaitic sources of any idea that the Messiah himself was an antemundane creation, or that he was regarded otherwise than as a man of human kind" (*Judaism,* II, 349), is also substantially true of the Jewish medieval writers, except for the *Merkabah* visionaries and such occasional homilists as the compiler of *Pesiqta rabbati* (XXXIII, XXXVI., ed. by M. Friedmann, fols. 152b, 162ab). It applies even to most medieval apocalypses, which in this respect differ sharply from their ancient counterparts. This reduction in the stature of the future Redeemer from that approximating a demigod to one of a mere superman was probably owing less to the direct Christian challenge than to the general refinement of Jewish monotheistic teachings achieved in the debates with Christians and Jewish sectarians. On the ancient background of the debates concerning the *Torah in the Messianic Age,* see also W. D. Davies's recent monograph under this title.

9. B.B. 122a; Sanhedrin 91b, 99a; and many passages quoted by Klausner in *Ha-Ra'ayon ha-meshiḥi,* pp. 241 ff.; Maimonides' *Iggerot,* ed. by Baneth, p. 66. Cf. also *infra,* n. 26; and *supra,* Vol. II, pp. 312 f. The very rationalist leaders, as we shall see, were hard put in trying to square the exalted expectations of a final redemption with a mere political return to the ancient homeland. Some of them may also have heard of the gibes by the Christian apologists, Aphraates and Chrysostom, who contended that the Isaianic prediction "that the Lord shall set his hand again the second time to recover the remnant of his people" (11:11) meant that He would not do it for the third time (Aphraates' *Homilies,* XIX.4, ed. by W. Wright; in G. Bert's German trans. in O. von Gebhardt and A. Harnack's collection of *Texte und Untersuchungen zur altchristlichen Literatur,* III, 305 ff.), or that the Jews had futilely tried to reestablish their shattered political fortunes under Hadrian, Constantine (!), and Julian and would fail again in the future (Chrysostom's *Adversus Judaeos,* V.11, in *PG,* XLVIII, 900 ff.). Certainly, such a limited liberation of their people appeared to the Jewish masses, as well as to most of the intellectual leaders, as but a part of the great divine scheme of redemption. They all, and particularly the mystically minded among them, confidently expected the messianic age to bring about not only the ultimate individual salvation, but also some basic transformations in the established order of the universe. Cf. also A. Spijkerman, "Afrahat der Weise und der Antisionismus," *Studii biblici franciscani,* V, 191–212.

10. *Nistarot* (Mysteries) of R. Simon ben Yoḥai, ed. by Jellinek in *Bet ha-Midrasch,* III, 80; ed. by Ibn Shemuel, pp. 196 f. The *Ziv,* mentioned in Ps. 50:11, was connected in one of the stories of Rabbah bar bar Ḥana (see *supra,* Vol. II, pp. 396 n. 5, 433 n. 18) with a mythical bird whose claws were immersed in deep waters while its head reached to the sky (B.B. 73b). All three gigantic monsters, representative of the world of land animals, fish, and fowl, had played a great role in Near Eastern eschatology ever since the ancient Babylonian epics, and became part and parcel of the vivid poetic imagery of the Bible (esp. Job 40:15–41:34). Through Judaism these ancient mythologies deeply colored both Christian and Muslim expectations of the Hereafter, but there was little reciprocal influence of these faiths on the already fully formed eschatological concepts of the mother creed. Even in the messianic doctrines themselves the Islamic influences were quite negligible by contrast with the impact of the Christian challenge. Only the Jewish Armilus legend may have received some new hues from the fearful *Dajjal* myths of Islam, whose mixed Zoroastrian-Jewish origin appears incontrovertible. Even the description of Armilus' ears—he is supposed to turn his healthy ear only to speakers of evil and

his dumb ear to those bringing good tidings—which appears for the first time in the late *Midrash va-yosha'* (cf. Jellinek's *Bet ha-Midrasch,* I, 56; Ibn Shemuel, pp. 93 ff.), may well reflect the pre-Islamic ethical biases of these two religions. By a curious inversion, this demonic anti-Messiah was to make his appearance, according to widespread Muslim legends, in the Jewish quarter of Isfahan, and was to attract 70,000 armed Jewish followers. Cf. A. J. Wensinck's numerous source references in *A Handbook of Early Muhammadan Tradition,* pp. 50 f.; G. Vajda's data in *JA,* CCXXIX, 112 f.; and D. S. Attema's dissertation, *De Mohammedaansche Opvattingen* (The Muslim Conceptions of the Era of the Last Judgment and Its Omens), especially pp. 152 f. Cf. also the older but still useful studies by James Darmesteter, Gerhold van Vloten, and C. Snouk Hurgronje (see *supra,* Chap. XVIII, n. 6), and others reviewed by I. Friedlaender in "The Messianic Idea in Islam," *Past and Present,* pp. 139–58, and the more recent essay on "Ahmad, the Promised Messiah and Mahdi," *Review of Religions,* XLVIII, Part 10, pp. 24–34. We must bear in mind, however, that the material for most of these studies is derived from either the authoritative sources of the *ḥadith* or the renowned works of Muslim theology, and hence is not quite comparable with the Jewish apocalyptic writings, stemming mainly from folkloristic and mystic circles. How much would we learn about the Jewish messianic teachings from the major philosophic works by Ibn Gabirol, Ibn Daud, Maimonides, and even Halevi? See *infra,* nn. 15, 27. A reexamination of the messianic doctrines in the now amply available body of early Muslim mystical writings, both orthodox and sectarian, may yet yield some remarkable new insights into their Jewish antecedents and later interrelations. Cf. also the general semipopular survey of W. D. Wallis, *Messiahs: Their Role in Civilization,* pp. 82 ff., 186 ff.; and *infra,* n. 30.

11. *Nistarot, loc. cit.,* with reference to Isa. 24:23, 54:10, 60:21; Hos. 6:2. So deeply rooted became the talmudic periodicization of history into six thousand years, of which the last two thousand were to constitute the messianic age (cf. 'A.Z. 9b; and Rashi's comment thereon *s.v. U-shene*), that the attribution of but 400 or 1,000 years to the messianic era, quite common in the ancient apocalyptic literature, as well as the various tannaitic estimates ranging from 40 to 7,000 years, were now completely overshadowed. Only Judah the Patriarch, otherwise a far from extravagant homilist, is quoted in *Pesiqta rabbati* as computing from the Isaianic prediction, "And my year of redemption is come" (63:4) a figure as high as 365,000 years for the duration of the messianic age, since a divine day, according to the psalmist, equals a thousand years. Cf. Ps. 90:4; Sanhedrin 99a; *Pesiqta rabbati,* ed. by Friedmann, fol. 4ab; W. Bousset's remarks in *Die Religion des Judentums,* 3d ed., p. 288 n. 2 (denying Persian origins); and on the general relations between the Persian and the Jewish world eras, *supra,* Vol. II, pp. 318, 435 f. n. 31. It is remarkable that the Samaritans, too, accepted that Jewish scheme of the world's duration for 6,000 years. Cf. their book *Asatir,* IV.19–21; XI.20, ed. by M. Gaster, pp. 213 ff. 283; in Z. Ben-Hayyim's Hebrew trans. in *Tarbiz,* XIV, 117, 124, 184; XV, 82. Because of the late date of this book (see *supra,* Vol. II, p. 339 n. 35), Samaritan adoption of this Jewish concept during the Middle Ages appears likely, although its roots in pre-Christian antiquity can by no means be ruled out.

12. The strict injunctions against "counting the end" began with R. Jose ben Ḥalafta and R. Nathan of the disillusioned generation after Bar Kocheba. Cf.

Sanhedrin 97ab; Mekhilta Vayassa' VI, ed. by Lauterbach, II, 125; Derekh Ereṣ rabbah, XI.13, ed. by M. Higger under the title *Tosefta Derekh Ereṣ,* with an English trans., in his *Masekhtot Derekh Eres* (The Treatises Derek Erez), pp. 313 (Hebrew), 117 (English). In "Ein polemischer Ausspruch Jose b. Chalaftha's," *MGWJ,* XLII, 505–7, W. Bacher ingeniously suggested that this entire utterance of R. Jose must be understood as a rejection of contemporary Judeo-Christian trends. Perhaps because of that temporary incentive, this prohibition was to be often disregarded in the subsequent more optimistic ages. Certainly, that Persian Jewish soldier who produced a Hebrew scroll indicating that the world would come to an end in the year 4291 (531 C.E.) seems to have found widespread credence and little opposition (*supra,* Vol. II, p. 318). We shall also presently see that some of the leading Jewish thinkers of the posttalmudic period ventured to defy that old prohibition. But the apocalyptic writers did not have to indicate any specific date, since the various hints and names thrown out in their visions must have impressed the more informed readers with the immediacy of the forthcoming redemption.

13. Saadiah's *Siddur,* ed. by I. Davidson *et al.,* pp. 62 f. Even statements like, "We daily grow weaker and weaker, and dwindle away in the course of years," inserted in a similar second poem (*ibid.,* pp. 87 f.), reproduce a standardized complaint rather than a reflection of contemporary realities. During the tenth-century anarchy the total number of Jews probably showed little diminution, although communities like that of Baghdad undoubtedly suffered severely. There, too, the situation deteriorated toward the end of Saadiah's life, rather than in the 920's and early 930's when he seems to have written most of these poems. Cf. the editors' intro. to his *Siddur,* pp. 22 f.; and *supra,* Chap, XVIII, n. 2. On the difference between the ordinary Jewish liturgy, ancient and medieval, and the *piyyuṭim,* see *supra,* Vol. II, pp. 119 f., 376 f. nn. 34–35.

14. Eleazar Qalir's prayers, *Yered ke-maṭar* (May Descend Like Rain), and *Adon mi-shamekha* (O Lord, from Thy Skies), published by I. Elbogen in his "Kalirs Geschem-Komposition mit unbekannten Einlagen," *Kohut Mem. Vol.,* pp. 165, 170 ff.; and his *Ba-yamim ha-hem* (In Those Days), long known from the editions of the Roman *Maḥzor* (prayer book for holidays) and reprinted by Ibn Shemuel in *Midreshe,* pp. 113 ff. Cf. also his poem, *Oto ha-yom* (On That Day, When the Messiah Son of David Will Come), in Ginzberg's *Ginze Schechter,* I, 310; and Joseph Marcus's ed. of *Ginze shirah u-fiyyuṭ* (Liturgical and Secular Poetry of the Foremost Mediaeval Poets), I, 28 f., 128. This is rather a conclusion (*silluq*) of a triumphant description of the glories of the restoration of the Temple services in Jerusalem, beginning with *Aron ha-tiferet* (The Ark of Glory). Following the general assumption of students of Jewish liturgy that Qalir and his confrères merely restated in poetic fashion what had previously been said by a homilist, Ibn Shemuel considers Qalir's description but a repetition of the visions of Elijah and Zerubbabel, although he admits that the poem reveals some significant deviations and omissions. But the absence of any reference to an Arab threat to Byzantine Palestine would be truly amazing if the poet had become familiar with the imagery of the book of Zerubbabel only after 636. However, as we shall see, the basic assumption of the poets' exclusive indebtedness to homilists may have to be revised and the former given much more credit for independent hermeneutic derivations from Scripture, as well as visions of their own. Cf. *infra,* Chap. XXXI.

15. Amittai ben Shefaṭiah's poem, *Ekh mi-kol ha-ummot* (How from All Nations), reprinted in B. Klar's ed. of *Megillat Aḥimaaṣ* (The Chronicle of Aḥimaaz), pp. 113, 135 (the same messianic theme, in its numerous variations, appears also in several other litanies of that early European author; cf. *infra,* Chap. XXXII); *Ibn* Gabirol's poems, *Shelaḥ minzar* (Send the Prince), *Shenotenu safu* (Our Years Have Drifted Away), *Shekhulah akhulah* (Bereaved and Devoured), and *Shoresh beno Yishshai* (Scion of Jesse's Son), in his *Shire,* ed. by H. N. Bialik and J. H. Rawnitzky, III, 7 No. 5, 11 No. 9, 28 f. No. 22, 33 No. 25; and his *Selected Religious Poems,* ed. by I. Davidson, with an English trans. by I. Zangwill, pp. 23 f., 71. In some of these liturgical pieces Ibn Gabirol showed considerable indebtedness to the apocalyptic writings. For instance, in his *Be-ṭal aṣur* (With Stored-Up Dew, in *Shire,* III, 124 ff. No. 94), he enumerated, like Qalir, the blessings provided for each month and foretold the redemption to come, not in the usual month of Nissan, but in Shebat, as did the author of the "Book of Elijah" (in Jellinek's *Bet ha-Midrasch,* III, 66; in Ibn Shemuel's *Midreshe,* p. 45). Many of these poems by Gabirol and Halevi, as well as statements by Bible commentators, are quoted by J. Sarachek in *The Doctrine of the Messiah in Medieval Jewish Literature.* Although not always precise in his quotations (for instance, in Ibn Gabirol's poem, cited p. 73) and almost wholly devoid of interpretation, this volume offers a useful collection of materials for the messianic theme.

In his poem, *Shebiyah 'aniyah* (Miserable Captive, in *Shire,* III, 5 No. 4), Ibn Gabirol compared the situation of the Jewish people to a ship grounded in a swamp, with no one to help pull it out. Halevi, too, drew a parallel between Israel and "a pilotless ship abandoned on high seas." Cf. his poem *Ekhah kelilat yofi* (How an Accomplished Beauty) in his *Kol Shire* (Collected Poems), ed. by Zemorah, III, Part 8, p. 332; and his *Selected Poems,* ed. by H. Brody with an English trans. by N. Salaman, p. 104. Cf. also his *So'arah 'aniyah* (Bewildered and Poor), ed. by Zemorah, p. 388, which referred to Israel as a sunken ship to be rescued by Elijah and the Messiah. This image is perhaps unconsciously derived from the ancient Jewish and Christian symbolism of the Jewish people, or the Church, plying its course toward the messianic goal in defiance of the Roman Empire's ship of state. Cf. E. Peterson's brief data on "Das Schiff als Symbol der Kirche: die Tat des Messias im eschatologischen Meeressturm in der jüdischen und altchristlichen Ueberlieferung," *TZ,* VI, 77–79; and K. Goldammer's observations thereon, "Des Schiff der Kirche. Ein antiker Symbolbegriff aus der politischen Metaphysik in eschatologischer und ekklesiologischer Umdeutung," *ibid.,* pp. 232–37. See also, more generally, K. Dreyer's data on *Die religiöse Gedankenwelt des Salomo ibn Gabirol,* esp. pp. 50 ff.

16. Ibn Gabirol's aforementioned poem, *Shoresh beno Yishshai.* Cf. Davidson's remark in his ed., p. 131 n. 37; E. Bertola's more recent Italian biography of *Salomon ibn Gabirol* (*Avicebron*), pp. 13 f.; *supra,* Chap. XVIII, nn. 5–6. Writing in the midst of the constant wars among the "petty princes" and at the inception of the great crusading movement, which already in the 1060's engulfed some Spanish communities (these were spared much grief by Pope Alexander II's intervention, see *supra,* Chap. XXI, n. 4), Ibn Gabirol nevertheless expected Israel's redemption to be attained by peaceable means. In an imaginary trialogue between the synagogue reader, the congregation, and God, the poet makes the reader urge the congregation to "Sow charity, and kindness shall be carted, / Who trusts in force is

ignorantly dreaming. / Oppression passes, trampled by oppression, / And violence breeds violent succession." Perhaps the meaning of the last verse is better reproduced by "He who loves violence, shall have no succession." But apparently a few words are missing here; perhaps they were omitted by a copyist fearing Gentile reprisals. Cf. the poem, *Shezufah nezufah* (Tarnished and Scolded), in *Shire,* III, 13 No. 10 (with the note thereon, *ibid.,* IV, 8); in Zangwill's trans., pp. 25 ff. No. 19.

17. Halevi's poems, *Ototenu hitmahmehu* (Our Portents Linger), and *Ya'avor 'alai reṣonkha* (May Thy Grace Pass Over Me), in *Kol Shire,* III, Part 8, p. 381; Part 7, p. 276; in *Selected Poems,* pp. 136 ff., 109. Cf. also various other editions, including the additions to the former poem by a later lyricist, in I. Davidson's *Oṣar ha-shirah,* I, 97 No. 2077; II, 401 No. 3117. Although writing considerably after Ibn Gabirol, Halevi, too, occasionally reflected the hope and the millennary disillusionment of the previous generation. In a poem *Yonati lailah* (My Dove . . . at Night), he complained, "She has counted a thousand [years], and her yoke still rests upon her." In *Yonat reḥoqim* (A Dove Afar, echoing Ps. 56:1), he described the fluttering dove of Israel, seeking relief from her beloved. "She deemed a thousand years the limit of her appointed time, / But now she is ashamed of all her reckonings." *Kol Shire,* III, Part 7, p. 222; Part 9, p. 527; *Selected Poems,* p. 118.

Moses ibn Ezra often addressed his liturgical poems to the worshipers, rather than to God. For example, in a lengthy poem exhorting the deaf, the thoughtless, and the blind of Israel, he includes the admonition "Ye blind, before your God stand prayerfulwise, / Seeking redemption." Cf. his *Ha-ḥershim shime'u* (Ye Deaf, Hear), lines 89 ff., in *Selected Poems,* ed. by H. Brody with an English trans. by S. Solis-Cohen, p. 163. Abraham ibn Ezra, too, composed merely several standardized *ge'ulahs* and petitions for the restoration of the Jewish people. The pious ending, however, of his aforementioned litany on the destruction of several Spanish and North African communities apparently stems from a later hand. See also *supra,* Chaps. XVIII, n. 6; XXI, n. 54.

18. Pseudo-Saadiah's *Commentary* on Canticles, reprinted in Lewin's *Otzar ha-gaonim,* VI, Part 2, pp. 70–72 (on Sukkah 52b); and by Ibn Shemuel, pp. 129 f. Although Saadiah was a fairly common name among the Near Eastern Jews of that period, later copyists and readers felt doubly prompted to ascribe his work to the author's famous namesake, as many mystical-messianic interpretations were included in the gaon's genuine commentary on Daniel, of which only portions are available in print. Cf. *infra,* n. 21. But here many legendary features are missing. Cf. also A. F. Gallé's French trans. of *Daniel avec commentaires de R. Saadia, Aben-Ezra, Raschi, etc. et variantes de versions arabe et syriaque;* and H. Malter's *Saadia Gaon,* pp. 321 ff. Incidentally, some messianic interpretations current among the medieval Bible commentators were derived from the older Aramaic translations of Scripture, especially the Palestinian Targum, with its plethora of aggadic elaborations. Cf. *infra,* Chap. XXIX. On the other hand, in his "Lc 2^{49} and Targum Yerushalmi," *ZNW,* XLV, 145–79, P. Winter pointed out that the Targum's rendition of Exod. 15:2 should warn the reader against giving that passage in the Gospel a christological interpretation.

19. Cf. Rashi's Commentaries on the respective passages; and his *Teshubot,* p. 16 No. 21, with reference to Megillah 12a; Rashi's Commentary thereon *s.v. Qobel;*

and *supra,* n. 8. The computation of 1352 for the advent of the Messiah was supported also by Rashi's interpretation of Dan. 8:14, although in his Commentary on Sanhedrin 97b, *s.v. Va-tashkemo,* he interpreted the psalmist's complaint "And given them tears to drink in large measure [*shalish*]" (80:6) as meaning that the exile under Edom would have three times the combined duration of the 400-year sojourn in Egypt and the 70-year Babylonian Exile, or 1410 years in all. Hence the Messiah was due to arrive in 1478. (The concluding phrase in this passage, "They [these years] have already passed and it did not happen, I have thus found written in the name of R. Samuel bar David," is an interesting example of an insertion by a copyist, possibly referring to a remark made as late as in the seventeenth century by Samuel bar David Moses ha-Levi, author of the well-known legal formulary, *Naḥalat Shibe'ah.* Its deletion was already suggested by Elijah Gaon of Vilna in his gloss on that comment by Rashi.) In his immediately preceding explanation, however, Rashi himself interpreted Daniel's prediction of "a time and times and half a time", as meaning three and a half times 400 years, that is that the redemption was to be expected in 1468. Cf. also S. Sarachek's *Doctrine,* pp. 59 f. By these contradictory statements Rashi obviously wished to impress upon his readers that, although computations of the end of days were not necessarily to be shunned, they would have to choose among many plausible alternatives suggested by the ancient rabbis. In any case, all these dates were still some three or four centuries away. Hence Rashi's contemporaries and immediate successors need not be seriously concerned about establishing the precise moment in history when God would sound the clarion call to their freedom.

20. Ibn Ezra's and Qimḥi's Commentaries on the respective passages (especially M. Friedlaender's ed. of *The Commentary of Ibn Ezra on Isaiah,* III, 64, 98, 104); *The Arabic Commentary of Yefet ben 'Ali the Karaite on the Book of Hosea,* ed. by P. Birnbaum, pp. xlviii f., 26 f.; and *The Commentary of Rabbi David Kimhi on Hosea,* ed. by H. Cohen, p. 17 (quoting Targum Jonathan). The compilation *Sharkh al-'atidot* (Explanation of the Future) was found among the Leningrad manuscripts by A. Neubauer. Cf. his brief communication in *JA,* 6th ser., V, 549; and his *Aus der Petersburger Bibliothek,* p. 7 n. 1, where he also refers to similar messianic interpretations by Jephet's Karaite predecessors, Benjamin Nahawendi and Salmon ben Yeruḥim. At the same time Jephet himself sharply repudiated the idea that one could compute the date of the Messiah's arrival. Cf. his *Commentary* on Dan. 12:9, ed. and trans. by D. S. Margoliouth, pp. 146 ff. (Arabic), 81 ff. (English). Cf. *infra,* Chap. XXVI, n. 41; and, more generally, W. J. de Wilde's dissertation, *De messiaansche Opvattingen der middeleeuwsche Exegeten Rasji, Aben Ezra en Kimchi* (The Messianic Conceptions of the Medieval Exegetes Rashi, Ibn Ezra and Qimḥi; with special reference to their commentaries on Isaiah). This volume includes both a systematic analysis of messianic concepts and translations into Dutch of many relevant statements by these three commentators and others.

21. Saadiah's *Beliefs and Opinions,* VIII, esp. 3, 5–6, pp. 234 ff. (Arabic), 120 ff. (Hebrew), 299 ff. (English); and especially his Commentary on Dan. 8:14, 11:2, in the excerpts published from a Bodleian MS by S. Poznanski in *MGWJ,* XLIV, 415 f., 511 f. So popular was this chapter of Saadiah's philosophic work that a Hebrew paraphrase thereof was often reprinted separately under the title *Sefer ha-Pedut ve-ha-purqan* (Book of Redemption). See the bibliographical data, supplied by H.

Malter in his *Saadia Gaon,* pp. 367 ff.; with the Hebrew supplements thereto by I. Werfel in *Rav Saadya Gaon,* ed. by Fishman, pp. 652 f. The sources of many of these views may be found in the aforementioned ancient and medieval writings, including the peroration in *Pesiqta rabbati* cited *infra,* Chap. XXVIII, n. 14. Cf. also L. Thorn's dissertation, *Das Problem der Eschatologie und der transzendenten Vergeltung bei Saadia ben Josef aus Fayum;* M. N. Zobel's summary, in the light of views held by Saadiah's predecessors and successors, of "The Computation of the End and Description of Redemption in the Book of Beliefs and Opinions" (Hebrew) in *Rav Saadya Gaon,* pp. 172–90; and A. Marmorstein's analysis of "The Doctrine of Redemption in Saadya's Theological System" in Rosenthal's *Saadya Studies,* pp. 103 ff. Marmorstein points out that the combination of the predestined "end" and "repentance" of the people is found already in IV Ezra (4:35), as well as in some *aggadot.* In view of the gaon's excellent familiarity with such apocryphal works as the *Megillat Bene Ḥashmona'i* and the sources of the *Chronicle of Yeraḥmeel,* he probably also saw IV Ezra. Cf. S. Atlas and M. Perlmann, "Saadia on the Scroll of the Hasmonaeans," *PAAJR,* XIV, 1–23; F. Rosenthal's comments thereon in his "Saadyah's Introduction to the Scroll of the Hasmoneans," *JQR,* XXXVI, 297–302; and *infra,* Chap. XXVIII, n. 44. His attempted computation of the end, a procedure frowned upon already by some ancient sages, called forth a sharp rebuttal by the Karaites, Salmon, Jephet and others. Cf. *supra,* n. 20; and Salmon's *Commentary* on Ps. 102:14 reproduced by Poznanski in *MGWJ,* XLIV, 519 ff.

22. Hai's *resp.,* first published in 1855, was reprinted in Lewin's *Otzar ha-gaonim,* VI, Part 2, pp. 72 ff. No. 194 (on Sukkah 52a); and Ibn Shemuel's *Midreshe,* pp. 135 ff. A slightly different version is reproduced in Abraham bar 'Azriel's *Sefer 'Arugat ha-bosem* (Bed of Spices; a commentary on *piyyuṭim*), ed. by E. E. Urbach, I, 256 ff.; it is provided by the editor with a number of pertinent notes. Remarkably, no serious question of the authenticity of that responsum had been raised by modern scholars, despite the presence of many spurious responsa attributed to Hai and his well-known independence in handling aggadic materials. Cf. *infra,* Chaps. XXVII, n. 131; and XXVIII, n. 29. If our interpretation of the contemporary background should prove correct, it would further support Hai's authorship. On that background, see *supra,* Chap. XIX, n. 11. In answer to a query which seems to have disturbed many contemporaries, namely, why Armilus should be allowed to vanquish and slay the Messiah son of Joseph, both geonim replied that this was a divine device to test the fidelity of the remaining Jews. Many would indeed despair of redemption and abandon their faith, only the staunchest holding out in the desert. This remnant would then be rewarded with the ultimate blessings of the messianic age.

23. Maimonides, *M.T.* Melakhim XII.2. Ibn Gabirol's computation is known to us only through the aforementioned indirect reference in Abraham ibn Ezra's Commentary on Dan. 11:30. Cf. Bar Ḥiyya's *Megillat ha-Megalleh, passim;* his *Sefer Hegyon ha-nefesh* (Contemplation of the Soul), ed. by E. Freimann, fols. 40 ff.; and his letter to Yehudah bar Barzillai published by A. Z. Schwarz in *Schwarz Festschrift,* Hebrew section, pp. 23–36. It was probably this powerful opposition and Bar Ḥiyya's partial retraction that Maimonides had in mind when he wrote of the miscalculation of "one of our keen minds in the province of Andalusia,"

and contended that "every one of our distinguished scholars made little of his declaration, discounted what he did and censured him sharply for it." Cf. his *Epistle to Yemen,* ed. by Halkin, pp. 76 f. (Arabic and Hebrew), xv (English); and the editor's comments in his intro., p. xxv n. 247. One wonders whether Bar Ḥiyya knew of Rashi's proposed alternatives and hoped to blunt the edge of his foes' attack by following that example. Cf. A. Poznanski's intro. to his ed. of Bar Ḥiyya's *Megillat ha-megalleh;* and, more generally, the comprehensive studies by A. H. Silver, *A History of Messianic Speculation in Israel: From the First through the Seventeenth Centuries;* and by J. Sarachek, *The Doctrine of the Messiah.* The general philosophic and scientific context of Bar Ḥiyya's "astrological conception of history" will become clearer *infra,* Chaps. XXXIV and XXXV.

24. Ibn Khaldun's *Muqaddima,* ed. by Quatremère, II, 142 ff., 163; in De Slane's French trans. II, 158 ff., 188; Halevi's *K. al-Khazari,* IV.23, ed. by Hirschfeld, pp. 264 ff. (English, pp. 226 f.), evidently based on the parable in Pesaḥim 87b; Maimonides' *Commentary* on M. Sanhedrin x, Intro., Principle XII, ed. by J. Holzer, pp. 28 f.; and his *M.T.* Melakhim XI.3–4. The latter text, frequently subjected to deletions by censors, is best preserved in a quotation by Naḥmanides in his *Derashah* (Dissertation über die Vorzüge der Mosaischen Lehre), ed. by A. Jellinek, p. 5. Cf. D. Cassel's note in his ed. of the Hebrew trans. of Halevi's philosophic tract, p. 343 n. 2. The Maimonidean view that the "false" messiahs of the other faiths nevertheless paved the way for the arrival of the final and true Redeemer is not controverted by his occasional outbursts against Christian trinitarianism which, in accordance with an opinion widely held in Muslim lands, closely approximated a polytheist doctrine. Cf. especially Maimonides' *Epistle to Yemen,* ed. by Halkin, pp. 92 ff.; the editor's notes thereon and in his introduction, p. xiv; and my remarks in *PAAJR,* VI, 71 n. 139. On the messianic idea in Islam and the Jewish influence thereon, cf. I. Friedlaender's essay and other literature mentioned *supra,* n. 10.

25. Maimonides, *Epistle to Yemen,* pp. 64 ff., 80 ff. (Arabic and Hebrew); xii ff., xv f. (English). Cf. Halkin's intro. thereto, pp. xii f., upholding the authenticity of that passage. We must note, however, the difference between Saadiah's confident assertion and Maimonides' communication of the family tradition out of a sense of duty. He clearly intimated his own doubts by concluding that paragraph with a pious shrug: "But God knows best what is true." Even that was too much for a critical historian like the sixteenth-century Mantuan, Azariah de' Rossi, who used for Maimonides the same expostulation the latter had employed in behalf of Saadiah. Cf. De' Rossi's *Me'or eynayim* (Light of the Eyes), section *Imre binah,* XLIII, ed. by D. Cassel, pp. 367 ff., 375 f. That this problem was not purely academic at any time may be seen from my comments on "Azariah de' Rossi's Attitude to Life," *Abrahams Mem. Vol.,* pp. 30 f.

26. Saadiah's *Beliefs and Opinions,* VIII.6, pp. 241 ff. (Arabic), 123 ff. (Hebrew), 304 ff. (English); Maimonides *M.T.* Melakhim XII.1, 4–5; his *Guide,* III.11, in Friedlaender's trans., p. 267; Abraham Maimuni's *Milḥamot,* in Maimonides' *Qobeṣ,* III, fol. 16b. Without being quite so outspoken, the elder Maimonides, too, interpreted away even the biblical descriptions of the messianic glories as mere allegory.

This moderation was wholly in line with his general biblical exegesis aimed at reconciling the biblical text with the demands of reason. Cf. *infra,* Chaps. XXIX, nn. 85–86; and XXXIV.

27. Saadiah, *loc. cit.;* Maimonides' *Commentary* on M. Sanhedrin, x (Ḥeleq), ed. by J. Holzer, pp. 1 ff., 18, 28 f. (the five opinions here controverted did not represent five historical schools of thought); 1.3, ed. by M. Weisz, p. 4, annotated p. 11 nn. 14, 14a; his "Treatise on Resurrection," ed. by Finkel, p. 18; his letter to Ibn Jabir in *Qobeṣ teshubot,* II, fol. 16bc; and his Credo, Art. XII–XIII. On the Covenant of 'Umar, cf. *supra,* Chap. XVIII, n. 12; and on Maimonides' attitude toward music *infra,* Chap. XXXI. It should also be noted that, long before Maimonides, Ḥananel ben Ḥushiel of Kairuwan had declared the messianic hope to be a cardinal principle (one of four) in Judaism. See his *Migdal Ḥanan'el* (Ḥananel's Tower; fragments from various commentaries), ed. by D. Z. Hoffmann, p. 35 (on Exod. 14:31).

A similar dichotomy may be observed among the other medieval thinkers. Ibn Daud's aloofness from the messianic theme in his "Exalted Faith" contrasted with Joseph ibn Ṣaddiq's encyclopedic compendium which dealt rather extensively with the messianic problem in philosophic terms. Joseph believed that, on the arrival of the redeemer, the pious Jews, and they alone, would be restored to a blissful life, while the revived bodies of the wicked would be made to burn anew. The bliss of the righteous, however, would consist in no earthly enjoyments, but merely in their basking in the divine light. Cf. his *'Olam qaṭan,* IV, ed. by Horovitz, pp. 59 ff. The absence of pertinent discussions in Maimonides' and Ibn Daud's major philosophic works was neither the result of hidden doubts, however, nor intended to arouse such doubts in the minds of readers between the lines. The general context of these works called for no more special consideration of this problem than did many other topics carefully analyzed in the ultrapietistic works by Baḥya and Abraham Maimuni. Of course, a fuller understanding of the interrelated doctrines of the messianic redemption, resurrection of the dead, and life in the Hereafter in the outlook of the medieval Jewish philosophers can only be secured by a consideration of their general philosophic theories, including their crucial teachings concerning prophecy and miracles. Cf. *infra,* Chap. XXXIV.

28. 'A.Z. 9b (with Ḥananel's, Rashi's and the Tosafists' comments); Sanhedrin 97b; Ibn Shemuel's intro. to his *Midreshe ge'ulah,* pp. 44 ff. As here pointed out, there were also computations based upon the duration of the First and Second Temples of 410 and 420 years respectively, according to the accepted chronology of *Seder 'olam rabbah.* Assuming that the Exile could not last longer than either era of freedom, some Jews expected the Messiah to arrive on or before 478 or 488. All these dates fell within the 85th jubilee cycle. We recall that the then regnant Christian chronology, too, by setting the birth of Jesus at approximately 5,500 A.M., postulated the end of the world at the end of the sixth millennium, that is about 500 C.E. See Hippolytus' *Commentary* on Daniel, Fragments IV–VI, in *PG,* X, 645 ff.; and *supra,* Chap. XVI, n. 15. Cf. also *infra,* Chap. XXXV.

29. Socrates Scholasticus, *Historia ecclesiastica,* VII.38, ed. with a Latin trans. by R. Hussey, II, 822 ff. (taken over verbatim into the *Historia ecclesiastica tripartita,* compiled from Socrates, Sozomenus, and Theodoret by Cassiodorus or

Epiphanius, XII.9, ed. by W. Jacob and revised by R. Hanslik, pp. 677 f.). Understandably, the Christian chronicler seized this opportunity to heap ridicule on Jewish gullibility, and he claimed that all survivors accepted baptism. Hence, some verification from an independent and more impartial source would be doubly welcome.

30. H. Z. Hirschberg's "Messianic Vestiges in Arabia during the Fifth and Sixth Centuries after the Fall of Jerusalem" (Hebrew), *Vienna Mem. Vol.*, pp. 112–24; and his *Yisrael ba-'Arab*, pp. 175 ff. These messianic expectations were, of course, but part of the much-debated impact upon the rise of Islam of Judaism, Christianity, and the various syncretistic Judeo-Christian trends discussed *supra*, Chap. XVII, n. 15. Despite the availability of considerable monographic literature (see *supra*, n. 10), a careful reexamination of the similarities of and the divergences between the Jewish, Christian, and Muslim messianic teachings, as reflected not only in the recognized theological works, but also in the more obscure domains of folklore, still is likely to prove rewarding. According to Ta'labi, for instance, a Muslim legend, current in the eleventh century or earlier, attributed to a young Jew, Baluqiya, a role resembling that of Moses and Mohammed. He was supposed to traverse the world's seven lands and seven seas in search of the miraculous spring which had allegedly enabled Alexander (Du'l Qarnayim) to survive to the days of Mohammed. Baluqiya thus hoped to await the ultimate day when all men would worship the true God. See M. Asín Palacios's data in *La Escatologia musulmana en la Divina Comedia*, pp. 315 f.

31. The story of the Samaritan uprisings and their repression by the government has long been known from the descriptions of such Byzantine contemporaries as Procopius and Malalas, and from the ever more stringent anti-Samaritan legislation, included in the codification of Justinian, esp. his *Codex*, I.5.17–18, 21, ed. by Krüger, pp. 56 ff.; and his *Novellae*, Nos. 129 and 144, ed. by Schoell and Kroll, pp. 647 ff., 709 ff. Further details have been supplied by such later Byzantine historians as Theophanes, and particularly by the Samaritan chroniclers themselves. Although these compilations date from a much later age and are even more heavily overlaid with legendary embellishments than are the Byzantine narratives, they furnish both new data and better insights into the factors underlying these desperate attempts. These reports in the so-called Book of Joshua, the chronicle of Abu'l Fatḥ, and the anonymous chronicles ed. by A. Neubauer, and by E. N. Adler and M. Séligsohn, respectively (see below and *supra*, Vol. II, p. 339 nn. 34–35) have been frequently analyzed, and need not be repeated here. According to Séligsohn (*REJ*, XLIV, 190) the Paris MS of Abu'l Fatḥ's chronicle continues to the year 933 C.E., whereas Vilmar's ed. stops at about 800. Cf. especially J. A. Montgomery's summary in *The Samaritans*, pp. 110 ff.; and S. Krauss's *Studien zur byzantinisch-jüdischen Geschichte*, pp. 1 ff. Cf. also *supra*, Vol. II, pp. 27 ff.; Chap. XVI, particularly n. 71; and A. M. Schneider's "Römische und byzantinische Bauten auf dem Garizim," *Beiträge zur biblischen Landes- und Altertumskunde* (*ZDPV*), LXVIII, 211–34.

The problem of the Samaritan Temple on Gerizim still awaits elucidation, however. Destroyed by John Hyrcanus, it (or perhaps another sanctuary) was rebuilt by Baba Rabbah according to Abu'l Fatḥ's *K. at-Tarikh* (Annales Samaritani, ed. by E. Vilmar, pp. 130 ff.) and "Une nouvelle chronique samaritaine," ed. by Adler and Séligsohn in *REJ*, XLV, 90 f. The existence of such a sanctuary is confirmed by

Chronicon Paschale, ed. by L. Dindorf, I, 603 (the author calls it a "synagogue"), but denied outright by Procopius, in *De aedificiis,* v.7, in his *Works,* ed. by H. B. Dewing and G. Downey, VII, 348 ff. A native of Caesarea during that period and generally a fairly reliable reporter, Procopius may perhaps be given most credence. Some of these contradictions, which have long puzzled scholars, disappear if we assume with A. Reifenberg that they refer to two different buildings, a temple and an altar, erected by the Samaritans on two different peaks of Mt. Gerizim. Only the latter still existed and was destroyed under Zeno. Cf. the data, supported by two coins and aerial photography, in Reifenberg's "Mount Gerizim" (Hebrew), *Eretz Israel,* I, 74–76. Similarly divergent are the reports on the date of the uprising under Justus. The Samaritan chroniclers place it under Emperor Martian (450–57), the *Chronicon Paschale* in 484, and Procopius (inferentially) in 490. The latter two dates may perhaps be reconciled by the assumption that the revolt was not finally suppressed until the end of Zeno's regime, to break out again under his successor.

32. Al-Baladhuri's *Futûḥ al-Buldân,* ed. De Goeje, p. 141 (in Hitti's English trans., I, 217); Abu'l Fatḥ's *K. at-Tarikh,* pp. 179 ff.; Ya'qubi's *K. al-Buldān* in G. LeStrange's English trans. in his *Palestine under the Moslems,* p. 303; A. Neubauer's ed. of "Chronique samaritaine" in *JA,* 6th ser., XIV, 405 ff. (text), 443 ff. (trans.); Adler and Séligsohn's ed. of "Une nouvelle chronique samaritaine" in *REJ,* XLV, 253; Benjamin's *Massa'ot,* ed. by Adler, p. 22 (English trans. p. 20). Cf. E. Mittwoch, "Mulimische Fetwas über die Samaritaner," *OLZ,* XXIX, 845–49 (although written in 1670 and later, these responsa of Muslim jurists reflect the well-established policy of treating Samaritans as Jews); B. Z. Segal, "On the History of the Jewish Settlement in Ramleh" (Hebrew), *Ṣiyyon,* V, 13 f., 17; Mann, *Jews in Egypt,* I, 18 n. 2. "The Alleged Samaritan Influence on Mohammed and Islam," postulated by M. Gaster, is rightly denied by D. Künstlinger in his Polish essay on the subject in *Rocznik orientalistyczny,* III, 269–75 (with a French summary, p. 345). The number of Samaritans in Caesarea in the 630's is raised to 80,000, while that of Jews is lowered to 100,000, in Yaqut's quotation from Yazid ibn Samara. Cf. *Sefer ha-Yishub,* II, 54 ff. The absence from this volume of any recorded entry under "Schechem" indicates that, even before the Crusaders' ravages, there were few if any permanent Jewish settlers in the city. M. Benayahu's "Documents to the History of the Jewish Settlement in Schechem" (Hebrew), *Sinai,* XIX, No. 227, pp. 102–14, belong to a later period.

In view of the great paucity of extant sources, however, one must often refer not only to later sources but also to events recorded in the thirteenth century and after in order to shed some light on conditions in the High Middle Ages as well. During the Mongolian siege of Jerusalem in 1260, for example, we are told, many Jews escaped to Nablus, but most of these refugees probably returned to the Holy City in 1267–68 at Naḥmanides' prompting. Cf. his letter to his son in A. Yaari's *Iggerot Ereṣ-Yisrael,* p. 85. Some Samaritan converts to Islam, like their Jewish counterparts, achieved high positions in government service. Abu'l Ḥasan ibn abi Sa'id even became vizier, although after one of the then frequent turns in political fortunes he was executed in 1251. See Jacob ben 'Uzzi ha-Kohen's brief biographical sketches of twenty-five Samaritan scholars of various periods in his "Old-Time Samaritans and the Arabic Works of their Scholars" (Hebrew), *Keneset,* IV, 321 ff. See also, in general, J. A. Montgomery's *Samaritans,* pp. 125 ff.; I. Ben-Zvi's *Sefer ha-Shomeronim,* pp. 29 ff.; and other literature cited *supra,* Vol. II, pp. 339 ff.;

and in L. A. Mayer's "Outline of a Bibliography of the Samaritans" (Hebrew), *Eretz Yisrael,* IV, pp. 252–68.

33. Qirqisani's *Kitab al-Anwar* (Book of Lights and Watchtowers), I.5, ed. by L. Nemoy, I, 40 f.; and in the excerpt translated by Nemoy into English in "Al-Qirqisani's Account of the Jewish Sects and Christianity," *HUCA,* VII, 362 f.; M. Gaster, "Die 613 Gebote und Verbote der Samaritaner," *Festschrift . . . des Jüdisch-Theologischen Seminars Fraenckelscher Stiftung* (Breslau), II, 393–404 (German), 35–67 (Hebrew); Maimonides' *Commentary* on M. Berakhot VIII.8, ed. by E. Weill, pp. 31 f. On the Jewish computation of the 613 commandments and their controversial formulation among the leading medieval rabbis, see *infra,* Chap. XXVII, nn. 103 ff. In their observance of biblical laws of purity the Samaritans exceeded even the equally rigid Karaites. Cf. P. R. Weis's "Abu'l Ḥasan Al-Ṣūri's Discourse on the Rules of Leprosy in the Kitab al-Tabākh," *BJRL,* XXXIII, 131–37 (on the basis of a John Rylands MS). The total excommunication of Samaritans, allegedly proclaimed by Ezra in the presence of 300 priests, 300 children, and 300 scrolls of law and with the accompaniment of 300 trumpets, is recorded in *Tanḥuma* on Va-Yesheb, II end; and *Pirqe de-R. Eliezer,* XXXVII [XXXVIII], ed. by Higger in *Horeb,* X, 214 (in G. Friedlander's English trans., p. 301; some texts omit the 300 children). To be sure, both these compilations date from the early Muslim period, and in "Les Dosithéens dans le Midrasch," *REJ,* XLIII, 51 ff., A. Büchler has argued for the origin of this ban in the geonic age. However, one would be at a loss in explaining the outburst of such extreme enmity soon after 640, whereas the bloodthirstiness of the internecine struggles in Palestine during the last century before the Muslim conquest would much better account for this sharp separation. Cf. also the tractate *Kutim,* II.7–8 in M. Higger's *Sheva masekhtot,* pp. 66 f. (English trans., p. 46); J. Starr's remarks in *JPOS,* XV, 282, 291 f.; my comments in *PAAJR,* VI, 58 n. 116; and, on Saadiah's eloquent silence, A. S. Halkin, "The Relation of the Samaritans to Saadiah Gaon," *Saadiah Anniv. Vol.,* pp. 271 ff.

34. Cf. Qirqisani's *K. al-Anwar,* I.5, 16, ed. by Nemoy, I, 40 f., 57 (in English trans., *HUCA,* VII, 362 f. 289); the theologico-polemical work ed. by Mann in *HUCA,* XII–XIII, 436; A. S. Halkin's "Samaritan Polemics against the Jews," *PAAJR,* VII, 40 ff., 57 f. (text); and J. Jeremias, *Die Passahfeier der Samaritaner.* On the date of Abu'l Ḥasan, left open by Halkin (in *PAAJR,* VII, 18 f.), cf. P. R. Weis's observations in his "Abu'l-Ḥasan al-Ṣūri's Discourse on the Calendar in the Kitab al-Tabakh," *BJRL,* XXX, 156 ("existed sometime between the years 995–1130 and wrote his book about the middle of the eleventh century"; the date 1130–40 given on p. 154 is evidently a misprint for 1030–40). Baladhuri likewise divides the Samaritans into *ad-Dustan* (Dositheans) and *al-Kushan* (Cutheans). Cf. his *Futûḥ,* I, 158 (English trans., p. 244). He is followed therein by Mas'udi and Shahrastani (1086–1153); the latter writes about the *Dusitaniya* in terms of a still existing schism, which insisted on reward and punishment only in this world, while the *Kusaniya* believed in the Hereafter. See his *K. al-Milal,* ed. by Cureton, pp. 170 f. (in Haarbrücker's German trans., pp. 257 ff.). But it is possible that this distinguished student of comparative religion merely quoted here a literary source, rather than contemporary testimony. Cf. also Montgomery's more general data in *The Samaritans,* pp. 252 ff. Qirqisani counts Malik among Jewish sectarians. That he was a Samaritan, however, seems evident not only from his denunciation of Jerusalem, which the

Karaite student of religion dismissed uncomprehendingly as "the action of a stupid person," but also from his origin in Ramleh with its strong Samaritan community (see Ya'qubi's statement antedating Qirqisani's by half a century, cited *supra,* n. 32). Generally, Qirqisani seems to know of Samaritans only from heresay. Of course, Samaritans as a rule avoided Jerusalem. According to another Karaite, Salmon ben Yeruḥim, they declared every Samaritan visitor there impure for seven days. See his *Commentary* on Lam. 1:13.

From 1832 on, the Samaritans seem to have regularly performed their rites at Gerizim, though apparently not in the original location. See Montgomery's *Samaritans,* pp. 37 f., 140 f., 234 ff. Their Passover celebration, particularly, has attracted tourists for many generations. It has been described at length in numerous traveloques and, more recently, by the Samaritan priest, Jacob ben 'Uzzi, in his *Qorban ha-peṣaḥ eṣel ha-Shomeronim* (The Celebration of Passover by the Samaritans; has appeared in both Hebrew and English).

35. The names of two Samaritan high-priests of 1048–49 (Eleazar) and 1205–6 (Ittamar ben Amram) have become known through two inscriptions analyzed by Z. Ben-Hayyim and I. Ben-Zvi in *BJPES,* XII, 74–82, 82–84. Cf. also Ben-Zvi's earlier data on "A Samaritan Inscription of the 5th Century A.H." (Hebrew), *Qobeṣ* (Journal) of the Jewish Palestine Exploration Society, I, 108–12 (dated 1038–39, it relates to a Samaritan synagogue, probably of Be'r Ya'kov and mentions the high-priest Eleazar ben Aaron). On the red heifer, see the addition to Abu'l Fatḥ's chronicle trans. from a MS by M. Gaster in his *Samaritan Oral Law,* I, 195 f.; and the reply given by the priest 'Abd Ḥasda, in 1937, to Gaster's detailed questionnaire concerning the "Rites and Beliefs of the Samaritans Relating to Death and Mourning," ed. by T. H. Gaster, in *JPOS,* XIX, 193 (Question v).

Little information is as yet available about the medieval Samaritan synagogues, but much may be reconstructed from their modern houses of worship, whose architectural and liturgical forms are carefully reviewed by I. Ben-Zvi in his Hebrew study of "Samaritan Treasures" in *Sinai,* V–VII (Vols. IX–XIV), esp. V, Nos. 51–56, pp. 323–33; and Nos. 57–62, pp. 100–106, 215–22. Apart from their intrinsic significance for the Samaritan religion, these synagogues, rather than cemeteries, have been the main locale of Samaritan inscriptions discovered over the years. These have been of interest not only to students of Samaritan history, but also to biblical scholars. Certainly, the inscriptions reproducing the Ten Commandments have added some significant textual variants to those preserved in the Samaritan Hexateuch or reconstructed from the Samaritan Arabic version. On the other hand, not all the variants represent genuine deviations from the Masoretic text. At times the Decalogue inscriptions differ not only from the Samariticum, but also among themselves to such an extent that they cannot be explained by diversity of underlying traditions. Many alterations, especially the abridgment of certain individual commandments, seem to have been dictated by such prosaic causes as spatial limitations in generally small buildings. In addition to the texts listed *supra,* Vol. II, p. 339 nn. 34–35, see in particular J. Bowman's analysis of "The Leeds Samaritan Decalogue Inscription," *Proceedings* of the Leeds Philosophical-Literary Society, VI, 567–75 (mentioning also two other inscriptions he saw at the Palestine Museum in old Jerusalem and at Bir Ya'qub [B'er Ya'kov], each containing fresh variants, pp. 573 ff.); and I. Ben-Zvi's even more recent find of "A Samaritan Inscription" at Kefar Bilu near Rehovoth, which he published and analyzed in Hebrew in *BIES*

(*BJPES*), XVIII, 223–29. All these inscriptions seem to date from Byzantine times, although the general conservatism characterizing sacred epigraphy in all fields may have induced the writers to follow closely the older patterns for centuries after these had become hallowed by usage. On the textual divergences, see also A. Alt's pertinent observations in his note, "Zu den samaritanischen Dekaloginschriften," *VT,* II, 273–76 (listing also other publications).

36. Munajja, quoted by Halkin in *Saadia Anniv. Vol.,* pp. 204 f.; Abu'l Ḥasan cited by him in *PAAJR,* VII, 50 f. (with reference to Lev. 22:24); S. J. Miller's introduction to his edition of *The Samaritan Molad Mosheh,* pp. 26 ff. One ought not to dismiss lightly the varying influences of the Muslim environment even on such intimate and tenacious forms of religious life as the synagogue liturgy. Just as the Jews yielded to environmental pressures in regard to ablutions, and the like, so did the Samaritans adopt the verse "For I call upon the name of the Lord" as the stereotyped opening for all their prayers. This was a clear emulation of the Arabic *bismillah,* much as its Qur'anic prototype may have been indebted to still older Jewish models. Cf. M. Gaster's *Samaritan Oral Law,* I, 59, 72. Similarly, in his inscription of 1205–6, high-priest Ittamar ben Amram writes, "The Lord is One and Only and Moses ben Amram is his servant"—clearly but a variant of the Muslim credo. Cf. Ben-Zvi's reading in *BJPES,* XII, 82 ff.

37. *Asatir,* XII.24–26, ed. by Gaster, pp. 52 f. (Samaritan), 318 ff. (English), with Gaster's comments thereon in his intro., especially pp. 87 ff.; and in Ben-Hayyim's Hebrew translation in *Tarbiz,* XV, 86 (explaining the total of twenty-six princes which corresponds to the total number of prophets since Moses; both series are the numerical equivalent of the Tetragrammaton); A. S. Halkin's ed. of "The Scholia to Numbers and Deuteronomy in the Samaritan-Arabic Pentateuch," *JQR,* XXXIV, 47 (Arabic), 50 f. (English); Epiphanius' *Adversus Haereses,* IX, in *PG,* XLI, 225; and Shahrastani's statement cited *supra,* n. 34. On the medieval, rather than ancient, provenance of *Asatir,* see the debate summarized *supra,* Vol. II, p. 339 n. 35. Going even beyond B. Heller, Ben-Hayyim considers its date as approximating 1000 C.E. A similar absence of far-reaching eschatological expectations connected with the advent of the Samaritan *taheb,* has already been noted by Merx in his monograph mentioned *supra,* n. 6. We must not lose sight, however, of the similar old, though equivocal, Jewish distinction between the "days of the Messiah" and the "World to come"; see *supra,* n. 26. The internal divisions affecting the Samaritan eschatology and the latter's gradual, though reluctant, evolution in the direction of the Jewish doctrines concerning the end of days are succinctly discussed in J. Bowman's "Early Samaritan Eschatology," *JJS,* VI, 63–72.

38. Abu'l Fatḥ's *K. at-Tarikh,* p. 74; Benjamin's *Massa'ot,* pp. 22 (Hebrew), 21 (English); Mann's ed. of the "Theologico-Polemical Work" in *HUCA,* XII–XIII, 437 f., with reference to Deut. 7:7, 28:64. Very likely Benjamin referred to a thousand Samaritan families, rather than souls. Cf. the scanty medieval population data assembled by Ben-Zvi in his *Sefer ha-Shomeronim,* pp. 40 f. Ezra's alleged fabrication of the new Hebrew alphabet for the purpose of enhanced segregation had already been mentioned by Epiphanius in his *De XII gemmis rationalis summi sacerdotis Judaeorum,* LXIII–LXVI, in *PG,* XLIII, 356 ff. (extant only in a Latin trans.). On the Samaritan Hebrew dialect, see the literature, listed *supra,* Vol. II, p. 340

n. 36, to which add the following recent linguistic studies: Fuad Hasanein (Foad Hassanein) Ali, "The Hebrew of the Samaritans," *Bulletin of the University of Egypt,* Faculty of Arts, VI, 55–71 (reprinted 1955); his "Beiträge zur Kenntnis der hebräisch-samaritanischen Sprache, I–II," *ibid.,* VIII, Part 2, pp. 19–37; IX, Part 2, pp. 17–84; Z. Ben-Hayyim, "The Samaritan Tradition and the Use Thereof for the Study of Hebrew and Aramaic" (Hebrew), *Leshonenu,* XVII, 133–38; and "The Samaritan Vowel-System and Its Graphic Representation," *Archiv Orientalni,* XXII, 515–30 (revised and enlarged from his earlier Hebrew study in *Tarbiz,* XX, 215–24). Of considerable interest, theological even more than linguistic, is also Ben-Hayyim's Hebrew essay, "On the Pronunciation of the Tetragrammaton by the Samaritans," *Eretz-Israel,* III, 147–54 (denying the pronunciation according to the spelling and controverting earlier opposing evidence).

Much pertinent linguistic, exegetical, and historical material, however, still is buried in the numerous Samaritan manuscripts scattered in the world's libraries. Although for the most part copied in modern times, many have retained older traditions. The recovery of these old memories from among the vast later accretions has been the main stumbling block in all Samaritan research. Even where catalogued, as in the case of the important collection assembled at the John Rylands Library in Manchester, they leave much room for further exploration. See for instance, T. H. Gaster's review of E. Robertson's *Catalogue* of the Manchester collection in his "Samaritan Manuscripts," *Journal of Jewish Bibliography,* II, 127–38. The much larger Moses Gaster collection, which includes some 300 Samaritan manuscripts, has thus far been utilized almost exclusively by Gaster himself, but should now be available to general research. See the brief communication by N.N., "The Gaster MSS," *BJRL,* XXXVII, 2–6. Needless to say, even dates supplied by the manuscripts themselves have to be taken with considerable skepticism. For one example, the famous Abisha Scroll, which had turned up in the fourteenth century and most of which was almost immediately destroyed by an earthquake, is still believed by many Samaritans to have been written in remote antiquity. Abu'l Fatḥ himself had evinced no doubts about its having been composed by Abisha ha-Kohen, great-grandson of Aaron, in the thirteenth year of the occupation of Canaan by the ancient Israelites. Cf. the modern critiques by F. Pérez Castro, "El Sefer Abiša," *Sefarad,* XIII, 119–29 (with a facsimile of the text of Deut. 5:25–13:19); and P. Kahle, "The Abisha Scroll of the Samaritans," *Studia Orientalia Joanni Pedersen . . . dicata,* pp. 188–92. The early medieval developments in the Samaritan Hebrew language and Bible exegesis will have to be more fully considered in connection with their Jewish counterparts, *infra,* Chaps. XXIX–XXX. Among the numerous Samaritan Bible commentaries we need here but turn the reader's attention to G. Rosen's Columbia University dissertation (in microfilm) containing the text and translation of *The Joseph Cycle (Genesis 37–45) in the Samaritan-Arabic Commentary of Mashalma ibn Murjan.*

39. A. N. Poliak in his well-documented essay on "L'Arabisation de l'Orient sémitique," *Revue des études islamiques,* XII, 55 f.; Mann, *Jews in Egypt,* I, 14 (citing Abu Salih's *Churches and Monasteries in Egypt*); Maimonides' *Responsa,* No. 46 (also pp. 359 ff.). Although it was an Egyptian "Cuthean," whose letter to Scaliger aroused the West's scholarly curiosity and laid the foundation for ever more detailed and careful investigations of this remarkable phenomenon in the

history of religion, most of the attention of both scholars and tourists was rightly concentrated on the district of Nablus.

40. S. Pinsker's *Lickute kadmoniot,* II, 31 f.; *Sha'are teshubah,* Nos. 23, 86, ed. by Leiter, fols., 2d f., 9b; Ibn Daud's *Sefer ha-Qabbalah,* in *MJC,* I, 65. In his *Karaimer* (Karaites: A Medieval Jewish Movement for Deliverance), pp. 57 ff., R. Mahler has assembled many data on the socioeconomic tensions within the Jewish communities of the early Islamic age. He went too far, however, in trying to explain the rise of all sectarian movements, including the Karaite schism, through the deterministic operation of these materialistic factors alone. See also his incisive critique of "Religious Sects and Cultural Trends in Dubnow's Interpretation" (Hebrew), in *Sefer Shime'on Dubnow* (Simon Dubnow in Memoriam: Essays and Letters), ed. by S. Rawidowicz, pp. 89–135 (with asides on Jost, Graetz, and Ahad Haam); and *infra,* Chap. XXVI, n. 14.

41. Qiddushin 49b, 71b. Cf. A. Büchler's aforementioned study of *The Political and Social Leaders . . . of Sepphoris;* and *supra,* Vol. II, pp. 278 f., 405 f. n. 41.

42. In his *Geschichte,* 4th ed., V, 168 f., H. Graetz has pointed to the Jewish refugees from Arabia as a major source of heterodoxy. His view was repudiated by A. E. Harkavy and I. Friedlaender principally because of these refugees' alleged ignorance of rabbinic letters and because most of the recorded names of the heterodox leaders reveal their Persian origin. Cf. *ibid.,* p. 169, n. 1; Friedlaender's "Jewish-Arabic Studies," *JQR,* I, 209 ff.; and *infra,* n. 44. As if paucity of learning had ever been a serious obstacle to heterodox leanings! On the contrary, impatience of uneducated individuals and groups with the formalistic interpretation of authoritative sources of tradition by its learned guardians has often proved a powerful stimulus to sectarian deviations in Judaism and other world religions. Most of the heresiarchs under early Islam, too, were unlearned men. We shall see that some made a virtue out of necessity. Nor does one have to postulate direct origins of a particular sect from among the Jewish refugees from Arabia in order to recognize that the latter's presence amidst the older Jewish communities with their diverse mores and traditions injected another catalyst into the social and spiritual turmoil. The fact that the small surviving North Arabian communities later addressed some inquiries to Sherira and Hai (cf. *Teshubot ha-geonim,* ed. by Harkavy, Nos. 201–3, pp. 94 f. [Arabic], 308 f. [Hebrew]; Ginzberg's *Geonica,* II, 61; and Friedlaender's comments thereon in his "Jews of Arabia and the Gaonate," *JQR,* I, 249–52) proves nothing with respect to the earlier, more turbulent period. Moreover, if the responsum in Harkavy's ed. No. 202, pp. 94 (Arabic), 308 (Hebrew), was also addressed to the Wadi al-Qari, as is indicated in the heading, the Babylonian teachers were evidently disturbed by the inquirers' unfamiliarity with the talmudic laws of inheritance (this "ignorance" may have been dictated by the Arabian tribesman's concern for the preservation of tribal rather than individual property), and took pains to steer them away from the heretical interpretation of "our opponents." The Karaites (cited by Harkavy, p. 392) were not the only sectarians to deny the husband exclusive rights to the estate of his predeceased wife. Cf. also H. Hirschfeld's remarks, hardly controverted by Friedlaender's reply, *JQR,* I, 447 ff.; H. Z. Hirschberg's *Yisrael ba-Arab,* p. 156; and *infra,* nn. 45, 49.

43. J. Mann's "'Chapitres' de Ben Bâboi," *REJ,* LXX, 142; Ginzberg's *Ginze Schechter,* II, 571, paraphrasing an older homily on Ps. 14:1, and Prov. 11:22. Mann is doubtless right in suggesting that this homily stemmed from geonic rather than talmudic times. Similarly medieval, though pre-Karaite, and based upon talmudic concepts doubtless was also an interesting homily on Num. 7:54, recorded in the *Pesiqta rabbati,* III, ed. by Friedmann, fols. 8b f. Koheleth's advice, "And furthermore [*me-hemah*], my son, be admonished: of making many books there is no end" (Eccles. 12:12) is interpreted as a warning to pay heed to the words of the scribes even more than to those of the Torah, for if all the Oral Law were to be written down, there would be no end to books and the ensuing confusion (*mehummah*). In fact, the new insistence on oral law vividly contrasts with most talmudic injunctions on the study of law generally; for instance, in B.B. 78b–79a.

44. Qirqisani's *K. al-Anwar,* I.2.12 ff., ed. by Nemoy, I, 12 ff. (in his English trans., *HUCA,* VII, 328 ff.). Cf. J. Rosenthal's convenient Hebrew summary "On the History of Heterodoxy in the Period of Saadiah," *Horeb,* IX, 21–37, which discusses, however, mainly the contemporary gnostic and dualistic trends. Cf. *supra,* Chap. XXIV, n. 30; and *infra,* Chap. XXIX, nn. 87 ff. We may note that Al-Baqillani, writing about half a century later, still took the 'Isawites with sufficient seriousness to count them among the four principal Jewish sects, together with Rabbanites, 'Ananites, and Samaritans, and to combat some of their arguments. Cf. his *K. aṭ-Ṭamhid,* p. 131; and R. Brunschvig's comments thereon in *Homenaje a Millás,* pp. 226 f. Minor bits of information about these Jewish sects have also been preserved later by Shahrastani. Cf. his *K. al-Milal,* I, 163 ff. (in Haarbrücker's German trans., I, 247 ff.). On the seventy-one sects see *infra,* n. 53. Equally important as these stray items is the general knowledge of the sectarian controversies raging within the Muslim majority which may be derived from these and other Arab students of comparative religion. Cf. H. Ritter's brief survey of the "Muhammedanische Haeresiographien," *Der Islam,* XVIII, 34–55. Of course, the number of Muslim sects and the intensity of their struggles far exceeded anything known in Judaism. According to a Shi'ite tradition, a long list of Muslim sects had already been prepared by the police for Caliph Mahdi (775–87) for guidance in the administration's repressive legislation. These political aspects played a far lesser role in Jewish sectarianism. Nevertheless students of the latter may yet learn a great deal from these internal controversies under both Islam and Christendom.

On the other hand, Jewish influences were often a significant factor in the rise and development of both Muslim and Christian heresies. The early converts K'ab al-Aḥbar and 'Abdallah ibn Salam seem to have been particularly impressive teachers. Wahb ibn Munabbih (died about 732), himself classified as a forbidden historian by the fifteenth-century historian of history, As-Sahawi, claimed that they were "the most learned men of their times, and that he collected what they knew." Cf. F. Rosenthal's trans. in *A History of Muslim Historiography,* p. 265. This is true even if we discount the exaggerations inherent in the epithet "Jew" freely attached to religious opponents. Of the vast modern literature, see esp. W. Thomson's study of "The Character of Early Islamic Sects," *Goldziher Mem. Vol.,* I, 89–116; B. Lewis's "Some Observations on the Significance of Heresy in the History of Islam," *Studia Islamica,* I, 43–63; F. Frade Merino's more comprehensive study of *Sectas y movimientos de reforma en el Islam;* as well as, mainly on the

Western evolution, S. Luciano's bibliographical survey of "Studi recenti sulle eresie medievali (1939–1952)," *Rivista storica italiana,* LXIV, 237–68; and the symposium on "Movimenti religiosi popolari ed eresie nel medioevo" by R. R. Betts *et al.* at the Tenth International Congress of Historical Sciences in 1955, summarized in its *Relazioni,* III, 305–541. As Lewis pointed out, Arabic had no term for heresy until modern writers borrowed it from the West. Hence the legal concept, too, was equivocal and full of often arbitrary nuances. The same holds true for Jewish terminology, where the term *kofer* (older than the Arabic *kafir*) likewise had many shades of meaning. Even "La Concezione di eretico nelle fonti giustinianee," as analyzed by A. Berger in the *Rendiconti* of the Accademia Nazionale dei Lincei, 8th ser., X, 353–68, though more sharply defined, still oscillates between the narrower range given it in the earlier sources, which is limited to Christian dissenters, and the broader scope employed in the codification of Justinian, which embraces also Jews and Samaritans.

45. Friedlaender in *JQR,* I, 207 f. The former conception that the Shi'a was exclusively the reaction of the Iranian spirit against Islam was greatly modified when J. Wellhausen, I. Goldziher, and others proved that the 'Alite movement had genuinely Arabian origins. However, it cannot be denied that soon thereafter Persia, together with Babylonia, became the classic territory of the great sect. Cf. also M. G. S. Hodgson's "How Did the Early Shī'a Become Sectarian?" *JAOS,* LXXV, 1–13. In the case of the Jewish sects, the battle certainly had to be carried on in Babylonia and Palestine, the centers of Jewish life, but the antirabbanite opposition even in those countries was steadily reinforced by the numerous immigrants and travelers from the Iranian Plateau. Persia's influence on the Jewish sectarian movements was first suggested by Harkavy and elaborated by Poznanski, Friedlaender, and others. Little effort, however, has thus far been made to relate these movements to Parsee teachings, whether orthodox or sectarian, except in so far as these had already been assimilated by Muslims. The direct Judeo-Parsee interrelations, reaching back to the Achaemenid empire, must have been greatly intensified during the last two centuries of Sassanian rule, when the counterpoise of Babylonian Jewry's effective control over the provincial communities had been greatly weakened. Cf. *supra,* Vols. I, p. 341 n. 1; II, pp. 317 f., 435 f.; and Chaps. XVI, n. 74; XXIV, nn. 31–32. The priority of some such Jewish adaptations of Parsee concepts and their influence on similar early Muslim synthesizing efforts is, therefore, wholly within the realm of probability.

46. Anonymous chronicle, ed. and trans. into Latin by I. Guidi in "Un Nuovo testo siriaco sulla storia degli ultimi Sassanidi," *Actes du VIIIe Congrès international des Orientalistes,* Section Semitique, pp. 1–36; and in *CSCO,* Scriptores Syri, 3d ser., IV, 33 (text), 27 f. (trans.); with T. Nöldeke's comments thereon in *SB* Vienna, CXXVIII, Part 9, p. 36 (the chronicle seems to have been written by a Nestorian author about 670–80). On the identification of Pallughta with Pumbedita, see J. Obermeyer's observations in *Die Landschaft Babylonien,* pp. 219 ff. The latter's effort, however, to connect this commotion with the upheaval under Mar Zuṭra II is very questionable. See *supra,* Vol. II, pp. 182 f., 196 f., 399 n. 15; and *infra,* Chap. XXVIII, nn. 60–61. The pseudo-messiah Severus will be more fully discussed *infra,* n. 58.

47. Quirqisani's *K. al-Anwar,* I.2 (12–13), II, 12, ed. by L. Nemoy, I, 12 f., 51 ff. (English trans. in *HUCA,* VII, 328, 382 f.); Shahrastani's *K. al-Milal,* I, 168 ff. (in Haarbrücker's trans., I, 254 ff.). Shahrastani does not mention the names of the previous four messengers. But in view of Abu 'Isa's relative recognition of Jesus and Mohammed (see *infra,* n. 49), their inclusion together with Abraham and Moses appears most likely. The doctrine of the "return of the messiah," mentioned in Cant. r. II.9 and other aggadic sources, and its importance to Muslim and Jewish sects, is discussed by Friedlaender in *JQR,* II, 481 ff.; and in his "Messianic Idea in Islam" in *Past and Present,* pp. 139 ff. On Maimonides' apparent assumption that Abu 'Isa had claimed Davidic descent, the equally erroneous contention of some later "Iṣbahaniyya," reported by a Muslim apologist of the sixteenth century, As-Su'udi, that Abu 'Isa "was a prophet sent prior to Moses," and Friedlaender's own rather forced connection between Abu 'Isa's *five* messengers, and the number *seven* prominent in both Jewish and Muslim soteriology, see the latter's observations in *JQR,* III, 246 ff., 251 n. 37, 272 n. 348.

48. Daniel al-Qumisi, ed. by J. Mann in "A Tract by an Early Karaite Settler in Jerusalem," *JQR,* XII, 285; and *Texts and Studies,* II, 5 ff.; Sahl ben Maṣliaḥ, *Iggeret mokhaḥat* (Epistle of Admonition) to Jacob ben Samuel in Pinsker's *Lickute kadmoniot,* II, 31; Joseph ibn Megas' *Resp.,* No. 186. Cf. also S. Assaf's data on Spanish Jews in Palestine of that period in his *Meqorot u-meḥqarim,* pp. 103 ff. "Mourners for Zion," a term going back to Isaiah (61:3), are recorded under various designations in many countries and periods. A particularly interesting messianic sermon on Isa. 61:9 alluding to them was preserved by an early medieval homilist in the ninth-century compilation, *Pesiqta rabbati,* XXXIV, ed. by M. Friedmann, fols. 128 f. This particular sermon probably stems from an earlier period. Cf. H. Albeck's note on L. Zunz's *Ha-Derashot be-Yisrael,* pp. 119 ff., 389 nn. 65–66; Mann, *Jews in Egypt,* I, 47 f. While sometimes ridiculed as excessively idealistic and pietistic, these Mourners' ascetic self-abnegation so long as the Temple lay in ruins greatly impressed the masses. Even in far-off eleventh-century Germany, a liturgical poet, Meir bar Isaac of Worms, was generally known under the honorable designation, "representative of the people [synagogue leader] from among the Mourners for Zion." Among that author's numerous poems the Aramaic *Aqdamut millin* (Introduction to the Recitation of the Targum) is still read in many synagogues on the first day of the Festival of Weeks. Cf. the literature listed in I. Davidson *Oṣar,* I, 332 No. 7314; the numerous other poems by that author listed *ibid.,* IV, 432; and I. Elbogen's data in *Der jüdische Gottesdienst,* pp. 334 f. A number of like-minded ascetics were said to have been encountered in Germany a century later by Benjamin of Tudela who definitely found a large group of "Mourners for Zion" also in the Yemen. *Massa'ot,* ed. by Adler, pp. 47, 72 (Hebrew), 48, 80 (English). The latter passage, probably interpolated, may date from an even earlier age. Cf. especially, S. Schechter's "Jewish Saints in Mediaeval Germany" in his *Studies in Judaism,* 3d ser., pp. 6 ff.

Benjamin's description of the life and external appearance of the Yemenite Mourners probably applied also to other Diaspora communities. But their main center remained in Jerusalem, where they lived a saintly life, supported by benefactors from various lands. For example, Aḥimaaz, ancestor and namesake of the chronicler, made three pilgrimages to the Holy City and each time donated 100 gold pieces (dinars) for the support of "those who were engaged in the study of

His law, and those who mourned the ruined house of His glory." Aḥimaaz' example was followed by Palṭiel and his son Samuel. Cf. the *Chronicle of Ahimaaz,* ed. by Salzman, pp. 4, 19, 21 (Hebrew), 65, 95, 97 (English); ed. by Klar, pp. 15 f., 44, 47. Extolling the beauties of Palestine and expatiating on the people's yearning for restoration thereto served also as a constant refrain in the liturgical poetry of the period. See, for one example, M. Zulay's "Palestine and Holiday Pilgrimages in the Liturgical Poetry of R. Phinehas" (Hebrew), *Yerushalayim,* I, 51–81. We also recall the legal fiction adopted by the geonim for commercial transactions, whereby each Jew could theoretically transfer his inalienable share of four ells in the Holy Land. Cf. *supra,* Chap. XXIII, n. 29; *infra,* Chap. XXVII, n. 152; and other data discussed by R. Mahler in his *Karaimer,* pp. 120 ff., 144 ff.

49. Qirqisani's *K. al-Anwar,* 1.11, ed. by Nemoy, I, 51 f. (English trans. in *HUCA,* VII, 382 f.); Ibn Ḥazm's *K. al-Fiṣal,* 1.14, pp. 99, 112, 114 (in Asín Palacios's trans., II, 211 f., 231, 234); Baqillani's *K. aṭ-Ṭamhid,* pp. 147 f.; and R. Brunschvig's comments thereon in *Homenaje a Millás,* pp. 226 f. On the Karaite mixture of theological broadmindedness with ethnic exclusivity, see the next chapter. Qirqisani doubtless exaggerated the opportunistic motivations of Abu 'Isa's almost "henotheistic" attitude which culminated in his injunction to his followers to study carefully both the Gospels and the Qur'an with their commentaries. The Kharidjites themselves, as well as many other Muslim sectarians, looked forward to the advent of a Redeemer who would then become the real "seal of prophecy." On their negative attitude toward the state, which revealed many similarities to, and probably influences from, the predominantly apolitical contemporary Judaism, and their general acceptance of a *dhimmi's* qualified recognition of Mohammed as a messenger sent only to the Arabs, see G. Levi della Vida's "Kharidjites," *EI,* II, 907; and M. Guidi's "Sui Ḫārigiti," *RSO,* XXI, 1–14.

50. The medieval testimonies in favor of the historic continuity from the ancient Sadducees to the Karaites are well assembled in Harkavy's supplementary note on Graetz's *Geschichte,* 4th ed., pp. 472 ff.; and, with minor additions, in Z. Cahn's *Rise of the Karaite Sect,* pp. 13 ff. Cf. especially Qirqisani, 1.2.7, p. 11 (*HUCA,* VII, 326); and the Karaite commentary on Exodus as well as a comment by Ben Mashiaḥ, cited by S. Poznanski in his "Anan et ses écrits," *REJ,* XLIV, 176 f. That the author of the former commentary was Ḥasan ben Mashiaḥ, or Sahl ben Maṣliaḥ, was timidly suggested by Harkavy and accepted by Poznanski, *ibid.,* and in *The Karaite Literary Opponents of Saadiah Gaon,* pp. 16, 32 f. Both stress the fact that "the Sadducean writings are known to all." True enough, no Sadducean or even pro-Sadducean medieval documents have as yet come to light. Schechter's original attempt to identify as such his *Fragments of a Zadokite Work* has rightly been rejected by later scholars on both ideological and chronological grounds. See *supra,* Vol. II, pp. 52 ff., 348 ff. In the heat of their victorious battles against the Sadducean character of these fragments, however, these scholars, especially L. Ginzberg, went too far in altogether denying any historic connection between the ancient Sadducee doctrines and the medieval heresies. Somewhat inconsistently, Ginzberg himself was prepared to admit on occasions the survival of ancient apocalyptic teachings, even when he could not document them from any older source other than the Gospel of John. Cf. his *Ginze Schechter,* I, 310, 547; II, 470, 478. The very survival of some Sadducee literary remnants, asserted by the two Karaite

authors, appears the more probable as we seem to possess evidence for the existence as late as the ninth and tenth centuries of some Philo manuscripts, possibly in Syriac translation. Cf. S. Poznanski's "Philon dans l'ancienne littérature judéo-arabe," *REJ*, L, 10–31.

The likelihood that some ancient sectarian letters were rediscovered in the early Muslim age has been greatly enhanced by a report of the Nestorian patriarch Timothy I of Baghdad (780–823) that in his day ("ten years ago"), Palestinian Jews had discovered precisely such a hoard of ancient writings in one of the Judaean caves. See O. Braun's ed. of "Ein Brief des Katholikos Timotheos I," *Oriens christianus,* I, 301–11. The attention of the scholarly world to this important report was first drawn by O. Eissfeld in "Der gegenwärtige Stand der Erforschung der in Palästina neu gefundenen hebräischen Handschriften," *Theologische Literaturzeitung,* LXXIV, 595–600; followed by Guy de Vaux in "À propos des manuscrits de la Mer Morte," *RB,* LVII, 420 ff. (connecting this story with Qirqisani's description of the Magharians); H. Grégoire in "Les Gens de la caverne, le Qaraïtes et les Khazars," *Le Flambeau,* XXXV, 477–85; and others. An historical reminiscence that ancient writings had been hidden in caves after the destruction of the Temple was preserved in Spain and became part of the inquiry addressed by Ḥisdai ibn Shapruṭ to the king of the Khazars. Because of that hiding place for their books, the Jewish statesman explained, the ancient refugees had "taught their children to pray in the cave on mornings and evenings, until after the passage of time their descendants forgot the reason for that ancient custom." Cf. Ḥisdai's letter in Kokovtsov's *Perepiska,* p. 17; and S. Segert's comments thereon in "Ein alter Bericht über den Fund hebräischer Handschriften in einer Höhle," *Archiv orientalni,* XXI, 263–69. This query must have struck a familiar chord in Khazar circles, since worship in caves had a long and venerable tradition in the Crimea and neighboring lands. See *supra,* Chap. XIX, n. 36. On the Rabbanite-Karaite controversy on this score, see *infra,* Chap. XXVI, n. 54. Regrettably, these stray tidbits do not yet allow for any far-reaching hypotheses concerning the underground links, if any, between the ancient Magharians or Qumran sectarians and their medieval successors. Cf. also *infra,* n. 56.

51. The main argument to the contrary, namely the prolonged absence of any reference to Sadducean teachings before the tenth century, is inconclusive because of the general paucity of extant Jewish sources in the preceding half millennium. Even if we were to assume that some of these ancient letters had reemerged not long before Qirqisani by a lucky find in one of the Palestinian caves (see *infra,* n. 56), we could not rule out the underground survival of Sadducean and other sectarian teachings in oral transmission.

52. Naṭronai's responsum in *Sha'are ṣedeq,* VI.10, fol. 24b (on its date, see *infra,* n. 58); Qirqisani, I.11, p. 52 (*HUCA,* VII, 382); L. M. Epstein's *Marriage Laws,* p. vii. Poznanski's identification of Jacob ben Ephraim with Jacob ben Samuel was rejected by Mann in *Texts and Studies,* II, 26. On the far-reaching implications of the Karaite marriage laws, and the frequent disregard by Rabbanites of the ensuing endogamous provisions, see *infra,* Chap. XXVI, n. 67.

53. Shahrastani's *K. al-Milal,* I.171 (in Haarbrücker's German trans., I, 259). Cf. I. Goldziher's "Dénombrement des sectes mohamétanes," *RHR,* XXVI, 129–37; and

I. Friedlaender's data on *The Heterodoxies of the Shi'ites according to Ibn Ḥazm,* p. 6.

54. Qirqisani, I.2 (11–13), 11–12, ed. by Nemoy, I, 12 f., 51 ff. (*HUCA,* VII, 328 f., 382 f.); Shahrastani, I.168 f. (Haarbrücker, I, 254 ff.); Yehudah Hadassi's *Eshkol ha-kofer,* No. 97, fol. 41c. The identity of Yudghan with the author Yehudah the Persian, mentioned by Abraham ibn Ezra and Elijah Bashyatchi, appears dubious. So does the equation of his followers with the Shadghanites, mentioned by Jephet ben 'Ali in his Commentary on Deut. 30:2 (Pinsker's *Lickute,* pp. 25 f.). Cf. Graetz's *Geschichte,* V, 212 f. (Hebrew trans., III, 217 f.). Yudghan's surname, "the Shepherd," bitingly paraphrased by Hadassi as "herder of thy camels," is explained by Qirqisani and all his successors as having had the semimessianic connotation of "shepherd of the people." However, it would seem strange that these sectarians should have selected this particular epitheton from among all possible messianic designations, without some direct provocation. The people at large had certainly not forgotten the Talmud's reiterated disparagement of the shepherd's calling. See *supra,* Vol. II, pp. 264, 418 n. 40. On the other hand, it would not have been at all incongruous for Yudghan, a native of the Persian highlands around Hamadan, to have started life as a shepherd and for his followers to rationalize this occupation as a symbol of his divine mission. L. Nemoy is quite right in ascribing the rise of some of these heterodoxies, though not necessarily as he assumes of the Karaite schism, to the "uncouth pioneers" from the Iranian Plateau. See his "Early Karaism (The Need for a New Approach)," *JQR,* XL, 307–15. Cf. also the Muslim parallels cited by Friedlaender in *JQR,* III, 282 ff.; and on the prohibition of meat and wine as well as on Abu 'Isa's additional prayers, *ibid.,* pp. 293 ff., 298 ff. Graetz's description of the medieval sects, particularly in his Notes XIV–XVIII, together with Harkavy's comments thereon, as well as the latter's excursus "On the History of Jewish Sects" in the Hebrew edition of Graetz, III, 493–511, still are the best general summaries based on full documentation. S. A. Poznanski's careful survey of "Founders of Jewish Sects in the Geonic Period" (Hebrew), *Reshumot,* I, 207–16, was unfortunately never completed.

55. Only one writer, Jephet ben 'Ali (in Pinsker, *Lickute kadmoniot,* pp. 25 f.), claims that the Yudghanites believed that all commandments had lost their binding force in the dispersion. For this reason they "relaxed many commandments and permitted the Jews Gentile food and the consumption of abominable things." If true, this report would merely indicate that some later Yudghanites more liberally interpreted the practical implications of their founder's theories.

56. Both Qirqisani, I.2(8).7, pp. 11 f., 41 f. (*HUCA,* VII, 326 f., 363 f.); and Shahrastani, I, 169 f. (Arabic), 257 (German), offer brief descriptions of the Magharians, which have long intrigued scholars. Since they are placed by Qirqisani before Jesus, and since Shahrastani reports a tradition that Arius (died 336 C.E.) had borrowed his doctrine of the Messiah as the Lord's angel from these sectarians "who had lived 400 years before Arius and had laid great stress on continence and a simple mode of life," Harkavy's hypothesis that we deal here with an offshoot of the Essenes or Therapeutae found wide acceptance. Harkavy's explanation, however, that their name of Cave Men was derived from the Essenes' predilection to live in deserted regions is not only controverted by the ancient records about the

dispersed, in part even urban, Essenian communities, but also by Qirqisani's etymology that "they were called so because their (sacred) books were found in a cave." Clearly this description fits far better the New Covenanters and their spiritual kinsmen of Qumran. Cf. *supra,* n. 50; Vol. II, pp. 52 ff., 349 n. 61; and the ever growing literature on the Dead Sea Scrolls which has been accumulating since.

Even with these new materials we are still unable safely to identify the Magharian writings mentioned by Qirqisani. "One of them," writes this Karaite historian, "is the Alexandrian whose book is famous and (widely) known; it is the most important of the books of the Magharians. Next to it (in importance) is a small booklet entitled 'The Book of Yaddua',' also a fine work. As for the rest of the Magharian books, most of them are of no value and resemble mere tales." Poznanski's alluring hypothesis (following Harkavy) that Qirqisani referred to some works by Philo the Alexandrian, whether or not he assumed that the latter's Hebrew name was Yaddua' (*REJ,* L, 23 ff., 28), encounters the almost insuperable barrier of the lack of evidence for the survival of any Philonic writings considered "famous and widely known" in the tenth century. The description here also gives the impression that Qirqisani referred to Hebrew, or possibly Arabic, works, whereas no such medieval translations of Philo are mentioned anywhere else. At best there may have been extant some Syriac translations. Cf. *supra,* n. 50. Neither does the mere fact that the Magharians believed in an intermediary angel who created the world necessarily link them directly to the Philonic *logos.* The doctrine of a *demiurge* had been much alive in the Christian, as well as Jewish, gnosis long before it was turned into a vehicle of anti-Jewish propaganda by Marcion of Pontus. Cf. *supra,* Vol. II, pp. 167 f., 394 n. 50; and, on Muslim parallels, Friedlaender's data in *JQR,* III, 254 ff. It is barely possible that Qirqisani referred here to some Hebrew, Aramaic, or Arabic version of the pseudo-Philonic *Liber Antiquitatum Biblicarum* which, in its Latin garb, was soon to make such a strange career in the West. See *infra,* Chap. XXVIII, n. 56.

57. The figure of hundreds of thousands combatants under Abu 'Isa is mentioned only in the Sulzberger MS of the relatively late *Epistle to Yemen* by Maimonides, ed. by Halkin, pp. 98 ff. (Arabic and Hebrew), xviii f. (English). This number evidently is a gross exaggeration; it is reduced to 10,000 in other MSS and old versions. Although the sage of Fusṭaṭ had at his disposal many since forgotten sources, and his general description of the messianic movements is distinguished by both lucidity and general reliability, he himself expressed doubts about the veracity of the traditions concerning Abu 'Isa, whom he failed to mention by name. His emphasis, too, that "they reached, according to the information I received, the vicinity of Baghdad. This happened in the beginning of the reign of the 'Umayyads," is pointless in so far as Baghdad was not to become the imperial capital until more than half a century after Abu 'Isa's downfall. Maimonides himself drew the distinction between this episode which he had "learned from oral reports" and the following incident which "we have verified and know to be true." Cf. also J. Mann's "Messianic Movements in the Period of the First Crusades," *Hatekufah,* XXIV, 355.

58. Naṭronai's resp. in *Sha'are ṣedeq,* VI.7 and 10, fol. 24ab; and the sources listed *supra,* n. 46. These sources for the story of the pseudo-messiah Severus

(Serene, Zonaria), in themselves confused and contradictory, have given rise to endless hypotheses. They have been subjected to renewed careful and judicious scrutiny by J. Starr in "Le Mouvement messianique au début du VIIIe siècle," *REJ*, CII, 81–92. Here the name Severus seems definitely established, whereas Serene, mentioned in Naṭronai's responsum, should be read, according to Friedlaender's suggestion, *Suryani* (the Syrian). "Zonaria" is merely a corruption of the latter. Starr goes too far, however, in denying the spread of that movement to Spain and Gaul. The pertinent passage in the chronicle of Pseudo-Isidorus Pacensis (cf. the version cited by T. Mommsen in his ed. of the *Continuatio Byzantia-Arabica* to St. Isidore's *Historia Gothorum*, in *MGH*, Auct. ant., XI, 359 n. 1) may indeed be a later interpolation. Yet the interpolator's substitution of the name of an oriental Arab governor by the western Emir Anbasa, without some backing by an older authority, would require a far more cogent explanation than has hitherto been offered. The term *volari* (fly), rather than the purely conjectural *nolari* (transport in ships), is likewise genuine. Cf. Friedlaender's comments in *JQR*, II, 503 ff.; and *infra*, n. 69.

Some of the chronological difficulties may be eliminated if we assume that Severus' agitation continued for a number of years. It probably started about 721–22 (according to our relatively oldest source, Theophanes) and continued into the reign of Hisham (724–43). In the meantime Severus may have been apprehended by Maslama, brother and active collaborator of Caliph Yazid ibn 'Abd al-Malik (720–24), but he seems to have been released after Maslama had "confiscated all his property." Cf. the anonymous chronicler's report, ed. by J. B. Chabot, in *CSCO*, 3d ser., XIV, Part 1, p. 308. This outcome of the prosecution hardly discouraged Severus from resuming his lucrative undertaking, or his excited followers from continuing to believe in his divine mission. Only when, to put an end to the disturbance, Hisham executed the messianic pretender, did most, or all, of the latter's adherents repent their delusion and apply for readmission to the regular community. Their acceptance was sanctioned by Naṭronai I (bar Nehemiah) whose regime, according to Sherira's Epistle (p. 102), began in 719 and lasted until some time before 739. The repeated efforts since E. H. Weiss to ascribe the crucial responsum to Naṭronai II (bar Hilai) after 853 have not met with success. The principal argument for the ninth-century date advanced, for instance, by L. Ginzberg (in his *Geonica*, I, 50 n. 1), that in the second responsum by that gaon (No. 7), "a plain reference is made to the Karaites" founded by 'Anan some three decades after Naṭronai I's death, is but the result of the unawareness of the strong protokaraite trends before 'Anan and the usual exaggerations concerning the impact of Karaism on the contemporary community. Cf. *infra*, Chap. XXVI. This assumption is controverted by the entire tenor of the responsum, which refers to opponents of the written, as well as the oral, Law. In fact, the language of the informed questioners, even more than that of the gaon, tends to indicate that these sectarians lived in sexual promiscuity (*peruṣin ba-'arayot*), a term which would hardly have been used for any Karaite misinterpretation of the legal impediments to marriage. We probably have here some early Jewish counterpart to the Qarmatian schism and later the followers of Ibn ar-Rawandi among the Muslims, which took over some of the Mazdakite teachings concerning the community of women and property. Cf. Friedlaender's *Heterodoxies*, p. 37; *supra*, Vol. II, p. 399 n. 15; and Chap. XVI, n. 69. To what extent Platonic teachings in their neo-Platonic garb contributed to the theoretical justification of these doctrines is yet to be examined.

Certainly neo-Platonism had started to exert a growing influence on the Arabic-speaking intelligentsia, through literary media, as well as through the Mazdakite heritage. Cf., for the time being, F. Altheim and R. Stiehl's "Mazdak and Porphyrios," *Nouvelle Clio,* V, 356–76. Certainly, such sectarian extremism fits much better into the turbulent Muslim and Jewish community life of the eighth century than into the somewhat better organized communal structure of the ninth century. The attribution of both these responsa to Naṭronai II would also encounter the insuperable barrier of Qirqisani's and the other heresiologues' total silence about the movement initiated by Severus. An ephemeral commotion led by a self-seeking adventurer could easily be ignored. But a sectarian group which lasted for more than a hundred and thirty years, almost to the lifetime of David Al-Muqammiṣ, would certainly have been recorded by him and, through him, by Qirqisani and Hadassi. Our harmonization of the existing records may not quite suit the tastes of supercritical scholars, but it seems to offer the most acceptable reconstruction of the actual events.

59. Ibn 'Abd Rabbihi's *K. al-Iqd al-Farid* (Collar of Unique Pearls); Shahrastani, *supra,* n. 56; and the sources cited by Friedlaender in *JQR,* III, 286 ff. Friedlaender raises the intriguing question as to whether the number nineteen had any of the mystic connotations it possessed among some Zoroastrians and Muslims.

60. Qirqisani, I.2.15–19; I.15–17, ed. by Nemoy, I, 13 f., 56 ff. (*HUCA,* VII, 329 f., 388 ff.); and the sources analyzed in Graetz's *Geschichte,* 4th ed., pp. 512 ff. Qirqisani's complaint that "there are no scholars or theologians among" the Mishawayhites is rather curious. As if the other non-Karaite dissenters had been distinguished by learning. Cf. S. Poznanski's searching investigation of "Meswi al-Okbari, chef d'une secte juive du IXe siècle," *REJ,* XXXIV, 161–91.

61. Shahrastani, *loc. cit.;* Jephet ben 'Ali, cited in Ewald and Dukes, *Beiträge zur Geschichte der ältesten Auslegung und Spracherklärung des Alten Testaments,* II, 30 f.; Tobiah ben Moses' legal compilation *Oṣar neḥmad* (Lovely Treasure) in the excerpt cited from MS by Poznanski in *REJ,* XXXIV, 182; Maqrizi's *Al-Khitat* in De Sacy's *Chrestomathie arabe,* I, 174 (Arabic), II, 184 f. (French). On Abu 'Imran's polemics against the sharp Bible critic, Ḥivi (Ḥayyawayh) of Balkh, see *infra,* Chap. XXIX, n. 88. Mishawayh's nihilist but, in practice, rather innocuous approach to the Jewish calendar is well illustrated by his pithy apothegm, "All money is unreliable; stick, then, to the counterfeit coin that you have on hand," that is, observe the holidays together with the orthodox majority. Cf. Qirqisani, I.17, pp. 57 f. (*HUCA,* VII, 390; there is no need for Nemoy's hesitant interpretation that he or Abu 'Imran wished to enjoin his partisans to follow in these matters the "general body *of the sectarians*").

62. Cf. A. S. Halkin's Hebrew and abridged English introductions to his edition of the *Epistle to Yemen;* and J. Mann's comprehensive analysis in *Hatekufah,* XXIII–XXIV. Mann, who reprinted here the Hebrew originals or translations of most pertinent sources, had at his disposal also the relevant portion of the Arabic original of the *Epistle,* then being prepared for a critical edition by I. Friedlaender, together with the latter's English translation. His interpretation, however, of these successive movements left many questions open. While fully realizing the great

impact of the Crusades, he failed to supply the reasons for the outbreak of each particular mass psychosis. Cf. also J. Shapiro's more popular restatement of the story of the Jewish messianic movements in his *Bi-shebile ha-ge'ulah* (On the Paths of Redemption), which, however, adds but little to the previously known facts.

63. Maimonides' *Epistle to Yemen,* pp. 102 f. (Arabic and Hebrew), xx (English). *Al-Afranj* does not necessarily mean France in the Arabic letters of that period, but like the term "Franks" or "Ashkenazim," included all the successor states of the Frankish empire, or even all of western Europe. Although probably not quite of the size of the Lyons community, that of Spanish Leon was likewise both old and substantial, and was later to give birth to the famous Kabbalist, Moses de Leon. One Jacob of Leon is recorded to have brought back from a pilgrimage to Palestine an important philological work by Abu'l Faraj Harun. Cf. Abu'l-Walid Merwan (Jonah) ibn Janaḥ's *K. al-Luma'* (Livre des Parterres fleuris; grammaire hébraïque), ed. by J. Derenbourg, pp. 322 f. (in Yehudah ibn Tibbon's Hebrew trans., entitled *Sefer ha-Riqmah,* ed. by M. Wilensky, II, 338; in M. Metzger's French trans. the geographic designation is omitted); and *supra,* Chap. XX, n. 40. Even to a native Spaniard like Maimonides, the northern city of Leon with its immemorial connections with the Frankish empire may well have appeared as a large city in the Frankish possessions, though not perhaps in their "center," a term, questionable even in the single Arabic text and totally absent from the other Arabic and all Hebrew versions. Cf. also H. Gross's *Gallia judaica,* pp. 306 f., which shows that, while both cities were often spelled in Hebrew in the same manner, Lyons often had the added "s" as in English, or else was spelled in some derivative from the Latin *Lugdunum.*

64. Cf. the sources listed *supra,* Chap. XXI, nn. 7, 24; Tobiah ben Eliezer's *Midrash Leqaḥ ṭob* (Good Lesson) on Lev. 22:32–33, ed. by M. Padwa, p. 123; and on Cant. 1:3, ed. by A. W. Greenup, pp. 15, 24. Cf. *infra,* Chap. XXVIII, nn. 26 ff. Of course, it is possible that the Tobiah of the messianic missive was not the author of the Midrash, or else that in retrospect he viewed the Balkan repercussions as but a tempest in a teapot. The events in the Rhinelands, however, made a deep and lasting impression on the Jews of all lands, and especially on Tobiah, who may himself have been of Western origin. Cf. the debate on this score summarized in Zunz and Albeck's *Ha-Derashot,* pp. 145 f., 441 n. 40; and J. Starr's *Jews in the Byzantine Empire,* pp. 215 ff. The first person plural in Solomon's chronicle is taken over from the basic contemporary source so eloquently postulated by Y. Baer in *Sefer Assaf,* pp. 130 ff. But even in the conclusion of his chronicle, triumphantly relating the severe losses sustained by the Crusader bands on their march through Hungary and the Balkan countries, Solomon makes no mention of the Balkan agitation. Despite the numerous messianic references in his commentaries on the Bible, and especially on Psalms, largely composed in the overheated atmosphere of crusading France after 1096, Rashi likewise fails to hint at any messianic upsurge in Byzantium. See especially the searching reconstruction of the meaning of a number of these messianic passages against the background of contemporary Judeo-Christian polemics in Y. Baer's aforementioned essay in *Tarbiz,* XX, 328 ff. If the reading "Khorasan" rather than "Khazaria" should prove correct, as is likely, the manifold speculations about the seventeen Khazarian communities would become meaningless. Cf., for instance, A. N. Poliak's *Khazariyyah,* pp. 231 ff.; and D. M. Dunlop's *History of the Jewish Khazars,* pp. 255 f.

65. Maimonides' *Epistle to Yemen, loc. cit.* On the Almoravid threat see *supra,* Chap. XVIII, n. 5. Maimonides fails to mention here any connection with that threat, but rather blames these events on some Cordovan Jewish students of astrology (there must have been many) who subsequently detected in their dreams signs that the Messiah was to be found in Cordova. But he does not explain why these particular horoscopes were taken more seriously than many others, and why the populace, unsolicited, chose a local man as its messiah, despite the long accepted legends that he was to reside in Rome or Constantinople. Maimonides' silence with respect to the urgency behind this frantic quest may readily be explained by his general peeve against the "science" of astrology, and by the intervening disappearance of the semimillennial threat. Certainly, in countries outside the reach of Almohades, the status of the Jews had undergone no major change in the first seven decades of the sixth century A.H.

66. Maimonides' *Epistle to Yemen,* pp. 100 ff. (Arabic and Hebrew), xix (English); and *supra,* Chap. XXIV, n. 22. Maimonides did not deny the fact that Al-Dar'i's several predictions had come true. By explaining that such occurrences were by no means "inconsistent with the tenets of the Torah, for prophecy will return to Israel before the messianic advent," he even intimated that Al-Dar'i may indeed have been endowed with the gift of prophecy and in this way have served as the harbinger of redemption. Cf. *infra,* Chap. XXXIV.

67. Cf. the fragment from Obadiah's scroll, republished with corrections from the Adler MS by Mann in *Hatekufah,* XXIV, 336 f. (by mentioning that the episode of the Karaite messiah occurred nineteen years after his conversion to Judaism, Obadiah dated it precisely in Ellul, or August–September, 1121); and S. D. Goitein's publication and analysis of an Oxford Genizah fragment containing "A Report on Messianic Troubles in Baghdad in 1120–21," *JQR,* XLIII, 57–76. On the difficulties encountered even by Egyptian Jewry, including some Palestinian communities still under Egyptian domination, toward the end of Al-Afdhal's regime, see Mann's *Jews in Egypt,* I, 210 ff. The appearance of this first Karaite pseudo-messiah and his revival in practice of the ancient sectarian idea of a priestly messiah whom Karaite teachers had long equated with Elijah, reveal a degree of messianic tensions which would be difficult to explain without some such overwhelming fears, as were nurtured by the approaching end of the solar half millennium. Cf. N. Wieder's data on "The Doctrine of the Two Messiahs among the Karaites," *JJS,* VI, 14–25, also referring to the Manual of Discipline among the Qumran scrolls, analyzed by K. G. Kuhn in "Die beiden Messias Aarons und Israels," *New Testament Studies,* I, 168–79. Cf. also D. Barthélemy's edition and interpretation of the pertinent passage in his and J. T. Milik's *Discoveries in the Judaean Desert, I: Qumran Cave I,* pp. 110 f. (Hebrew), 117 f. (French, lines 11 ff.); and its reinterpretation, with a new English rendition, by F. M. Cross, Jr. in his review article on that volume, "Qumran Cave I," *JBL,* LXXV, 124 f. One must also bear in mind some later reminiscences of that theory, discussed *supra,* n. 6, where L. M. Silberman's reservations on Kuhn's interpretation of the Qumran passage are also mentioned. Cf. also *supra,* Chap. XXIV, n. 45; and *infra,* Chap. XXVI, n. 61. On Dan-Baniyyas, a frontier fortress in the vicinity of Damascus, which was to play a considerable role in the wars between the Latin Kingdom and the Muslims, see William of Tyre's *Historia,* XIV.17, 19, etc., in *RHC,* I, 650, 654; and in Babcock and Krey's English

trans., II, 74 ff., and *passim.* Cf. also the excerpts and literature relating to the Jewish settlement there in *Sefer ha-Yishub,* II, 50 f. The obscure Baghdad events may have been stimulated also by some letters received at that time from leaders of a similar movement in a none-too-distant mountain region. See *infra,* n. 68; and Chap. XXVI, n. 67.

68. Benjamin's *Massa'ot,* pp. 51 ff. (Hebrew), 76 ff. (English); Samau'al ibn Yaḥya's *Ifḥam al-Yahud,* cited and analyzed by Schreiner in *MGWJ,* XLII, 410 f.; and the Genizah fragment, first published by Mann in his "Obadia le prosélyte," *REJ,* LXXI, 90 f., and republished with additional comments in *Hatekufah,* XXIV, 347 f. Only the latter mentions the beginning of that movement under Solomon ben Duji in the days of Al-Afdhal. Nevertheless we have no reason to doubt the essential truth of that report showing that the movement extended over a considerable period of time. It is noteworthy, however, that in his enumeration of the previous messianic failures Maimonides did not even hint at the eastern disturbances, which had occurred about the time of Al-Dar'i's appearance in Morocco and again a quarter century later. Perhaps he simply assumed that the Yemenite leaders' familiarity with events transpiring in Baghdad and Palestine—he himself had still been a relative newcomer in those regions—was greater than with the more or less local happenings under western Islam.

69. See especially A. N. Poliak, "David Alroy" (Hebrew), *Ha-Kinnus,* I, 404–6, whose succinct analysis comes closest to our reconstruction of the events from the three often contradictory sources. Poliak also points out the difficult situation of the Jews of Khazarian Daghestan and its vicinity around 1120. The greatest difficulty consists in dating that movement, which seems to have extended intermittently from about 1120 to 1147 and beyond. Its *terminus a quo* is given by Al-Afdhal's death in 1121. The final date is more questionable. Benjamin's reference to "ten years ago," or close to 1160, seems definitely erroneous, and may be due to an easy scribal error, which replaced *'esrim* (20) by *'eser* (10) and *shanah* by *shanim* (years). His mention, in this connection, of Alroy's teacher Ḥisdai underscores that error, since Ḥisdai had died in 1135. Cf. S. Abramson's "R. Joseph Rosh ha-Seder" (Hebrew), *KS,* XXVI, 93. Mann's effort to connect the appearance of Alroy with the Second Crusade of 1146 (*Hatekufah,* XXIV, 343 f.) has more in its favor than the mere *terminus ad quem* of 1149 or the death of Zif ad-Din of Mosul, mentioned by Benjamin himself. In fact, Zif, like his brother Nur ad-Din (Nureddin), achieved power only after the assassination of their father, Zangi, on September 14, 1146. It is to this assumption of power by Zif that Benjamin clearly alludes. On Zangi's use of Jewish settlers in Edessa, see *supra,* Chap. XXI, n. 33. On the other hand, the date of "about 4895" (1135) given by David Gans in his chronicle *Ṣemaḥ David,* fol. 38b, and accepted by Poliak, is, like his entire account of Alroy's agitation, entirely unreliable. Avowedly based on Ibn Verga's chronicle, it even confuses Alroy with the Yemenite pretender of Maimonides' *Epistle.* Certainly, the news about the leading monarchs in Europe preparing an invasion of the Near East must have nurtured new hopes among the Asiatic Jews. To be sure, the story of the attempted flight from the roof tops caused particular skepticism among modern scholars such as Schreiner. But, apart from being an ancient ingredient of the messianic hope (R. Levi had already interpreted Isa. 60:8: "Who are these that fly as a cloud" as referring to worshipers from all over the world being brought on clouds to Jerusalem on every

Sabbath and New Moon; cf. *Pesiqta rabbati,* I, ed. by Friedmann, fol. 2a), it is also borne out by the belief of the followers of Ibn-Rawandi, reported by the historian Ṭabari (III, 418) and mentioned also by Schreiner himself, that they would be able to fly. In fact, we are told that the distinguished lexicographer Abu Naṣr Isma'il al-Jauhari died some time between 1003 and 1010 in a futile attempt to fly from the roof of his home or of the chief mosque in Nishabur, Khorasan. Cf. Brockelmann's *Geschichte der arabischen Literatur,* rev. ed., I, 133; and other data supplied by A. Zeki in *L'Aviation chez les Musulmans.*

70. Maimonides' *Epistle to Yemen,* pp. 84 ff., 92 ff. (Arabic and Hebrew), XVI, XVIII (English); and A. Marx's ed. of "The Correspondence between the Rabbis of Southern France and Maimonides about Astrology," *HUCA,* III, 357. Although such demonstration of one's veracity is a rather frequent theme in international folklore (we recall the somewhat related stories of the Persian-Christian girl martyr, Shirin, and the Cordovan rabbi Hanokh's wife who resorted to similar subterfuges in order to save their virtue; *supra,* Chaps. XVI, n. 72, XXIII, n. 56), we must accept this particular narrative as historically authentic. It stems from a critical writer, permanently in touch with Yemen and doubtless evincing a healthy curiosity about the final outcome of his previous correspondence.

Another letter, however, attributed to the Fusṭaṭ sage and produced by one Isaac bar Nathan of Fez at the end of 1187, was but a pious fabrication, doubtless intended to instill courage in the struggling remnant of Moroccan Jewry under the Almohades. Here Maimonides allegedly gave an affirmative testimony to the existence of a messiah in Isfahan, whom he had personally contacted through his brother David and who had satisfactorily answered fifteen of eighteen legal problems left open by the ancient sages for ultimate resolution by Elijah. The fabricator knew something about Maimon's family who had spent several years in Morocco, but he had apparently not learned about David's death in a shipwreck in 1166–67. He also had heard rumors about David Alroy and perhaps invented for him a son, Abi Sa'id ben Dawudi, but placed him in the city of Isfahan. There is no record that Alroy ever was in Isfahan, but this prominent Jewish community, as we know, long played a major role in Muslim folklore as the place of origin of the awesome *dajjal.* See *supra,* Chap. XXIV, n. 64. Cf. the text published by A. Neubauer in his "Documents inédits, I: Une pseudo-biographie de Moïse Maimonide," *REJ,* IV, 174 ff. (Hebrew) 181 ff. (French); and republished by Halkin in his ed. of the *Epistle to Yemen,* pp. 108 ff. Neubauer, followed by D. Kaufmann, rightly sensed the spurious nature of the Fez letter. If in his brilliant essay on the messianic prediction for 1186 (see *supra,* Chap. XXI, n. 45), F. Baer tried to salvage some historic kernels of truth, he succeeded only in furnishing additional proof that the years preceding the Third Crusade were fraught with messianic expectations, which were likely to produce such fabrications. The only astonishing feature in his reply to the southern French rabbis was Maimonides' misreading of their inquiry as relating to his *Epistle to Yemen,* rather than to one about a messiah in Isfahan. But such an error could easily arise in the correspondence of an extremely busy man with respect to a tangential detail. Moreover, he may have been familiar with the unauthorized use of his name in the spurious letter, and yet felt too sympathetic with the plight of his former compatriots in Fez publicly to disavow it. He deftly sidetracked the issue, therefore, without directly accusing the Moroccans of circulating a forgery. On the messianic tensions under the government of Saladin himself, see E. Ashtor-Strauss's observations in *HUCA,* XXVII, 317.

71. Some recent students of Karaism have advanced the notion that all the sectarian trends between the seventh and the ninth century were part and parcel of the Karaite movement. L. Nemoy, in particular, to whom scholarship is greatly indebted for making available the Arabic text of Qirqisani's major work, which includes most of our first-hand information about these heterodoxies, has given currency to that view without anywhere offering a fully documented substantiation. In his *Karaite Anthology,* for example, he writes without much ado about the various sectarian leaders who arose after 'Anan, and adds, "The surnames quoted above indicate the territorial expansion of Karaism during the ninth and early in the tenth century" (p. xix). There is no justification for thus lumping together entirely heterogeneous elements. Even Qirqisani, who describes them in their chronological sequence, nowhere intimates that he considers them all subdivisions of Karaism, any more than he counts Jesus or Mohammed among the Karaites. (No Karaite before the nineteenth century claimed Jesus for his sect; cf. *infra,* Chap. XXVI, n. 56.) True, in his description the contemporary Karaites, too, appear as anything but a homogeneous group. But his analysis of the teachings of these sects, however brief, does show the great difference between movements, primarily inspired by messianic pretenders, with neither the ability nor the desire to propagate major changes in the existing legal system, and the primarily legalistic changes introduced by 'Anan, Benjamin or their distinguished scholarly successors, including Qirqisani himself. In the spiritual effervescence, which characterized the first two or three centuries of Islamic rule, all sorts of individual, as well as group manifestations of questioning and discontent came to the fore, of which Karaism may have become the major beneficiary, but for which it can claim no credit: 'Isawites or Mishawayhites doubtless repudiated the rigid Karaite interpretation of Scripture even more vigorously than they did the masses' warm and colorful adherence to talmudic law. In short, most of them preached an emotional, prophetic-messianic brand of Judaism; Karaism, as we shall presently see, espoused a rational, legalistic-scholastic reform.

CHAPTER XXVI: KARAITE SCHISM

1. Curiously, this story, so vital for the understanding of the origins of the Karaite schism, is preserved only in a biased anti-Karaite account by a Rabbanite controversialist (probably Saadiah Gaon) as cited in the Karaite apologia, *Ḥilluq ha-Qara'im ve-ha-Rabbanim* (The Difference between the Karaites and Rabbanites). See the text reproduced in Pinsker, *Lickute kadmoniot,* II, 103. This tract seems to have been written by Elijah ben Abraham, a twelfth-century Byzantine scholar, according to S. Poznanski's plausible arguments in his *Karaite Literary Opponents of Saadiah Gaon,* pp. 72 ff. It is essentially confirmed by the cryptic statement in Qirqisani's older and well-informed account (1.2, p. 14; in Nemoy's trans., *HUCA,* VII, 329) that "the Rabbanites did all they could to kill him ['Anan] but God let them not get hold of him." This had nothing to do with either any attempt at assassination, or any formal trial by a Jewish court. Hence S. Poznanski's objections to some details of this account in his "Anan et ses écrits," *REJ,* XLIV, 162, are unwarranted.

Even less justified is L. Nemoy's extreme skepticism with respect to the entire story of 'Anan's candidacy and imprisonment. Cf. his "Anan ben David: A Reappraisal of the Historical Data," *Löw Mem. Vol.* pp. 239–48, briefly repeated in his *Karaite Anthology,* pp. 6 f. His arguments from the silence on this score of both Naṭronai Gaon (see *infra,* nn. 10, 79) and Qirqisani are not only mutually contradictory, but are even more precarious than other *argumenta a silentio.* It is well known that the writers of that period evinced little interest in biographical details, and mentioned them as a rule only if they helped drive home a juridical or philosophic reasoning. How much do we know about the life of Naṭronai himself, or about Qirqisani and the other Karaite worthies? Moreover, in the very first mention of 'Anan, Qirqisani calls him "exilarch" (*ras al-jalut*), clearly hinting at his "noble lineage and his candidacy for the office of exilarch." Cf. his *K. al-Anwar, loc. cit.* Cf. also Sherira's *Iggeret,* ed. by Levin, p. 107. While, because of its late date and inherent bias, one may legitimately doubt the details of a narrative preserved only in Elijah ben Abraham's quotations from a Rabbanite author (whether or not this author was Saadiah) and Abraham ibn Daud's chronicle (*Sefer ha-Qabbalah,* ed. by A. Neubauer, in *MJC,* I, 63 f.), it is difficult to explain away its fundamental facts in view of the persistent Karaite traditions concerning 'Anan's and his descendants' claims to the exilarchic succession buttressed by lengthy genealogical lists (see *infra,* n. 14). Nor has any valid reason been offered as to why a later Rabbanite author should have invented such a claim and conceded that 'Anan had been the older and more learned candidate. Skepticism *à outrance* can, indeed, be self-defeating. Of course, in the century and a half between 'Anan and Saadiah and, to a lesser extent, in the two centuries between Saadiah and Elijah, the story may have undergone many modifications. It has nevertheless retained a sufficiently authentic ring not to be relegated into the limbo of legend.

The name of 'Anan's Muslim fellow-prisoner is not mentioned in the source, but A. Harkavy and others have long agreed to consider Abu Ḥanifa as the most likely choice. In fact, Harkavy built around the personality of this distinguished jurist an attractive, though debatable, theory concerning certain methodological, as well as substantive, Ḥanifite influences on 'Anan's teachings. Cf. especially Harkavy's brief summary, "Anan, der Stifter der karäischen Secte," *JJGL,* II, 107–22. If true, this identification furnishes us, through Abu Ḥanifa's arrest and death in prison in 767, a more precise date for 'Anan's breach with the Rabbanites than the otherwise loosely documented period of some time between the foundation of Baghdad in 763 and Caliph Jafar al-Manṣur's death in 775. On Abu Ḥanifa, see also C. C. Adams's remarks in *MW,* XXXVI, 217 ff.

2 'Anan's treatise on metempsychosis is unfortunately lost, and we do not even possess any significant citation therefrom. Nevertheless the tradition, preserved by Qirqisani that such a work had existed, deserves credence despite the latter author's evident inability to secure a copy, and the fact that he devoted several chapters in his *Book of Lights,* III.17–18 (in Nemoy's ed. II, 307 ff.) to the combating of this doctrine. Cf. Poznanski's remarks in the second part of his "Anan et ses écrits," *REJ,* XLV, 190 f.; and his earlier edition and interpretation of the Qirqisani chapters in *Semitic Studies in Memory of Alexander Kohut,* pp. 435–56.

3. Modern students of Karaism have recovered a few significant segments of 'Anan's *Book of Commandments.* Half a century ago Harkavy made available in his *Zikhron la-rishonim,* Vol. VIII, a fairly large fragment of the Aramaic original, accompanied by a Hebrew translation and notes, and in addition, assembled a large number of citations from this work (in the original or in a Hebrew trans.) which had appeared in the subsequent literature, both Karaite and Rabbanite. Other fragments were published between 1910 and 1936 by S. Schechter in his *Documents of Jewish Sectaries,* Vol. II; J. Mann in *Journal of Jewish Lore,* I, 348–51; M. N. Sokolov in the *Izvestia* (Bulletin) of the USSR Academy of Sciences, Class of Humanities, 7th ser., 1928, pp. 243–53; and J. N. Epstein in *Tarbiz,* VII, 283–90. Much in these new fragments covers the same ground as Harkavy's citations and hence bears eloquent testimony to the general faithfulness of later writers in their verbatim quotations. Together, therefore, fragments and citations give us a fair idea of 'Anan's original composition, although they still leave open such vital literary problems as the scope and arrangement of the entire work, its possible revisions by author or copyists, and the kind of readers to whom it was initially addressed. Cf. also L. Nemoy's excerpts in English trans. with explanatory notes in his *Karaite Anthology,* pp. 11 ff., 322 ff.

4. This significant injunction is mentioned only by the tenth-century Karaite, Jephet ben 'Ali (in his commentary on Zechariah) and by Moses Ibn Ezra, who evidently copied it from Jephet. It may, therefore, be but a rationale developed in the tenth century for the then rampant individualism of Karaite exegesis. This seems particularly true with respect to the second half of that quotation from 'Anan, "And do not rely on my opinion," whose Hebrew phrasing (*ve-al tisha'anu 'al da'ati*), contrasting with the Aramaic of the former sentence (*ḥapisu be-oraita shappir*), appears doubly suspicious if Jephet took it, as is usually assumed, from 'Anan's introduction to the Aramaic Book of Commandments. Cf. Harkavy's *Zikhron,* VIII, 132, 139. Nevertheless, the first half of the statement well summarizes the Karaite founder's approach to the Bible which differed radically in tone and aim, if not in formulation, from the parallel Ben Bag Bag injunction (M. Abot v.25), and

even from Shafi'i's statement cited by J. Schacht in *The Origins of Muhammadan Jurisprudence,* p. 6. Freedom from authority had nothing to do, of course, with rationalist freedom of thought, since everything ultimately depended on the conformity of each new interpretation with the entire context of biblical legislation.

5. Cf. Harkavy, *Zikhron,* VIII, pp. xi f.; Moses Bashyatchi's *Maṭṭeh Elohim* (Divine Rod; on the Karaite-Rabbanite differences), cited from a MS in Graetz's *Geschichte,* V, 492 f. According to I. D. Markon, however, Moses Bashyatchi wrote this work in 1545, but did not die until 1572. See his brief Hebrew analysis of "Karaite Manuscripts from the Collection of Abraham Geiger," *Essays Hertz,* Hebrew section, pp. 96 f. On the Muslim *qi'as,* see A. J. Wensinck's analysis in *EI,* II, 1051–52; J. Schacht's brief comments in his "Foreign Elements in Ancient Islamic Law," *Journal of the Society of Comparative Legislation,* 3d ser., Parts 3–4, p. 14; and M. Zucker's fuller discussion of the conflicts over the *qi'as* in Islam and Judaism in his "Fragments from Rav Saadya Gaon's Commentary on the Pentateuch from Manuscripts" (Hebrew), *Sura,* II, 323 ff.; and on Aḥai of Shabḥa's work, *infra,* Chap. XXVII. The Karaite equation of Prophets and Hagiographa with the Pentateuch as sources of equal rank for Jewish law evoked the sharp reaction of such Rabbanite leaders as Saadiah. Cf. the latter's introduction to his translation of the Pentateuch, ed. by J. Derenbourg, in *Oeuvres complètes,* I, 3.

6. Harkavy, *Zikhron,* VIII, 40, 67 f., 78 f., 82 ff., 129 f., 133, 141, 149 f.; Qirqisani, *K. al-Anwar,* 1.13, in Nemoy's ed., I, 53 f. (*HUCA,* VII, 384 f.). 'Anan clearly went far beyond anything suggested by the rabbis in the case of Gentiles already circumcised who wished to adopt Judaism, from whom one had to extract but a drop of the "blood of the covenant." Cf. Shabbat 135ab; Simon of Qayyara's *Halakhot gedolot,* ed. by J. Hildesheimer, p. 107; and the standard codes. We need not discount, as does Harkavy (p. 83 n. 8), the version that, according to 'Anan, anyone failing to perform the prescribed ritual of circumcision in full, "has become liable to capital punishment." This was an accepted talmudic metaphor which 'Anan, who had no hesitation in adopting the talmudic idiom while rejecting the talmudic law, had the less reason to avoid, as he recognized that the Jewish people had long lost the authority to execute criminals. It is questionable, however, whether he meant to inflict upon the transgressor all the dire consequences attached to a real capital crime. See *infra,* n. 13. The extent to which 'Anan made use of such good rabbinic authorities as the Targum and the Talmud itself may be seen in his translation of the word *dukhifat* (Lev. 11:19). By a misunderstanding of Onkelos' version and a talmudic passage (Giṭṭin 68b), he identified this prohibited bird (the lapwing or hoope?) as the simple household chicken. He forbade, therefore, the consumption of any fowl other than pigeons, calling forth the facile ridicule of Ibn Ezra (on Lev. *ad loc.*). There was nothing wrong, however, with the Karaites making use of the accumulated lore of ages concerning the Hebrew vocabulary, without accepting the reasoning and juridical derivatives therefrom of the talmudic sages.

7. Cf. the geonic *Resp.* in *Sha'are teshubah,* No. 153 (the gaon's attack may have been aimed at a pre-'Ananite rejection of phylacteries); Harkavy, *Zikhron,* VIII, 102 f., 105 ff. (taken from 'Anan's summary, the so-called *Fadhālika* of the laws of incest), 129, 170 ff., etc.; Poznanski in *REJ,* XLIV, 173 ff. The alleged misinterpreta-

tion of the biblical passages pertaining to the levirate marriage by "ignorant Rabbanites" called forth a sharp outburst also on the part of a later Karaite. Cf. the Commentary on Ruth 1:13, attributed to Salmon ben Yeruḥim, but really stemming from Jephet ben 'Ali, and ed. by I. D. Markon in *Poznanski Mem. Vol.*, Hebrew section, p. 84 (the problem of its authorship will be discussed *infra,* Chap. XXIX, n. 73). On the influence of ancient sectarian deviations on Karaism, a cornerstone in Abraham Geiger's much-disputed theory of the origins of the Old Testament canon, as well as on the numerous similarities between Philo and 'Anan, see B. Revel's *Karaite Halakah.* See also his Hebrew essay on the "Differences between the Babylonians and the Palestinians and the Sources of Karaite Law," *Horeb,* I, 1–20. It may also be noted, in this connection, that the modern catechism *Moreh ṣedeq* (Teacher of Righteousness), published in Cairo in 1948, counts the Septuagint translators among the Hebrew prophets. Cf. S. Szyszman's description of "Une Visite au Caire," *VT,* IV, 202 f. More recently, H. H. Ben-Sasson has argued convincingly, though without documentary evidence, for the assumption that much of 'Anan's and Benjamin's legislation can be understood only as a rationalization of existing practices. Cf. "The First of the Karaites—the Trend of Their Social Conception" (Hebrew), *Zion,* XV, 42–55. Unfortunately, almost nothing is known about the early religious life and observances in the countries east of Babylonia which doubtless influenced both men far more deeply than the somewhat more familiar Western patterns.

Of course, one must beware of postulating influences where similarities can easily be explained through similar biases or even pure chance. Harkavy seems to have gone too far in his pan-Essenian quest (see *supra,* Chap. XXV, nn. 50, 56), when he postulated 'Anan's dependence on the Essenian laws of physical cleanliness (pp. 200 ff.). There is no more need to look for Essenian influences on 'Anan's detailed regulations concerning the location of a toilet and man's behavior after visiting it, than there is to trace back his prohibition of cohabiting with a pregnant wife until three months after the birth of the child to any ancient precedent (Harkavy, *Zikhron,* pp. 51, 60, 130, 135). In his own day there seem to have been Rabbanite Jews who forbade intercourse with wives for forty days after the birth of a son and for eighty days after that of a daughter. Maimonides placed the blame on Karaite influences, but unwittingly admitted that he had found a discussion thereof in geonic responsa. None such seem to be extant, but they apparently stemmed from the earlier geonic period, the records of which still survived in the Maimonidean age. Cf. *M.T.* Issure biah XI.15; and A. Schwarz's groping in the dark in his comments in Jacob Guttmann *et al., Moses ben Maimon,* I, 353 f. Cf. also Qirqisani's discussion of these sexual restrictions during pregnancy, placed on a par with pederasty, under capital sanction in his *K. al-Anwar,* VI.77, ed. by Nemoy, III, 740 f., and analyzed by him in his "Contributions to Gynecology and Embryology" (Hebrew with an English summary) in *Harofé Haivri,* [XII], 1939, Part 2, pp. 35–41, 167–73. In any case, 'Anan went further than any known ancient sectarian in prohibiting sexual intercourse "during daytime; he also forbade having more than one cohabitation in a day and a night" (Qirqisani). At the same time he insisted that if a man married a second wife, his first wife could neither refuse nor be refused her due share of sexual satisfaction. Cf. Harkavy, pp. 134 f. (from Levi ben Jephet), 207. In fact, 'Anan so frequently discussed the intimate aspects of life, not only like most rabbis with no trace of prudery but with obvious delight in graphic detail, that he might be a fit subject for psychoanalytical investigation.

8. Harkavy, *Zikhron,* VIII, 40, 69, 163 (Elijah Bashyatchi); Schechter, *Documents of Jewish Sectaries,* II, 29; Midrash Tanḥuma on Noah beg., with reference to M. Shabbat II.6; b. 31b f. ʻAnan himself demanded that a light burning on the Sabbath be extinguished, but he was controverted therein by some of his successors mentioned by Qirqisani (I.19; HUCA, VII, 395 f.) and by Yeshuʻa ben Yehudah. Cf. also the discussion in Elijah Bashyatchi's *Adderet Eliyahu* (Code), fols. 50d f. On the other hand, to underscore the obligatory nature of the kindling of Sabbath lights, as taught by the ancient Rabbanites (Shabbat 25b), Maimonides insisted that a poor man ought to go begging, if need be, to secure the necessary oil (*M.T.* Shabbat V.1). The seventy-day fast, briefly alluded to by ʻAnan and mentioned by Qirqisani as "established" by him, seems to have found so little acceptance in the Karaite community that Qirqisani did not even mention it as a subject of controversy among ʻAnan's successors. Levi ben Jephet, to whom we owe fuller information concerning ʻAnan's biblical derivation of this fast, treats it as an obvious antiquarian reminiscence (Harkavy, p. 133).

9. Harkavy, *Zikhron,* VIII, 7 ff., 12, 36, 38, 140, 151 f., 158; Schechter, *Documents,* II, 26; and Sokolov's fragment (see *supra,* n. 3). On the rabbinic attitude toward sexual intercourse on the Sabbath, see the early responsum cited from a MS Adler by A. Marmorstein in his "Spuren karäischen Einflusses in der gaonäischen Halacha," *Schwarz Festschrift,* p. 469; Maimonides' *M.T.* Ishshut, XIV.1. Karaite opposition is elaborated by Qirqisani, V.13–14, ed. by Nemoy, III, 511 ff. See the Hebrew translation of that passage by Nemoy and J. J. Schwarz in their "From Al-Qirqisani's Chapters on Sabbath" (Hebrew), *Horeb,* I, 200–206. While interpreting away the commandment of *mezuzah,* like that of phylacteries, by the simple expedient of differently explaining the pertinent biblical passages (cf. Abraham ibn Ezra's succinct comments on Deut. 6:6, 8), ʻAnan went to great lengths in elaborating the laws of showfringes. According to Ibn Ezra (on Deut. 22:12), the "negators" (Karaites), probably going back to ʻAnan himself, distinguished between two kinds of showfringes for use by day or by night. Cf. Harkavy, pp. 7 ff., 142 f.; and B. Revel's pertinent arguments against D. Chwolson's attempt to connect these views with traditions of the allegedly Sadducean "people of the land" (*Karaite Halakah,* p. 14 n. 30). Similarly ʻAnan was so sharply opposed to the use of alcoholic beverages that he declared anyone entering a synagogue after indulging in intoxicating drink (even if not in a state of inebriation) as liable to capital punishment (Harkavy, pp. 4, 21). Not surprisingly, the marriage of two brothers to two sisters irked the Karaites as a particularly drastic illustration of Rabbanite aberration. It was singled out for opprobrium by the Karaite controversialist (Yeshuʻa ben Yehudah or a Byzantine writer in 1088) in a pamphlet cited in Pinsker's *Lickute,* II, 75. On its authorship, see Z. Ankori's "Some Aspects of Karaite-Rabbanite Relations in Byzantium on the Eve of the First Crusade," *PAAJR,* XXIV, 7 n. 17.

10. Harkavy, *Zikhron,* pp. 12, 17 f., 36 ff.; and the fragment published by Mann (see *supra,* n. 3); Weiss, *Dor Dor,* IV, 97, 182 n. 9. Rabbanite reactions were evidently directed against non-Karaite opponents as well. Although it is likely that ʻAnan himself, or some of his early successors, had eliminated from the Passover Haggadah all the numerous passages taken from talmudic literature and substituted for them biblical verses, the fulminations of Naṭronai bar Hilai against such practice (859) were apparently aimed at other "heretics," as well as at Karaites.

Cf. Amram Gaon's *Seder,* ed. by Frumkin, II, 206 f. Certainly, his awesome declaration that such a transgressor "denies the words of our sages and holds in contempt the provisions of Mishnah and Talmud" would have been completely lost on outspoken enemies of the Talmud. See also *infra.* n. 79.

11. Maqrizi, *Khiṭaṭ,* in A. I. Silvestre de Sacy's excerpt with a French trans. in his *Chrestomathie arabe,* I, 162 (Arabic), II, 177 (French); Ibn Ezra's *Commentary* on Exod. 21:2. See *supra,* Vol. I, pp. 302 f. n. 5; and *infra,* n. 63.

12. Harkavy, *Zikhron,* pp. 3 f., 6 f., 7 f. (compared with Menaḥot 42a), 79, 193; Epstein's fragment in *Tarbiz,* VII, 287; and *supra,* Vol. II, pp. 148 f. Under these circumstances 'Anan's, or some later 'Ananite's, statement that the Torah did not impose any obligations on the Gentiles may have been but a tacit denial of the so-called Noahide commandments postulated by the rabbis—a denial which but further widened the breach between the Jewish and the outside worlds. In its context, however, as reported by Levi ben Jephet, this seems to have been only an answer to a philosophic objection. If the Torah placed any obligation on pre-Mosaic non-Jews, opponents had queried, it must have existed from the days of Creation and, hence, why should it be called the Torah of Moses? Without discussing the problem of the Torah's preexistence—a subject which was soon to be debated heatedly, particularly in Muslim circles with reference to the parallel Qur'anic origins—the 'Ananite reply was that the commandments were named by those for whom they were obligatory (the emendation suggested by Harkavy, p. 134 n. 7, is unnecessary). Just as some were given to Jewish priests alone, so was the whole Torah called the Torah of Moses to indicate that only Moses' successors, the Jews, were obliged to submit to all of it. If this interpretation is correct, it would appear that some later disciple, rather than 'Anan himself, was concerned with such an apologia.

13. Harkavy, *Zikhron,* pp. 14 f.; Maimonides' *Commentary* on M. Ḥullin 1.2; and *supra,* Chap. XXIII, n. 14. Naṭronai bar Hilai had stated at least with respect to a "murderer in the presence of witnesses that he is to be excommunicated until he dies." Cf. S. Assaf's "Fifteen Short Responsa by R. Naṭronai" (Hebrew), *GK,* IV, 97, 99, No. 90 (completing, from a Leningrad MS, missing pages of the same MS now in Cambridge and published in Ginzberg's *Ginze Schechter,* II, 103 ff.); and the sources listed *ibid.,* p. 97. It is indeed unlikely that the sage of Fusṭaṭ, despite his relative mildness in the treatment of these schismatics (see *infra,* n. 83), should have consciously taken over from them such an important regulation. He speaks of it as being "a tradition with us and a universally accepted practice." Probably he and 'Anan went back to some unknown common source.

14. Pinsker, *Lickute kadmoniot,* II, 51 n. 2 end. Cf. Mann, *Texts and Studies,* II, 131; Schechter, *Documents,* II, 23 end. Unfortunately, Mann's list (stemming from another branch of 'Anan's descendants) breaks off in the middle and shows some variants. It probably also traced 'Anan's descent all the way back to David or some other biblical figure. In their quest for the social background of political and intellectual movements, modern scholars have tried to furnish some economic and social reasons for the rise of the Karaite schism. R. Mahler, especially, built his entire structure of Karaite origins around the theory that its founders pursued

a comprehensive program of social and national liberation. Cf. his "National and Social Foundations of 'Anan's Religion" (Yiddish), *YB,* IX, 31–62; and his comprehensive work on *Karaimer.* However, the evidence marshaled in support of this thesis is extremely meager. That 'Anan was an ardent nationalist has long been recognized, but his brand of nationalism obviously was of the quietist kind. Like other Jews, he doubtless dreamed of an early supernatural liberation of the people, and, even more than the others, tried to isolate it from contact with the outside world, but this can hardly be called a national *liberation movement.* One might, on the contrary, find one of the clearest differentials between 'Anan and the other sectarian leaders of the day, in that he did *not* endeavor to alter the status of Jewry through direct political action. Nor is there any evidence that he advocated the cause of the poor as such. His insistence on unleavened bread made of barley, his demand that tithes be paid also from metal ores dug from the ground (we hear little about Jewish mining enterprises at that time) and his turning over of the levitical dues to the synagogue (Schechter, *Documents,* II, 3; Harkavy, *Zikhron,* pp. 131, 135), were but reflections of the same ascetic literalism which colored so many of his other teachings. Nor is his reiteration of the prohibition of usury and injunction to lend even more readily to poverty-stricken coreligionists (Schechter, p. 27) in any way a departure from accepted views. Similarly his restoration of the old law concerning the cancellation of debts (only in so far as these originated from loans, not from sales or services) during the Sabbatical year (Harkavy, pp. 10 f.) was but an obvious application of the biblical law, concurred in by many talmudic sages themselves even after Hillel's reform (see *supra,* Vol. II, p. 262). On the other hand, he went further than any contemporary Rabbanite leader in his hostility to the illiterate masses from whom, as we recall, he tried completely to segregate his own group of followers. In fact, an excellent case can be made to show that, while Karaism generally cut across class lines, 'Anan's and, even more, Benjamin's legislative measures pursued a decided policy of *not* altering the established economic order, and of upholding the economic interests of the upper classes. See the examples cited by H. Ben-Sasson in "The First of the Karaites," *Zion,* XV, 42 ff.; and particularly *infra,* n. 34. On Nemoy's theory that Karaism owed its origin to the uncouth eastern mountaineers, see *ibid.* and *supra,* Chap. XXV, n. 71.

15. Harkavy, *Zikhron,* pp. 109, 113, 119. The gradual further emancipation of the Jewish woman from the talmudic era (cf. *supra,* Vol. II, pp. 235 ff., 412 f.) may be gleaned from stray extant records. The increasingly urbanized Jewish ladies must have caught something of the spirit of the ever freer Roman matrons in the legally monogamous Byzantine society. The leeway given them even with respect to the dissolution of marriage found expression in the Palestinian *Sefer ha-Ma'asim* at the turn from the Byzantine to the Muslim age, where a special sanction was inserted against a man inciting a married woman to secure divorce from her husband, so that they might marry (in the fragment ed. by J. Mann in *Tarbiz,* I, Part 3, p. 12). Finally, it led even in Babylonia to the "reform in behalf of the rebellious woman" of 687 (see *infra,* Chap. XXVII, nn. 71, 153). As elsewhere, 'Anan seems to have but supplied a new rationale for existing trends, although his permission for a woman to demand divorce clearly ran counter to the biblical law. Modern scholars were at a loss to find for it any biblical backing (see Harkavy, p. 119 n. 1). Nemoy's suggestion that it may have stemmed from 'Anan's equation of husband and wife

as "one flesh" and hence as enjoying the same rights (*Karaite Anthology*, p. 325) is unlikely, as it would logically lead to a degree of equality between the sexes undreamed of by any Karaite author.

16. The identity of Daniel, the exilarchic pretender against David ben Yehudah has long been in doubt. See *supra* Chap. XXIII, n. 6. However, we have the clear statement of Barhebraeus, our main source, that he was an 'Ananite and that he was supported by the "Babylonians" (Baghdadians). With a fair degree of success I. D. Markon identified him also with Daniel mentioned obliquely in Naṭronai bar Hilai's aforementioned responsum cited in 'Amram Gaon's *Seder*. Cf. Markon's "Wer ist der in einem Responsum von Natronai Gaon II erwähnte Karäer Daniel?" *Moritz Schaefer Festschrift*, pp. 130–36. J. Mann's main objection to this identification, namely that no self-respecting members of either Babylonian academy would have supported the candidacy of a sectarian leader (see his *Texts and Studies*, II, 128 ff.) presupposes a clearer line of demarcation between Rabbanites and 'Ananites within half a century after the initial conflict, than is anywhere indicated in the sources, or otherwise seems likely. We certainly have no right to dismiss an explicit statement by Barhebraeus on the basis of that hypothetical rigid separation.

17. In his letter to Babylonia Ben Meir relates not only his own sufferings at the hands of the "descendants of 'Anan, the princes," but also mentions that one of his ancestors, Musa, had lost his life in the Temple yard "at the hand of the seed of 'Anan." See Bornstein's edition in *Sefer ha-Yobel . . . Nahum Sokolow*, pp. 106 f.; and Mann's comments thereon in his *Jews in Egypt*, I, 57 ff., and *Texts and Studies*, II, 7 f., 128 ff. Here Mann reconstructs a fairly complete list of Karaite *nesi'im* of the Holy Land from the ninth century on. Cf. also the earlier compilation by Poznanski in his *Babylonische Geonim im nachgaonäischen Zeitalter*, pp. 125 ff.

18. Compare Benjamin's *Mas'at Binyamin* (Civil Code), fols. 2ab, 3ad, 5ab, 6ab with 'Anan's statements in Harkavy, *Zikhron*, VIII, 12 ff.; Qirqisani, I.14 (*HUCA*, VII, 386 f.). Cf. also the excerpts from Benjamin's Book of Commandments assembled by Harkavy, VIII, pp. 175 ff.; a passage cited by Tobiah ben Moses in Pinsker's *Lickute kadmoniot*, II, 95; and other data cited by Ben-Sasson in *Zion*, XV, 50 ff. More sweepingly than the rabbis, Benjamin denied wives any control over their property and declared, "The wife's property belongs to her husband during her lifetime and after death." He also unconditionally disqualified women from testimony in court and forced husbands to divorce childless wives after ten years (*Mas'at Binyamin*, fols. 3a, 4ad, 5ac). The husband's unrestricted right to inherit his wife's property was challenged, however, by such later Karaites as Qumisi. Cf. Qirqisani's *K. al-Anwar*, XIII.9, ed. by Nemoy, V, 1275 f.; and the latter's *Karaite Anthology*, p. 326. The very fact that Benjamin found it necessary to compile a special manual for civil law, the *Mas'at Binyamin*, published by later Karaites in Gozlowo-Eupatoria, 1834, in addition to the more customary ritualistic Book of Commandments, is revealing. Evidently, as a judge he had considerable experience with the administration of justice in civil affairs. He never tired of reiterating that Jews must appoint judges in every city even in the dispersion and that "only a Jew can judge another Jew." The Jewish judge, on his part, ought to be available for sitting in judgment "at any time" (*Mas'at Binyamin*, fols. lab, 3a). Benjamin was the first to give the sect the designation "Karaites," in contra-

distinction to "'Ananites." This is the very opposite of the express avowal of allegiance to Jesus through the name *Christianus* selected by Paul and his associates in Antioch. *See supra,* Vol. II, p. 366 n. 44.

19. Qirqisani, I.14 (*HUCA,* VII, 387); Elijah Bashyatchi's code, *Adderet Eliyahu* fol. 163b; *Mas'at Binyamin,* fols. 5d, 6ad; Harkavy, *Zikhron,* VIII, 176 ff. Although accepted by Hadassi, Benjamin's informal method of breaking an engagement was rejected by Bashyatchi and others, while his radical calendar reform is barely mentioned in later Karaite letters. Benjamin's insistence on the subjection of children to the whole burden of the law was likewise abandoned, although Ḥasan aṣ-Ṣuri, the Samaritan, still berated the Rabbanites for their neglect on this score. Cf. the summary of Aṣ-Ṣuri's *Kitab aṭ-Ṭabakh* in E. Robertson's *Catalogue of Samaritan MSS in the John Rylands Library,* p. 112.

20. See Joseph al-Baṣir's statement in Pinsker's *Lickute kadmoniot,* II, 199; Yehudah Hadassi's *Eshkol ha-kofer,* fol. 25c. We shall see that Benjamin's concern with the doctrine of intermediaries arose, not like that of Philo, from the query as to how a perfect Creator could have created such an imperfect universe, but rather from a studied endeavor to explain away the anthropomorphisms of the Bible. Cf. *infra,* Chap. XXXIV. On Benjamin's Bible commentaries—we have later quotations from, but no real fragments of, his exegetical works on the Pentateuch, Isaiah, Canticles, Ecclesiastes, and Daniel—and their composition in Hebrew, rather than in Arabic, cf. Mann's *Texts and Studies,* II, 11 f., 17 n. 32. The mystic emphases of Benjamin's commentary on Eccles. were contrasted with his own more directly exegetical approach by Salmon ben Yeruḥim, Benjamin's admiring, but critical, follower. Cf. Neubauer's *Aus der Petersburger Bibliothek,* p. 107; and the Hebrew translation in Pinsker's *Lickute,* II, 109.

21. Mann, *Jews in Egypt,* I, 52 ff.; II, 41 f.; and *supra,* Chap. XXIII, n. 35. That such appeasement of Palestine was only temporary is evident from the subsequent Saadiah–Ben Meir controversy. The intervening growth of the Karaite center in Jerusalem may well have convinced the Babylonians even before Saadiah that the best way to safeguard the people's unity was to accentuate the hegemony of their country in all matters of law and ritual. Cf. *supra,* Chap. XXIII, n. 33.

22. Benjamin's address to the whole diaspora is even less suspect than the claim of later Karaite leaders to be the heads of the "whole diaspora of Israel." See Mann, *Jews in Egypt,* I, 176. For no good reason, therefore, A. Neubauer suggested that this formula was inserted by some copyist. Cf. his *Aus der Petersburger Bibliothek,* p. 6.

23. Pinsker, *Lickute kadmoniot,* II, 104 ff. On the author and date of this significant pamphlet, see Poznanski, *Karaite Literary Opponents,* pp. 72 ff. On the quest for unity vs. minority status in the Byzantine Karaite community, see the illustrations cited by Z. Ankori in *PAAJR,* XXV, 166 f.

24. Pinsker, *Lickute kadmoniot,* II, 2 ff.; Bashyatchi, *Adderet,* fols. 78c ff.; Solomon ben Aaron's *Appiryon 'asah* (Survey of Karaism) in Neubauer, *Aus der Petersburger*

Bibliothek, pp. 16 ff. Cf. D. Sidersky's brief analysis of "Le Caraïsme et ses doctrines," *RHR,* CXIV, 210 ff. In his *Aḥar ReSheF le-baqqer be-sifrut ha-Qaraim* (A Critique of Firkovitch's Studies in Karaite Literature), pp. 19 ff., P. (F.) Frankl has convincingly argued, however, for Hadassi's priority over Nissi ben Nuḥ's spurious tract. On the exclusive use of Hebrew in prayers, see Aaron ben Elijah of Nicomedia's *Gan 'Eden,* fol. 70b, trying to minimize even the biblical Daniel's Aramaic prayers. Qirqisani first reported objectively Benjamin's view of the "angel who created the entire world, sent out the prophets and commissioned the messengers, performed miracles and issued orders and prohibitions." But subsequently he devoted an entire paragraph to the combating of this doctrine. Cf. his *K. al-Anwar,* I.14, III.3 (in Nemoy's ed. I, 55; II, 190 ff.; his trans. in *HUCA,* VII, 386; and "A Tenth Century Criticism of the Doctrine of the Logos," *JBL,* LXIV, 523 ff.). That Daniel and his disciples apparently went the whole length of denying the very existence of angels may be deduced from the tract emanating from his school and published by Mann in *JQR,* XII, 261, 275 f., 447, 458; XV, 367, 387 f.

25. Qirqisani, *K. al-Anwar,* I.2 (21), 18 (I, 14, 59; *HUCA,* VII, 330, 391); Jacob ben Reuben in his *Sefer ha-'Osher* (Bible commentary) cited in Pinsker's *Lickute kadmoniot,* I, 22. On the date of this author, see Poznanski's *Karaite Literary Opponents,* pp. 66 ff. Understandably, these disagreements and inconsistencies lent themselves to facile ridicule by enemies. In his polemical poem, *Essa meshali* (see *infra,* Chap. XXXII, n. 12). Saadiah heaped scorn upon the daily changes of mind by Karaite leaders. Cf. the text republished by B. M. Lewin in *Rav Saadya Gaon,* ed. by J. L. Fishman, p. 512. Even a Samaritan glossator on the Samaritan Pentateuch (to Lev. 18:6) spoke disparagingly of the "erroneous combinations" of the Karaites and the fact that "they themselves contradict one another." Cited by S. Munk in his *Notice sur Abou'l-Walid Merwan ibn-Djana'h,* p. 8 n. 1 (in *JA,* 4th ser., XIV, 304 n. 1).

26. Cf. Yeshu'a ben Yehudah's *Sefer ha 'Arayot* (Book of Prohibited Degrees in Marriage), ed. by I. Markon, pp. 131 f., previously known from a Leiden MS described by M. Steinschneider in his *Catalogus codicum hebraeorum Bibliothecae Academiae Lugduno-Batavae* (Leyden), p. 194. David ben Boaz' commentary is known to us only from some brief citations by subsequent authors, beginning with Joseph al-Baṣir's *Sefer ha-Mo'adim* (Book of Festivals) in Pinsker's *Lickute kadmoniot,* II, 199. This neglect is doubly noteworthy as five generations later, his descendant Solomon ben David took pains to extol him in the aforementioned genealogical list (see *supra,* n. 14) for having "explained and illumined the words of the living God" (Pinsker, *Lickute,* II, 51 n. 2). Stressing the importance of the eastern sectarians for the rise of the new schism, L. Nemoy protested against the "oversimplification" of the accepted view of 'Anan as the "founder of Karaism." See his remarks in *Löw Mem. Vol.,* pp. 239 ff., his "Social and Economic Factors in Early Karaism" (Yiddish), *YB,* XXXIII, 95–112, 251, and his "Early Karaism (The Need for a New Approach)," *JQR,* XL, 307–15 (both with reference to Mahler's *Karaimer*). On the other hand, his own contention, mentioned above, that Karaism was "really founded by these uncouth pioneers" of the Iranian Plateau (*ibid.,* p. 310) is no less an oversimplification at the opposite end. It required, as we have tried to show, the impetus given to Karaism by a heresiarch of the status

and stature of ʿAnan to channelize into a mainstream most of the forces of discontent found in great profusion in the Jewish communities from the Mediterranean to the borders of India.

27. Salmon's Arabic Commentary on Psalms (69:1), cited in Hebrew trans. in Pinsker, *Lickute kadmoniot,* I, 21 f. On "Karḳisiya," see M. Streck's pertinent article in *EI,* II, 765 f. Qirqisani wrote two complementary works in 937–38: the oft-quoted code of laws, *K. al-Anwar* which, apart from legal problems and the history of Jewish sects, contains a number of important excursuses on doctrinal subjects; and a vast commentary on the nonlegal portions of the Pentateuch, likewise picturesquely entitled *K. ar-Riyad w-al-ḥadayiq* (Book of Gardens and Parks). Only the former is now available in a comprehensive edition by L. Nemoy. Since the editor has refrained, however, from adding explanatory notes (only partially replaced by his articles quoted here in various connections), the older publications of fragments by Harkavy, Hirschfeld, and Poznanski, as well as the more recent textual studies and translations by Vajda, Zucker, and others have retained independent value. Cf. the list in M. Schloesinger's review of Nemoy's edition in *Journal of Jewish Bibliography,* II, 101–3. Cf. also *infra,* Chap. XXXIV; and, on excerpts from the *Book of Gardens, infra,* Chaps. XXIX–XXX. A contemporary of both Saadiah and Qirqisani, Salmon ben Yeruḥim seems to have been born between 909 and 914, according to I. Davidson's computation in the introduction to his edition of Salmon's *Sefer Milḥamot Adonai* (Book of the Wars of the Lord), pp. 4 ff. The distinction between Karaites and ʿAnanites was still mentioned as a matter of course by the author of the Karaite polemical fragment published by S. Assaf in *Tarbiz,* IV, 48.

28. Some interesting excerpts for the history of the early Karaite community of Jerusalem are assembled in *Sefer ha-Yishub,* II, 41 f., 43 ff. Cf. also Mann, *Texts and Studies,* II, 3 ff., 1469 ff. On David ben Abraham al-Fasi's Palestinian residence see the plausible arguments presented by S. L. Skoss in the introduction to his edition of David's distinguished lexicographical work, *K. Jamiʿ al-alfaẓ* (Agron), I, p. xxxvi; and *infra,* Chap. XXX, n. 18. On Daniel's growing animosity toward the founder of the sect, see *infra,* nn. 29, 57. The status of the Karaites under the conquering Crusaders is discussed *supra,* Chap. XXI, n. 30. After 1099, Jerusalem and its academy ceased to function as the world center of the Karaite movement. Even a century earlier Salmon had already voiced the fear that, were the Christians to secure power over Jerusalem, they would drive the Jews out. This comment was doubtless elicited by the approach of the Byzantine army under John Tsimiskes in 972–74. The days of Byzantine intolerance were clearly far from forgotten. Cf. Mann, *Jews in Egypt,* I, 46 f., 200 n. 1; his *Texts and Studies,* II, 18 f., 42, 120 ff.; and *supra,* Chap. XIX, n. 11. His doubts as to whether Salmon was still living in 972, or even in 968–69 (p. 19 n. 34) are hardly justified, since the Karaite author had apparently not yet reached the age of sixty then.

29. Poznanski, *Karaite Literary Opponents,* pp. 59 f. (citing a British Museum MS). Some important aspects of the life and work of Tobiah ben Moses the Translator and his part in the newly arising Karaite center of Constantinople have been elucidated by Z. Ankori's searching analysis of "The Correspondence of Tobias ben Moses the Karaite of Constantinople," which is to appear in *Baron Jub. Vol.* Cf.

also his more general observations in "Some Aspects of Karaite-Rabbanite Relations in Byzantium," *PAAJR,* XXIV, 1 ff.; XXV, 157, 168 f., 178 ff.; and particularly his Columbia University dissertation, *Karaites in Byzantium: the Formative Years (970–1100).* The works of the later Byzantine Karaite writers have long been known through the publications of Karaite presses, particularly that of Gozlowo-Eupatoria in the 1830's. Yehudah Hadassi's encyclopedic work, *Eshkol ha-kofer,* has long served as a particularly rich source of information for all students in the field, although its text is in need of critical reexamination. Some portions had actually been omitted so as not to offend Christian sensitivities, especially in that period of Russian censorship and a general Russo-Karaite rapprochement. See the section recovered by A. Scheiber in his "Manuscript Materials for the Literary Work of Yehudah Hadassi," *Bernhard Heller Jubilee Volume,* pp. 101–29. That is why the earlier analyses by scholars, both Rabbanite and Karaite, pertaining to that period, are less obsolete than those regarding Karaite origins. Unfortunately, partisan bias has colored most of the descriptions of the Karaite past. Already Bashyatchi, Karaism's leading codifier, was quite hazy about the early phases of his own community four centuries before. The distorted picture drawn by him has misled generations of scholars. Cf. now Z. Ankori's "Elijah Bashyachi: an Inquiry into His Traditions concerning the Beginnings of Karaism in Byzantium" (Hebrew), *Tarbiz,* XXV, 44–65, 183–201 (with a good English summary; also reprint). S. I. Lucki's *Oraḥ Ṣaddiqim* (The Road of the Righteous); or his larger work *Me'irat 'Eynayim (The Enlightening of the Eyes;* only the interesting tenth chapter of the second part was published by J. Mann in his *Texts and Studies,* II, 1409–43); and M. Sultanski's *Zecher Caddikim (The Memory of the Righteous),* ed. by S. Poznanski, may be regarded as typical of modern Karaite historiography. Cf. Poznanski's illuminating introduction. On the Rabbanite side, the publications of Jost, Fürst, Graetz, Gottlober, and particularly Pinsker, Harkavy, and Poznanski have laid foundations for a really scientific investigation of the early history of the schism. See, for example, Poznanski's *Karaite Literary Opponents;* and his bibliographical survey of *Die karäische Literatur der letzten dreissig Jahre, 1878–1908.* More recently J. Mann and others have published many valuable documents. Cf. I. Markon's "Das Karäertum (Wesen, Entstehung und Entwicklung)," *Jeschurun,* XIII, 603–10, XIV, 25–32, 139–43 (incomplete); J. Mann's "New Studies in Karaism," *Yearbook CCAR,* XLIV, 220–41 (in part summarizing the content of the numerous documents published in his *Texts,* II); and S. Assaf's "New Material on the History of the Karaites in the Orient" (Hebrew) in his *Be-Ohole Ya'aqob,* pp. 181 ff.

30. See the sources cited in B. Revel, *Karaite Halakah,* pp. 17 ff.; 'Anan's statement in Schechter, *Documents,* II, 5; Mann, *Texts and Studies,* II, 13, 19 f.; Sahl's *Sefer Dinim* (Civil Code), cited by Samuel ben Moses al-Maghribi in his *Kitab al-Murshid* (Book of Precepts), XI, ed. by Julius Cohn, pp. 1 (Arabic), 11 ff. (German); and Qumisi's commentary on Leviticus partly recovered in Ginzberg's *Ginze Schechter,* II, 476, 481. Purely theoretical was also the postulate of some later Karaite authors that a high priest be allowed to marry only the daughter of a priest, and that the tithe of animals, which Rabbanite law had treated on a par with the "second tithe," be given to the priests. As Geiger and Revel pointed out, these opinions are also found in Philo and the Apocrypha (Jubilees, Tobit), for whom, of course, these still were living issues. Cf. Revel's *Karaite Halakah,* pp. 77 f., 79 f. On the Karaite leaders' uncertain attitude toward the contemporary

application of the laws governing the ancient Temple ritual, cf. also *infra,* n. 47. On the other hand, they almost unanimously adhered to the monogamous interpretation of the term "sister" in Lev. 18:18. See, for instance, Qirqisani's lengthy discourse in his *K. al-Anwar,* XI. 19, ed. by Nemoy, V, 1141 ff.; and Nemoy's English trans. thereof in his "Al-Qirqisani on Leviticus 18:18," *Bernhard Heller Jubilee Volume,* pp. 258–64.

31. Mann, *Jews in Egypt,* I, 176 ff.; his *Texts and Studies,* II, 43 ff., 128 ff.; Jephet's statement cited by Aaron ben Joseph in *Sefer ha-Mibḥar* (Commentary on the Pentateuch), fol. 42b; Samuel al-Maghribi's *Murshid,* VII, ed. by S. Gitelson, pp. 21 f. By equating without much ado the designation *ahl al-kitab* (people of the book), widely used in Muslim circles since Mohammed for all Jews and Christians, with *bene miqra* (followers of Scripture), by then a synonym for Karaites, Salmon cleverly insinuated the ancient origin of the Karaite schism. The Karaite teachers were far from consistent, however. In the same commentary on Ruth which begins with the glorification of genuine piety as greatly superior to genealogical distinction, Jephet ben 'Ali concludes with the statement that the descendants of Zerubbabel were destined to serve as chiefs (*nesi'im*) until the coming of the Redeemer. Cf. the text ed. by Markon in *Poznanski Mem. Vol.,* Hebrew section, pp. 81, 96; and on its authorship see *supra,* n. 7. Mahler's suggestion that these *nesi'im* were not recognized by the Karaites until the eleventh century (*Karaimer,* pp. 374 f.) is untenable.

32. Cf. Mann, *Texts and Studies,* I, 372 ff., 383 ff.; Pinsker, *Lickute kadmoniot,* II, 51 n. 2. On the various extant genealogical lists, including one of 1838, which traced the descent of the Karaite *nesi'im* back to 'Anan, see E. Strauss, *Toledot ha-Yehudim be-Miṣrayim,* II, 559 ff.

33. Samuel's *Murshid,* XI, ed. by Cohn, pp. 16 ff. (Arabic), 45 ff. (German). Cf. also Hadassi's *Eshkol,* fol. 127b. On 'Anan's attitude to proselytes, see *supra,* n. 12.

34. Pinsker, *Lickute kadmoniot,* II, 31 f.; Jephet's *Commentary* on Isa. 55:2, in Neubauer, *Aus der Petersburger Bibliothek,* pp. 17, 112; Hadassi's *Eshkol,* fol. 59c; Ginzberg, *Ginze Schechter,* II, 435, 438 f. Sahl's authorship of this liturgical fragment is hesitantly suggested by Ginzberg. As a matter of fact the entire interpretation of this section is principally based on the contrast between the "repentant sinners" and the "evil men of Israel" in which Ginzberg sees allusions to the struggle between Karaites and Rabbanites. In his *Karaimer,* pp. 323 ff., Mahler has meritoriously culled from the older Karaite literature a considerable number of passages attacking the social inequalities in the contemporary Jewish community and the abuses by the ruling Rabbanite circles. One must bear in mind, however, that much of this material stems from Karaite commentaries on Scripture, which naturally caught something of the spirit of the prophetic denunciations of ancient society. Homilists of all faiths, commenting on the memorable prophetic exhortations, could not refrain from chastising their own contemporaries for similar transgressions. Few of these, however, actively promoted social change such as was reflected in the ancient Deuteronomic legislation. The Karaites, too, who in their partisan ardor attacked the Rabbanites on every count—their denunciations of alleged Rabbanite ritualistic transgressions far transcend in number and intensity of feeling

those directed at social inequities—ardently championed a total revamping of the existing ceremonial law, but had little to suggest in the way of new social legislation. All they preached was renunciation of worldly goods and a more righteous application of the existing laws governing human relations. It suffices to compare Benjamin's (or any other Karaite's) civil code with its minor modifications of the existing civil law, with the radical departures in the whole realm of ritual and religious practice championed by the same man in his Book of Commandments. Almost all the denunciations, moreover, of trade morals, communal oppression and lack of charity could, and often were, delivered with equal vehemence by Rabbanite preachers. Curiously, some of the choicest morsels taken by Mahler (p. 347 n. 1, 342 n. 34) from "Daniel al-Qumisi's Homilies," published by A. Marmorstein in *Ṣiyyon,* III, 31 ff., are almost certainly not of Al-Qumisi's authorship. Cf. Mann, *Texts and Studies,* II, 18. Probably of later medieval origin, they may even be, despite the frequent use of the term *maskil* (enlightened person) by Karaites, of Rabbanite provenance. In fact, the distinction between Rabbanite and Karaite social ethics is so tenuous that, when Marmorstein undertook to locate traces of Karaite concepts in the Midrash (see his aforementioned essay in *Schwarz Festschrift,* pp. 455–70), he could do so only on the basis of ritualistic divergences, rather than of differences in social outlook. See also *supra,* n. 14.

35. Cf. P. Birnbaum's ed. of *The Arabic Commentary of Yefet ben 'Ali the Karaite on the Book of Hosea,* pp. xxxi, 50 f.; Ginzberg's *Ginze Schechter,* II, 456 ff. (this fragment is poorly preserved and its meaning quite obscure); a commentary on Hos. 12:9, ed. by Mann in *JQR,* XII, 496; Qumisi's commentary on Lev. 21:7, *ibid.,* p. 477 (cf. also the sources cited *ibid.,* pp. 469 f. n. 16); Samuel al-Maghribi's *Murshid,* XI, ed. by Cohn, pp. 5 ff. (Arabic), 21 ff. (German); Maimonides' *M.T.* Matnot 'aniyyim, X.17, with the comments thereon in my *Essays on Maimonides,* p. 248. Cf. also *infra,* n. 39.

36. Benjamin's *Mas'at Binyamin,* fols. 1c, 2acd; Qirqisani, *K. al-Anwar,* I.3.32 (*HUCA,* VII, 344); Ben Zuṭa's debate with Saadiah reported by Abraham ibn Ezra in his *Commentary* on Exod. 21:24; Hadassi's *Eshkol,* fols. 102c, 104cd, 105abcd, 149c; and later sources cited in Revel's *Karaite Halakah,* pp. 51 f., 56 f., 61 f., 65, 70 f., 74 f. Revel quotes also ample Philonian and Samaritan parallels. On the meaning of *karet,* see also Ibn Ezra's pointed remarks in his *Commentary* on Gen. 17:14.

37. L. Nemoy, "A Tenth Century Disquisition on Suicide according to Old Testament Law," *JBL,* LVII, 411–20 (an English trans. of, and commentary on, Qirqisani's *K. al-Anwar,* VI.47, in his ed. III, 683 ff.). Even some slower forms of suicide to beg God's forgiveness for sin were discouraged here, "for his [the sinner's] suicide merely wipes out one of his sins, whereas repentance would undo all of them." On the importance of these injunctions, see *infra,* Chap. XXVIII, n. 51.

38. Harkavy, *Zikhron,* VIII, 113, 118 f.; Benjamin, *Mas'at Binyamin,* fols. 5ab, 6c; Hadassi, *Eshkol,* fol. 121ab; Levi ben Jephet cited by Aaron ben Elijah in his *Gan 'Eden,* fol. 155a. According to Qirqisani (I.10, 7, pp. 50 f.; *HUCA,* VII, 381), Babylonian Jews outlawed betrothals during the jubilee year—as if jubilee years had ever been observed in the Euphrates Valley. Neither is B. Revel's suggestion that the Karaite author may simply have mistaken a Palestinian for a Babylonian

custom (*Horeb,* I, 2 n. 4) borne out by the Palestinian sources. On the far more humane treatment by the Rabbanites of a raped married woman see Ketubot 51b; and Ibn Ezra's comment on Lev. 20:10. Although the "bridegroom's benediction" used to be recited in the presence of ten adult men already in talmudic times (see T. Megillah IV.14, 226; b. Ketubot 8b), medieval rabbinic opinion was greatly divided on the required quorum at weddings. Cf. my *Jewish Community,* III, 46 f. n. 36.

39. Qirqisani, *K. al-Anwar,* I.3 (38), 4 (12), pp. 26, 35 (*HUCA,* VII, 346 ff., 355), with reference to Ḥagigah 16a; cf. *supra,* Chap. XVIII, n. 27. On the "best men," see the pertinent section of a Karaite prayer book containing formularies for betrothal and divorce, written in 1334–35 (not 1423–24; cf. E. Strauss's *Toledot,* II, 548) by the Egyptian scholar, Abu'l Fakhr ibn 'Imran and published by Mann in his *Texts and Studies,* II, 189 f., together with Mann's comments, *ibid.,* pp. 162 n. 8a, 1127 n. 142. Qirqisani's strictures on Rabbanite sex life included, on the one hand, his deprecation of the Rabbanite requirement that, after consummation of marriage, the couple should abstain from cohabitation for seven days, and, on the other hand, his censure of the alleged local custom of the "people of Syria" (Palestine) who "prescribe depucelation by means of a finger." According to him, the latter feared that, if after a natural intercourse the bridegroom discovered lack of virginity and annulled the marriage, he would already have committed the sin of illicit cohabitation. Qirqisani's own advice was no less strange, namely to interrupt the coitus on the first sign of the bride's premarital indiscretion.

40. Cf. Samuel al-Maghribi's *Murshid,* IX, ed. by D. Weiss in his *Incestgesetze bei den Karäern,* pp. 1 (Arabic), 14 (German); Elijah Bashyatchi's *Adderet,* section on 'Arayot (fols. 144 ff.). Here (especially Chap. V, fols. 148c ff.) the contradictory views of the leading Karaite authorities are well summarized. Cf. also the pertinent texts of Yeshu'a ben Yehudah's *Sefer ha-'Arayot,* ed. by I. Markon. Otherwise modern scholarship has more often debated than added substantially to our understanding of the ramified Karaite doctrine of these staggered relationships. Cf. L. M. Epstein's brief summary in his *Marriage Laws in the Bible and the Talmud,* pp. 263 ff.

41. Qumisi cited by Jacob ben Reuben in Pinsker, *Lickute kadmoniot,* II, 85 (Jacob himself opposed that interpretation with reference to Num. 27:9); his commentary on Lev. 22:12 in the text published in Ginzberg, *Ginze Schechter,* II, 481 (a continuation of Mann's text in *JQR,* XII, 479; cf. also the sources discussed by Ginzberg, p. 475); Qirqisani, *supra,* n. 39; David ben Boaz cited (and repudiated) by Aaron ben Elijah in *Gan 'Eden,* fols. 165d–166a; Elijah Bashyatchi's *Adderet,* fols. 172b f.; Ibn Daud's chronicle in *MJC,* I, 79. Cf. also Ginzberg, *Ginze Schechter,* II, 470 ff.; the polemical text ed. by Assaf in *Tarbiz,* IV, 45 ff. (Arabic), 197 ff. (Hebrew); and, more generally, Z. Karl's survey of "The Daughter's Inheritance in Israel" (Hebrew), *Ha-Peraklit,* VI, 211–17. On the opinions of the Muslim schools of jurisprudence, largely derived from the Qur'anic injunction that women receive only half of the men's inheritance (4:11–12), cf. e.g., T. W. Juynboll's *Handbuch des islamischen Gesetzes nach der Lehre der schafi'itschen Schule,* pp. 246 f. It may be of interest to note that Jacob ben Reuben also reports (Pinsker, *loc. cit.*) Sahl ben

Maṣliaḥ's deduction from Num. 27:9 that maternal and paternal brothers must be treated equally with respect to inheritance. One wonders whether Sahl was prepared to press this equality to the extent of safeguarding the claims of a maternal half-brother. If so, the estate of a father, whose only son had predeceased him without leaving children, might go to a stepson. This conclusion, however, would not be surprising for Sahl who, as one of the extreme exponents of the catenary doctrine (*rikkub*), doubtless postulated almost blood relationship between a stepfather and a stepson. Cf. Pinsker, *Lickute,* II, 65 n. 3, 200.

42. Qirqisani, *K. al-Anwar,* I.3 (7 ff.), 19 (1 ff.), pp. 17 ff., 59 ff. (*HUCA,* VII, 333 ff., 392 ff., 397). On the unceasing Karaite debates on the issue of kindling and extinguishing lights on Sabbath, see *supra,* n. 8; and Elijah Bashyatchi's *Adderet,* fols. 50 ff. Elijah reports here (fols. 52d f.) that his grandfather and father were the first to permit candles lighted before the sunset on Friday. With a broad overstatement he also claims that this reform was accepted by all, "except a few who had come from a distant land and remote islands." Cf. the sources cited by Ankori in *Tarbiz,* XXV, 58 n. 47, 183 n. 66. But even these Constantinople "liberals" outlawed the Rabbanite practice of having Gentiles kindle lights and perform other chores for Jews if the Gentiles did them for their own benefit. "According to our law," Bashyatchi informs us, "no Israelite may make use of any work done by a Gentile on Sabbath, whether the latter did it for himself or for an Israelite."

43. Salmon ben Yeruḥim's *Milḥamot,* ed. by Davidson, pp. 84, 105 f.; Ginzberg, *Ginze Schechter,* II, 541 f.; the Karaite fragments, ed. by Mann in *JQR,* XII, 463 f., 473 f. (on Lev. 16:31); XV, 388; and Ibn Saqawaihi's views reconstructed by M. Zucker from the additional fragment of Saadiah's polemical tract against this mysterious Karaite spokesman (whose identity with Salmon is here again effectively denied), published by Zucker in his "Two Anti-Karaite Fragments" (Hebrew), *PAAJR,* XVIII, 12 n. 12. Cf. also Hadassi's *Eshkol,* fol. 56d (distinguishing between private fasts forbidden on Sabbath and those occasioned by "the desecration of the Lord's honor, the desolation of His sanctuary" and other national misfortunes which must invariably be observed); and Samuel al-Maghribi's *Murshid,* in N. Weisz's ed. of the *"Traktat" über den Sabbat bei den Karäern, passim.* The extreme latitude given by Hadassi, "the Mourner," to the term *'innui* (affliction) in Lev. 16:29 (*Eshkol,* fol. 95ab) appeared exaggerated even to a moderate Karaite like Elijah Bashyatchi (cf. *Adderet,* fol. 74cd). In his personal debate with a Karaite on the meaning of the prohibition in Exod. 35:3, Ibn Ezra pointed out that, were one to take the phrasing of this passage literally, one would forbid the kindling of fire only on the day (*be-yom*) not the evening of the Sabbath. Since we depend on tradition to broaden the meaning of this term, *yom,* we may rely on it also with respect to the definition of the prohibited act. Cf. Ibn Ezra's short commentary *ad loc.,* ed. by L. (J. L.) Fleischer, pp. 337 ff.; and P. R. Weis's remarks thereon in *Melilah,* I, 53. Cf. *infra,* Chap. XXVII, n. 76.

44. Qirqisani, *K. al-Anwar,* I.10 (8), p. 51 (HUCA, VII, 381 f.). The "special work" on these differences from which this Karaite theologian admittedly derived his information is probably identical with the *Sefer ha-Ḥilluqim,* ed. by M. Margulies, and discussed *supra,* Chap. XXIII, n. 25.

45. Harkavy, *Zikhron,* VIII, 189. Such dependence on the natural Spring (*Abib*) in Palestine caused many complications for the Byzantine and other distant communities living under different climatic conditions. They had to rely upon news from the Holy Land arriving on time for the celebration of their Passover, an expectation frequently frustrated by the precarious communications in the eastern Mediterranean, particularly in periods of heightened international tensions. Cf. the illustrations cited by Ankori in *PAAJR,* XXIV, 25 ff.; XXV, 157 ff. Cf. also n. 46. The Karaites also went further than the Rabbanite jurists in outlawing work on the half-holidays of Passover and the Feast of Tabernacles except for men living in dire poverty who could not sustain the loss of so many working days. Cf. Samuel al-Maghribi's *Murshid,* in F. Kaufmann's ed. of the *Traktat über die Neulichtbeobachtung und den Jahresbeginn,* pp. 10 f., 15 f. (Arabic). 15 ff., 24 f. (German). Only with respect to the observance of the Festival of Weeks there seems to have been no difference of opinion among the various Karaite groups, as indeed among most sectarians. Cf. *infra,* n. 81. Perhaps by design Abraham Firkovitch inscribed a dedication of a copy of his *Mibḥar Yesharim* (Selection of Righteous [Works], now in possession of Columbia University) on Sivan 6, 5612 (1852), which happened to fall on a Tuesday.

46. Qirqisani, *K. al-Anwar,* I, 10 (1, 8), 19 (2), pp. 48 ff., 51, 60 f. (HUCA, VII, 377 ff., 381, 393); Mann, *Texts and Studies,* I, 49 f.; J. Starr, *Jews in the Byzantine Empire,* pp. 183 ff.; Hadassi's *Eshkol,* fol. 76a; Maghribi's *Murshid,* III, ed. by Kaufmann, pp. 16 f. (Arabic), 26 f. (German). Similarly in the question of fallowness and Jubilee years such later Karaites as Aaron ben Elijah departed from the general principle that the years were to begin in Nisan, and acknowledged the Rabbanite starting point with the New Year in Tishre. Cf. Aaron's comment on Lev. 25:9 in his *Keter Torah,* III, fol. 70b. Notwithstanding all these inconsistencies, calendar computation on the basis of observation became a major uniting link between the diverse Karaite groups. It also was one of the main issues in the Karaite-Rabbanite debate, such as was conducted between Saadiah and several Karaite scholars. Later Karaite jurists also devoted much space to the rules and regulations governing the calendar, although, relying on observation, they did not require those complex computations which absorbed the attention of mathematically trained Rabbanite jurists. Samuel al-Maghribi, for example, assigned the entire third chapter of his *Murshid* to this subject. Despite all these efforts, the Karaites often differed among themselves with respect to the celebration of holidays, offering facile targets to their opponents. Cf. Bartenora's observations on his journey in Yaari's *Iggerot Ereṣ Yisrael,* pp. 119 f.; and, more generally, with particular reference to more recent Karaite discussions, A. S. Halkin's analysis of the "History of the Sanctification of the New Moon in the Karaite Community" (Hebrew), *Horeb,* II, 87–93, 208–36. Cf. also *infra,* n. 82.

47. Harkavy, *Zikhron,* VIII, 17 f., 37 ff., 203; fragments ed. by Mann in *Journal of Jewish Lore,* I, 348 ff.; Qirqisani, *K. al-Anwar,* I.3 (35), p. 25 (*HUCA,* VII, 345); Hadassi's *Eshkol,* fols. 10a ff., 15b; Ginzberg, *Ginze Schechter,* II, 435 ff. Ginzberg assumes (p. 436) that in the early days the right of uttering additional prayers was restricted to wise and understanding persons, but that subsequently greater freedom was given to any individual. This is unlikely. Generally speaking liturgical evolution tends to standardize prayers and to restrict individual creativity. The latter

probably was at its peak in the early period of greatest Karaite legal diversity. Hence, all that the anonymous author discussed by Ginzberg meant to say (p. 440) was that any person capable of composing another prayer was free to do so.

48. Benjamin cited in Harkavy, *Zikhron,* VIII, 180; Hadassi's *Eshkol,* fol. 135a; Ginzberg, *Ginze Schechter,* II, 120, 122 f.; Neubauer, *Aus der Petersburger Bibliothek,* p. 37. On the *kapparot* ceremony, cf. also *infra,* Chap. XXVII, n. 143. On the other hand, even such Karaite rationalists as Hadassi could not completely escape the impact of their "superstitious" environment. Cf. A. Scheiber's review of the "Elements fabuleux dans l' 'Eshkol ha-Kofer' de Juda Hadasi," *REJ,* CVIII, 41–62 (includes French translations of selected passages). It took some time before the Karaite communities agreed on any kind of uniform liturgy. 'Anan's selections of biblical passages, his requirement of two daily recitations from the Scroll of Law, his semiannual cycle of reading the whole Torah, and other liturgical innovations partially reconstructed by Mann (in *Journal of Jewish Lore,* I, 329 ff.), seem to have enjoyed but limited acceptance even among his early followers. The existing prayer books, like the one published in Vienna, 1854, are all evidently of relatively recent origin. For this reason little can be confidently asserted about the liturgical evolution of medieval Karaism. Both new discoveries and much intensive research will be needed before a critical and comprehensive history of Karaite liturgy will emerge from the realm of scholarly desiderata.

49. Harkavy, *Zikhron,* VIII, 187 f.; Hadassi's *Eshkol,* fols. 89c, 114c. Cf. Revel, *Karaite Halakah,* p. 46 n. 73. Social separation was also promoted by Karaite prohibitions of food in any way originating from Gentiles. Going beyond, though not necessarily conflicting with, 'Anan's aforementioned restrictions (see esp. Harkavy, p. 3), later Karaites forbade the consumption of fish caught or salted by Gentiles. Cf. Hadassi, fol. 89d; H. Hirschfeld's "Arabic Portion of the Cairo Genizah at Cambridge, XIV," *JQR,* [o.s.] XIX, 138, 143 (Arabic), 154 (English). Whether or not following Samaritan precedents (cf. L. Wreschner's *Samaritanische Traditionen,* p. 51), this prohibition made it impossible for conscientious Karaites to partake of a typical Rabbanite Sabbath meal without first ascertaining whether the fish served had been caught by Jews. We certainly hear little of Karaite, or even Jewish, fishermen in the Middle Ages. Conversely, the Karaite disregard of the meat-and-milk taboo and the different forms of slaughtering prevented pious Rabbanites from eating anything cooked in ordinary dishes at Karaite homes.

50. Hadassi's *Eshkol,* fol. 10d; T. Yadaim II.20, 684; a Bodleian manuscript quoted by Poznanski in *REJ,* XLV, 194 ff.; S. Schechter's ed. of "The Oldest Collection of Bible Difficulties by a Jew," *JQR,* [o.s.] XIII, 358 (with reference to Job 30:31). As Ginzberg pointed out (in his *Geonica,* II, 39 f., 370 f.), the geonim still preserved a vestige of the ancient ablutions in the case of a menstruating woman and a *ba'al qeri* (a man after a nightly pollution), but otherwise refused to continue these ancient taboos during the Exile. Cf. also Qirqisani's tirade against the rabbinic ambiguities with respect to the laws of purity (I.3 [16 ff.], pp. 18 ff.; *HUCA,* VII, 336 ff.).

51. A Rabbanite quoted by Qirqisani, II.12.3; in Nemoy's ed. I, 113; Hadassi's *Eshkol,* fol. 64d; Bashyatchi's *Adderet,* Introduction, unnumbered fol. 3a, and fols.

9d, 109bc. Here the Karaite codifier also summarized the hermeneutic methods accepted by his coreligionists under seven categories of *heqqesh,* including the *heqqesh qol va-ḥomer,* or the long-accepted rabbinic *a fortiori.* Even this classification was far from exhaustive. On the acceleration of these adjustments under the impact of the new needs of the nascent Byzantine communities, cf. Z. Ankori's pertinent observations in *PAAJR,* XXIV, 7 ff.

52. Salmon's commentary on Ps. 69:1 in Pinsker, *Lickute kadmoniot,* I, 21 f.; the interesting commentary on the Decalogue attributed to Nissi ben Nuḥ, which, in truly Philonian fashion, interprets the Ten Commandments as containing the entire body of Jewish law (*ibid.,* II, 13; on its date see *supra,* n. 24); and G. Margoliouth's "Ibn al-Hītī's Arabic Chronicle of Karaite Doctors," *JQR,* [o.s.] IX, 433 (Arabic), 439 (English). In the same introduction to his Code in which he cited Exod. 24:12 in support of the Karaite thesis that only the written Torah was revealed and severely censored both Saadiah and Ibn Ezra for their twisted interpretation of that verse, Bashyatchi also quoted Nissi ben Nuḥ's advice and referred more generally to the Karaite sages' opinion concerning the Karaite origins of most of the Mishnah and Talmud (unnumbered fol. 3a). Saadiah's comment is not extant, and Bashyatchi knew it probably only from the derogatory quotation by Tobiah ben Moses, who in turn had probably learned it from David ben Boaz or Jephet ben 'Ali. Cf. Tobiah's commentary, *Oṣar neḥmad,* with Poznanski's comments thereon in his *Karaite Literary Opponents,* pp. 62 f.; and Ankori's observations in *Tarbiz,* XXIV, 49 n. 19, 188 f., 201. We must bear in mind, however, that many Rabbanite jurists, too, recognized the nexus between the Decalogue and the traditional system of 613 biblical commandments. See *infra,* Chap. XXVII, n. 103.

53. Pinsker, *Lickute kadmoniot,* II, 26, 35. The personality of Ibn Saqawaihi, whose treatise unfortunately is known only from a few brief quotations by later authors, has long intrigued scholars. Geiger's suggestion that he was identical with Salmon ben Yeruḥim found a staunch supporter in I. Davidson (in his ed. of Salmon's *Milḥamot,* pp. 21 ff.) and an equally determined opponent in J. Mann (in his *Texts and Studies,* II, 1469 f.). Ultimately, especially in quieter surroundings, Karaite students often evinced a great, and from the Rabbanite standpoint unhealthy, curiosity about Rabbanite letters. In fifteenth-century Constantinople an aroused Rabbanite congregation prevailed on Chief Rabbi Moses Capsali to acquiesce in the pronouncement of a ban against any talmudic instruction of Karaites. This ban was very short-lived, however. Cf. the complementary descriptions of these events by Capsali's successor in the chief rabbinate, Elijah Mizraḥi (in his interesting *Resp.,* No. 57) and by the Karaite Joseph ben Mose Beghi (in his epistle, ed. in part and commented on by Mann in *Texts and Studies,* II, 294 ff.).

54. See the historical theories of Jephet ben 'Ali and Elijah ben Abraham in Pinsker, *Lickute kadmoniot,* II, 100 ff., 185 n. 3; Yehudah Halevi, *Kitab al-Khazari,* III.65, ed. by Hirschfeld, pp. 210 ff. (in his English trans., pp. 186 ff.); Moses ben Ḥisdai Taku, *Ketab tamim* (The Unblemished Work), ed. by R. Kirchheim, in *Ozar nechmad,* ed. by I. Blumenfeld, III, 62. S. Lieberman, who first called attention to this passage, rightly observed that, although a Western rabbi of the early thirteenth century, Moses must have had earlier traditions at his disposal. Moses himself claims to have heard that accusation from his teachers. Cf. Lieberman's

"Light on the Cave Scrolls from Rabbinic Sources," *PAAJR,* XX, 402 f. On the general relations between Karaism and the ancient scrolls, see the literature listed *supra,* Chap. XXV, nn. 50, 56; and the studies by S. Szyszman, "À propos du Karaisme et des textes de la Mer Morte," *VT,* II, 343–48 (with comments thereon by P. Kahle, "The Karaites and the Manuscripts from the Cave," *ibid.,* III, 82–84); and "La Communauté de la Nouvelle Alliance et le Karaïsme," *Actes du XVIe Congrès de l'Institut International de Sociologie,* 1954. Jephet and Elijah disagreed in many significant details among themselves, as well as with Qirqisani, and the Rabbanites, including Halevi, were quick to point out these inconsistencies. In his anti-Karaite harangue (III.34 ff., pp. 182 ff.; English, pp. 166 ff.) Halevi's representative emphasized the insufficiency of Scripture, unaided by oral traditions, to furnish guidance in simple, as well as the more intricate, domains of law. He attacked the Karaite reliance on human reasoning alone. The result was that their doctrines varied with the reasonings of each person. "Not one individual would remain constant to one code. For every day he forms new opinions, increases his knowledge, or meets with someone who refutes him with some argument and converts him to his views" (III, 38). Despite this adverse criticism, the later Karaites were glad to cite this outstanding Rabbanite testimony against the equation of Karaism and Sadduceeism, and were generally much impressed by Halevi's daring historical reinterpretation. Cf. Poznanski's intro. to his ed. of Sultanski's *Zecher Caddikim,* pp. 22 ff.; and Ankori's remarks in *Tarbiz,* XXIV, 183 nn. 72–73, 199 ff. (somewhat overstressing the *conscious* misuse of Halevi by the Karaite sages of Constantinople). So determined were the Karaites to secure a legitimate ancestry that they extolled any minority party recorded in earlier history. Even the ninth-century Masorite, Moses Ben Asher, spoke glowingly of the Sons of Batirah, "the heirs of the prophets," perhaps because they were opposed to the offering of Passover lambs on Sabbath. Cf. Moses Ben Asher's "vine poem," first published by B. Klar in "Ben-Asher" (Hebrew), *Tarbiz,* XV, 44 f., evidently with reference to Pesaḥim 66a. On Ben Asher's much-debated Karaite sympathies, see *infra,* Chap. XXIX, n. 15. Cf. also N. Wieder, "The Qumran Sectaries and the Karaites," *JQR,* XLVII, 97–113, 269–92, continuing his study mentioned *supra,* Chap. XXV, n. 67.

55. Cf. Qirqisani's slur on Ḥanukkah (I.3 [49], p. 30; *HUCA,* VII, 349: "What is more strange than a person pronouncing a blessing over a Sabbath-eve lamp and saying in the blessing that God commanded it? Likewise, over the lamp of Ḥanukkah"); and the Karaite attack on Saadiah's chronological computations concerning the growth of the Mishnah in Harkavy's *Zikhron,* V, 194 f., together with Poznanski's comments thereon in his *Karaite Literary Opponents,* p. 41 n. 1. The miracle tales connected with the Maccabean revolt and the Talmud's reference to them as the chief reason for the festival of Ḥanukkah must likewise have antagonized the early Karaite rationalists. They could not possibly know the hidden motives behind the talmudic attitude, discussed *supra,* Vol. I, 400 n. 30. We shall see, however, that Karaite rejection achieved the opposite result and greatly heightened the dignity of this festival among the Rabbanite majority.

56. Jephet ben Sa'id's *Shalshelet ha-qabbalah* (Chain of Tradition) in Lucki, *Oraḥ ṣaddiqim,* fol. 26a. The main purpose of these chronological discussions was, of course, to prove Karaite priority over the Rabbanites, or as Elijah ben Abraham stated it, that "we were before them" (Pinsker, *Lickute kadmoniot,* II, 101). The

Rabbanites were but "contentious innovators," according to Samuel al-Maghribi in his *Murshid,* IX, in D. Weiss's ed. pp. 1 (Arabic), 14 (German). Cf. Poznanski's comprehensive analysis of the vicissitudes of Karaite historiography in his aforementioned introduction to Sultanski's *Zecher.* This analysis could be amplified, but not substantially changed as a result of more recent discoveries. The climax of Karaite perversions of history was reached in the works of the notorious Abraham Firkovitch who contended, for example, that both Jesus and Philo had been Karaites. Cf. his *Mibḥar Yesharim,* fols. 2a, 54a, 56a. These extreme views, alongside of many more meritorious ones, of this (despite all his faults) very noteworthy scholar, will be discussed in their modern context.

57. Qirqisani, *K. al-Anwar,* I.1 (*HUCA,* VII, 321); Elijah ben Abraham's *Ḥilluq* in Pinsker, *Lickute kadmoniot,* II, 104; Mann, *Texts and Studies,* II, 4. In the memorial liturgy included in the modern Karaite prayer book (Vilna ed., 1891, I, 399) 'Anan is extolled as "prince, man of God and exilarch who opened up the way of the Torah, enlightened the eyes of the children of Scripture, brought many back from sin and [divine] anger, and led us on the righteous path, may the God of Israel place him in a good abode." There is no way of telling when that prayer was composed and made part of the Karaite ritual. From time immemorial, however, a list of Karaite worthies which bears all the earmarks of a semiliturgical composition was circulated among the faithful. See Elijah's *Ḥilluq* in Pinsker, *Lickute,* II, 106 (curiously here 'Anan's name is preceded by those of Abu Nissi and Obadiah, probably already then a misspelling of the name of the forgotten sectarian, Abu 'Isa-Obadiah who indeed preceded 'Anan by some three quarters of a century); and Joseph Beghi's epistle in Mann, *Texts and Studies,* II, 303.

58. Mann, *Jews in Egypt,* I, 141 n. 1; II, 157; Bartenora in Yaari's *Iggerot Ereṣ Yisrael,* p. 131; Joseph Beghi's epistle in Mann's *Texts and Studies,* II, 300, 314; the Genizah fragment from the Kaufmann Collection, ed. by S. D. Goitein in *Tarbiz,* XX, 196 ff.; *supra,* Chap. XVIII, n. 43; and *infra,* nn. 73–74. The social structure of the Karaite communities in the various stages of their evolution has never yet been examined in detail. Admittedly Karaite scribes of later generations, and for that matter also most modern investigators, were so exclusively preoccupied with the normative, exegetical, and polemical aspects of the earlier literature that they paid little attention to any factual material that might have survived the ravages of migrations, persecutions, and general neglect. However, a determined effort to examine the extant documentation with the view of extracting therefrom every shred of pertinent evidence may yet bring forth some worthwhile data to justify at least some tentative hypotheses.

59. Mann, *Texts and Studies,* II, 100 f.; Salmon's *Milḥamot,* ed. by Davidson, p. 113. Cf. also Pinsker, *Lickute kadmoniot,* II, 18 f., 32; and the tract published by Mann in *JQR,* XII, 276 f. Ironically, the graves of some of the Karaite controversialists became themselves centers of pilgrimages. We have the testimony of the fifteenth-century Karaite chronicler Ibn al-Hiti that Salmon ben Yeruḥim's grave "is known to this day in Aleppo, and among the Gentiles and others as the grave of the righteous one, and vows are made to him to the present day." Cf. the text ed. by G. Margoliouth in *JQR,* [o.s.] IX, 434 (Arabic), 441 (English). Despite the editor's hesitation, the word "others" doubtless refers to Rabbanites whom Ibn

al-Hiti had the better reason not to mention by name, as he probably realized the ironical implications of his statement. Equally paradoxical was the query addressed to Maimonides on whether the *She'ur qomah* had been composed by Karaites or other heretics. Cf. his *Resp.,* No. 373. This entire controversy over real or alleged superstitious beliefs and, particularly, the legitimacy and boundaries of anthropomorphism will be more fully discussed in the broader context of medieval mysticism and philosophy.

60. Harkavy, *Zikhron,* VIII, 148, 189; Mann, *Texts and Studies,* II, 75 f., 80 ff.; Qirqisani, *K. al-Anwar,* I.1 (Vol. I, p. 1; *HUCA,* VII, 321), VI.12 (Vol. III, pp. 593 ff.); Nemoy, "Al-Qirqisani's Criticism of 'Anan's Prohibition of the Practice of Medicine" (Hebrew), *Harofé Haivri* [XI], 1938, Part 2, pp. 73–83 (Hebrew), 198–207 (English); Neubauer, *Aus der Petersburger Bibliothek,* pp. 13, 109 f.

61. Qirqisani, *K. al-Anwar,* I.1, pp. 3 f. (*HUCA,* VII, 321), VI.14 (Vol. III, pp. 600 ff.); L. Nemoy, "Al-Qirqisani's Essay on the Psychophysiology of Sleep and Dreams," *Harofé Haivri,* 1949, Part 2, pp. 88–95 (Hebrew), 158–65 (English); G. Vajda, "Etudes sur Qirqisani," *REJ,* CVI, 115 ff.; *Sharḥ al-'atidot,* cited *supra,* Chap. XXV, n. 10; 'Anan's benedictions in Harkavy, *Zikhron,* VIII, 19 ff.; Jephet's Zionide poem published in Mann, *Texts and Studies,* II, 31 f. (in English trans. in Nemoy's *Karaite Anthology,* pp. 107 f.); Menahem ben Michael's elegy, *Ṣiyyon teqonen* (Zion Weeps) in the Karaite prayer book, Vilna ed., I, 134 f. (Poznanski's argument for its dependence on Halevi in *Karaite Literary Opponents,* p. 12, appears dubious); and Sahl's exhortation in Pinsker, *Lickute,* II, 36. On Solomon ha-Kohen, cf. *supra,* Chap. XXV, n. 67. On the absence of the messianic doctrine in later Karaite writings, see E. Mainz's edition of the brief tract by Israel ben Samuel ha-Ma'arabi in "The Credo of a Fourteenth-Century Karaite," *PAAJR,* XXII, 55–63; S. Szyszman's critical observations thereon in *VT,* IV, 201 ff.; and Mainz's reply in his "Comments on the Messiah in Karaite Literature," *PAAJR,* XXV, 115–18. Mainz's explanation that Israel's silence was owing to his fear of Mameluk authorities is neither plausible in itself, nor does it make clear the similar silence of Aaron ben Elijah or the modern catechism. In his suggested formula for a marriage contract Hadassi insisted on the insertion, next to the date according to the era of creation, of the year since the destruction of the Temple, "the era which we use while submerged in Exile . . . we the Karaites that sigh and that cry far from our country" (*Eshkol,* fol. 13b; cf. also Mann's data in *JQR,* XII, 281, 518 f.; and *Texts and Studies,* II, 158 n. 8, 164 n. 14). Mann points out that in Palestine the era of King Jehoiachin's exile was used, perhaps in honor of the Karaite "princes" who claimed to be descendants of that king.

62. Qirqisani *K. al-Anwar,* I.2(5), 5, 15, pp. 10 f., 40 f., 56 f. (*HUCA,* VII, 325, 362, 388); Hadassi's *Eshkol,* fol. 41bc (citing Al-Muqammiṣ who doubtless was also Qirqisani's main source); Estori Farḥi, *Kaftor va-feraḥ,* (Knop and Flowers; Topography of Palestine), v end, Venice, ed., 1549, fol. 20b. Hadassi only added the remark that the Samaritans "to your eyes" take off their clothes when contaminated by the touch of unbelievers. This practice, however, need not have been derived from either observation or hearsay, for Hadassi often made such gratuitous additions for the mere purpose of maintaining his artificial rhyme. Conversely, Samaritan attacks on Karaism were equally rare. Apart from the aforementioned gloss to the Samaritan Pentateuch (see *supra,* Chap. XXV, n. 26), one need refer only to Abu'l Ḥasan

aṣ-Ṣuri's polemics against the scriptural quotations adduced in support of the Karaite calendar. Cf. his *K. aṭ-Ṭabakh,* described on the basis of a John Rylands MS by E. Robertson in his *Catalogue of Samaritan Manuscripts,* pp. xxx f., 112; and A. S. Halkin's data in *PAAJR,* VII, 22 n. 54, 25, 44 ff.

63. Shahrastani, *K. al-Milal,* ed. by Cureton, I, 167 (in Haarbrücker's trans., I, 253 f.); Maqrizi's *Khitat* (*supra,* n. 11); Qirqisani, *K. al-Anwar,* I.2 (9), 4 (16), 8ab, ed. by Nemoy, I, 12, 37, 42 (*HUCA,* VII, 327, 358, 364 ff.); III.16 (III, 301 ff.; cf. the text previously published in H. Hirschfeld's *Arabic Chrestomathy in Hebrew Characters,* pp. 116 ff.); Ibn al-Hiti's register in *JQR,* [o.s.] IX, 434 (Arabic), 441 (English). On Ben Mashiaḥ and Ibn Zar'a, cf. also Steinschneider's *Polemische . . . Literatur,* pp. 148 f.; and Poznanski's *Karaite Literary Opponents,* pp. 15 f. Salmon's evil forebodings concerning the fate of the Karaite community of Jerusalem in the eventuality of Christian occupation (see *supra,* n. 28) did not necessarily imply any more universal fears of Christian intolerance. Living under Christian Byzantium, Hadassi could actually take cognizance of the Christian Easter in fixing the date of Passover. Of course, the Karaite celebration of Pentecost on Sunday could also be viewed by Rabbanite opponents as a form of catering to the Christian rulers. Cf. Hadassi's *Eshkol,* fols. 76b–77a; other sources quoted by Ankori in *PAAJR,* XXIV, 22 f. n. 51; XXV, 159 n. 87; and *supra,* Chap. XVI, n. 9. On the other hand, Caleb Afendopolo's very sympathetic comments on Jesus reflect the then rather unique atmosphere of religious tolerance in fifteenth-century Constantinople under the Ottoman regime. While arguing against the chronology of the Gospels and insisting that Jesus had been a contemporary of R. Joshua ben Peraḥiah and Alexander Jannaeus (see *supra,* Vol. II, pp. 148, 387 n. 27), Caleb conceded that "in the opinion of the lovers of truth Jesus the Nazarene was a great scholar and a righteous, pious, and God-fearing man." Only the Apostles had departed from orthodox Judaism. Cf. the text published by M. Steinschneider in his *Catalogus . . . Academiae Lugduno-Batavae* (Leyden), pp. 127 ff., 393 ff.

64. Qirqisani, *K. al-Anwar,* III.15–16; IV.53–57 (in Nemoy's ed., II, 292 ff., 441 ff.; cf. *HUCA,* VII, 373); Pinsker, *Lickute kadmoniot,* II, 42 f., 75 f. Cf. also I. Friedlaender's brief comments on Qirqisani's anti-Muslim chapter (first published by him from a British Museum MS) in his "Qirqisani's Polemik gegen den Islam," *Zeitschrift für Assyriologie,* XXVI, 93–113; and R. Brunschvig's summary of the arguments in IV, 53 ff. in *Homenaje a Millás,* pp. 239 f. (pointing out how frequently Al-Baqillani later reverted to the same lines of reasoning).

65. Cf. Steinschneider's brief survey in *Polemische Literatur,* pp. 341 ff.; and Neubauer's *Aus der Petersburger Bibliothek,* pp. 13, 109. Among other derogatory terms applied to Mohammed stands out the designation *pasul* (disqualified), used already by Qirqisani. According to G. Margoliouth's plausible suggestion, this was but a popular Jewish parody of the Muslim glorification of the *rasul* (Messenger). Cf. Friedlaender's communication in *Zeitschrift für Assyriologie,* XXVI, 97 n. 3. Nor was the equally facile mispronunciation *qalon* (shame) for Qur'an absent from Karaite letters. Karaite leaders residing in Palestine doubtless shared the then prevalent Palestinian pronunciation of the word *qolon,* lending it even greater phonetic resemblance to the Muslim Scripture. See *infra,* Chap. XXX, n. 23. Of considerable interest also is the story of the forced conversion to Islam and ultimate escape

of the Karaite Moses ben Samuel, a government official in fourteenth-century Damascus. Dramatically narrated by him in poetic prose and including a satirical description of the author's "enforced" pilgrimage to Mecca, the story unfolds in the documents published and commented on by Mann in his *Texts and Studies,* II, 201 ff.; and in Nemoy's English trans. in his *Karaite Anthology,* pp. 151 ff., 356 ff. Mann's overcredulous acceptance, however, of Moses' assertions of unwavering loyalty to Judaism and his constant yielding to irresistible pressures needs some rectification. In any case his story is far from typical, especially for the earlier, more tolerant periods.

66. Pinsker, *Lickute kadmoniot,* I, 158 f.; II, 32, 42; Ginzberg, *Ginze Schechter,* II, 475, 477, 482; the text of the Karaite-Rabbanite marriage contract of 1028, first published by A. M. Luncz and reprinted in A. Gulak's *Oṣar ha-sheṭarot* (Collection of Deeds Used by Jews), pp. 56 f. No. 53. Karaite resistance to appeals to Muslim courts is further exemplified by the proclamation of the Damascus community of 1500 threatening all culprits with burials on isolated spots in the cemetery. Cf. Neubauer, *Aus der Petersburger Bibliothek,* pp. 28, 118.

67. Cf. the texts published by S. Schechter in his "Geniza Specimens," *JQR,* [o.s.] XIII, 220 f.; and by Mann in his *Texts and Studies,* II, 171, 173. Cf. also S. Assaf's succinct analysis in his *Be-Ohole Ya'aqob,* pp. 182 ff. Of course, one cannot draw far-reaching conclusions from the ratio of 4:2 in favor of Rabbanite men marrying Karaite women among the six couples of the eleventh and twelfth centuries whose marriage contracts happened to be preserved. Yet it stands to reason that the obstacles to intermarriage placed by the more powerful, and perhaps also more implacable, Rabbanite authorities, could be overcome with less difficulty by Rabbanites wishing to marry Karaite women.

68. Cf. Maimonides' *Resp.,* ed. by Freimann, No. 162; Estori Farḥi's *Kaftor,* v end (Venice ed., fol. 20b); David ibn Abi Zimra's *Resp.,* I, No. 73 (Sudzilkov ed., fol. 10bc); Benjamin of Tudela's *Massa'ot,* ed. by Adler, pp. 31 (Hebrew), 30 (English; in the latter passage, however, Benjamin may merely have referred to the mutual endogamous exclusion of Karaites and Samaritans only); Joseph Karo in his *Bet Yosef* on *Ṭur,* Eben ha-'ezer IV end (citing R. Simson of Sens); Moses Isserles in his marginal note on Karo's *Shulḥan 'arukh,* IV.37. Cf. also Mann's *Texts and Studies,* I, 425 f.; Assaf's *Be-Ohole, loc. cit.; infra,* n. 83; and Chap. XXVII, n. 155.

69. Sahl ben Maṣliaḥ cited by Aaron ben Joseph in *Sefer ha-Mibḥar* (Commentary on the Pentateuch), Part 5, on Deut., fol. 19b (Aaron himself disagrees); Hadassi's *Eshkol,* fols. 140b, 148d; and other sources cited by Revel in his *Karaite Halakah,* pp. 66 f.; Solomon ben Aaron's aforementioned *Appiryon 'asah,* cited from a MS by Assaf in *Be-Ohole,* p. 190 (not in Neubauer's *Aus der Petersburger Bibliothek,* Hebrew section, pp. 4 ff.). Assaf's assumption that Solomon invented this allegedly 'Ananite tradition for the benefit of the Riga rector, Johann Pufendorf, so as to explain to this Christian student the existing separation between Rabbanites and Karaites, is more than questionable. After all, for purposes of prestige he would have stressed principally Karaite objections to intermarriage even after conversion similar to those raised by Rabbanite authorities. Understandably, however, Karaites wished to preserve Karaite estates for the benefit of their community. For this

reason they not only adopted the old Jewish ruling that "he who in his father's lifetime turned to evil ways [became an infidel] does not inherit his father's money" (Benjamin Nahawendi in *Mas'at Binyamin,* fol. 6a), but also reiterated that no inheritance shall go outside the tribe. Rabbanites, like Maimonides, following talmudic precedents, simply assumed that every Jew would leave behind some heirs. Cf. *M.T.* Naḥlot I.3; and *Commentary* on B.Q. IX.11, invoking an ancient tradition. The small size of the Karaite communities made the apprehensions of their leaders perfectly realistic.

70. Cf. H. Hirschfeld's "Karaite Conversion Story," *Jews' College Jubilee Volume,* pp. 81–100, largely summarizing the story told by As-Suyuti. Needless to say that, despite all legal obstacles, there were occasional conversions of Muslims to Karaism, as to Rabbanite Judaism or Christianity. No less a figure than Yeshu'a ben Yehudah was accused by a fellow Karaite, Sahl at-Tustari, of slandering the son of a Muslim convert and thereby forcing him temporarily to renounce Judaism. See Mann, *Texts and Studies,* II, 40.

71. Pinsker, *Lickute kadmoniot,* I, 111 ff., 168 f.; II, 24 f., 27 ff., 37 ff., 91 ff., 99 ff.; Salmon's *Milḥamot,* ed. by Davidson, p. 67; Maqrizi's *Khitat, loc. cit.* (*supra,* n. 11). Cf. also Poznanski's *Karaite Literary Opponents, passim.* A detailed monograph on the Karaite propaganda, its methods, successes and failures should prove highly rewarding.

72. Ibn Ḥazm's *K. al-Fiṣal,* I, 14 (in Asín Palacios's Spanish trans., II, 211); Ibn Daud's chronicle in *MJC,* I, 79. Cf. also I. Loeb's brief discussion of "Les Caraïtes en Espagne," *REJ,* XIX, 206–9; and *supra,* Chap. XX, n. 47. The fact that few new data have come to light in the last sixty years since this essay was written is itself proof of the paucity and relative insignificance of Karaite settlements on the Iberian Peninsula.

73. Benjamin, *Massa'ot,* ed. by Adler, pp. 31 (Hebrew), 30 (English); R. Gottheil's ed. of "A Decree in Favour of the Karaites of Cairo dated 1024," *Festschrift Harkavy,* pp. 115–25; S. D. Goitein, "A Caliph's Decree in Favour of the Rabbanite Jews of Palestine," *JJS,* V, 118–25; and *infra,* n. 82. The fact that the Cairo Karaites at one time paid as much in taxes as the Rabbanites (cf. *supra,* n. 58) probably indicates their greater economic prosperity, rather than equality in numbers. On the small size of the Karaite community in Egypt see also the sparse data collected by E. Strauss in his *Toledot,* II, 548 ff. It was an expression of hope, rather than an antiquarian reminiscence, when a Karaite commentator pointed out the difference between the first two books of Psalms and declared, "At first only individuals will return to the Lord, but later they will become a large congregation." Cf. Mann, *Texts and Studies,* II, 111.

74. Benjamin, *Massa'ot,* pp. 16 (Hebrew), 14 (English); Starr, *Jews in the Byzantine Empire,* pp. 242 ff.; Solomon ben Aaron's *Appiryon* in Neubauer, *Aus der Petersburger Bibliothek,* Hebrew section, p. 4; and in the larger version in Mann, *Texts and Studies,* II, 1444 f. Benjamin's awkward phrase *u-me-hem,* from among them (the MSS register here no variant) might indicate that there were 2,000 families in all, that is 1,500 Rabbanite and 500 Karaite. Ibn Daud's curious geographic

designations (in his chronicle, *MJC,* I, 79) are explained, though with excessive freedom, by S. Krauss in his *Studien zur byzantinisch-jüdischen Geschichte,* pp. 77 f. Evidently familiar with this statement, Simon Duran merely added the remark, "But we have heard that they [the Karaites] all died out and that not one has remained in that locality [Warjalan]." Cf. his *Magen abot,* II.3; and Mann's comment in his *Texts and Studies,* II, 139 n. 19. The Karaite feeling of inferiority seems to have motivated also those medieval Karaite informants, from whom almost all Muslim students of religion derived their basic data about the history of the sect. Rabbanites, far more sure of themselves, were decidedly more restrained in discussing with outsiders such "internal" Jewish affairs.

75. Solomon Cohen's *Resp.,* III, No. 15 fol. 25d. Apart from Jerusalem and Ramleh, only Ascalon and Gaza and possibly one or two smaller communities had Karaite settlers. The petition of the community of Ascalon (published in Mann, *Jews in Egypt,* II, 198), however, although referring to the Karaite elders of Cairo as "our elders," probably was written by the main Rabbanite community. Only during the Crusades did Benjamin find in that city which had been occupied by the Crusaders merely during the years 1153–87, 40 Karaites alongside of 200 Rabbanites and 300 Samaritans. Cf. *Massa'ot,* pp. 29 (Hebrew), 28 (English). Neither is the name, Al-Gazzi (Alghazi), mentioned in the eleventh-century colophon of a Karaite Bible as that of the father of the scribe, by itself evidence of Karaite settlement in Gaza. Cf. P. Kahle, *Masoreten des Westens,* I, 74. Cf. also *Sefer ha-Yishub,* II, Introduction, pp. 50 ff.; the sources listed in the Index there, p. 152; and *infra,* Chap. XXIX, nn. 13 and 16.

76. Levi ben Jephet cited by Bashyatchi in *Adderet Eliyahu,* fol. 31c (the Constantinople jurist tried to explain the discrepancy by identifying the "land of Shine'ar" with "Khazariah and Russia in the far north" where the moon was of course visible at different times); Aaron ben Elijah's *Gan 'Eden,* fol. 8d; Jacob Castro's commentary *'Erekh leḥem* on *Tur,* Y.D. No. 268, fol. 48cd; Tobiah ben Moses' *Oṣar neḥmad* cited from a Bodleian MS by P. (F.) Frankl in his *Aḥar ReSheF le-baqqer,* p. 18. The aforementioned cases of intermarriage likewise show that the boundaries between the two groups could be crossed easily and without attracting too much public attention. Similarly, the reiterated explanations by Maimonides and other rabbis that such and such customs had crept into Rabbanite life under Karaite influence (cf. e.g., *M.T.* Issure biah XI. 15; and *infra,* n. 83) can only be understood because of these easy and inconspicuous forms of transition from one to the other group.

77. See Mann, *Jews in Egypt,* I, 141 ff., 149 ff.; II, 161 f., 172 f.; his *Texts and Studies,* I, 325 ff.; D. H. Baneth's "Ibn Kammuna," *MGWJ,* LXIX, 309 f. Cf. also Mann's *Jews in Egypt,* II, 376 ff. Jewish charities were, as one may well understand, even less discriminating. One of our oldest records pertaining to Byzantine Jewry relates to the ransom, by the Jewish community, of four Rabbanite and three Karaite captives from the city of Attaleia in 1028. Cf. the text published by Cowley in his "Bodleian Geniza Fragments, IV," *JQR,* [o.s.] XIX, 250 ff. Evidently no distinction was drawn between orthodox and heretics in cases of great need. Similarly a distinguished Jewish leader like Palṭiel, the reputed founder of the office of Egyptian *nagid,* did not hesitate to provide in his will for charities to be dis-

tributed in Jerusalem among the poor of both denominations. He did not mention the Karaites by name but by donating 1,000 dinars to "the mourners of the sanctuary" in Jerusalem (*abele bet ha-'olamim,* a variant of *abele Ṣiyyon*), he must have wished to provide for the Karaite ascetics, too. Cf. *The Chronicle of Aḥimaaz,* cited *supra,* Chap. XXV, n. 48; and on the Egyptian *nagid's* control over the Karaites as well, *supra,* Chap. XXIII, n. 49. Ibn Kammuna, incidentally, could the more readily serve as a sort of impartial chairman, as he was generally moderate in his religious views and an advocate of the status quo. See *supra,* Chap. XXIV, n. 28; and L. Nemoy's recent "Remarks on Ibn Kammuna's Treatise on the Differences between the Rabbanites and the Karaites" (Hebrew), *Tarbiz,* XXIV, 343–54 (correcting the text, ed. by H. Hirschfeld).

78. Cf. Saadiah, *Oeuvres complètes,* IX, 91, No. 4 with reference to Yebamot 121a; and *supra,* Chap. XXIII, n. 15. This is not to deny that Saadiah, keenly aware of the existing controversies in the Jewish community, was probably more ruthless in issuing bans than his confrères living in more quiescent periods. Hence perhaps also his general severity in deciding questionable problems of Jewish law in which he did not wish to be outdone by the sectarians. See my remarks in *Saadiah Anniv. Vol.,* p. 56 n. 105. Some of Saadiah's Karaite contemporaries indeed accused the rabbis of having, for purely opportunistic reasons, lowered the requirements of Jewish law.

79. Qirqisani, *K. al-Anwar,* I.2 (14), p. 13 (*HUCA,* VII, 328 f.). Al-Baṣir's version is not recorded in Nemoy's ed. (I.13 ll. 5–6) and probably is a later rationalization. The authenticity of Qirqisani's story has rightly been questioned by Harkavy and Ginzberg. Cf. I. Davidson's *Maḥzor Yannai,* pp. xli f. But even if true, this report does not prove that Hai ben David wished to legitimize 'Anan's deviations but rather that he wished to place at the disposal of students of Jewish law unfamiliar with Aramaic—such doubtless existed only in the provinces east of Babylonia, in Egypt and other North African countries and to a lesser extent in Palestine—some helpful hints for their debates with the heretics. There is in fact no other trace of that document in our extant sources, Karaite or Rabbanite.

80. Of Saadiah's anti-Karaite pamphlets, the *Kitab ar-Radd 'ala 'Anan* (Refutation of 'Anan; only a small fragment is available through B. M. Lewin's ed. in *GK,* V, 147–52) was written in 905. This was an important year in the restoration of the caliph's direct authority over Egypt and Palestine, and Saadiah's memorandum was probably intended to aid some Rabbanite officials in the steps then taken to reestablish Rabbanite supremacy in these provinces. As such it was clearly intended for confidential use by the Rabbanite negotiators. Cf. my remarks in *Saadiah Anniv. Vol.,* pp. 17 ff. The considerably more ambitious *Kitab al-Tamyiz* (Book of Distinction), written in 926–27, shortly before Saadiah took over the gaonate of Sura, is known to us chiefly from fairly lengthy quotations by Karaite opponents, especially Jephet ben 'Ali, who would naturally select passages relating to some focal points in the Karaite-Rabbanite debate. Neither these passages, nor similar excerpts from his subsequent "Refutation of Ibn Saqawaihi," give us a real inkling of their general purpose and intended circulation. Cf. the extensive discussion and literature cited by Malter in his *Saadia Gaon,* pp. 260 ff., 380 ff., with I. Werfel's supplementary notes in *Rav Saadya Gaon,* ed. by Fishman, pp. 655 f.;

and the additional fragment published by M. Zucker in *PAAJR,* XVIII, Hebrew section, pp. 1 ff. On the other hand, Saadiah's main philosophic treatise fully available to us is remarkably free of any overt polemics against Karaism. Evidently many other issues far overshadowed the struggle against these sectarians in the mind of the Rabbanite leader. On the date of his poetic pamphlet *Essa meshali,* see Chap. XXIX, n. 15.

81. Cf. Qirqisani's lengthy exposition in his *K. al-Anwar,* VIII.1–10, ed. by Nemoy, IV, 851 ff. Among the latest exponents of this traditional view have been P. R. Weis in "The Anti-Karaite Tendency of R. Saadya Gaon's Arabic Version of the Pentateuch" in *Saadya Studies,* ed. by E. I. J. Rosenthal, pp. 227–44; and especially M. Zucker. Cf., for instance, his essay on "Saadiah Gaon's Share in the Controversy over 'On the Morrow of the Sabbath'" (Hebrew), *PAAJR,* XX, 1–26 (also citing in full Saadiah's statements). Here Zucker even makes the sweeping claim with respect to the gaon's Bible commentaries that "whenever he [Saadiah] reaches a passage which, directly or indirectly, impinges on the Karaite-Rabbanite controversy, he enters the debate and endeavors to dispose of the Karaite views" (p. 2). Cf. also Zucker's "Fragments from Rav Saadya Gaon's Commentary" (Hebrew), *Sura,* II, 316 ff. On the basis of the published commentaries, Zucker's sweeping assertion sounds like an overstatement, although we must suspend judgment until the publication of his projected volume on Saadiah's legal and philosophic teaching as reflected in the Bible commentaries, which is to be based on many hitherto unpublished texts. But even if his thesis should be confirmed, such purely intellectual discussions would prove little concerning any sense of danger from this quarter to the community and its fundamental institutions among the contemporary Rabbanite leaders. Cf. also the excerpts assembled in B. M. Lewin's older "Chapters from R. Saadiah Gaon's Struggles" (Hebrew), *Sinai,* III, Nos. 32–38, pp. 36–47, 147–51; and *GK,* VI, 3–21.

82. Mann, *Jews in Egypt,* I, 134 ff., 169; II, 152 ff., 198 f.; his *Texts and Studies,* I, 325 ff.; II, 43 ff., 67 ff.; and *supra,* n. 73. The reader of these documents is struck by the fact that in all these squabbles neither leaders nor the rank and file of both groups behaved as if they belonged to wholly separate communities. If, as Mann assumes, the writer of the Ascalon letter was a Karaite speaking "in the name of the whole community . . . which seems to have united the followers of both sections," such employment of a Karaite spokesman by what must have been a Rabbanite majority would doubly confirm the absence of any bitter struggle among the two factions in eleventh-century Palestine. Cf. the documentation pertaining to the Ascalon community, almost exclusively Rabbanite, which is assembled in *Sefer ha-Yishub,* II, 4 ff.; and the "petition" cited *supra,* Chap. XXIII, n. 42.

83. Maimonides' *Resp.,* Nos. 46, 47 (pp. 359 ff.), 99, 162, 178, 371 (in part citing precedents established by Hai Gaon); and Abraham Maimuni's *Resp.,* Nos. 63, 80. Cf. A. H. Freimann's note on his edition of the latter, p. 67 n. 12; and my remarks in *PAAJR,* VI, 84 f. Of course, if Karaite law differed from the Rabbanite practice, as in questions of a required quorum, Maimonides opposed the participation of sectarians holding contrary beliefs. Cf. his *Resp.,* No. 14. He also led in the issuance in 1176 of a sharp ordinance against those Rabbanite women who, in emula-

tion of Karaite practice, performed their ritualistic ablutions in ways contrary to talmudic law. Cf. I. Friedlaender's ed. of "Der arabische Original der anti-karäischen Verordnung des Maimonides," *MGWJ,* LIII, 469–85; Maimonides' *Resp.,* pp. 91 ff. No. 97; and *infra,* Chap. XXVII, n. 155.

84. See the midrashim cited by A. Marmorstein from a British Museum MS in *Schwarz Festschrift,* p. 462 n. 4; and by L. Ginzberg from a Genizah fragment in his *Ginze Schechter,* I, 21 f.; also Tanḥuma on Noah, III, p. 30; Buber ed., pp. 27 f. and note 6. The latter homily on Num. 19:14 is, of course, only a variant of the old talmudic peroration, cited *supra,* Vol. II, p. 277. However, the change in emphasis is revealing: the Talmud speaks of the need of self-sacrifice for the study of the Torah generally, the author of Tanḥuma relates it to that of Oral Law specifically.

85. Cf. Shabbat 25b with the comments thereon by the *Tosafot s.v. Ḥobah;* B. M. Lewin, *Otzar ha-gaonim,* II, 27; Simon Qayyara's *Halakhot gedolot,* ed. by Hildesheimer, p. 612 (in the name of Yehudai Gaon or his son? cf. also Abraham Simon Traub's comments in the Warsaw ed., fol. 8ab); Naḥmanides' commentary on Maimonides' *Sefer ha-Miṣvot,* I; Saadiah's *Siddur,* p. 155; Simon Duran's commentary, *Magen abot,* II. 1 (Leipzig ed., fol. 19a); *Sha'are teshubah,* No. 187. The requirement of warning a prospective woman proselyte that she must strictly observe the rabbinic laws concerning behavior during the menstrual period, the separation of priestly *ḥallah* from dough, and the kindling of Sabbath lights, evidently also had an antiheretical point. Compare the medieval tractate *Gerim,* I, 1 (in Higger's ed. of *Sheva masekhtot qeṭanot* [Seven Minor Treatises], p. 68) with its tannaitic source in b. Yebamot 47b. On the use of rings at weddings, see *supra,* Chap. XXIII, n. 33. One should bear in mind, however, that the Karaites did not reject the title "rabbi" as such. Hadassi called 'Anan himself by the honorific title *rabbenu,* while the thirteenth-century memorial ritual, as well as Aaron ben Elijah, used rather indiscriminately the designation "rabbi" for many of their own scholars. Cf. I. M. Jost's *Geschichte des Judentums und seiner Sekten,* II, 381. We may see therein but another illustration of the irresistible impact of the majority customs on those of the minority group.